THE LIBRARY OF LIVING PHILOSOPHERS

Volume II

THE PHILOSOPHY OF GEORGE SANTAYANA

THE LIBRARY OF LIVING PHILOSOPHERS

PAUL ARTHUR SCHILPP, *Editor*

Already Published:

THE PHILOSOPHY OF JOHN DEWEY (1939)

THE PHILOSOPHY OF GEORGE SANTAYANA (1940)

In Preparation:

THE PHILOSOPHY OF BENEDETTO CROCE

THE PHILOSOPHY OF G. E. MOORE

THE PHILOSOPHY OF BERTRAND RUSSELL

THE PHILOSOPHY OF ERNST CASSIRER

THE PHILOSOPHY OF LÉON BRUNSCHVICG

Other volumes to be announced later

George Santayana in 1940

THE LIBRARY OF LIVING PHILOSOPHERS

Volume II

THE PHILOSOPHY OF GEORGE SANTAYANA

Edited by

PAUL ARTHUR SCHILPP

NORTHWESTERN UNIVERSITY

1940

NORTHWESTERN UNIVERSITY

EVANSTON AND CHICAGO

THE PHILOSOPHY OF GEORGE SANTAYANA

Printed in the United States of America

FIRST EDITION

L-B

GEORGE BANTA PUBLISHING COMPANY, MENASHA, WISCONSIN

GENERAL INTRODUCTION*

TO

"THE LIBRARY OF LIVING PHILOSOPHERS"

ACCORDING to the late F. C. S. Schiller, the greatest obstacle to fruitful discussion in philosophy is "the curious etiquette which apparently taboos the asking of questions about a philosopher's meaning while he is alive." The "interminable controversies which fill the histories of philosophy," he goes on to say, "could have been ended at once by asking the living philosophers a few searching questions."

Perhaps the confident optimism of this last remark goes too far. Living thinkers have often been asked "a few searching questions," but their answers have not stopped "interminable controversies" about their real meaning. It is none the less true that there would be far greater clarity of understanding than is now often the case, if more such searching questions had been directed to great men while they were still alive.

This, at any rate, is the basic thought behind the present undertaking. The volumes of *The Library of Living Philosophers* can in no sense take the place of the original writings of great thinkers. Students who would know the philosophies of such men as John Dewey, Henri Bergson, Alfred North Whitehead, George Santayana, Benedetto Croce, G. E. Moore, Bertrand Russell, Léon Brunschvicg, Ernst Cassirer, Martin Heidegger, *et al.*, will still need to read the writings of these men. There is no substitute for first-hand contact with the original thought of the philosopher himself. Least of all does this *Library* pretend to be such a substitute. The *Library* in fact, will spare neither effort nor expense in offering to the student the best possible guide to the published writings of a given thinker. We shall attempt to meet this aim by providing at the end of each volume in our series a complete bibliography of the published work of the philosopher in question. Nor should one overlook the fact that the essays in each

* This *General Introduction*, setting forth the underlying conception of this *Library*, is purposely reprinted in each volume (with only very minor changes).

volume cannot but finally lead to this same goal. The interpretative and critical discussions of the various phases of a great thinker's work and, most of all, the reply of the thinker himself, are bound to lead the reader to his work and thereby to the philosopher himself.

At the same time, there is no blinking the fact that different experts find different things in the writings of the same philosopher. This is as true of the appreciative interpreter and grateful disciple as it is of the critical opponent. Nor can it be denied that such differences of reading and of interpretation on the part of other experts often leave the neophyte aghast before the whole maze of widely varying and even opposing interpretations. Who is right and whose interpretation shall he accept? When the doctors disagree among themselves, what is the poor student to do? If, finally, in desperation, he decides that all of the interpreters are probably wrong and that the only thing for him to do is to go back to the original writings of the philosopher himself and then make his own decision—uninfluenced (as if this were possible!) by the interpretation of any one else—the result is not that he has actually come to the meaning of the original philosopher himself, but rather that he has set up one more interpretation, which may differ to a greater or lesser degree from the interpretations already existing. It is clear that in this direction lies chaos, just the kind of chaos which Schiller has so graphically and inimitably described.[1]

It is strange that until now no way of escaping this difficulty has been seriously considered. It has not occurred to students of philosophy that one effective way of partially meeting the problem is to put these varying interpretations and critiques before the philosopher while he is still alive and to ask him to act at one and the same time as both defendant and judge. If the world's great living philosophers can be induced to coöperate in an enterprise whereby their own work can at least partially be saved from becoming merely "desiccated lecture-fodder," which on the one hand "provides innocuous sustenance for ruminant professors," and, on the other hand, gives an opportunity to such

[1] In his essay on "Must Philosophers Disagree?" in the volume by the same title (Macmillan, London, 1934), from which the above quotations were taken.

ruminants and their understudies to "speculate safely, endlessly, and fruitlessly, about what a philosopher may have meant, nay must have meant," (Schiller) they will have taken a long step toward making their intentions clearly comprehensible.

With this in mind *The Library of Living Philosophers* expects to publish at more or less regular intervals a volume on each of the greater among the world's living philosophers. In each case it will be the purpose of the editors of *The Library* to bring together in the volume the interpretations and criticisms of a wide range of that particular thinker's scholarly contemporaries, each of whom will be given a free hand to discuss the particular phase of the thinker's work which has been assigned to him. All contributed essays will finally be submitted to the philosopher with whose work and thought they are concerned, for his careful perusal and reply. And, although it would be expecting too much to imagine that the philosopher's reply will be able to stop all differences of interpretation and of critique, this should at least serve the purpose of stopping certain of the grosser and more general kinds of misinterpretations. If no further gain than this were to come from the present and projected volumes of this *Library*, it would still seem to be fully justified.

In carrying out this principal purpose of the *Library*, the editor announces that each volume will conform to the following pattern:

First, a series of expository and critical articles written by the leading exponents and opponents of the philosopher's thought;

Second, the reply to the critics and commentators by the philosopher himself;

Third, an intellectual autobiography of the thinker whenever this can be secured; in any case an authoritative and authorized biography; and

Fourth, a bibliography of the writings of the philosopher to provide a ready instrument to give access to his writings and thought.

Future volumes in this series will appear in as rapid succession as is feasible in view of the scholarly nature of this *Library*. The editor hopes to publish at least one new volume each year.

It is a real pleasure, finally, to make grateful acknowledgment for the financial assistance which this project has already received. Without such help the work on this *Library* could never have been undertaken. The first three volumes have been (and are being) made possible in part by funds granted by the Carnegie Corporation of New York. Additional financial assistance, especially for the first volume, came from the Alumni Foundation Fund of the College of Liberal Arts of Northwestern University. To these donors the editor desires to express his sincere gratitude. The Carnegie Corporation and the Northwestern University Alumni Foundation are not in any sense the authors, owners, publishers, or proprietors of this *Library* and they are therefore not to be understood as approving by virtue of their grants any of the statements made in this or in any succeeding volume.

PAUL ARTHUR SCHILPP
Editor

302 HARRIS HALL
NORTHWESTERN UNIVERSITY
EVANSTON, ILLINOIS

TABLE OF CONTENTS

PREFACE

WITH this volume on *The Philosophy of George Santayana* the series, of which this is Volume II, ceases to be a mere experiment and gives promise of becoming a tradition. The reception which the philosophical world accorded our first volume in *The Library of Living Philosophers* has justified the faith which some of us had in this project from its inception. No one, however, could have foretold the degree of coöperation which great men and eminent thinkers would be willing to give to an enterprise of this sort. Men like John Dewey, George Santayana, Bertrand Russell, G. E. Moore, and others of their philosophical stature, have already given unsparingly of their time, effort, energy, and good will in order to make the volumes of this *Library* the thorough and authoritative documents which they need to be if they are to fulfill the major purpose for which they are being called into existence. Looked at from this angle, the work on this undertaking has been a great satisfaction.

Permit me to be specific. I have never had the personal privilege of meeting Professor Santayana. When, therefore, I first wrote to him in the hope of securing his consent to and coöperation in a volume on *The Philosophy of George Santayana,* I must confess that I wrote with considerable trepidation and doubt, not to say fear. I shall never be able to describe the sense of elation which came to me on the reading of Mr. Santayana's first letter in reply to my original invitation and request. Not as if Mr. Santayana had seemed over-anxious to agree to my proposal; far from it! What he did write, however, was so kind, so considerate, so gracious, and so full of sympathetic understanding of the nature of my problem and of the meaning of this project, that all my trepidations very quickly vanished into thin air. Moreover, the correspondence which ensued upon that first letter of

December 16th, 1938, has more than fulfilled the unwritten promises contained in the spirit of that original reply.

The ultimate proof of all this the reader of this volume will be able to test for himself. For, the "*Apologia Pro Mente Sua*" herein contained, which offers us Mr. Santayana's reply to his commentators and critics, will be recognized by every student of philosophy to be a thorough-going, detailed, and exceedingly carefully prepared piece of philosophical writing; a piece of polemics which is far more than that. It is our Philosopher's sincere attempt to answer questions, to help students of his works over difficulties, and—in general—to make more precise and specific the statement of his position. As such Mr. Santayana's *Apologia* in itself would be quite sufficient reason for this volume. I am very certain, therefore, that in expressing to him here my sincere thanks and heart-felt editorial appreciation I am merely speaking as the mouthpiece of thousands of Santayana readers, students, and admirers.

At the same time, there is nothing in the present volume which would cause me to take back what I wrote at the close of my Preface to the Dewey volume concerning the meeting of philosophical minds.

Here, as there, however, I desire to express my gratitude to the contributors to this volume who, by their kind coöperation, by the incisiveness of their criticism, and by the careful preparation of their essays, gave Professor Santayana his opportunity to reply in such a happy vein and in a manner of such lasting philosophical importance. Although the brevity of the comments from the pen of Mr. C. A. Strong would hardly cause them, under ordinary circumstances, to be singled out here, it is only fair to say that we are particularly proud to have his two pages in this volume because they constitute, so far as is known, the last piece of philosophical writing in which Mr. Strong engaged before he passed away, at the age of 77, on January 23, 1940, at Fiesole, Italy. There are two others to whom the editor owes a special debt of obligation. One is Miss Shohig Terzian, of New York City, who, simply as an admirer of Santayana, undertook the arduous task of compiling the bibliography and who, not satisfied with her signal achievement of this task, also prepared the special index to the bibliography for the present volume. The other is Mr. Arturo Fallico, of Chicago, who used his artistic genius to furnish the pen-drawings of both Mr. Dewey and Mr. Santayana for the jackets of the Dewey and of the Santayana volumes. To both these persons I wish to express my sincere gratitude and appreciation for work well done.

The reader's attention is called to two points at which this second volume in our *Library* is even more complete than was Volume I. In the first place, due to the fortunate circumstance that Mr. Santayana composes his literary work with pen and ink (whereas Mr. Dewey does his composing directly at the typewriter) we are enabled to present to the reader a facsimile reproduction of the first page of Mr. Santayana's *Apologia* in his own handwriting. This facsimile page will be found facing the first printed page of Mr. Santayana's "Rejoinder."

The second novel addition consists of a Special Index to the bibliography of Mr. Santayana's writings, aimed to enable the student of Santayana to locate any specific item among Santayana's writings immediately without having to search through the voluminous and chronologically arranged bibliography itself. In the case of our first volume on *The Philosophy of John Dewey* the necessity for such an index was obviated by the publication of a separate volume on *A Bibliography of John Dewey: 1882-1939*, published in 1939 by the Columbia University Press and edited by Dr. Milton Halsey Thomas, who provided his volume with a detailed index.

The publication of a volume like this in a time like the present seems to be particularly significant. It proves that the realm of ideas and of scholarship knows no national boundaries and is above the noise of strife and warfare. Three of the contributors to this volume wrote and sent their essays from Italy, another from Switzerland. All European contributions had to brave British censorship and cross international boundaries under "total-war" conditions. This has, at times, been none too easy on the editor, especially when one of the contributed essays at one time during the process was lost in trans-Atlantic transit for over three months. Finally, however, the MS. did turn up and everyone was happy again. Perhaps one should be even more elated over the fact that, though nations may fall and maps may be re-drawn, though hunger, epidemic, and war stalk through nation after nation, the process of intellectual understanding and of scholarly coöperation not only can but does go on with as little interruption as war-mad officials of the various warring nations will permit. May the time never come when true scholarship and intellectual endeavor themselves fall prey to the inhuman cries of hyper-nationalistic hysteria and murderous intent!

P. A. S.

Department of Philosophy
Northwestern University
Evanston, Illinois
October 1940

ACKNOWLEDGMENTS

GRATEFUL ACKNOWLEDGMENT is hereby made to the publishers of all of Professor Santayana's books as well as to the editors and publishers of philosophical and literary journals and magazines for their kind permission to quote from the works of Professor Santayana as well as for their courtesy in not insisting upon a detailed enumeration of the books and articles quoted. Such grateful acknowledgment is further made to the publishers of other works quoted in the following pages, who have also been kind enough not to require the specific enumeration of the works thus quoted. In a few instances special permission to quote is given in the footnotes.

George Santayana

A GENERAL CONFESSION

A GENERAL CONFESSION*

I

HOW came a child born in Spain of Spanish parents to be educated in Boston and to write in the English language? The case of my family was unusual. We were not emigrants; none of us ever changed his country, his class, or his religion. But special circumstances had given us hereditary points of attachment in opposite quarters, moral and geographical; and now that we are almost extinct—I mean those of us who had these mixed associations—I may say that we proved remarkably staunch in our complex allegiances, combining them as well as logic allowed, without at heart ever disowning anything. My philosophy in particular may be regarded as a synthesis of these various traditions, or as an attempt to view them from a level from which their several deliverances may be justly understood. I do not assert that such was actually the origin of my system; in any case its truth would be another question. I propose simply to describe as best I can the influences under which I have lived, and leave it for the reader, if he cares, to consider how far my philosophy may be an expression of them.

In the first place, we must go much farther afield than Boston or Spain, into the tropics, almost to the antipodes. Both my father and my mother's father were officials in the Spanish civil service in the Philippine Islands. This was in the 1840's and

* Part I of *A General Confession* appeared originally as "Brief History of My Opinions," in *Contemporary American Philosophy*, edited by G. P. Adams and William P. Montague (1930), II, 237-257, and is reprinted by permission of The Macmillan Company, New York. Part II is an excerpt from Mr. Santayana's Preface to Volume I of the Triton Edition of *The Works of George Santayana* (1936), and is reprinted by permission of Charles Scribner's Sons, New York. Part III is the Preface to Volume VII of the Triton Edition (1936), also reprinted by permission of Charles Scribner's Sons.

Whatever minor changes from the original articles appear in the above text were made by Mr. Santayana himself. The new title for this newly combined autobiography was also furnished by Mr. Santayana.—*Ed.*

1850's, long before my birth; for my parents were not married until later in life, in Spain, when my mother was a widow. But the tradition of the many years which each of them separately had spent in the East was always alive in our household. Those had been, for both, their more romantic and prosperous days. My father had studied the country and the natives, and had written a little book about the Island of Mindanao; he had been three times round the world in the sailing-ships of the period, and had incidentally visited England and the United States, and been immensely impressed by the energy and order prevalent in those nations. His respect for material greatness was profound, yet not unmixed with a secret irony or even repulsion. He had a seasoned and incredulous mind, trained to see other sorts of excellence also: in his boyhood he had worked in the studio of a professional painter of the school of Goya, and had translated the tragedies of Seneca into Spanish verse. His transmarine experiences, therefore, did not rattle, as so often happens, in an empty head. The sea itself, in those days, was still vast and blue, and the lands beyond it full of lessons and wonders. From childhood I have lived in the imaginative presence of interminable ocean spaces, coconut islands, blameless Malays, and immense continents swarming with Chinamen, polished and industrious, obscene and philosophical. It was habitual with me to think of scenes and customs pleasanter than those about me. My own travels have never carried me far from the frontiers of Christendom or of respectability, and chiefly back and forth across the North Atlantic—thirty-eight fussy voyages; but in mind I have always seen these things on an ironical background enormously empty, or breaking out in spots, like Polynesia, into nests of innocent particoloured humanity.

My mother's figure belonged to the same broad and somewhat exotic landscape; she had spent her youth in the same places; but the moral note resounding in her was somewhat different. Her father, José Borrás, of Reus in Catalonia, had been a disciple of Rousseau, an enthusiast and a wanderer: he taught her to revere pure reason and republican virtue and to abhor the vices of a corrupt world. But her own temper was cool and stoical, rather than ardent, and her disdain of corruption had in it a touch of elegance. At Manila, during the time of her first marriage, she had been rather the grand lady, in a style half Creole, half early Victorian. Virtue, beside those tropical seas, might stoop to be indolent. She had given a silver dollar every morning to her native major-domo, with which to provide for the family and the twelve servants, and keep the change for his wages. Meantime she bathed, arranged the flowers, received visits, and did embroidery. It had been a spacious life; and in our narrower circumstances in later years the sense of it never forsook her.

Her first husband, an American merchant established in Manila, had been the ninth child of Nathaniel Russell Sturgis, of Boston (1779-1856). In Boston, accordingly, her three Sturgis children had numerous relations and a little property, and there she had promised their father to bring them up in case of his death. When this occurred, in 1857, she therefore established herself in Boston; and this fact, by a sort of pre-natal or pre-established destiny, was the cause of my connection with the Sturgis family, with Boston, and with America.

It was in Madrid in 1862, where my mother had gone on a visit intended to be temporary, that my father and she were married. He had been an old friend of hers and of her first husband's, and was well aware of her settled plan to educate her children in America, and recognized the propriety of that arrangement. Various projects and combinations were mooted: but the matter eventually ended in a separation, friendly, if not altogether pleasant to either party. My mother returned with her Sturgis children to live in the United States and my father and I remained in Spain. Soon, however, this compromise proved unsatisfactory. The education and prospects which my father, in his modest retirement, could offer me in Spain were far from brilliant; and in 1872 he decided to take me to Boston, where, after remaining for one cold winter, he left me in my mother's care and went back to Spain.

I was then in my ninth year, having been born on December 16, 1863, and I did not know one word of English. Nor was I likely to learn the language at home, where the family always continued to speak a Spanish more or less pure. But by a happy thought I was sent during my first winter in Boston to a Kindergarten, among much younger children, where there were no books, so that I picked up English by ear before knowing how it was written: a circumstance to which I probably owe speaking the language without a marked foreign accent. The Brimmer School, the Boston Latin School, and Harvard College then followed in order: but apart from the taste for English poetry which I first imbibed from our excellent English master, Mr. Byron Groce, the most decisive influences over my mind in boyhood continued to come from my family, where, with my grown-up brother and sisters, I was the only child. I played no games, but sat at home all the afternoon and evening reading or drawing; especially devouring anything I could find that regarded religion, architecture, or geography.

In the summer of 1883, after my Freshman year, I returned for the first time to Spain to see my father. Then, and during many subsequent holidays which I spent in his company, we naturally discussed the various careers that might be open to me. We should both of us have liked the Spanish army or diplomatic service: but for the first I was already too old, and our means and our social relations hardly sufficed for the second. Moreover, by that time I felt like a foreigner in Spain, more acutely so than in America, although for more trivial reasons: my Yankee manners seemed outlandish there, and I could not do myself justice in the language. Nor was I inclined to overcome this handicap, as perhaps I might have done with a little effort: nothing in Spanish life or literature at that time particularly attracted me. English had become my only possible instrument, and I deliberately put away everything that might confuse me in that medium. English, and the whole Anglo-Saxon tradition in literature and philosophy, have always been a medium to me rather than a source. My natural affinities were elsewhere. Moreover, scholarship and learning of any sort seemed to me a means, not an end. I always hated to be a professor. Latin and Greek, French, Italian, and German, although I can read them, were languages which I never learned well. It seemed an accident to me if the matters which interested me came clothed in the rhetoric of one or another of these nations: I was not without a certain temperamental rhetoric of my own in which to recast what I adopted. Thus in renouncing everything else for the sake of English letters I might be said to have been guilty, quite unintentionally, of a little stratagem, as if I had set out to say plausibly in English as many un-English things as possible.

This brings me to religion, which is the head and front of everything. Like my parents, I have always set myself down officially as a Catholic: but this is a matter of sympathy and traditional allegiance, not of philosophy. In my adolescence, religion on its doctrinal and emotional side occupied me much more than it does now. I was more unhappy and unsettled; but I have never had any unquestioning faith in any dogma, and have never been what is called a practising Catholic. Indeed, it would hardly have been possible. My mother, like her father before her, was a Deist: she was sure there was a God, for who else could have made the world? But God was too great to take special thought for man: sacrifices, prayers, churches, and tales of immortality were invented by rascally priests in order to dominate the foolish. My father, except for the Deism, was emphatically of the same opinion. Thus, although I learned my prayers and catechism by rote, as was then inevitable in Spain, I knew that my parents regarded all religion as a work of human imagination: and I agreed, and still agree, with them there. But this carried an implication in their minds against which every instinct in me rebelled, namely that the works of human imagination are bad. No, said I to myself even as a boy: they are good, they alone are good; and the rest—the whole real world—is ashes in the mouth. My sympathies were entirely with those other members of my family who were devout believers. I loved the Christian epic, and all those doctrines and observances which bring it down into daily life: I thought how glorious it would have been to be a Dominican frair, preaching that epic eloquently, and solving afresh all the knottiest and sublimest mysteries of theology. I was delighted with anything, like Mallock's *Is Life Worth Living?*, which seemed to rebuke the fatuity of that age. For my own part, I was quite sure that life was not worth living; for if religion was false everything was worthless, and almost everything, if religion was true. In this youthful pessimism I was hardly more foolish than so many amateur mediævalists and religious æsthetes of my generation. I saw the same alternative between Catholicism and complete disillusion: but I was never afraid of disillusion, and I have chosen it.

Since those early years my feelings on this subject have become less strident. Does not modern philosophy teach that our idea of the so-called real world is also a work of imagination? A religion—for there are other religions than the Christian—simply offers a system of faith different from the vulgar one, or extending beyond it. The question is which imaginative system you will trust. My matured conclusion has been that no system is to be trusted, not even that of science in any literal or pictorial sense; but all systems may be used and, up to a certain point, trusted as symbols. Science expresses in human terms our dynamic relation to surrounding reality. Philosophies and religions, where they do not misrepresent these same dynamic relations and do not contradict science, express destiny in moral dimensions, in obviously mythical and poetical images: but how else should these moral truths be expressed at all in a traditional or popular fashion? Religions are the great fairy-tales of the conscience.

When I began the formal study of philosophy as an undergraduate at Harvard, I was already alive to the fundamental questions, and even had a certain dialectical nimbleness, due to familiarity with the fine points of theology: the arguments for and against free will and the proofs of the existence of God were warm and clear in my mind. I accordingly heard James and Royce with more wonder than serious agreement: my scholastic logic would have wished to reduce James at once to a materialist and Royce to a solipsist, and it seemed strangely irrational in them to resist such simplification. I had heard many Unitarian sermons (being taken to hear them lest I should become too Catholic), and had been interested in them so far as they were rationalistic and informative, or even amusingly irreligious, as I often thought them to be: but neither in those discourses nor in Harvard philosophy was it easy for me to understand the Protestant combination of earnestness with waywardness. I was used to see water flowing from fountains, architectural and above ground: it puzzled me to see it drawn painfully in bucketfuls from the subjective well, muddied, and half spilt over.

There was one lesson, however, which I was readier to learn, not only at Harvard from Professor Palmer and afterwards at Berlin from Paulsen, but from the general temper of that age well represented for me by the *Revue Des Deux Mondes* (which I habitually read from cover to cover) and by the works of Taine and of Matthew Arnold—I refer to the historical spirit of the nineteenth century, and to that splendid panorama of nations and religions, literatures and arts, which it unrolled before the imagination. These picturesque vistas into the past came to fill in circumstantially that geographical and moral vastness to which my imagination was already accustomed. Professor Palmer was especially skilful in bending the mind to a suave and sympathetic participation in the views of all philosophers in turn: were they not all great men, and must not the aspects of things which seemed persuasive to them be really persuasive? Yet even this form of romanticism, amiable as it is, could not altogether put to sleep my scholastic dogmatism. The historian of philosophy may be as sympathetic and as self-effacing as he likes: the philosopher in him must still ask whether any of those successive views were true, or whether the later ones were necessarily truer than the earlier: he cannot, unless he is a shameless sophist, rest content with a truth *pro tem.* In reality the sympathetic reconstruction of history is a literary art, and it depends for its plausibility as well as for its materials on a conventional belief in the natural world. Without this belief no history and no science would be anything but a poetic fiction, like a classification of the angelic choirs. The necessity of naturalism as a foundation for all further serious opinions was clear to me from the beginning. Naturalism might indeed be criticized—and I was myself intellectually and emotionally predisposed to criticize it, and to oscillate between supernaturalism and solipsism—but if naturalism was condemned, supernaturalism itself could have no point of application in the world of fact; and the whole edifice of human knowledge would crumble, since no perception would then be a report and no judgment would have a transcendent object. Hence historical reconstruction seemed to me more honestly and solidly practised by Taine, who was a professed naturalist, than by Hegel and his school, whose naturalism, though presupposed at every stage, was disguised and distorted by a dialectic imposed on it by the historian and useful at best only in simplifying his dramatic perspectives and lending them a false absoluteness and moralistic veneer.

The influence of Royce over me, though less important in the end than that of James, was at first much more active. Royce was the better dialectician, and traversed subjects in which I was naturally more interested. The point that particularly exercised me was Royce's Theodicy or justification for the existence of evil. It would be hard to exaggerate the ire which his arguments on this subject aroused in my youthful breast. Why that emotion? Romantic sentiment that could find happiness only in tears and virtue only in heroic agonies was something familiar to me and not unsympathetic: a poetic play of mine, called *Lucifer*, conceived in those days, is a clear proof of it. I knew Leopardi and Musset largely by heart; Schopenhauer was soon to become, for a brief period, one of my favourite authors. I carried Lucretius in my pocket: and although the spirit of the poet in that case was not romantic, the picture of human existence which he drew glorified the same vanity. Spinoza, too, whom I was reading under Royce himself, filled me with joy and enthusiasm: I gathered at once from him a doctrine which has remained axiomatic with me ever since, namely that good and evil are relative to the natures of animals, irreversible in that relation, but indifferent to the march of cosmic events, since the force of the universe infinitely exceeds the force of any one of its parts. Had I found, then, in Royce only a romantic view of life, or only pessimism, or only stoical courage and pantheistic piety, I should have taken no offence, but readily recognized the poetic truth or the moral legitimacy of those positions. Conformity with fate, as I afterwards came to see, belongs to post-rational morality, which is a normal though optional development of human sentiment: Spinoza's "intellectual love of God" was a shining instance of it.

But in Royce these attitudes, in themselves so honest and noble, seemed to be somehow embroiled and rendered sophistical: nor was he alone in this, for the same moral equivocation seemed to pervade Hegel, Browning, and Nietzsche. That which repelled me in all these men was the survival of a sort of forced optimism and pulpit unction, by which a cruel and nasty world, painted by them in the most lurid colours, was nevertheless set up as the model and standard of what ought to be. The duty of an honest moralist would have been rather to distinguish, in this bad or mixed reality, the part, however small, that could be loved and chosen from the remainder, however large, which was to be rejected and renounced. Certainly the universe was in flux and dynamically single: but this fatal flux could very well take care of itself; and it was not so fluid that no islands of a relative permanence and beauty might not be formed in it. Ascetic conformity was itself one of these islands: a scarcely inhabitable peak from which almost all human passions and activities were excluded. And the Greeks, whose deliberate ethics was rational, never denied the vague early Gods and the environing chaos, which perhaps would return in the end: but meantime they built their cities bravely on the hill-tops, as we all carry on pleasantly our temporal affairs, although we know that to-morrow we die. Life itself exists only by a modicum of organization, achieved and transmitted through a world of change: the momentum of such organization first creates a difference between good and evil, or gives them a meaning at all. Thus the core of life is always hereditary, steadfast, and classical; the margin of barbarism and blind adventure round it may be as wide as you will, and in some wild hearts the love of this fluid margin may be keen, as might be any other loose passion. But to *preach* barbarism as the only good, in ignorance or hatred of the possible perfection of every natural thing, was a scandal: a belated Calvinism that remained fanatical after ceasing to be Christian. And there was a further circumstance which made this attitude particularly odious to me. This romantic love of evil was not thoroughgoing: wilfulness and disorder were to reign only in spiritual matters; in government and industry, even in natural science, all was to be order and mechanical progress. Thus the absence of a positive religion and of a legislation, like that of the ancients, intended to be rational and final, was very far from liberating the spirit for higher flights: on the contrary, it opened the door to the pervasive tyranny of the world over the soul. And no wonder: a soul rebellious to its moral heritage is too weak to reach any firm definition of its inner life. It will feel lost and empty unless it summons the random labours of the contemporary world to fill and to enslave it. It must let mechanical and civic achievements reconcile it to its own moral confusion and triviality.

It was in this state of mind that I went to Germany to continue the study of philosophy—interested in all religious or metaphysical systems, but sceptical about them and scornful of any romantic worship or idealization of the real world. The life of a wandering student, like those of the Middle Ages, had an immense natural attraction for me—so great, that I have never willingly led any other. When I had to choose a profession, the prospect of a quiet academic existence seemed the least of evils. I was fond of reading and observation, and I liked young men; but I have never been a diligent student either of science or art, nor at all ambitious to be learned. I have been willing to let cosmological problems and technical questions solve themselves as they would or as the authorities agreed for the moment that they should be solved. My pleasure was rather in expression, in reflection, in irony: my spirit was content to intervene, in whatever world it might seem to find itself, in order to disentangle the intimate moral and intellectual echoes audible to it in that world. My naturalism or materialism is no academic opinion: it is not a survival of the alleged materialism of the nineteenth century, when all the professors of philosophy were idealists: it is an everyday conviction which came to me, as it came to my father, from experience and observation of the world at large, and especially of my own feelings and passions. It seems to me that those who are not materialists cannot be good observers of themselves: they may hear themselves thinking, but they cannot have watched themselves acting and feeling; for feeling and action are evidently accidents of matter. If a Democritus or Lucretius or Spinoza or Darwin works within the lines of nature, and clarifies some part of that familiar object, that fact is the ground of my attachment to them: they have the savour of truth; but what the savour of truth is, I know very well without their help. Consequently there is no opposition in my mind between materialism and a Platonic or even Indian discipline of the spirit. The recognition of the material world and of the conditions of existence in it merely enlightens the spirit concerning the source of its troubles and the means to its happiness or deliverance: and it was happiness or deliverance, the supervening supreme expression of human will and imagination, that alone really concerned me. This alone was genuine philosophy: this alone was the life of reason.

Had the life of reason ever been cultivated in the world by people with a sane imagination? Yes, once, by the Greeks. Of the Greeks, however, I knew very little: the philosophical and political departments at Harvard had not yet discovered Plato and Aristotle. It was with the greater pleasure that I heard Paulsen in Berlin expounding Greek ethics with a sweet reasonableness altogether worthy of the subject: here at last was a vindication of order and beauty in the institutions of men and in their ideas. Here, through the pleasant medium of transparent myths or of summary scientific images, like the water of Thales, nature was essentially understood and honestly described; and here, for that very reason, the free mind could disentangle its true good, and could express it in art, in manners, and even in the most refined or the most austere spiritual discipline. Yet, although I knew henceforth that in the Greeks I should find the natural support and point of attachment for my own philosophy, I was not then collected or mature enough to pursue the matter; not until ten years later, in 1896-1897, did I take the opportunity of a year's leave of absence to go to England and begin a systematic reading of Plato and Aristotle under Dr. Henry Jackson of Trinity College, Cambridge. I am not conscious of any change of opinion supervening, nor of any having occurred earlier; but by that study and change of scene my mind was greatly enriched; and the composition of *The Life of Reason* was the consequence.

This book was intended to be a summary history of the human

imagination, expressly distinguishing those phases of it which showed what Herbert Spencer called an adjustment of inner to outer relations; in other words, an adaptation of fancy and habit to material facts and opportunities. On the one hand, then, my subject being the imagination, I was never called on to step beyond the subjective sphere. I set out to describe, not nature or God, but the ideas of God or nature bred in the human mind. On the other hand, I was not concerned with these ideas for their own sake, as in a work of pure poetry or erudition, but I meant to consider them in their natural genesis and significance; for I assumed throughout that the whole life of reason was generated and controlled by the animal life of man in the bosom of nature. Human ideas had, accordingly, a symptomatic, expressive, and symbolic value: they were the inner notes sounded by man's passions and by his arts: and they became rational partly by their vital and inward harmony—for reason is a harmony of the passions—and partly by their adjustment to external facts and possibilities—for reason is a harmony of the inner life with truth and with fate. I was accordingly concerned to discover what wisdom is possible to an animal whose mind, from beginning to end, is poetical: and I found that this could not lie in discarding poetry in favour of a science supposed to be clairvoyant and literally true. Wisdom lay rather in taking everything good-humouredly, with a grain of salt. In science there was an element of poetry, pervasive, inevitable, and variable: it was strictly scientific and true only in so far as it involved a close and prosperous adjustment to the surrounding world, at first by its origin in observation and at last by its application in action. Science was the mental accompaniment of art.

Here was a sort of pragmatism: the same which I have again expressed, I hope more clearly, in one of the *Dialogues in Limbo* entitled "Normal Madness." The human mind is a faculty of dreaming awake, and its dreams are kept relevant to its environment and to its fate only by the external control exercised over them by Punishment, when the accompanying conduct brings ruin, or by Agreement, when it brings prosperity. In the latter case it is possible to establish correspondences between one part of a dream and another, or between the dreams of separate minds, and so create the world of literature, or the life of reason. I am not sure whether this notion, that thought is a controlled and consistent madness, appears among the thirteen pragmatisms which have been distinguished, but I have reason to think that I came to it under the influence of William James; nevertheless, when his book on *Pragmatism* appeared, about the same time as my *Life of Reason*, it gave me a rude shock. I could not stomach that way of speaking about truth; and the continual substitution of human psychology—normal madness, in my view—for the universe, in which man is but one distracted and befuddled animal, seemed to me a confused remnant of idealism, and not serious.

The William James who had been my master was not this William James of the later years, whose pragmatism and pure empiricism and romantic metaphysics have made such a stir in the world. It was rather the puzzled but brilliant doctor, impatient of metaphysics, whom I had known in my undergraduate days, one of whose maxims was that to study the abnormal was the best way of understanding the normal; or it was the genial author of *The Principles of Psychology*, chapters of which he read from the manuscript and discussed with a small class of us in 1889. Even then what I learned from him was perhaps chiefly things which explicitly he never taught, but which I imbibed from the spirit and background of his teaching. Chief of these, I should say, was a sense for the immediate: for the unadulterated, unexplained, instant fact of experience. Actual experience, for William James, however varied or rich its assault might be, was always and altogether of the nature of a sensation: it possessed a vital, leaping, globular unity which made the only fact, the flying fact, of our being. Whatever continuities of quality might be traced in it, its existence was always momentary and self-warranted. A man's life or soul borrowed its reality and imputed wholeness from the intrinsic actuality of its successive parts; existence was a perpetual rebirth, a travelling light to which the past was lost and the future uncertain. The element of indetermination which James felt so strongly in this flood of existence was precisely the pulse of fresh unpredictable sensation, summoning attention hither and thither to unexpected facts. Apprehension in him being impressionistic—that was the age of impressionism in painting too—and marvellously free from intellectual assumptions or presumptions, he felt intensely the fact of contingency, or the contingency of fact. This seemed to me not merely a peculiarity of temperament in him, but a profound insight into existence, in its inmost irrational essence. Existence, I learned to see, is intrinsically dispersed, seated in its distributed moments, and arbitrary not only as a whole, but in the character and place of each of its parts. Change the bits, and you change the mosaic: nor can we count or limit the elements, as in a little closed kaleidoscope, which may be shaken together into the next picture. Many of them, such as pleasure and pain, or the total picture itself, cannot possibly have pre-existed.

But, said I to myself, were these novelties for that reason unconditioned? Was not sensation, by continually surprising us, a continual warning to us of fatal conjunctions occurring ouside? And would not the same conjunctions, but for memory and habit, always produce the same surprises? Experience of indetermination was no proof of indeterminism; and when James proceeded to turn immediate experience into ultimate physics, his thought seemed to me to lose itself in words or in confused superstitions. Free will, a deep moral power contrary to a romantic indetermination in being, he endeavoured to pack into the bias of attention—the most temperamental of accidents. He insisted passionately on the efficacy of consciousness, and invoked Darwinian arguments for its utility—arguments which assumed that consciousness was a material engine absorbing and transmitting energy: so that it was no wonder that presently he doubted whether consciousness existed at all. He suggested a new physics or metaphysics in which the essences given in immediate experience should be deployed and hypostatized into the constituents of nature: but this pictorial cosmology had the disadvantage of abolishing the human imagination, with all the pathos and poetry of its animal status. James thus renounced that gift for literary psychology, that romantic insight, in which alone he excelled; and indeed his followers are without it. I pride myself on remaining a disciple of his earlier unsophisticated self, when he was an agnostic about the universe, but in his diagnosis of the heart an impulsive poet: a master in the art of recording or divining the lyric quality of experience as it actually came to him or to me.

Lyric experience and literary psychology, as I have learned to conceive them, are chapters in the life of one race of animals, in one corner of the natural world. But before relegating them to that modest station (which takes nothing away from their spiritual prerogatives) I was compelled to face the terrible problem which arises when, as in modern philosophy, literary psychology and lyric experience are made the fulcrum or the stuff of the universe. Has this experience any external conditions? If it has, are they knowable? And if it has not, on what principle are its qualities generated or its episodes distributed? Nay, how can literary psychology or universal experience have any seat save the present fancy of the psychologist or the historian? Although James had been bothered and confused by these questions, and Royce had enthroned his philosophy upon them, neither of these my principal teachers seemed to have come to clearness on the subject: it was only afterwards, when I read Fichte and Schopenhauer, that I began to see my way to a solution. We must oscillate between a radical transcendentalism, frankly reduced to a solipsism of the living moment, and a materialism posited as a presupposition of conventional sanity. There was no contradiction in joining together a scepticism which was not a dogmatic negation of anything and an animal faith which avowedly was a mere assumption in action and description. Yet such oscillation, if it was to be justified and rendered coherent, still demanded some understanding of two further points: what, starting from immediate experience, was the *causa cognoscendi* of the natural world; and what, starting from the natural world, was the *causa fiendi* of immediate experience?

On this second point (in spite of the speculations of my friend Strong) I have not seen much new light. I am constrained merely to register as a brute fact the emergence of consciousness in animal bodies. A psyche, or nucleus of hereditary organization, gathers and governs these bodies, and at the same time breeds within them a dreaming, suffering, and watching mind. Such investigations as those of Fraser and of Freud have shown how rich and how mad a thing the mind is fundamentally, how pervasively it plays about animal life, and how remote its first and deepest intuitions are from any understanding of their true occasions. An interesting and consistent complement to these discoveries is furnished by behaviourism, which I heartily accept on its positive biological side: the hereditary life of the body, modified by accident or training, forms a closed cycle of habits and actions. Of this the mind is a concomitant spiritual expression, invisible, imponderable, and epiphenomenal, or, as I prefer to say, hypostatic: for in it the moving unities and tensions of animal life are synthesized on quite another plane of being, into actual intuitions and feelings. This spiritual fertility in living bodies is the most natural of things. It is unintelligible only as all existence, change, or genesis is unintelligible; but it might be better understood, that is, better assimilated to other natural miracles, if we understood better the life of matter everywhere, and that of its different aggregates.

On the other point raised by my naturalism, namely on the grounds of faith in the natural world, I have reached more positive conclusions. Criticism, I think, must first be invited to do its worst: nothing is more dangerous here than timidity or convention. A pure and radical transcendentalism will disclaim all knowledge of fact. Nature, history, the self become ghostly presences, mere notions of such things; and the being of these images becomes purely internal to them; they exist in no environing space or time; they possess no substance or hidden parts, but are all surface, all appearance. Such a being, or quality of being, I call an essence; and to the consideration of essences, composing of themselves an eternal and infinite realm, I have lately devoted much attention. To that sphere I transpose the familiar pictures painted by the senses, or by traditional science and religion. Taken as essences, all ideas are compatible and supplementary to one another, like the various arts of expression; it is possible to perceive, up to a certain point, the symbolic burden of each of them, and to profit by the spiritual criticism of experience which it may embody. In particular, I recognize this spiritual truth in the Neo-Platonic and Indian systems, without admitting their fabulous side: after all, it is an old maxim with me that many ideas may be convergent as poetry which would be divergent as dogmas. This applies, in quite another quarter, to that revolution in physics which is now loudly announced, sometimes as the bankruptcy of science, sometimes as the breakdown of materialism. This revolution becomes, in my view, simply a change in notation. Matter may be called gravity or an electric charge or a tension in an ether; mathematics may readjust its equations to more accurate observations; any fresh description of nature which may result will still be a product of human wit, like the Ptolemaic and the Newtonian systems, and nothing but an intellectual symbol for man's contacts with matter, in so far as they have gone or as he has become distinctly sensitive to them. The real matter, within him and without, will meantime continue to rejoice in its ancient ways, or to adopt new ones, and incidentally to create these successive notions of it in his head.

When all the data of immediate experience and all the constructions of thought have thus been purified and reduced to what they are intrinsically, that is, to eternal essences, by a sort of counterblast the sense of existence, of action, of ambushed reality everywhere about us, becomes all the clearer and more imperious. This assurance of the not-given is involved in action, in expectation, in fear, hope, or want: I call it animal faith. The object of this faith is the substantial energetic thing encountered in action, whatever this thing may be in itself; by moving, devouring, or transforming this thing I assure myself of its exisence; and at the same time my respect for it becomes enlightened and proportionate to its definite powers. But throughout, for the description of it in fancy, I have only the essences which my senses or thought may evoke in its presence; these are my inevitable signs and names for that object. Thus the whole sensuous and intellectual furniture of the mind becomes a store whence I may fetch terms for the description of nature, and may compose the silly home-poetry in which I talk to myself about everything. All is a tale told, if not by an idiot, at least by a dreamer; but it is far from signifying nothing. Sensations are rapid dreams: perceptions are dreams sustained and developed at will; sciences are dreams abstracted, controlled, measured, and rendered scrupulously proportional to their occasions. Knowledge accordingly always remains a part of imagination in its terms and in its seat; yet by virtue of its origin and intent it becomes a memorial and a guide to the fortunes of man in nature.

In the foregoing I have said nothing about my sentiments concerning æsthetics or the fine arts; yet I have devoted two volumes to those subjects, and I believe that to some people my whole philosophy seems to be little but rhetoric or prose poetry. I must frankly confess that I have written some verses; and at one time I had thoughts of becoming an architect or even a painter. The decorative and poetic aspects of art and nature have always fascinated me and held my attention above everything else. But in philosophy I recognize no separable thing called æsthetics; and what has gone by the name of the philosophy of art, like the so-called philosophy of history, seems to me sheer verbiage. There is in art nothing but manual knack and professional tradition on the practical side, and on the contemplative side pure intuition of essence, with the inevitable intellectual or luxurious pleasure which pure intuition involves. I can draw no distinction—save for academic programmes—between moral and æsthetic values: beauty, being a good, is a moral good; and the practice and enjoyment of art, like all practice and all enjoyment, fall within the sphere of morals—at least if by morals we understand moral economy and not moral superstition. On the other hand, the good, when actually realized and not merely pursued from afar, is a joy in the immediate; it is possessed with wonder and is in that sense æsthetic. Such pure joy when blind is called pleasure, when centred in some sensible image is called beauty, and when diffused over the thought of ulterior propitious things is called happiness, love, or religious rapture. But where all is manifest, as it is in intuition, classifications are pedantic. Harmony, which might be called an æsthetic principle, is also the principle of health, of justice, and of happiness. Every impulse, not the æsthetic mood alone, is innocent and irresponsible in its origin and precious in its own eyes; but every impulse or indulgence, including the æsthetic, is evil in its effect, when it renders harmony impossible in the general tenor of life, or produces in the soul division and ruin. There is no lack of folly in the arts; they are full of inertia and affectation and of what must seem ugliness to a cultivated taste; yet there is no need of bringing the catapult of criticism against it: indifference is enough. A society will breed the art which it is capable of, and which it deserves; but even in its own eyes this art will hardly be important or beautiful unless it engages deeply the resources of the soul. The arts may die of triviality, as they were born of enthusiasm. On the other hand, there will always be beauty, or a transport akin to the sense of beauty, in any high contemplative moment. And it is only in contemplative moments that life is truly vital, when routine gives place to intuition, and experience is synthesized and brought before the spirit in its sweep and truth. The intention of my philosophy has certainly been to attain, if possible, such wide intuitions, and to celebrate the emotions with which they fill the mind. If this object be æsthetic and merely poetical, well and good: but it is a poetry or æstheticism which shines by disillusion and is simply intent on the unvarnished truth.

II

The liberal age in which I was born and the liberal circles in which I was educated flowed contentedly towards intellectual dissolution and anarchy. No atmosphere could have been more unfavourable to that solidity and singleness of conviction to which by nature I was addressed. I suffered from a slack education, conflicting traditions, deadening social pressure, academic lumber, and partisan heat about false problems. The pure philosophy to which, in spirit, I was wedded from the beginning, the orthodox human philosophy in which I ought to have been brought up, has never had time to break through and show all its native force, pathos, and simplicity. I ought to have begun where I have ended.

Would it be possible to indicate, in a page or two, what I conceive orthodox human philosophy to be? Perhaps: because the thing is not unknown. The ancients came innocently upon it in various fields. Yet not even Aristotle, much less the moderns, ever conceived it in its entirety, with a just balance of its parts. I seem to recognise three orthodox schools of philosophy, each humanly right in its own sphere, but wrong in ignoring or denying the equal human rightness of the other two.

The Indians are orthodox in transcendental reflection. They take systematically the point of view of the spirit. For there is an invisible and inevitable moral witness to everything, not a physical or psychological self, but a higher centre of observation to which this world, or any world, or any God, is an imposed and questionable accident. Being morally inspired, being the voice of a living soul, this spirit has dramatic relations with the world which it encounters. The encounter may occasionally turn into a passionate embrace in which the spirit and all things seem merged in utterable unity. But that is a dramatic episode like any other: the tragic spirit revives and recovers its solitude. It would not be an actual spirit at all if it were not a personal moral being subject to fortune and needing to be saved. Spiritual philosophy would therefore not be orthodox if it were not ascetic and detached from the world.

The Greeks before Socrates reached orthodoxy in natural philosophy, which was re-established later in Spinoza and in modern science. Natural philosophers quarrel among themselves just because they are engaged in a common task with the issue undetermined. Yet they are all conspiring to trace and conceive the structure and history of this natural world in which everyone finds himself living.

The Greeks after Socrates founded orthodoxy in morals. I have endeavoured to retrace this theme in *The Life of Reason* and in my entire criticism of literature and religion. The principles of orthodoxy here were most clearly laid down by Plato in the *Philebus* and in the First Book of the *Republic;* but unfortunately, contrary to the modesty of Socrates himself, these principles were turned instinctively into a new mythology, in the effort to lend power and cosmic ascendency to the good: a good which is *good* only because, at each point, life and aspiration are spontaneously directed upon it. Ethics, as Aristotle said, is a part of politics, the foundation of this art being human nature, and its criterion harmony in living. But how should harmony be achieved in living if the inward spirit is distracted and the outer conditions of existence are unknown? Soundness in natural and in spiritual philosophy therefore seems requisite to soundness in politics.

That is all my message: that morality and religion are expressions of human nature; that human nature is a biological growth; and finally that spirit, fascinated and tortured, is involved in the process, and asks to be saved. What is salvation? Some organic harmony in forms and movements is requisite for life; but physical life is blind and groping and runs up continually against hostile forces, disease and death. It is therefore in the interests of life to become more intelligent and to establish a harmony also with the environment and the future. But life enlightened is spirit: the voice of life, and therefore aspiring to all the perfections to which life aspires, and loving all the beauties that life loves; yet at the same time spirit is the voice of truth and of destiny, bidding life renounce beauty and perfection and life itself, whenever and wherever these are impossible.

III

In *Winds of Doctrine* and my subsequent books, a reader of my earlier writings may notice a certain change of climate. There were natural causes for this change. I was weathering the age of fifty. My nearer relations were dead or dispersed. I had resigned my professorship at Harvard, and no longer crossed and re-crossed the Atlantic. I have explained the effect of these changes in the Preface to the later edition of the *Life of Reason*, and in what has already preceded here. My *Soliloquies in England* contain clear indications that, in spite of the war then raging, fancy in me had taken a new lease of life. I felt myself nearer than ever before to rural nature and to the perennial animal roots of human society. It was not my technical philosophy that was principally affected, but rather the meaning and status of philosophy for my inner man. The humanism characteristic of the *Sense of Beauty* and *Life of Reason* remained standing; but foundations were now supplied for that humanism by a more explicit and vigorous natural philosophy; a natural philosophy which, without being otherwise changed than as the growth of natural science might suggest, was itself destined to be enveloped later by the ontology contained in *Realms of Being*. These additions are buttresses and supports: the ontology justifies materialism, and the materialism justifies rational ethics and an æsthetic view of the mind.

Certainly materialism cannot justify moral ideals *morally*. Morally a sentiment can be confirmed only by another sentiment, for whatever that may be worth. But materialism justifies the life of reason martially, as a fighting organisation, and explains its possible strength and dominance. What from the moral point of view we call the instruments of reason are primarily the ground and cause of reason: and reason can control matter only because reason is matter organised, and assuming a form at once distinctive, plastic, and opportune. Unity of direction is thus imposed on our impulses; the impulses remain and continue to work and to take themselves most seriously; things tempt and hurt us as much as ever. Yet this very synthesis imposed upon the passions has brought steadiness and scope into the mind. The passions seem less absolute than before: we see them in a more tragic or comic light; and we see that even our noble and civilised life of reason is bought at a price. As there were wild animal joys that it has banished, so there may be divine insights that it cannot heed.

I had begun philosophising quite normally, by bleating like any young lamb: agitated by religion, passionately laying down the law for art and politics, and even bubbling over into conventional verses, which I felt to be oracular and irresistible. But my vocation was clear: my earliest speculation was at once intimate and universal, and philosophically religious, as it has always remained; yet not exclusively on the lines of that complete Christian system which first offered itself to my imagination. I was always aware of alternatives; nor did these alternatives seem utterly hostile and terrible. My enthusiasm was largely dramatic; I recited my Lucretius with as much gusto as my Saint Augustine; and gradually Lucretius sank deeper and became more satisfying. What I demanded unconditionally was dramatic wholeness. I wanted to articulate each possible system, to make it consistent, radical, and all-embracing. Hesitation and heresy were odious to me in any quarter; and I cared more for the internal religious force of each faith than for such external reasons as might be urged to prove that faith or to disprove it. What indeed could such external reasons be but corollaries to some different system, itself needing to be believed?

A judicial comparison of various systems of life and morals was therefore not possible for me until I had found a sure foothold for criticism, other than the histrionic convictions between which my youthful sentiment could so easily oscillate. This foothold was supplied to me by human nature, as each man after due Socratic self-questioning might find it in himself, and as Plato and Aristotle express it for mankind at large in their rational ethics. There is nothing unalterably fixed in this moral physiognomy of man, any more than in his bodily structure; but both are sufficiently recognisable and constant for the purposes of medicine and politics. The point of chief speculative interest is that morality, like health, is determined by the existing constitution of our animal nature, and the opportunities or denials that materially confront us; so that we are much deeper and more deeply bound to physical reality than our wayward thoughts and wishes might suggest. The potential, in an organic being developing through time, is necessarily richer and more important than the actual. The actual is superficial, occasional, ephemeral; present will and present consciousness are never the true self. They are phenomena elicited by circumstances from a psyche that remains largely unexpressed. Yet this psyche, this inherited nature or seed, flowers in those manifestations, filling them as they pass with beauty and passion: and nothing will be moral or personal in ideas except what they borrow by a secret circulation from the enduring heart. There, and not in any superstitious precepts, lies the root of duty and the criterion of perfection.

In saying this I am far from wishing to attribute a metaphysical fixity or unity to the psyche, or to claim for my own person an absolute singleness and consistency. Some passive drifting and some fundamental vagueness there must be in every animal mind; and the best-knit psyche still participates in the indefinite flux of matter, is self-forgetful in part, and is mortal. But this only proves that no man can be wholly a philosopher or an artist, or wholly himself. We are moral individuals, we exist as persons, only imperfectly, by grace of certain essences kindly imputed to us by our own thoughts or by the thoughts of others. There is always a moral chaos, though it be a dynamic mathematical order, beneath our rationalised memory or criticism: a chaos which is an indispensable support and continual peril to the spirit, as the sea is to a ship. Yet in our nautical housekeeping we may disregard the background. The deluge keeps our rational ark afloat, and our thoughts follow our treasures.

Yet not necessarily all our thoughts. The need of keeping a look-out may generate a disinterested interest in the winds and tides, and we may end by smiling at the moral reasons which we first assigned for the deluge. In my later writings I speak of something called the spiritual life; of a certain *disintoxication* clarifying those passions which the life of reason endeavours to harmonise. Is spirit then hostile to reason? Is reason hostile to spirit? Neither: but within the life of reason there is incidental rivalry in the types of organisation attempted, in their range, and in the direction in which the inevitable sacrifices are accepted. Spirit and reason, as I use the words, spring from the same root in organic life, namely, from the power of active adaptation possessed by animals, so that the external world and the future are regarded in their action. Being regarded in action, absent things are then regarded in thought; and this is intelligence. But intelligence and reason are often merely potential, as in habit, memory, institutions, and books: they become spirit only when they flower into actual consciousness. Spirit is essentially simpler, less troubled, more lyrical than reason: it is not specifically human. It may exist in animals, perhaps in plants, as it certainly exists in children; and in its outlook, far from being absorbed in tasks and cares, like reason, it is initially universal and addressed to anything and everything that there may happen to be.

Between the spiritual life and the life of reason there is accordingly no contradiction: they are concomitant: yet there is a difference of temper and level, as there is between agriculture and music. The ploughman may sing, and the fiddler at times may dig potatoes; but the vocations pull in different ways. Being ready for everything, and a product of vital harmony, spirit finds an initial delight in art and contrivance, in adventure and discovery, for these are forms of order and enlarged harmony: yet in the midst of business, spirit suspends business, and begins to wonder, to laugh, or to pray. A family quarrel may easily arise between these mental faculties; a philosopher sympathises naturally with speculation; but the ethics of this conflict are the same as in other conflicts: to know oneself, and to impose on oneself or on others only the sacrifices requisite to bring one's chosen life to perfection.

I have always disliked mystics who were not definite in their logic and orthodox in their religion. Spirit is not a power: it comes to fulfil, not to destroy. By understanding the world we may in a certain ideal sense transcend it; but we do not transcend it by misunderstanding it: on the contrary, we remain in that case dupes of our own flesh and our own egotism. Every temperament and every vocation, even the highest, engages us in a special course that imposes sweeping renunciations in other directions. But these renunciations would not be true sacrifices if the things sacrificed were not admittedly good. Marriage and wealth, sport and adventure, dominion and war are not condemned by the spiritual man in being renounced. They are left benevolently or sadly for the natural man, who is generously and inevitably engaged in them. The passions are the elements of life; nevertheless they are deceptive and tragic. They fade from the mind of the old man who can survey their full course; unless indeed he makes himself a shrill and emasculated echo of them, forgetting the dignity of years. Sometimes these passions shock and repel a young soul even at their first assault: and then we have the saint or seer by nature, who can transcend common experience without having tasted it; but this is a rare faculty, abnormal and not to be expected or even desired. Thus there is a certain option and practical incompatibility between spirituality and humanism, between poetry and business, between sheer logic and sound sense; but the conflict is only marginal, the things are concentric, and spirit merely heightens and universalises the synthesis which reason makes partially, as occasion requires, in the service of natural interests. To make this synthesis is itself a natural interest, as the child loves to look and to explore: and spirit, the conscience of nature that sees the truth of nature, is the most natural of things.

My later philosophy, then, on the moral side, merely develops certain ultimate themes of the inner life which had run in my head from the beginning: they had dominated my verse, and had reappeared in my early accounts of poetry and religion, of Platonic love, and post-rational morality. The developments in no way disturb the biological basis assigned to all life; they do not make my naturalistic ethics dogmatic. They are proposed merely as optional. They are confessions of the sentiment with which the spectacle of things and the discipline of experience can fill a reflective mind.

Within the same naturalistic frame my later philosophy has also elaborated the analysis of perception, of belief, and of "ideas" in general; and in this direction I have come to discriminate something which seems strangely to irritate my critics: I mean, what I call essence and the realm of essence. These words, and my whole presentation of this subject, were perhaps unfortunate. I have advanced an emancipating doctrine in traditional terms; the terms excite immediate scorn in modern radical quarters, while the emancipating doctrine horrifies those conservatives to whom the terms might not give offense. I am sorry: but this accident after all is of little consequence, especially as the same doctrine—loaded, no doubt, with other accidental lumber—is being propagated by various influential writers in uglier and more timely terms. The point is to reduce evidence to the actually evident, and to relegate all the rest to hypothesis, presumption, and animal faith. What I call essence is not something alleged to exist or subsist in some higher sphere: it is the last residuum of scepticism and analysis. Whatsoever existing fact we may think we encounter, there will be obvious features distinguishing that alleged fact from any dissimilar fact and from nothing. All such features, discernible in sense, thought, or fancy, are essences; and the realm of essence which they compose is simply the catalogue, infinitely extensible, of all characters logically distinct and ideally possible. Apart from the events they may figure in, these essences have no existence; and since the realm of essence, by definition, is infinitely comprehensive and without bias, it can exercise no control over the existing world, nor determine what features shall occur in events, or in what order.

Indeed, it might seem idle to have mentioned these pure essences at all, which living thought traverses unwittingly, as speech does the words of one's native language; yet the study of grammar is enlightening, and there is a clarifying and satiric force in the discrimination of essences. For the irony of fate will have it that these ghosts are the only realities we ever actually can find: and it is rather the thought-castles of science and the dramatic vistas of history that, for instant experience, are ghostly and merely imagined. What should mind be, if it were not a poetic cry? Mind does not come to repeat the world but to celebrate it. The essences evoked in sensation and thought are naturally original, graphic, and morally coloured. Consciousness was created by the muses; but meantime industrious nature, in our bodily organisation, takes good care to keep our actions moderately sane, in spite of our poetic genius.

Thus as in my younger days in respect to religions, so now in respect to all experience and all science, critical reflection has emancipated me from the horrid claim of ideas to literal truth. And just as religion, when seen to be poetry, ceases to be deceptive and therefore odious, and becomes humanly more significant than it seemed before; so experience and science, when seen to be woven out of essences and wholly symbolic, gain in moral colour and spirituality what they lose in dead weight. The dead weight falls back from sensuous images and intellectual myths to the material fatality that breeds and sustains them.

This fatality itself, in proving wholly arbitrary, seems to oppress us less; it inspires courage and good humour, rather than supplications and fears. Perhaps what the realm of essence, in its mute eternity, chiefly adds to our notion of nature is the proof that nature is contingent. An infinite canvas is spread before us on which any world might have been painted. The actuality of things is sharpened and the possibilities of things are enlarged. We cease to be surprised or distressed at finding existence unstable and transitory. Why should it have been otherwise? Not only must our own lives be insecure, as earthly seasons change, but perhaps all existence is in flux, even down to its first principles. *Dum vivimus vivamus.* Everything, so long as it recognisably endures, is free to deploy its accidental nature; and we may lead the life of reason with a good grace, harmonising as well as possible our various impulses and opportunities, and exploring the realm of essence as our genius may prompt.

The exposition of my philosophy is still incomplete, and in many directions, as for instance in mathematical physics, the development of it is beyond my powers. Yet virtually the whole system was latent in me from the beginning. When in adolescence I oscillated between solipsism and the Catholic faith, that was an accidental dramatic way of doing honour both to rigour and to abundance. But the oscillation was frivolous and the two alternate positions were self-indulgent. A self-indulgent faith sets up its casual myths and rashly clings to them as to literal truths; while a self-indulgent scepticism pretends to escape all dogma, forgetting its own presuppositions. With time it was natural that oscillation should give place to equilibrium; not, let us hope, to a compromise, which of all things is the most unstable and unphilosophical; but to a radical criticism putting each thing where it belongs. Without forgetting or disowning anything, myth might then be corrected by disillusion, and scepticism by sincerity. So transformed, my earliest affections can survive in my latest.

G Santayana

I

Baker Brownell

SANTAYANA, THE MAN AND THE PHILOSOPHER

I

SANTAYANA, THE MAN AND THE PHILOSOPHER

I

TO many Americans Santayana is the Mona Lisa of philosophy. Though eloquent and penetrating, he finally brings forth what seems to them only an enigmatic smile. This is the popular reputation of Santayana's work, to be sure, as it is of Leonardo's picture, but it may have its grain of justice. I suspect that even his more erudite critics may be rather uncertain about their knowledge of him.

Here is disillusionment, he says, take it and be happy. For those who must find bread by means of their philosophy, or the sawdust that often passes for it, this is strange food. Or he may say, addressing now another grade of people, your illusion is my disillusionment, let us each hold his own to his heart and be content, for each in its way interprets the kinds of experience appropriate to it and gives them form. For those who seek in philosophy a final fixation of their cosmos in universal terms this has little weight. For others it will seem a subtle case of special privilege and snobbery, as if ideas rode in first or second classes and were valid according to the status of the men who had them. When philosophy, however, like poetry and like religion, is thought of as a way to give flexible patterns and values to experience and to make it intelligible in one form or another, Santayana's enigmas become, not enigmas, but deep illuminations in that mist and dream of immediate life of which he is always conscious.

In reading and rereading Santayana's books—and I have done this more or less for thirty years since I was a student in his classes—I have tried to capture this elusive quality in his thought. That I have not entirely captured it is in part my own fault—of that I am well aware—but the material has also some part in the difficulty. For Santayana's work is many colored, like a drop of water in the sun, and shifts without due notice from one aspect or interest to another. In my youth I read the books then written, *The Sense of Beauty*, *Three Philosophical Poets*, *Poetry and Religion*, *The Life of Reason*, for the poetry there, for I was tuned to that frequency, and in the classroom listened less to the smooth progressions of his argument than to the golden hum and overtone. The poetry came to meet me, and though I could "get by" in other aspects of his work with at least some conceptual knowledge when examination time came, they were in the background for me, hidden reticently behind the lyric voice.

Poetry was, and still is, the main value of his work to me, and I see now that the delicate and involved dialectic, the turning over and over of lovely abstractions, as one might turn a jewel in the hand, is also a kind of poetry, or as Santayana might call it in another's work, a myth. I learned in those earlier days to recognize the sort of thing that Santayana offered. It was, as he says, "an invitation to think after a certain fashion,"[1] and I sensed, if I could not describe, what that fashion was. This interest more in a fashion of thinking than in a system of conclusions and this variegation in the quality of his work, now sensuous, now poetic, now logical or prophetic, makes it hard to pin this philosopher down. Not conclusions but the exercise of ideas, is central in Santayana. Not consistency of opinions through the years but consistency of philosophical mood, not content and belief, eternal fixations, but the color and poetry of thought always created anew.

He was a poet with the inherent mystery of the poet's mind, but the Santayana that I knew during my college days was not a personal mystery or enigma. He seemed fairly appropriate within the purlieu of Emerson Hall, where Harvard's philosophy was ensconced, of Quincy street, of the Colonial club for faculty folk, over by the Union, where one could stand before the fire in the late afternoon with his dish of tea steaming on the mantel. Santayana was younger, to be sure, than his great colleagues, James, Royce, Palmer, and I do not know whether

[1] *Reason in Science*, 133.

he saw much of them, but he was no mysterious stranger among students or staff. He had his friends, the Münsterbergs, for example, and Charles Eliot Norton, and if he did not see much of the faculty as a group, he saw a good deal of the students. At football games he would wander along the upper colonnade of the stadium, classically framed, wearing his smart, if exotic, European cape and overcoat, looking at the game no doubt from a Greek background. On his way to classes he may have carried the usual green bag for books, I do not remember, but his figure on the street as he turned from Massachusetts avenue into the yard was not particularly arresting nor in any way odd.

While Royce would loaf in the doorway before class, a cigar in his mouth, his great white head lolling to one side, and James would flit in and out along the hall on some business or other, Santayana would come to class and then go away, and that was all. He had no periphery there outside of the class room. Once on his way down the hall, he paused before the bronze, seated Emerson for whom the hall is named. He looked at it a moment and turned to me standing near by. "How do like it?" he asked me; and to my rather indefinite reply, he said, "The upper part is all right, but those shanks are too prominent." I walked on with him to Phil 10; it is the only time I saw him dally outside of the class room.

He was a dark, gentle looking man, unobtrusive, medium sized. He was quietly dressed, neither arty nor academic, and usually, as I remember, wore fastidious, faintly trans-Atlantic black. Within his quietness one discerned a distinguished manner, grace, reticent pride; and he had beautiful eyes. He was bald, rather tragically so, we students thought, but he had a handsome and philosophic beard that later gave way to more handsome though less philosophic mustaches without a beard. His lectures were quiet, gently spoken. He rarely paced the stage. Usually he sat in his chair, his musing hands before him, gave his lecture or carried on a leisurely class discussion, and when the bell rang, stopped. Certainly the so-called enigma and evanescence of his philosophy was not in personal flightiness or whim. It was, if anywhere, in the natural texture of his thinking.

To a Mediterranean mind enigma and elusiveness are not welcome characterizations, and when applied to a philosophy written with such delicate precision of language as Santayana's, they deserve perhaps more than passing discussion. It is not his intention to elude his readers, and the reasons that he does so often elude them may be in themselves more virtues than they are faults. One may track down his philosophy as if it were a doe in the forest. Here the trail is clear and sharp along a well-known stream; here it turns across a prairie and enters the woods, leads to the stream again and is lost in the water; here it emerges, suddenly clear again, far down the bank. I shall describe this philosophical doe very briefly, at least as I see it, and then suggest some of the reasons why it is so hard to follow.

Santayana's philosophy is mainly moral in interest and is concerned with the conditions of life, the emergence of values and the possibilities of happiness. The conditions of life are established in the realm of matter. The causes of life, the activities, and, indeed, the actuality of life are in matter. This realm of matter is mechanical in its order and indifferent in its attitude. It is the whole of nature and of natural things.

Santayana, however, is not interested in nature from its own point of view, as the scientist is or thinks he is, but in the bearing of nature on man, on his possibility of knowledge and on his chances for happiness. So far as knowledge of nature is concerned, we know these existing things only in our assumption and animal faith. Nature is a kind of emotional necessity, as God once was. It is a matrix in which our lives find a kind of security and relevance to something other than themselves. So far as happiness is concerned, we may be happy in our existence, if we do not trust it. We may find a way to live well within the fictions of life.[2] We must assume the natural world of existing things, he says, under the compulsion of practical necessity; these naturalistic constructions are no less speculative and hypothetical than the idealists' dreams, but they are legimate and fruitful fictions and obvious truths, and their truth, like all truth,

[2] *Soliloquies in England*, 93.

lies in their being verifiable hypotheses and stable inferences.[3]

Having said this much it is hard to say more about matter. Having presumed something corresponding to the word *that*, the rest of philosophy must concern itself mostly with the realm of *this*. A unique relevance and amenability would seem to distinguish *this* from *that;* one may be known, in other words, the other not. Thus the infinite realm of essences: and I well remember the persistent hours that Santayana gave to them before our somewhat stubborn and obfuscated class in metaphysics. Essences are, briefly, the features of any fact that distinguish it from other facts. They are all such characteristics or features that may possibly be distinguished in sense, thought or fancy; and, Santayana hastens to add, they have no existence apart from the events that they figure in.[4] The diversity of animal experience, he says, exhibits sundry qualities or forms of being, which (whether revealed to anybody or not) are the realm of essence.[5] This is simple enough, but for our class of hopeful undergraduates it was not at all easy. So tough was it for me that, after creditably completing the work of the course, I returned to it the following semester—which proved to be Santayana's last at Harvard—and "audited" those essences again.

Essences are the characters of facts both of existing things and of our thought. Thus they are in a sense the nexus between thought and things. Only essences are present to us, only essences can we know, and only in essences is the reason for values though not their source. The natural world of existing things in its contact with us arouses the flux of experience and, since thought is inherently representational, we assume that this flux of essences stands for substance in flux. It is the wild data of sensation that we spend lifetimes in organizing.

This substance in flux, or matter, sustains organic equilibrium, says Santayana, and from organic equilibrium ideal form arises. To this ideal form consciousness corresponds, and consciousness raises ideal form to existence. Thus comes the creative function

[3] *Reason in Common Sense*, 201.

[4] Preface to Vol. VII of the Triton Edition of *The Works of George Santayana.*

[5] *Realm of Essence*, viii.

of man and of *The Life of Reason* as developed in this great early work. "But ever since substance became at some sensitive point intelligent and reflective," he says in an eloquent passage,

> ever since time made room and pause for memory, for history, for the consciousness of time, a god, as it were, became incarnate in mortality and some vision of truth, some self-forgetful satisfaction, became a heritage that moment could transmit to moment and man to man. This heritage is humanity itself, the presence of immortal reason in creatures that perish. Apprehension, which makes man so like a god, makes him in one respect immortal; it quickens his numbered moments with a vision of what never dies, the truth of those moments and their inalienable values. . . . It is imperishable simply because it is ideal and resident merely in import and intent.[6]

Nature is reason's basis and theme, says Santayana; and reason is nature's consciousness. From the point of view of that consciousness when it has arisen, reason is also nature's justification and goal.[7]

As a metaphysics in the rigorous sense this, as Santayana well knows, can probably be punched full of holes. It is a descriptive myth more than an analysis. Abstractions have a delicate way of becoming things, and things, abstractions; and what should be functionally simple and monosyllabic, as it were, appears concrete and many sided. His doctrine of Platonic love, which is just this mystical deliquescence of concrete things into universals, tinctures most of his thinking. These universals in turn are unconsciously endowed by the poet and mystic with a concreteness and kind of power that give them a status not unlike natural things. But punching holes, even were I an expert in such matters, is a mean and futile business; in regard to Santayana's work, as in all poetry, it is particularly irrelevant. As a kind of moral metaphysics, or a metaphysical epic of man's creation of the eternal, his work is unassailable.

Two other great terms in Santayana's philosophy are truth and spirit. The one indicates "valid ideation, verified hypothesis, and inevitable, stable inference."[8] It refers to the complete de-

[6] *Reason in Religion*, 263.

[7] *Reason in Common Sense*, 205.

[8] *Reason in Common Sense*, 201.

scription ideally, of natural structure and process. From this the truth becomes not only the description of natural structure but the determinate character of those structures themselves. It is thus a juncture of essence and matter.

Spirit is a kind of universalization of values in the same way that truth is of structural fact. But universalization of values is tantamount to the disintoxication from them, for values are by nature local in interest. Spirit is seeing things as eternal, and the spiritual life is the disintoxication from the local passions and the pressures that assail our lives. It is a realm of noble peace. Thus the spirit, particularly in his later thinking, stands in contrast to the struggles and hopes of living, or, as Santayana once said in a letter to me " 'Consummation' is what I call spirit, the rest being all 'action' or matter in motion."

Why this philosophy of Santayana, here so briefly indicated, has been difficult and elusive for most Americans may be attributed partly to accidental idiosyncracies of Santayana's method but far more to certain textural characteristics of his thought itself. Because his thinking is plasmic, like a vital organism expanding on all sides from the center, it is hard for him, if not impossible, to make his material neatly consecutive. To be an easy currency in the class room or in the annual meetings of the philosophical association a philosophy needs to have sequence, clear and narrow specification, a well defined choice, and because Santayana's thought is not conveniently packaged and labeled it is not prominently displayed in those meager show windows of philosophical goods. He has few disciples. His school of critical realism, if it be a school, is more a way of approach than a net of theory. This is not a serious disadvantage; but when thoughtful readers, lost delightfully in a vegetation of fancy and spontaneous ideas or among pulsing expositions of different points of view, say that he has no philosophy the matter is of more concern. Really his fashion of thinking is about the only one in this modern culture that can be fairly called philosophical, rather than scientific, technological, mathematical, educational, sociological, theological or what not; but the philosophical public is not always aware of it.

Some of the more external reasons for the elusiveness of this philosophic doe on its shadowy way through the wilderness have often been pointed out. For one thing people are less interested in it than in more domestic meat. Our corrals after all are full of more specific, more pressing and seemingly more pertinent problems; why go into an alien woods for a creature that sportsmanship in any case would not permit us to kill? There is also Santayana's episodic style. Again, there is his confusing way of undermining criticism by anticipating it, admitting it and including it, as it were, in his original position. The critic thus is left uncertain which Santayana he is attacking. Even more disconcerting is the astonishing versatility of his understanding, his ability to dramatize both sides of a situation, both pro and con. This is less the objectivity that usually is attributed to him than a kind of cosmic sympathy for all the forms and variations of being. What he repudiates in Whitman he has to some extent himself, though, unlike Whitman, he does make his choice. As his thought passes through its materials it becomes them, or they become it. It absorbs their color. His words are used for what they really are, mere shifting, glittering points in the stream of thought. But such lingual naturalism makes a fixed and crystalline philosophy impossible. This lingual naturalism and sympathy, this poetic understanding of each moment of being, whatever its character, is a great and unusual virtue in philosophies. But the reader may lose the trail.

More important as factors in the so-called Santayana mystery, however, are two textural qualities of his thinking that usually are unrecognized or ignored as merely accidental. Still, they are central in the unique nature and personality of his thought. They are his interest in contextual quality and the union in his work of poetry and dialectic.

Because his interests are more in contexts than in denotations, more in the savoring of each drop than in getting the drink down, the general aspect of his philosophy seems to shift and change with each new internal emphasis. At one moment it is confidently naturalistic, at another, subjective, at another pragmatic or fictional. This sense for the context of things, or connotation, gives to his books an inner illumination that no other philosopher's possess. He can enter an idea or a philosophy and make it glow from within. He can identify himself even with objects that he dislikes, such as protestantism, secular mysticism, German idealism, forgetting for the moment their outer references, and make them incandescent with any innate authority that they may have. From these contextual matrices, warm and plastic as they are, the universals that he is always using emerge. They are literary universals, not mathematical, and they arise in concrete, imaginative material, or crystallize from it, as they should. Rarely are they imposed from without, after the mathematical or hypothetical fashion, and since contextual colors and suggestions change with every breath, shimmering and moving like the surface of a sea, the universals arising in them are temporary—if such a paradox may be permitted—practical, as it were, good in the present situation and for the present purpose, but not always consistent with a later universal of the same name.

Santayana's universals, in other words, do not quite detach themselves from their concrete background. What would a poet do, indeed, without his universals, stately, beautiful, unimpugned by any rumor of relativism or qualification during the period of their service! They are fragile, to be sure, and not to be bandied about or held valid under all circumstances, like pi or the logical symbolists' *O* relation, but they serve their purpose, as cloud castles do, then give way to another. If we were safe in our plastic existence, like nature and the gods of nature, says Santayana,[9] change would not be ill-omened, and what disappears would never narrow the range of what is yet to be.

But these inconstant universals make a systematic philosophy, or any philosophy as a structural whole, difficult both to construct and to understand. Because they are close to the nature of life perhaps, they lack the rigid artifice, hypostasis and abstraction necessary to such structures. They are natural words. Where most philosophers try to fixate words in frozen files or to make them definite and denotative, Santayana seems to think of them merely as terms in a fluid discourse that change with every change of scene or movement. Truth, for example, is it a description of or a characteristic of natural structure? Consciousness,

[9] *Soliloquies in England*, 19.

is it a passing product of the self-reflecting flux of existences, or an active agent in it? And what is its status in respect to reason? It would seem that existence and reason in Santayana's philosophy always are committing incest, or are on the point of it in spite of rigorous separation, like an Oedipus, or a Barclay in a tragedy by Jeffers, under some structural compulsion.

An object,[10] again, such as an apple, is it a concretion of perceptions of redness, hardness, sweetness, roundness—in a way that the modern Gestalt school of psychology would denounce most vigorously—or is it existential? For cssences are infinite in number, and there are essences not only of the apple's redness, roundness, but of its weight, its inertia, and presumably of its existence too. The "actual" existence of the apple thus seems to become quite as superfluous to knowledge, and perhaps to life, as Kant's shadowy noumenon. The apple's existence depends indeed on a psychic factor, an animal faith, to the extent that it enters experience at all. And so far as Santayana's method can decree, it seems to be only that in reality. And even further than that, he says, if I may trust my notes of his lectures thirty years ago, "Existence is merely the fixation of essence in non-dialectical ways." It is one of the company of heaven, Lucifer, rebelling against the others. "It stands out; it is other than intellectual." Santayana's transcendentalism, in a word, returns to consume him. Only by raising another fiction by fiat, the fiction of material existence, and setting it over against the first does he escape.

Or, on the other hand, the emphasis may lie on the naturalistic realm of material things. In that case the realm of essence, as a separate pattern of being, seems to be an impertinent interjection into a normal, natural system. A physical object, says Santayana, is

> conceived by fusing or interlacing spatial qualities, in a manner helpful to practical intelligence. It is a far higher and remoter thing than the elements it is compacted of and that suggest it; what habits of appearance and disappearance the latter may have, the object reduces to permanent and calculable principles.[11]

[10] *Reason in Common Sense,* 164.

[11] *Reason in Common Sense,* 162.

This is clear enough to the average, intelligent reader. So also is the naturalistic background, which seems to recede into a greater distance as Santayana leaves American shores. But what of the two together?

Santayana is, of course, aware of this difficulty. From early 'til late in his work he has concerned himself with the answer. The answer, to an average reader at least, is not very clear, and once answered, the difficulty seems to raise its head again unashamed, only to be answered in another way. Perhaps Santayana uses categories to which we are not accustomed, or relates them together in unaccustomed ways. "Matter, dialectically studied," he says,[12]

> makes consciousness seem a superfluous and unaccountable addendum; mind, studied in the same way, makes nature an embarrassing idea, a figment which ought to be subservient to conscious aims and perfectly transparent, but which remains opaque and overwhelming. In order to escape these sophistications, it suffices to revert to immediate observation and state the question in its proper terms: nature lives, and perception is a private echo and response to ambient motions. . . . Consciousness, then, is the expression of bodily life and the seat of all its values. Its place in the natural world is like that of its own ideal products, art, religion, or science; it translates natural relations into synthetic and ideal symbols by which things are interpreted with reference to the interests of consciousness itself.

But even here the transition from existence to symbol, though refined, is not made clear or wholly plausible. The whole matter, I imagine, comes down to some form of the simple fact that we behave towards the material symbol such as a sound or a mark on paper, or the representation of a thing, as if it were the thing, thus economizing and at the same time amplifying our living activity; but so crude an answer only partially fits into the pattern of Santayana's philosophy. It ignores his projection of ends and values into these representations.

It is hard indeed to find in his philosophy other than impermanent answers, answers that lie in the changing and plastic context of the moment. They shift to the subjective and back again, or move in other ways. The tendency of empiricism to

[12] *Reason in Common Sense,* 206f.

become transcendental, which Santayana often points out, is a tendency which the average reader will find in Santayana's own naturalism. But the shifting, the contextual iridescence of his philosophy has its own validity and virtue. Rigorous consistency is of merit only in some situations, and those perhaps local ones. In this clamoring world we must face many ways or meet disaster. A philosophy of aspects, of the varying visions of life, is probably the only naturalism possible in the pluralistic culture of today.

The exotic union of poetry and dialectic in Santayana's work is another virtue that adds to an innocent reader's difficulties. In a modern world where philosophy, so far as it is consciously desired at all, is desired in its bare mechanism or is skeletal form, ideas having the gratuity and abundance of living things may not easily be recognized as philosophical. Santayana's mind is poetic and essayistic in character, if not in purpose. His ideas are clothed in life. Comment and fancy, not always mathematically relevant, attend them. Sometimes his philosophy retires wholly into life and fancy and forgets or abandons dialectic and its skeletal abstractions. His native interest in the quality and inner tune of things sometimes belies his chosen emphasis on structural reason.

Once he had no metaphysics, or so he claimed,[13] and the dialectic in his work was mainly in the interest of clarifying reflection and in giving *The Life of Reason* an inner harmony consistent with a happy life. It was subordinate and piece-meal. Though the assumption that dialectic—which for Santayana is an order of essences—or reason, or anything else of the sort can harmonize life and make it happy unless the impulses that lie behind the various elements of the situation also happen to be in harmony is far-fetched and overly optimistic, it may be allowed to pass because it is the starting point of all classical ethics and hope for a better world. Though intelligence does indeed clarify impulse and purpose and define their end, it may as easily clarify them for purposes of more effective conflict as for peace, for reason is a harmonizer only in a homogeneous culture. In cold fury no conflicts exceed dialectical ones

[13] *Soliloquies in England,* 251; *Scepticism and Animal Faith,* vii.

such as the conflict between the Marxists and the Catholic church, but reason in a tradition that goes back to the days of the quarreling Sophists of Greece, has usually been called the arch harmonizer nevertheless. In Santayana's four autumnal books, introducing a system of philosophy with well defined realms of being, the emphasis on reason and its dialectical accessories as both a moral instrument and end is replaced to some extent by more ontological interests. Dialectic remains, but has another function. It becomes metaphysical.

I doubt whether Santayana has the confidence in a rigorous dialectic that, say, Russell has. Dialectic no doubt seems to him strangely nude and helpless when stripped to its bare essentials. Its authority for Santayana and his readers is, I think, fully as much in the persuasions of attendant poetry and feeling as in the directness of its logic. But the dialectic is there. So much is it there that Santayana's philosophy, a deliberate league, as it were, of logic and lyric, becomes bilingual so far as its expression is concerned. Unless the reader is highly sensitive both poetically and intellectually, a rare and often contradictory combination, he may find the reading difficult. Nor am I sure that Santayana himself is entirely successful in making the synthesis.

In a better world than this these languages and limitations might not have separate authorities; for the doom of man seems to be the distintegration that accompanies the growth and refinement of his various functions and abilities. Friendly enough with each other in their youth as playful cubs, his interests become solitary, morose, and fratricidal as they mature. Nature, it seems, cannot support them all in their maturity. Their community disintegrates. Many die. In a better world human reflection and representation might endow their objects not with poetry *or* dialectic, not with concrete context *or* abstract structure, but somehow with both, as naturally integrated things in our experience always do. In such a world, strange as it seems, a musician might be found reading a book, an engineer might have social responsibility, a philosopher might be a good dancer, a poet might be a dialectician. In such a world, in other words, the indigenous integrations of life and nature might also be found in discourse, and we could talk about the skyline from

Jackson Lake without disintegrating its perceptual wholeness into aesthetic, geologic, economic, and political aspects. If discourse, as it seems to me, is inevitably disintegrative, inevitably in conflict and at cross purposes with things, or on the contrary, if discourse, as Santayana would say, is inevitably of a different associational order from things and in value higher than things, then perhaps a better world would have either less discourse or more, according to one's disposition.

In Santayana's case, however, the incomplete union of poetry and dialectic—and also of naturalism and dialectic—may not be entirely due to the inevitable character of discourse. Naturally he is a poet, a man of insight; the flame burns in every line that he writes. Nor does he lack, when he wishes to use it, an adept hand at dialectic. He commands dialectic to his purpose, and no Greek sophist or scholastic Catholic can pink an adversary more deftly, or justify a predisposition more manifestly. He can use dialectic, like the touch of Circe, to transform into swine ideas for which he has a native distaste. Thus, for example, German transcendental ideas, hopes, sacrifice, including even the categorical imperative, become forms of egotism. Or, on the contrary, he can raise in the interests of fair play or courtesy things that he dislikes to eminences of plausibility.

Santayana's dialectic, for all its skilfulness, does not belong to him, I think, in the same way that his poetry does. It is not a creative instrument for him. It is not a surveyor's transit running a line through the woods, as it seems to be for Russell, nor a club as for the Marxists, nor a factor in growth and production as for Dewey. Santayana does not use it, so far as I can see, as a vehicle for advancement to new ground. His impulses and native intuitions perform that function. His conception of dialectic, as well as of its form comes over from the sophists and the scholastics. It retains a primness and antique authority, a classical pattern and conception of function, a quaint purity, that modern disciplines and techniques, such as long years in experimental science, mathematics, practical education, would rapidly wear away. Dialectic for Santayana,[14] is an order of essences that differs from calculation in that the latter must always return

[14] *Reason in Science*, 78.

to sensation and the flux of existing things for its sanction whereas dialectic soars free on its own wings without that mundane necessity. It is, one might say, the free play and exercise of essences controlled only by their own natures. They are discursive, or at least consecutive, not poetic.

This contrast between Santayana's dialectic and his poetry, and their exotic union, is also the contrast, as I have suggested, between his dialectic and his naturalism. For in this respect the poetic and the natural thing may be considered the same. In their concreteness and irrationality they are the same. In their source and their bearing towards dialectic they are the same. They arise, both of them, in the dense and uncontrollable experience of life. They press up irresistably. They are concrete, or many sided, stubborn, integral in themselves. They are not easily amenable to the linked consecutiveness of dialectic, nor can they be broken down into single, thin, successive essences. They are lyrical, both of them, mystical rather than logical in the sense that they are gratuitous, spontaneous songs as it were in our experience. Poetry flows from the concrete, contextual richness of natural things, or rather they both flow from the same spontaneous source. Essence and dialectic belong elsewhere. As students in Santayana's classes we recognized this poetry and this naturalism and many of us sensed that they belonged together. His doctrine of essences was harder for us. Internally lucid though it was, clear as water, this doctrine nevertheless seemed alien to us. We had difficulty in making it relevant to our other ideas and to our impulses.

Essences and their order in dialectic were difficult because we could not easily clear away certain modern predispositions that were deep in our youthful outlook. We were habituated more to calculation than to dialectic, and it was hard for us to take seriously a realm of possibility which was given a status, though not an existence, that for all we could see was independent of the natural world of life and things. It was a ghost world improperly wavering, as ghosts will do, into realms of potential power and implicit causation. It was a reminiscence of classical divisions between ideal reality and material reality, and what turned out to be only a methodological analysis of discourse, seemed inevitably metaphysical and effective in events.

And our greatly admired teacher was not entirely guiltless of causing our confusion. Throughout his work he says repeatedly that essences do not exist, but he continually treats them as if they do exist. He gives them aesthetic objectivity, which no methodological abstractions have a right to possess; he speaks of them, playfully no doubt, as sources of action and influence. He makes them concrete. Indeed his sceptical reduction of spiritual existences to the realm of essence is sometimes betrayed and subverted by his poetry, for his vision of essences does not always correspond to his definition of them. When a philosopher says that something does not exist while at the same time he acts as if it did exist, we may in general hold that his actions, and his operational objects, speak louder than words.

But "these ghosts," says our naturalist,[15] "are the only realities we ever actually can find;" thus it is no wonder that we students were somewhat confused as we listened to the music of his lectures on metaphysics. For this is not the naturalism to which we were accustomed, dialectically irrefutable though it be. We were not entirely wrong, perhaps, in thinking it a naturalism honestly docile to obvious facts, but so tortured by scholastic memories that the face of it is hardly recognizable. For the naturalism to which we were inured does not segregate essence from existence, as Santayana does in his philosophy, nor does it

[15] Preface to Vol. VII of the Triton Edition of *The Works of George Santayana*, xiii. If essence means "distinction, infinitely minute and indelible distinction of everything from everything else"—*Scepticism and Animal Faith*, 129—it should remain distinction, it seems to me, and solely that; it should remain a simple, analytic unit of discourse, that cannot be treated as a moral or aesthetic matter of interest, a concrete concern of spirit or of life, or anything else except pure distinction, without abandoning the primary logic of the definition. Essence, which has only one face, seems to lose its necessary ghostliness when such such things are done. It becomes Platonic. To avoid confusion I should also explain that the word *concrete* to me means the many-sided, obvious tangibility or perceptibility of a particular thing as it is found in common sense experience. For Santayana, on the other hand, *concrete* seems to mean merely definiteness and singularity—*The Realm of Essence*, 32f.—and thus can be applied by him to an essence. I have also called an essence abstract because I think it is derived methodologically from whole, concrete things, although Santayana denies vigorously that essence is in any significant sense abstract. And I have referred to essence in one case as the realm of possibility, following in this Santayana's earlier lectures, though in his later work he repudiates this attribution.

treat dialectic as having any self-sufficiency in value or important status of its own. Essence and dialectic are merely bits of method and are kept within the naturalistic whole, submerged there as analytic details. In our dumb and embarrassed youth, we were perhaps nearer to modern scientific naturalism than is Santayana.

Though modernism is not necessarily a virtue, it is probably true that modern naturalism is more nearly an effective and sound adjustment to the realities that impose themselves upon us and in which we live than any naturalistic theory of the past. In this respect Santayana is less a modern, perhaps, than he is Greek or scholastic. He still separates essence from existence. He clings to the old and indeed tries to superimpose it on the new as a kind of evolutionary flowering. Santayana is a true modern and a naturalist in many ways, far more so, for example, than his older colleague, Royce, but he is also classical in his love of ideas, and as one reads him one is inconsistently grateful for it.

This modern poet and philosopher is in a sense the end of the season, the last bright autumn of the old philosophy, the Indian summer of dialectic and of faith in dialectic. The old philosophy in its closing movement is inevitably aesthetic, inevitably moral and post-rational. It becomes articulate once more in him. At the same time he recognizes the new and tries to harmonize it with the old. But Santayana's slightly anachronistic logic is not wholly congruous with his poetry and naturalism. Books and pride in his Latin tradition gave him, I imagine, the former; life and America gave him the latter.

Santayana's philosophy in another sense is vernal, like a flowering apple tree. Its effortless blooming adorns each Spring, and if the blossoms are like last year's, why not? Why should they progress? Why must a philosophy go somewhere or solve something? Why must it be more than expressive? Santayana's philosophy is beautifully static like a temple of the Greeks. Although he recognizes process, flux, evolution, dynamics, he recognizes them as natural facts, to be accepted, of course, but also in a measure to be escaped by the invention of essences and ideals. He calls this escape disillusionment and, on a remoter plane, the disintoxication from values, or the spiritual life. His best selling novel, *The Last Puritan*, illustrates this escape to essences, though what is a virtue in a philosophy may be a fault in a novel. True essences are his men and women there, eternal and unchanging, but they don't know what action is, nor the change of character through action. There is no principle of advancement, no cumulative movement. It is a novel naturalistic enough in its way, or in Santayana's way, but the essences supervene upon it and their touch is cold; it is frozen. Reading it is like a visit to Madame Tussaud's Waxworks; everything is there but life.

The innocent but thoughtful reader of Santayana's books may appreciate their poetic intonation. He may sense their delicate fire and mysticism—though Santayana would not admit this. He may wonder at their penetrations into the timeless immediacies of the moment. Such a reader may also accept the naturalism, the existences, the world of things in those books. He may also recognize the discourse, the orders of ideas over against existence. But even down to the latest book, the reader may not be clear in thinking of these worlds in reference to each other. Now one predominates as he reads, now another. Now one seems to be derivatory, now another. This lack of clearness is hardly a fault in organization, for Santayana repeats over and over that existence is prior in time, ideas prior in value, while the immediate flux and faith is prior in experience. The confusion is more a matter of variable emphasis and plausibility, a pluralism of culture, a divided or a synthesized loyalty in Santayana himself.

There is of course no good reason why his loyalty should not be divided. Nevertheless they stand there: his poetry, mysticism, naturalism on the side of concreteness; his dialectic and the harmonies of reason on the side of essence. Each one traditionally is monopolistic, mutually exclusive; each one is universal in its way. Santayana, it is true, thrusts relativity upon them, for he abhors absolutes, but it remains difficult, so far as philosophical offspring are concerned, to breed long separated species together.

This of course is the problem of all modern philosophy struggling with its diverse inheritances. The philosophical dilemmas of today are really translations of cultural conflicts and contradictions in the more general world of life and affairs. Nor does Santayana escape. His philosophy hesitates, I think, not between solipsism and abundance, as he suggests of his early work, but between a naturalistic, dynamic culture and a classic culture. The former is empirical, concrete, poetic. The latter has its dialectic, its essences, its ideals. Santayana's American present and his classic past make a difficult team to drive together.

II

What is this American present that I have attributed to Santayana, and what does he think of it? Though he lived in America forty years from childhood to middle age, was educated there in kindergarten, public school, college and university, held the famous Walker travelling fellowship from Harvard two years, wrote eleven of his books and earned his living there as a teacher of philosophy until he was fifty, Santayana never admits that he was more than an alien in our midst, a friendly observer without ties or burdens, an Athenian exiled by practical compulsions in Syracuse.[16] He retired from teaching in January, 1912, left these shores immediately, and, I believe, has never returned.

Santayana pictures himself in respect to America as a kind of unmoved mover, a modest one to be sure, but nevertheless a being that in its way emanates influences upon the environment without accepting reciprocal influences in return. In a society that possesses its members in a unique and personal way and in turn is possessed by them, Santayana refuses possession in either sense. In a democratic culture where social behavior and individual behavior are diffused into each other in a kind of spiritual immanence, Santayana prefers transcendence. He does acknowledge a debt and educational influence to individuals such as James, Royce, Palmer, but one feels that these men are hardly symbols or forces of America but three good men, namely, William James, Josiah Royce and George Herbert Palmer. Towards America as a culture, a society, an ample land, San-

[16] Preface to *Character and Opinion in the United States,* v-vi.

tayana is friendly, far more generous than most European intellectuals, but, in his books at least, carefully remote.

I do not know what lights, what emotions, what personal patterns lie behind this detachment towards America. Inherent pride, defensive sensitiveness, a boyhood among strange folk speaking a strange language, a youth without natural roots, moving always back and forth across the ocean, a young man recalling the old, recalling it perhaps more poignantly during our war-year with Spain, recalling Spain, Spain, but always leaving it again to live in the new; these no doubt are some of the more obvious influences behind it. I have seen the gay light of humor and friendship in his face, as he talked to another, flashing out suddenly and, indeed, rather surprisingly to one accustomed to his demure classroom manner, and I have seen his eyes wide and misty as he turned hastily to the door during the applause at the close of one of his courses. I was thrilled and made grateful in my youth by his enquiries as to my own pattern and personality and difference amid the casual crowds of the college world, though I knew of course that he would forget me when our ways parted. Santayana, indeed, is far from indifferent to people; nevertheless I doubt if he ever felt himself "one of the boys," or wished to, particularly in America. Possessive Americans may be a little resentful, a little amused and piqued at this sort of thing. They had perhaps expected the poet and philosopher to marry and settle down in Cambridge. When he perversely chose Olympus, or at least Rome, they very likely said, "We didn't raise him for this." The she-wolf was aggrieved, no doubt, when the fateful twins deserted her and went to found a city.

America from 1872 to 1912, the forty years that Santayana lived here, had not reached the obvious eminence of power and influence of a few years later, nor had the new flowering in the arts and sciences occurred. Emerson and Whitman, it is true, were still alive during Santayana's youth. William James was his colleague at Harvard. But America and its cultural landscape may have seemed rather dreary to the dark-eyed young Spaniard. He had been a lonely boy in his American home among much older children, and at kindergarten among much younger ones. He had gone through the routine of American education, finding now and then a good or a passable teacher. The boys in Boston were wont to tease him in high school, his schoolmate, James Houghton Woods, once told me; but a sharp tongue and a fiery temper made him well able to take care of himself. College, where he was already a local literary light, college magazines, one of which, *The Harvard Monthly*, he helped to found, poetry, graduate work, a thesis on Lotze, teaching, writing, teaching, with many trips abroad: thus had the she-wolf suckled the poet.

He missed in America the brilliant movement in poetry that began with the founding of *Poetry, A Magazine of Verse*, in 1912, the year that he left, but I am not sure that his tradition-tinted literary values would have been congenial to it anyhow. Sandburg, Frost, Masters, Lindsay, Stevens, Jeffers were just coming into the sunlight. He missed most of the new American dancing and wild music, the bands, the jazz, a massive Dionysian folk movement that would have influenced him even in his resistance. He missed much of the modern architecture and its drive towards cleanness and functionalism. Frank Lloyd Wright that year had just published his architectural designs in Germany. The Progressive rebellion against the old line interests burst forth that year and has continued intermittently down through Wilson and the second Roosevelt. But these liberal vitalities in the arts and in society might well have left him cold even had he been here. His own vitality was of another sort.

America, however, was also producing at this time its Henry James, who in 1912 was living abroad, and many another person of lesser consequence who felt that American soil was insufficiently manured to nourish his genius. Ezra Pound of Idaho, T. S. Eliot of Missouri, Gertrude Stein of California, Hilda Doolittle of Pennsylvania, are some of the many more. Though Santayana, along with James, had a more authentic cultivation and far more ability than the general run of expatriates, he belongs, I think, to the same group—to the same group in the sense that his flight was of the same order as theirs. Though his Spanish birth and blood and closely maintained European tradition obviously gave him more cause for leaving America, the flight was more American in quality, at least overtly, than it was alien.

For flight from America was an authentic phase of American culture of that period. Where another society might impose on its members a sense of the acceptance of fate or resignation, America may impose a desire to get out. It is in its way an expression of American character and life, and a nation of former frontiersmen should not be surprised when some of its intellectuals become nomadic too. It was in part a romantic phase of revolt not unconnected with the concurrent revolt at home in poetry and politics, in architecture, music, morals, manners and philosophy. It was a revolt now against the genteel tradition, now against the massive barbarism of an industrial age, and now against the presentness and thrust of things themselves, a revolt, indeed, against existence. But the revolt nevertheless found its source in strains of protestantism and democratic freedom, and, in the case of the expatriates at least, was turned against the culture that gave it birth. We children of America have always assumed the right to abuse our mother. Puritanism, in other words, had the seeds within itself of counteraction. At this time no other culture seemed to have even that vitality.

To this American tradition Santayana belongs; his revolt and his social criticism associated with it remain usually within the American cycle. It is noteworthy, for example, that he directs no criticism, or at least very little, on the cramping conventions, the dogmas and barbarities of the Catholic customs of his inheritance. These he takes for granted, or considers a gracious myth, nor does he seek to escape them. These are not the theme of his rebellion and escape. The attack, rather, is on the genteel tradition of the Calvinists and the musty smell of duty over New England. The reason for this is less in prejudice and sectarianism than in the fact that the Catholic culture gave little freedom to social and institutional self-criticism. We may grant the musty smell of duty over New England; certainly it was once there, though now perhaps replaced somewhat by the smell of incense in Catholic churches; we may grant the chill and silent censorship of the genteel tradition; but Santayana rebelled against these rather than against equally depressing rigidities elsewhere because the sources of freedom and revolt lay more in the American life that he was criticizing than perhaps in any other. There is a place for revolt there, a kind of recognition of its function, as there was not in other no less burdensome cultures.

Europe was not, of course, a "traveller's rest" for Santayana, as it is for many of our expatriates, a pleasant place for consumption or enjoyment only, with the grim problems of production, finance, sales, earning a living or getting a patron confined to the western side of the ocean. After all, Santayana's infancy was spent in Europe and his father lived in his native Spain. But the poet's flight from America was fully as much American in spirit, supported of course by these other facts, as it was an unreconstructed European's longing for home.

This may have importance, not merely as related to Santayana's personal life, of which I know little, but as a clue to his philosophical association of naturalism and classical dialectic. The biographical assumptions here may well be all awry, for who can know the inner strains and growth of so subtle and so defensive a mind? But aside from this there is a certain interpretive interest in the situation itself that may have bearing on his philosophy. The American presentness in Santayana's work is perhaps greater than he realizes. He found there the mass and power of life, the sense of a world in motion over which he had little control. His naturalism came not from Lucretius or Spinoza, for no naturalism can be in the past tense. No naturalism can be in other than impact and movement. It lies in the encounter with things, not in the history of them. It is reflective, if reflective at all, on the naturalist's own engagements with things, not in secondary reports. Santayana's naturalism came from the massive presentness of America. Thence come also, it seems to me, his independence and wilfulness in repudiating other aspects of America.

For not even the Spanish pride of this poet and philosopher could prevent his life during those long years from being influenced and indeed penetrated through and through by the powerful influences of the American present. No longed-for past with its books and ghosts could hold out against it. No poetic, desperate pose, no illusion of disillusionment, no romantic escape to lands more friendly to the mind—at least to the visitor's—or more hospitable to beauty and ideals could obscure that vast American fact of existence, power, poetry, love. From this came the naturalism of Santayana's doctrine.

To Santayana ours is a gay, barbaric folk, like playful Goths in Rome, wearing the classic robes of a post-rational morality. A strange melange it is to him of violent men and last Puritans, of glad hearts and simple, animal faiths, and of sallow, failing hopes. Those of us who know America, the city, the country, Boston, Chicago, the far west, the south, know that this is at least partly true. For America is complex and diverse, with many qualities of life and many cycles of culture moving concurrently but in different stages all in the same system. It is a universe, in valid metaphor at least, with past, present, future, with life and death, youth and senility, with hope and disillusionment all concomitant in its great moment of being. The Spanish poet is himself an example of this American diversity.

Spanish in blood and grace, Mediterranean and Catholic in intent, if not wholly in culture and belief, with an exact beauty in style, with disillusionment and some color of indifferentism in the passions and enthusiasms of the soul, at least superficially, it might seem that this philosophical poet has little in common with America or even with New England. But America is infinitely versatile and productive. Strange fruit that he is, Santayana is a product of the American tree.

He is indeed a kind of educated Emerson. Like Emerson the quality of his mind is mystical and alchemic, transforming the lumps and details of experience into eternal gold, and like Emerson he is more interested in the gleam of this transformation than in systems and rational relationships. I have long sensed this mystical quality in Santayana's thought and feel confident that I am not wrong in noting the similarity in this respect to Emerson. In an examination paper in one of Santayana's courses I once accused him of flagging mysticism on his passage to ideal ends, but the remark, I imagine, did not go further than the young Doctor Kallen, who at that time was his reader.

So, after thirty years, here it is again, true now, I think, as it was then, but still phrased, I am afraid, as indefinitely as before. Though Santayana dwells on reason, its harmonizing activity, its beauty, its creativeness of value, he actually operates within this rational and formal field relatively little. The hidden flame of insight is the light that really captures his eyes, the mystical identities and fusions of things, the combustion of this bit of experience or that in a pure flame. He associates things in imagination not by similarity, not by contiguity, but by a kind of contextual identity or transubstantiation. This is mysticism. And this is like Emerson.

Santayana is not a mystic in theory—if mystics can have theory—he is not mystical in the large, in fact he dislikes it; but in the poetic quality of his observation he is imaginatively mystical. This may be called a distributive mysticism. It is diffused through his work. He is a mystic saddened, sometimes almost to tears, I think, by a rationalism that perversely makes illusions of what would otherwise be real; and in his later turning to the spiritual life, he seems to recognize this dilemma. Mysticism is in his temper, though he refuses almost violently to let it enter the structure of his thought. Instead he veers towards scepticism and disillusionment. But the sceptic, at least some sceptics, and the mystic are alike. Both are seeking more than the conventional absolutes and relativities of the world, and both find, in a sense, the same thing in their respective empyreans. The difference between them is in the attitude towards what they find. At the fork in the road Emerson went one way, Santayana the other. But in wise and lovely insight into the context of things Santayana, like Emerson, is at his best. No other philosophers that I know have this quality to this degree.

Santayana reveals things to you by his insight; this is his inspiration; he does not stimulate you by his purpose. He is not immersed in will. Though Emerson and Santayana both have a formal idea of the good life, leaving it neither to chance, impulsive decision, nor to the natural development of the growing animal, Santayana is less the preacher. Happiness in principle, he says,[17] "is spontaneous life of any sort harmonized with

[17] *Soliloquies in England*, 70.

circumstances" and happiness is primary in the evaluation of life. It requires not drive or ambition but recognition. This comparative willessness is an aspect of Santayana's disillusionment. For, he might be imagined saying: Willing, so far as it is defined, is over and done with. Does not all the world of willing and all achievement that can be actually defined and made intelligible lie in the past behind us; is not the past alone able to define the will and make it real? Let the memory then encompass the realms of will and let there be no escape beyond the confines of the past, for beyond that the will is a vague surge into inarticulate mist. In his demand for measurable definition and form, such as lies only in the past, arises, it may be, Santayana's love of antiquity.

Santayana considers the sunset and the bright day that has been lived; Emerson was primitive and lived in a world of perpetual dawn. He rejected tradition, says Santayana,[18] and thought as one might think if no man had existed. But Santayana embraces tradition. He loves antiquity and thinks as one might think if all men had lived and all thinking had been done. He is retrospective in philosophy. His is the epilogue as Emerson's was the prologue of discourse. The two in their extremes, one in a sense pre-rational, the other post-rational, in mood if not in theory, meet in their common insight, their immediacy of vision. Movement or discursiveness of thinking, the progression of ideas, is not characteristic of either one, though it is more prominent in Santayana, of course, than in Emerson.

Santayana has also the advantage—or disadvantage—of a sophistication and diversity of culture that Emerson never dreamed of. Emerson was a profound but innocent man. He found the universe almost literally in his own back yard, and in that back yard were his roots. His acquantance with the patterns and techniques of the philosophically publicized systems of thought was surprisingly small for a man of his influence. It is more than possible that he could not have grasped some of them had he been acquainted, nor himself have made systems had he wished. His wisdom was not historically articulate nor theoretically defined. Santayana, on the other hand, is deeply

[18] *Poetry and Religion*, 220.

conscious of his philosophical background, passionately aware of the past. Tradition becomes articulate in him. His mind and his sensibilities are experienced and maturely formed. What men have thought and what men of art have formulated, at least in the great tradition from Greece, Rome, the Catholic church, to modern works of philosophy and art, he knows. His mastery of these overt materials of his work far exceeds that of Emerson.

And he is an older man than Emerson in his feelings and enthusiasms, older in his loves and disillusionments. He retains his metaphysical emotions, for example; they thrill and sing over the orb of all reality in a way that Emerson would recognize as spiritually akin; but Santayana, unlike Emerson, discards the orb of all reality. He clings only to poetic or emotional absolutes, or, in other words, mythical absolutes, and relinquishes the metaphysical ontologies that often go with them. He sings less of being than of recognition. Santayana is an educated Emerson, a less naïve and, in outward aspect at least, a colder Emerson. His love and warmth are more contained in aesthetic objects and less diffused over the material, moral and human world.

In spite of these differences Santayana has much more in common with Emerson than not. A thinker capable of hardness, even of cruelty if it be necessary, a traditionalist who says, "No," a philosopher without massive social impulse and compassion, a poet who loves beauty more than man, is not an Emerson, it is true, but he is what an Emerson might become with the burden of fifty modern years of sophistication. That particular cycle of moral evolution that begins in Puritanism and moves on through Unitarianism to Emerson, might well move still onward to Santayana. He is the only man with Emerson's quality of genius who has carried on to more mature conclusions the American tradition, or some part of it, that Emerson embodied.

They are thus spiritually akin. The difference between them in social attitudes and intellectual articulation is more or less the accident of history, of inheritance, of the cultural cycle. Santayana's intellectual insistence on the separation of the ideal and of existence, for example, leads him to envision an Aristotelian world graded in value, with upper and lower levels and various well defined degrees of excellence. Thus he comes early to an aristocratic conception of society, a timocracy,[19] or government by eminent men, though, as usual in such cases, he says little as to how these men shall be selected and given power; he comes to some measure of racialism, and to other doctrines of privilege that probably would not accord with Emerson's more democratic respect for the human being as such. Nor is Santayana's insight into social situations as profound or as comprehensive as into other fields. His *Reason in Society* and the social essays in *Soliloquies in England* though beautifully written are not much more than personal and are the least mature of his works. Santayana's Englishman, for example, is the well-worn stereotype, the comfortable "gentleman." Of the masses and millions of other Englishmen, on whom many of these "gentlemen" live fatly, Santayana says little and probably knows less. Socially he does not escape class limitations or Victorian sentiments of gentility. He is indeed more Greek than Catholic, more Aristotelian than Christian in his social attitudes, for he has little interest in people in general but much interest in cultivated persons about him. Though one may grant that love of all men is on analysis not much more than a vague sentimentality, it nevertheless seems to be effective. Jesus or Lincoln could hardly be Santayana's ideals; they might well have been such for Emerson.

Accidents though they may be, the differences between the two men are of course important. The subtlety of Santayana's work, its many-sidedness, its sophisticated defensiveness and delicate aplomb are in great contrast to Emerson's innocence. His mind is urban in contrast to Emerson's bucolic temperament. Nor does he care for nature as Emerson does, nature without frame, without human foregrounds. Emerson loves nature more for herself, the mother of motion and life, but he is less naturalistic in theory. Santayana loves nature, as Socrates does in the *Phaedrus*, as a pleasant place for discourse or meditation, but on the other hand is frankly naturalistic in theory, at least in his earlier and more American work. Santayana again has

[19] *Reason in Society*, 128.

seen many people, many places; his mind is experienced, sceptical and he sees happiness as the natural desire of individual, limited life. Happiness for him is relative, made by human hands. Emerson on the contrary thinks of goodness as a kind of destiny. For him value is central in reality, but for Santayana it is supervening.

But the two philosophers are alike in their humanistic treatment of material. Like most of the men in America's tradition, they deal less with things than with the bearing of things on man, less with problems than with men's ideas of problems. And the two philosophers are alike in their serenity: they are not philosophers of struggle. Though they come to that serenity by different paths, the one by implicit faith and joy in being, the other by scepticism and gentle disillusionment, they find at the end the same thing. Their serenity hangs above their heads like the mild sun.

I need not carry this casual comparison further, since its only value here is in evoking the uniquely magical pattern of life and ideas that is called a man and his philosophy. As I said at the beginning of this essay, I am not sure that I have captured the elusive philosophy of Santayana, and I have given some of the reasons why I am not sure. Nor am I sure that my notion of the man as seen mostly in his writing and teaching is sound or just. At best a person attempting such a task can do little more than create another fiction. It may be relevant to the early invitation made by Santayana "to think after a certain fashion," but can never hope to make articulate completely the deeper suggestions of a life and its formulation in ideas.

I have tried to look through the fire and dream of this poet's work, which in a sense have no time or place, and see the Santayana that I knew at Harvard in his relation to those forty years in America that were so powerfully present in his life, and I have suggested how that great present affected him and why he responded as he did. Santayana is American. At least so it seems to me.

Baker Brownell

Department of Philosophy
Northwestern University

2

Celestine J. Sullivan, Jr.

SANTAYANA'S PHILOSOPHICAL INHERITANCE

2

SANTAYANA'S PHILOSOPHICAL INHERITANCE

EVERY man's philosophy is his own. But just as his thought must be expressed in some current language or other and never in the pure object of his intent, so the very character of this thought is likely to show affinities to traditional forms or to express current drives and through such media to find understanding in the minds of men nurtured in the same traditions or participating in the same drives. A philosophy completely novel and divorced from the radical interests of men might have a cogency and unity all its own, might even be true, if that was its pretension, but it would be as incomprehensible to all but its author as Chinese characters are to the majority of Americans. But a philosophy such as Dewey's, for example, steeped in an idolization of the flux of things coupled with a faith in man's power to master this idol just by partaking of its ceaseless pulsations, by living in and with it, turning every accomplished end into a means to some further accomplishment, this is so expressive of the life and faith of so many in this distracted age, that it might well be said that if the flux is their God, Dewey is its prophet. And, on the other hand, a philosophy such as Santayana's, reminiscent equally of Greek idealism, materialism and scepticism, of Indian, neo-Platonic and medieval mysticism, of medieval scholastic distinctions and modern psychology, is certainly as steeped in tradition as Dewey's philosophy is expressive of contemporary temper.

These obvious observations are open to misunderstanding. I do not mean to imply that Dewey's philosophy is just an image of present day distraction or Santayana's but a shadow of the past cast across the present. Each is obviously a philosophy in its own right and to be understood in its own terms if at all. But how understand these terms—I do not mean the words but what they intend—if one has not thought or felt something similar to them in one's own reflections? And what would a man who knew nothing but distraction think and feel but distraction? True, if he does not relish such distraction he will be driven to seek a refuge from it, and he may find a deliverance in his own soul, but in what terms will he express this new insight? Very likely in none at all, unless he finds some expression congenial to his new feeling in the literature of the present or past. This being true of the least imaginative publican is no less true of the greatest philosophers. Certainly in Occidental philosophy ever since the days of Heraclitus and Parmenides originality has not consisted in absolutely new insights but in new syntheses. There has, for example, been no philosopher more original than Spinoza and none more traditional in his thought. Even Dewey, when he would give expression to the drives of the present, called upon the past to witness to its own error, and by this error to delimit and define the truth, for past philosophy he claimed sought certainty in antecedent reality whereas this can only be found in man's own work, in his own measure. So likewise said Protagoras.

It is not to criticize Santayana's originality then that I write of his philosophical inheritance, but rather, by presenting certain elements in his thought that are traditional, to remind the reader how he has handled these themes, what he has taken from them and what not, and how he has brought them together in his own philosophy. However, both the spatial limitations of this essay and the difficulty of the subject cause me to limit the traditional themes I shall consider to three: Platonism, materialism, and scepticism, so that I might better have entitled my essay, Platonism, materialism, and scepticism in Santayana's philosophy; only I hope it will be agreed that these *are* the dominant themes in this philosophy, and that while much even that is traditional in Santayana's thought does not fall under these three headings, especially as I shall treat them, broadly and in general outline, and much else going to the make-up of this scheme of things is also totally neglected here, still the synthesis of these three traditional themes forms the skeleton framework, the bare bones, over which is organized the body of a living philosophy.

Let us begin then with Platonism, and in Santayana's philosophy with the theory of essence. The principle of essence, Santayana says, is identity, and each essence is by being identical and individual and therefore distinguishable from every other essence, and consequently universal since "it contains no reference to any setting in space and time, and stands in no adventitious relations to anything," and is therefore eternal.[1] The properties of essence then are identity, individuality, distinguishability, universality and eternity, and all of these but the first follow from it, which is the principle of essence.

Here it might be well to observe that, whatever his critics may say, Santayana is perfectly clear that none of his many statements about essence and essences, in general and in particular, are meant to be statements of fact. The realm of essence, he says, is not an object of belief but a conceptual distinction and category of logic among others constituting "one of many languages in which the nature of things may be described" and anyone who wishes is free to discard these categories and employ others—if he can get on with them.[2] By a trick of language essence is seemingly hypostasized by being made the subject of a statement, as though it were some thing or other that I might find among the tables and chairs and books in my own room or at least among the things in the universe about me, like God sought by a telescope in the broad heavens, or the soul by a microscope in the pineal gland. But an essence is not something lying in wait to be discovered by an enquiring or a brooding mind, and unrealized essences are not laid up in a heaven beyond the stars. Yet Santayana writes of them, as some unrealized, some embodied here and not there, some intuited now and not then, of essences evoked by the Psyche or swimming into her ken; and literal-minded men want to know if these essences are not changed by these events, or where they are when they are not in existence, or else they boldly assert that if they do

[1] *Realm of Essence*, 18, 25.
[2] *Realm of Truth*, 47.

not exist, why then of course they are not, that what does not exist, being no substance, therefore can be no subject of any statement. However, it seems to me that we must, at least in describing his own philosophy, take Santayana at his word. The principle of essence is simply identity; an essence is not an existent and changing thing.

There is, however, one other important property of essence that follows from its definition which we have not as yet mentioned. The realm of essence is infinite. To deny this is to assert it, for the denial must designate that which is denied.[3] Therefore, it is either meaningless to assert or deny the infinity of the realm of essence, or this realm is infinite. Consequently there is a vast background for the setting of existence constituted by unrealized essences; the principle of identity is not limited to the character of what exists, for essence is eternal and does not come into being and pass away with the generation and corruption of its object, nor is it affected if this object never exists or if the essence itself is never thought of. Suppose I assert, for example, that all the numbers that have never been and never will be thought of are over 100, I intend these numbers though I do not think of them, and in the same way even in denying the infinity of the realm of essence I designate and therefore intend it.

Such in bare outline is Santayana's theory of essence. How Platonic is it? Let Santayana himself speak.

> I might almost say that my theory is a variant of Platonism, designed to render Platonic logic and morals consistent with the facts of nature. I am afraid, however, that this readjustment unhinges Platonism so completely that I have no right to call my doctrine Platonic. In the realm of essence as I conceive it, the sphere of Socratic Ideas is infinitely extended and freed from all confusion with natural forces. I am no pupil of Plato's in all that phase of his thought in which he seems to supply the lack of a cosmology by turning moral and ideal terms into supernatural powers.[4]

Santayana conceives that the Platonic Forms are essences but are limited in extent and are confused with natural forces,

[3] *Realm of Essence*, 22.

[4] *Realm of Essence*, 155.

whereas the realm of essence is infinite and from the identity of any essence nothing follows but that essence, so that essences cannot be natural forces. The Platonic Ideas are limited, he says elsewhere, to "only such essences as expressed the categories of Greek speech, the perfections of animals, or the other forms of the good," specifically not the objects of aesthetic intuition, the data of sense,[5] and again he says that "the Ideas originally were really nothing but values."[6]

There are two main points then, according to Santayana, on which the Platonic theory of the Ideas differs from his theory of essence, the limited extent of the realm of Ideas and the attribution of natural force to at least some of them. Let us consider each of these points in the Platonic tradition separately, and first the extension of the Ideas. (Note: In the Platonic references that follow I am obviously indebted to Burnet and Taylor.)

In the *Parmenides*, Parmenides asks Socrates what is the content of the world of forms and Socrates replies that he is certain there are forms of Right, Good and Noble but doubtful about forms of organisms and physical things, Man, Fire and Water, and in the case of such things as mud, dirt and hair, sensible things which do not appear to have a recognizable type of structure, he is inclined to think that there are no forms, though consistency with the theory of participation of forms and things would demand that these things have forms too. But Socrates feels that to give forms to everything would lead him into "abysmal nonsense."[7] Here the ethical emphasis of Socrates at least is plain. As Taylor says, "the main point is, that though Socrates is not certain about the contents of the system of forms, the forms of which he is most certain are those which correspond to our ethical ideals."[8]

Whereas Socrates, then, is primarily interested in ethical forms, it is fairly clear now that the theory of the forms was first developed as the Pythagorean theory of numbers. Numbers

[5] *Scepticism and Animal Faith*, 225.
[6] *Platonism and the Spiritual Life*, 21.
[7] *Parmenides* 130 b-d, cited in A. E. Taylor, *Plato*, 354.
[8] Taylor, *Plato*, 354.

were the forms of all things, the geometrical figures of which the world was constructed. But when this view was shattered by Zeno's paradoxes and the discovery that the diagonal and side of a square are incommensurable, the Pythagoreans resorted to a sharp division of the world of thought from the world of sense, the numbers from geometrical figures which are henceforth treated by them as only likenesses or imitations of numbers. As Burnet said, "the fateful doctrine of two worlds, the world of thought and the world of sense, in fact originated from the apparent impossibility of reconciling the nature of number with continuity as the Eleatics called it, or the unlimited as the Pythagoreans said."[9] And although mathematics was not of primary concern to Socrates, it should be observed that even in such a recognizably Socratic dialogue as the *Phaedo* "three" and the other numbers are spoken of as forms, and that in the *Republic* the study of numbers is made an integral part of the training of the philosopher-kings. But whatever may have been true of Socrates, it is certain that mathematics was of fundamental importance to Plato, for according to Aristotle[10] Plato called the forms numbers, thereby returning to the ancient Pythagorean doctrine, but evidently with a new theory of number and of the relation of arithmetic to geometry.

I have called attention to Plato's doctrine of forms as numbers and its Pythagorean background in order to point out that as I see Platonism in Plato the world of forms is both wider in some respects and narrower in others than Santayana seems to allow Plato—wider, for it takes in the whole range of numbers, as Plato understood these, integers, rational numbers and real numbers, including surds, and ideally, I suppose, whatever might be defined as a number whether or not known to Plato—but also narrower, for it would exclude anything about a man, for example, which could not be expressed in numbers, whereas the Socratic ethical norms, on the other hand, are redolent of other forms than numbers. I do not mean to say that Plato failed to observe other forms or essences than numbers, but that, consistently with his doctrine of the identity of the forms with

[9] John Burnet, *Thales to Plato*, 89-90.

[10] *Metaphysics* A 987b, 18-25, cited in Taylor, *Plato*, 508.

numbers, he would have to hold either that the ethical norms distinguished in the Socratic dialogues are numbers or they are not forms, just as Hobbes, for example, denies that color is anything but motion, for motion produces nothing but motion. Of course one form or essence cannot be another and to assert that color is motion or man is a number or round is square is simply to indulge in self-contradiction and to mean nothing at all, though such confusions are themselves real and quite understandable.

Since there are an infinite number of numbers, the realm of form is for Plato infinite, but only under the category of number, so that it is not absolutely infinite in Santayana's sense. But this infinite pluralism is commonly overlooked in Plato, both because of the priority of the Form of the Good in the *Republic* and the common identification of this form with the creator in the *Timaeus*, and because of what was made of Platonism by the neo-Platonists. Surely Socrates, as presented by Plato, distinguished many forms and in making the Good the one source of them all, he never meant to deny their essential diversity, even, I venture to say, in the case of the four virtues. Each virtue to be sure implies every other, but on this ground to deny their difference, one would be required to claim that the definition of one is the same as the definition of another, which it is not. It is only the mystics who deny difference, who swallow up all diversity in the sense of existence at one extreme or the intuition of pure being at the other, and the infinite pluralism of Platonism is thus swallowed up in the pantheistic neo-Platonism of Plotinus.

The orthodox Christian view however returned in part to a traditional Platonism, viewing the forms as the Ideas of God, but thereby introducing a psychologism into the theory of forms foreign to Plato, and also conceiving the content of the realm of forms more as Socrates apparently did than as Plato. But with the revival of learning and the scientific revolution of the seventeenth century a curious thing happened. Aristotle, who in the thirteenth century had become the symbol of a new interest in this world as opposed to the other-worldliness of medieval Platonism, had become by the sixteenth and seventeenth centuries the symbol of conservative natural philosophy, and an appeal was made by the new philosophers to the authority of Plato against the conservatism of the Aristotelians, and quite rightly, I think, if authority was needed at all for their radical temper and new insights; for, compared with Plato's tentativeness in natural philosophy, Aristotle errs on the side of dogmatism, especially in astronomy, though compared with his Renaissance defenders he is the essence of open-mindedness.

However, let us turn now to Santayana's contention that Platonism attributes natural force to at least some of the forms. In the *Phaedo* Socrates argues that the reason or cause for anything being what it is, why a beautiful thing is beautiful, for example, is the presence of its form to it or its partaking of its form. And in the *Republic* he states that there is one supreme form, the source of all the others, the Form of the Good, which is grasped only by a mystical and ineffable insight by the philosophical student after the completion of his studies in dialectic. It is this Form of the Good which is made the One of neo-Platonism and the *ens realissimum* of medieval Platonic realism, and as such it is conceived as the one source of all reality, playing as form the rôle of Pure Being in Santayana's philosophy but usurping, as supposedly existent, the rôle of what Santayana calls matter, the natural and dynamic force at work in the world, the nature of existence itself. It is the one being with respect to which the medieval distinction of essence and existence breaks down, the only being whose essence it is to exist. Hence it is true that in the Platonism of the neo-Platonists and the medieval realists form is operative, is conceived as a natural force, in the case of this one form at least whose essence implies its existence.

But, as De Wulf observes in his *History of Medieval Philosophy,* such realism, which he calls exaggerated, leads to pantheism because Being or God, the most universal and most real, includes everything else under it. Consequently, the orthodox realists, orthodox as Christians that is, drew a sharp distinction between God and his creation and between God and his Ideas, or models of creation. Thus Anselm claims that God before creating the world possessed in His infinite nature and knew the *ratio* of everything which was to exist, and that the truth of things has its foundation in God who willed things to be what they are, which I interpret to mean that God is a living force, not a form, who knows the forms or essences of things and wills their realization in existence, and is other than what he knows and wills. Therefore, while God's essence implies his existence, these are not identical, else God would only be the Idea of Himself present to His own mind.

This conception of God as other than an Idea or Form to whom the forms were present as His Ideas or Thoughts, as the models of creation, was not only held by the orthodox realists, but was the commonly accepted view in the twelfth century of God's relation to the forms and to created things, as witness a selection from a poem by Alain of Lille. (The translation is that of Henry Adams, in his *Mont-St.-Michel and Chartres.*)

> "God Himself pursues the task and sets in act
> What He promised. So He calls Noys to seek
> A copy of His will, Idea of the human mind,
> To whose form the spirit should be shaped,
> Rich in every virtue, which, veiled in garb
> Of frail flesh, is to be hidden in a shade of body.
> Then Noys, at the King's order, turning one by one
> Each sample, seeks the new Idea.
> Among so many images she hardly finds that
> Which she seeks; at last the sought one appears.
> This form Noys herself brings to God for Him
> To form a soul to its pattern. He takes the seal,
> And gives form to the soul after the model
> Of the form itself, stamping on the sample
> The figure such as the Idea requires. The seal
> Covers the whole field, and the impression expresses the stamp."[11]

Nor was this conception strange to Platonism, for it may be found in the *Timaeus*, the first two-thirds of which was known throughout the Middle Ages. In this work the Demiurge is definitely distinguished from the model of the sensible world.

[11] Pp. 357-358. (Reprinted by permission of the Houghton Mifflin Company, publishers.)

He is a craftsman who works with an eternal model in the realization of the sensible world as a copy of this. Of course it has been argued that the craftsman of the *Timaeus* is simply a mythical symbol for his own model. But this is not what is written in the *Timaeus,* where the craftsman and his model are explicitly distinguished, just as God and his Ideas are distinguished by Alain of Lille. And in such a typical Platonic myth as that of the cave in the *Republic* there is maintained a one-to-one correspondence between the terms of the myth and that which it is meant to symbolize, whereas if this distinction between craftsman and model was indeed itself meant to be mythical, a distinction in the symbols must have been meant to stand for the absence of any such distinction in what was symbolized, a form of mythology that seems very strange to me indeed.

To be sure, in the *Republic* the Form of the Good is said to be the source of all the reality and being of everything, and this may mean that, in Aristotelian terms, it is the formal cause of everything, as the presence of the form of Beauty to a beautiful thing is said by Socrates in the *Phaedo* to be the reason or cause why the thing is beautiful. Then how the Form of the Good came to be present to all things would require a further explanation, namely, that offered of the origin of order in the sensible world which is given in the *Timaeus* and the *Laws,* and on this interpretation, as Taylor says, "the activity of God as producing a world 'like' the forms is the one explanation Plato ever offers of the way in which the 'participation' of things in forms is effected."[12]

In any case, there were two Platonic traditions on this point, one that of the neo-Platonists followed somewhat hesitantly by the medieval realists, in which the Form of the Good as the One and the *ens realissimum* is made operative, generating all things out of itself, and the other, the orthodox Christian view, in which the forms came to be interpreted as the Ideas of the Christian God, the models of His creation.

So much then for the extension of the realm of forms in Platonism and the question as to whether some at least of these

[12] Taylor, *Plato,* 442.

forms are operative, or, in Santayana's terms, are confused with natural forces. As to the former point, the forms for Plato were probably infinite in number, but only of one kind, that is as numbers and not absolutely infinite. As to the second point, there are, as I have indicated, two Platonic traditions, logically opposed, though confused perhaps by some medieval realists, but as for Plato, it is fairly clear that he did not hold that any of the forms were operative.

Let us consider now the question of the relations of forms or essences. The realm of essence, as conceived by Santayana, is infinite in extension and each essence, being self-identical, is different from any other essence.

> Since any essence is an eternal form of being, each is grounded in itself without reference to any other. Thus the realm of essence is an infinite plenum or continuum, in which every essence is surrounded by others differing infinitesimally from it in character. This realm is an absolute democracy by virtue of the indefeasible right of every member to its self-made place in it; and whereas in earthly democracies it suffices to be born in order to acquire every civic right, in this celestial republic even those who have not taken that risk and trouble possess full citizenship. Nor is any one threatened here by the pressure of the hard-hearted majority, or by any rude government. Here is perfect anarchy in perfect peace. The population is infinite, no legislation is possible, and everybody is safe.[13]

How Platonic is this theory of the absolute democracy of the realm of essence?

In the *Sophist* Plato is led to consider the meaning of "not-being." Briefly his conclusion is that "not-being" is "the different," and that since everything is different from all other things, we may boldly assert that "not-being" is thoroughly real. Thus, of the five Platonic categories or forms considered in this section, being, motion, rest, identity and difference, "non-being" may be asserted of all of them, even of being itself, since each of them is different from any of the others, and thus is not any of the others. This democracy of the forms, however, does not preclude the possibility that some may combine with others, just as some letters can be combined to form syllables. Regarding

[13] *Realm of Essence*, 78.

this question of combination of the forms there are three logical possibilities, either all, or none, or some of them can combine, and Plato's conclusion is that some but not all can combine; thus motion can and does combine with being, since motion *is*, but not with rest, since motion *is not* rest. But this is not to say that motion is identical with being; here too it *is not*, it is not being.

This is the extent of what Plato has to say in the dialogues of the difference and combination of the forms. But now let us take "motion" and "being." They combine, for motion *is*. But is this combination, "motion plus being" therefore something different from "motion?" No, because motion *is;* "motion" is itself "motion plus being." Is "being" then within "motion;" is "motion" made up of "being" and "motion without being?" But motion *is*, so that "motion" cannot be composed of "motion without being" and "being." It is obvious that the theory of combination, and its co-relative, analysis, is not precisely fitted to the theory of the democracy of the forms, and yet that Plato held that every form is different from every other form is not only clear from the *Sophist* but follows also from Plato's identification of the forms with numbers, for each number is different from every other number.

Whether Plato saw clearly or not that the difference of every form from every other form precluded in any case the strict application of combination and analysis to the forms, he evidently did see this in the case of numbers. For, according to Aristotle, Plato said that "there is a first 2 and a first 3, and the numbers are not addible to one another."[14] That is, the number "m plus n" is not analyzable into two other numbers "m" and "n" nor a combination of these. For example, 2 plus 3 equals 5, but 5 is not a 2 and a 3 but *one* 5.

What then are we to say of Plato's view? He held that the forms are numbers and that the numbers are not addible; therefore, the forms cannot be combined. But in the *Sophist* he states that some forms will combine and others will not, just as some letters can be combined to form syllables and others cannot. Are we to explain this contradiction by the device of attributing

[14] *Metaphysics* M 1083a 32, cited in Taylor, *Plato*, 506.

one view to Socrates and another to Plato? While this would relieve Plato of contradiction, it would not do the same for Socrates. For that the forms cannot combine to make other forms nor be analyzed into combinations of other forms, as letters can combine to form syllables or syllables be analyzed into combinations of letters, is a necessary consequence of the difference of every form from every other, which is asserted in the *Sophist* to hold of everything.

All that I can say, then, is that the theory of combination and separation does not follow from the theory of the difference of the forms and that Plato evidently realized this with respect to numbers, which in his final philosophy are the only forms, so that on this point he is in agreement with Santayana, though not, as I have previously observed, on the extension of the realm of forms.

What then is to be said of the account of combinations of the forms in the *Sophist* I do not know. A very real problem is raised here of course, the problem that Santayana deals with in his chapters on complex essences, implication, and the basis of dialectic in *The Realm of Essence*, the problem of how, if each essence is different from every other essence, we can speak intelligibly of complex essences, of implication between essences, and of a logic or logics of such implication. The only answer to this problem that Plato offers in the dialogues is the theory of combination given in the *Sophist*. This theory is not followed by Santayana, nor is it consistent with the theory of difference presented in the same dialogue or that of the non-addibility of numbers attributed to Plato by Aristotle. In the field of numbers Plato evidently devoted a great deal of effort to the development of a satisfactory number system from which it would follow that while the number 5 was not composed of the numbers 2 and 3, 2 plus 3 would equal 5, so that 5 would be a "complex essence" as Santayana uses this term. The establishment of such a system would of course be an instance of a solution of the problem of the One and the Many in the realm of forms, but even if attained it would not in its own terms state what in the most general terms was involved in such a solution, that is, as applied to any forms, as forms, whether or not they are numbers. Since, however, for Plato there are no forms that are not numbers, he may have seen no need for a more general statement, or such a statement may simply have been lost. In either case this does not excuse the contradiction in the *Sophist*, whether or not this be Plato's own contradiction.

As for Santayana's theory of complex essences, this is simple in principle but goes beyond anything in Plato or Platonism. It is briefly, as I understand it, this, that though each essence is *one*, some essences may be surveyed or defined in terms of their parts. Such an essence would be from this point of view complex, that is, many in one, but not essentially complex, for then it would be many essences and not one. Consider a triangle, for example. It is a three-sided figure and may be analyzed into these parts in certain specified relations, but the triangle is one essence and not a mere list of its parts and relations. Or take a number, 6, for example. This may be analyzed as the product of 1 and 2 and 3, or the sum of 3 and 3, or 10 minus 4, etc. But 6 is clearly *one* number, 6, and not any of these analyses of it. If this is obvious even in the case of number, where it would be most easy to mistake one essence for a combination of others, then it is certainly clear in a case where the rules of number operations are not applicable. Consider the example we selected from the *Sophist*. In the form of motion there is both the form of being and the form of motion; the form of motion may be so analyzed. But it would be absurd to say that the form of motion is the form of being plus the form of motion.

If then a complex essence is not any analysis of it, why are some analyses incorrect? If 3 and 3 is not 6, why is this analysis correct and the statement that 3 and 4 is 6 incorrect? 3 and 4 is not 6, but neither is 3 and 3. What analyses are correct is determined by the definitions of the terms, not just of the term analyzed but of the terms of the analysis as well. The whole number system is so defined that certain operations with certain numbers will be correct and certain ones not. As Kant observed, 12 *is not* 7 plus 5, but 7 plus 5 equals 12, not because, as Kant thought, this is a synthetic *a priori* truth but because 7 and plus and 5 and "equals" and 12 are so defined that this expression is correct. The whole number system as an essence includes in its analysis all numbers and all their relations, by definition, but each one of these is likewise an essence, by definition. An essence excludes from its analysis only such terms as by definition of it and of them would be so excluded. Thus the form of motion excludes the form of rest by mutual definition.

One consequence of the unique character of each essence is that no part of a complex essence can be an essence as that part, for an essence is a whole and not a part. 2 and 3 equals 5, but the number 5 is not composed of the numbers, or essences, 2 and 3; the numbers are not addible. They are not parts of other numbers, but each is the number it is in itself.

> Thus logical implication is unilateral; every essence involves its parts, considered as the elements which integrate it; but these elements, considered as separate essences and individual units (which all essences are) do not in turn imply any whole into which they may enter elsewhere; for they may enter into all sorts of concretions, and their only essential being is their own and what is intrinsic to their individuality.[15]

Consequently, it follows that any logic is only a chosen set of implications within a complex essence, and that dialectic is "the conscience of discourse" holding the mind to its assumptions as players hold one another to the rules of their game, all of which does not preclude a different elaboration of some of these same terms in a different logic with a different dialectic, just as players may play with the same cards differently in a different game. The only limitations which must be adhered to by any logic are those laid down by the definitions of all the terms.

Thus the theory of the difference of every essence from every other essence follows from the principle of essence, identity, and from this it follows that no essence defined as complex can be composed of other essences and that therefore there is no logic of the internal implications of an essence that excludes any other logic, except that of the whole realm of essence which excludes nothing. But beyond the principle of difference, which was itself not strictly adhered to by Plato in the *Sophist* and was flagrantly violated by the neo-Platonists, these consequences were not drawn by Plato and the Platonists, primarily because they had

[15] *Realm of Essence*, 86.

not grasped the absolute infinity of the realm of forms even when, as in Plato's case, they did not attribute natural force to any of the forms, but conceived the realm as limited to one intelligible system exhibiting a logos they would impress upon all of nature excluding any other.

However, just as the theory of essence is not the whole of Santayana's philosophy so the theory of forms is not the whole of Platonism. Platonism points on the one hand to a theory of value and on the other to a theory of force, the ultimate ground or grounds of values, forms and everything else. The Platonic theory of force I shall consider briefly in dealing with Santayana's materialism, that of value I want to say a few words about now.

In *Platonism and the Spiritual Life* Santayana observes that Platonism is not a disinterested idealism, a self-forgetful love of essence for the sake of essence alone. The very selectivity of the Platonic realm of forms is proof against this. He is probably right here, though I would question the degree of emphasis on political morality he attributes to Plato. "To this descendant of Solon," he says, "the universe could never be anything but a crystal case to hold the jewel of a Greek city."[16] However, I think a close reading of the *Republic* alone will show that, austere though Plato's ideal state may seem to a democrat, the interests it was meant to serve were those of its members, and specifically, in the case of the rulers, their interest in pure science, in mathematics and dialectic. Such studies are an end toward the realization of which the state is a means. To be sure, for the privilege of such study the rulers must pay with their rule, but are in turn rewarded not in gold but with the means of sustenance and the leisure to study. That state is ruled best, says Plato, in which the rulers are least eager to rule.

This emphasis on the pursuit of science as the highest end is in keeping too with what we learn of Plato's final philosophy from Aristotle. It is a philosophy of number and all things are viewed in a mathematical light. It is here I think that Plato's spiritual bias is to be found. Form is mathematical and what is formal in the material world expresses number; all else is but

[16] *Platonism and the Spiritual Life*, 27.

dire necessity, mere brute fact. But the good soul, a ghostly visitor in the realm of matter, is akin to form; it loves harmony as its natural goal, its appropriate expression, and in the soul of the philosopher this love is conscious, for he seeks not only to realize a harmony in his own life but to know harmony itself. Thus all value, the end of life, is harmony, form, number, and, in the philosopher, the knowledge of this.

For Santayana too value is harmony, the good natural to each living thing; and the good for spirit, itself alive, is the contemplation, the union with essence, disinterested in pure spirit, as far as any spirit becomes pure, but biased by animal exigencies and animal faith in any actual living Psyche. Pure spirit is addressed to the realm of essence for Santayana, as the soul of the philosopher is addressed to the realm of forms for Plato. The difference between the two lies in the different extensions of the realms of their respective objects, the absolute infinity of the realm of essence and the limited infinity of the realm of forms or numbers.

Beyond this of course is a more fundamental difference between Platonism and the philosophy of Santayana, namely in their respective theories of the origin of the embodiment of form, for the one is spiritualistic, the other materialistic. I have seen reason to suppose that Plato himself, whatever might be said of some of his followers, did not attribute natural force to the forms; but when he came to explain why some forms are realized he had recourse to a theory of souls, active spiritual forces working with the forms as models and shaping the world in accordance with their purposes. A soul, for Plato, is a self-moved mover, and the proof he gives for the existence of souls in Book X of the *Laws* is that motion must at some point be spontaneous, and a spontaneous source of motion is a soul. It cannot be physical, for physical motion is always mechanical or communicated, a motion which can only move other things and supposes a spontaneous motion as its source. Therefore, the movements of soul, "tempers and wishes and calculations, true beliefs, interests and memories" are the source and cause of all physical movement.[17]

[17] *Laws* 896d, cited in Taylor, *Plato,* 491.

Thus the issue between ancient materialism and Platonism is clearly indicated. It has nothing to do with any picture of the elements of matter, whether these be conceived to be earth, air, fire and water, or the opposites beneath these, or one of the elements to the exclusion of the others, or indivisible atoms, or Pythagorean solids; it turns solely on the source of motion, conceived so widely as to include all change. The materialists held a dynamic conception of matter, Plato a static one; that is, he attributed the source of all material change to a force from without coming in and stirring up dead matter, like a mighty whirlwind, such as those I have seen advancing across the dry plain of the valley of Mexico, a mysterious spirit gathering its body about it as it moves. The materialists, on the other hand, were quite conscious that they conceived matter as dynamic. Democritus held that this world was created by no one and no thing, that its eternal motion was as native to it as the atoms and the void they moved in. It was in fact to circumvent the dialectic of Parmenides that the atomists drew such a sharp distinction between the atoms and the void, in order that the atoms would have space in which to move.

To be sure, Plato varies his story in the *Timaeus*. Here the receptacle in which the Demiurge realizes the cosmos is given random chaotic movements of its own, but movements capable of being organized by the Demiurge into the order of the cosmos. The Demiurge is responsible only for order and orderly motions. This does not claim as much for soul or rob matter of as much as does the *Laws*, where disorder and irregularity are attributed to a bad soul or souls; but in either case what Plato said not to be native to matter the materialists attributed to it, and so does Santayana.

Such materialism holds that change is spontaneous in existence (for Santayana it is the very principle of existence) and that whatever order there is in existence is an expression of matter itself. Materialism holds, that is, that change and order are not imposed on matter from without but constitute its very nature. Of course the mechanists of the seventeenth century, much more than the ancient atomists, tended to substitute a picture of matter, an essence intuited or intended, for the thing itself. The first law of motion seemingly excluded all spontaneity from matter; yet force, obvious and marvelous, was everywhere. What was more natural, therefore, than to see in its manifestations God's presence in space, as Newton did, or, more radically, having shorn matter of all activity, to deny the very reality of matter as Berkeley and Leibnitz did in their different ways. Seventeenth century mechanism was a very valuable tool in its time but paradoxically enough it worked havoc with philosophical materialism, not that mechanism and spontaneity are contradictory, but a scent for external causes and general laws and simple pictures of nature did make them appear so at that time. And now in our own time, when nature is once again sensed to be at heart dynamic, there are those who see in this revival of a view common to ancient materialists a refutation of materialism itself.

I know of no term more abused than this term "materialism." Suffice it to say that in the sense in which the ancient materialists were materialists Santayana is a materialist. Thus Santayana calls the "concrete but ultimate elements in the web of existence, within which there is no change or variation of essence"[18] *natural moments* and to each natural moment he attributes a *forward tension* which is "whatsoever corresponds, within a natural moment, to the external fact that it occurs between two others,"[19] that it is continuous with them in an actual progressive continuum. But, further, this universal flux "is many-voiced, like the sea of Homer."[20] There are many natural moments collateral with one another "if, when traced backwards or forwards according to their inward tensions, they terminate in identical ulterior moments,"[21] so that "a natural moment arises and exists only by virtue of external supports; first a parent to launch it and determine its initial character, and then collateral moments to control that heritage and determine what, and how long, it shall be in act."[22] Thus the ground is set for a possible

[18] *Realm of Matter*, 88.
[19] *Ibid.*, 91.
[20] *Ibid.*, 95.
[21] *Ibid.*
[22] *Ibid.*, 97.

universal mechanism in which the lateral tensions of collateral natural moments determine the existence and the forward tension of every part, but it is just as true, if this is the case, that the forward tensions of these same parts, taken together and meeting, compose the lateral tensions at work at that time, so that "material existence, though everywhere conditioned externally, is everywhere spontaneous."[23] And as matter is spontaneous, so it takes on whatever forms it may. That matter is the source of its own forms follows from its spontaneity, so that granted this it follows that order is not imposed from without.

Santayana's objections to Platonic spiritualism, to the Platonic notion of spiritual force, are two—one, which we have noticed, that Platonism makes of some forms natural forces, and two, that a Platonic "soul" is simply a material force. I think that Plato himself may be absolved of the first charge; the second is more to the point. Depending on which version we take, that in the *Laws* or that in the *Timaeus*, the Platonic "soul" is made responsible either for all change or only for orderly change. If we take the first version, then matter becomes simply a static picture or model of the world, a form or essence that is, and the Platonic categories have been turned topsy-turvy, for originally it was the forms that were eternal and changeless and the world of visible things that made up a Heraclitean flux never for two moments the same with itself; and now this flux is stopped in its course, like the sun stayed by the hand of Jehovah, and good and bad souls are called in from without to stir it up, like angels the waters of Bethesda. But if we take the second view, the flux is restored to matter, but only in part. Intelligence is made responsible for the realization of intelligible form and intelligence is not material; but since it would be hard to make out what forms are not intelligible, this view would on analysis tend to collapse into the first. However, let us take it on its own grounds. What then is to be understood by the creative force of intelligence? Intellectual apprehension is properly addressed to the forms; this as Santayana says is the essence of spirit. But the forms

[23] *Ibid.*, 99.

are not themselves operative; this is granted and is even a cardinal point with Plato. However, by the activity of the intelligence either Plato means a precluded activity of the forms apprehended in intuition or intended in thought, what in Aristotle is the seeming identification of formal and final cause, or he means to intend the native force of the flux itself which takes on and supports, when it does, forms congenial to the apprehension and interests of a mind adapted to its material environment; either, that is, he means a formal or material principle, and the former he has explicitly excluded.

Now I do not mean that Plato would grant this conclusion. This is the dialectic of his position. Undoubtedly, however, in spite of his great devotion to the pursuit of knowledge as an end in itself, and his consequent pure conception of the nature of form in his chosen field of study, in mathematics, he was also at heart, as Santayana maintains, a moralist, and for Plato the moralist, as for the Manichaeans after him, the categories of good and bad take metaphysical precedence over both form and matter and divide the world along moral lines. Thus the dualism of the good and bad souls in the *Laws* cuts across the dualism of form and matter and makes of the Platonic philosophy a strange and unresolved discord. Are there two Platos then? Are Plato the moralist and Plato the scientist at odds with one another? Or is the moralist simply playing the part of the good ruler, the good shepherd of the *Republic*, who sees fit at times to lie to his people in their own interests, or at least in the interests of the philosopher-kings? I do not know, but I sometimes wonder.

Santayana in any case is both a Platonist and materialist, which is to say that he recognizes both the categories of form and matter, the principle of identity and the principle of change, an Aristotelian in fact, minus the Aristotelian teleology, which may or may not be the heart of Aristotle. And Santayana has himself given a delightful presentation of this purified, or denuded, Aristotle in *Dialogues in Limbo*. But Santayana is also a sceptic and I pass at last to the tradition of scepticism and its place in Santayana's philosophical inheritance.

Ancient Scepticism was in origin a cult of indifference; it

was an ivory tower or escape philosophy, at one in this respect with Epicureanism and Stoicism. As the Epicureans and Stoics found escape from a collapsing world in the conviction of the necessity of all things, which taught the Epicureans not to fear death and to seek content in the milder pleasures, and the Stoics the virtue of living according to nature, so the Sceptics found solace in the conviction that nothing was certain, for if this is the case, what need we fear when the wisest of men can know nothing? To be sure, the world is collapsing about us, and we are helpless in our ignorance and cannot put things right, but then we are no worse off than other men, for this is the natural state of man, to know nothing. Thus it is curious and interesting to note that the Epicurean and Stoic belief in necessity and the ancient Sceptic doctrine of uncertainty have much in common in their influence on, or revelation of, a human attitude. They are all doctrines of the powerlessness of man in the midst of a nature so much greater than he, so far beyond his control; they are all forms, albeit exaggerated in their several ways, of natural piety. The Sceptics in denying knowledge did not deny nature; by implication they asserted her Sphinx-like majesty. Ignorance is not ignorance if of nothing, and in their absolute scepticism the Pyrrhonists saluted what they could not embrace, a nature independent of them, a power vast and inscrutable. A sceptic is necessarily a naturalist, for he refuses to attribute to the world at large a solicitous interest in his own destiny, which indeed might be a very unlikely hypothesis.

But likelihood and unlikelihood presuppose a mitigated scepticism, like that of the Middle Academy, which Santayana claims to be closer to his own scepticism than that of the Pyrrhonists. It is well to acknowledge our ignorance, but it is foolish and superstitious to make of ignorance itself a cult. Santayana's scepticism, then, like that of the moderns, is no end in itself but a clearing the ground of ancient debris that man might build more securely. Unlike the moderns and like the ancients, however, he is thorough in his scepticism; in this rebuilding he does not reinstate as certain what he had previously found dubious, like Descartes, or claim that the object of his belief is some construction of his own mind, like Hume, or in a more radical way, Kant and the German Idealists.

Among the moderns Hume is closest to Santayana in scepticism. His scepticism stops short only at the claim that the existence of "perceptions" is certain; but this contention vitiates his whole positive philosophy for it led him to attempt to build the world in which we believe out of these perceptions as elements, as a man might build a house with bricks. That an assumption such as this attempt implies, namely, that what we are most certain of constitutes the elements of the world we believe in, that such an assumption is absolutely gratuitous, and, on the face of it, contrary to the very nature of our belief in an external world, Hume seems to allow when he leaves the investigation of the causes of our sensations to physical philosophers, but just as obviously forgets, when, in a section of the *Treatise* ironically entitled "Of scepticism with regard to the senses," he constructs a world supposedly believed in out of the data of the senses.[24]

Santayana criticizes Hume's doctrine of "tendencies to feign" on the ground that proof of a genesis of our beliefs is no proof of their falsity; "the truth of beliefs hangs on what they assert, not on their origin."[25] In this contention I would certainly agree with Santayana. But if we pause to consider what Hume thought we had a tendency to feign, namely the continued and independent existence of our perceptions when we do not perceive them, or the *identity* of all our *different* perceptions as constituting our personal identity, we might well agree with Hume that such beliefs would indeed be but tendencies to feign what in the nature of the case is absurd; but we might also question whether any sensible person, including Hume, ever entertained such beliefs, precisely on the grounds of the patent absurdity of what they assert. I realize that these grounds are not sufficient in themselves, considering the absurd *credos* that human beings have prated from time immemorial; but then there seems little cause for absurdity regarding what we mean by an external world or our personal identity, though,

[24] Curiously enough, most of Hume's real and enduring sceptical analysis in the *Treatise* is to be found in Book I, Part III, "Of knowledge and probability" and some of his most dogmatic doctrines in this section of Book I, Part IV, "Of scepticism with regard to the senses."

[25] *Scepticism and Animal Faith*, 296.

from this point on, as to the constitution of that external world and the destiny of our own precious selves, there is no limit to what men may believe.

In any case, Hume seems most weak to me in what he claimed we had a tendency to feign rather than in any contention that a genesis of our beliefs proves their falsity, which I am not aware that Hume holds, since he rests his case for the feigned character of those beliefs he regards as feigned on their obvious absurdity. And he was led to this contention that we must feign absurdities because of his gratuitous assumption that since what we believe in is something supposedly existent, it must be constructed out of perceptions, the very bricks of existence. This opinion that perceptions constituted the very stuff of existence resulted from Hume's identification of the *terminus ad quem* of sceptical analysis with the object of animal faith, of essence with existence. This was Hume's fatal error, from which proceeded his strange and absurd accounts of the nature of men's fundamental beliefs in an external world and in their own selves.

(Note: I have not here considered Hume's account of the nature of our belief in the case of causal inference. There is nothing absurd of course in our expectation of the future or inference of the past, and Hume does not claim that these are feigned; but it may be noted that even here Hume would have our belief consist merely in the vivacity of some present idea without any reference to its transcendent object. In fact, he fails to distinguish the object of the belief from the belief itself. But it is quite clear, for example, that the sun I believe will rise tomorrow is not my idea of it tonight, no matter how vivacious this may be, and should I claim it to be so, I would certainly be most confused in my temporal orientation. The plain fact is that there is no place in Hume's scheme for anything but the perceptions of the moment, so that not only the meanings of the external world and of the self are reduced to perceptions, but the past and future are reduced to the present, making even causal reasoning indistinguishable from the heated dreams of a madman. All this however does not touch in the least the value of Hume's scepticism, which is quite independent of the dogmatic psychologism he constructed in place of the rationalistic dogmas he destroyed.)

Finally the question might be raised, why Santayana supposes that a thorough scepticism is one of the best approaches to essence, how through scepticism the distinction between essence and existence is made clear and obvious. I do not propose to present a summary of Santayana's account of this process as given in *Scepticism and Animal Faith,* but to indicate very briefly why, as I see it, he supposes that a thorough scepticism will lead inevitably to a distinction of essence from existence.

Since the principle of essence is identity and the principle of existence change, if I am certain of anything, I am certain of what it is, of its identity, of its essence; but, by the same token, in being certain of it, I am not certain of its coming to be, its duration and its passing away, in a word, of its existence. Thus, grant the certainty of anything and it is the essence of that thing, not its existence, supposing it to exist, of which I am certain. Thus does scepticism ferret out and distinguish essence from existence. Why may not the object of which I am certain, then, be the coming to be, the duration or the passing away of something, and in this case at least my certainty be a certainty of the existence of something, with no need to distinguish its essence from its existence? Such an object I may intend, of course; but to grasp real change in an indubitable intuition I should have to perform an impossible feat, grasping at once, in one intuition, what by hypothesis is itself not one but divided into parts coming before and after. The form of this succession I might perchance intuit, but then it would not be as the form of the real succession, in that embodiment, but as existing in my intuition that I would grasp it, and it would always be questionable whether the form so grasped was the same as the form of the real succession. Thus not only if I am certain of anything am I certain of essence, but this alone I can be certain of, never of existence. Had Hume understood this he would not have been tempted, it seems to me, to construct a world out of the data of experience, and thus his scepticism would not have been vitiated by a psychologism the end of which, in German Idealism, he could not possibly have foreseen and would surely have disavowed, for he was a man of great common sense as well as a great philosopher.

One, like Santayana, who is a thorough sceptic realizes that out of the residua of scepticism nothing can be constructed, not even a language about these data. To label the essence of something and to return to what we call the same thing with what we call the same label is to perform an act of faith. The identity of essence is certain, by definition; but that this essence intuited or intended today is the same as that of yesterday is by no means certain, and yet faith in such identity is necessarily presupposed in the employment of any stable language. And such faith works pretty well, of course, for general terms, such as those of mathematics, used judiciously. But when we come to indicate the full variety of the world we experience, the world of trees and flowers, of blue skies and dark nights and stars overhead, no man of sense expects language to correspond literally with the wealth of this variegated world. Here all is equally obvious and equally beyond anything like an exhaustive indication in language, and yet here, likewise, is the touchstone of all our language and all our thought, without which all would be but the One Absolute of Schelling, the dark night in which all cows are black, and not even this as distinct and different from the day.

The end of scepticism is silence in the presence of the simplest fact. If we would be thorough sceptics we must pause now and then before the data of our world in simple wonder at them. If I see a sunset I love, as here in Oregon, a land of much cloud and sky, I often do, or a flower, or wind moving over the grass, I have no desire then to speak; only later, as now, I may call upon language to remind me or others of such things, to call them up in memory or imagination, not by any literal description, which would be impossible, but by indicating in a general way the circumstances of the experience and, by a turn of phrase or other form of expression, suggesting a mood. All language about the full character of the immediate is inevitably poetic, if it is not to be wholly inadequate to the purpose in hand.

Thus does a thorough scepticism bring us around to wonder and poetry, and so it does not seem strange to me that Platonism and scepticism are united in Santayana's philosophy, the careful delineation and definition of essence in language with the love and wonder of it in sceptical silence. It may be remembered, moreover, that for Plato himself philosophy was always a quest, a love of wisdom, not a pretense to it as it has been so often in later days; and it is the pretense and not the quest that modern scepticism when thorough denies.

Thus I have completed this brief survey of three traditional themes in Santayana's philosophy, his Platonism, materialism, and scepticism. In so doing I have analyzed the complex form or essence of this philosophy, like a triangle, into three main parts; and just as three lines taken one by one do not make a triangle, but only the union of the three in one form, so these three themes, one by one, do not make this philosophy, but only their unity does this. Even this bare unity is, as I have said, but the skeleton framework of this philosophy; like a triangle rich with geometrical implications, or better yet, like that triangular form much used by painters in diverse and intricate works, this framework supports a vast and subtle organic philosophy with many secret springs and strange unpredictable motions, a living philosophy that is a joy to observe.

CELESTINE J. SULLIVAN, JR.

DEPARTMENT OF PHILOSOPHY
UNIVERSITY OF OREGON

3

Daniel M. Cory

SOME OBSERVATIONS ON THE PHILOSOPHY OF SANTAYANA

3

SOME OBSERVATIONS ON THE PHILOSOPHY OF SANTAYANA

IT was my original intention to contribute a long and detailed essay on the later philosophy of Mr. Santayana. At the outbreak of the war, however, I found myself stranded in Switzerland with hardly any books to refer to either for information or for purposes of quotation. So, frankly, under the circumstances, I was in no mood to compose the kind of essay I had promised the Editor. I decided instead to set down some random observations on certain refinements, or shifts of interest, that have occurred in the philosophy of Mr. Santayana since he left America over twenty-eight years ago. On the epistemological issues involved, I shall speak with a certain measure of confidence: if at the end I make bold to say something about the *moral* quality of Mr. Santayana's work—I am merely airing the prejudices of an unevenly educated man with a happy-go-lucky temperament. It is essential to remember, however, that the movement of Mr. Santayana's mind is so comprehensive that even his theory of knowledge has a certain moral complexion, and his moral considerations are tinged by his epistemology. One feels that the whole man, rather than an exclusive area of the cerebral cortex, is behind the written word. But let me begin with a few observations on the treatment of knowledge in *The Life of Reason,* in order that we may appreciate the later variations on this problem in *The Realms of Being.*

I. Realism in an Idealistic Climate

If the initial task of epistemology is always an investigation of that original fund of unclarified knowledge that is presupposed as an inevitable starting-point for discussion, then we may say that the first volume of *The Life of Reason* is chiefly concerned with an attempt to trace the historical growth of this knowledge. Sometimes the description is in terms of the mental history of the individual mind, at other times it refers to the general dawning of knowledge in the collective consciousness of the race. It is obvious, however, that our primary knowledge of things is overlaid and distorted by many spontaneous illusions about the real world in which we live and have our material being. So perhaps the most interesting theme in *Reason and Common Sense* is the effort to sketch the difficult flowering in the human mind of the *idea* of a natural world. There is a clever diagnosis of the psychological birth-pangs experienced before the *meaning of matter* is born stripped of its grosser superstitions. Of course it is inevitable that this *idea* should remain wrapped in certain symbolic swaddling-bands: otherwise our proud intuition would hold nothing but some anemic mathematical construction.

A philosopher, however, can hardly expect to recover the epistemological innocence of a new-born baby in order to observe at first hand just how our crude notions of things flower in experience. By the time we begin to investigate the nature or history of our primary knowledge we are adults already possessed of a fund of practical if somewhat unrefined information. A philosopher may also resort to an external observation of the early behaviour of babies or young monkeys, and thereby gather some pertinent hints as to the growth of knowledge; but it would be extremely difficult to determine, for example, at exactly what epistemological crisis in the mental history of a child or monkey the notion of the *independent* existence of a physical object arises: a wild yell or a sudden burst of chattering are inadequate evidence to establish the point in question. If it would be desirable, then, to observe at first hand just how our original notions of things evolve in experience (either within my own immediate field of experience, or that of another mind) there is, unfortunately, no direct opportunity for such an ideal kind of observation.[1]

[1] For a fuller treatment of this dilemma, I must refer the curious reader to my article entitled "The Origin in Experience of the Notion of a Physical Object," *Analysis*, I (May, 1934).

Let us be content, however, to take Mr. Santayana's description of the flowering of intelligence as a work of the *imagination*, as a rough sketch fitting rather loosely the elusive facts he was trying to follow. It was his laudable desire to transplant the fantastic dialectical cosmology of Hegel onto a naturalistic basis and to offer us instead a sober description of the birth and development of reason in man. He pursued a rather ambitious ideal with enthusiasm, and if I find his epistemology a little "in the air," it is only because the manner, the *historical manner* of his investigation does not permit of a closer description of our original knowledge of things. But in so far as he, or Bertrand Russell, or any other philosopher, is under the illusion that it is quite possible to trace closely the flowering of knowledge in the nascent mind, I can only shake my head at his confidence.

If the dominant theme of *Reason and Common Sense* is the extrication of the idea of a natural world from the lavish mythology of the human mind, there is of course in the ensuing volumes the general epistemological position to be considered. Now Mr. Santayana has always been a *realist* in theory of knowledge; that is to say, he has accepted the independent existence of things, of fellow-minds, and of natural causation, as the inescapable presuppositions of any sincere inquiry into the conditions of experience. And one must admire the intellectual courage and soundness required to be an unfashionable realist at a time when the high-tide of German idealism was sweeping over all official philosophy; when the lofty guns of Bradley and Royce were booming respectively at Oxford and Harvard, and one had only the watery phenomenalism of J. S. Mill and William James for a sanctioned alternative. I am not astonished, then, to find passages that reveal a certain hesitation, a tendency to stammer, when it comes to stating unambiguously the precise nature and extent of our knowledge of the external world. But an unfortunate complication of this uneasiness in theory of knowledge is a rather loose employment of such key-terms as *reality*, *appearance*, *property*, *the ideal*, etc. For instance, I recall that Mr. Santayana has written somewhere in *The Life of Reason* as if "appearances" might be the "properties of reality." This would *appear* to be flatly contradicting his own official view. If, however, we substitute the word "effects" for "appearances," and take "reality" as a blanket term to cover all those dimensions of being that he was later to distinguish so exactly, the difficulty is at least mitigated. It is not my intention, however, to try and justify the utter consistency of Mr. Santayana's philosophy over a stretch of some forty years: it is enough to remark again that his basic realistic allegiances have never been abandoned, and that the later refinements in theory of knowledge are due much more to a shift in interest and manner of investigation, than to any radical change in doctrine. When he gave up teaching at Harvard he became free of the idealistic *climate* (I am including phenomenalism and moral idealism in the metaphor we owe to Dr. Whitehead) that permeated that seat of learning: he could now make a fresh start and allow to develop unhampered by the routine of lectures, or unconscious academic pressure, those philosophical affinities that have found full expression in his *chef d'œuvre—The Realms of Being*. Stimulating conversations with Dr. Moore and Bertrand Russell in England, and the interest in the *non-existent* that had come from Meinong in Austria, certainly played a part in a general spring-cleaning of the entire house of thought. I have always felt, however, that even the subtle distinctions of his mature theory of knowledge are somehow *there* in *The Life of Reason:* hidden from the full light of intuition, perhaps, but waiting, like patient seeds, a late summer of intense contemplation. And after all, the *Parmenides* and the *Theaetetus* were available before the advent of Meinong.

Mr. Santayana told us all long ago that "knowledge is a salutation, and not an embrace." There is nothing in his later pronouncements to contradict this perfect epistemological statement, although one may feel that the possibility of embracing the external world in *sensuous* perception has become even more remote in his mind. But if we are content to take our knowledge of things for what it is—an appropriate human version of the facts—, and cease to insist that it ought to be something different—a more literal acquaintance with things—, perhaps we will have learned our fundamental lesson in theory of knowledge from Mr. Santayana.

II. In the Steps of Descartes

I turn now to the later manner of investigating our primary knowledge of things adopted in *Scepticism and Animal Faith.* In this prolegomena to *The Realms of Being* there is no further attempt made to trace the history of our original fund of knowledge; but instead we have an initial sceptical investigation of the latent presuppositions involved in all immediate experience that claims to be a *knowing* of something other than and beyond itself. Essentially, this is the way of Descartes (only more radical in execution), the way of any conscientious philosopher who desires at a certain stage in his development to render explicit, to lay bare the anatomy, as it were, of those cardinal assumptions that he is compelled to make at every turn of his argument, or with every inquiry that he undertakes in the world. Such a deliberate dissection of knowledge enables a philosopher not only to clarify the precise nature of these inevitable assumptions, but also, by a kind of self-correction within scepticism itself, to realize the vital compulsion of the animal side of the mind in making its cognitive claims. Now the compulsion I speak of is at bottom *physiological,* rather than Fichtean: when I am hungry and remember a loaf of bread, the compulsion to posit that object is probably due to some organic condition, and not the innate constitution of the Ego.

I am aware, however, that the ultimate step in Mr. Santayana's relentless scepticism, the arrival at a "solipsism of the present moment," and the subsequent declaration that "nothing given exists," have been questioned in various quarters, and the usual stricture is that *essences* are abstractions from simple perceptual propositions entertained by even the doubter himself, and therefore highly artificial. The possible force of such an objection is mitigated, however, by the fact that not all our immediate experience is of the assertive type expressed in such a statement as "this friar is fat." Indubitably a large part of our perceptual life is of this character; whenever, for example, we *recognize* an object in the world: but there are also moments of pure intuition or feeling—moments untroubled by any form of assertion—that *supersede* the more practical work of the senses and judgment, and flood the mind with joy. It is not my intention to imply, however, that sense-perception and discourse are necessarily distracting and full of anxiety: I merely wish to call attention to the obvious fact that there are states of consciousness in which nothing ulterior is asserted or believed in. But the academic mentality (especially in England) is inclined to be too verbal and finical: it often betrays an inveterate impotence to escape the superficial tangle of statements and rest on a level of disinterested awareness.

I am prepared, then, to accept a "solipsism of the present moment" as the logical outcome of any deliberate sceptical investigation that is thoroughly carried out. I think it should be emphasized, however, that the ultimate datum left to a pure solipsist is *not* the asserted significant sense-datum of ordinary perception, seen at a certain distance and direction from the body: it is rather the isolated residuum of a special state of consciousness from which all belief and assertion have been *deliberately* banished. Aesthetic intuition, on the other hand, is never *enforced:* it supervenes upon the function of the senses in locating a material object, and turns a posited substance in the realm of matter into its ideal counterpart in the realm of essence. In the spiritual man, this clarification of everything in the work-a-day world into its essential *form* is spontaneous and habitual, because he is a lover of essence and not of matter.

Another and different kind of objection is sometimes urged against an initial scepticism of such a radical type. Even if the logic of solipsism is admitted to be flawless, it is felt that the *morale* of a subsequent system of philosophy is somehow weakened. After a philosopher has almost committed intellectual suicide at the outset, it is a difficult task to return again to the real world. As a matter of fact, however, it is only a metaphor to speak of either a "departure" from, or "return" to, the world of common sense. Scepticism is a method, a manner of investigating the latent original assumptions of discourse and experience in the light of their own results. The so-called "return" to common sense indicates only the cessation of our initial inquiry, and the *enlightened acceptance* of our primary body of knowledge—or "animal faith." We all know that unacknowledged presuppositions are like subterranean mines in the sea of philosophy, and the thorough scepticism of Mr. Santayana has probably had a salutary "sweeping" effect on modern thought. An initial mortification of even the most instinctive claims to knowledge should not stultify a courageous thinker, but purify the recognized necessity of his future assertions. He will henceforth be dogmatic with a *difference.*

III. A Platonic Variation

Unfortunately, the embarrassment that has been occasioned in some minds by Mr. Santayana's relentless scepticism seems to have been only heightened by the subsequent volume on *The Realm of Essence.* This modern refinement of the Platonic doctrine of Ideas, dispossessing them on the one side of any magnetic influence over the flux of existence, and on the other extending them so as to cover such undignified objects as dung and scurfy hair, has received a somewhat mixed reception. From the standpoint of theory of knowledge it is said that the difficulties (created by the critics in question) of overcoming the symbolic complexion and "lamentable" relativity of human perception are only increased by "erecting an ontological barrier" between an epistemologist (rather than a layman) and the external world. I must confess that I find such an objection quite astonishing: it seems obvious to me on the contrary that if the essence of 4, which is presumably embodied in the four legs of the material chair, is *identical* with the essence given to intuition, then the requirements of the strictest definition of knowledge have been fully satisfied. A critical realist need not claim that the literal shape or size of the four material legs is presented in immediate experience: it is sufficient for the purposes of effective motor responses, and for the application of mathematics to nature, that the chair should have *four* material legs, rather than two or three.

However, the tendency to frown upon the doctrine of essence arises also from the curious trick that the learned have of conceiving an "essence" as a kind of *quasi-existential* entity, and the infinite realm of essence as a *subsisting* world of being overhanging, like some enormous petrified shadow, the realm of matter. If this is the cause of the dissatisfaction in question, permit me to disabuse the perplexed Ph.D. of such a misreading of the doctrine. I understand perfectly that there are two familiar pigeon-holes in the professional letter-box marked respectively EXISTENCE and SUBSISTENCE—but *The Realm of Essence* was not addressed by Mr. Santayana to either of these holes.

"Very well," the reader may protest, "but if—and you seem to be rather sure of yourself—an essence is not a *subsistent* entity, will you be so kind as to inform me just what an essence is?"

Now many fruitless conversations with English philosophers have taught me that it is not very conducive to illumination to reply by trotting out a long string of general "words of the trade." I know that Mr. Santayana has said that essences are "eternal," "universals," "logical and aesthetic terms," etc. But I always find that if I use such technical language it merely serves to open the doors to a fierce bout of wrangling along well-established lines. At the risk of appearing rather naïve and mystic, therefore, I invite the reader to consider the following illustration drawn from my own immediate experience.

On a late afternoon recently, I was coming down the mountain road from Caux towards Montreux. I rested for a few minutes on a stone wall, as I was somewhat weary from a long climb earlier in the day. Over on my right in the direction of Geneva, a marvelous sunset was blooming like a colossal rose in the western sky, and the placid lake was flushed with a kind of subdued crimson excitement. Gradually the lovely color faded from sky, mountainside and lake; a greyness came over all, and the night-wind blew up from the valley of the Rhone. On the way down to Montreux, I thought to myself,—"What a pity that fine crimson has changed into all this depressing grey!" Then suddenly it dawned on me, with an overwhelming conviction, that in a very fundamental sense I was *mistaken*. How could the intrinsic nature—the wonderful peculiarity of that crimson shade—literally *change* into anything other than its own inalienable loveliness? Crimson is crimson and grey is grey. It is not the *essences* of things that grow, alter, or are subject to decay, but the pulses and congeries of existence that borrow these qualities, and give them a local vicarious notoriety in some mind—or secretly exemplify them in nature. I must confess that at that moment Mr. Santayana's distinction between essence and matter seemed the most simple and inevitable point for a philosopher to make. Surely it must be other considerations, our manner of approaching essences, of labelling and comparing them with incompatible things, that prevented us from seeing once and for all their *obviousness*.

The realm of essence, then, is simply a name for that inexhaustible fund of possible characters, both simple and complex, that may or may not be exemplified in either intuition or the external world.[2] One may employ the categories of existence, such as space and time and causation, in order to define essences indirectly, by saying what they are *not;* but in strictness it is adventitious to their proper nature to claim that they can be antecedent to, contemporaneous with, or future to, any phase or moment of existence. All these temporal modes of speaking have nothing to do with essences: they only reveal the distracted relativity of the mind looking out from its human station. Because an essence does not *subsist* like a kind of arrested physical event, or prolonged pulse of existence, waiting for something to catch up to it: an essence simply *is*. And lastly, the realm of essence is not something to be "believed in." Essences are never the objects of belief or "animal faith," for the simple reason that they are not *things*.

It is better, however, not to worry one's head too much over this question of a realm of essence. If the reader finds that it does not help to clarify his own intellectual climate, but strikes him as being the far-fetched reflection of some repressed longing for a different—a more ideal—world, he had better forget "essences" all together. As an Irishman might put it—"the obvious is easy to overlook." The realm of essence does not require of us an official acknowledgment or denial of its

[2] I remember an occasion some years ago when I was playing billiards with my friend S., a layman in philosophical matters. Suddenly, during a pause in the game, he turned to me and said: "Just imagine all the *possible* strokes that you or I or anyone else has never made in a game of billiards!" Well, I suggest that my innocent companion at that moment had a rather clear intuition of the infinite nature of the realm of essence.

being. And in the nature of the case, I cannot say that I *believe* in a realm of essence: I *believe* in a realm of matter. But I thank Mr. Santayana for having called my attention early in life to a variation on Plato that has made a peculiar *difference* in the quality of all my thinking and experience.

IV. Substance Revindicated

The Realm of Matter is substantial evidence of the return of Mr. Santayana to more mundane considerations. Here at long last a sincere effort is really made by a contemporary philosopher to overcome the "dominance of the foreground" (the phrase is his own) and to understand the natural conditions of the mind. Other thinkers may style themselves as "naturalists," but a scrutiny of their works generally discloses that there is no *natural* explanation of anything—least of all the conditions that govern the birth and movement of the human mind.[3] Now the reluctance that some people display to accept such a general description of the external world as Mr. Santayana has given us, arises, I believe, from certain phenomenalistic presuppositions that are popular today. If knowledge is so defined that I can only be said to know, or even speak about, a "world" that is immediately presented to, and verified by, sense-experience, it follows, of course, that physical objects and causal processes must somehow be constructed out of "families" and sequences of sense-data.[4] The usual consequence of this line of reasoning is simply to ignore those antecedent and controlling conditions that put this whole "foreground" of experience on the human stage.

I should have thought, however, that even a smattering

[3] If Mr. Dewey accuses other philosophers of a mere "manipulation of ideas" divorced from some "indeterminate situation" in which all genuine inquiry must arise, it is necessary to ask oneself the further question: What possible difference can it make to Nature at large whether she is "indeterminate," chaotic, or an orderly system of events? Does Mr. Dewey honestly believe that Nature herself is *confused* or *doubtful* about anything? Is the Rock of Gibraltar, *qua* rock, "on edge" over the present European situation?

[4] If I use the term "sense-data" instead of "given essences" in this section, it is because I am thinking of the *instances* of essences, rather than their characters. Also I would avoid possible contention.

of physiology would have been sufficient to convince anybody that *sense-data are not things.* This simple distinction granted, it might be deemed prudent to relax the severity of the phenomenalistic notion of knowledge, so that students could be permitted to realize that human perception is not a literal acquaintance with the external world, but a symbolic interpretation of things in the language of sense-data. The interesting discovery that our immediate experience has a certain dream-like complexion is hardly a source of dismay to anybody but an inveterate phenomenalist with a narrow notion of knowledge to defend: a layman would consider it a true advance in intelligence. Now *sense-data*—as I have remarked on another occasion—

> —are not like brick walls that stand between the mind and its external objects: they are complex spontaneous signals in the field of active perception enabling us *to know appropriately* (we are not God) physical objects. As Professor Sellars has put it, we "think through our sense-data" to real things. In ordinary perception we do not mean or intend our private sensuous constructions—as phenomenalists seem to maintain. When I am hungry and reach for a loaf of bread, I doubt very much if I only reach for some "family" of sense-data that phenomenalists mistake for a nourishing object: I know a loaf of bread through, or by means of, the symbolic data of experience. And if my hunger is appeased, I think I am entitled to regard this as at least a *virtual* knowledge of a loaf of bread, even if I do not possess a *literal* knowledge of all its intrinsic properties. It is only because so many philosophers are haunted by a misleading ideal of what knowledge ought to be that they fain would substitute in their learned arguments a sophisticated analysis of the external world in terms of sense-data for *that object* [viz., the *real world*] *itself.*[5]

The Realm of Matter is an attempt, then, to say something more about Nature, the background of immediate experience, than simply that she is "the influences, of whatever nature, to which the mind is subject from whatever is without and independent of itself."[6] It is a sober and reasoned plea for a recog-

[5] From an article on "The Private Field of Immediate Experience," *Journal of Philosophy,* XXXVI (1939), 422-423.

[6] I. A. Richards, *Coleridge on Imagination,* 157.

nition of those inevitable properties that any world must possess if it is to be *a world.* Now there is a natural principle of explanation to account for the discernible order in our perceptual fields, and for the appositeness of mathematics and experiments to the structure of things. The principle I speak of is *substance.* It is scarcely an exaggeration to say that all modern philosophy has been, and still is, an attack on substance—or rather, on the *definition* of substance: because for the most part the critics have been tilting, in a somewhat Quixotic manner, at figments of sense or logic or grammar. But the substance I believe in and presuppose in all my daily actions is not "a subject-predicate form of statement," a complication of syntax, or a cluster of abstracted sense-data: it is the loaf of bread that relieves my hunger and enables me to analyze the concept of substance. I think, moreover, that we must go to the homely arts for illustrations of the use and workings of substance, instead of going to logic and grammar.

I remember when as a young man in London about thirteen years ago, I attended lectures under Bertrand Russell at the Institute of Philosophy. After learning a great many things about perception, and about public and private space, that I have never forgotten, I listened eagerly one afternoon when he analyzed with great acumen the problem of substance. However, it all left me strangely cold and dissatisfied; so that at the end of the lecture I held up my hand:

"Excuse me, sir," I said, "but the cook tells me that from a given number of apples she can only make just so much applesauce. Now that is what I mean by *substance,* and not that unintelligible mathematical formula you have marked on the blackboard."

I am afraid that my distinguished lecturer thought that I was joking, or merely trying to be clever, because he only laughed and complimented me on my sources of information. As a matter of fact, however, I was in earnest; and thirteen years of reflection have only served to increase my respect for the homely wisdom of the Cockney cook. Nothing could have persuaded her, and nothing can persuade me, that by juggling with sentences or sense-data you can transform apples into applesauce, or flour into bread.

Now I think that Mr. Santayana would be the first to admit that his description of a realm of matter *is a description*—or, if you will, an intellectual construction. But it does not follow that just because all our descriptions of Nature are human versions of her inmost structure and movement, *therefore* (a) she does not really exist "on her own;" (b) she must somehow be absorbed into and exhausted by the stream of sense-data, or babble of words, that she provokes in experience; (c) all our descriptions of Nature are *equally* misleading or inappropriate. The question is rather for the *common intelligence* of mankind, as manifested in the past, the present, or the future, to decide which description is the most faithful translation of the facts in human language, and the freest from gross superstition. It is to this radical strain of sanity, running through all ages and races, that *The Realm of Matter* was addressed by its author.

In the meantime, the appropriate faithfulness, and the inevitable shortcoming, of any human attempt to describe the nature of things are recorded in that gigantic complex essence of the world that Mr. Santayana has called *The Realm of Truth*. The truth is simply that standard to which we all appeal, that presupposition which we all make, when we exclaim, for instance, "Heaven only knows!" I realize that truth is not popular at the moment; or rather that it is circumscribed to propositions of sense-perception: e.g., *if* I have certain experiences tomorrow morning, I shall *verify* the efficacy of the medicine I take tonight. But this vulgar circumscription of the truth to human interests is probably a passing fashion in philosophy.

V. The Sense of Joy

It is with a certain diffidence that I venture to round off this essay with a few personal observations (probably trivial and beside the point) on the moral significance of Mr. Santayana's work—both earlier and later. This is the first time I have touched on the subject of moral philosophy, and in so doing I break a vow made not only to myself, but to some of my best friends. When we come to morals we come to prejudice and sentiment: we approve or disapprove of a fellow moralist according to the degree with which he flatters either the manners of the region in which we live, or the idiosyncrasies of our own nature. Here all is local, relative and, therefore, passionate. Any attempt to transcend these geographical or personal limitations is usually misunderstood and regarded with grave suspicion.

Now the moral complexion of *The Life of Reason* has been more appreciated (at any rate in America) than any other aspect of Mr. Santayana's philosophy. *One* of the sources of its appeal is not difficult to ascertain if we refer to physical space and time. The turn of the century found many conscientious professors and other intellectual energies in a very receptive mood for a brilliant series of books not only expounding the philosophy of naturalism, but at the same time supplying a felt need for a certain moral elevation—for a reaffirmation of the threatened dignity of "the thinking reed." Albeit the theological interpretation of *heaven,* for example, was questioned by an enlightened minority of earnest Puritans, one could still, and in fact *ought* to, appreciate the quality of the furniture in those many imaginary mansions beyond the world of the senses. If the streets of Boston were not paved with gold, and the average American youth but a pale reflection of the Idea of an Angel, all the more reason to call attention to these imperfections, and aim at something "higher." Seriously speaking, however, many a sensitive intellectual youth of fifty years ago was as passionately obsessed with the challenge to revealed religion issued by Darwin, as he is today with the challenge to love issued by Freud. And religion and love are not easy things for susceptible youth to avoid: they are the perennial fountains of all that matters in life.

The early Mr. Santayana was primarily interested in religion. It was his desire, on the one hand, to defend the value of the religious imagination in the face of a crude protestant impatience accentuated by an exaggerated respect for science and industry; on the other hand, he wished to substitute truth for fiction in placing human life in a natural setting. Although familiar with all the orthodox theological puzzles, he had by nature an intuitive rather than analytic mind: it was the Christian imagination, and its expression in ritual and architecture, that gripped him. At Harvard he knew what it was to be a favourite member of an inner circle devoted to religion and poetry, and interested in a good society with beauty and friendship in it. But the wider America that lay around him left much to be desired, both in the quality of living then exemplified, and in the dubious goals of life to be pursued. What might be, what ought to be, the quality and goals of life became uppermost in his thought. It was only by living in the light of some appropriate preconceived ideal, and subordinating one's random impulses to a single-hearted if vain pursuit of that distant goal, that life could acquire any true meaning;—nay, could become even tolerable to a spirit by nature addressed to better things, and imaginatively acquainted with more satisfactory periods of human history.

As I have said, however, this moral complexion of *The Life of Reason* is so well-known, and other people are so much better qualified to delineate its features, that I do not propose to dwell upon it any longer. One may admire the incidental graces and epigrammatic curves of thought to be found in these five volumes and yet be somewhat bored by the moral burden (in both senses of "burden"). Perhaps I am incapable of feeling the lure or necessity to remodel things nearer to the heart's desire: I have never thought of life as expressly an opportunity to improve one's self—or other people. A man must be a born reformer, or a born poet; but these dark tricks of destiny are not of our spinning.

The reading of the spiritual (rather than moral) life[7] that the later Mr. Santayana has given us is not so likely to meet with a popular or sympathetic understanding. If I have succeeded at all in grasping its central message, it is not because of any agonizing scrutiny of the written word. But there are

[7] The moral life is so bound up with manners and laws—is so hopelessly *relative*—that I distinguish between the inner education of the spiritual life, and its inevitable locus in a given society.

times when even the adept have only the light to go by—and we must trust the light as it falls on us. Putting the matter in my own way, then, I should say that the *highest good* open to the spirit of man is not to be found in a striving after some exclusive ideal, for here there is usually an element of anxiety concerning personal profit: it is rather to be found in those moments of life in which the *joy of awareness* is so perfect that the proper objects of either action or thought are loved only for their essences, and the illusion of exclusiveness or profit is dissolved in *gladness*. Now this joy or gladness I speak of is by definition (that is, in virtue of its intrinsic essence) incompatible with any element of anxiety or sense of evil: therefore I claim that it is the certain touchstone for the purity of the spirit at any instance. The *good* is simply this unique quality of experience which any object, or state of affairs, may conspire to minister to and sustain. Such moments of pure liberation from the friction and compulsion of life do not presuppose for their occurrence a lonely pilgrimage into some high mountain, or a mingling with camels in the desert: one can be alone with the Alone on the golf links. Of course a sound body is important for the free play of intuition (at least there must be a central integrity), and a sane upbringing will help to knit the organism firmly and so avoid conflicting impulses—a terrible source of anxiety. In other words, there are natural conditions that either hinder or foster the desire of the spirit to realize its true vocation: the immediate joy of seeing or doing or understanding anything with utter impartiality. *In so far* as our spirits are pure, then, heaven lies all around us; in the words of that child of light—Francis Thompson: "Turn but a stone and start a wing."

It may be objected, however, that it is dangerous to morality as a whole to find a criterion and apex of the spiritual life in the *sense of joy*. It will be said among other things that such a spiritual touchstone, or watchword, has a tendency to favour Mary rather than Martha; that it is somehow irreconcilable with "the doing of good deeds." Now if such an imputation were necessarily true, it would indeed be a serious one. But I am told on good authority that there is a way, a *spiritual* way of going about in the world and doing practical acts of mercy that is known to the few who are called to such a vocation. And the *joy* that these people experience in their work is (according to their own reports) "unutterable," and radically incompatible with any considerations of personal profit or safety. For the average Englishman, it is doubtless impossible to love *all horses equally;* he is interested in the special animal that he has put his pound on and hopes will win the race; therefore an element of anxiety about possible profit will contaminate to a certain extent his genuine love of horses. And, indeed, so it is with most of us in our public acts of mercy. Whether we admit it or not, there are ulterior factors at work, motives behind our ostensible philanthropic gestures, that are alien to the essence of *charity:* which is simply the desire to see all forms of life as joyous as we are ourselves, *in so far* as our spirits are pure and liberated. Naturally, if we have seldom experienced moments of perfect gladness—moments that are final and point to nothing beyond themselves, it is difficult for us to appreciate the enthusiasm of the initiated. I am too much of a worldling ever to have endured even a minor "dark night" of the spirit: but there have been times in my life when I have experienced a certain "change of heart," and it became possible—

> —to serve the Lord with gladness;
> And come before His presence with a song.

VI. A Last Observation

Of course there is a great deal more in the spiritual life than I have expressed in a few random paragraphs, and the reader must turn to Mr. Santayana for correction and further instruction. If I have been a little impatient with the moral complexion of *The Life of Reason,* and slightly caricatured some of its features, or sources of appeal, doubtless there will be more able critics to defend it stoutly, sketch it aright, and sing of its excellence. *Chacun à son goût.* But as I consider that the radical investigation of knowledge carried out in *Scepticism and Animal Faith,* and the subsequent ontological distinctions, are clarifications of that early epistemological fog that clings to *The*

Life of Reason: so also I venture to predict that the later interpretation of the spiritual life is destined to be estimated as the summit of an extraordinary philosophical career. I am not sure, however, that Mr. Santayana will agree with me that *joy* is, from the spiritual point of view, the crown of life, and the only *moral* justification for existence. But if the birth of spirit is itself the best testimony to an intermittent tendency on the part of Nature to rise above herself and overcome a profound indifference, then in certain moments of consciousness, when the sheer gladness of seeing or doing or understanding something is *final,* Nature has justified herself morally—albeit she soon exhausts an occasional curiosity to apprehend the form of her body.

DANIEL M. CORY

VEVEY, SWITZERLAND

4

Sterling P. Lamprecht

ANIMAL FAITH AND THE ART OF INTUITION

4
ANIMAL FAITH AND THE ART OF INTUITION

THE doctrine of essence is the most prominent of the themes which appear with some novelty in the later writings of Santayana. Doubtless it is anticipated in the earlier writings; but it comes to such prominence in *Scepticism and Animal Faith* and subsequent volumes that it seems a new theme. Essence is the datum, which, when we have sceptically discarded all the accretions of undemonstrated beliefs, remains aesthetically immediate and unquestionably present to our minds. And the event in which essence is viewed is the act of intuition.

Santayana himself regards his earlier and later philosophical writings as different in emphasis but compatible in ideas. And he is here doubtless correct.[1] In the earlier works, of which *The Life of Reason* is the most notable, he sought to develop that humanism in moral philosophy which, derived from the Greeks, received its finest contemporary expression in his statement of it. From this humanism he has never departed, though he has overlaid it with distracting embellishments, thus making its classic form somewhat obscure in its new decorations. In the later works, in addition to furnishing these embellishments of the original humanism, he has sought to define the ontological and epistemological principles which would support and justify the humanism. Thus he has given us the naturalism and the critical realism with which *Scepticism and Animal Faith* and later writings are primarily concerned. In the earlier period he quite properly tended to view things, and even the cosmos as a whole, in terms of the part they played in human action and imagination, and even resorted to questionably subjectivistic

[1] I intend my statement to be a correction of an exaggerated version of the contrast between the early and late writings of Santayana which I gave in an article "Santayana Then and Now," *Journal of Philosophy*, XXV, 533-550.

terminology in carrying out this task. But he never identified things with the notions men entertain of those things; he never forgot, even when he did not explicitly mention, the natural world which, apart from human experience, conditions human life and, in its very blindness to good and evil, yet provides a check upon our moral programs and ambitions. In the later period, while his humanism remains unabated, the inexorable drive of material substance and the difficulties of human knowledge come into the foreground of his reflections and discussions. And the moral achievements of man which are exalted in the humanistic period are now taken to be cosmically indifferent and trifling. This shift of interest is accompanied with emergence of the doctrine of essence to a prominent place in the later writings. Instead of inviting men to spirited pursuit of their highest good, he rather deals with the possibility of a passive and quiescent contemplation of essence. For from the point of view of the indifferent cosmos, must not the most noble of human aspirations and the most glorious of human achievements seem but curious accidents that have ephemeral existence in the course of nature's shifting events?

The doctrine of essence enters into the discussion of many different problems in the delicate nuances of Santayana's thought. Among the many aspects of the doctrine three are here selected for comment. These three together do not give an exhaustive analysis of the subtleties of Santayana's treatment of his doctrine. But they are concerned in turn with the ethical, ontological, and epistemological bearings of the doctrine; and hence they touch on all three of the main fields within which the doctrine has significance.

We may begin then with the significance which the doctrine of essence has for ethical theory. Certainly the intuition of essence is very different from the practical solution of a moral problem: rapturous and disinterested contemplation of some pure datum is very different from heroic and zealous struggle for some special end chosen from among the many possibilities of nature. Yet the detached intuition of essence has its place in the political life; and the moralist can never allow any type of human experience, however unconcerned it may in intent seem to be with moral issues, to go uncriticized and unevaluated for its consequences on the course of affairs and for its own intrinsic worth. Sheer disinterestedness, or "disintoxication" with the world as Santayana sometimes expresses it, has important relations to other human attitudes and ventures; it earns, if it does not expressly pay, interest in the clash of human desires, ambitions, and ideal programs of action. Even the taking of a moral holiday is itself justifiable on moral grounds if indeed it is justifiable at all. There is thus an intimate and curious interplay between absorption in and aloofness from affairs. On the one hand, absorption in affairs furnishes men with themes for contemplation which might never occur to men who were not entangled in the furious play of rival forces, as efforts to measure distance and to find one's way around in the world direct attention to those essences which constitute the system of Euclidean geometry. On the other hand, aloofness from affairs enables men to achieve a balance, perhaps a justice, of judgment without which the light of moral wisdom would quickly degenerate into the heat of arbitrary passion or petulance.

Santayana has given striking names to the two different ways in which human intelligence may be directed. When human intelligence is directed to solution of practical problems and the achievement of specific human ends, it gives rise to the life of reason. When it is turned away from all such tasks and cares, smiles indulgently at all moral programs, and is free from all animal bias in moments of pure contemplation of essences for their own sake, it leads to the spiritual life. The latter term seems to me a rather bad one: I should prefer to use the term spirituality for that quality which life has when it is most sensitive to the varied goods available within the movement of the life of reason.[2] Yet terms are but terms; however important terms may be (for without attention to them and analysis of their use, there can be no clarity of thought), they are but counters for the exchange and development of ideas. And furthermore, the contemplation of pure essence involves some of that radical justice of appraisal without which sensitivity to the relative

[2] Santayana himself taught me this usage of the term. Cf. *Reason in Religion*, 193ff.

worth of alternative goods would not be possible. In any case, and here we return to exposition to Santayana's meaning, the spiritual life is one of the expressions of human intelligence. In his earlier writings Santayana distinguished natural and free and ideal society. Natural society is a name for the particular form of our human entanglements in the course of affairs. Free society is a name for the reconstructions of nature which, in our institutions and our social customs, safeguard the achievements of the life of reason. Ideal society is a name for detached contemplation (in religion or art or science) of those ideas which, while they may also happen to be true of nature, are enjoyed for their own sake, that is to say, for the sake of the ideal possibilities they open up to the detached imagination. Is anything more added to this conception of ideal society when Santayana comes in his later works to commend the spiritual life? Certainly there is heightened emphasis upon it. This heightened emphasis may be due in part to Santayana's conviction that the world would be more tolerable to man if he entered into ideal society more readily and more often. Yet one always feels like apologizing to Santayana when one attributes to him any concern to reform the world or to render men's lives more excellent. The emphasis may have had its philanthropic bearing; but it was surely due primarily to a desire to make the point entirely clear. Santayana remarks himself that he stressed the doctrine in his later works "for the sake of rendering the conception of essence perfectly unambiguous."[3] And perhaps it is best to leave the matter there. It is always gratuitous to seek a moralistic purpose back of an honest effort to think clearly and to express one's thought lucidly.

The enjoyment of ideal society or the intuition of essence or the practice of the spiritual life (however the matter be designated in one or another of Santayana's phrases) is but the limit of one movement in the life of reason. It is the carrying out to its logical goal of that effort to achieve objectivity which is biased by other considerations in the normal course of the life of reason. Perhaps it is, at least in many cases, morally justifiable that the effort to understand be biased by other con-

[3] *Scepticism and Animal Faith*, 131.

siderations; for we need to sweep aside what interferes with the quick pursuit of our given ends. But kinder fortunes may release some men at some times from some of this urgency; and then the intellectual life may well be more dispassionate. One may argue endlessly over the place which sheer intellectual curiosity may legitimately play in a world as full as is ours of pressing problems, of wars, of racial persecutions, of economic disasters, of deadly disease and pain. One can not solve the question in any general formula; for here as in all other matters we must seek the right amount at the right time in the right way, and we can only estimate what is right in each case as it comes along. But even in the midst of war there is room for the free intellect. Indeed the unescapable insistence of war may make the free intellect the only available form of salvation for some men at some times in their lives. However much other legitimate enterprises preoccupy men's minds, there will always be some little room for some few men to practice such emancipated contemplation as Santayana describes. Thereby they may gain an increased balance of soul; they may even at times save their souls from the fury of a destructive world.

The relative degrees of sympathy which Santayana himself has for the engaged life of reason and the detached life of the spirit are not easy to state with hope of accuracy. Perhaps his forthcoming book on *The Realm of Spirit* may make this point clearer. The point has, indeed, no philosophical, only biographical, interest, and hence some might object that there is no reason why the point ought to be made clearer. Yet readers of Santayana are bound to have their attention directed to the biographical question by what seem like conflicting statements in the text. Perhaps the degree of interest in the two ways of living, the more engaged and the more detached, will vary with changing moods: such would be neither surprising nor improper. Santayana seems in one mood when he writes: "I frankly cleave to the Greeks and not to the Indians, and I aspire to be a rational animal rather than a pure spirit."[4] He seems in quite another mood when he writes: "I myself have no passionate attachment to existence, and value this world for the intui-

[4] *The Realm of Essence*, 65.

tions it can suggest, rather than for the wilderness of facts that compose it."[5] But to reconcile such statements by saying that both moods are legitimate in turn is to risk confusion of moral insight with passing currents of fancy or inclination.

In any case, and a matter of general theory, Santayana does at least recognize that the spiritual life falls within the life of reason. If the spiritual life is, in its pure and extreme form, entire disintoxication with existence, it still remains a life. And therefore with it, as with the business life, the aesthetic life, the sexual life, or any other kind of life, we must always revert to morality and must consider the healthfulness and relative worth it has for the entire course of living. That is, we are bound to recognize that the spiritual life falls within the political life, in the Greek sense of politics. Now, as Santayana says, a family quarrel may occur at times between different interests such as attention to some pressing care of the life of reason and some desire to retire into detached contemplation. "In the midst of business, spirit suspends business, and begins to wonder, to laugh, or to pray."[6] And business may, from the standpoint of the collective interests of a human animal, deserve prior attention. Faced with peril of shipwreck, the captain of a vessel may pour his valuable cargo of oil upon the stormy waters. Retreating before an enemy, a general may burn forest and villages the possession of which would strengthen the foe for further attack. "It is sweet," sang Lucretius, "when on the great sea the winds trouble the waters, to behold from land another's deep distress." But those in the tossing of the waters have more pressing business than to share the pleasure of those safe on the rocky shore.

Intuition, therefore, is an art to be practiced, as are other arts, in accord with the jurisdiction which reason enacts for the sake of the whole course of animal life. Perhaps it is the noblest of all the arts; for all the other arts may be regarded as contributing occasions for intuition. "The world is always classical," writes Santayana,

> the truth of human destiny is always clear, if only immersion in our

[5] *Scepticism and Animal Faith*, 171.

[6] Preface to Vol. VII of the Triton edition of *The Works of George Santayana*, xi.

> animal cares does not prevent us from seeing it. Lifting the eyes would be so easy, yet it is seldom done; and when a rapt poet compels us to do so, we are arrested, we are rebuked, we are delivered.[7]

Such deliverances it has been Santayana's rôle to effect for many of his readers.

The ontological bearings of Santayana's doctrine of essence are closely connected with the ethical purport of the doctrine. The notion of essence, Santayana tells us, adds to our notion of nature a proof that nature is contingent. Doubtless the realization that nature is contingent can be reached in other ways; for many philosophers from Aristotle to our own day have maintained the position without reliance upon the doctrine of essence. But Santayana, developing the doctrine of essence chiefly for other reasons, came to exploit this possible bearing of the doctrine too. The realm of essence is infinite in range: it contains not simply the essences that happen to be the natures of all existing things, but also the essences of all non-existent things. "It is far more garrulous than nature, herself not laconic."[8] Thus the realization is enforced that what exists must be accepted in its actuality but can not be demonstrated from *a priori* necessity: no ontological argument is possible, no demonstration can be given which validly proceeds from essence to existence. When we survey the infinite realm of essence, we are forced humbly to recognize the difference between the vast possibilities of many conceivable worlds and the limited actualities of any single existing world. Through the doctrine of essence "the actuality of things is sharpened and the possibilities of things are enlarged."[9]

It is doubtful whether one can properly classify Santayana as an empiricist. For Santayana holds that empiricism assumes naïvely the accessibility of given facts, and that this assumption can never meet the transcendentalist criticism of knowledge. But empiricism is a theory of knowledge which, even if it have implications for ontology, may best be considered later in con-

[7] Foreword to Iris Origo, *Leopardi: a Biography.*

[8] *Scepticism and Animal Faith,* 78.

[9] Preface to Vol. VII of the Triton edition of *The Works of George Santayana,* xiv.

nection with the epistemological bearings of Santayana's doctrine of essence. Suffice it here to point out that Santayana recognizes and accepts one implicit tenet of an empirical philosophy, namely, that facts, on whatever ground they may be believed in, are yet irrational surds. Empiricists may disagree with Santayana when they suppose that before rational discourse begins they possess many assured facts; but at least Santayana agrees with empiricists in holding that (in the words of Thomas Hobbes) "no discourse whatsoever can end in absolute knowledge of fact." The function and rôle of discourse are not, by its own unaided powers, to establish matters of fact, but to explore implications and develop meanings; and discourse must join forces with something beyond itself if it would become effective inquiry and eventuate in discovery of truth. Empiricists would naturally find this something in direct observation of facts; and Santayana, seeming to rebuke the credulity of empiricists, finds it in what he calls animal faith. But however different observation of facts and animal faith may or may not be (a question to be examined below), at least empiricists and Santayana ground their position on the same ontological principle. They both treat existence as an indemonstrable kind of factuality. Facts may be a compulsory factor in the universe; but there is an irresolvable distinction between particular things (or facts) and definable natures (or essences).

Santayana presents the ontological bearings of his doctrine of essence in a form which, I confess, seems to me indefensibly whimsical. Ontology was not his concern in *The Life of Reason* and so receives but incidental treatment there. It becomes more prominent in the various volumes of his *Realms of Being*. Indeed the book *Scepticism and Animal Faith*, which at once serves as introduction to the series and is surely the most comprehensive, perhaps the most important, volume in the series, rests its argument on a metaphysical *tour de force*. In this respect (if in no other) it resembles Descartes's *Meditations*. Scepticism in both Descartes and Santayana is a methodological device whereby, in effect if not in intent, their readers are startled into premature acquiescence in the subsequent favored metaphysical doctrines. In both cases the scepticism is a dramatic, even an histrionic, approach to a determined exposition of the authors' convictions, convictions which the authors entertained from the start but could make more plausible by exhibiting them as the only refuge from the calamity of a far-reaching ontological despair.

The ontological bearings of Santayana's doctrine of essence are not dependent in any way upon this methodological scepticism. Indeed they are clear and they are evidently sound wherever and whenever the Aristotelian doctrine of "matter" is accepted. They are requisite in any philosophy which does not resolve existence into essence or "form." They are not necessarily tied up, even if in Santayana they happen to be entangled, with certain epistemological theories.

And thus we are naturally driven on to a consideration of the epistemological bearings of Santayana's doctrine of essence. In dealing with these epistemological bearings of the doctrine of essence I wish to grant at the outset a diffidence because I am not certain what exactly Santayana means to say. I must therefore give a preliminary exposition of what his position seems to be and then proceed to distinguish two interpretations of this position, to decide between which would seem to me to require some further comment from Santayana himself.

The epistemological bearings of Santayana's doctrine of essence are tied up with the oft-quoted phrase "Nothing given exists."[10] This contention, whatever it may also be, is at least a definite warning against excessive credulity, against taking first and hasty opinions as settled truths. Essence is, as Santayana himself puts it, "the last residuum of scepticism and analysis."[11] We need prolonged criticism of our beliefs. And criticism serves to teach each of us in turn "the contrast between what I find I know and what I thought I knew."[12] Attention to any existing fact which we think we encounter will bring about the more careful analysis of that fact; the greatest respect for fact will be required to enable any one to separate out the nature that fact

[10] This phrase is the title of chapter VII of *Scepticism and Animal Faith*, but occurs frequently through the later writings of Santayana.

[11] Preface to Vol. VII of the Triton edition of *The Works of George Santayana*, xiii.

[12] *Scepticism and Animal Faith*, 4.

really has from suppositions as to what it might be but perhaps is not. No allegation about fact is indubitable, and all assertions about fact need refinement in the fires of ceaseless investigation. This sceptical caution it is certainly Santayana's intent to enforce; and herein he is eminently sound. One hears throughout the pages where this caution is given echoes of Bacon's discussion of the "idols of the mind," of Locke's warnings against the dangers lurking in the indiscriminate use of words, of Hume's advice against taking our ideas, derived from past experience, as a sure guide to future experience. Eternal vigilance is the price of knowledge.

So far, so good. But what more is intended when it is said that "nothing given exists"? It may be that Santayana means to say that, when once we have abstracted some character from a given fact and come to contemplate this character as an ideal term of discourse, we are embarked on a venture from which return to existence is not easy. That nothing given exists would then mean that none of the detached items of regard in the act of intuition can be affirmed, at least without some basis which intuition does not afford, to be the nature of existent fact. Tables and chairs, substances in general, are then never "given." The choir of heaven and furniture of earth are substantial, not essential, and belong to the realm within which we animals move and act, not to the realm of essence. The art of intuition involves departure from the facts of existence, and precludes return to its involvements. When one is engaged in intuition he is apart from existential materials and deprived of any valid technique for their determination.

But existence may yet be given in some other sense of the term "given." And the doctrine of "animal faith" may be Santayana's way of recognizing this fact. That we are animals that move and act, that something of the choir of heaven and furniture of earth are visibly present to us as animals, that things may be observed through the senses even if not in intuition, these are themselves facts that can not be demonstrated to the utterly sceptical mind but are none the less assuredly so. Were we pure spirits whose entire life consisted of intuition, we should never know existence at all. But it is doubtful whether such a possibility as a life consisting entirely of intuition can be considered without contradiction; for intuition is itself a life and life is itself an animal affair. "Scepticism," Santayana himself says, "is an exercise, not a life."[13] And in our living we find much to be true that could not be derived from the most expert technique of intuition. Santayana tells us that facts are sometimes "discoverably" disclosed.[14] The ever-present distinction between intuition and animal faith may then be Santayana's way of showing how much more is involved in knowing a fact than in contemplating passively an essence. The art of intuition, useful to free men's minds from prejudice in morals and to bring them to grant the selective (hence arbitrary) nature of existence, is then useless for reaching knowledge. Knowledge is another sort of affair. "An animal is aware that something is happening long before he can say to himself what that something is, or what it looks like."[15] And this awareness, needing criticism, needing searching criticism, yet furnishes the subject-matter with which knowledge is concerned. Knowledge is always of this subject-matter: it never produces its own subject-matter or proceeds without subject-matter. It can not demonstrate its own right to deal with this subject-matter. But this right can not be challenged by any animal aware of his own existence or of his involvement in an existing world.

There is much in Santayana's theory of experience which fits in with this fashion of interpreting his doctrine of essence. Experience, he tells us, is "a fund of wisdom gathered by living."[16] Experience is not for Santayana as for Locke a subjective realm of "ideas" that are existential yet without locus in nature. Santayana is not a dualist of the type that makes a sharp distinction between the realm of nature and the realm of mind. He is rather the Aristotelian naturalist for whom mind is one of the strange and inexplicable but yet obvious and assured things

[13] *Ibid.*, 69.
[14] *Ibid.*, 173.
[15] *Ibid.*, 188-189.
[16] *Ibid.*, 138.

that happen in the course of nature's changes.[17] The man of experience is the man whose mind is well equipped with ideas that furnish him with interpretations of the materials of the natural world of which we as animals within that world are more or less aware.

> Experience brings belief in substance (as alertness) *before* it brings intuition of essences; it is appetition *before* it is description. . . . Experience, at its very inception, is a revelation of *things;* and these things, before they are otherwise distinguished, are distinguishable into a here and a there, a now and a then, nature and myself in the midst of nature.[18]

It brings belief in substances before it brings intuition of essences, because the art of intuition is a specialized activity for which even fairly intelligent animals need training and sophistication. And prior to such training and its consequent sophistication, human beings have to deal with substances, have to be alert to find food and avoid attack, have to arrange many affairs in their contingent, yet unescapably insistent, world of looming forces. The cognitive life will arise soon; yet it arises in a natural context. The art of intuition, Santayana has said, may make the cognitive life more effective by inducing sceptical caution and by opening up many vistas into ideal possibilities. But knowledge is not the outcome of bare intuition. Knowledge is rather the outcome of animal necessities when approved methods have been adopted to guide inference, to check hypotheses, to discipline the otherwise too hurried credulities of timorous minds. Knowledge can never explain *why* things are as they are found to be; but if a man accepts the world around him because animal necessity compels him to do so, knowledge may give him some reliable information as to *what* things are. To pure spirit such knowledge remains but one of the myriad possibilities of the free imagination; but to the rational animal

[17] Mind is here used in the sense in which mind is "a determinate form of being, a distinguishable part of the universe known to experience and discourse, the mind that unravels itself in meditation, inhabits animal bodies, and is studied in psychology" (*Reason in Common Sense,* 125). It has of course other senses, as Santayana goes on to say; but what is said above might not be true of mind in these other senses.

[18] *Scepticism and Animal Faith,* 188-189.

such knowledge may finally become "true belief grounded in experience," that is, "controlled by outer facts."[19]

That such is the epistemological position which Santayana means to assert is indicated by many passages in his earlier and later writings. It is indicated, for example, by the sub-title of Volume I of *The Life of Reason—Reason in Common Sense.* Common sense can never be established with that kind of complete logical substantiation which certain rationalists seek. It rests upon a prior acceptance of an existential subject-matter, which acceptance is not a reasoned matter at all but a matter of "animal faith." The life of reason is not the basis of man's existence any more than of nature's ways: it is the outcome which, once man's entanglement in nature is granted, is most to be desired. To read reason back into the basis of life is to abandon the life of reason for a vain mythology. And the philosopher is not a whit more privileged than other men. "A philosopher is compelled to follow the maxim of epic poets and to plunge *in medias res*."[20] He must plunge *in medias res*, not merely in the sense that his reflections begin after much of life has already long been going on and has committed him for better or for worse to beliefs which, however much criticized, remain unavoidable to the same judgment, but also in the sense that his reflections can never verify the existential actuality of the subject-matter he seeks to investigate and perhaps comes partly to know. Santayana is here in accord with Hume. At least he realizes that the best-grounded rationalities of life rest on what, to reason itself, remain arbitrary assumptions and unverified claims.

Yet is this all that Santayana means to assert? I confess I am not sure. I have thought that he means to assert more, and with that more I happen to find myself in fundamental disagreement.[21] I am troubled by the alliance Santayana seems to make with Herbert Spencer's doctrine of the Unknowable; by the

[19] *Ibid.*, 180.

[20] *Ibid.*, 1.

[21] I have expressed my views already in an essay on "Naturalism and Agnosticism in Santayana," *Journal of Philosophy*, XXX, 561-574. I have not been able to withdraw the criticism there made and so resubmit it here in hopes of learning how just or unjust it really is.

assertion that "images in sense," like "love in youth, and religion among nations," are part of "normal madness;" and by the favor Santayana has shown to "critical realism."[22] Possibly I am guilty of taking metaphorical language in a sense not intended. But the difficulties I find are perhaps worth stating; and if they are due to misunderstanding, they can be easily met and removed.

My difficulties might be reduced to one central difficulty; but I should like to consider three critical points. In the first place, what is the relation of the art of intuition and the exercise of animal faith to sense experience? The object of intuition is essence, and the exercise of animal faith involves adjustment to and manipulation of substance. But the art of intuition is a discipline which many people practice but rarely and no one can practice without frequent interruption. And when one is not practicing the art of intuition is one not immediately confronted with "things?" Would Santayana regard ordinary sense-experience as the occurrence of intuition? Do we not see colored things as well as intuit colors and believe in things? Do we not find sense-qualities existentially occurring even when no intuition is going on? And if we come to discover that colors and other sense qualities are existentially conditioned in their occurrence (not wholly, but in part) upon the organs and nervous structure of the percipient organisms, do we then have to conclude that they are not genuinely qualifications of the things before us? Is not sense experience different both from belief (however inevitably it may lead to belief) and from intuition (however much it may at times lead to intuition)? And is not sense experience instructive of nature and nature's ways? In other words, how lacking in direct and empirically indisputable evidence is "animal faith?" Is the procedure of *Scepticism and Animal Faith* an adroit argument by which to make the extreme sceptic ashamed of his philosophical pose? Or is it a serious effort to convince us all of the existence of things on grounds than which there are no others available?

Santayana gives much attention to intuition and to animal

[22] Cf. Santayana's essay, *The Unknowable; Dialogues in Limbo*, 46; and *Essays in Critical Realism*, 163-184.

faith. And he omits any description of what I should regard as the more normal kind of experience, namely, sense experience of existing things. Is he assuming that we know about sense experience and thus need no description of it? Or is he supposing that it is only a part of the contemplation of essence which he calls intuition? If the latter, I am compelled to disagree. In *Scepticism and Animal Faith* Santayana presses scepticism as far as he can, and then proceeds to show that we come sanely to belief in demonstration, then to belief in experience and substance, finally to belief in nature. Is this ordering of his material a semi-poetical development of a chosen theme, or a necessary line of argument without which a belief in nature could not validly be reached? Do beliefs in existential things depend on the fact that we are interrupted in our intuitions of essence? Or are they not rather due to noting what is immediately present to us in sense experience whether we ever intuit essences or not? Doubtless men do not readily understand in what sense observed things may be called substances, nor to what degree observed things so fall into a system that they may be said to be parts of nature. But even if we have to be taught what substance and nature mean, have we not initially an existential subject-matter present before us from which both the practice of the art of intuition and the development of animal faith may depart. Even an organism which was incapable of intuition and which had no beliefs at all might yet see things and have sense experiences; and if we human beings are capable of intuition and also entertain beliefs, we ought not to overlook the fact that we also have direct awareness of things in a much more indisputable way than Santayana seems to include in his account of human life and in his theory of knowledge.

And then, in the second place, do we not have immediate awareness *that* things occur as well as awareness of *what* things in part are? I should not wish to question the claim that any of the characters of things may be isolated in intuition and contemplated in their essential nature apart from all existential locus, relationships, and indications. Nor should I be so simple-minded as to suggest that all the secrets of existence are open to our immediate inspection in sense awareness or in any other awareness. I should wish to insist, however, that we have direct awareness of the "thatness" of things. However exciting we find it to turn in intuition to some item of the whatness of things, however elaborate our philosophical proof be of the impossibility of dealing forever with such detached essences, we ought never to lose sight of the initial experience of the empirical factuality (or "thatness") of things. It is one thing, and it is a correct thing, to say that existence can not be demonstrated. It would be quite another thing, and it would be an incorrect thing, to say that existence is an inference. Things are present in their thatness (and in some of their whatness) as directly as essences are present in their ideality. The existence of atoms, or of angels, or of the glacial age, or of some alleged future is indeed a matter of inference, and in making such inferences we may at times be correct and at other times incorrect; for whether such things are may always be questioned. But that *some* things exist about us can not be questioned except in some philosophical fantasy, or rather in some imaginative caprice. If I say that I see a man across the field from me and if what I call a man is rather a tree stump or a shadow of a passing cloud, I have at least been confronted with existential fact. The existential factuality or thatness of things can not be before us in intuition; but it is none the less before us. And on our dealings with it, rather than on the interruptions of our intuitions, rests our belief in an existential world. If animal faith be a name for the way in which every assertion concerning the character of existence may be challenged and, even after prolonged investigation, remains open to some theoretical doubt, well and good. But if it be a name for the way in which beings to whom only essences are immediately given yet come to believe in existence, then criticism seems to me to be requisite.

It was said above that it is doubtful whether one can classify Santayana as an empiricist. Let me return to this consideration in a further comment along the same line. Empiricists, both classic and contemporary, have often assumed naïvely that some knowledge is sure because some facts are given to inspection; they have even at times regarded sense awareness as a kind, even as the best kind, of knowledge. In these claims empiricists seem to me mistaken. Santayana's theory of knowledge would be useful as a corrective of this overly naïve empiricism. Knowledge is different from seeing and hearing and touching; knowledge always involves inquiry and issues in opinions which, however well established, lack complete certainty. But knowledge is uncertain because it is an interpretation of a subject-matter; and recognition of this truth does not then require that we assert that our subject-matter be absent from sense awareness. Of course it *may* be absent from sense awareness: we may seek to know the chemical composition of the core of the earth or the history of the pre-glacial age or the outcome of the war. But it *need* not be absent; and in many cases it *is* not absent. Hence we must be cautious in generalizing. Santayana said long ago: "Knowledge is recognition of something absent; it is a salutation, not an embrace."[23] The last part of this statement seems to me sound. But is the first part? Of course knowledge is an effort to determine what, until determined, is not cognitively present; but it may well be the investigation of what is both physically and visually present. We do not need to deny that we really see and touch existent things in order to explain that knowledge involves more than seeing and touching.

The whole of nature is of course not present to sense; and the whole character of even one single substance is not revealed in any sense experience. But it would be dangerous to conclude that nature is "external" to sense; and it would be false to assert that what we perceive in sense is not part of the existential materials of which nature is the inclusive system. If things are not "given" in some specialized sense in which "given" means present to intuition, then things are yet given in another and important sense. Both the empirical actuality of things (which, in at least one possible interpretation of the *Metaphysics*, is what Aristotle meant by "matter") and also something of the character of things (which surely falls within what Aristotle called the "form" of things) are indubitably present in normal experience. So good an Aristotelian as Santayana ought not to omit recognition of this truth. Animal faith then ought not to mean faith in things transcendental to experience.

[23] *Reason in Common Sense*, 77.

It does not lack empirical grounds (in a broader sense of empiricism than that criticized above). It would be unfounded belief only to one who first made the rationalistic claim that all subject-matter is illusory until its existence be demonstrated by logic. I accept the doctrine of animal faith if it be a poetic name to designate the position that in all our knowledge of existence we begin by accepting a subject-matter we can not logically justify and by positing conclusions we can not guarantee to be theoretically free from possible error. But I reject the doctrine of animal faith if it mean that man, confined to essence in all his immediate materials of direct awareness, yet manages to postulate another realm of being never truly observed at all.

My criticism of Santayana can, in the third place, be expressed in terms of an examination into the meaning of the phrase "realms of being." This phrase which serves as the general title of the recent series of Santayana's writings perplexes me and leaves me in doubt as to their author's ultimate intent. The realm of essence is one possible realm into which we may enter when we neglect all but the rapturous appeal of some "given" item of sense or the intriguing meaning of some entertaining discourse. And the realm of matter is one possible realm we may consider when we seek to analyze certain aspects of the existential world, to treat qualities in terms of quantities, or to explain the transient or (in Aristotle's sense) accidental characters of things in terms of their more permanent or (again in Aristotle's sense) essential characters. Similarly we may define the realm of truth and the realm of spirit. Indeed we could define as many other realms as we could make important and interesting distinctions. Santayana himself says exactly this. "My system," he writes, "is *no system of the universe*. The Realms of Being of which I speak are not parts of a cosmos, nor one great cosmos together: they are only kinds or categories of things which I find conspicuously different and worth distinguishing."[24] We could have the realm of color, the realm of music, the realm of politics, the realm of error, etc., etc. The four realms of being in Santayana's books are, however, of

[24] *Scepticism and Animal Faith,* vi.

fundamental import: they rest on distinctions that *must* be noted if philosophic wisdom is to replace vain prejudice.

Yet, as I just said, I am perplexed. I am perplexed by what Santayana omits rather than by what he includes, and I am perplexed by what he means to indicate concerning the relation to each other of the realm of matter and the realm of essence. He works out his theory of knowledge without bringing in any other realms than those of matter and essence: the art of intuition introduces us to the realm of essence and animal faith keeps us sanely rooted in the realm of matter. But all the empirical material by which ideas are sorted and theories are tested belong to neither of these realms. Sense qualities do not qualify "matter" even though they do qualify material things. They do not belong to the realm of essence, even though they can be so taken apart from events as to become detached essences. Actually and originally they occur as existential items in the nexus of natural events; and their status is indicated by none of Santayana's realms. Yet without taking them into account no adequate theory of knowledge can be framed. Has Santayana fallen into the error of taking the realms of matter and of essence as together exhaustive of nature's richness? According to explicit statement he has not; but according to the implications of his epistemological theory he seems to have done just this. Where silence in regard to so important a consideration is complete, denial of the pertinence of that consideration is naturally to be suspected. My perplexity is over Santayana's omission of much that seems to me requisite to any adequate theory of knowledge. If we grant that no theory of knowledge can be demonstrated (for knowledge is a fact, and no fact can be demonstrated), yet a theory of knowledge is not plausible that is left without other support than an animal urge. Has Santayana possibly assumed that a theory which can not be demonstrated can not be substantiated? Theories can be substantiated by evidence even if the evidence can not be logically demonstrated. But evidence is factual occurrence; and the kind of evidence needed for a theory of knowledge is neither within the realm of essence nor within the realm of matter.

The difficulties I have expressed are variants of one criticism. I am more than ready to acknowledge that phrases in Santayana's books anticipate and forestall the grounds of my criticism at the same time that other phrases lead me to renew the criticism. So the criticism is presented more as a question than as a declaration of opposition. Perhaps I might be permitted to say in closing that, for purposes of philosophical adequacy, we need more than intuition of essence and assurance of animal faith. We need an exposition of the factual grounds whereby, under severe criticism, animal faith can be transformed into reasoned assurance. As Santayana shows that the art of intuition falls within the movement of the life of reason, so one might show that, on grounds of evidence if not of logic, the "shrewd orthodoxy" of animal faith gradually becomes a well-substantiated disclosure of part of nature's actual structure and form.

Sterling P. Lamprecht

Department of Philosophy
Amherst College

5

Charles Hartshorne

SANTAYANA'S DOCTRINE OF ESSENCE

5

SANTAYANA'S DOCTRINE OF ESSENCE

I. The Possible Doctrines

IF EVER there was a philosopher with whose exposition of his own ideas one would not wish to compete, this philosopher is Mr. Santayana. The combination, in his writing, of poetic vividness with logical neatness and sharpness would be the despair of anyone making such an attempt. I shall therefore devote much of this essay to an attempt to show what the doctrine of essence is not, that is, I shall evaluate it in relation to alternative doctrines, particularly such as seem to me neglected in Santayana's own discussion. I shall also try to reduce the doctrine to its bare logical bones; since the defect, if there is one, of his exposition is to clothe his ideas so richly in concrete imagery, examples, applications, that criticism is at a disadvantage in trying to locate the crucial questions. I shall therefore try to sum up the doctrine in three main points, one of which seems to me logically not to imply the other two, although these two themselves appear reducible to one, so that the question, "Is the doctrine true?" turns out to be several questions: "Are both of the two main portions of the doctrine true, are both false, or is one only true, and which one?" If I am wrong in this, if the doctrine is really all of a piece and must be accepted or rejected as a whole, then my attempt will have failed. My own belief, to reveal it at once, is that the "first portion" of the doctrine is true, the other not. This is, of course, compatible with a high appreciation of the manner in which both portions are developed and defended.

The doctrine of essence appears to consist of the following tenets or propositions, with their consequences and applications.

(1) There are *two modes of being*, *existence*, consisting of

events and enduring substances, and *essence*, consisting of the characters by which events or substances are or might be qualified. The two modes are *non-coextensive*, for though every existent has character, not every character has existence, characters being what they are whether or not they are embodied in existence. Existence may be infinitely varied, but it does not enjoy all possible kinds of infinity at once; it is not, like the realm of essence, "absolutely infinite." Existence is more or less exclusive, essence is strictly all-inclusive. "It contains with perfect placidity, and without begging leave either of God or man, everything whatsoever."[1] (This paragraph states, perhaps, several tenets rather than one, but I shall not try to distinguish them.)

(2A) The proposition, characters are what they are whether or not they are the characters of any existent, is to be taken as without exception. *All characters are on the same level* with respect to existence, the realm of essence is *completely* separable from existence, existence being thus wholly accidental (since, devoid of essence, existence would be indistinguishable from bare nothing). There is then no one privileged essence ("essences are all primary"[2]) such as might constitute the identifying character of a necessary being; and not even the disjunctive embodiment of essences, "some essences or other, any you choose, but at any rate some," is necessary. Not only of *each* essence is it true that it might not exist ("no essence has an essential lien on existence anywhere"[3]), but apparently of *all* it is true also (a logically independent assertion, just as to have a choice among possibilities is not the same as to be free to choose none of them). It is to be remarked, however, that if no essence whatever is necessarily the character of an existent, then the distinction made above between "each" and "all" would not hold; for this distinction, to have any significance, implies that existence has some basic essence which necessarily attaches to it, an essence which implies the disjunctive, though

[1] See p. 143. (All page references are to *The Realm of Essence*, unless otherwise specified.)

[2] See pp. 138 ff.

[3] P. 25.

not conjunctive, necessity of all the others (subject to a qualification to be noted later).

(2B) All characters, even apart from their embodiment in existence, are absolutely *determinate*, "individual," devoid of "intrinsic generality," vagueness, abstractness, or mutability. Like the Thomistic God they cannot be acted upon (although unlike Him neither can they act). This postulate adds to (1) above (that there are actually or potentially disembodied characters) the further assertion that such characters are determinates not determinables (in W. E. Johnson's terms). The denial of (2B) does not imply denial that there are non-actual characters (1), or that there are determinate characters, but only that the two can coincide. "Every essence is perfectly individual. There can be no question in the realm of essence of . . . vagueness."[4]

> This inalienable individuality of each essence renders it a universal; for being perfectly self-contained and real only by virtue of its intrinsic character, it contains no reference to any setting in space or time. . . . Therefore without forfeiting its absolute identity it may be repeated or reviewed any number of times.[5]

The last quotation suggests the logical equivalence of (2A) and (2B). For if a character, in its detachment from existence, is wholly determinate (that is, assuming [2B]), then since there is no room for degrees in absolute determinateness there is no room for degrees of the detachment, no basis for a distinction between relative and absolute detachment, or between postulates (1) and (2A). Or, if a character is absolutely detachable from existence (that is, assuming [2A]), then again there being no degrees of absolute detachability there will be no degrees of determinateness correlated with degrees of detachability. And the two must be correlated, for, as Santayana points out, to be determinate is to have whatever can possibly be required for being, since any addition to the determinate could only destroy its identity. What Santayana does not remark here is that while no relations could be added to the determinate, they might be

[4] P. 18.
[5] *Ibid.*

already involved in its determinateness, so that the characters as detachable from existence would be, just in so far, non-determinate characters, and the only fully determinate ones would be those in existence, already in possession of all their existential relations. (Change would then be not the addition to these characters of new relations but the addition to the substances having these characters of new characters with their intrinsic relations to the previously existent characters. More of this later.)

In order to see the problems I wish to consider the reader must understand the first proposition as *not* implying the other two. If, as he interprets the proposition, it does imply the second and third, then I ask him to try a different interpretation. On the other hand, as just indicated, I have no objection if he interprets the second and third propositions as each implying the other. I believe Santayana is brilliantly right, where many have erred, in putting these two doctrines together. And of course, from either the second or third the first is a mere corollary or tautological consequence. The main point, however, I wish to develop is that the first proposition might be true while the others were false, and that we find rather little in Santayana's writings that could be considered an answer to the question, "Are (2A) and (2B) supported by any evidence?" I confess that I do not believe they are, and naturally I will try to recommend this disbelief as best I can. But I wish also to emphasize that, in accepting (1), I am accepting what we might call the first half, or the weaker form, of the doctrine of essence. In addition I admire the skill with which the implications of both halves of the doctrine are drawn out, and the numerous matchless details of exposition and application. Moreover, in differing from Santayana in regard to essence I am aware of being in the uncomfortable position of differing also from many other important writers, past and present. The axiom of determinacy is widely held. For instance, Whitehead's "eternal objects" appear to involve it, or at least not to avoid it in a manner that I can understand.

The point at issue is not, it will already be plain, the division of being into two modes, actual existence and something else.

That the actualities of nature, or any and all actuality (including any purely actual God) do not exhaust the real (what is, independently of any finite mind's thinking it is) I wholly grant, even though Santayana is here combatting many illustrious precedents. But assuming that actuality is not everything, it does not seem to follow that the non-actual is absolutely determinate and individual, nor that it is independent of all existence. In addition to actual existence there may be potential existence, and potential existence may be the indeterminate but determinable aspect, as actuality is the determined aspect, *of existence,* the two aspects together making up existent substances. Thus substance would be all inclusive, as Aristotle held, and yet it would be true that not all that is determinable is determined (actual), and further the absolute infinity of the determinable may be a correct conception, provided there exists some substance whose determinability is absolute in its range.

One objection to this view needs to be met at once. Against the idea of determinable characters it might be held that prior to determination of the determinable the determinations must have been there as possibilities, one for each determinate character that can ever arise. This may seem self-evident. It can, however, reasonably be denied, as follows. A determination, prior to coming into existence, was neither possible nor impossible, it was nothing, for there was no such "it," and only of what in some sense is can anything be predicated, even possibility or impossibility. *After* being constituted in existence, the "it" may then have the retrospective relation of absence from antecedent existence, but this relation is external to such existence. In this view it is part of any determinate, existent event, as such, to be just where it is in reality and not anywhere else. It is, on the contrary, not inherent in the other portions of the real to exclude the event, *unless these portions are subsequent in time* (and even then the exclusion is only from that aspect of the present which is the mere present, not that aspect which includes the past as *its* past). Retrospective contrast is inherent in being, but prospective contrast is not, except for the contrast between the present and the more or less general and indeterminate schema which is all that there is to the future until it is no longer future. This view of the relations of characters to time will become clearer as we proceed. If it is false, then I have little idea where the truth of the matter lies. I am aware that Santayana would probably think it false, on several counts, and these will receive attention.

Perhaps the reader is asking, "Do you really deny that a character eternally is what it is, and do you really assert that x-ness, say, could ever have been other or less than x-ness?" I reply, "Of course, it could never have been other than it, provided 'it' was anything and not nothing, provided the word had a referent." But "it" may very well have no referent in that part of the universe we call the past (sheer eternity as neither in the past nor present being meaningless on the view here suggested).

Of every determinate character it is true that it, as an essence, "involves its existence," and yet that existence is contingent. The paradox is not serious, since to exist is a contingent qualification, not of *what* exists (even possibilities must in a manner exist to be at all), but of *existence,* as contingently enjoying that particular addition or member or determination. We ascribe qualities to their place in the universe as capable of being without those qualities, that is, of having others in their place, rather than a place or function in the universe to qualities as capable of being without such place or function. Determinate qualities have a determinate cosmic function, without which the universe, indeed, but not they, would have being (a somewhat different being) as determinate. Similarly, determinable qualities have determinable cosmic functions without which (unless we are speaking of the ultimate or generic determinable, the "primordial nature" of the cosmos) the universe, but not they, as those determinables, would have being (or even non-being or any definite status whatever).

Of course it is easy to think of objections to this doctrine, of arguments for Santayana's alternative to it. I shall consider these in the course of the essay. I suggest, however, that Santayana has not adequately argued his case against the alternative just proposed (which I shall accordingly call the Neglected Alternative), but has argued it chiefly against alternatives which I can only agree with him in regarding as erroneous.

The alternative I propose is, to restate it, that while there is a real duality of "actuality" and something else, it does not follow that there is anything over and above *existence.* For possibility is possible-*existence* if it is anything, and the duality we really need is that between actual and possible existence. Take any existing individual, say a man. This man actually is in this or that state. He actually is in pain, or in ecstasy, or in some intermediate state; he actually has done such and such deeds. But is it not a part of what we mean by his existence that he *can* or *could* do or suffer many things which he in fact has not done or suffered, and perhaps never will? This can or could is not just a piece of the realm of possibility in general, for what one man can, another man cannot. Potentiality is a part of the individual essence of an existent, and it varies from one unit of existence to another. You cannot describe individuals in terms of certainties, of what they are and will be; you must also indicate that which is peculiar in what they may or are likely to be and do. A man's "character" is not an affair of sheer actuality, but a system of possibilities and impossibilities (or—a distinction I shall ignore—of probabilities and improbabilities), a system different for each person. Of course, if probabilities and possibilities are nothing but words for our ignorance, then this account is false. But are they? If, for instance, probability is relative frequency, it may be objectively real, and there may be in reality no inevitability of individual events but only of classes of events.

You may, however, object that existent individuals might not have existed, and that this potentiality for non-existence cannot be regarded as a property of the individuals; for the state of non-existence would hardly be a state of the individual not existing, since it would rather be (on our assumption that substance is the inclusive mode of being) the non-being of the individual with all of his states. Moreover, when an individual comes into existence, this event must, on the foregoing account, realize a potency, determine a determinable, previously in existence and still existing. The upshot is that there must be one existent (it can be shown that it must be only one) which has never come into existence and never can cease to exist, since all "coming into" or "going out of" existence can only be the realization of the anterior determinability of this existent through its posterior determinations. This is, I believe, the correct idea of the necessary being, though it is not the traditional idea. For the latter took for granted that *all* of the character of a necessary being must be necessary, hence complete and perfect (since unachieved potency is excluded), whereas the logic of the situation implies rather that nothing in the necessary being is necessary (or perfect in the sense of unincreasable) except the most general determinable, the one eternal feature in possibility, including the general character of having always *some* determinations or other of the determinable. It is necessary that the necessary being should have accidents, though of course it could not be necessary that it should have the accidents it happens to have. Moreover, the necessary being will not only have accidents, it will have *all* accidents, since all that happens will happen to it. (Even evils will qualify it, except moral evil as such, for moral evil as happening *to* one is not moral, but aesthetic, as one's friends' wickedness may make one suffer but not, *ipso facto*, make one wicked. This is about all that there is space to say concerning this problem. The necessary being can be exempt from no suffering, but evil choices in others it may merely endure, without itself making any.)

This conception of the necessary being I find scarcely discussed in Santayana, although in his essay on Bergson in *Winds of Doctrine* he does parody it, without a very clear statement of what is logically involved.[6] This essay is a fine and most brilliant example of how to exhibit all the weaknesses of a man, without distinguishing very adequately between those weaknesses and such of his doctrines as do not imply them. The notion of a literally changing God with an unchanging necessary essence as one side of his character is infinitely more important than Bergson's philosophy, or the philosophies of any dozen

[6] For a similarly ambiguous discussion see *The Realm of Matter,* 170 or 124; or *Scepticism and Animal Faith,* 130 ff; or *The Realm of Truth,* 136-137.

men. It is one of the few major formally possible doctrines—one of which must be true. Moreover, if Bergson's philosophy is romantic, without solidity, good sense, and so on, as this essay says it is, there are also those, even among Santayana's strongest admirers, who think the doctrine of essence is too obviously fantastic to be taken seriously. I am not one of these. The doctrine, or something like it, is one of the chief alternatives among which we have to choose. So is the Bergsonian view of deity as only dimly grasped by Bergson himself, especially in his earlier writings. Bergson is one of the first of those to realize that the "without shadow of turning" of religion need not be taken as a complete description of the relation of God to time. (As the context clearly shows, the phrase indicates His reliability of character; but we rely on individuals who change in an unchangingly right way, not on those who unchangingly fail to change, and so fail to exist in any significant sense.) Existence is temporal or nothing, as Santayana himself insists; but the way to secure this insight is to explore the possible forms of existence in time, including whatever deity may conform to the requirements.

It may seem that the necessary being as involving the ultimate determinable could not be the righteous God of religion. Yet we must remember that any state of existence must be *a* state, any universe must be *a* universe, and that the ultimate being must fulfill two requirements. It must include all actual states, including values, and yet it must preserve its own identity in the midst of all this diversity of determinations. I suspect that this is "rightness" of action, to take all values that exist, or are potential in existence, into account in forming one's own unitary state. To harmonize the fullness of life into one life, so far as possible without sacrificing the real individuality and initiative of the many lives, that is what cosmic benevolence would be, to my understanding. Who asks God for something else asks for unrighteousness. (A non-benevolent God would be one who either failed to feel our values, or who had the split personality of a cruel person who, as Spinoza said, can only torture others while torturing himself.) Such a cosmic unity, patient of individuality in lesser lives, seems also the only idea that conforms to the requirements of existence as involving change and potentiality and everlasting identity.

Against the idea of potentiality as a real aspect of existence, Santayana has some words to say.[7] He suggests that either possibility is material possibility (compatibility with the course of nature) or it means the imaginable, and that depends upon whose imagination and at what time. The only objective factor in the case of the imaginable must be the realm of essence as "there" to be imagined if some one able to imagine it exists. Nor does the test of consistency change this conclusion; for any essence is consistent with itself, so that the totality of things consistently conceivable would only be the realm of essence over again.

Thus "possible" either means belonging to actual nature, past or future, or belonging to the realm of essence, or it means something subjective and varying with our ignorance or lack of imagination. Santayana even says,

> "in the actual universe, its essence being completely determined by the events which compose it, all that is actual is necessary and all else impossible. But this of course does not preclude the possibility of any different world; and so long as the complete essence of the actual universe is unknown to us. . . ."[8]

In *The Realm of Matter* also Santayana makes it clear that he regards the future as determinate no less than the past, although he is not a determinist in the sense of holding to the idea of absolute patterns or laws by which future portions of the world-essence could be known precisely from past portions. Now the doctrine which I am opposing to Santayana's holds that "actual nature" means nature up to now, since futurity is "essentially" a kind of relative inactuality or indeterminateness, so that it is an inalienable aspect of the determinate actuality of the world now that its next stage is not wholly determinate but determinable in certain directions and to a determined extent, the extent in the various directions being different for each

[7] Pp. 26-28.

[8] P. 28.

now. Thus the doctrine of essence calls for something more than existence only, I suggest, because it sees but one aspect of existence.

It is remarkable that Santayana says that other universes, taken as wholes (with all their moments of time doubtless included), than the existent universe (or universes) are possible. In what sense "possible," if possibility only means presence either in an existent universe or in the realm of essences? Doubtless the latter is here intended. Yet isn't something more implied, in spite of the doctrine? Can we escape the intuitive idea that the non-actualized essences "might have been" actualized, and that this refers to something else than the mere negative principle that nothing in an essence could *prevent* its coming into actual existence? Take the realm of essence, as complete and separate in itself, and then ask, "What could effect the transition from essence to existence?" Not essence itself, surely. (Essences, according to Santayana, are not dynamic, they do nothing.) Not existence, for that there is any existence presupposes that the transition has been made. Granting that the world has got under way, or at any rate is under way, we can then say that existence, or matter, or spirit, "selects" essences. But this selection presupposes existence. Had no world, by bad or good luck, existed, then no selection could have taken place. This is what I call a supernatural view of possibility. There is nothing in the world corresponding to the word "can" but only to the words, "has done," "does," "will do." But also, in the doctrine of essence, there is nothing even out of the world corresponding to the word "can." Essences are what they are, and so are actualities. What they "might" be is nothing to either of them.

Suppose, on the contrary, that at every moment nature, actuality, is confronted with a more or less vague aspect of itself which it has to make more definite as its next state, this making-definite constituting the fundamental nature of process, of reaching the next state. If we then ask, "What is materially possible?" the answer may be: allowing for all moments of time, everything is materially possible, in that either there was a time when it could, materially speaking, have been chosen, or there will come a time when it will be materially possible. The other possible universes are simply *all the unchosen (and incompletely determinate) alternatives* that once were or once will be "open" to choice by or in the universe, in infinite time. This doctrine is the only one that can fully naturalize possibility. Its price includes the admission that all laws of nature (except such sheer generalities as the law that there shall be laws) are subject to indefinitely great alteration within indefinitely great lapses of time, so that physics is not the study of what electrons, say, will always do or have always done, but only of what they have done and will do so long as electrons corresponding to our definitions and laws exist, this "so long" not being forever. All possible laws of nature other than the actual ones are then laws which the universe at some time could have assumed, in some cases no doubt did assume, or in the future may assume, and the present laws are to be conceived as flexible enough to allow for gradual development away from the modes of behavior they prescribe to any mode you please, given time enough. In short, like habits of animals, they can be changed and are changed, and although there is a habit of taking and developing habits, this is subject to limitations or to an "uncertainty principle" of infinite magnitude with respect to infinite time, so that the development of habits is even less rigidly predictable than are single actions as based on the habits. This view is not an eccentricity of mine. A host of great men, including Peirce, James, Boutroux, Whitehead, Bergson, have been developing the theory of real potentialities in just this sense (although Whitehead's eternal objects seem to me to involve excessive concessions to a Platonism of Santayana's type).

In Santayana's early essay on Bergson (in *Winds of Doctrine*) we find him arguing that the presumption is in favor of a fairly thoroughgoing mechanism, since the smallest and the largest processes known to us, the astronomical and the chemical, are both deterministic, and therefore probably the intermediate processes are so also. Here we may pose two objections. The large-scale changes are not those of individuals but of masses of particles with no sign of organized integrity. We realize today that there is no reason to believe that, could we deal with individual particles, they would exhibit strictly deterministic behavior. The only macroscopic masses of particles, short of the universe as a whole, that appear to act as dynamic units, rather than mere masses, are not known to act in a predetermined manner. These are the living organisms. And of these, one kind, the human, is directly given to us as a unit, in the unity of experience as such. For Santayana it is "literary psychology" to take this unity (which, as given, seems far from determinate) seriously as a sample of what substance fundamentally is, although it is, I should suppose, the only sample given to us with any great distinctness.

Be this as it may, we have the dilemma: there is or there is not a determinate total essence of actuality, past and future. If there is, then possibility is purely supernatural, and the other possible worlds have no natural basis whatever. If there is not, then possibility has a natural basis in the character of what exists, since to that character belongs an indeterminateness as to future alternatives (for surely the character cannot determinately exclude such alternatives, since then nothing could happen). Consequently there is no need for a separate realm of essence to house non-actualized possibilities, and these so far as eternal can be housed in the eternal or necessary aspect of the character of the universe, and so far as emergent can be housed in the *pro tem.* contingent character of the universe and the finite substances which this character includes.

The dilemma is such only if one assumes the validity of another dilemma: that a necessary being must either be necessary in all its being, and so coincide in actuality with the realm of possibilities (thus destroying the meaning of both actual and possible) or else have no rationale whatever. It is clear, however, that the alternative to the affirmation of a being necessary in all its characters is not the denial of a necessary being, but rather the disjunction: either there is no necessary being, or there is one whose existence, as qualified by certain (non-determinate, or general) characters, is necessary, although as qualified by other (less general) characters it is contingent. If not *all* characters attach necessarily to existence, still *some*, or *one*, may do so, and all other characters may attach, not by absolute necessity, but potentially and by hypothetical necessity, that is, should they exist, to the same existent as is qualified by the necessary character, or that character by virtue of which this existent *constitutes existence as such* for itself and for all other things.

Clearly this view involves the division of characters into two kinds, whereas Santayana has much to say in favor of the thesis that all essences are equally primary (postulate 2 A). He would doubtless suspect that the refusal of the Neglected Alternative to put all characters on a level could only spring from the desire to make an arbitrary exception, say in favor of God, or of some other allegedly basic conception. This would be a conclusive objection if the axiom of determinacy had been established. But if it can be held that characters, as separable from actuality, are intrinsically indeterminate or general, each such determinable requiring, for its actualization, the veritable creation of some form of definiteness, in advance specified (beyond a certain point) only negatively as "not identical with any now in being"—if all this can be defended, then of course characters are not on a level. For, since there are degrees of indeterminateness or intrinsic generality, the realm of characters will be a hierarchy, with the most general characters or character enjoying a unique status such that it can, in entire consistency, be viewed as the only really eternal character, at all times necessarily given *some* embodiment, some determination, or expression of its character as a determinable; while the other, less general or more determinate characters would be relevant, not to all time, but to stretches of time proportional to their generality (except that all characters, once actualized, would be relevant to all the future because of the "immortality of the past" according to Whitehead, immortality being of course infinitely other than eternity). Thus "color" (as a quality of sensation) might, prior to the emergence of organisms with eyes, have had no such definiteness as it has now, but "pain" may well have characterized organisms long before this emergence. And such characters as "being," "relation," "quality" (and perhaps also "experience as such") can never have emerged but must always have been embodied in some fashion in the past of the universe. Thus we would have no arbitrary exceptions to the principle that universality has all degrees between the absolute coextensiveness with space-time, or all existence as such, which constitutes necessity of existence, and the localization at a given time and place which characterizes the quite particular contingent.

Even to say of particular characters that they have no necessary relation to existence is misleading. Always a particular character is covered by some range of possible diversity (rather than a mere diversity of possibilities, strictly speaking) within which range something *must* happen. This must is conditional, that is, granting the state of the world up to now. At an earlier moment, taking the world up to then, a different range was open for compulsory decision. Going back far enough, all conditions are removed except those imposed by the essence of existence as such, or by that character by which the necessary factor in existence is identified as the same individual substance in spite of all its real changes. The necessity of this character is its coincidence with the universal factor in *both* actuality and potentiality, that unity pervading all alternatives or ranges open for decision which therefore itself has no alternative and could not, by virtue of any decision or the lack of it, fail to exist.

(Incidentally, ordinary objections to the ontological argument gaily assume either that there is no hierarchy of characters with a maximal instance, or that the maximal instance need present no unique problems.)

It may well be that the older formulations of the idea of necessary existence are untenable, indeed self-contradictory. A "most real being" (one which actualizes all possibility, enjoys completed all-round perfection, and thus contradicts the postulate of the relative independence of the two modes of being, and of the greater extent of the realm of unactual characters over actual) may fail to exist, not because there can be no necessity of existence, but because there can also be a necessity of non-existence, namely, with reference to the absurd. All that Santayana says of this traditional metaphysical notion of the absolute or of God seems to me a sound application of postulate

(1), which we know to be true if we know anything in philosophy.[9] It is important to note, however, that it is *only* the first portion of the doctrine of essence, postulate (1), that is required to bring out the weakness of the idea of a being complete as well as necessary. For if there is any distinction between characters and actuality, if the two are ever contingently related in a non-necessary actuality, then all existents sharing in actuality with the non-necessary must undergo contingent relations to it, and so have non-necessary properties, since purely necessary relations to the contingent would be self-contradictory. In any case, the necessary being is needed precisely as the presupposed subject of all accidents; so that to deny accidents of it is an error.

I have stated the alternative against which I propose to attempt an estimate of the doctrine of essence because I doubt if criticism in philosophy amounts to much apart from a clear statement of the view in contrast to which the one criticized is being estimated. Against a vacuum anything may seem good or bad, for one reads into the vacuum any merit or demerit one chooses. One may cling to a view because one dimly supposes anything else would be devoid of the attractions of the view under consideration (whereas it might, as a higher synthesis, include them), and could not offer any less serious difficulties (there is always the explanation of these, is not the human mind limited?); or one may, at the opposite extreme, suppose that there must be some alternative which would make everything easy, and so at the first sign of difficulty give up the proposed line of thought. Also I am firmly convinced that the great philosophers have made their most serious mistakes in their conception of the views between which one would have to choose if some doctrine of theirs was rejected. It could be shown that over and over again they have sought to show the inevitability of their proposals by exhibiting the weaknesses of *some,* rather than all, of the chief possible alternatives. This is a formal fallacy, and of all formal fallacies the most serious, so far as philosophy is concerned. It is not necessary for my argument that the philosopher in question (for example, Santayana)

[9] See, e.g., pp. 22, 58, 161f.

should *never* entertain the neglected possibility; it is enough that he should have given to it far less careful consideration than to the others. For only his prejudices can assure him that it is worth a merely casual inspection. If matters in philosophy were as simple as such procedure implies, we should be nearer agreement than we are.

It will perhaps be clear that the Neglected Alternative identifies the eternal aspect of characters with that "intrinsic nature" of matter which Santayana says is unknown[10]—or at least identifies it with so much of this nature as is the same at all times and places. To matter, says Santayana, all things are possible. I suspect that this is even truer than it was quite intended to be; but with David of Dinant and Bruno I hold the doctrine (called "crazy" by Aquinas) that prime matter, the ultimate potency which all change whatever actualizes, is an aspect of God, His power to form himself and so create form. I differ from them (and agree in effect with Santayana) in denying that this, if true, can mean the *identity of actuality and potency* in God, or the unreality of change (Bruno).

The existent, whether man or God, has power-to-take-form as part of its actual form, and if one asks, what is the form of this power to take form, the answer is that it is, or includes, the form of partial indefiniteness with respect to form.

Santayana himself gives a hint supporting this idea of a form of indefiniteness with respect to form. He says that if we are in a muddle or vague with respect to essences, this muddle or vagueness itself has a "perfectly possible" and "individual" essence. Well, that is the principle that the Neglected Alternative makes use of to explain all non-actual form. Non-actual forms, in proportion to their remoteness from actuality, are definitely indefinite to a given degree. Santayana tells us that "degrees of articulateness" are themselves all, as essences, perfectly distinct. One objection here is that these degrees form a continuum and, as we shall urge presently, continuity cannot exclusively consist of distinct parts. But it is true that if there are degrees of indefiniteness, the degrees themselves cannot

[10] P. 140.

be infinitely indefinite. Articulateness has various stages of completeness, and the Neglected Alternative holds that in the realm of non-actual characters even the most articulate essence is always less articulate than any actual character that "realized it." The most nearly articulate essences would be those whose realization was possible in the immediate future.

A striking feature of the doctrine of essence is the denial that characters do anything, the rejection of Platonic teleology. Now very likely characters do not themselves act, but perhaps they are actual or potential actions of substances which in and through them do or would act. And the ultimate determinable may be only the ultimate range of possible action and passion of the cosmic agent, the ways in which it could influence and be influenced. Plato may have been right enough here for anything Santayana seems to me to prove. For the aesthetic influence exerted in and through essences as embodied in our experience upon each other and the course of experience seems to me at least a patent fact. And absolutely disembodied essences, essences as not even determinable aspects of substance, cannot, as we shall argue in the next section, be shown to have being. Of course, what is not is also not powerful. It is nothing, there is no such "it." But an essence embodied as a facet of aesthetic attraction and repulsion, as a concrete portion of that search for novel integrated contrasts which *is* "spirit," that is the very essence, if you will, of power.

Power of one substance over another is of course not explained by the foregoing account, unless it can also be shown that aesthetic attraction and repulsion occurs not in a solitary substance, but in a substance immediately social, immediately participant in the being of other substances. Here is where the body comes in; for it consists of many substances, not one, and with these we are *immediately* in rapport, this rapport, a largely unconscious direct social interaction, being the mind-body relation, even though Hume, Kant, and many others have failed to see it.[11]

[11] Santayana's refutation of panpsychism turns on his implicit denial of the immediately social nature of feeling, volition, and thought. See *The Realm of Matter*, 183-87.

The Neglected Alternative is not an easy conception. I pay the doctrine of essence the compliment of supposing that it has no easy alternative, that only a view comparably worked out can offer any competition with this doctrine. We must pay all philosophers the compliment, moreover, of supposing that existence is not readily understood, and that consequently we have only to elaborate any doctrine to find it is not equally clear, for any one of us, at all points, nor infinitely clear at any point. I claim only to have given a more definite picture than our author of the possibilities confronting one who rejects one main portion of his doctrine while accepting the other. Such an one is not quite the inhabitant of a sterile island in the sea of thought that the readers of Santayana's truly magic words might be led to suppose.

II. Determinacy and Repetition

To illustrate how Santayana's doctrine really poses two questions, not one, I shall now try to show that the evidence which supports the first postulate—in my opinion very good evidence—lends no support to the axiom of determinacy, and is in no need of support from that axiom.

First, there is the argument that we can and do know characters without having any basis for knowing just what actualities do or do not embody them. To understand "whiteness," and to know all the things that ever have been or ever will be white, are two things different in principle. This is, it can be claimed, the very meaning of universality, without which we should have no rational knowledge. It is the definition of the universal that it does not involve all its instances. To deny that there is universality in this sense is *ipso facto* to deny all knowledge, as Bradley admitted, though he could not consistently adhere to the admission. It was the fallacy of Spinoza, isolated by an act of genius, that dramatized this issue for all time. Particulars cannot follow from the nature of being as such, for then being would be no more fundamental or universal than the least particular, and you might as well say that Spinoza's own acts, say, "follow necessarily" from the nature of God as a modification of Spinoza, as to say that they follow from Spinoza (and other finite things) as a modification of God, both God and Spinoza being, by hypothesis, absolutely, and therefore equally, necessary to being.

This argument supports (1) but it does not support (2A) or (2B). The reason is that no universal there is reason to think we can know or conceive is a wholly determinate character.[12] Redness we know, but redness is a somewhat indefinite range of qualities, not just one quality. There is no reason to think that we can divide the color scale into a definite set of absolutely distinct items, each a species of quality with no subspecies. (See section III.)

Another form of the evidence for the detachability of essence from existence, and so for its at least relative independence from the latter, is the experience of repetition. If the identical character can appear in more than one thing, or in more than one event, this at least proves that it does not depend upon any one thing or event. Curiously, it may seem, Santyana has doubts about such reappearance within human experience, perhaps even in the universe. He says it is improbable that precisely the same essence ever occurs twice in human experience.[13] This means that, so far as perception is concerned, we have no direct evidence that essences, as determinate, are detachable from their substances, not to mention from all existence.

Santayana, however, seems to make the claim that we can in imagination intuit an essence as unembodied in substance.[14] But this depends upon his view of the mind-body relation—which defenders of the Neglected Alternative are not likely to grant—the view that the body as a substance, or set of substances, is not immediately intuited, but, like all substances, "posited in action" by animal faith. Thus imagination reaches essences directly, in their independence of substance. But imagination may, on the contrary, be construed as only one special way of being aware of what is going on in the body and nervous system, as composed of a number of real substances, such bodily processes being taken by us, and indeed by animal faith, as signs of actual or possible processes elsewhere.

[12] On the indeterminateness of mathematical universals, see section III.

[13] P. 91.

[14] Pp. 129ff., 176.

Even were we not, in our imaginings, aware of the body, we should be aware of ourselves as actually containing the intuited essence, which colors our momentary personality. Santayana, however, in the passage above referred to, denies this. He says that an essence may be objective to spirit without being "formally" actualized in spirit as an existent. One may think of God or matter without thereby requiring them to exist with the essences thought of. I should think rather that either divinity is an indefinite or pseudo-idea, or (divinity as a mere potency being meaningless) there is a divine existent directly involved in my experience (without "my" personal character thereby becoming divine, experience being not merely private and personal in its immediate contents but also social). It is clear to me that to have a really *determinate* idea of red or pain it is necessary to have the required feeling or sensation as a property of one's actual experience. One may have signs of qualities without embodying the qualities in any way, but not intuitions of the qualities, not the full cash-value of the signs.

Santayana also contrasts practical concern with existence as past and future, and "timeless" spiritual contemplation of essences as eternal.[15] But is the contrast absolute? The limit of concern for time is interest in the ever-identical aspect of changing substance, and this is the eternal in the only sense, I venture to say, for which there is any spiritual or other need. Furthermore, complete contemplation, one may urge, would see in the essence of the present situation all that is real of the future.

We read often in Santayana that given essences are only indirectly relevant to action as adjustment to and control of the extra-bodily environment, but still they are directly relevant to the total problem of control, which includes control of the qualities of our human experience as the crucially important matter. All control is ultimately aesthetic in goal and criterion. And the ultimate beauties, I suggest, are forms *of* process, not mere forms *in* process. The dualism between changing existence (actual and potential), as the concern of action, and immutable essence, as the concern of spirit, seems an overstatement of the difference between activity directed toward immediate and probable results in terms of contemplation (including self-

[15] *Scepticism and Animal Faith*, 161f.

contemplation of its own changes), and that which is freer in its range. To wish to translate that form of variety which is change into a set of forms capable of a merely eternal being is to wish to diminish the variety of being, contrary to the supreme aesthetic criterion of unity in variety. A mind that experienced music all at once, without any contrast between expectation and its fulfillment, (such as would exist even with perfect memory of the past) would, to speak dogmatically and in spite of what Mozart seems to have said, experience less than music. (Mozart was scarcely speaking the language of literal science.) The eternal which is worth contemplating is the general outline and cause of possible change as involved in changing existence itself. (Mathematics is an aspect of this outline, in its admission of open alternatives and so far as it is expressible in formal language.)

We must return to the problem of repetition. When we look at an object and say that it has the same quality as certain objects previously experienced, do we mean anything absolute by this sameness? Santayana shrewdly suggests that we do not (whereas most philosophers seem, without thinking much about it, to assume that we do). Suppose two objects, as immediate objects of experience, are judged to exhibit the same shade of red. By what criteria do we distinguish between cases in which the objects have nearly, and those in which they have exactly the same color? We are relying upon memory or upon an act of comparison in which one object is in the focus and one in the fringe of attention, or in which both objects are out of the focus, which falls between them. In all three cases it seems reasonable to say that the judgment is fallible or of approximate accuracy only. Psychologists find that there are all degrees between "complete" inability to distinguish and complete ease of distinguishing. Statistical methods bring out the absence of any absolute line between inability and ability to make distinctions; for if the subject thinks he is merely making an arbitrary guess he may agree with himself and other subjects, upon the direction of the difference he says he can't detect, far too well for there to be any explanation other than that his sensitivity to difference is too fine for his introspection to keep track of it.

You may say that introspection is the absolute authority as to immediate experience, so that if one thinks that sensation A is not different from sensation B, and that B is not different from C, yet that nevertheless A is different from C, this means, not a contradiction, but that, when the third comparison is made, A or C or both, as data, have changed. Doubtless they have, but does that really make reasonable the assumption that we have the faculty of absolute introspective accuracy? Hardly, when the change itself probably escapes introspection!

Of course, one may ask what use there is in a notion of accuracy that apparently we can never employ? However, perhaps we do in a sense employ it as the abstract limit or ideal of a series of increasingly "fine" comparisons. In any case, it is he who defends the notion of a possible absolute identity of quality, in spite of existential change, who has the obligation of justifying the idea of a comparison which alone could furnish the meaning of such an absolute.

Santayana himself seems to furnish several good reasons for not affirming absolute repetition of essences, though insisting it cannot be logically impossible. For he holds to infinite gradations of essences.[16] Now too obviously our comparisons are not infinitely fine. Q.E.D., as to *verifiable* repetition. Also, there is an essence of the cosmos, and every essence of a part of the cosmos has to correspond uniquely to some aspect of the cosmic essence. Now how, in the absolute unity of the latter (see section IV) could there be bare repetition at different points? The relations of the repeated aspects could not all be repeated, and they are not external relations, since nothing literally in the essence can be external to anything else, the essence being one. This really, I think, proves that repetition is impossible in this universe, or even between universes.

Santayana does not, it is true, ground the theory of essence upon the experience of repetition. He apparently holds that we can see directly that a given essence is what it is, whatever its relations in existence may be. But this appears to be an illicit passage from "we are able to think explicitly about the essence while allowing its existential relations to drop from the focus to the

[16] P. 78.

fringe of consciousness," to "we are able to think what the essence would be if it had no existential relations." The problem of marginal or subconscious awareness has to be faced here, and the doctrine of degrees of awareness would have to be rejected by the defender of essences in favor of the doctrine that with every change in degree of awareness there is merely a shift to a different qualitative object. This would, however, result in the admission of indeterminate essences, and so in inconsistency.

One point will probably be admitted (it is fully conceded by Santayana). We do not in ordinary life draw any distinction between absolute and approximate qualitative similarity. We select or match colors, we describe the qualities of landscapes, animals, persons, or works of art, with no serious notion of achieving perfect accuracy. We designate by the musical scale those tonal qualities which a singer or performer is to produce, but no informed person imagines that anything but close similarity between different productions of the same composition is thereby obtained. For *all* practical questions whatever, what is repeatable is not a quite determinate essence, but a universal of a more or less high degree of specificity, or perhaps an *infima* species, where "*infima*" has no absolute meaning but indicates only the unavailability of any convenient method for further subdividing the species, "convenient" itself having no absolute meaning but varying with the purpose. Thus the pragmatic import of the doctrine of essence appears to be *nil*. Even where we appear to set a value upon real qualitative identity, as in holding that no copy of a painting can be strictly equivalent to it aesthetically, or in preferring the mechanical repetition of a favorite musical performance through the phonograph to a performance by other artists who will necessarily create slightly different tones, even here, it is not really absolute identity of qualities that we are valuing. For the experienced color depends upon the lighting as well as the canvas, and it depends partly also upon the inner state of the organism, the functioning of attention, and other factors whose absolute constancy is vastly if not infinitely improbable. Even the effect of different performances of the same record upon the same phonograph upon the same organism at different times cannot be known as identical at any qualitative point. All probability is in favor of slight differences, due to temperature and other physical, physiological, and psychological conditions.

One may go even further. Not only is there no human purpose which could be served by absolute qualitative repetition, there is no conceivable purpose, however superhuman. To an omniscient being—and nothing short of that could verify absolute qualitative sameness—nothing would be gained by the ability to enjoy the same quality at different times. An omniscient mind would have no need to repeat the identical qualities it had once experienced, for being omniscient it would never lose the experience in question but must either preserve it "immortally" (in Whitehead's phrase), in absolute memory, or else possess it eternally from a standpoint above time (whatever that might be). There would be no need to "play the record over again," since the one playing would be an absolute possession, forevermore (or eternally) available.

Yet it may seem a paradox to say that close similarity has a value, while absolute similarity has none. I think, however, there is no paradox except on the surface. It is valuable to have friends who think much as we do, or even who quite agree with us concerning certain more or less general conceptions. But what value would there be in exact qualitative coincidence with someone else? Since most or practically all of the relations of the identical "individual" quality would be different, it follows from the principle of organic unity which governs aesthetic value, the principle of *Gestalt*, that the alleged qualitative sameness would be useless or meaningless. The "same" quality could not have the same function; so to what avail its sameness?

On the other hand, high degrees of similarity have quite obvious value. If all qualities were simply the same or simply different, organic unity would be impossible. There could be no degrees of value, which seem to depend upon degrees of contrast balanced by equally striking degrees of similarity. Slight change of context may call for slight change of quality, greater change of context for great change of quality, but absolute sameness seems called for by nothing except absolute sameness of context, that is, not repetition but simply the original instance of the quality. However, there is such a thing as the same quality in different contexts in just the sense and to the extent that the past is that which will be involved in all future events, with relations which will be internal to the future but external to the past. The past, being fixed, does certainly get itself related to each new present. The omniscient mind has no need to play the record over, but for it the one playing is put in relation to each moment in existence as it comes into existence.

I know that Mr. Santayana holds that through the timelessness of truth all moments of time are in eternally fixed relations to past and future moments,[17] so that the total context of every instance of a given quality is the same. But, however the relations of truth and time be viewed (and the subject will recur—see section V), the notion of repeatable but absolutely determined qualities is a functionless notion. If the absolutely same quality could be appropriate in different parts of the total context (except as the past is always as such appropriate to the context of each subsequent present), then how could any difference of context, however great, call for varying degrees of difference of quality? If a considerable difference of context makes *no* difference in quality, why should still greater difference in the one make a finite difference in the other? Given an organic relation, the degrees of its effects may vary; but if organic unity is absolutely denied by the assertion of the absolute independence, at any point, of constituent essences, then there is no basis for variation in degrees of dependence, no ground for inserting such dependence at one point more than at another.

In short, I conclude that if there be no essences in the sense of postulate (2B), absolutely no conceivable purpose is in the least affected by this negative truth. We seem forced to agree with Mr. Munitz: the doctrine of essence (in its stronger form, or so far as going beyond postulate one) is irrelevant to a philosophy of life,[18] not only in its practical but in its most purely contemplative aspects. Even omniscience could enjoy essences, not as apart from the actualities and potencies of existence, but

[17] P. xv; *The Realm of Matter*, 64-79; *The Realm of Truth*, 79-96.

[18] See Milton Karl Munitz, *The Moral Philosophy of Santayana* (Columbia University Press, 1939).

only as contributory to actual or potential, determinate or determinable, existential states. Anything else would by definition be irrelevant to its enjoyment, or to that of any being for whose enjoyment it was concerned.

III. Determinacy and Continuity

The idea of wholly definite yet detachable, and so general, essences seems to go back to Plato and to have been derived in part from reflection upon mathematics. Mathematical ideas seem general and yet definite. Their definiteness, however, is not unqualified, but rather the most drastically qualified, in a sense, of all. To say of a group of entities that it is "two" is to convey the minimum of information about this group. The information is definite in just the sense that it is as definite as it wishes to be or is (except by philosophers) in danger of being taken to be. The indefiniteness, though infinite, is itself definitely bounded. Anywhere within the confines of the class "pairs of objects," anywhere you please, quite indefinitely, is the group of objects in question, and definitely not outside that class. Mathematics is the only science which can thus render its degree of indefiniteness entirely definite. Another way of putting the matter is this: to know a mathematical character of an object is to have definite information about other mathematical characters, though completely indefinite information about any non-mathematical characters. That is, the definiteness is all on one plane, that of mathematical abstraction. In relation to a more concrete level there is no definiteness whatever.

Even in relation to other mathematical ideas, however, a mathematical concept is perhaps not wholly definite. Mr. Santayana himself says that "triangle" is not strictly the same essence when combined, say, with equality of angles as otherwise.[19] It is mere multiple similarity between any definite sort of triangle and triangle by itself. I believe we must distinguish two quite different cases. Triangle in general and red triangle are related somewhat as our author suggests, except that I should say the identity of triangle in the two instances is literal and absolute if the determinable as such is intended. Of course the determinable

[19] Pp. 83f., 82f.

as determined (to be red) is different from the determinable as merely determinable; nevertheless, it is the identical determinable that is now determined in one way, now in another. But it would not do, I fear, to regard "even number" as determinable and "two" as determinate, if by that were meant that one might understand the former without seeing the possibility of the latter; whereas the Neglected Alternative holds that "triangle" can be understood without even knowing that "red triangle" is even possible. The ultimate eternal logos, the real essence of existence as such, includes all the generic factors necessary to knowledge, such as relation, time, plurality, number, quality, and the generic interrelations of these. Thus in a sense "2" seems as general as "number," in that the idea of number *is* the idea of pairs of classes, and a class is the idea of something which might be paired with something else as similar, thus involving the ideas of twoness and threeness or synthesis, as Peirce has worked out in his scheme of the categories.[20] It is noteworthy, however, that geometrical ideas are strictly generic only when taken algebraically, for what is meant by "right-angle," "equal length," etc., depends upon physical factors entering into measurement which can be surveyed distinctly *a priori* only in their purely algebraic and ordinal aspects. Nor do I see any reason for supposing that such "essences" as redness must be involved distinctly in the generic ideas.

Mathematics itself suggests the above distinction between eternally definite and, from the eternal standpoint, non-determinate characters, in so far as the views of some mathematicians concerning the nature of continuity are accepted. From postulate (1)—rather than from postulate (2)—follows the absolute infinity of the realm of possible characters. Any conception that could distinguish at all between actual and possible would have to allow infinity in every direction to the possible. Thus, for example, we can indicate the possibility of colors redder than any red we experience, taking red here as a quality or datum of experience. The judgment that a red is "pure" is a comparative judgment. It means that any reddish color closer to gray or blue or yellow will seem slightly grayed or purple or

[20] See his *Collected Papers*, Vol. I.

orange to us. But for all we know there *could* be a sensation in comparison to which even our pure red would seem gray or purple or orange. That is, the color scale might, for some being, be divided more finely, or it might extend farther out into the—for us—empty color space beyond the limits of the double cone of color sensations as we have them. This defines certain regions of possible but, for all we know, non-actual sensory qualities. These regions can contain as many different qualities as you please, for there is no ground for setting a limit to the merely possible subdivisions or extensions of the actual, once the non-coincidence of possible and actual is granted at all.

In the above case the infinity and the continuity of essences are two aspects of the same thing. This seems sound as a general principle. For what is continuity or absence of gaps, as Peirce said, but the totality of possibilities in a certain direction? Gaps represent what might be there between two terms but is not there. Furthermore it has been proved that the multitude possible to a continuum is without any limit among transfinite numbers. Any number, not only infinite, but of any order of infinity whatever, can be included in a continuum. This seems to show that possible variety cannot be too great for continuity, which can be as multitudinous as you please both in dimensions and in items on each dimension. So when Santayana says that the realm of essence is "a plenum or continuum in which every essence is surrounded by others differing infinitesimally from it,"[21] he says something which is well supported by any reasonable evidence for there being non-actual characters.

What, then, is the relation of continuity to postulate (2B), to determinacy? It seems clear that determinates need not be continuous. The whole numbers seem (mathematically) determinate but discontinuous. And it is by no means certain that everything required to make the whole numbers part of a continuum will be as determinate as the whole numbers. Can a continuum consist of wholly determinate parts or subdivisions, or must it not consist rather, as Aristotle said, of inexhaustible subdivisibility, rather than of inexhaustible divisions? Santayana's essences are points in his essence-space, and it is no-

[21] P. 78.

toriously still a moot question today among mathematicians and logicians whether a point is or can be a determinate entity in a space, and not rather a way of looking at the possible divisions of the space, a way that is determinable rather than determinate. Applying the Whiteheadian notion of extensive abstraction to the space of possible qualities (including Whitehead's own eternal objects!) it would turn out, apparently, that the realm of non-actual characters, together with actual ones, is composed not of indivisible parts, but of slices, potentially as small as you like, of the space. Now such slices would possess precisely the intrinsic generality denied by postulate (2B). Thus the slices of reds between very obviously purple and very obviously orange hues is not any absolutely determined or specific hue but an infinity of possible hues too little different for the difference to strike us. If the slice is so small that we *cannot*, except statistically or uncertainly, detect differences, we say that all the parts are equally pure red, but this sets no absolute attainable limit or point.

Not only do present-day extremists among the intuitionist school, such as Brouwer, deny that a continuum can have extensionless parts, but the more moderate thinker Peirce stoutly insisted that since, as Peirce hoped he had proved and Zermelo (on the basis of his usually accepted axiom) is now recognized to have done, continuity admits of any multitude, and since further a maximal multitude is impossible, and anything less than a maximal multitude of points on a line must omit something which could have been there, it follows that the continuum of possibilities cannot be any distinct set or multitude at all, but is rather something beyond multitude and definite variety, an inexhaustible *source of variety* rather than variety itself.[22]

How could absolute "individuals" compose a continuum, since each would be, like a point, without any internal complexity or distinction of ends to unite it to its neighbors (I do not say, its next neighbors, for of course there are none in a continuum)? Must not absolute individuality be a limit of thought, like a point, a limit having no being apart from the

[22] See *The Collected Papers of Peirce*, ed. by Charles Hartshorne and Paul Weiss (Harvard University Press, 1931-35), I, 499; III, 563-70; VI, 185ff.

process of which it is the limit, or ideal? An individual event may have a determinate quality by comparison to events earlier than itself in time; for the previously-effected divisions of the continuum are immortal. But future divisions are the mere general possibility of further division. Nothing in the continuum is eternal except certain ultimate dimensions, or dimensions of possible dimensions, or something of the sort. It would take another Peirce to discuss the matter adequately; here I can scarcely do more than propose the problem.

Santayana once said that pure being is a sort of space to the other essences. If the foregoing account of continuity is correct, then pure being is the only essence that is eternal, the continuum of undifferentiated potentiality (the bare power of God) that alone precedes every event whatever.

IV. Some Consequences of Determinacy

From the axiom of determinacy Santayana, with notably rigorous logic, deduces certain consequences. Among these is the denial that "complex essences" have separable parts.[23] For parts which were detachable but not detached would introduce determinability into the determinate and so destroy it as such. Hence the most "complex" essence is so only in a peculiar sense. It is, though this is not Santayana's phrase, a *Gestalt* with multiple relations of similarity to simpler essences which nevertheless are not contained in it. Thus a pattern of colors as one essence is in different moments of its organic unity similar to but not absolutely identical with these colors taken separately. From this it seems to follow that the whole quality of any experience or of its object is always but one essence, and that it is impossible simultaneously to intuit two or more essences. I am not aware, I confess, how from this situation we could ever really derive the idea of a plurality of essences or know what is meant by the similarity of a complex essence to simpler ones. Santayana says that the entire realm of essence is one essence of absolutely infinite complexity;[24] but he can only mean that there is one complex essence which has maximal multiple similarity, through

[23] Pp. 88ff.

[24] P. 71.

its aspects, to all less complex essences. This complex essence itself will be a member of the realm; and this suggests an infinite regress and paradoxes such as those which gave rise to the theory of types. I do not, however, undertake to found a refutation upon this point, although I suspect it could be done, even though Santayana might say that the problem of types concerns "discourse," not essences in themselves. A similar question arises concerning the essence of the universe.

Granted indeterminacy of detachable essences, the problem is eased immediately. For then there is indeed but one determinate essence in experience at one time (except, as we shall see in the next section, for the multiplicity of past events). But there are many determinable essences at one time, for the single determinate essence of the given event has aspects which determine diverse determinables, thanks to which the aspects can be recognized as diverse aspects. These determinables, by virtue of their incomplete determination, have a certain margin of freedom with respect to their interrelations. Redness of such and such a fairly definite sort admits of a wide variety of shapes in its embodiment, although not so wide as might be thought if it were forgotten that the shape of the embodiment includes the structure of the organism and of the stimulus, without which, so far as psycho-physics can show, there may be no such quality as redness. The dimensions of determinability are as open to external relations as they are themselves indeterminate. Thus they can function as parts independent of their wholes, and so enable us to be aware of multiplicity. However, all such determinability is merely an aspect of the essence of futurity which itself is an aspect of time as "objective modality" (Pierce).

The axiom of determinacy means that no essence is intrinsically general. For, the general being the partially indeterminate, the intrinsically general is the intrinsically partially indeterminate. Thus redness in general is less definite than "light red with a purplish cast." Color is less definite than red or green. Sensory quality is less definite than color. The order of decreasing definiteness is the order of increasing generality. Santayana affirms this truth, but couples it with the to me almost baffling acceptance of pure being as an essence quite as determinate as any other.[25] That is, to say of a thing that it "is" is to say something no less definite than to say exactly what its quality is! But, if pure being is an essence then why not pure color, and pure sensory quality, and pure redness, all the intermediaries between "just this determinate red now given to me" and being in general? And if these are all equally determinate and individual, then, so far as I can see, anything is anything. This is the point where I find the doctrine of essence almost weird. But perhaps I have simply lost my way among the subtleties of the doctrine. For Santayana admits that pure being is not really the same as contained in one essence, say that of light, and as contained in another, say that of darkness. Indeed, how can being literally be contained in any essence if no essence has real parts (doctrine of the *Gestalt*)? Yet Santayana also says that being is contained in every essence. Evidently this is not meant quite literally, but in accordance with the doctrine of multiple similarity. Santayana also says that being is the entire realm of essence "implicitly." If this meant, by its determinability rather than by its determinations, then I should understand; but then being would be intrinsically abstract and general (as, to say truth, I am almost sure it must be). As it is, I feel lost in a forest of ambiguities. Being is the realm of essence determinately but implicitly; there is also an essence corresponding to the whole realm of essence in its explicit character; and there is finally the irreducibly plural realm of essence itself, no one of whose members can literally be in any other.

If essences are determinate and complete apart from existence, then all relations of essence to existence, or by virtue of existence, are external to essence. Its relations to existence are purely contingent. But can the determined receive a relation, even contingently? What relevance could the relation possibly have? It could make no difference to the essence that it has the existential relation. In short, "it" would not have it. Existence would have both the essence and "its" relations to existence. The essence would thus be like the Thomist's God, who is said not to be related to the world (lest He be relative) although the world is related to Him. This Thomistic doctrine is para-

[25] P. 49.

doxical, to put it mildly. For since a relation is a unity embracing its terms (a mere *type* of relation includes only *types* of terms, as in "xRy"), the term that includes the relation necessarily includes the other term within itself, and thus the world is the Thomistic "absolute" God and more besides! (The paradox disappears in the Neglected Alternative, since the world as including the relations of the eternal determinable to its determinates *is* God in His total being as including a contingent aspect, and as thus more than Himself as merely determinable.) In the doctrine of essence, it is not indeed stated that essence is in every sense absolute; so perhaps it seems a tolerable outcome that existence should prove to be more inclusive than the absolutely infinite realm of essence (since existence alone owns the relation of this realm to existence). Still, is it not the same paradox substantially? Are not the relations of the two realms of being homeless in both realms? To the paradox of denying an inclusive unity for relations, Santayana adds the further paradox of a plurality of absolutes, which is one of the doctrines upon whose impossibility thinkers have most nearly agreed.

The alternative here is the view that the externally related is abstract or indeterminate to the extent of its external relatedness. Not that externality is unreal, but that indeterminacy or abstractness is real. Let us consider a concrete case. A white thing is a whole to which whiteness is internal, although the white thing is external to whiteness. Now the white thing is a unity. If it were simply a set of items, then indeed one item might be abstracted unchanged, determinately the same whether in or out of the whole. But a mere set, not in any further sense a whole, is a mere limit of thought, a fiction. A real thing, as Santayana himself seems to hold, is more than just the co-being of items; and the universe as a real thing must be more than this, or knowledge of one thing through another would be impossible. Now it follows that when we single out for attention features of reality, including our own experience, and consider them "apart" from their relations, we alter them in some way. If we simply changed them into different qualities, then abstraction would be mere falsification, and knowledge impossible. But if abstraction generalizes, or substitutes for the given qualities somewhat less determinate equivalents (with boundaries marked out by the limits of accuracy of our comparisons) then, since absolute accuracy is not the reasonable goal of human knowledge, there is no harm done. Hence the way to justify abstract knowledge is to admit that the abstractable or detachable features of existence are never fully determinate.

In any case, it seem to be a fact that experience presents no such thing as the determinate possibility of what has not yet happened. Take any anticipated event as anticipated, and you will never find it to be determinate. It is not simply that we are in doubt as to what it will be, we are even in doubt as to what it could possibly be. The exact flavor is not even imagined. Indeed, a determinately imagined experience and an actual experience could not be distinguished. Dreams may be determinate enough, but only so far as they are not merely possible events but real ones. The very distinction between actual and possible is effected in experience only because the present involves generic rather than absolutely specific qualitative indications of the future.

Were possibility a set of determinate alternatives, then the process of selecting those to be actualized would be futile, since it could only exclude some qualities already in being and add to the others the meaningless dignity of "existence," which would contribute nothing determinate whatever, all determinateness having been already ascribed to the realm of possibility. It does not answer this to say that actuality brings the qualities within reach of an actual subject and its real enjoyment. For all the possible qualities of subjectivity and enjoyment would, as possible, be there anyway, and again we have only the meaningless compliment of "actuality" to distinguish the two realms. Experience shows the value of actualization to be rather that of sharpening contrasts and thereby enhancing harmonies which in possibility, as we know it at least, are only vaguely there among other vague possibilities. Some of this vagueness is our ignorance, since other minds may be less vague in the matter. One who has never known parenthood has a less definite notion of the possible qualities of this experience than one who has known it. It is, however, equally apparent that the qualities of each case of parenthood are in subtle ways unique, and there is some burden of proof on the assertion that any mind whatever, or any realm of essence, contains a complete set of determinate qualities from which each actualized quality will turn out to be a mere selection. Creation may be more than such mere mechanical selection, it may be creation, the determination of the somewhat indefinite, as well as the decision between alternatives.

Let us take an example of choice. I may choose to try to be kind rather than injurious to a person who has injured me. But the actual word or deed must be more definite than anything such choice can envisage prior to action. Choice is among "intrinsically general alternatives," although what is done is never general in the same degree. This is the meaning of choice: it is determining which determinable to particularize through further determinations not yet in being. No God can choose otherwise, Leibniz and others to the contrary notwithstanding. Our horror of anthropomorphism does not entitle us to play fast and loose with concepts. The process of time is known to us as the bringing of particular quality into being, not as its transfer from God to the world, or from essence to existence.

The basic meaning of the axiom of determinacy in relation to existence is identical with the doctrine of Hume that "what is distinguishable is separable" and that experience consists of factors distinguishable in this sense, or as Santayana puts it, "Essences are the only data of experience."[26] From this atomism follows all Hume's scepticism. Of course causality is for Hume objectively groundless, for the succession of events has no unitary character which is essential to the separate items in events and therefore has authority over them. No God or self can help, for the items are by hypothesis completely independent of any and all relations, hence even of relations to God. The unity of mind has been declared a non-entity on the plane of experience. How can it be rescued on the plane of inferential thought? Thus personal self-identity is a riddle and nothing more. And thus of course, as is suggested in Hume's *Dialogues*, dead matter could as well explain cosmic order as God; since, by hypothesis, nothing could explain or intelligibly constitute order. Order means

[26] *Scepticism and Animal Faith*, 91.

internal relations at some point or in some direction. Any terms exempt from dependence upon all but themselves are simply and absolutely non-causal. It is Santayana's discovery that Platonism, if taken as the theory of determinate separable forms, coincides with Hume's doctrine.

The alternative is to make experience in its unity a single *Gestalt* character, whose full determinateness is what is meant by its "existence." This determinateness or existence can never be reached by mere description, but only by concrete experiential contact, by pointing, and then it is not reached with full consciousness but with an intuitive grasp that is mostly faint background rather than clear focus. The path to existence and to determinateness is thus the same, and to us human beings it is a path that expresses our human limitations.

V. Essences and the Structure of Time

If characters are completely determinate, they are of course immutable. For what is wholly determined lacks nothing it could ever acquire. It would become simply another "it" were anything added to it. The Neglected Alternative, which takes actuality and determinateness as coincident, accordingly regards the actual aspect of existence as immutable, but can admit change with reference to the potential aspect, this being more or less indeterminate in character, though not simply without character.

The doctrine of determinate essence, on the other hand, must perform the logical miracle of reconciling change with the denial of determinable characters, of intrinsically general essences. Santayana says, "In the essence of change we have given together, in a single image, the successive phases of an event which, when change is enacted, are necessarily alternative."[27] But, remembering the denial of real parts in essences, we see that the essences belonging to the successive phases cannot literally be embraced in a single essence. The essence given to the present experience must simply exclude all other essences, and it may then be doubted if memory or the awareness of time could ever arise.

To quote Santayana again, "Events, if they are to be successive or contiguous, must be pervaded by a common medium, in

[27] P. 77.

which they may assume relations external to their respective essences; the internal or logical relations between these will never establish any succession or continuity among them."[28] The suggestion is that if events involved essential relations, relations of character, only, there could be no real change. Surprisingly, however, this does not follow, provided one regards the relations as asymmetrical with respect to past and future. The *Gestalt*-essence, to which what is new in the present belongs, may literally embrace the past essences also, but not essences which have not yet occurred. When new *Gestalten* occur, they will be included in the essence of the present, but it will be a new present. Time is thus a series of *Gestalten*, each containing the series up to and including itself, somewhat as four contains one, two, and three, with an addition. (The analogy is not perfect, because numbers are abstractions, not concrete, determinate characters.) This is the Bergsonian or Whiteheadian view of time as growth, creation without any destruction of the same ultimacy. What is "destroyed" is merely lines or trends of creation, which may break off at a certain stage, although as effected up to that stage they are indestructible. A man may die, but his having lived up to that moment can never die, can never be less than it has been.

Since asymmetry is itself a character, the combination of internal and external relations above indicated makes change itself something with a specifiable character, whereas Santayana's account makes the character of change identical with the blank mystery of a "matter" which is a mere surd to character, rather than a system of more or less general or determinable characters.

The reason we do not have to make inclusion in the essence of the present apply to future events in their determinate individuality is simple: they have no such individuality. The past has actually occurred as it has occurred, and hence the present, as soon as it is in being, must have determinate, not merely determinable, relations to it; but the future is that which will be determined, exactly *how* being not determined. A and B must involve definite relations so far as A and B are both definite, but only so far. In this way we can make relations really relate,

[28] *The Realm of Matter*, 16.

be something to, their terms, and yet avoid the block universe that would eliminate all distinctions. (How spatial diversity is dealt with must be left undiscussed here.)

The chief alternative to essence is thus Bergsonian. *The immortality of the past is the immutability of essences as determinate.* They will always have been just what they have been. This immortality of the past, though in a manner admitted by Santayana, is not for him a datum of experience. He speaks of "the ghost of the murdered past,"[29] and of the "fading" of an event into an essence—presumably meaning only that for our limited human vision the past is less than present reality. The human limitation, however, he takes in the extreme form. He says, "My recollections . . . are only essences which I read . . . as signs."[30] Thus the past as such is a pure inference from timeless essences. This inference is said to be supported by the "habits" latent in the body and somehow also in the mind.[31] Still, the paradox remains concerning what "time," the present, the future, the past, could mean were there no direct intuition of the distinctions between them. The basis of the view, one may suspect, is that our intuition of the past is faint and is overlaid with generous elements of imaginative construction not clearly distinguishable introspectively from the intuition. When we speak of recalling what in the interval had been forgotten, this involves a drastic shift in the vividness with which certain parts of the intuited past are intuited, plus elements that do not belong to the datum of the intuition but are not sufficiently different from that datum to betray their foreignness.

Difficult as this notion of faint though direct intuitions of clear experiences may be, the alternative is not necessarily less difficult. For the alternative is that everything about experience that is given at all is given absolutely, just as it is, and then I believe nothing can ever explain how error is possible. If to intuit and to be able to know that you intuit were one, then the line between datum and inference could offer no trouble. All essences considered by us, however slightly differ-

[29] P. 25.

[30] *Scepticism and Animal Faith,* 155.

[31] *Ibid.,* 156.

ent, would be for us exactly that, slightly different, and all confusions would be excluded. The difficulty is not wholly ignored, nor yet, I feel, really surmounted, in Santayana's analysis.

Santayana speaks sometimes as though all vagueness or confusion were due to discourse. But intuition itself gives nothing wholly clear; indeed, it may be urged that such clarity of intuition is what ought to be meant by deity, although even in that supreme instance not every sort of vagueness (say, of the future as such) must be considered lacking.

Santayana's theory of *truth* is stated as an account of what everyone means by "truth," hence as needing no argument. Nevertheless an argument suggested for it is that "what will happen will happen," that *something* definite must be true about the future.[32] The law of excluded middle appears to necessitate that every proposition, even about the future, have a definite truth value. This I accept, but it does not follow that the future must be determinate. For to be "definitely indefinite to a certain extent" is a state which allows every proposition a determinate truth value. Thus either "x *is* definitely-going-to-occur," or "x *is not* definitely-going-to-occur." But suppose x *is not* definitely-going-to-occur. It does not follow that x must then "definitely be going-not-to-occur." It may rather be definitely "not decided either to occur or not to occur." A proposition asserting that it is decided will be definitely false. There are, indeed, three possible cases, each of which may be asserted or denied, such assertion or denial being always at a given time determinate in truth value. (1) x definitely *is going to* occur, or, the non-occurrence of x is, given the actual (that is, present) state of the world, impossible; (2) x definitely *is going not to occur*, or, the occurrence of x is, given the actual state of the world, impossible; (3) the occurrence and the non-occurrence of x are both, in view of the actual state of the world, possible. In short, *all* the possibilities, or *none* of the possibilities, or *some and only some* of them, as real potentialities involved in actual existent things, involve the occurrence of x. Each of these three cases, if asserted in a proposition, will yield definite truth or falsity. For

[32] See *Scepticism and Animal Faith*, 268f.; also *The Realm of Matter*, 71ff.; and *The Realm of Truth*, 94f.

a state of indeterminacy *in actuality* with respect to the future is, according to the Neglected Alternative, a real state and the *only* state, when it exists, by virtue of which propositions about certain aspects of the future could be true or false, but thanks to which they all are either true or false: false if they assert the positive determinateness of the universe with respect to the future in the given aspect; false equally if they assert its negative determinateness; true if they assert, what is in fact the case, that the universe, not the truth values of propositions, is, in truth, indeterminate in the aspect in question. Thus all attempts to settle the ontological question about the character of the future by the purely formal law of excluded middle, or by an appeal to "truth," are real cases of the fallacy wrongly charged against the ontological argument for God, of an illicit passage from thought to reality. What will be will be, but maybe there is no one definite thing which will be, although there will be *something* definite or other. I can know that the author of an anonymous book is definitely male or definitely female, without knowing definitely which it is. Similarly, the world can be determined to select between the occurrence and the non-occurrence of "x tomorrow" without being determined to select the occurrence or determined to select the non-occurrence. I am aware that Santayana thinks truth about the future refers to the future directly and not via any determination in the present. This, however, is the only point at issue: is the future determinately real while it is future? (The very question will seem to Santayana to imply a confusion between "sentimental" and real time, but that too is the point at issue, even granting that there may be a valid distinction between *human* and cosmic time.)

Another argument might be that when an event, said not definitely to be going to occur, does occur, this verifies the assertion, if previously made, that it was definitely going to occur. Now the occurrence of the event does prove it was not impossible, and may suggest that it was probable; but that its non-occurrence was impossible at the time the prediction was made no single occurrence of the event can prove or strongly support. Only the "verification," not of a single prediction but of many, as deducible from some general law, would really give evidence that the non-occurrence of the event had all along been at least highly improbable.

In one of the rather rare passages in Santayana's writings which state, or almost state, the new type of theistic metaphysics, Santayana speaks of it as an alternative to the view of an "omniscient" deity.[33] But the view is rather, for nearly all its adherents, including Bergson, that concerning the future there is nothing to know except the limited extent to which future events are already determined in various directions, and beyond this the bare general truth that it will be determined *somehow* or other, that its indeterminations are to be removed.[34]

In one criticism of Bergson, Santayana seems definitely mistaken. He cannot properly say that the identification of time with what is given in the present logically or necessarily reduces time to an eternal changeless now. For why should not immediacy be aware of itself as perpetually acquiring new determinations, additional to those which, once acquired, are never lost? True, the past portions of time do not change, once they have occurred, except to get farther into the past portion of time as a whole, farther from that end of the past which is the present as contrasted to the past; but the total present, as inclusive of the past, changes always, since increase is a change if anything is. However, Bergson's phrase about "interpenetration," if taken without qualification, would justify Santayana's objection. Here we must choose between making nonsense of Bergson, and improving upon his expression.

VI. The Necessary Being

In a criticism of Leibniz, who, as he says, "had a marvellously clear head," Santayana suggests that any God choosing among possible worlds would Himself be the actuality of one possible world.[35] Astute as it is, this remark must, I think, be taken with careful qualification. It is one thing to say—as many theologians now would say—that to exist God must have one among various

[33] *Winds of Doctrine*, 97.

[34] Bergson has shown that, in spite of, or even thanks to, relativity, it is possible to conceive a cosmic present, past, and future, to which our doctrine of a world determinate up to the present but no farther could apply. See his *Duration and Simultaneity*.

[35] P. 163.

possible forms, and thus actualize in Himself some possible world. It is another thing to say that God is simply identical with such a world. For this second assertion assumes that the other possible worlds are something other than possible states of God. On the contrary, that there are unexhausted and inexhaustible possibilities for further worlds is, for the Neglected Alternative, identical with the indeterminate determinableness of God's power as the supreme existent. Santayana holds, however, that the *goodness* of God is merely one among possible forms or worlds. Now the particular goodness of particular acts of God is certainly subject to alternatives. But the generic goodness, the common quality of all actual or possible acts of God, is not subject to an alternative since it is, on the theistic notion, the very thing that makes each and every possible world *a* possible unitary world (or rather, that would produce such unity, were "it" to have being—merely "possible worlds" not having individual unity). If existence is inseparable from a certain degree of order, so that things can coexist rather than nullify each other, then the goodness of God may be simply God as causative of such order. Santayana says:

> . . . this gallery of possibles present to the Creator's mind is not the realm of essence at all, but an emanation of his particular existing nature; just as it is not the realm of essence in its entirety that swims before a novelist when he debates what conclusion to give to his novel; but the alternatives that suggest themselves are only a few, such as lie within his experience and conspire with his purpose and are compatible with the plot of the novel so far as it has gone. The Creator would then be a perfectly contingent existence, a particular being finding himself already at work. He could not have asked himself, before he existed, whether he would be the best possible God. The fabled problem of creation must already have been solved before it could be proposed; and a mind considering which world to choose is a world existing without ever having been chosen. The notions of the possible and the best, otherwise unintelligible, become significant in reference to the accidental potencies and preferences of that existing being. His creations, like those of any living artist, would then be naturally in his own image, and it would turn out that of all those possible worlds only the best was really possible, since a motive for creating one of the others would necessarily be wanting. . . . I need not enter into the moral difficulties which this rigid monotheism involved.[36]

[36] Pp. 162-63.

In this most brilliant even if somewhat playful passage, I believe Santayana has made an excellent, if unintentional, contribution to theology. Certainly the Creator, as at a moment creating the world of the next moment, is not considering all that at *some* moment or other would be possible, but only all that is relevant to that moment. He is asking how the plot *as so far developed* may suitably be continued. This plot being God's concrete history and empirical nature to date, naturally its continuation will be "in His own image." For the concrete character of God and the concrete unity of the cosmos are the same. No deliberate continuation of the world-plot which is inferior to some possible one is a possible divine preference. However, it does not follow that it cannot happen (and here the "rigidity," inimical to morals, drops out); for what God *prefers* is not the same as what He *permits to happen*. God has two intentions in mind, what He prefers, should the creatures freely coöperate to produce it, and what He will infallibly bring to pass by setting limits, if necessary, to such freedom, in order to guarantee *a* world, even if not the best possible. The sinner is not perhaps the only factor making for the non-coincidence of these two aspects of the divine plan. Even non-rational creatures need some range of spontaneity, and it is a question of luck or of statistical probability what harm they do with it.

Also it need not be thought that even God's preference is uniquely determined by His history and generic character. For it is impossible that a particular—and any world state must be particular—should follow as a conclusion from anything as premise, whether something universal or something particular, unless the latter be a particular whole of which the conclusion is a part. And that the future (except as indeterminate) is a part of the existing whole which embraces the past, is just what is not to be taken for granted. So whatever God prefers will be indeed such that nothing better, more apt to continue the plot, is possible, but not such that nothing equally good would have been possible.

The conclusion from the foregoing is not quite that God is a "perfectly particular being." He is a generic and the only strictly generic or necessary being; but it is involved in this necessity that He contain an ever-growing infinity of contingent particulars.

God is not metaphysically compelled to exist with the particular contents of experience which He actually has, but He is compelled to exist (that is, the idea of an alternative is meaningless) as having *some* contents or other, as a man may be compelled to pay his taxes *somehow*, though not necessarily in cash or by check on a certain specified bank.

So of course God does not ask Himself whether or not to be the most benevolent possible God, but only how to *continue* His existence, which from the beginningless past is already there, in conformity with His character as the best possible being, ethically and cognitively. (It is not aesthetically the best possible, since, as Santayana points out,[37] infinite perfection of beauty—or happiness—is meaningless; a neglected negative truth of great theological importance. Although no other individual could equal God in happiness, He can surpass Himself, that is grow, in this respect. Such growing happiness may in a sense be infinite, but not "absolutely infinite.") God, as considering "which world to choose," is indeed "a world existing," but yet not one which has never been chosen. For the moment earlier is the locus of that world's choice, and so on for every past moment. God has forever been choosing Himself, and forever He has already chosen Himself up to the moment of any given self-choice—which is partly acquiescence in the choices of the creatures. (Of course, Santayana's criticisms remain valid against Leibniz, who denied contingency and change to God.)

It seems obvious enough that there must be a generic variable in existence whose identity is more than the mere words "being" or "the universe," but that to which these words refer. Granted such a cosmic unitary generic essence, then all more determinate and specific determinations can be provided for through more or less general universals, analogous to the specific purposes which are from time to time adopted as determinations of a man's generic life-purpose, down to the actual achievements of purpose which are always concrete, particular events with their unique qualities only *specifically* identical with the qualities of even the most specific purposes, but not identical with them determinately or individually. This scheme of generic or outline

[37] *The Sense of Beauty*, 36.

purpose running through life, special purposes running through portions of life, and unique moments of actual achievement whose determinate qualities no anticipatory purpose quite envisaged, seems to fit experience and to end the stubborn quarrel between being and becoming in a manner to do justice to all real interests except that of prolonging some verbal tradition.

The alternatives which Santayana most clearly saw he decided, I believe, correctly, as great philosophers are privileged to do. The most hopeful criticism is to find the alternatives that he dealt with chiefly by implication. The new type of theology that is being built up by Whitehead, Montague, Hocking, Brightman, Tennant, and numerous other philosophers and theologians, a type of doctrine whose very existence is practically ignored by Santayana (as it is by Dewey), is able to employ most of Santayana's negative arguments without necessarily adopting most of his positive conclusions. I think it is an example of the human tragedy that Santayana has been so sure that men like James and Bergson have had little to teach him. No issues can be permanently decided except explicitly and on their merits.

In Santayana's writings some of the most pervasive errors of philosophers are remorselessly and resourcefully combatted. Particularly grateful to him should be those philosophers who believe in metaphysics as the attempt to deal rationally with our sense for the ultimate and everlasting, for the necessary aspects of being, and who nevertheless do not wish to limit the possibilities for metaphysical thought to certain prevailing tendencies in the great tradition. Without turning philosophy into a mere handmaid of physics, Santayana has been able to reject some of the most hallowed metaphysical dogmas. His eloquence is thus a force on the side of philosophy as a study enslaved neither to the past nor to the sciences whose success can be measured by so obvious an act as switching on an electric light or crossing a bridge. The subtler human interests are also to be considered, and they are not forgotten by our great poet-philosopher.

Charles Hartshorne

Department of Philosophy
University of Chicago

6

Milton K. Munitz

IDEALS AND ESSENCES IN SANTAYANA'S PHILOSOPHY

6

IDEALS AND ESSENCES IN SANTAYANA'S PHILOSOPHY

SANTAYANA'S writings call repeated attention to the ultimate significance which form possesses for human experience in giving meaning and value to our activities. Unless a man is interested in the characters which things have or might have, he can hardly be said to live at all, in any morally significant sense. This theme is given a wealth of illustration and examined in a variety of contexts from *The Sense of Beauty* to *The Realms of Being*. The analysis of its implications involves a considered treatment of all the traditional branches of philosophic interest, morals, metaphysics, aesthetics, and the theory of knowledge. I have selected ideals and essences in Santayana's philosophy for discussion, because they seem to me to crystallize two dominant yet divergent ways in which this principle is justified and its consequences drawn in terms of a total philosophy. The analysis of these concepts provides, therefore, not only a suggestive means for the examination of a controlling interest in Santayana's thought, but also the opportunity to raise, from a critical point of view, certain crucial difficulties that are present in their combined use.

One strain of Santayana's thought, as I have suggested elsewhere,[1] consists of a combination of naturalism in metaphysics, humanism in morals, and realistic methodology in the theory of knowledge. These doctrines receive dominant expression in the works of the middle period,[2] especially in *The Life of Reason.* The latter work is an acknowledged classic, one that at the time of its composition was unique in its presentation of a point of

[1] See my *Moral Philosophy of Santayana,* (New York, 1939), 10-12.

[2] For the arrangement of Santayana's works into three periods, its reason and significance, cf. *ibid.,* 8-10.

view that has since become widely accepted in its major outlines. By its effective synthesis of the principles just mentioned, a significant alternative was pointed to the moribund idealism and impoverishing mechanistic materialism which nineteenth century speculation bequeathed as its fruits.

The natural setting for a life of reason is found to consist of a network of objects and events related to one another in multitudinous ways, of which human experience is but a special instance.

> Human nature has for its core the substance of nature at large, and is one of its more complex formations. . . . Nature and evolution, let us say, have brought life to the present form; but this life lives, these organs have determinate functions, and human nature, here and now, in relation to the ideal energies it unfolds, is a fundamental essence, a collection of activities with determinate limits, relations, and ideals.[3]

Moral idealism is simply a general name for that force in human activity that would stimulate and sustain our interest in converting those elements of our experience which flounder in ignorance, ugliness, or maladjustment into their opposites. Moral idealism acts as a leaven to naturalistic philosophy in upholding the value of pursuing rational interests. Nature understood and controlled, beauty discovered and created, social harmony and a total personal health achieved, are the ideal ends recurrently and incessantly sought, that give purpose to our activity and afford intrinsic satisfactions in their specific, plural realizations.

It should be well recognized by now, however, primarily as a result of the direction in which his later philosophy has been moving, as indeed from a careful scrutiny of certain undercurrents in the earlier writings, that there is another side to Santayana's thought. In important ways these other doctrines annul or cast doubt upon the naturalism and humanism of his philosophy. Santayana's early attachment to the other-worldliness of Platonism, the Catholic tradition, and the philosophy of Schopenhauer was submerged and corrected by the dominant theory of *The Life of Reason.* His underlying affinity for this general type of thought, however, is revivified and supported by a novel architectonic in the latest writings. Here it appears in

[3] *Reason in Common Sense,* 289, 277.

the guise of a theory of essence. The scepticism and agnosticism of the later theory of knowledge, the mystical and post-rational character of the spiritual life, and the theory of the ontological independence and priority of the realm of essence to the other "realms," are all intimately related, yet collectively at the opposite pole from a naturalistic and humanistic philosophy. Since essences may be examined in relation to the "problem" of knowledge, aesthetic experience, and their significance for a spiritual life, we shall find it profitable to compare the manner in which essences function in these contexts as over against ideals. We may then find that the conception of an independent ontological realm of essence, far from being an original metaphysical sanction for these other matters, is rather a consequence of an attitude involving a mystical abandonment of moral idealism. The metaphysical dislocation of forms into a separate realm will appear as a technique for "justifying" such an attitude. It is only because our author has exposed with remarkable lucidity and force the inherent weakness of this general type of thought, that one who has benefited by the rich insights of *The Life of Reason* need not look elsewhere for critical principles in an estimation of similar tendencies in Santayana himself.

I

Santayana's discussions of the nature of knowledge may be considered as they fall into two broad divisions, methodological and epistemological. The methodological analysis is concerned with understanding the conditions, materials, procedures, types, and ideals of science. It elucidates and confirms the underlying assumptions of a controlled pursuit of knowledge. In terms of the epistemological approach, Santayana takes over the problem with which philosophy ever since Descartes has been concerned, namely, how the mind in being confined to its own "ideas" can possibly know the external world. Here Santayana proposes a transcendental criticism of our assumptions with regard to the acquisition of knowledge that, when carried through, results in a "disillusionment" with science and a serious challenge to the ultimate validity of its ideals. Both concerns are present with varying degrees of emphasis in the earlier analyses, *Reason in*

Common Sense and *Reason in Science*, as well as in the later work *Scepticism and Animal Faith*. In the earlier analysis the methodological approach is predominant, in the later treatment the epistemological. Taken together, however, these are incompatible, since they operate with contrasting assumptions about the nature of experience, the one affirming its adequacy to disclose the traits of our environment, the other insisting upon its inevitable illusory and fictitious character.

From a methodological point of view science is recognized as an elaborately controlled operation that develops out of and has its original basis in common sense. The acquisition, systematization, and increase of knowledge are parts of a process that has no absolute beginning. They constitute transformations in the direction of the ideal of the materials (concepts and beliefs) already in existence. To further this enterprise it is not necessary to call into question, by a wholesale scepticism, the validity of *all* beliefs at once. The ideal as an outgrowth of natural conditions, in the case of knowledge signifies a reworking of the crude, unorganized mass of established beliefs. This is accomplished through weeding out the true from the false, through systematizing, making more precise and extending the limits of those judgments that can be empirically verified. Since science, though an advance upon common sense, is nevertheless continuous with the latter, it employs the same human faculties, however supplemented or corrected by special instruments and techniques, that are employed in our everyday conscious responses to the world.

> Science differs from common knowledge in scope only, not in nature. ... Its validity is of the same order as that of ordinary perception, memory, and understanding. ... The validity of science in general is accordingly established merely by establishing the truth of its particular propositions, in dialectic on the authority of intent and in physics on that of experiment. It is impossible to base science on a deeper foundation or to override it by a higher knowledge.[4]

The ideal product of empirical investigation consists of true propositions. The truth in this sense is not something antecedently or metaphysically given; it is a property of discourse

[4] *Reason in Science*, 18, 37, 318.

won through verification. Nature is constituted of objects and events related to one another in multiple ways, physical, biologic, and social; these compose natural existence in its diversity and complexity. Intelligence is itself a complication in nature and a unique type of activity. When it is present, other facts as well as its own powers can be understood. The understanding of natural phenomena, as an ideal of science, involves transforming into actuality the potential intelligibility of the world (since the latter exhibits some order and not a total chaos); and this is accomplished through the operation of sound procedures.

Far from lumping all modes of interpretation into one class and asserting that they are all mythical or fictional in character, though of different degrees of "practical" value and applicability (as is done in the later writings), Santayana takes pains, in *Reason in Science*,[5] to distinguish science from myth. For the capacity which science has to reveal the intelligible structure of nature comes through formulating by means of hypotheses the functional interconnections among objects and events. These hypotheses can be ultimately verified through the prediction, identification, and experimental control of the instances to which they apply. Myth on the other hand is, when properly understood, a poetic symbolization of events, not a literal report of their exact properties. Its intent and value is dramatic, not cognitive.

Science, morever, as a method of articulating the structure of things, exhibits a distinctive manner of dealing with nature. One cannot legitimately demand that science be reduced to the immediacy of sensation or to some other form of non-discursive existential relation, and expect it to retain its own distinctive essence. For in that case we should simply have abandoned the intellectual essence of science—life *understanding* its own conditions—in order to substitute for it the blindness of existence itself, unconscious and brute.

What commonly escapes speculative critics of science, however, is that in transcending hypothesis and reaching immediacy again we should run a great risk of abandoning knowledge and sympathy altogether; for if we *became* what we now represent so imperfectly, we should evidently no

[5] Pp. 8-18, 23f.

longer represent it at all. . . . Knowledge is not eating, and we cannot expect to devour and possess *what we mean.*[6]

The ideal results of science are achieved in two main types of investigation, in those where the interest is that of discovering the structure of some portion or level of natural existence, and in those where, in abstracting certain forms and symbolically recombining them in novel relations, analysis is performed in order to discover their logical implications. In the first case our interest, as an empirical one, is to verify hypotheses through perception; in the second, as in the case of mathematics, the interest is one of finding what consequences are necessarily entailed, as a matter of sheer consistency, by the original assumptions. The one demands verification by sense, the other logical cogency and compatibility with original intent.

I think a theory of knowledge as presented in *Reason in Science* that has the direction and contours just briefly outlined, is essentially sound. In terms of it, we avoid making knowledge an insoluble or falsely stated problem, but supply instead, a fruitful methodologic guide for the interpretation and criticism of actual contributions to the body of science.

Santayana, however, despite all his earlier condemnation of mysticism and transcendentalism as diseases that disintegrate the healthy instincts of a life of reason, has himself adopted these methods in *Scepticism and Animal Faith* and emerged with conclusions that challenge the adequacy of science. His theory sanctions the pursuit of science for practical reasons, but proclaims nevertheless its ultimately fictional character. The abandonment of the ideals implicit in scientific inquiry is made evident in Santayana's adoption of total scepticism as a method and of doctrinal agnosticism as a conclusion. A certain element or type of scepticism, is, of course, involved in every genuine scientific inquiry; but, as we shall see, it is not of this that Santayana is speaking. Rather scepticism, for him, involves a retrogression to the antecedent conditions of the ideal products of science, and agnosticism the confession that the ideal, when supposedly achieved, is not genuine. In the one case we eliminate all pretensions to have knowledge of anything and reduce all beliefs

[6] *Reason in Science*, 21; *Reason in Common Sense*, 77.

to the materials of which they are ultimately constituted. These, for Santayana, are taken to be immediately present, certain, non-signifying, luminous, non-existent, universal essences. In the other case, we are asked to admit that the formulations and descriptions of science are mere symbolic devices for the designation of objects in the "external world," objects whose existence is postulated on the grounds of animal faith. These symbols provide the basis for practical adjustment to outlying objects, but give us no ultimate insight into their properties. Scepticism, seeking absolute *certainty*, finds none in any and all claims to knowledge, but only in the immediate presence of some essence. Agnosticism, concerning itself with the *reality* or adequacy of presumptive knowledge, finds an inevitable dichotomy and discrepancy between the opaque pictorial terms of description used by the mind and the hidden, underlying "real essences" of things in themselves.

For one who is concerned with furthering the discovery of true beliefs or with understanding the methods for securing them, there is no opportunity nor necessity to adopt the method of scepticism. Santayana's use of this method is not itself an instrument for advancing science; it is not a demand for more adequate evidence for specific beliefs. It is rather a total disintegration of all beliefs to that level of experience in which no assertions are made, no claims to information are offered, and no interpretations of the connections of natural or logical entities are proposed. We are to abandon the perspectives and contexts in which intelligence operates and stop short at what is there for brute sensation or simple imagery. This mystical retrenchment, it is claimed, will yield an intuitive contact with essences that are at once indubitably certain and non-existent.[7] Ordinary knowledge is neither; it is always open to doubt and correction, and it has reference to the actual course of natural events.

Why does Santayana consider it necessary to adopt the method of scepticism as the initial step in the presentation of his philosophy? Why indeed would a "philosopher today . . . be ridiculous and negligible who had not strained his dogmas through the utmost rigours of scepticism, and who did not

[7] Cf. *Scepticism and Animal Faith*, 42-8, 74, 110.

approach every opinion . . . with the courtesy and smile of the sceptic?"[8] For, if scepticism amounted simply to a critical scrutiny of the evidential value of any specific belief or system of beliefs, surely such scepticism is nothing other than a phase of any philosophic or scientific inquiry that demands consistency and empirical corroboration for its assertions. Obviously, however, scepticism does not, in such a situation, involve distrusting at once already relatively established beliefs, a relevant portion of which must, in fact, serve as the basis for continued investigation of some new problem. For, as Santayana remarks in a passage preceding the one quoted above, to the extent that scepticism is identified with the specific criticism of a particular belief, it itself involves the use of some opinion in countering the one being challenged. Genuine doubt, in short, is always relative to some context in which established meanings and beliefs are taken for granted and used. The fact that no empirical proposition is absolutely indubitable but rather is always corrigible, does not mean, therefore, as Peirce has well emphasized, that continued investigations cannot take place until every proposition is established as absolutely indubitable. Just as we cannot choose honestly to doubt everything at once, since genuine doubt is occasioned only by some felt difficulty at a given cross-current in the ongoing activities of thought and conduct, so too, fruitful progress involves the use of previously settled opinions as the context and means for aiding in the settlement of some fresh difficulty. Santayana's scepticism is at one with all types of artificial scepticism, including the Cartesian, that presume to discover the irreducible and absolute foundations of all knowledge. Santayana's system, like Descartes' (the one finding these irreducible elements in essences, the other in self-evident axioms), is to be sharply contrasted with a realistic theory of knowledge which emphasizes, on the one hand, the self-corrective, cumulative advance of science, and, on the other, the impossibility of "reconstructing" a given product (in this case knowledge itself) after having dissolved it into its elements. The wholesale scepticism that Santayana's method would seem to imply contributes nothing whatsoever to the furthering of any specific inquiry or,

[8] *Ibid.*, 9.

indeed, to an understanding of scientific procedure in general.

Santayana's theory of knowledge as presented in *Scepticism and Animal Faith* is, in effect, a subtle attack on science and an attempt to justify a subjective retreat to the immediacies of indubitable, eternal, and aesthetically rewarding essences, while leaving science to a subsidiary, action-rewarding task of representing the "hidden" material conditions and environment of life. Scepticism makes possible the mystical escape from the tentative, hypothetical, and plodding course of scientific inquiry and opens the mind to a realm where it can possess immediately and all at once the joy of beholding pure forms.

> There are certain motives . . . which render ultimate scepticism precious to a spiritual mind, as a sanctuary from grosser illusions. . . . A mind enlightened by scepticism and cured of noisy dogma, a mind discounting all reports, and free from all tormenting anxiety about its own fortunes or existence, finds in the wilderness of essence a very sweet and marvellous solitude. The ultimate reaches of doubt and renunciation open out for it, by an easy transition, into fields of endless variety and peace, as if through the gorges of death it had passed into a paradise where all things are crystallised into the image of themselves, and have lost their urgency and their venom.[9]

We may ask, however, can it truly be said that a retreat to those levels of experience in which intelligence no longer operates yields a paradise, and one, moreover, in which we suddenly come upon forms that are non-existent and certain? We may grant at once the possibility of the sceptical exercise, but is it anything more than the forsaking of one level of experience in order to fall back on a more primitive one? Such an exercise, if it does make available an intuition of essences, gives us merely such as result from the type of experience proper to the faculties and instruments which we have retained after having abandoned all the rest. In stopping short at brute sensation or at some immediate image, we have simply withheld the activities of interpretation and analysis that intelligence adds in normally supervening upon these in a rational life. A reversion to this stage of mental experience out of which intelligence originally develops, as Santayana tells us in *Reason in Common Sense*, is "an

[9] *Scepticism and Animal Faith*, 40, 76.

exercise in mental disintegration, not a feat of science."[10] From the point of view of the life of reason such reversion, while always possible, is never fruitful, if what we are interested in is enlightenment and not the meaningless sensations of animal existence. "The immediate is not God but chaos . . . it is that from which all things emerge in so far as they have any permanence or value, so that to lapse into it again is a dull suicide and no salvation."[11] Essences exhibited at the level of immediate sensation or imagination are not ideal products; they are rather the material for rational understanding and interpretation.

Consider again Santayana's insistence that what intuition discloses is a non-existent essence.

> A datum is by definition a theme of attention, a term in passing thought, a visioned universal. The realm in which it lies, and in which flying intuition discloses it for a moment, is the very realm of non-existence, of inert or ideal being. . . . The notion that the datum exists is unmeaning, and if insisted upon is false. That which exists is the fact that the datum is given at that particular moment and crisis in the universe; the intuition, not the datum, is the fact which occurs. . . . That which is certain and given, on the contrary, is something of which existence cannot be predicated. . . .[12]

Is not this denial of existence to the qualitative *products* of the operation of an organism in its environment, while affirming existence of the terms in the relation, the consequence of an extremely arbitrary use of the term existence? Is it not entirely contrary to that common sense which a clarifying metaphysics would take for its starting point? For, can it be seriously maintained that when I drink a cup of tea, for example, my tongue and the cup of tea exist, but the taste does not? Or when I look at the moon, my eye and the moon exist, but the yellow which I see does not? Santayana would perhaps reply that he is using the term existence as applying only to the causally effective, underlying material substance of things, not to the qualities of things as they appear to us. But this usage and this restriction is false to a genuine naturalistic theory, for it would confer exist-

[10] *Reason in Common Sense*, 40.

[11] *Ibid.*, 42.

[12] *Scepticism and Animal Faith*, 54-5, 45.

ence upon the conditions or causes of a relation and deny it to its products or effects, whereas both in fact are equally involved and continuous with one another. The qualities resulting from the activity of sensation are no less naturally existent than the act itself or the object upon which it is directed. What Santayana has done is to cut off the products, the forms actualized when the appropriate conditions are present, and set them up in an independent realm, conferring essential being upon them apart from such connection with natural conditions as they must necessarily have. Far from matter being an accidental occasion for their appearance, it is their only possible condition of existence. When, therefore, Santayana tells us that "nothing given exists," we may say that even after scepticism has done its worst, such essences as are experienced nevertheless exist on the minimal levels of sensation and imagination. Forms which in the presence of intelligence exist in a context wherein they are employed in description, belief, and prediction, now exist in a different context. What has happened has been a disclosure of forms on another, lower level of experience, not an escape through such experience to objects having no existence at all.

Furthermore, in what meaningful sense can certainty be predicated of forms thus beheld? Instead of recognizing certainty to be an ideal of science, one to be progressively approximated, Santayana's method would reverse the process and attempt to find it in the immediate intuition of essences, the disintegrated residuum of beliefs that have been purged of their claims to knowledge.

> When by a difficult suspension of judgement I have deprived a given image of all adventitious significance, . . . then an immense cognitive certitude comes to compensate me for so much cognitive abstention. My scepticism at last has touched bottom, and my doubt has found honourable rest in the absolutely indubitable. . . . I have absolute assurance of nothing save of the character of some given essence; the rest is arbitrary belief or interpretation added by my animal impulse.[13]

But does not this reversal of direction in the search for certainty —from the accumulation of objective evidence for hypotheses

[13] *Scepticism and Animal Faith*, 74, 110.

to blank stares at meaningless qualities,—actually fail in its results? For consider the simple intuition of some color; *what* as a matter of fact is it that is certain here? Surely not the mere *having* of the experience, since we must distinguish such having from assertions *about* it. The assertion "I am seeing a color" is different from the immediate experience to which it makes reference. The seeing of a patch of color is something brute; the moment one hazards an interpretation, either out of curiosity, habit, or need that, for example, this color is ocher or vermilion, the realm of knowledge-claims has been entered and the certainty of the assertion must be established since it is not initially given. Certainty is either a psychological feeling attending the belief in the truth of some proposition (a feeling that is of no logical value in determining its actual truth) or the scientific ideal wherein any given proposition or set of propositions would be established through having obtained all possible, verified, objective evidence. In any case, certainty has reference to the truth value of some *assertion* or *belief*. Until some predication is present, the mere having of a sensation or an image is neither certain nor uncertain, it simply is. Santayana's search for certainty in the wrong direction not only does not make it available in any significant sense, but neglects consideration of the way in which it actually functions as an *ideal* for science.

Santayana's transcendental method has two results; it removes knowledge as an ultimate ideal to make room for an aesthetic intuition of essences; and, by virtue of the very attempt to extricate oneself from these pure immediacies and re-establish the belief in an external world, if only because of the animal necessity of doing so, it ultimately develops a dualistic theory of knowledge. The only consequence of the latter is agnosticism, an admission or insistence that no disclosure of the structure of things is possible. For, according to Santayana, empirical knowledge is merely the leap beyond given essences, a leap or transcendence necessitated and justified by animal faith. Precisely because essences are taken as fictional or poetic creations (not merely in the literal sense of being products resulting from the activity of the mind in perceiving and understanding the world, which is a perfectly naturalistic notion, but in the disparaging sense of being illusory figments), the only alternative left is to try to fit the picture to some already existent real essence of objects themselves. Thus the shades of the Kantian *Ding-an-sich* and Lockean *Unknowable* rear their heads once more.

> The pride of science should turn into humility, . . . it should no longer imagine that it is laying bare the intrinsic nature of things . . . the forms of science are optional, like various languages or methods of notation. One may be more convenient or subtle than another, according to the place, senses, interests, and scope of the explorer; a reform in science may render the old theories antiquated, . . . but it cannot render them false, or itself true. Science . . . yields practical assurances couched in symbolic terms, but no ultimate insight.[14]

The impasse is inevitable; if once we designate the qualities of experience as mere appearances by means of which we symbolize an underlying, hidden substance, we can never elude the suspicion that what is thus postulated to exist by animal faith is indeed something of which we can have no understanding at all. Consider the following statement as an illustrative consequence: "To me the opinions of mankind," says Santayana, "taken without any contrary prejudice (since I have no rival opinions to propose) but simply *contrasted with the course of nature*, seem surprising fictions, and the marvel is how they can be maintained."[15] Let us ask ourselves what it means to judge the "opinions of mankind" (which presumably include those of common sense and science) to be fictions. If such judgment does not involve sifting and specifying *which* opinions are fictions, in the sense of being erroneous or misleading, by contrast with *other* judgments that have received the best available confirmation and, therefore, are accepted as true until disproved by still other judgments, what then does it involve? "Contrast with the course of nature?" However, does not such a phrase cloak the tacit assumption that we are already in possession of certain true *beliefs* as to the character of "the course of nature?" Otherwise, what does it *mean* to compare beliefs with nature, how can we ever get to "nature" without already having some ideas as to

[14] *Some Turns of Thought in Modern Philosophy*, 79.

[15] *Scepticism and Animal Faith*, 7; *italics* mine.

its structure? But if we do possess such beliefs, how can it be said that these are *all* fictional? The application of such an epithet to all judgments simply removes the meaning it might otherwise have as a discriminated opposite of truly verified judgments.

An object is what an object does. The expectation that we can have knowledge of what things or events are, apart from the way in which they exhibit their powers or traits through connection with other things, is doomed to failure. Certainly, in order to understand things and have knowledge in a significant sense, it is necessary to transcend immediacy. Such transcendence does not, however, require the attempt to dive behind appearances in order to measure their correspondence with the "real essences of things." The sort of transcendence required, rather, is that involved in the very operation of intelligence itself in making clear and intelligible the connections of things as these are presented in observation. Nor is it necessary to explain how such a transcendence is possible by making an initial mystery of it, unless we are willing to make a mystery of every naturally produced fact. That reason has the power to understand the order of things is something which we must accept as part of our data. Nature gives us eyes that can see and an intelligence that can understand; this must be set down to the total miracle that is nature. We can, of course, investigate and lay bare the antecedent conditions or causes of some natural fact. But we can see no reason why just such consequences do eventuate from their operations. This is a point, I take it, that Hume showed conclusively. Given an eye and given an object in the light, the eye can see its color and shape. Given intelligence and given some order in the world, the former can understand the latter. Moreover, just as there is a legitimate problem and need for improving, correcting and modifying our vision through attention to the conditions, instruments, and accuracy of seeing, so too we may take pains, as in science, to control, improve, and correct our methods of understanding things. Understanding, however, like vision, is a power we possess, and we cannot question the possibility of its operation or account for its creation. It is on these, or closely similar lines, that Santayana criticized Kant in

Reason in Common Sense.[16] Yet he would seem to have abandoned those very principles of criticism in his own later theory of knowledge and to have developed a point of view that, despite its many important differences from Kant, ultimately has much in common with it.

In turning to the formal sciences, again a noticeable shift in Santayana's views is to be observed. In the one case mathematics, for example, is said to deal with those abstracted forms of empirical subject matter that find their original suggestions in such subject matter, but whose status is that of ideal constructs or imaginative combinations in the realm of discourse itself. In the other, Santayana would make mathematics deal with an antecedent realm of essence that has no necessary connection with nature or human experience. A naturalistic interpretation, such as is suggested in brief outline in the chapter on "Dialectic" in *Reason in Science*, exhibits the continuity of mathematical knowledge with the rest of empirical knowledge, at the same time that it points to its important differences in procedure and outcome. For the data of mathematics, the abstract forms constituting the material operated upon and the various rules employed in their connection and manipulation, are ultimately derived, by a process of successive abstraction to a high order of generality, from the material provided in experience.[17] Yet the ideal products of mathematics, those resulting from the deductive elaboration of the systematic consequences of an original set of assumptions, are validated solely through adhering to the intent implicit in our definitions and rules of procedure. And their status as ideal products is not revelatory of a realm whose constitution is established already in advance of any investigation. It is simply expressive of the necessary implications to which we are committed in the realm of discourse. Such a theory, if elaborated and refined, is capable of accounting for the basic continuity of mathematical data with empirical data, for the possibility of setting up various alternative systems of "pure" mathematics (as linguistic calculi), and for exhibiting the use to which such systems may be put when their terms and

[16] Cf. 94-7.

[17] Cf. *Reason in Science*, 189.

relations are given specific empirical denotations and made to function as empirical hypotheses. It is a theory based on an analysis of the *procedures* of mathematical inquiry.

In his later writings, however, Santayana would give an ontologic support for mathematics by referring its investigations to the realm of essence, whose constitution already eternally and unchangeably determined makes possible its systematic exploration and discovery. The selection of particular ideas (postulates) for examination, the detail and thoroughness with which they are elaborated, and the applications of their results to empirical description, are all functions of some selective interest and are accidental, not essential to the matters investigated. All this is, in effect, a direct reversal of the earlier naturalistic theory. By dissociating the ideal products of mathematical inquiry from the procedures and instruments through which they are made actual in human discourse, and by postulating the eternal subsistence of all those "systems" (mathematical essences) that have not even been formulated, Santayana's theory has inverted the relations between natural conditions and their ideal result. Possibility is now the ontologic ground of actuality; what is said has been miraculously divorced from the conditions of its saying, and imaginative discourse, that instrument through which novel constructions in the realm of ideas are in fact created, is now taken to be a mere accidental occasion for their "disclosure."

II

There is a significant and perhaps profound sense in which we may regard all of Santayana's philosophy as derivative embellishments or supports in epistemology, morals, and metaphysics, of an initial and persistent attachment to experience in its aesthetic dimensions. Even without his explicit statement that "the decorative and poetic aspects of art and nature have always fascinated me and held my attention above everything else,"[18] the most superficial acquaintance with Santayana's writings, their character and emphases, could confirm this fact.

[18] "Brief History of My Opinions," in *Contemporary American Philosophy*, II, 256.

In the earliest of his philosophic works, *The Sense of Beauty*, Santayana finds in the experience of beauty a standard of all ultimate value. The mind possesses an intrinsic and self-sufficient reward in the aesthetic perception of realized perfections. "Beauty seems to be the clearest manifestation of perfection, and the best evidence of its possibility. . . . [it] is a pledge of the possible conformity between the soul and nature, and consequently a ground of faith in the supremacy of the good."[19] While the characteristic emphasis in that work is upon the psychology of aesthetic enjoyment rather than upon the creative process of art or the interfunctional connections of the fine arts with other areas of culture in a moral economy, the analysis given of the ground of such enjoyment as consisting of a delicate adjustment of the perceiving organ to its subject matter, is, nevertheless, important for the hints it contains of Santayana's general moral philosophy as contained in *The Life of Reason*.

For, in the latter work, the scope of investigation was broadened to include all types of human value. Attention to natural conditions, processes of intelligently instituted adjustment, and the status of ideals as intrinsic standards and marks of perfection, has been extended and deepened. In the *Life of Reason* one finds the categories relevant to the creative processes of *art* used as the dominant guides for analysis. Indeed, using the term art in a broad sense to cover the deliberate and intelligent transformation of available raw materials in the interest of achieving a consciously enjoyable perfection of those materials, one may say that the life of reason is "the sum of art."[20] The so-called fine arts exhibit in principle and in miniature scale the conditions and ideals of all human good. In them contemplative enjoyment is consequent upon and continuous with the artful fashioning of matter in accordance with some finite ideal, one that is grounded in some specific medium, subject, and interest. Dilettantism, aestheticism, and romanticism are diseases that mark the dislocation of the rationally valid function which art and aesthetic experience have in a totally integrated life. For they would dissociate appreciation from their vital roots in human

[19] *The Sense of Beauty*, 269f.

[20] *Reason in Common Sense*, 6.

experience, from the processes of the creative act itself, and from the necessity of envisioning the ideal as some selected form and not as located in a limitless and indeterminate realm of fancy. One of the recurrent points made in *Reason in Art* is that the aesthetic good present in the delightful exercise of sense or imagination cannot be arbitrarily divorced from the broader moral, intellectual, or social context in which it appears as an element or strand. Condemnation of a sharp separation between the industrial and fine arts, or between the arts themselves and the current needs and interests of a cultural life, is but the obverse side of a positive insistence on their essential continuity. The arts and aesthetic experience become "brief truancies from rational practice" only when they are, in effect, not the fruition of workaday materials of experience, but the by-play of vagrant and irresponsible fancy. To relegate the products of art to museums, "mausoleums rather in which a dead art heaps up its remains," or to draw a distinction between morality and art as consisting of the attention in the former to the necessary labor involved in the elimination of evil and, in the latter, to the free and positive enjoyment of spontaneous, "useless" play, is to mistake the true rôle of art in a rational life. In the fine arts or in the art of rational living as a whole, the refined forms embedded in or realized through a selected medium are the *results* of intelligent labor.[21] They are internal to a selected subject matter or moral economy, not escapes from these to some independent and external sphere.

In Santayana's later writings one finds only scattered references to and treatments of art and aesthetic experience. Such incidental statements as do occur, however, are significant for the hints they contain of a shift in perspective and theory. It is true, of course, that one does not find a complete and absolute replacement of one set of views by its direct opposite. There are undeniable continuities and recurrent emphases. Yet the latter

[21] Yet this distinction between morality as the sphere of negative values and art as the holiday life of positive ones, is made by Santayana himself in *The Sense of Beauty*, 23-5. It is a separation that is discarded and healed in *The Life of Reason*, but one that reappears in a new dress and with more refined elaboration in the latest writings as the distinction between morality and the spiritual life, public art and the activities of an "aesthetic soviet."

are now mixed with and set in a different light because of subtle changes in doctrine.

Among these changes we find, for example, a marked emphasis upon aesthetic experience as intuitive rather than upon appreciation as an ideal result of the creative process of intelligent organization of materials in perception. Essences present to aesthetic intuition, we are told, are to be contrasted with the manner in which active intelligence deals with a world of facts.

> As I was jogging to market in my village cart, beauty has burst upon me and the reins have dropped from my hands. I am transported, in a certain measure, into a state of trance. I see with extraordinary clearness, yet what I see seems strange and wonderful, because I no longer look in order to understand, but only in order to see. I have lost my preoccupation with fact, and am contemplating an essence.[22]

The value of such a sharp separation between fact and essence, between understanding and aesthetic intuition is a questionable one. For the identification of aesthetic appreciation with immediate intuition fails to indicate the necessary contributing groundwork and labor of which aesthetic enjoyment is a concomitant fruition and with which it is at all points continuous. Just as the process of artistic production involves an active manipulation of external raw materials into a finished product and pattern, so on the side of appreciation a like re-integration of perceived elements is necessary. It is true, of course, that such appreciation may often have the character of instantaneous insight into a complex unity of elements. But such immediacy of insight is again but the fruit in telescoped awareness of prior gestation and interpretation, one having as much worth, indeed, as the thoroughness, scope, and depth of these activities themselves. In any case contemplation, if it is to be significant and not merely a blank stare or rapt swooning, depends upon some active understanding of the sequence, suggestions, and patterning of the complex of elements perceived.

Just as intuition, therefore, would constitute a phase of intelligence and not a faculty sharply distinct from it, so again, on the side of the objects involved, a distinction of emphasis or function rather than of ontological character would seem to be

[22] *The Realm of Essence*, 6-7.

more appropriate. Instead of contrasting facts and essences, we might recognize instead a difference in the controlling interest taken in facts themselves. The degree or extent of this interest will determine whether the facts are being attended to for practical reasons as material means for reaching some end beyond themselves, as subject matter for scientific analysis in terms of their constitutive elements and relations, or, finally, as objects of intrinsic aesthetic enjoyment, because of their arresting qualities and expressive content.

It is not only in appreciation, but in the creation of works of art themselves, that one cannot introduce a sharp separation into mutually exclusive domains among these interests unless violence is to be done to all. Yet just as in our consideration of Santayana's later theory of knowledge we found a greater spiritual value attributed to scepticism (even though animal necessity forces a return to a practical concern with adjusting symbols to facts), so too it may be questioned whether Santayana does not attribute greater spiritual value to the activities of "irresponsible aesthetes . . . the children of light"[23] or to the "artist himself [who] lives only in his own labour, irresponsible, technical and visionary."[24] An "aesthetic soviet," it is suggested,[25] would afford spiritual release from preoccupation with the problems and interests inherent in a culturally oriented art. The sheer exploitation of the resources of a medium and its emancipation from any functional use in representation or construction, would permit a spiritual freedom not otherwise obtained when tradition, need, or social interests are the dominant contexts and motivational sources of artistic creation. But that one cannot wholly abstract essences as the sole concern of aesthetic contemplation or be devoted ideally to a purified and abstracted technical exploitation of media, while eliminating all reference to intelligence, need, or desire, has been so admirably stated by Santayana himself, that the following, written in 1903 in a review of Croce's *Aesthetics*, must be quoted as the best possible criticism of such tendencies.

[23] "An Aesthetic Soviet," *Dial*, LXXXII (May, 1927), 369.

[24] *Platonism and the Spiritual Life*, 40.

[25] "An Aesthetic Soviet," *Dial*, LXXXII (May, 1927), 361-370.

The pleasures of sense, the charm and functions of objects, even if denied an aesthetic status, will endure in the mind that judges and feels, unless indeed, that mind has been reduced to a state of affected aestheticism and unintelligence. Ulterior judgment, practical and moral, will inevitably color every perception given to a rational creature. To say that such simultaneous human reactions do not affect aesthetic feeling is to walk the tight rope of artificial distinctions. . . . Man does not feel without thinking and knowing. Life is sure in these matters to take its revenge upon scholasticism and the more punctiliously a department has been cut off from the general society of the mind, the more will that department be reduced to insignificance. If intuition has nothing to do with sense or with reason, so much the worse for intuition. An art which is nothing but an irresponsible and private exercise of fancy on every occasion becomes a visionary indulgence, a trick not of genius but of incapacity halting in the middle of life.[26]

In certain passages of the later writings, one may also note, in connection with a theory of the beautiful, an ontologic separation of forms beheld from their material embodiments, a contrast between essences eternally inhabiting their own realm, and the temporary, accidental, material or psychologic occasions for their exemplification or selection. Consider the following as an example:

Not the marble which a man without any sense of beauty might see, is the seat of beauty; the contrary quality may be as truly attributed to it. The only Venus which is inalienably beautiful is the divine essence revealed to the lover as he gazes, perhaps never to be revealed to another man, nor revealed to himself again. . . . In a form felt to be beautiful an obvious complexity composes an obvious unity: a marked intensity and individuality are seen to belong to a reality utterly immaterial and incapable of existing otherwise than speciously. This divine beauty is evident, fugitive, impalpable, and homeless in the world of material fact; yet it is unmistakably individual and sufficient unto itself, and although perhaps soon eclipsed is never really extinguished: for it visits time, but belongs to eternity.[27]

But, we may ask, if neither the marble nor any other external material substance nor any organs nor perspectives of the observer are the seat of the "divine essence," what meaning can it have to

[26] *Journal of Comparative Literature*, I (April, 1903), 191-195.
[27] *The Realm of Essence*, 153-4.

attribute independence to the latter? Is not the distinctive mark of a work of art the relatively unique instance it presents of matter formed in a manner able to arouse our admiration and attention? And does not the form realized in, expressed by, and communicated to us by the object have its sole being precisely in these activities of realization, expression, and communication? To give prior and independent status to the form of a work of art, as it exists for an observer, is surely to have arbitrarily cut off the *result* of a creative process, to have conferred antecedent being upon it and thus to have reversed the actual order of connection. Far from temporal and material conditions serving as adventitious occasions for the "eternal" and formal, if any meaning or status at all can be given to the latter, it is as refined products of the former that we must take them.

III

The clearest evidence, in its most general form, of a radical shift in Santayana's views, is to be found in his moral philosophy. Stated most simply and in the terminology which Santayana has made current, we may say that his own moral philosophy has passed from rational ethics to post-rational morality, from the moral idealism of the life of reason to the disintoxication of values of the spiritual life. One may find expressions of the latter in the early works just as one may point to passages in the later writings that carry over the doctrines of *The Life of Reason.* The dominant doctrines, however, are so noticeably different that Santayana himself has recognized the changes. These changes are regarded by him as representing an advance in depth of insight, a correction given to one set of principles through setting them in the context of a wider and more satisfactory theory. The humanism of the life of reason is to remain standing but is to be enveloped by a theory of the spiritual life. The principles are not inconsistent, Santayana claims, but supplementary.

The life of reason, as Santayana describes it, represents a union of intelligence and natural impulse in the interest of achieving ideals. If we look for an analysis or definition of the spiritual life in the later works, however, we cannot find a clear and unequivocal statement of its meaning. Indeed a careful comparison of his various statements will reveal, I think, the presence of three distinct positions. It is by continually shifting from one to the other, sometimes in the course of a single paragraph, that Santayana is able to leave the whole discussion in solution, as it were, and thereby claim for the entire presentation the virtues that in fact come from only some of its parts. If these different conceptions of the spiritual life were to be severally precipitated and examined for their worth, we might find them not totally compatible when taken together, nor worthy of our complete assent. These three positions consist of an identification of the spiritual life with (1) the contemplative enjoyment of ideals achieved in a life of reason; (2) an "intellectual" disintoxication from values, a detachment from action and passion that takes the form of a stoic absorption in sheer understanding of the "inevitable" structure of the world; and (3) a complete mystic intuition of Pure Being. These last two conceptions of the spiritual life mark distinguishable stages in a progressive abandonment of the morality of the life of reason. Spirituality involves the gradual and ultimately the complete undoing of humanism and in that accomplishment exhibits its own final bankruptcy and futility.

In the case of the first position, Santayana's distinction in the later writings between intelligence and spirit is simply a distinction between method and result, between the techniques involved in securing adjustment and the conscious enjoyment of ideals when achieved. In this sense the spiritual life consists of that dimension of a total life of reason which contains the "intuitive" appreciation of formal values realized in and by (and only so) their material conditions and instruments, when the latter have been thoroughly perfected in their use and function. The method of intelligence, when successful, effects a transition from raw impulse, material imperfectly formed, interests not yet or not thoroughly satisfied, habits conflicting with novel demands, to the ideal resolution, use, satisfaction, or adjustment of these materials, interests, or forces. Where the active transformation of interests or materials has received some relatively enduring expression, the finished and funded work of intelligence serves as a stay for the spirit. From this point of view, spirit is simply the actualization in moments of enjoyed awareness of the perfections achieved. Far from the perfection or adjustment of natural interests resulting in unconscious automatism, the self-justifying fruit of all effort is precisely the enjoyed consciousness of the forms expressed through the intelligently expert use of the given medium. These peaks of realized form are the rewards of intelligence and the content of spiritual activity. "Without such vision realised at each of its stages, life would be a mere fatality, automatism at odds with itself, a procession of failures."[28] This is a phase of rational ethics which Santayana emphasized in *The Life of Reason.* By embodying references to this point in the later writings, he would seem merely to have reformulated it in a new terminology. In this sense, obviously, there is no incompatibility between reason and spirit; indeed, for rational conduct, each taken singly is necessary but not sufficient. The first insures the second, the latter justifies the former.

Santayana, however, does not maintain this position consistently in the later writings. He advances in addition certain ideas which, if adhered to in practice, would involve the abandonment of moral idealism and the retrenchment of not only the several animal and social bases of moral life but the very use of intelligence in their disciplined development and organization. Whereas the life of reason consists of a harmonization of the passions, the spiritual life, he tells us, represents a disintoxication from their influence.[29] Unlike intelligence which consists of the attempt to give natural impulses disciplined expression, spirituality involves their deliberate repression and disillusioned surrender. It is to be achieved

> religiously by the disciples of the inner man, so that a part of him is weaned from the passions and interests which distract the world and is centered upon purely intellectual or spiritual aspiration. Religion is hard

[28] *The Realm of Essence,* 11; cf. *Reason in Common Sense,* 229-31.
[29] Cf. *Platonism and the Spiritual Life,* 30ff.

for external events to defeat, since ill-fortune stimulates it as much at least as good fortune.[30]

Spirituality, as thus described, does not depend upon the surrender of all the passions; like all post-rational moralities, Santayana's retains some passions while overthrowing all the rest. The disillusionment is with respect only to the interests of the "natural" or "worldly" man. By retaining an intellectual love of truth, at the same time renouncing all other loves, by claiming to have transcended and escaped the illusions of ordinary human pursuits in understanding them in "their intrinsic character and relative value, in their transitiveness and necessity, in a word in their truth,"[31] Santayana has at this stage of the analysis salvaged one ideal from the flood of despair. With the Stoics this consists of taking intellectual refuge in the inevitable structure of things, to win release from the importunities of the moment or from exclusive allegiance to some specific ideal of action. For, although spiritual minds "may survey or foresee action, they do not live in action, because they see it in its wholeness and in its results; as a spectator who sees the plot of a play understands the emotions of the characters; but does not succumb to them."[32]

A good instance of Santayana's lack of definiteness, on this subject of the relation of spirit to passion and action, is to be found in the first chapter of *The Realm of Essence.* A few pages after the sentence just quoted, we find the statement that "the passions insofar as they quicken the mind are favourable to the discernment of essence; and it is only a passionate soul that can be truly contemplative."[33] But again Santayana also insists that "the passions are the elements of life; nevertheless they are deceptive and tragic."[34] Spirituality marks a "gift of transcending humanity in sympathy with the truth;" it detaches itself from allegiance to animal interests having "with-

[30] *The Realm of Essence,* 12.

[31] *Platonism and the Spiritual life,* 33.

[32] *The Realm of Essence,* 10.

[33] *Ibid.,* 16.

[34] Preface to Vol. VII of the Triton Edition of *The Works of George Santayana,* xi.

drawn into the absolute and reverting to them only with a qualified sympathy, such as the sane man can have for the madman or the soul in general for inanimate things."[35] In thus introducing a separation between action and contemplation, Santayana's analysis has simply abandoned a naturalistic psychology and the omnimodal interests of a rational life. For contemplation, if it is to be significant, must be recognized as itself a type of action, being the deliberate analysis of some situation; and if any action is to partake of rationality, it must involve likewise the use of intelligence as the method internal to its perfection and enjoyment. Yet, as Santayana conceives it, contemplation functions to effect an attitude of passive resignation rather than to clarify and guide the expression of natural impulses or to celebrate their ideals when achieved.

Santayana tells us that the contemplative attitude of spirit

> evidently finds a freer course in solitude than in society, in art than in business, in prayer than in argument. . . . Spirit finds an initial delight in art and contrivance, in adventure and discovery, for these are forms of order and enlarged harmony; yet in the midst of business spirit suspends business and begins to wonder to laugh or to pray.[36]

But, we may ask, is not solitude that consists of having severed oneself from society precisely one in which significant material even for reflective contemplation has been excluded? Can solitude feed on its own substance without having first or rather continually grounded that substance in society? And is not art itself a form of "business" on its own scale and in its own medium, one that has become rationalized so that it incarnates and liberates intrinsically satisfying forms; and is not "business" something which needs to be transformed through intelligence in those areas where it exhibits servility to means, drudgery, or desperate conflict between those engaged in it? Finally, can any "prayer" be significant that is not a summation of, or an imaginative stimulus to a controlled investigation of some specific human ideal with respect to its genuine desirability and the means of its achievement? Are not wonder,

[35] *Genteel Tradition at Bay*, 65.

[36] *Platonism and the Spiritual Life*, 33; Preface to Vol. VII of the Triton Edition of *The Works of George Santayana*, xi.

laughter, and prayer appropriate only as they come to celebrate or express the ongoing activities and concerns of human enterprise rather than as interruptions of or escapes from them? Unless the cloister and ivory tower, since still part of the world, serve as footholds for renewed realization of human goods in the arts, in social living, and in scientific inquiry, they mark failures of adjustment in the normal world of affairs and an escape from the interest or responsibility faced by intelligence in meeting the problems and needs of that world.

If, further, it is the mark of spirit not to dwell on the machinery which may control its destiny and to "live in the moment, taking no thought for the morrow,"[37] may we not say that it represents the very antithesis of a rational attitude? For it is precisely attention to machinery that insures a controlled liberation of genuinely spiritual goods, and a representative concern for the future consequences of our present actions that prepares the ground for continuing fruition of spiritual satisfactions. Not to emphasize the continuity of means and ends, but to make the former at most accidental occasions for the latter, is either to confess defeat and to accept such crumbs of enjoyment as blind fate, entrenched forces, or chance may throw to us, or to live, perhaps unaware of the fact, on the interest of a capital once honestly won through intelligent perseverance and deliberate art. In any case, to dissociate contemplation from its connection with the procedural or natural forces necessary to its realization, is covertly to admit a constriction and disparagement of intelligence. In this direction we turn not to the Olympian attainments of a God but to the pathetic surrender of all that is distinctively human and ultimately worth caring for.

The final abandonment of rational ethics comes when not even a contemplative absorption in the "truth" identifies the spiritual life so much as a flight to the infinity or essential individuality of Pure Being itself. Here mysticism functions to loosen all allegiances and to overthrow all standards of selection and preference. For the finite concerns of a rational ani-

[37] *Platonism and the Spiritual Life*, 85.

mal it will substitute a sense of the infinite realm of possible forms. For the discriminating investigation of the specific laws of nature it will substitute a simple intuition of the widest of all possible categories, Being. "The force of insight would thus have to vanquish all will and transcend all animal limitations, cancelling every fear, preference, or private perspective which a station now and here would involve."[38] The aspired result of this total disintegration of finite cognitive and moral perspectives will yield a selfless absorption in Pure Being. The austerity, candor, and impartial vision of spirit make it ready to accept and contemplate *anything* whatsoever, since in its virtual omniscience it will avoid giving accidental preeminence to one form rather than another. From the point of view of God there are no preferences.

Santayana disclaims complete personal sympathy with the ideal implied by this last stage of spiritual attainment. He tells us, "I frankly cleave to the Greeks and not to the Indians, and I aspire to be a rational animal rather than a pure spirit."[39] But the logic of his position nevertheless drives to the other conclusion. Santayana himself admits as much.

> Spirit . . . is ultimately addressed to pure Being. . . . The Platonic philosophy opens a more urbane and alluring avenue towards spiritual enlightenment than does the Indian, although the latter runs faster towards the goal and attains it more perfectly. . . . Ultimate good is . . . realized by the contemplative intellect absorbed in pure Being.[40]

If we refuse to be impressed by the sublime afflatus and seeming profundity of the concept of Pure Being, however, and take it as Santayana describes it, either as the explicit infinity of all possible forms or as the limit of all abstraction and thus as an individual essence itself, it will appear that what we have in fact are two distinguishable errors. In the one case we have a bald hypostasis of anarchic atoms of a disintegrated human consciousness into a metaphysical realm to serve as the counterpart of a romantic attitude and limitless charity. In the other case we have the erection into an entity in its own right of a participial term from which all significant content and specifica-

[38] *The Realm of Essence*, 47.
[39] *Ibid.*, 65.
[40] *Platonism and the Spiritual Life*, 47, 69; *The Realm of Essence*, 61.

tion has been removed, and which, therefore, cannot serve to designate the subject matter of some *specific* inquiry. Neither aspect of Pure Being is something with which a rational animal is concerned. The pursuit of rational ideals involves the rejection of any attempt to attend to the infinite as a locus of salvation. For if by the infinite is meant a literally unending succession of determinate forms, then not only is such an infinite incapable of being surveyed in a given life, but even the very attempt to do so is a romantic indulgence that forfeits any possibility of achieving some specific ideal, which latter would of necessity have to be sacrificial, finite, and restrictive. The genuine value of devotion to essences as the realm of possible meanings is that it serves to broaden ideals and ideas that are otherwise stifling or unfruitful. By opening our minds to a wealth of new possibilities scope is given for more comprehensive, enlightened thought and conduct. The serious fault with Santayana's formulation of the realm of essence is that it does not function in this way as a source of ideals for rational living. To spirit the mere recognition of the selective finitude of any specific idea or ideal becomes an occasion, not for its correction and deepening, but rather for an ironically detached recognition of it as part of an infinite remainder. The realm of essence functions as in post-rational morality as a refuge of salvation that is nevertheless specious since genuine salvation can arise only with the intelligent ordering of relevant materials of observation and conduct. But again, if by the infinite is meant not an inexhaustibleness of determinate forms, but simply the indeterminate itself, then to lapse into absorption in it is to abandon the interest in form altogether and to reduce experience to sheer flux and chaos. The sense of the infinite and its sublimity then becomes truly unutterable because what is present is a feeling of complete vagueness and incoherence, a diffused emotion accompanying a total and radical inability to conceive or accomplish anything definite.

IV

In the first chapter of *The Realm of Essence* Santayana summarizes the various approaches to essence through scepticism, dialectic, contemplation, and spiritual discipline. In the second chapter he analyzes the properties of essences that belong to the latter as independent ontologic entities; these include identity, universality, infinity, and non-existence. Essences, we are told, possess these properties and their own independent being apart from all connection with nature and human experience. The latter offer merely accidental or incidental occasions for their temporal, material exemplification or discovery. Although Santayana thus offers his doctrine of the metaphysical status of essences as capable of standing on its own feet and as not dependent upon such approaches as may be had to them in human experience, it may be questioned whether the relation between these two aspects of the doctrine of essence is what is thus claimed for them.

For, if we look closely, the ontology of essence, instead of being an antecedent locus for its exploration by human experience, bears the marks, on the contrary, of its original human incidence and genesis. Like all forms of supernaturalism and other-worldly idealism, the realm of essence reflects in its constitution the properties and attitudes which lie at the bottom of its conception. When faith in intelligence is at low ebb, either through being overwhelmed by irrational forces that disregard its operation, or because of an internal withering of natural impulses that sustain and give direction to its problems, barbarism in the one case and mysticism in the other takes its place. The one arrogates a blind and relentless egotism in which no just perspective of the relativity of its interests could be had; the other withdraws into a selfless, Olympian absorption in a "total" background in terms of which the "foreground" of finite perspectives, interests, and preferences are to be renounced and overcome. The realm of essence may be regarded as an evident ontological duplication, extension, and "justification" of the latter of these tendencies, since it reflects the results of a mystical disintegration of ideals in thought, appreciation, and conduct.

One may thus say of the realm of essence what Santayana has said of the supernaturalism of Platonism and Christianity: "There is a sort of acoustic illusion in it; the voice that reverberates from the heavens is too clearly a human voice."[41] Yet the analogy is not complete. For the religious conception of heaven or the Platonic world of Ideas, while both metaphysical transcripts of human ideals, have this much to recommend them, when the myth is appreciated for its true meaning and the vision re-instated in its proper place as an imaginative expression of ideals, we have at least a formula for certain selected human goals. For, indeed, as Santayana himself asserts in *Reason in Religion:*

> If we once launch, as many metaphysicians would have us do, into the hypostasis of qualities and relations, it is certainly better and more honest . . . not to render our metaphysical world unmeaning as well as fictitious by peopling it with concepts in which the most important categories of life are submerged and invalidated.[42]

Santayana's own metaphysics of essence, however, although equally a myth, does not even serve to express a genuine moral ideal. For it is the ontologic analogue of experience that has been mystically dissolved into an infinite catalogue of unselected, meaningless forms, and is a notion that needs to be discarded not merely as metaphysics but even as a metaphoric expression of a possible moral ideal as well.

MILTON K. MUNITZ

DEPARTMENT OF PHILOSOPHY
COLLEGE OF THE CITY OF NEW YORK

[41] *Genteel Tradition at Bay*, 43.
[42] *Reason in Religion*, 162.

7

Stephen C. Pepper

SANTAYANA'S THEORY OF VALUE

7

SANTAYANA'S THEORY OF VALUE

A WISDOM emanates from Santayana's words and from between his words and between his lines which is more essentially his philosophy than anything he explicitly says. His philosophy has an aroma. It can be distinctly smelled, as he once said of another philosophy, where it cannot always be clearly seen. This impresses me as particularly true of his theory of value. For his whole philosophy is a theory of value, or rather an attitude distributing values among things.

To single out one set of assertions from his writings and analyze these as his theory of value is accordingly not very satisfactory. It subjects the critic to the danger of being called pedantic, and of actually being so. Yet in the end I see nothing else to do.

Santayana's philosophy contains a criticism of criticism which tantalizes the critic whichever way he turns. For the critic cannot point to the existential facts since "perception *is* faith,"[1] and the critic cannot compare his own theory of the facts with Santayana's, since he is then only comparing one essence with another. Existential fact resolves itself evidentially into "shock" or "punishment," whereas all content freed from "the unintelligible accident of existence"[2] is essence. If the critic disagrees with Santayana, he merely disagrees, or possibly he will be punished. There seems to be no argument.

Nevertheless, Santayana has written many volumes of argument. The literal thinking critic finds it hard to know how this argument should be interpreted, how to make meaning out of it, or even how not to make meaning out of it. Santayana himself expresses his reader's perplexity through the Stranger in the "Secret of Aristotle:"

[1] *Scepticism and Animal Faith*, 69.

[2] *Ibid.*, 73.

Allegory has its charm when we know the facts it symbolizes, but as a guide to unknown facts it is perplexing; and I am rather lost in your beautiful imagery. Am I to understand that matter alone is substantial, and that the other three principles are merely aspects which matter presents when viewed in one light or another?

To this Avicenna replies (and is it Santayana speaking through Avicenna, or is it Santayana writing a fascinating theory? Is it Santayana in existence or Santayana in essence? How may a poor literal reader know?):

Matter? If by that word you understand an essence, the essence of materiality, matter would be something incapable of existing by itself, much less could it be the ground of its own form or of its own impulses or transformations: like pure Being it would be everywhere the same, and could neither contain nor produce any distinctions. But the matter which exists and works is matter formed and unequally distributed, the body of nature in all its variety and motion. So taken, matter is alive, since it has bred every living thing and our own spirit; and the soul which animates this matter is spontaneous there; it is simply the native plasticity by which matter continually changes its forms. This impulse in matter now towards one form and now towards another is what common superstition calls the attraction or power of the ideal. But why did not a different ideal attract this matter, and turn this hen's egg into a duckling, save that here and now matter was predisposed to express the first idea and not the second? And why was either idea powerful over the fresh-laid egg, but powerless over the same egg boiled, except that boiling had modified the arrangement of its matter? Therefore my benefactor boldly concluded that this habit in matter, which is the soul of the world, is the only principle of genesis anywhere and the one true cause.

The Stranger answers:

I see: 'Tis love that makes the world go round, and not, as idolatrous people imagine, the object of love. The object of love is passive and perhaps imaginary; it is whatever love happens to choose, prompted by an inner disposition in its organ. You are a believer in automatism, and not in magic.

And Avicenna answers, "Excellent."[3]

So now we are perhaps justified in believing that we have the clue to value in existence, value in fact. "'Tis love that

[3] *Dialogues in Limbo*, 185-186.

makes the world go round," and not, observe especially, "as idolatrous people imagine, the object of love." And yet "it is whatever love happens to choose, prompted by an inner disposition in its organ." I think I catch the aroma. Value in existence is an impulse of choice based on some natural pattern. Even to say so much, however, is to say more than can be said without faith, for this is value in existence.

What is value in essence? Only of value in essence can we speak freely, have discourse and theory and then perhaps take the great risk of belief. As a literal critic, I cannot but feel a little foolish at this transition. Yet as a critic of Santayana's *theory* of value, I cannot do otherwise than make this very transition since it is about this essence, his theory, that I must discourse.

As it seemed wise to lead up to the clue of Santayana's value in existence through a section of a dialogue, I will enter upon Santayana's value in essence through a parable. This parable is spoken by the Stranger as a summary of a long argument by the shade of Democritus. I trust my own reader will have an understanding of the course of my own argument through the beauty of these quotations. For these quotations and their very beauty are a part of my argument. I believe Santayana is most serious when he appears least so. This parable seems to me to contain the essence of Santayana's theory of value and to be more serious and significant than many other things he has said with more apparent seriousness—like another parable of a cave by another philosopher.

Once upon a time, so the story runs, the whole world was a garden in which a tender fair-haired child, whose name was Autologos, played and babbled alone. There was, indeed, an old woman who tended the garden, a goddess in disguise; but she lived in a cave and came out only at night when the child was asleep, for like the bat and the astronomer she could see better in the dark. She had a sharp pruning-hook on a very long pole, with which she silently pruned every tree and shrub in the garden, even the highest branches, cutting off the dead twigs and shaking down the yellow leaves in showers; and often, muttering surly words to herself which were not intelligible, she would cut off some flower or some bud as well, so that when the child awoke he missed them and could not imagine what had become of them. Now the child in his play gave names to everything that he liked or disliked; and the rose he called Beauty, and the jasmin Pleasure, and the hyacinth Sweetness, and the violet Sadness, and the thistle Pain, and the olive Merit, and the laurel Triumph, and the vine Inspiration. He was highly pleased with all these names, and they made those flowers and plants so much more interesting to him, that he thought those names were their souls. But one day, having pricked himself with the thorns of a rose, he changed her name to Love; and this caused him to wonder why he had given those particular names to everything rather than quite different names; and the child began to feel older. As he sat brooding on this question, for he had stopped playing, a man in a black gown came into the garden who was a botanist, and said: "It matters little what names you give to flowers because they already have scientific names which indicate their true genera and species; the rose is only a rose, and is neither Beauty nor Love; and so with all the other flowers. They are flowers and plants merely, and they have no souls." Hearing this the child began to cry, very much to the botanist's annoyance, for being a busy man he disliked emotion. "After all," he added, "those names of yours will do no harm, and you may go on using them if you please; for they are prettier than those which truly describe the flowers, and much shorter; and if the word soul is particularly precious to you, you may even say that plants and flowers have souls: only, if you wish to be a man and not always a child, you must understand that the soul of each flower is only a name for its way of life, indicating how it spreads its petals in the morning and perhaps closes them at night, as you do your eyes. You must never suppose, because the flower has a soul, that this soul does anything but what you find the flower actually doing." But the child was not comforted, and when the wind had dried his tears, he answered: "If I cannot give beautiful names to the plants and flowers which shall be really their souls, and if I cannot tell myself true tales about them, I will not play in the garden any more. You may have it all to yourself and botanize in it, but I hate you." And the child went to sleep that night quite flushed and angry. Then, as silently as the creeping moonlight, the old woman came out of her cave and went directly to the place where the child was sleeping, and with a great stroke of her pruning-knife cut off his head; and she took him into her cave and buried him under the leaves which had fallen on that same night, which were many. When the botanist returned in the morning and found the child gone he was much perplexed. "To whom," said he to himself, "shall I now teach botany? There is nobody now to care for flowers, for I am only a professor, and if I can't teach anybody the right names for flowers, of what use are flowers to me?" This thought oppressed the poor man so much that he entirely collapsed, and as he was rather wizened to begin with, he was soon reduced to a few stiff tendons and bones, like the ribs of a dry leaf; and even these shreds soon crumbled, and he evaporated altogether. Only his black gown remained to delight the ragpicker. But the goddess in guise of that old woman went on pruning the garden, and it seemed to make no difference in her habits that the child and the botanist were dead.

I think we may surmise that the true name of this goddess must have been Dikè, the same that the wise Democritus was calling Punishment; and the botonist's name must have been Nomos, whom he was calling Agreement; and of course the child Autologos was that innocent illusion which was the theme of his whole discourse.[4]

I shall not particularly try to explain this parable. The same parable extended and placed in a realistic setting appears as the "Last Puritan." Like music it expresses itself. As a literal critic I merely point to it as the full denotation of Santayana's theory of value.

From now one I shall allow myself to become pedantic and turn to the set of technical propositions which can be picked out of the body of Santayana's writings and which may be regarded as his attempts to systematize what in this parable and in fact everywhere he richly expresses.

In technical terms, his theory of value appears to be an interest theory, and, I should say further, based fundamentally on mechanistic categories such as are presented in Chapters II and III of *The Realm of Matter* on the "indispensable" and "presumable" properties of substance. His theory of essence has surprisingly little effect on his theory of value. Essences merely furnish the scenery or the costumes of value, and might, so far as the values themselves are concerned, have any other ontological status, such, for instance, as images or sensations in a typical subjectivistic psychology characteristic of the traditional mechanists. My own conviction is that his philosophy was firmer and more fully empirical in *The Sense of Beauty* where he was following the natural movement of the mechanistic categories, than later when his doctrine of essences

[4] *Dialogues in Limbo*, 51-54.

began to creep in. This comment, however, is outside our present discussion, except as a side question to Santayana to explain (if he thinks the comment wrong) what difference it makes to his theory of value whether the "content" of an interesting, satisfying, or pleasant situation is an eternal essence or a momentary and fugitive sensation, image, or feeling.

In an interest theory of values, two problems are posed: (1) What is the locus or unit of value? (2) What is the means of making judgments or comparisons of value? This latter question resolves itself into the determination of a standard or set of standards of value, and leads to a subsidiary problem of the relation of the standard to the unit of value. I shall attempt to examine statements with respect to these two problems and their relationship.

The sources in Santayana's works which appear to bear most directly on these problems are the last few chapters of Volume I of the *Life of Reason* (*Reason in Common Sense*), the last two chapters of Volume IV (*Reason in Art*), the chapter on Rational Ethics in Volume V (*Reason in Science*), the essay on *The Philosophy of Bertrand Russell*, and, as an early work, *The Sense of Beauty*. This last book has to be referred to with care, not because the doctrine of essences has not yet emerged, which, as just remarked, seems to be a minor consideration in this context, but because the doctrine of reason does not seem to have appeared, and this is a major consideration.

It is rather surprising that in Santayana's more recent writings, from *Scepticism and Animal Faith* on, I find nothing new or particularly pertinent to the theory of value as a technical problem. During all his later period Santayana seems to have been absorbed in the problem of knowledge, which certainly becomes acute as a result of his committing himself to the doctrine of essence. If there is anything pertinent to the theory of value in these later writings which I have missed, and which supplements his earlier statements, I hope it will be pointed out.

Let us begin with the question of the locus of value. It is perhaps too much to have expected that Santayana should be precise in this matter when the need for precision has only lately been fully exhibited. Santayana's chief merit in this respect perhaps lies in his wisdom in abstaining from precision. How conscious this was it is hard to say, but his numerous criticisms of the narrowness of such earlier attempts at precision as were made by the traditional Cyrenaics, hedonists, and utilitarians, suggest he was not unconscious of the problem, and preferred to denote the locus of value with a broad gesture rather than risk pointing specifically with one finger.

The term "interest" which he frequently uses is a blanket term, so abstract as to cover most any concrete act. Without further specification, it is only a little better than the term "good," which he so skillfully criticizes for its abstractness in his essay on *The Philosophy of Bertrand Russell.* The only advantage of "interest" over "good" is that it connotes the act of an organism or self and is to that extent less easily hypostatized. It cannot be said that Santayana hypostatizes interest. His method is to use a great variety of terms with varying connotations—pleasure, enjoyment, impulse, instinct, desire, satisfaction, preference, choice, assertion—which a literal reader can only gather together under such a term as interest.

Now all of these denoted acts have a certain common form. They are acts relative to an organism and relative to a content or an object. They have the form SRO, where S is the subject interested and O the object or content in which he is interested, and R, thereby, the relation of interest. This pattern may then be defined as a unit of value concretely located among all those acts denoted by the various terms above.

This does not take us very far, however. We can, it is true, develop a calculus from this unit, show that two of these units are more than one unit, that one unit is equal to another unit if the values of the variables are identical ($SRO = SRO$), and that if two subjects are exactly similar (if $S_1 = S_2$), then the units of value for similar objects ($O_1 = O_2$) will be equal ($S_1RO_1 = S_2RO_2$). We can then show that two units of value for one subject are equal to the same two units for another subject $[(S_1RO_1 + S_1RO_1) = (S_2RO_2 + S_2RO_2)]$ and, then, the important principle that a unit of value for one subject plus the same unit of value for another subject is equal to those same two units of value for the same subject $[(S_1RO_1 + S_2RO_2) = (S_1RO_1 + S_1RO_1)]$. This is all very pretty and entirely rational. The question is, does it apply to the actual pleasures, satisfactions, and desires of actual persons?

Santayana emphatically states in his dealing with Russell that it does not:

> In the real world, persons are not abstract egos, like A and B, so that to benefit one is clearly as good as to benefit another. . . . Actual egoism is not the thin and refutable thing that Mr. Russell makes of it. What it really holds is that a given man, oneself, and those akin to him, are qualitatively better than other beings; that the things they prize are intrinsically better than the things prized by others; and that therefore there is no injustice in treating these chosen interests as supreme. The injustice, it is felt, would lie rather in not treating things so unequal unequally.[5]

So, it appears, that for Santayana an abstract interest theory would be as untenable as Russell's abstract theory of good-indefinable. What we must deal with is concrete interests and the way they concretely behave. At least, this must be our starting point, wherever we may end.

If we start with concrete interests, we find that they have great variety, and are not apparently comparable even within the same subject. If Santayana disagrees with this, it would be very enlightening to learn why. Take a few illustrations like these: the sweet taste of a liqueur on the tongue, a man suffering from a variety of vague aches (later diagnosed as influenza), a child running away from a bee, the dread of a dentist's appointment, the anticipation of dinner, running at the dinner call, satisfaction after the dessert, the choice of an apple instead of a pear, jumping at a clap of thunder, a boy's awareness of a girl. Here we have pleasure, discomfort, aversion, dread, anticipation, desire, conation, satisfaction, preference, instinct and impulse.

Am I correct in assuming that these would all be instances of value for Santayana? But clearly they differ materially in their structure. The pleasure is a localized feeling with a sense quality.

[5] *Winds of Doctrine*, 150.

The discomfort is a diffused feeling vaguely localized. In both whatever object there is, is immediately present. In the dread and the anticipation, a feeling is intensely present and rather diffused but the object is distant in space and time. In the running *away* there seems to be little feeling, but vigorous kinaesthetic sensations, actions, and the object is in the distance and in the past with a vague objective of safety in the future. In the running *to* there is little feeling, much activity, and the object is in the future. In the satisfaction there is a rich feeling based on previous desire and the object seems to be in the past. In the preference, there is perhaps little feeling and there are two objects which receive their respective values apparently *subsequent* to the act. In instinct and impulse there may be little conscious feeling, but when it is present, even when it is intense, it seems to shadow the act rather than substantiate it, and the object may be present or absent.

Suppose we restrict our consideration to three of these offerings—pleasure, desire, and preference. It is very hard to see how these can be combined into a single unit without violent distortion or neglect of features essential to their value structure.

Pleasure seems to be a value in its own right with its natural opposite, pain or unpleasantness. It does not seem to require any object. If there are disembodied pleasures and pains, they would be positive and negative values in themselves. It may be plausibly held, however, that empirically these feelings never do occur except as modifying or infusing some sensuous or imaginal content. The content thus modified would be the object of value and the pleasure would be the factor instituting the value. Moreover, environmental stimuli producing pleasurable perceptions would in a secondary sense become objects of value, on the judgment that they are instruments for the production of value.

Desire has a very different structure. It is by no possibility self-complete. It involves an activity initiated at one time towards a supposed object which is to terminate the activity at another and a future time. Since the object that is supposed to terminate the desire frequently does not exist, the status of the object of desire is a difficult one to define. It is, however, generally agreed that if an object exists which can terminate the desire, that object acquires value in virtue of the desire for it.

Preference involves still a third structure. Here at least two objects must be actually present to the organism, either as conscious content or as physical stimuli. By some psychological or physiological mechanism (descriptions differ widely) the subject accepts one object and rejects the other, whereupon automatically the accepted object acquires positive and the rejected object negative value. Or, if there is a whole series of preferences, the objects may receive differential values according to their location in the preference series.

The selection of one of these three units as definitive of value would constitute a type of interest theory of value. If one of these types of unit could be shown to be the *real* source of value, and values found in the other two could be shown to be derivative from this *real* source, then the problem of the interest theory, so far as the unit of value is concerned, would be solved. For then we should have one basic, common unit of value and what is meant by value would be unambiguous, and comparisons of value could be freely made over the whole field.

If this solution is not advocated, however, what sort of solution can be suggested? Santayana does not seem to advocate this solution. The nearest he comes to it is in his aesthetic theory as developed in his *Sense of Beauty* and perhaps in his *Reason in Art*. In *The Sense of Beauty* he defines the field of beauty as pleasure objectified and exhibits the sensuous, formal, and expressive contents in which such pleasure is found. On the whole, he stays, while treating questions of art and beauty, within his defined field. But not altogether. For in examining this field in its wider contexts with life he trespasses upon other fields of interest. He writes in the concluding chapter of *Reason in Art*, "The fine arts are seldom an original factor in human progress. If they express moral and political greatness, and serve to enhance it, they acquire a certain dignity; but so soon as this expressive function is abandoned they grow meretricious."[6] This is the theme of the whole chapter, as well as of the earlier chapter on the "Justification of Art." The ex-

[6] P. 217.

pression of moral and political greatness, however, is the satisfaction of interests quite different from objectified pleasure. These interests may indeed be objectified pleasurably in the work of art, but the intent of the passage is to show that the greater value of such works of art consists not in the greater amount of pleasure objectified in them, but in the political and moral interests satisfied there, interests more in the nature of desires and preferences than immediate pleasures. For instance, there is no evidence that a "meretricious" work of art may not contain as much objectified pleasure as a dignified one, but it will lack the satisfaction of the political and moral interests which may not be intensely pleasant. So even in aesthetics Santayana does not confine himself to one type of interest. What, then, does he propose to do with the diversity of interests?

I think he would say that the locus of value is among them all. I do not think, however, he would wish to say that they were incomparable, for this conclusion would be incompatible with his dominant theme of rationality. How, then, are diverse interests to be compared or ordered? The principle of comparison seems clearly not to lie among the interests themselves. As between the pleasure of reading a novel now (assuming one is reading) and the desire to quench one's thirst, what shall determine the relative values of this pleasure and this desire? If we should answer, compare the pleasure of this reading with the pain of this thirst, the answer might seem obvious, on the assumption that pleasures and pains are in the same scale, and are the same type of interest. But Santayana himself questions this:

> Pleasures and pains are not only infinitely diverse but, even if reduced to their total bulk and abstract opposition, they remain two. Their values must be compared, and obviously neither one can be the standard by which to judge the other. . . . Thus when Petrarch says that a thousand pleasures are not worth one pain, he establishes an ideal of value deeper than either pleasure or pain.[7]

However, even if we could properly compare pleasures and pains, it is not empirically certain that the intensity of desire is

[7] *Reason in Common Sense*, 238-239.

equivalent to the pain of want, or to the predicted or the imagined pleasure of satisfying the desire, so that a comparison of these with the pleasure of reading is no sure test of the relative values of the pleasure and the desire. If we leave the matter up to preference, we have simply given preference to preference without solving the problem, because in terms of either pleasure or desire the preference may be arbitrary and impulsive.

It is clear that for the solution of this problem in such a way as still to recognize the intrinsic claims of these diverse types of interest, we are driven to another level of consideration. This is the level of our second technical problem, that of the judgment of value or the standard of value and its relation to the units of value.

Santayana's general attitude to this problem is as clear as was his general attitude to the other. He says, "The standard of value, like every standard, must be one,"[8] and he leaves no doubt that one such standard consists in the demand for "rationality" among the interests. But when we ask specifically what this "rationality" may be and what is its connection with these interests, we are again answered rather vaguely.

Let us follow through the paragraphs that succeed the one we have just been quoting. He says: "Nor can the intensity of pleasures and pains, apart from the physical violence of their expression, be judged by any other standard than by the power they have, when represented, to control the will's movement."[9] Here the standard seems to be the act of representing the interests from which a resultant act can be expected. The obligation seems to consist in giving the interests a fair chance to motivate conduct, and the conduct seems to be rational in so far as each interest has a chance to make its force felt in the resultant.

He then warns us of various corrections that need to be made to guarantee a fair representation of the diverse interests. "In estimating the value of any experience, our endeavor, our pretension, is to weigh the value which that experience possesses

[8] *Ibid.*, 238.
[9] *Ibid.*, 239.

when it is actual."[10] The ideal is to get the force of the *actual* interest. But in *representation,* he points out, the original value of the interest is "robbed" and a substitute value introduced. "This divergence falsifies all representation of life and renders it initially cruel, sentimental, and mythical. We dislike to trample on a flower . . . but we laugh at the pangs we endured in childhood."[11] These illusions of interest have to be corrected in order to attain a rational judgment of value, and this is done by seeking and sifting the evidence for the actual values of the interests:

> For although an impulsive injustice is inherent in the very nature of representation and cannot be overcome altogether, yet reason, by attending to all the evidences that can be gathered and by confronting the first pronouncement by others fetched from every quarter of experience, has power to minimize the error and reach a practically just estimate of absent values.[12]

As an intuitive assistance to this corrected estimate, Santayana in many passages makes a great deal of "sympathy." Sometimes he writes as if this were the standard itself and nothing more were necessary or possible. It is all he adduces as a ground of rationality in his criticism of Russell, for instance:

> In practice, values cannot be compared save as represented or enacted in the private imagination of somebody: for we could not conceive that an alien good *was* a good unless we could sympathize with it in some way in our own persons; and on the warmth which we felt in so representing the alien good, would hang our conviction that it was truly valuable, and had worth in comparison with our own good. The voice of reason, bidding us prefer the greater good, no matter who is to enjoy it, is also nothing but the force of sympathy, bringing a remote existence before us vividly *sub specie boni.* Capacity for such sympathy measures the capacity to recognize duty and therefore, in a moral sense, to have it.[13]

Here Santayana places one type of interest, sympathy, as a judge or standard over all others. The arbitrariness of this de-

[10] *Ibid.,* 240.
[11] *Ibid.,* 241.
[12] *Ibid.,* 244.
[13] *Winds of Doctrine,* 149.

vice from the point of view of *all* interests, or of a pure interest theory, must be patent. In the passages we are following this arbitrariness is there clear to Santayana also: "Direct sympathies, which suffice for instinctive present coöperation, fail to transmit alien or opposite pleasures," he writes, "they overemphasize momentary relations, while they necessarily ignore permanent bonds. Therefore the same intellect that puts a mechanical reality behind perception must put a moral reality behind sympathy."[14]

This "moral reality" seems to be composed of a consistency and harmony of interests. Speaking of fame, he says, "It would be rationalized in the only sense in which any primary desire can be rationalized, namely, by being combined with all others in a consistent whole."[15] And later, "We must buttress or modify our spontaneous judgment with all the other judgments that the object envisaged can prompt: we must make our ideal harmonize with all experience rather than with a part only."[16] Lest this ideal be thought too idealistic, Santayana hastily adds,

> A rational will is not a will that has reason for its basis or that possesses any other proof that its realization would be possible or good than the oracle which a living will inspires and pronounces. The rationality possible to the will lies not in its source but in its method. An ideal cannot wait for its realization to prove its validity. To deserve loyalty it needs only to be adequate to an ideal, that is, to express completely what the soul at present demands, and to do justice to all extant interests.[17]

We now wonder what may be the range of "extant interests" which "the soul at present demands." We learn that "a harmony and coöperation of impulses should be conceived, leading to the maximum satisfaction possible in the whole community of spirits affected by our action."[18] "The ideal has the same relation to given demands that the reality has to given perceptions."[19] Here we seem to be passing out of the confines of representation

[14] *Reason in Common Sense*, 245.
[15] *Ibid.*, 247.
[16] *Ibid.*, 254.
[17] *Ibid.*, 255.
[18] *Ibid.*, 256.
[19] *Ibid.*, 257.

of interests by a single agent to what in fact, in reality, the co-operation of impulses would be for "the whole community of spirits affected by our action." But we are promptly drawn back within the circle of an agent's interests by the remark that "if the ideal can confront particular desires and put them to shame, that happens only because the ideal is the object of a more profound and voluminous desire and embodies the good which they blindly and perhaps deviously pursue,"[20] unless perchance this "voluminous desire" were an over-individual desire or a society's desire—but that would be a solution opposed to the whole tenor of the passages we are following.

Yet what could a "voluminous desire" be for Santayana but one interest, no doubt an absorbing one, among all others? In the remaining pages of the chapter, he gropes for a solution of this difficulty. He again speaks of sympathy and of a resultant of forces—"One condition the ideal must fulfill; it must be a resultant or synthesis of impulses already afoot,"[21] and concludes with this paragraph:

> Reason as such represents or rather constitutes a single formal interest, the interest in harmony. When two interests are simultaneous and fall within one act of apprehension the desirability of harmonizing them is involved in the very effort to realize them together. If attention and imagination are steady enough to face this implication and not to allow impulse to oscillate between irreconcilable tendencies, reason comes into being. Henceforth things actual and things desired are confronted by an ideal which has both pertinence and authority.[22]

Now, as a sympathetic reader, I could import many plausible interpretations into this paragraph, but as a literal reader, I fail to see how this ideal has either pertinence or authority. If reason is a single interest, as Santayana states in the first sentence of the paragraph, then clearly this interest is impertinent to opposing interests of unreason. Santayana may call an interest in unreason madness, or any other conventionally disparaging name, as he frequently does, but what authority, on any grounds mentioned, has the formal interest of reason over an

[20] *Ibid.*
[21] *Ibid.*, 260.
[22] *Ibid.*, 268.

informal interest of unreason? The nearest he comes to an answer in the pages reviewed is the psychological observation that "when two interests are simultaneous and fall within one act of apprehension, the desirability of harmonizing them is involved in the very effort to realize them together." But if that desire is absent, what authority can invoke it? Moreover, at best this limits the judgment of value to instances where "interests are simultaneous and fall within one act of apprehension." Stupidity and carelessness and ignorance would never be irrational or bad, nor acts with hidden motives. Nor would there be any judgment of value possible in conflicts of interests between individuals when neither individual could understand the other, nor would there be any relevant authority requiring them to understand each other. If value judgment is limited to the chance of interests being simultaneously present or represented in one act of apprehension together with an interest in harmonizing them, then all we have is a description of certain complex acts of valuing. There is no good reason why these complex acts of valuing should be set apart from other complex acts of valuing otherwise constituted. A preference for harmonizing interests seems as immediate and as irrational a preference as one for fishing, stamp collecting, or missionary work. No standard is, in fact, set up at all. Moreover, the inference would be that Santayana believed none could be set up.

Yet the trend of his whole *Life of Reason* is that reason, in the sense of the harmony or integration of interests, is the standard of value. Yet I believe that no literal reader could find a valid justification of this standard among Santayana's discussions of interest.

If, however, the reader relaxes his literalness and seeks for the spirit rather than the letter of Santayana's view, he discovers something different which runs somewhat like this: We are to accept the main outlines of the mechanistic interpretation of nature by which matter through the action of natural forces forms into bodies, some of which attain life. "What mechanism involves in this respect is exactly what we find: a tentative appearance of life in many quarters, its disappearance in some, and its reïnforcement and propagation in others, where the physical equilibrium attained insures to it a natural stability and a natural prosperity."[23] This natural integrative process which produces states of equilibrium and "stability" and "prosperity" continues in the forms of life, in the evolution of species, in the evolution of forms of society, and in the development of social ideals. Santayana points out that "government neither subsists nor arises because it is good or useful, but solely because it is inevitable."[24] A set of mechanical forces blindly at work among living forms produces a resultant integration, which is relatively stable because of the equilibrium of forces embodied there. Then a social ideal emerges. The government "becomes good in so far as the inevitable adjustment of political forces which it embodies is also a just provision for all the human interests which it creates or affects."[25]

> It lies in the essence of a mechanical world, where the interests of its products are concerned, to be fundamentally kind, since it has formed and on the whole maintains those products, and yet continually cruel, since it forms and maintains them blindly, without considering difficulties or probable failures. Now the most tyrannical government, like the best, is a natural product maintained by an equilibrium of natural forces. It is simply a new mode of mechanical energy to which the philosopher living under it must adjust himself as he would to the weather.[26]

But the integrative drive of these natural forces still continues.

> Where there is maladjustment there is no permanent physical stability. Therefore the ideal of society can never involve the infliction of injury on anybody for any purpose. Such an ideal would purpose for a goal something out of equilibrium, a society which even if established could not maintain itself; but an ideal life must not tend to destroy its ideal by abolishing its own existence. In the second place, it is impossible on moral grounds that injustice should subsist in the ideal. The ideal means the perfect, and a supposed ideal in which wrong still subsisted would be the denial of perfection.[27]

The ideal, then, or the standard conception of value, will on

[23] *Reason in Science*, 94.
[24] *Reason in Society*, 71.
[25] *Ibid.*
[26] *Ibid.*, 111.
[27] *Ibid.*, 112.

this interpretation be an extrapolation in idea of the natural integrative processes of life which produce states of equilibrium and consequent stability in the preservation of forms of life either in the individual or in society. Reason is the name for this integrative drive working upon natural forms and especially upon living forms and more especially upon living interests. For

> the Life of Reason is the happy marriage of two elements—impulse and ideation—which if wholly divorced would reduce man to a brute or to a maniac. The rational animal is generated by the union of these two monsters. He is constituted by ideas which have ceased to be visionary, and actions which have ceased to be vain.[28]

"Reason is an operation in nature, and has its root there."[29]

The authority for this ideal of Reason, therefore, which Santayana unfolds in his chapter on Rational Ethics (*Reason in Science*, ch. IX) and which he explicitly states there is an idea only ["in lieu of a rational morality, we have rational ethics; and this mere idea of a rational morality is something valuable"[30]]—the authority for this ideal of Reason comes not from the interests but from the basic integrative drive in nature which passes right through the interests and makes for another stable equilibrium in nature, this time a social equilibrium, which simply uses individual interests as materials for this inevitable end. In actual societies, this end is only partially achieved, but the aim of nature is detected by the reflective philosopher who in the medium of ideas is also driven by the integrative force of reason and precipitates an ethical ideal which is indeed what rational or self-integrating nature is trying to do and may yet succeed in doing in the medium of living men and societies.

This, I think, is the spirit of Santayana's theory of value on the technical side. It explains some anomalies in his rational ethics considered as an interest theory. For a self-consistent interest theory would hold tight to the integrity of each interest and the integrity of each bodily individual who had interests. But Santayana says,

[28] *Reason in Common Sense*, 6.
[29] *Reason in Science*, 237.
[30] *Ibid.*, 239.

> For reason the person itself has no obstinate existence. . . . *The man's life*, the circle drawn by biographers around the career of a particular body, from the womb to the charnel house, and around the mental flux that accompanies that career, is no significant unity. All the substances and efficient processes that figure within it came from elsewhere and continue beyond; while all the rational objects and interests to which it refers have a transpersonal status.[31]

A man's body with its individual life and interests now appears to be just an incident or a locus for the integrative process of cosmic Reason.

> In a world that is perhaps infinite, moral life can spring only from definite centres, and is neither called upon nor able to estimate the whole, nor to redress its balance. It is the free spirit of a part, finding its affinities and equilibrium in the material whole which it reacts on, and which it is in that measure enabled to understand.[32]

I see no way of reconciling the spirit of Santayana's technical theory with the letter—or, if both are according to the letter, how to reconcile one with the other. Reason as a cosmic integrative process furnishes an excellent over-individual standard of value, but it presupposes a definition of value very different from one in terms of interest, and dispenses value far beyond the confines of interest. If, on the other hand, value is defined in terms of interest, no rational standard of the sort Santayana struggles for can be derived.

It is no doubt true to say that a society founded upon a purely individualistic interest theory would lack stability and endurance and that an integration of interests from vital centers is necessary to ensure an extensive endurance of interest itself. But why should any specific interest be interested in the endurance of interest in general? That is what no interest theory *in its own terms* has ever made clear—at least to me. Sympathetic interest and an occasional interest in rationality will not do it. The pressure of life processes themselves, however, may; not because they are interests (often probably they are not) but because, as Santayana says, they are inevitable. But when inte-

[31] *Ibid.*, 250.
[32] *Ibid.*, 261.

gration and equilibrium and self-preservation are appealed to as grounds of value, then value is not definable in terms of interest alone. Interest becomes then, at best, simply a factor or partial ingredient of value.

Thus, I find two different technical theories or definitions of value implicit in Santayana's writings. On one theory, value is defined in terms of interest. A strict adherence to this definition does not develop any standards of value beyond the prudence of individuals preferring the gamble for a long life of many satisfied interests to the assurance of a short life and a gay one. That preference is itself an individual affair, which can be weighted by conventional sanctions in education (or propaganda), social pressure, law, political compulsion, and religious dogma, and enlarged into a sort of social prudence, the origin of which can be anthropologically and sociologically described, but the *value* of which in terms of the satisfaction of specific concrete interests as they actually come is nothing more than the satisfaction immediately felt or predicted by the agent. If value is really the satisfaction of interest, no authority can demand that an individual *ought* not to have that interest or *ought* to have another. Conventional sanctions are not standards of *value* on the interest theory. They are simply environmental facts which interests have to cope with. That these sanctions have an origin in the conflict of individual interests and that "unsocial" individuals who prefer a short life and a gay one generally get the short life and those that prefer the long life tend to survive and propagate,—these are facts which explain the wider distribution of "social" as against "unsocial" individuals, but they do not establish the greater value of the "social" life *in terms of value defined as the satisfaction of interest*—unless interest is treated abstractly as a mere counter. But the empirical evidence for the interest theory is the actual interest immediately present in an actual individual, and if that evidence is abandoned for some abstraction, the appeal and justification for the interest theory is lost.

The second technical definition of value which I find implicit in Santayana's writings is that value is integration, or, somewhat arbitrarily restricted, the integration of interests. If this definition is accepted, it is obvious that we have an authoritative standard (assuming that the definition can be empirically supported) in conformity with which it is possible and requisite to say that some interests *ought* not to be and that individuals persisting in them *ought* to be eradicated, whereas certain other interests *ought* to be and individuals possessing them *ought* to be preserved and multiplied.

Both of these theories seem to me personally to have empirical weight, and they seem to me incompatible. I think it was wise of Santayana to carry the two along together but not particularly rational or clarifying. Would it not be wiser still to pull them clearly apart and examine their separate implications and evidences, and then see if a single better theory could be devised, or if perhaps "value" means two quite different things whose connections may be investigated, or, if not, whether some practical advice could not be given so that we might profit from the evidences of both of these theories without being confused or dogmatic about either?

STEPHEN C. PEPPER

DEPARTMENT OF PHILOSOPHY
UNIVERSITY OF CALIFORNIA

8

George Boas

SANTAYANA AND THE ARTS

8

SANTAYANA AND THE ARTS

ABOUT fifty years ago the author of *The Life of Reason* published a sonnet whose burden was the necessity of faith. In it occurred such phrases as, "It is not wisdom to be only wise, and on the inward vision close the eyes, but it is wisdom to believe the heart." The octave terminated on Columbus' trust in "his soul's surmise," and the sestet, in more abstract language, urged man to bid "the tender light of faith to shine," that he might be led "unto the thinking of the thought divine." A candidate for the doctorate, and several have already appeared to win diplomas by straightening our Mr. Santayana's ideas for him, will some day see in this sonnet a curious fusion of Franciscan mysticism and Dominican rationalism, of neo-platonic anti-intellectualism and peripatetic intellectualism. He will ponder over the difficulty of "reconciling," as he will call it, these two antithetical strains, and ask how by following the heart across "a void of mystery and dread," one can arrive at the thinking of any predictable thought, be it divine or merely human. He will not, probably, ask why so complicated a philosophic question should have been answered in fourteen lines of verse nor wonder at the willingness of a philosopher, even if in his twenties, to write sonnets rather than treatises, nor will the relation of art and philosophy—when one is used as a vehicle for the other—stir him.

If such a person should imagine that this fusion of diverse trends was a phenomenon of the philosopher's youth, he will have forgotten the *Dialogues in Limbo* and *The Last Puritan.* The latter, though not confined to fourteen lines, presents an opposition of philosophies as precisely as his early sonnet. The former contains conversations in which three opposing philosophers figure as protagonists: Democritus, Socrates, and Avicenna. And if one ask of the author, as one constantly asks of Plato, "Who speaks for you?" the answer appears in his conception of realms of being.

The Democritean element in Santayana's thought can no more be denied nor explained away nor reconciled nor reduced, than it can in the universe. Has he not always insisted that matter was the flux of substance out of which all else arose? Not only when discussing metaphysics, but also when dealing with epistemology, he has emphasized the material substratum of all change. In his early work on aesthetics, *The Sense of Beauty*, which dates from the period of the sonnet referred to above, we find him maintaining that "the most important effects" of works of art are attributable to their form and at the same time pointing out that, "Form cannot be the form of nothing. If, then, in finding or creating beauty, we ignore the materials of things, and attend only to their form, we miss an ever-present opportunity to heighten our effects."[1] Much later, when discussing the "selective principle" by which we fix our attention upon one essence rather than another, it turns out that "to thump existence with empirical conviction," though it direct the eye to an essence, is nevertheless a material gesture.[2]

That matter gives us the conditions of existence, though these conditions tell us nothing of the nature of what exists, must then be granted to Santayana. It is the strain which makes it possible for his critics to group him with the materialists and even for him, in some of his moods, to claim a share in the materialistic program. But the "inner nature" of matter can only be guessed at, so that if one stayed within the realm of matter, one would never know what one was talking about—nor could one, I imagine, even talk. Animal faith might orient us towards food and mates, but we should dwell in perpetual darkness and silence. Since we do not dwell in such a sensory void, and since we are not happy with unknowables, we complete our Democritean views by following Socrates into the realm of essence. If matter is irrational, the realm of our understanding must be nonmaterial. And if matter is the basis of all existence, the things we

[1] *Sense of Beauty*, 77.

[2] *Realm of Essence*, 15.

understand must be inexistent. But we begin our understanding with sensory data, which are, in spite of their incorporation, timeless qualities. The most precise statement of their relation to the rest of the world is to be found in *The Realm of Essence*, but their peculiar function in knowledge is perhaps more clearly expressed in *Scepticism and Animal Faith*. There we discover that if we dwell with Socrates in the world of forms, we shall never know that anything exists, but shall have to be satisfied with the bright radiance of eternity.

Life, however, is not all knowledge. We have "free expression," sensations, passions, "perpetually kindled and fading in the light of consciousness."[3] This is the realm of spirit. It is a realm whose praises are sung by Avicenna in his lament for this world. "Rather than be eternal, who would not choose to be young?"[4] For the young can feel the diversity of existence, and surround the godhead

> with beings able to die and to kill, able to dream, able to look for the truth and to tell themselves lies, able above all to love, to feel the life quickened suddenly within them at the sight of some other lovely and winsome creature, until they could contain it no longer, and too great, too mad, too sweet to be endured it should leap from them into that other being, there to create a third.[5]

It is this realm which contains literature, philosophy, "and so much of love, religion, and patriotism as is not an effort to survive materially."[6] This is the realm of those values for which matter and essence exist; the spirit feels terminal—or final—values, the necessity for which might be calculated by the reason, and the embodiment of which might be found in matter. But the reason, though it knows that terminal values are needed, can never feel their tang; our bodies, though they are prerequisite to the enjoyment of life, are but instruments for its enjoyment.

Each realm thus turns out to be incomplete and to give no

[3] *Ibid.*, x, xi.

[4] *Dialogues in Limbo*, 165.

[5] *Ibid.*, 165-166.

[6] *The Realm of Essence*, Preface, XI. Compare this notion of "realms" with what Santayana says about the various schools of philosophy in the "Preface" to Triton Edition of *The Works of George Santayana*, I, ix; also "Preface" to Vol. VII, x.

satisfactory picture in itself of the entire universe. A philosophy which was exclusively materialistic could never account for either "ideas" nor values; one which was exclusively idealistic could never account for matter nor for values; one which was exclusively spiritualistic, could never account for matter or ideas. For the discovery of the incompleteness of each realm is a real discovery; it is not a deduction. Only the collision with their boundary stones could reveal how limited they are. There is no reason within the realm of matter for either ideas or values to exist—and in fact materialists are here to testify to their non-existence. So it is with the realms of essence and spirit. There are no rational paths from one to the other. That is why when man is locked within the framework of knowledge, only animal faith and intuition will open the locks. One can see that the later Santayana is an expansion of the earlier.

The subject-matter of aesthetics is one which falls within the realm of spirit. In Santayana we have one of the few examples of philosophers who both write about art and create works of art. We shall discuss what he says about art, for two other papers in this volume discuss the works of art which might be expected to bear out the truth of his theory.

The first of these writings is *The Sense of Beauty*, published when its author was still best known as a teacher and poet. Its subject-matter and method were at that time—in the early nineties—somewhat unusual, as its author recognized. Its subject-matter was neither the exercise of aesthetic judgment nor the anthropology of the arts; it was "the nature and elements of our aesthetic judgments." Its method was neither didactic nor historical, but psychological. It kept close to the facts of feeling, to use the author's own words, for "to feel beauty is a better thing than to understand how we come to feel it."[7] It is the feeling which justifies the rest of life. Should one simply know about beauty without ever feeling it, the only value received would be the satisfaction of curiosity. This would not presumably be enough for the Santayana of 1896. For even then he maintained that there was a hierarchy of values and that the value of intel-

[7] *Sense of Beauty*, 11.

lectual satisfaction was not so elevated in the hierarchy as "that incommunicable and illusive excellence that haunts every beautiful thing."[8]

It was precisely that sense of the primacy of life's claims which so endeared Santayana to the generation of his students and which, especially when expressed in his musical style, made him an object of suspicion to his professional colleagues. If one was to preach the primacy of feeling, not in the logical or genetic sense—as that out of which other things are compounded or grown—but in the sense of value, one usually did it with a kind of neo-Darwinian sneer at these brutes who think themselves angels. Santayana not only insisted upon the primacy of feeling but also intimated that its animal roots were, like matter, the necessary conditions but not the limits of its worth. This was the period when materialism was usually coupled with the adjective "crass" and when an "avowed materialist" was expected to hang his head in shame. Santayana seemed to assure such people that there was nothing shameful about their doctrine and that the origin of a value or its condition had no influence whatsoever upon its place in the hierarchy. But, curiously enough, he never faced the psychological problem—except in his novel—that human beings do in reality depreciate things of whose conditions or origins they disapprove. The feeling of beauty, that is, might be as intense as you please; so long as one remained in ignorance of its source, one would be satisfied with its occurrence; but let one know from what unworthy ground it springs and one immediately suspects its "real" value. This could present no problem to an out and out rationalist who believed that values could all be thoroughly justified, not merely on the basis of feeling, but on the basis of rational evidence. For such a person could presumably give reasons why a value lost nothing when its origin was known. Even if everyone felt ashamed of a given value and began to devaluate it, it could theoretically be proved that everyone was simply wrong. But when one starts out by identifying value with feeling, then when the feeling goes, the value goes with it.

The irrationality of aesthetic preference was insisted upon by

[8] *Ibid.*, 12.

Santayana, but that did not mean that every preference for a work of art was automatically justified. He maintained, to be sure, that "values spring from the immediate and inexplicable reaction of vital impulse," but, should one's vital impulses react immediately to the "historical connexions or proper classification" of works of art, one would not be enjoying an aesthetic value.[9] Yet there are people whose enjoyment of a picture becomes enhanced, intensified, when they see it as the production of a certain tribe or epoch or religious group; they do not simply know in scientific detachment that it is such a thing but, knowing this, they enjoy it the more. The statue of Aristotle on the west portal of Chartres, for instance, would excite no great interest were it not the medieval version of a Greek theme. The more one knows about the survival of classical themes in medieval art, the more one enjoys, in the most literal sense of the word, the works of art in which these themes appear. They become more quaint, more picturesque, perhaps, and nothing more, but one's feelings towards them change, and if one's feelings are in any way indicative of value, the value has changed too. Similarly many a poem would seem characterless, were not the "proper classification" made. The complicated meters of the *langue d'oc* have to be known before the poems written in them can have their full effect. This does not mean that one could not divine the meter by reading the poem or that everyone who knows the names of the elaborate meters and stanza-forms derives any pleasure from his knowledge; it merely means that once one knows what the technical problem was which faced the author, one reads with increased admiration and hence pleasure.

It is admitted by Santayana that "facts have a value of their own," but he is satisfied with pointing out that their value is not sufficient. To argue that what used to be called realism is not the sole criterion of aesthetic excellence no longer requires debate; everyone will grant it. It is, however, of the greatest importance to recognize that in granting the possible contribution of realism to any work of art, one grants that aesthetic appreciation, however affective in its nature, may be modified by knowledge or ignorance. Such modification was called by Santayana

[9] *Ibid.*, 19-20.

an effect of "certain associations."[10] But, aside from simple colors and other sensory qualities, what emotion could be aroused by an experience with which one had no associations?

Every word, every pattern of line and color, every shape, every complexity of human relationship, every motion of the body, is a stimulus to emotion because of association. Were a person from another civilization to witness a play by Shakespeare, he might be excited by wonder, but hardly by pity and fear. Salvador Dali recently protested to his critics that if a woman with a fish's tail was beautiful, then a woman with a fish's head must be equally beautiful. And, other than our association with mermaids in poetry and painting, what answer could be made to his argument? The exclusion of all associated experiences from the aesthetic experience would remove the meaning of words, the subject-matter of paintings, the fitness of buildings from the field of aesthetics. One would arrive at what Mr. Prall has called "the aesthetic surface." It has, however, yet to be demonstrated (1) that the aesthetic surface has any emotional force in and by itself, and (2) that anyone ever has enjoyed a work of art for its aesthetic surface alone.

The point is not labored, however, by Santayana and it would be absurd to labor it here. He was more concerned with selecting certain common associations which in his opinion detracted from aesthetic enjoyment than in elaborating the theory of aesthetic purity. He wished to point out that aesthetics was neither the history of art nor anthropology, and his demonstration can be granted. But when he proceeds to demonstrate a more complete independence of art from life's other interests, his argument becomes less forceful. For, although he appreciates the fact that aesthetic values arise out of non-aesthetic—as when truth becomes a landscape, having lost its practical utility[11]—he does not face the question of whether any non-aesthetic value, regardless of its origin, can become aesthetic or the complementary problem whether an aesthetic value is self-justified simply because it is aesthetic. Honor, truthfulness, and cleanliness may be obvious examples of moral values which have become

[10] *Ibid.*, 20.
[11] *Ibid.*, 29.

aesthetic; but is their transmutation a proof that they need no further justification? The writer of this essay has maintained that even biologically harmful practices, when they have become habitual, will take on that air of necessity which is identical with "immediate authority." This would appear to have been recognized by Santayana, for he is as gently contemptuous of intuitionalistic ethics as he is of utilitarian. He seemed to maintain when he wrote *The Sense of Beauty* that the rise of immediate values out of instrumental was an unfortunate accident and that "real" aesthetic values were not to be explained in this way.

There followed in that early volume his famous definition of "beauty." The beautiful was a kind of pleasure; but it was neither physical—in the sense that bodily pleasure is physical—nor disinterested, nor universal, as various schools of aesthetics at the time maintained. The differentia of aesthetic pleasure lay in its objectification: it was "the transformation of an element of sensation into the quality of a thing."[12] It was, we were told, "the survival of a tendency originally universal to make every effect of a thing upon us a constituent of its conceived nature."[13] It is this tendency which causes us to regard pleasure as the quality of a thing.

The reasonableness of this definition, which was also a theory, must have seemed unusual to Santayana's students. Mr. George Washburne Howgate, in his dissertation on Santayana, indicates briefly how the book was received by the press. Apparently the definition of beauty met with most objections.[14] People were used to more mystical accounts of the matter, though Santayana was by no means the first to treat of aesthetics from the psychological point of view. However, beauty generally was held to be something almost supernatural. Did we not have it on excellent authority that it was a sensuous manifestation of the Absolute? To have presented it as something inherent in our nature, requiring no theological substantiation, was to have freed oneself from a long tradition that stemmed from Plato. It was a tradition, moreover, which Santayana wished to retain in part

[12] *Ibid.*, 44.
[13] *Ibid.*, 48.
[14] *George Santayana*, Philadelphia, 1938, 97f.

and, as a poet, he retained it almost in its entirety. Thus this objectification of pleasure became for him in his poetic moments the one thing which redeems the barrenness of life. When he wrote of Platonic love, he used the old terminology of Platonism, and we are told that "the imagination and the heart," like the senses and the "mind," extend beyond the given. Their extension produces "an absolute beauty and a perfect love."[15] How much of this was ill-considered and youthful enthusiasm—like his sonnet sequence of 1896—and how much serious philosophical reflection, there is no way of telling. There is evidence nevertheless that even at this date the Platonic and the Democritean Santayana were at play with each other. For though Democritus might well describe beauty as objectified pleasure, Plato would immediately ask questions about the beauty of actions, laws, and ideas.

It would seem as if that which is pleasure objectified would need no further qualification. It would seem as if one man's objectified pleasure were as good as another's. But to Santayana this was by no means the case. It turned out to be immediately true that only certain of our capacities were fruitful of beauty. Thus breathing and the passion of love contribute heavily to the object of aesthetic pleasure, whereas—and this is particularly interesting from the historical point of view—"social and gregarious impulses, in the satisfaction of which happiness mainly resides, are those in which beauty finds least support."[16] For in general they are not imaginable in definite form. Thus "home" may form an image of house and garden, but friendship, wealth, reputation, power, have no such potency. Yet surely love of country, loyalty, military duty, to take only a few obvious examples, have been presented in images which have seemed as concrete and moving as those even vaguer ideas presented in the form of pagan myths, and if one passes to arts less productive of beauty than of other aesthetic values, arts such as caricature, friendship, wealth, reputation, and power, they too have had their embodiment in striking image. It would

[15] "Platonic Love in Some Italian Poets," in *Interpretations of Poetry and Religion*, 145.

[16] *Sense of Beauty*, 63.

indeed appear not only that social impulses can be imagined in materialized form, but also that such imaginings, whether of social impulse or not, are not always productive of beauty.

Beauty then ought to reside in those objects the perception of which gives pleasure and which can be definitely imagined. Should one find senses whose objects do not meet these conditions, one would be faced with the aesthetically irrelevant. The "lower senses," touch, taste, and smell, were held by Santayana to fall into this category, though what the passion of love—which, it will be recalled, was one of the main contributors of beauty—would feed upon if it were confronted with only sights and sounds, must seem somewhat mysterious to those readers who grew up in the twentieth rather than in the nineteenth century. A purely visual and auditory world would be less fertile both in animal life and in ethical problems than one in which tactile, gustatory, and olfactory sensations had their place, but it is questionable whether anyone outside the genteel tradition would ever care to step into it. It might satisfy what Santayana called "the principle of purity;" could it satisfy "the principle of interest?" Santayana insisted upon the necessity of satisfying both. Yet if he inclined to one side more than to the other, it was to the side of purity. For not only are sight and hearing raised to a level of aesthetic importance above that of the other senses, but sight is elevated above hearing, and then, as if that were not enough, we were assured that beauty cannot be attributed wholly or mainly to pleasures attached to abstracted sensations; "by far the most important effects are not attributable to these materials, but to their arrangement and their ideal relations."[17] Why formal beauty should be more "important" than material, was not, to the best of my knowledge, ever demonstrated by the younger Santayana. Was it not simply a remnant of the traditional aesthetics, a bit of that somewhat frayed Platonism which appeared in what he himself would have called puritanism? That he asserted it so dogmatically is probably attributable to its apparent obviousness; in spite of one's materialistic sympathies, it was difficult in the Cambridge of 1892, one imagines, even to suspect that form was not more important than

[17] *Ibid.*, 77.

matter. The beauty of form nevertheless was simply the beauty of a combination of sensory elements which in themselves might be indifferent. Few would deny that such beauty exists; whether it is objectified pleasure in the sense that a beautiful color or sound is, might be questioned. Even if its existence were granted, however, there would be little more than the eulogistic connotation of the word "form" to make one believe it higher in the hierarchy of values than any other kind of beauty. What is of peculiar interest to-day, when formal beauty has become a commonplace not only of aesthetics but also of artistic criticism, is precisely the rank which Santayana conferred upon it. When he spoke of it, he sank to something close to oratory. Thus we find him saying,

> Beauty of form . . . is what specifically appeals to an aesthetic nature; it is equally removed from the crudity of formless stimulation and from the emotional looseness of reverie and discursive thought. The indulgence in sentiment and suggestion, of which our time is fond, to the sacrifice of formal beauty, marks an absence of cultivation as real, if not as confessed, as that of the barbarian who revels in gorgeous confusion.[18]

The first clause is a *petitio principii;* the rest is an *argumentum ad hominem.* It could all be rewritten from what might be called the "romantic point of view" and the question-begging epithets would argue to an entirely different conclusion. Could one not say with the same logical effect, "It is equally remote from direct contact with material excitement and from the emotional spontaneity of dreams and conversation. The appreciation of feeling and suggestion, of which our time has the secret, having abandoned the quest of cold formal beauty, marks an absence of self-conscious priggishness, whether we are aware of it or not, as that of primitive man who revels in the opulence of material beauty"?

Besides the influence of a Platonistic tradition, there was in his background an idealistic tradition which made one feel that the "mind" was somehow more intrinsically worthy than the body. This feeling appeared when he announced that the synthesis which constituted form was an "activity of the mind."[19]

[18] *Ibid.,* 96-97.
[19] *Ibid.,* 97.

Professor Loewenberg has freed the present generation from the fascination of "the apotheosis of mind,"[20] but in 1892 it was too much to ask a young professor to see mind detached from its rank in a hierarchy of values. To have doubted its superiority—not merely its difference—to body would have been to ally oneself with vulgar materialists and aesthetic hedonists. Santayana had already purged aesthetics of three of the senses; his world had become a visual map which gave off harmonious sounds to the sensitive ear. It could have cost him little to progress to the point where the mind entered as a unifying agent, producing uniformity in multiplicity.

However, in this early work formal beauty was not unique in conferring value upon works of art. There was also the beauty of "expression." Expression is the quality acquired by objects through association.[21] It is this beauty which will vary, one gathers, from observer to observer, for everyone's associations are more or less personal. Santayana pointed out in this connection that the value of a given experience in isolation in no way determines its value in association: a kind deed in certain relations may seem ludicrous, an evil deed seem beautiful. In the arts it is necessary that the material itself—and presumably the form—appear beautiful in order that associated experiences may take on beauty. It is thus that Santayana avoided the danger of attributing the aesthetic values to the associated terms. On the contrary, they take on beauty when associated with beautiful works of art. In this way utility, cost, fitness, become associated with aesthetics and their value heightened. A useful object, an expensive jewel, a neatly turned chair, take on a value which they would not have in themselves. And we say that the work of art with which they are associated expresses utility, rarity, and fitness.

The method of *The Sense of Beauty* was the method of introspective psychology. It was a method which necessarily tended to isolate works of art from other things and to isolate our reactions to them from our other reactions. A man as sensi-

[20] See "The Apotheosis of Mind in Modern Idealism," *Philosophical Review*, XXXI (May, 1922), 215.

[21] *Sense of Beauty*, 193.

tive to the arts and as fond of them as Santayana was bound sooner or later to feel the injustice of this method and within a decade of the publication of *The Sense of Beauty* appeared an article called "What Is Aesthetics?" The importance of this essay is its insistence upon the initimate relation of art to life's other interests.[22] While admitting the possibility of psychological aesthetics, the essay refused to admit its importance. For "aesthetic experience will . . . continue to elude and overflow psychology in a hundred ways, although in its own way psychology might eventually survcy and represent all aesthetic experience."[23] It will overflow psychology into the rest of life.

Aesthetic good is accordingly no separable value; it is not realizable by itself in a set of objects not otherwise interesting. Anything which is to entertain the imagination must first have exercised the senses; it must first have stimulated some animal reaction, engaged attention, and intertwined itself in the vital process; and later this aesthetic good, with animal and sensuous values imbedded in it and making its very substance, must be swallowed up in a rational life; for reason will immediately feel itself called upon to synthesize those imaginative activities with whatever else is valuable.[24]

This is decidedly the voice of Avicenna, rather than that of either Socrates or Democritus. It does not say that the experience of works of art and of beauty cannot be treated psychologically; nor does it say that beauty is not an ideal, as eternal in its way as the essence of mathematics; it says that, besides all that, beauty is something which may become attached to all experience and that its place in the realm of values is to be determined by the moral philosopher rather than by the scientist.

What else could have been expected from one who was both an artist and a philosopher? It would have been easy for the philosopher to insist—as his predecessors had—on the unique character of the beautiful, to have dwelt lovingly upon its eter-

[22] Cf. Howgate, *George Santayana*, 108. This paper was probably part of a symposium on the nature of aesthetics held by the American Philosophical Association in 1903. For an abstract of a paper read by Santayana in that symposium had the same argument and some of the same phrasing as the article. See *Philosophical Review*, XIII (Mar., 1904), 184f.

[23] "What is Aesthetics?," *Philosophical Review*, XIII (May, 1904), 323.

[24] *Ibid.*, 323-324.

nal nature or cynically to have dug its roots out of matter and held them up to dry. But the poet was there too. Santayana had the unusual opportunity of discussing the arts from the point of view of the artist and he seems to have seen the importance of art as a mode of expression. Having the equally unusual gift of appreciating works of art, he could at least insist that when art became divorced from life's other interests, it became impoverished.

The swallowing up of the aesthetic good, "with its animal and sensuous values," in a rational life was of course depicted in *Reason in Art.* Its argument was mysterious only to those who could not decipher its Greek epigraph. To an Aristotelian the secret was not so occult. The whole-heartedness of the *Nichomachean Ethics,* in which no human capacity is seen to lack its ideal form or the power to make some contribution to human felicity, appears rolled up in four simple Greek words. The "phases of human progress," this new phenomenology of the human spirit,[25] are not steps upwards towards the attainment of an eternal spirit, but the many aspects of a single process whose end is here on earth. This process might be called the integration of vital interests. That such integration may be impossible ought to occur to a philosopher, but it seldom if ever has. For philosophers have not "the tragic sense of life." The problem of one who believes in the possibility of integration is to integrate art into life's totality. From the very opening of *Reason in Art,* "The Basis of Art in Instinct and Experience," we are aware that we are not reading a document either in idealistic aesthetics or in "aestheticism." Neither Hegel nor Walter Pater was the source of this chapter heading. If one suspected that it was a text from some Darwinian, one was equally wrong. For Santayana still retained his belief in realms of being and apparently saw no more reason then than he does now of judging a thing's value by its origin. Art might arise from instinct and experience, but its aim was not a return to instinct and experience. His notion of art was fundamentally the notion of a *techne;* the arts are ways of doing things—they are nature's ways guided by reason. Thus though the thing to be done might simply be the

[25] See the preface to the revised edition of *The Life of Reason* (1922), I, x, xi.

satisfaction of a primordial hunger, yet the way of doing it was not primordial gulping. Man automatically feels the need of enlightenment. Some accidental insight gives him a glimmer of satisfaction and, following the glimmer, he arrives at illumination. He may think that he has kindled the flare; he has done nothing of the kind. On the contrary, since the road leads to enlightenment, he will say that he meant it to come out that way. So we say that we deduce certain conclusions from formal reasoning, instead of saying that we have demonstrated that they can be deduced. In both cases we have profited from a lucky accident.

However, what enlightenment means in this case is utility. All fine art emerges from what Santayana called "industry." And the emergence was fundamentally the burden of *Reason in Art*. The story was simple enough. Every art had its material and its task, and presumably the task was the idealization of material potencies. One had merely to indicate the material of each art—gestures, sounds, stone—and discover their limitations and their possibilities.

Thus, after a start which might have led to a radically novel aesthetics, Santayana fell back into the traditional classification of the arts on the basis of their materials rather than on the basis of their purpose. There need be no doubt about the justice of interpreting an art as the perfecting of an instinctive capacity—if the word "instinctive" is not objectionable—but simple fiddling with materials is only one of the human capacities which rise into art. One makes gestures at random, to be sure, and such random gestures may become beautiful in the eyes of others and be preserved as ritualistic dances. But one also makes gestures to communicate thoughts and emotions, to relieve oneself of bodily strain—as when one stretches and yawns—, to make love, to fight, to play games, to eat and to drink. The purpose is more important than the material used, for its satisfaction will measure the success of the act and consequently what act will be retained as the "right" act. There are, to be sure, material limitations imposed upon our acts: our verbal pictures do not have the same color as those which are painted. And the conquering of the limitations has become the technique of the various arts. It cannot be denied that much of the satisfaction coming to an observer of a work of art emerges from a knowledge of such limitations and a sympathy with the technical problems involved. At the same time, a knowledge of just what human capacity is expressing itself to terminate in a given work of art is even more important.

Thus a person who thought of drawing as the manipulation of line and mass, the composing of dark and light, however sensitive he might be to linear rhythms, representational exactitude, pattern and the like, would be far from appreciating a drawing by Daumier, if he knew nothing of the satirical intention. Whether making fun of our fellows is instinctive or not, I do not know; few people in any event seem to lack the desire to do so. One may satirize others in the dance, in painting, in sculpture, in literature, even in music. The problems of satire are perhaps more determinative of the end result than the problems resident in the materials used. Thus Daumier in the *Rue Transnonain* is more like Swift than he is like Constantin Guys, in spite of the latter's having been a contemporary caricaturist. Again, the classical ballet on points is certainly closer to Mozart in his sonatas than it is to the modern expressionistic ballet. One need not have recourse to some ineffable identity of "spirit" to justify this. The meaning is merely that in both cases—to justify only the comparison between Mozart and the classical ballet—the artistic purpose was the arrangement of certain elements into harmonious and balanced compounds. Whatever "meaning" one may read into a Mozart sonata or whatever title may be given to a classical ballet, the technical feat is identical. Mozart has principal themes and secondary themes; he proceeds from tonic back to tonic; he states figures, turns them upside down, sometimes plays them backward, and gives one music whose pattern is clear and open to verbal description. So with the classical ballet. Every position of legs and arms, the passages from one to the other, the groupings of the dancers, are as ritualized as mathematics. The choreographer's main function is the combining of these simple and elementary figures. He may be telling the story of Daphnis and Chloe or of Echo and Narcissus; his problem will be the same. His relation to his predecessors and successors in the history of the dance is genealogical, and there is no more nor less reason to maintain that their purpose is the same as there is to establish an identity between the businesses of fathers and sons.

It is unlikely that any artist ever said to himself, I will make a statue, or a poem, or a dance. His task is always more specific. It is always—at a minimum—to achieve a certain effect in sculpture or painting or dancing. If he be engaged in an art like literature, which may express ideas, or one like painting which may be representative, his purpose will specify what he is going to say or represent as well as how. But as soon as he has included in his statement of the problem something beyond the material he proposes to work, he will have made it impossible to give an adequate criticism of his work of art in terms of the material. Consequently the defining of arts on the basis of their materials, while telling us something of great technical interest, incurs the danger of setting up standards of workmanship which are in the long run only part of the story. Now Santayana does not in practice limit himself to such standards. His criticism could be as it is even if he had never heard of his theory of the rise of art in the manipulation of materials. But his theory nevertheless can account for no standard other than "truth of materials." It is akin to theories which defining, for instance, sculpture as the cutting of stone—or some other heavy material—then call cast bronze bad sculpture, or praise sculptures for preserving the stony quality of their material. There could be no question of the right of sculptors to limit themselves to stone and to cut stone. A critic who knew the technical difficulties of their craft would know standards for judging their success. But whether it be sculpture or non-sculpture, there is an art of cast bronze; it too has its problems and consequently its standards. There may, however, also be an art of casting bronze so that it looks like stone or of cutting stone so that it looks like bronze. One may laugh at such fancies, but some of the greatest triumphs of baroque sculpture consisted in making one material look like another.

The contribution of Santayana to aesthetics in America must be measured by what existed at the time he wrote. There were both Hegelian dealers in edifying abstractions who valued a work of art because of the spirit which infused it and psychologists who held up pieces of paper divided in two and asked their students whether the division was beautiful or not. Neither group had a very extensive knowledge of works of art. They accepted the judgment of standard books of criticism with the result that the new movement in poetry and painting and dancing and architecture which marked the beginning of the twentieth century received neither encouragement nor understanding from the universities. These scholars talked of eternal beauty until their pupils—of whom the writer of this paper was one—began to wonder whether their discourse was not simply an excuse for neglecting temporal beauties. To read one of Santayana's books at that time was like listening to a man of the world who knew by acquaintance what the others simply knew by description. The style in which these works were written had a kind of distinction which, if it seems a bit Brahmin now, then seemed sensitive and right. Perhaps the author's air of remoteness, his very snobbishness, the authority and self-confidence with which he spoke of barbarians and Philistines, which to-day, when we suffer so terribly from uncertainty and insecurity, would be inexcusable, at that time of academic self-satisfaction seemed just what was wanted. We were not used to professors who saw that Lucretius and Dante and Goethe were poets as well as philological problems. When we read literary criticism, it had oozed out of the pens of Hamilton Wright Mabie and Henry Van Dyke. Courses in literature were a mixture of superficial biography and cautious eulogy. That there was a world of contemporary artistry going about its business beyond the campus was never mentioned; that the great classics, as they were called, had any reason for being beyond the fact that someone had called them great classics, never leaked out. Though Santayana seldom mentioned contemporaries, what he had to say about the great classics gave them a kind of vitality which was, to say the least, novel. If any one man is responsible for the contemporary sensitiveness to the arts in American university circles, it is this man. For, besides his writing on aesthetics, it turned out to be possible for him to appear in such a magazine as *The Dial*. That he should have gone on to produce a novel then caused no surprise; and, what is more, no raising of brows.

One of the secrets of Santayana's power as critic and philosopher of art lies in the threefold nature of his philosophy. A lesser man would have felt the necessity of "reconciling" the realms of matter, essence, and spirit. He would have reduced two of them to the third and left us a universe so neat and orderly that the world we live in would have become inexplicable. But he has the gift of recognizing diversity and, whether or not he has been pained by it, he has never attempted to explain it away. That has had its effect in his aesthetics as well as in his metaphysics.

George Boas

Department of Philosophy
The Johns Hopkins University

9

Philip Blair Rice

THE PHILOSOPHER AS POET AND CRITIC

9

THE PHILOSOPHER AS POET AND CRITIC

I. Poetic Theory

MR. SANTAYANA'S poetry deserves attention for its own sake, and for other reasons. Among these is that he is the only philosopher by vocation, at least in modern times, who has come close to achieving excellence as a poet. He can be expected, then, to bring a special kind of penetration to the discussion of the nature of poetry, and of philosophical poetry more particularly; and his own verse should offer a valuable testing ground for his principles.

Santayana began his poetic career with three handicaps which he did not entirely overcome: he was a philosopher, he was addicted to Platonism, and he lived in the United States at the end of the nineteenth century. These handicaps were greater, I suspect, than the one on which he himself lays most emphasis, that English was not his mother-tongue, that he "never drank in in childhood the homely cadences and ditties which in pure spontaneous poetry set the essential key," that he knew "no words redolent of the wonder-world, the fairy-tale, or the cradle."[1] This circumstance would bar to him a certain kind of lyricism, but I cannot believe that such a master of English prose as Santayana has suffered severely from the linguistic difficulty. The chief defects that show in his poetry are not defects of the ear or the tongue but of perception and imagination.

A profound acquaintance with philosophy is not necessarily detrimental to a poet; in fact Santayana argues persuasively that the greatest poetry is philosophical. Yet each pursuit has its exacting craft; and though the whole mind is enlisted in both cases, the emphasis, the method and the daily discipline are radically different. If the philosopher is addicted to Platonism,

[1] *Poems* (1923), viii.

even with Santayana's reservations, the handicap is more serious. In *The World's Body* John Crowe Ransom has argued, with plausibility, that it was a kind of Platonism, conscious or unconscious, that set English poetry on a wrong track, late in the seventeenth century, from which it has not altogether returned to the main highway.

If this view is correct, then Santayana's Platonism was simply a part of his third handicap, his time and place. In suggesting that to write poetry in English at the end of the nineteenth century was the gravest handicap of all, I am assuming the fundamental soundness of the revolution in the conception of poetry that has occurred in the last twenty or twenty-five years. Like most revolutions, this one has consisted partly in a return to an earlier state of affairs, real or imagined, and consequently in the repudiation of a vested heresy. Recent critics have written voluminously on the subject, but I shall summarize the latest and one of the most brilliant (although not perhaps the most judicious) treatments of it, Cleanth Brooks' in his book *Modern Poetry and the Tradition.* The heresy in question, as Brooks argues with documentation, was shared in greater or less degree by all the leading arbiters of poetic taste since and including Dryden: by Addison, Pope, Dr. Johnson, Wordsworth, Coleridge, Arnold, and latterly A. E. Housman. Its central assumption is that metaphor or imagery in a poem is primarily an illustration or an ornament. That is to say, that metaphor is not an integral structural part of the poem. The core of the poem, according to this view, consists in its "subject," which may be a Platonic idea, a moral direction, or an emotion. But in any of these cases the imagery is merely instrumental: it explains the idea, or renders the moral teaching palatable and persuasive, or sets the emotion vibrating.

In opposition to this conception of poetry, the moderns have returned to the faith of the Elizabethans and seventeenth century "metaphysicals" in the structural character of metaphor. As Mr. Brooks puts it, "We cannot remove the comparisons from their [the metaphysicals'] poems, as we might remove ornaments or illustrations attached to a statement, without demolishing the poems. The comparison *is* the poem in a structural sense."[2]

I shall not stop here to elucidate or to defend this view of poetry. Instead, I shall state, with this preparation, the thesis of the essay. Namely, that Santayana, in his theory of poetry, and to a scarcely less extent in his criticism, was ahead of, or, if you prefer, in a certain sense behind, his time; that, with his wide knowledge of literature and his sure taste, he perceived many of the errors in the prevailing conception of poetry. If this were all, his writings would be of merely historical interest. I believe, however, that Santayana's statement of his poetics, despite certain omissions and mistaken emphases, is in many respects superior to those now current, and possesses the further advantage of being firmly grounded in his general philosophy. Finally I shall try to show that in his poetry he was less able to escape the limitations of his time, and that, as he is well aware, his verse falls below the requirements of his poetic theory not only in scope but in quality.

Santayana's theory of poetry was given its most summary statement in the essay, "The Elements and Functions of Poetry," published as Chapter X of *Interpretations of Poetry and Religion* (1900). The elements or functions of poetry are classified as four: "euphony," "euphuism," what we may call experimental immediacy, and what we may call rational imagination. Euphony is the most rudimentary and indispensable element; but poetry rises in the scale of value as it progressively incorporates the other three.

Euphony is defined as "the sensuous beauty of words and their utterance in measure."[3] All the arts, according to *Reason in Art*, originate in spontaneous impulse. At its beginning vocal utterance was sheer automatism, without ulterior purpose; that speech could be representative and could be used for purposes of communication was a later discovery, even though a very early one: "Memorable nonsense, or sound with a certain hypnotic power, is the really primitive and radical form of poetry,"[4]

[2] *Modern Poetry and the Tradition*, 15.

[3] *Interpretations of Poetry and Religion*, 257.

[4] *Reason in Art*, 90.

and poetry retains something of this character in its most developed state. *The Sense of Beauty* treated the aesthetic object as an organic whole analyzable into the three aspects of material, form, and expression. Euphony consists of the intrinsic pleasingness of the material of poetry, sound, but of sounds in relation to each other. That is to say, it is dependent on "form" as well as "material." And the form itself, as we shall see, is conditioned by the "expression."

It may be rather surprising that Santayana should dignify as a second element what he calls euphuism, "the choice of colored words and rare and elliptical phrases."[5] His own verse is not markedly precious, especially when it is compared with that of his contemporaries. That he should single out this quality is nevertheless revealing. Pope's verse, he says, although euphonious is not euphuistic; the Symbolists, on the other hand, exploited this element almost exclusively. Now in Santayana's student days and for several years after, the aesthetic fashion among the more advanced young men in Boston and New York, as well as in England, was Symbolism.[6] During these years, as M. Taupin says, America began to wish to acquire an artistic conscience. The Symbolist school was formed in Paris about 1880, and claimed for its own several writers of the previous generation, such as Baudelaire and Rimbaud, whom it was far from comprehending. As usually happens in such cases, the propagandists for the movement carried as their banners only the masters' outermost garments. The movement became more attenuated when it was acclimatized to England by Arthur Symons, and again progressively when it reached America. It is significant that Santayana's Harvard acquaintances and first publishers, Stone and Kimball, were the founders of the *Chap Book*, the movement's American organ.

The French writers who were advertised under the Symbolist label stood for the most diverse tendencies. The tendency which was most widely acclaimed was a continuation of one of the main strands of romanticism. It aimed to heighten and purify the emotional quality of poetry, and the emotion most prized was

[5] *Interpretations of Poetry and Religion*, 257.

[6] René Taupin, *L'Inflence du Symbolisme Français sur la Poésie Américaine.*

the "sense of mystery." The symbol, that is the concrete imagery of the poem, was not an end in itself nor a structural factor in the poem; its function, like that of the Imagination according to Wordsworth, was to suggest "the plastic, the pliant, and the indefinite." Euphuism, as Santayana defined it, would appear to be a purely verbal quality. It is evident, however, that Santayana is associating it with the Wordsworthian-Symbolist conception of the imagination when he goes on to say that euphuism takes us "out of the merely verbal into the imaginative region."[7]

Verse that is compacted of euphony and euphuism has its charm, according to Santayana, but it is poetry at rather a low level. It is in part his emphasis on the third element, which I have called experiential immediacy, that makes his conception of poetry akin to that of the better Symbolists, the metaphysicals and their twentieth century disciples. Poetry "has body; it represents the volume of experience as well as its form."[8] Whereas scientific prose seeks to establish and use conventional symbols, poetry "breaks up the trite conceptions designated by current words into the sensuous qualities out of which these conceptions were originally put together." It seeks "the many living impressions which the intellect rejected," and labors with the "nameless burden of perception."

> Our logical thoughts dominate experience only as the parallels and meridians make a checker-board of the sea. . . . Sanity is a madness put to good uses; waking life is a dream controlled. Out of the neglected riches of this dream the poet fetches his wares. He dips into the chaos that underlies the rational shell of the world and brings up some superfluous image, some emotion dropped by the way, and reattaches it to the present object; he reinstates things unnecessary, he emphasizes things ignored, he paints in again into the landscape the tints which the intellect has allowed to fade from it. If he seems sometimes to obscure a fact, it is only because he is restoring an experience.[9]

This is similar to the *dérèglement raisonné* of Rimbaud and Corbière, the dissociation preached by Rémy de Gourmont. It enriches the affective qualities of the poem, and on occasion can

[7] *Interpretations of Poetry and Religion*, 258.

[8] *Reason in Art*, 98.

[9] *Interpretations of Poetry and Religion*, 259-261.

correct the partial perspective of the scientific vision. But it does not represent the highest organization of which poetry is capable. The unifying factor at this level is feeling:

> The poet's art is to a great extent the art of intensifying emotions by assembling the scattered objects that naturally arouse them. . . . By this union of disparate things having a common overtone of feeling, the feeling is itself evoked in all its strength; nay, it is often created for the first time.[10]

The ultimate end of poetry is more than the accomplishment of a mystical disintegration, which would be its tendency if it remained here. The poet's analysis of experience into its immediate elements is for the sake of creation. Santayana's discussion of the fourth element, which I have called rational imagination, is not wholly satisfactory; the essentials of a complete theory are here, but they are not fully developed, and he includes so many things under this function that the result is a certain confusion. His definition of it is:

> to repair to the material of experience, seizing hold of the reality of sensation and fancy beneath the surface of conventional ideas, and then out of that living but indefinite material to build new structures, richer, finer, fitter to the primary tendencies of our nature, truer to the ultimate possibilities of the soul.[11]

The last phrase indicates at once the moral function of poetry, and it may even suggest that Santayana is saying that poetry must aim, in some direct and obvious way, at prettifying the world, at remolding it nearer to the heart's desire. Further scrutiny of his theory shows that this is not the case. He is referring in this definition to two, or perhaps three, aspects of poetry which are not wholly separable but which it is useful to distinguish more explicitly than he does. One we may call imaginative structure, in a sense in which it is an element of any fully realized poem. The second is the logical structure; the third is the moral or ideal import, which only the prophetic kind of poetry possesses in high degree.

Santayana is saying here that poetry can have more structure

[10] *Ibid.*, 263.
[11] *Ibid.*, 270.

than is supplied by a unity of feeling. The differentiation of the feelings themselves "depends on the variety of the objects of experience,—that is, on the differentiation of the senses and of the environment which stimulates them."[12] Feeling and imagination must be fed by sense-experience, and they remake their materials into a form that is as concrete as sense-experience itself. The glorious emotions with which a child or a poet bubbles over "must at all hazards find or feign their *correlative objects*."[13] The phrase which I have italicized will at once remind the reader who is versed in contemporary criticism of T. S. Eliot's rather barbarous key phrase (which he may very well have adapted from Santayana's better one), the "objective correlative" of an emotion; to find this is the chief business of poetry as poetry. The poem possesses full structural unity only when it has been achieved.

Such a notion is required by Santayana's definition of beauty or aesthetic value in *The Sense of Beauty:* "value positive, intrinsic and objectified. Or, in less technical language, Beauty is pleasure regarded as the quality of a thing."[14] The important word here is "objectified;" the questionable one is "pleasure" or "value." I am not questioning primarily the equation of value with pleasure; Santayana's developed theory of value makes many of the necessary qualifications. The disputable point is whether it is exclusively the pleasure (or value) that is objectified. If so, we are landed in a Romantic-Symbolist theory of art; art is the expression of feeling. By objectification Santayana means this: although the pleasure exists only in the act of perception, it exists as if in the object. Later in the same book the author presents a somewhat different and better view of what is objectified. This is explained in his theory of "expression," the third ingredient of the aesthetic object in addition to material and form. Santayana makes a very important distinction between "expressiveness" and "expression." He uses "expressiveness" to designate all the capacity of association or suggestion possessed by an ideal or symbol; as such it is not

[12] *Ibid.*, 278.
[13] *Ibid.*, 277.
[14] *The Sense of Beauty*, 49.

necessarily a function of aesthetic experience. "Expression," on the other hand, is limited to those suggestions or associations which are "incorporated in the present object."[15] It includes values, but more, for it includes other elements of meaning together with their values. Such meanings must be compressed into the immediate experience if the object is an aesthetic one rather than the occasion for a sentimental reverie.

What, then, is the aesthetic object in the case of a poem? Santayana's essay on the elements and functions of poetry gives us some clues. The correlative object, at rather a low level of invention, consists of the characters of the poem; at a somewhat higher level, of the figures against their physical and historical background, or the cosmic landscape; the poem is still more highly organized when it has a plot, when the characters belong to an imagined society, and move within a dramatic situation, implied or enacted. There are other possibilities before we go on. Santayana might have put in somewhere in this list a single physical object, such as Keats' Grecian urn or Marvell's garden, which focuses the poem and supplies a structure through its ramifications for experience. It is such imagined referents of the significant sounds in the poem, I believe, that constitute the phenomenal world, or segment of a world, recreated in the experience of the poem. The referent of the poem, in a famous one by Yeats, is at most a pseudo-Byzantium, and it may not copy very closely any real Byzantium that ever existed; but it should have the same *kind* of structure for experience as a real city, or it does not have the characteristically poetic structure. This is the gist of the distinction between poetry and music. Music in its sound patterns objectifies nothing if not the structure and quality of an emotional experience itself. Poetry, on the other hand, projects at a psychic distance an imaginatively reconstructed, particular referent—the garden, the urn, the pseudo-Byzantium, the court of Elsinore, Dante's whole imagined universe yearning for its imagined creator—in which the sounds and feelings have their locus. In a certain sense, poetry is an "impure" art: the poetic object is not, like the musical object, a mere pattern of sounds with their incorporated feelings. It

[15] *Ibid.*, 198.

contains two kinds of sensory elements, the sounds and the non-auditory images of which they are the signs. The non-auditory imagery constitutes the primary object, but it retains and fuses with the sounds themselves, which are not mere signs but enter reflexively into the complex referent. The poet's success in reinforcing the imagery with the sound is the measure of his success in exploiting his medium.

The "poetic object," or complex referent, must embody the logical implications or moral attitudes or socio-political directions of the poem, when it has any of these. The poem, we can say, may refer to universals as well as particulars, but the universals must exist *in re*, in the concrete experience of the poem, and not merely *ante rem* in the mind of the poet or *post rem* in the reflection of the reader.

Such a view of the poetic object is required, as I shall try to show, by Santayana's critical practice, although it does not rereceive adequate statement in his poetic theory.

It is through the act of the imagination, so conceived, that poetry may achieve its ideal function. The poet becomes a prophet, Santayana holds, when he "portrays the ideals of experience and destiny."[16] But this function is not accomplished exclusively through imagining Utopias, or even through feasible enhancements of the existing reality. Tragedy gives us a "glimpse into the ultimate destinies of our will;" through its invocation of a cosmic order, it creates the "sense of a finished life, of the will fulfilled and enlightened."[17] At its highest reaches poetry is metaphysical or religious in character: "The imagination . . . must furnish to religion and to metaphysics those large ideas tinctured with passion, those supersensible forms shrouded in awe, in which alone a mind of great sweep and vitality can find its congenial objects."[18] So far as their rational function is concerned, poetry and religion at their final limit of development become identical. Both are best when they are true as well as imaginative: "The highest ideality is the comprehension of the real."[19]

[16] *Interpretations of Poetry and Religion*, 286.

[17] *Ibid.* 281.

[18] *Ibid.*, 6.

[19] *Ibid.*, 284.

II. Poetic Practice

Santayana's theory must have been influenced by his poetic practice, as well as by his reading of other poets and by his general philosophy. Since he is a conscious artist, his poems in turn must have been subjected to scrutiny in the light of his principles. No genuine poet writes poems to exemplify a theory, but his theory can modify his attitude toward experience, can exercise suasion over the process of revision, can determine which poems he will publish and which he will withhold.

Within limits, Santayana is a skilful workman in respect of all that he includes under euphony—meter, rhyme, prosody. G. W. Howgate in his book *George Santayana* has made a very patient and sensitive analysis of such aspects of his poetry, and has treated them so thoroughly that I shall merely allude to them here. In a comparatively small total output of verse, Santayana has mastered a large variety of stanza forms and rhyme schemes, and even a considerable number of meters. In particular, he has used creatively his favorite form, the Petrarchan sonnet, achieving invention while remaining strict. Even in his schoolboy efforts we can see that he learned well what the Latin poets, and especially the satirists, seen through the English neoclassical tradition, had to teach: his language is always at least "felicitous," in the better sense of that word, and his joinery is neat. His formalism, however, often leads him to pad his lines with superfluous adjectives in phrases. While his phrasing never becomes in a high degree creative, it is usually precise. He uses words that poets have used before, or that one feels they might have used, and the context rarely elicits new or unexpected shades of meaning from them. Within the limits of a vocabulary that is almost completely bookish—that draws nothing from colloquial usage or linguistic experimentation—his language is free from the imitativeness of the dull poet; the phrase strikes one as hackneyed less often than its component words.

His musical effects rarely achieve more than well-patterned simple melody. They are varied enough to save the poem from monotony, and there is some degree of internal alliteration, assonance and consonance, although not enough to produce a strong illusion of musical counterpoint. With a marked preference for long vowels and liquid consonants, he avoids the poetic equivalent of musical discords and their resolutions, and prefers the smooth rhythm to the more complex and powerful one. Very infrequently does he attempt a harsh consonant effect or a plunging rhythm as in the opening of Sonnet XXVIII:

> The brackish depths of the blown waters bear
> Blossoms of foam. . . .

—perhaps because he knows that he cannot manage it superlatively. (I am impelled to juxtapose by way of contrast Yeats' line: "Arraigned, constrained, baffled, bent and unbent.")

I am not suggesting that Santayana should have tried to impose on his verse a richer and denser texture than it has. His music is altogether adequate to the imaginative structure of the poems, which is fundamentally simple, and he does not commit the errors in taste of many Elizabethan, Romantic and modern poets who try, by tricks of rhythm and sound, to give their verse a greater musical complexity than its imaginative framework and thought demand. Santayana's thought, as I shall try to show later, could well manifest itself in a more elaborate imaginative structure, but that is beside the present point.

His limitations are not primarily defects of euphony and euphuism, but of experiential immediacy and imaginative structure. This can best be shown by confronting the poetry itself. I shall choose Sonnet I from his longest sequence:

> I sought on earth a garden of delight,
> Or island altar to the Sea and Air,
> Where gentle music were accounted prayer,
> And reason, veiled, performed the happy rite.
> My sad youth worshipped at the piteous height
> Where God vouchsafed the death of man to share;
> His love made mortal sorrow light to bear,
> But his deep wounds put joy to shamèd flight.
> And though his arms, outstretched upon the tree,
> Were beautiful, and pleaded my embrace,
> My sins were loth to look upon his face.
> So came I down from Golgotha to thee,

Eternal Mother; let the sun and sea
Heal me, and keep me in thy dwelling-place.

This is one of Santayana's most interesting sonnets, although not one of his most nearly perfect. The intellectual content is more important than in many better poems. The "gentle music" of the first quatrain itself is appropriate to the theme; and in the last line the tonal quality and the repetition of the long vowel "e," with the resultant slowing of the rhythm, bring the poem to the kind of consummation that the thought demands.

Suppose, however, that one should come back to it immediately after reading these lines from Donne's third *Satyre:*

On a huge hill,
Cragged, and steep, Truth stands, and he that will
Reach her, about must, and about must goe;
And what the hills suddennes resists, winne so;

If this is compared with the second quatrain of the sonnet, the two are perceived to have certain similarities. In both, the theme is the search for religious faith, the "correlative object" is a hill, and the hill of Golgotha (for Donne is talking about the Truth of the Christian religion). The most striking difference in treatment is that Santayana tells us about the hill: Donne takes us there. We fall in behind him and try to climb it with him. The words "huge hill" themselves confront us with an obstacle; "Cragged, and steep, Truth stands" gives us its topography and its toilsomeness; the next line sets us at the obdurate ascent, not only by its rhythm but through the dramatic suggestions condensed in the words "about must, and about must:" the attitude is that of a weary but determined man. The phrase "And what the hills suddennes resists" likewise gives us the *object as experienced.* The tempo quickens at the beginning of the line, only to check us with the two stressed syllables "hills sud-" and to jolt us on the three following short syllables, bringing us up finally at the syllable "-sists," the whole managed with as much lashing by sibilants and grinding by double and triple consonants as we can bear. These effects would not give the line its power, if they were not fused with the dramatic suggestions of the word "suddennes." This is not the most exact word to describe literally the object as it is in itself—"steepness" or "sheerness" would be scientifically more accurate—but it is the right word to describe the hill for us; and its very unexpectedness creates the shock of coming up against a blank wall of stone. (It is a coincidence that Santayana has used an almost identical phrase in his fifth Sapphic Ode: "saw thy sudden mountains," but not with Donne's evocation of the three dimensions of space and the dimension of time.) Donne has conveyed the body of experience here as well as its content;

> . . . e la presente
> È viva, e il suon di lei.

The shortcoming of Santayana's poem does not consist in a failure to find concrete symbols for the experience. The garden, the hill, and the seashore are at least potentially appropriate images here, even though their particular qualities are not fully elicited. The structural use that is made of them is somewhat confusing, however. In a Petrarchan sonnet, one expects the principal structural units, as set by the rhyme scheme, to be the octet and sestet. So strongly does the convention of the Petrarchan form, as well as its logic, establish this expectation, that when I first read the sonnet I took the first quatrain, in conjunction with the second, to refer to a kind of aesthetic Christianity, whereas, of course, even a slightly less casual reading shows that the "garden" of the first quatrain is the pagan paradise by the sea of the last tercet. The structure of the poem, both logical and imaginative, divides therefore not 8-6 like the rhyme scheme but 4-7-3, with lines 1-4 and 12-14 forming a unit contrasted with lines 5-11. This defect is not explained away by the fact that the poem is the introductory one in a sequence of twenty, and that the first quatrain states the theme of the entire sequence. So I cannot overcome the conviction that the sonnet would have been better organized if the poet had been able to make lines 5-11 into the octet, and had put the rest into the sestet.

Although the structure is imperfect, the "correlative object"

—the descent from Golgotha to the sea—is valid for the ideas of the poem. That the poem is an adequate representation of Santayana's own spiritual experience is unlikely. I do not believe that the lines "But his deep wounds put joy to shamèd flight" and "My sins were loth to look upon his face" report accurately Santayana's rejection of Christianity, which was not an act of moral evasion. His true spiritual autobiography might have been more valuable, but apparently he could not find imaginative terms for it, or else found the form Procrustean, and so he let the poem follow its own process of growth. A little later I shall suggest what may be the fundamental reason for the inadequacy of Santayana's poetry to his philosophy.

Although experiential immediacy is wanting generally in his poems, a very large proportion of them have a structural use of the correlative object. Sonnet II, for example, achieves the specific organization of the Petrarchan sonnet:

Slow and reluctant was the long descent,
With many farewell pious looks behind,
And dumb misgivings where the path might wind,
And questionings of nature, as I went.
The greener branches that above me bent,
The broadening valleys, quieted my mind,
To the fair reasons of the Spring inclined
And to the Summer's tender argument.
But sometimes, as revolving night descended,
And in my childish heart the new song ended,
I lay down, full of longing, on the steep;
And, haunting still the lonely way I wended,
Into my dreams the ancient sorrow blended,
And with these holy echoes charmed my sleep.

The prosody here is also more consistently fused with the other elements than in the first sonnet.

Other sonnets in the sequence, such as IV, XII, XIII, XIV, XV, XVI, XIX, and XX, are equally strict in their organization. In some, however, such as VI and IX, the connection between octet and sestet is logical rather than imaginative. Still others are even less unified: Sonnet XI, for example, divides structurally into 8-2-2-2, and Sonnet V, organized 4-4-4-2, might have been better in the Shakespearean form. By way of compromise, however, it is rhymed *abbaabbaccdcdd*, ending with a couplet. In general, I think that Santayana is as strict in this respect as most of the great sonneteers; and his achievement of imaginative structure leads one to wonder why he did not place more stress on it in his theory.

The connections between the poems, as usually and tolerably in a sonnet sequence, are loose. The sequence is given some semblance of organization, however, in addition to the logical connections, by the motif of the descent, and by such thematic repetitions as in these lines from X, with their reference to the imagery of Sonnet I:

> Doth the sun therefore burn, that I may bask?
> Or do the tirèd earth and tireless sea,
> That toil not for their pleasure, toil for me?

The thought in this sequence is not too complex for the poet's imaginative resources; there is, however, metaphysical subtlety if not superlative poetry, in this passage:

> O martyred spirit of this helpless Whole,
> Who dost by pain for tyranny atone,
> And in the star, the atom, and the stone,
> Purgest the primal guilt, and in the soul.[20]

And the thought at times rises to such greatness that the simple and direct, although not always fresh, imagery is charged with the burden of high poetry;

> The soul is not on earth an alien thing
> That hath her life's rich sources otherwhere;
> She is a parcel of the sacred air.
> She takes her being from the breath of Spring,
> The glance of Phoebus is her fount of light,
> And her long sleep a draught of primal night.[21]

The best poems of this sequence, along with a few others, represent the peaks of Santayana's achievement. Among his other outstanding poems, "Cape Cod" strikes an unusual note

[20] Sonnet VIII.
[21] Sonnet XX.

of direct perception and has an exquisite music; slight as it is, it might be taken as Santayana's most flawless poem. "Sybaris" has decadent magic; "Avila" and "King's College Chapel" have fine passages which should earn them a secure place in the poetry of our language. In the third and fifth of his odes in an adaptation of the Sapphic stanza, Santayana achieves that topographical sense, that evocation of the historical and cosmic background, which he so much admired in Homer and which he ranked high in the list of structural devices. The unity is achieved in the two cases by the symbols of the American continent and of the Mediterranean, respectively. The poems are also among the best expressions of his naturalism and his social criticism.

Santayana's longer pieces, the essay in philosophical drama *Lucifer* and the narrative poem *Hermit of Carmel*, are much less successful. The poet is not able consistently to create dramatic characters or situations, the plot of *Lucifer* is ill-knit, and the versification often falls to the level of the usual academic translation of a Greek tragedy. *Lucifer* nevertheless has its fine passages which repay the reading of it.

The crucial question concerning the relation between Santayana's poetry and his philosophy is best treated by examining his second sonnet sequence, XXI-L. This contains several splendid poems, of which I should choose especially XXIV, XXXV, XLII and XLIX, and many memorable passages besides. A few possess a dramatic structure which Santayana failed to achieve in the other sequence; of these XXIV is, I believe, the best, though the first part of it is not remarkable:

> Although I decked a chamber for my bride,
> And found a moonlit garden for the tryst
> Wherein all flowers looked happy as we kissed,
> Hath the deep heart of me been satisfied?
> The chasm 'twixt our spirits yawns as wide
> Though our lips meet, and clasp thee as I list,
> The something perfect that I love is missed,
> And my warm worship freezes into pride.
> But why—O waywardness of nature!—why
> Seek farther in the world? I had my choice,

And we said we were happy, you and I.
Why in the forest should I hear a cry,
Or in the sea an unavailing voice,
Or feel a pang to look upon the sky?

This illustrates the principal theme of the sequence, which is dominated by Santayana's "Platonism," whereas the first sequence was primarily an expression of his paganism or naturalism. The sequence as a whole is more derivative and artificial than the first sequence, echoing the Italian poets whom he was reading at that time. It is also less adequate to its philosophical theme. The Platonic tradition, with its distrust of the senses, its worship of the abstract, is fundamentally anti-poetic; and Plato was quite consistent, great poet though he was, in excluding the poets from his ideal state.

Now Santayana's own philosophy is only metaphorically Platonic. His essences are not existences (except when they are embodied) but mere possibilities. And values or ideals for him belong only incidentally to the realm of essence. During the time when he wrote these sonnets, he was engaged in working out his theory of value, which is closer to Spinoza than to orthodox Platonism (if one excepts the *Philebus* and *Statesman* from orthodoxy). Values, as Santayana conceives them, are expressions of the living preferences of the organism. They are grounded in our irrational impulses, and represent an organization, purification and projection by reason and imagination of our spontaneous interests. The "things eternal" that Santayana celebrates in his poetry are sometimes mere essences—any characters whatever seen under the form of eternity—and sometimes the reflections in the realm of essence of moral ideals. In his philosophy, moreover, we are constantly reminded of the foundation of values in the realm of matter or nature. It is, in fact, precisely his explanation of the emergence of the ideal from the natural that constitutes the great originality of his theory of value, and the great superiority of his system to most other naturalisms and idealisms. In the sonnets, however, this natural basis of the ideal, and the irony and wonder of the emergence of values, are almost completely ignored. Instead of finding images that would express the dialectical intricacies of his own system, he is content to use the vehicles of traditional literary Platonism. The semantic scheme of the poetry then becomes as follows: the imagery of the poem symbolizes traditional Platonism, and traditional Platonism in turn becomes a symbol for Santayana's heretical Platonism. This will not do. In philosophical poetry, as in all poetry, the symbol must take us directly to its referent.

Santayana indeed never felt altogether at home with the Platonizers. In the original version of his essay, *Platonism in the Italian Poets* (1896), there is a revealing passage which was unhappily omitted when the essay was reprinted in *Interpretations of Poetry and Religion:*

> As for me, when I read the words of those inspired men and try to understand the depths of experience which is buried in them as in a marble tomb, I feel, I confess, very far away from them. I wonder if all their exaltation is not the natural illusion of a hope too great for any man; but at the same time I remember the story of Ruth and how she was impressed by that so strange and so passionate Jewish race into which she had come,—a race that lived on prophecy and hope, and believed in its transcendent destiny—and I envy her that she found it in her heart to say, what I would gladly say to the family of Plato, "Let thy people be my people and thy God my God."

Santayana himself always remained amid alien corn.

Especially conspicuous in his poetry is the absence of a quality that pervades his prose writings: irony. This consideration can supply, I believe, the principal answer to the question why Santayana's poetic vision is not as full and just as his philosophic vision. Cleanth Brooks, in the book I have cited, takes irony, or its synonym wit, to be the essential quality of metaphysical poetry. (He goes on to make it the essence of poetry *überhaupt,* which is an exaggeration.) Metaphysical poetry, through its exploration of all the ramifications of its object, achieves a synthesis of the most discordant and heterogeneous qualities. A mature apprehension of those things which we prize includes a recognition of their partial absurdity, ugliness and evil. These aspects are included in and heighten the total effect of the experience, just as an adult love includes, is even given an edge by, a full consciousness of the lady's blemishes. Santayana, however, turned away from his not wholly satisfactory bride to a heavenly one. The dominant tradition of the eighteenth and nineteenth centuries excluded the trivial and tainted aspects of experience from serious and ideal poetry, relegating them to the inferior sphere of "fancy," and recommending that the poetic imagination select an unqualifiedly beautiful or noble subject matter. (Plato here, as so often elsewhere, was better than the Platonists: in the *Parmenides* he makes fun of the young Socrates for refusing to admit Ideas of hair and filth.) In this respect Santayana's poetry is very much limited by its time. I am surprised to find no mention anywhere in Santayana of the English metaphysicals, since the quality of his own mind, as exhibited in his prose, is so much akin to theirs. It is agreeable to fancy how Donne or Marvell would have made this essentially poetic insight into a poem:

> Scepticism is the chastity of the intellect, and it is shameful to surrender it too soon or to the first comer: there is nobility in preserving it coolly and proudly through a long youth, until at last, in the ripeness of instinct and discretion, it can be safely exchanged for fidelity and happiness.[22]

Or this: "The tight opinionated present feels itself inevitably to be the center and judge of the universe; and the poor human soul walks in a dream through the paradise of truth, as a child might run blindly through a smiling garden, hugging a paper flower."[23]

The first quotation is from *Scepticism and Animal Faith*, the second from *The Realm of Truth*. Since such passages bloom everywhere in his later writings, I can only conclude that Santayana's poetic imagination became fully developed long after he had ceased to write verse. For his philosophic vision is also a poetic vision.

III. Critical Practice

Despite its unique merits, Santayana's verse could not conceivably alter the main currents of literary tendency. His criticism, on the other hand, has already had a considerable if quiet

[22] *Scepticism and Animal Faith*, 69-70.
[23] *The Realm of Truth*, 58.

influence on the critical fraternity. The time may not have come for it to be most profitably absorbed by creative writers or even by critics themselves. Poetry at the beginning of this century was not ready for the kind of guidance that Santayana had to offer. It needed to be rebuilt from the ground up. The influential criticism of the past two or three decades, that which helped to shape the creative movement in poetry, has been technical analysis of a closeness without precedent. The sustained attention to the craft of poetry which was called for could not have been found in Santayana's writings. Although he is not, like most philosophical critics of literature, insensitive to matters of technique, he has placed the emphasis elsewhere, on the intellectual and ethical attitudes which control the poet's sensibility and imagination. These considerations abstract from the total experience of the poem, and they are best discussed in close connection with its other aspects. Yet a complete analysis of any important work cannot omit them. The critic who approaches the poem from the technical side is forced, if he is thorough, to come to grips with philosophical issues, and for this his equipment is usually poor. The man of letters can learn much from a master moralist like Santayana, who has derived many of his most penetrating insights from literature itself.

Contemporary critics often exaggerate the extent to which the imaginative structure of the poem is independent of its logical structure, just as recent poets too often fail to make the poem a logical as well as imaginative unit. For purposes of analysis it is useful to separate the two types of structure, as I have done, yet a treatment of the imaginative in isolation from the logical may be just as dangerous an abstraction as the reverse. Such is Santayana's assumption. In the essay, "The Poetry of Barbarism" (*Interpretations of Poetry and Religion*), he insists that the poetry of the late nineteenth century must be treated in relation to both "the general moral crisis and the imaginative disintegration of which it gives a verbal echo."[24] The classic and Christian traditions had split apart at the time of the Renaissance, and in the succeeding centuries each went far toward

[24] *Interpretations of Poetry and Religion*, 169.

dissolution, without a new discipline having taken form to replace them. Santayana writes in 1900:

> We find our contemporary poets incapable of any high wisdom, incapable of any imaginative rendering of human life and its meaning. Our poets are things of shreds and patches; they give us episodes and studies, a sketch of this curiosity, a glimpse of that romance; they have no total vision, no grasp of the whole reality, and consequently no capacity for a sane and steady idealization. The comparatively barbarous ages had a poetry of the ideal; they had visions of beauty, order and perfection. This age of material elaboration has no sense for those things. Its fancy is retrospective, whimsical, and flickering; its ideals, when it has any, are negative and partial; its moral strength is a blind and miscellaneous vehemence. Its poetry, in a word, is the poetry of barbarism.[25]

Santayana's rigorous standards do not lead him, as they often led the neo-humanists who claimed him somewhat doubtfully as an ally, to deny all merit to those writers whom he considers "barbarians." Even a decadent literature has its charms and its characteristic insights. His treatment in particular of Whitman—who is almost the anti-poet by Santayana's criteria—is remarkably sympathetic, and a far juster estimate than had been achieved by any other critic at that time:

> Full of sympathy and receptivity, with a wonderful gift of graphic characterization and an occasional rare grandeur of diction, he fills us with a sense of the individuality and the universality of what he describes—it is a drop in itself yet a drop in the ocean. The absence of any principle of selection or of a sustained style enables him to render aspects of things and of emotion which would have eluded a trained writer. He is, therefore, interesting even where he is grotesque or perverse. He has accomplished, by the sacrifice of almost every other good quality, something never so well done before.[26]

Whitman's disregard for the craft of poetry, Santayana suggests, is wholly appropriate to his theme: "There is clearly some analogy between a mass of images without structure and the notion of an absolute democracy."[27] What Whitman digs up

[25] *Ibid.*, 168-169.
[26] *Ibid.*, 180-181.
[27] *Ibid.*, 181.

is the raw material of poetry rather than poetry itself. And his failure of imagination is associated with an intellectual defect, his failure to perceive the direction of the essential America that he was trying to express. Even around 1900 he was appreciated chiefly by Europeans, and because he gave them a caricature of America that fitted in with their preconceptions of it. The Jacksonian democracy that Whitman celebrated was not, as he believed, the "promise of the future" but the "survival of the past." Nor did Whitman succeed better in becoming the poet of the common man, from whom nothing is further than "the corrupt desire to be primitive," or the poet of the poor, who seek in the arts a picture of the form of life to which they aspire and not a representation of their present indignity. Santayana's whole discussion of Whitman, like his study of Shelley, deserves careful attention, among other reasons for his anticipation of recent politico-social criticism and also for his avoidance of the fallacies of its cruder practitioners.

To genteel literary circles at the beginning of the century, it would have been a severe shock to find Browning listed with Whitman as a poet of barbarism. If the net effect of Santayana's criticism was to raise Whitman to some extent above prevailing estimates, it supplied on the other hand a needed deflation of Browning. This despite the fact that Santayana on the whole rates Browning higher as a poet than Whitman, with whom disintegration had gone much farther. He calls Browning a great writer, a great imaginative force, and a master in the expression of emotion. But he continues: "What is not perhaps so obvious, but no less true, is that we are in the presence of a barbaric genius, of a truncated imagination, of a thought and an art inchoate and ill-digested, of a volcanic eruption that tosses itself quite blindly and ineffectually into the sky."[28] Browning's style, he says, is turgid except for brilliant flashes, his characters are mere sketches, neither his verse forms nor his dramatic structure are fully achieved. His moral and theological ideas are of course easy game for Santayana. Both this aspect of his poetry and his chief technical deficiencies are attributed by Santayana to the lack of a "rational imagination." Browning's art

[28] *Ibid.*, 189.

was in the service of the will. He had not attained, in studying the beauty of things, that detachment of the phenomenon, that love of the form for its own sake, which is the secret of contemplative satisfaction. . . . He was too much in earnest in his fictions, he threw himself too unreservedly into his creations. His imagination, like the imagination we have in dreams, was merely a vent for personal preoccupations. His art was inspired by purposes less simple and universal than the ends of imagination itself.[29]

Santayana did not fear to subject Shakespeare to an equally searching scrutiny, in the two essays, "On the Absence of Religion in Shakespeare" (1896) and "Hamlet" (1908). These were written at a time when a blind Shakespeareolatry was more prevalent than it is now, and when A. C. Bradley was convincing a considerable section of the scholarly public that Shakespeare was a great philosopher. Santayana does not call Shakespeare a barbarian, as did the pseudo-classicist Voltaire; he pays him due tribute as the poet who has given fullest expression to the many-sidedness of human nature, with the greatest variety in "style, sentiment and accent." He even indicates that he would choose the works of Shakespeare if he were allowed to select the one monument of civilization that was to survive to a future age; they contain "the truest portrait and best memorial of man."[30] Yet the memorial, he argues, would not be complete; Shakespeare's is the world of human society, largely cut off from its cosmic background and lacking a coherent view of life's significance and destiny. Shakespeare lived in a time when the religion of Western man and his culture had taken separate paths, and more especially in Northern Europe. Hamlet, if he also "expresses a conflict to which every soul is more or less liable,"[31] is peculiarly the symbol of human genius since the Renaissance; mature in the development of his separate faculties, he has youth's inability to unify them in a harmony of thought, feeling, and action. The Christian symbols in Shakespeare could no longer serve for more than incidental ornament, and since no new system had been achieved in their

[29] *Ibid.*, 194.
[30] *Ibid.*, 147.
[31] "Hamlet," in *Obiter Scripta*, 61.

place, the result is a fundamental chaos of the imagination: "What is required for theoretic wholeness is not this or that system but some system. Its value is not the value of truth, but that of victorious imagination. *Unity of conception is an aesthetic merit no less than a logical demand.*"[32] Recent scholarship, such as that of Caroline Spurgeon and G. Wilson Knight, has shown that Shakespeare's imagery supplied more of a pattern than Santayana discerned, but this type of unity is similar to that supplied by the Wagnerian leitmotiv; although it is a useful adjunct in literature, it cannot be relied upon to supply the principal structural element in poetry, or even the chief orchestration of the dramatic structure.

Santayana's fullest exposition of his idea of a rational poetry is *Three Philosophical Poets* (1910). The reasonings and investigations of philosophy, he says, are not poetic (although in *Interpretations of Poetry and Religion*, as in *The Life of Reason*, he had said that the distinction between intelligence and imagination is not absolute, that all scientific and philosophical ideas are imaginative in origin and function); where poetry and philosophy meet is in their vision. Both have fullness, suggestion, compression, perspective. Poetry is poetical not for its brevity but for its scope and depth. Give it these qualities in greater measure, "focus all experience within it, make it a philosopher's vision of the world, and it will grow imaginative in a superlative degree, and be supremely poetical."[33] The form of poetry should not be thrown over the substance of prose; Santayana objects to Lucretius' comparison of philosophical poetry to the mixture of wormwood with honey that physicians administer to small boys. The philosophical poet's problem,

> after having enough experience to symbolize, lies only in having enough imagination to hold and suspend it in a thought [in an image?]; and further to give this thought such verbal expression that others may be able to decipher it, and to be stirred by it as by a wind of suggestion sweeping the whole forest of their memories.[34]

[32] *Interpretations of Poetry and Religion*, 164 (italics mine).
[33] *Three Philosophical Poets*, 13-14.
[34] *Ibid.*, 14.

The detailed studies of Lucretius, Dante, and Goethe do not carry out this approach in as sustained a manner as one might wish. Santayana's analysis is devoted more to discovering and evaluating the philosophical ideas presupposed and implied by the poems than to exhibiting their imaginative realization. For anything like a balanced approach to Dante, for example, it would be necessary to supplement Santayana's essay by T. S. Eliot's little book on the author of the *Divine Comedy*. Yet Santayana's essays are indispensable to a complete understanding of these writers; and any literary scholar's treatment of their philosophies seems shallow and inept in comparison. Among the three of them, he holds, Lucretius, Dante, and Goethe supply the essential ingredients to make a complete philosophical poet. Goethe is the poet of immediacy; he seizes upon the iridescence of life, and presents experience for its own sake. Faust does not at the end earn the wisdom or salvation that his creator wishes upon him. Even his tardily acquired civic virtue, his supposed conversion to altruism, consists in building a colony like Holland with incurably leaky dikes, so that the citizens will have to spend their lives in the strenuous activity of repairing them. Faust remains essentially a romantic, a slave of his will, without a sense of the resignation imposed by knowledge of man's natural condition, or a coherent scheme of the ultimate good. Lucretius has a fundamentally sound vision of nature and of the limits of human life, but he perceives very inadequately the potentialities of experience, remaining a timid sage. Dante has, in one sense, a greater range than either of these poets. He presents a vision of the entire universe, rising to an ordered view of the final human good; he is thus "the type of a consummate poet." Unfortunately his vision lacks the merit of being *true*. His universe is not only an imaginative one—this is its great merit—but an imaginary one, with an anthropocentric physics and a conception of the human good which, for all its frequent profundity, is somnambulistic. The *altissimo poetà*, who would combine the partial insights of these three men,

should live in the continual presence of all experience, and respect it; he should at the same time understand nature, the ground of that experience; and he should also have a delicate sense for the ideal echoes of his own passions, and for all the colors of his possible happiness. . . . But this supreme poet is in limbo still.[35]

Whether this conception of the supreme poet is to be taken as merely an ideal standard by which the strict critic will judge existing poetry, or Santayana believes in him as a "real possibility" and is crying for him in the wilderness, is a point on which Santayana is not altogether consistent. In the conclusion to *Three Philosophical Poets* he says it is time that such a genius should appear, and in "The Poetry of Barbarism" he suggests that modern poets have not made the best use of their opportunities:

they have many arts and literatures behind them, with the spectacle of a varied and agitated society, a world which is a living microcosm of its own history and presents in one picture many races, arts and religions. Our poets have more wonderful tragedies of the imagination to depict than had Homer, whose world was innocent of any essential defeat, or Dante, who believed in the world's definitive redemption.[36]

There is also material for comedy in the modern social revolutions; and modern science has given the poets a new vision of nature to exploit. Elsewhere, however, Santayana implies that moral chaos and imaginative disintegration have gone too far to make the emergence of the supreme poet likely. In *Reason in Art,* he suggests that a rational art can only grow out of a rational society, which we are far from having dreamed of, let alone attained.[37]

A survey of the poetry written in the thirty years since Santayana made his proclamation would hardly justify expectation of such a poet's speedy arrival. Our poets have been engaged for the most part in merely trying to survive: in relearning their craft, in sharpening their blurred senses, and lately in trying to envision a social order which would make the supreme poet's advent possible. They have succeeded in assimilating the modern world to their sensibility; they are far from having

[35] *Ibid.*, 214-215.

[36] *Interpretations of Poetry and Religion,* 167-168.

[37] *Reason in Art,* 225.

ordered it by the imagination. The most successful efforts in English have been those of Yeats and Eliot, neither of whom would meet Santayana's requirements. (Bridges had the will, but not the gifts.) Yeats achieved imaginative order, or a simulation of it, by an eccentric scheme patched together from occultist lore. In *The Waste Land* Eliot sought to put his house in order by an eclectic assemblage of materials drawn from the human past; since then he has made an increasingly attenuating effort to recapture the Christian symbolism. Thomas Mann's Joseph story, which is still unfolding before us, seems to come closer to meeting Santayana's requirements; its imaginative rendering of the human tradition is, if prosaic in its form, poetic in structure and substance. These examples show, if nothing more, that Santayana's dream of a rational art has found a parallel impetus in our most serious and gifted writers. Whether the impetus is doomed to frustration, or augurs the epiphany of the *altissimo poetà*, it would be rash to prophesy.

PHILIP BLAIR RICE

DEPARTMENT OF PHILOSOPHY
KENYON COLLEGE

10

Irwin Edman

HUMANISM AND POST-HUMANISM IN THE PHILOSOPHY OF SANTAYANA

10

HUMANISM AND POST-HUMANISM IN THE PHILOSOPHY OF SANTAYANA

IT IS A striking fact that the philosophy of George Santayana, as distinguished from his style, has appealed to many writers and thinkers not generally concerned with the technical problems of philosophy. It is equally striking that technical philosophers have admired Santayana's philosophy for the same characteristic that has appealed to men of the world and to men of affairs: its humane wisdom. They have appreciated the humanity of its moral philosophy as well as the incidental contributions to technical analysis. Of the latter, indeed, they have been not a little critical and sometimes even suspicious. Technical philosophers have been willing to waive ambiguities they found in the enunciation of specific doctrines—those concerning essence and truth, for example—for the sake of the larger human sense Santayana's writings made. Even where they have found in him, especially in his later writings, an unamalgamated compound of Locke and Plato in epistemology, or of Aristotle and the Hindus in metaphysics, they have respected him for his sensitiveness to the human scene and to the human incidence of ideas, religions, mythologies and philosophies. And does not our author himself lend the weight of his own judgment to the wide treatment of him as a moralist and a humanist: does he not describe moral philosophy as his "chosen subject?"

What is the humanism which devotees and critics alike find in Santayana, that humanism which is perhaps his essential quality, his characteristic gift and his permanent claim to a place in Western culture, and, more questionably, in Western philosophy? What do they find in his later works, that are so much preoccupied with epistemological and ontological controversies, that qualifies Santayana as a humanist? What do they find even in his earlier writings that qualifies his intentions and that indicates that even from the first he was not altogether faithful to his own humanism, or that even at the last he has not been altogether unfaithful to it? That there are what seem to be infidelities to the humanistic ideal I think no attentive reader can doubt. Nor can a faithful reader remain unaware that such real or apparent infidelities are waverings or shifts of interest in the preoccupations of a humane wisdom that clearly belongs in the tradition of which Santayana frequently describes himself as the heir: that of the Greeks, and of what one may call (though he himself nowhere does so) the good Europeans, in French and English literature and philosophy.

An incidental but by no means trivial evidence of the humanist in Santayana is his style. He would, one suspects, like to have that limpid and graceful instrument taken for granted. But in this instance the style cannot be taken for granted. It is a model of conscious and deliberate art, and the art is that of a poet. It is the prose of a mind that thinks in images. It is characteristic that for him philosophies are views, religions metaphors, and works of art, embodied intuitions. The fact is that Santayana began his literary career as a poet, that his early prose writings were interpretations of poetry and religion, and that even where, as in *The Realm of Essence,* he tries to be most soberly analytic, the metaphors and the music keep breaking through. His thinking is characteristically contemplation, and his writing is predominantly that of a poet surveying the fortunes of the psyche, the poetic images it generates and the dramatic perspective it focuses in this existence, so "polyglot, interrupted, insecure." The prose dress of this philosopher is a habit, in more than one sense. It is a habit worn and gained from a poet's taste and a poet's tradition. Santayana might have said these things quite differently, but had he said them differently, he might never have said them at all. Myth, metaphor, dramatic perspective, sentimental space and pictorial time, literary psychology, poetic truth, ideal immortality—such terms occur by the dozens in his writings. They are not simply epithets into which he falls, but terms deliberately used as philosophical distinctions. The style is the man and the man is here predominantly the poet. And in this instance the philosopher is predominantly a poet, too. His view of philosophy in general and our view of his philosophy must be colored by that fact. What one means, then, by calling Santayana a humanist is that he is speaking as a philosopher-poet. He never forgets and never allows us to forget that "the vision of philosophy is sublime," and that "for each philosophical poet the whole world is gathered together."

If in his own temper Santayana is a poet, in his approach to philosophy he may be described a humanistic critic, understanding philosophies and, indeed, largely estimating them by the evocative power and dreaming suasion of their intuitions of nature and man. He had, he says, from earliest childhood "a habit of poetic sympathy with the dreaming mind, whatever it might dream." He developed also a criterion of sanity, health, and wholesomeness in philosophy, and it is indeed therein that the core of his critical humanism lies. But he is a humanist before he is a critic, a humanist in the sense of having an imaginative sympathy and a singular gift for dramatically or transcendentally taking the perspectives of others, even when they are not his own and when, as in the case of Hegel in philosophy or Whitman in poetry, these are antipathetic to him.

Santayana's incidental comments on other and other-worldly philosophies constitute a wonderful body of ironically sympathetic perspectives. He himself says that *The Life of Reason* might have been called *The Romance of Wisdom*. In that "presumptive biography of the human intellect," he finds episode after episode to which he can lend a half-persuaded ear, and to which, save for the smiling malice of a phrase or a paragraph, he almost converts the reader. The irony is usually half affectionate, for even in systems of thought or religion or society that seem to him erroneous or perverse, he sees some human ideal struggling to expression, or even sober good sense partially and gaudily expressed. He can sense the ideal from its own standpoint of primitive tribal religions or of "Buddhistic morality, so reasonable and beautifully persuasive, rising so willingly to the ideal of sanctity." He can say of the last that it is "as far above the crudities of intuitionism as the whisperings of an angel are above a schoolboy's code."

A poet's sensibility and a cultivated tolerant sympathy with all the expressions of human interest and human frailty, of human insight and human error are not, however, the chief claim of Santayana to the title of humanist. Humanism is not only his temper, it is his philosophy and it is the core and substance of *The Life of Reason.* It is best stated in his own words:

I was not studying history or psychology for their own sake: my retrospect was to be frankly selective and critical, guided by a desire to discriminate the better from the worse.[1]

He found this criterion in the possible conditions and the possible forms of human happiness, the former being found in the mechanical conditions explored by physics, the latter in the examination of intent by dialectic.

The humanism of *The Life of Reason* is both that of a sympathetic retrospect and of a moral judgment. What is the moral judgment that is delivered upon the histories of human enterprise and the varieties of human feeling and thought? What are the criteria upon which those judgments are based? The judgments take the form of condemnation. A philosophy is postrational, religion is superstitious, a kind of art is barbarous, a morality is egotistic, a physics is mythical. Approvals take the opposite form. A morality is rational, a religion is the rational expression of an ideal, an art is classic, "idealizing the familiar and expressing the ultimate," a society is ordered, a life is healthy, a psyche harmonious. The criterion is Aristotle's mean, and the ethics is Aristotle's ethics. The retrospect of past philosophies is made with a realistic and circumspect malice. Each large episode in human experience, each view of the world, each religious myth, each artistic style, each form of government, each is examined with respect to what it does or does not contribute to *The Life of Reason.* Or in Santayana's own words:

Starting with the immediate flux, in which all objects and impulses are given, to describe the Life of Reason; that is, to note what facts and purposes seem to be primary, to show how the conception of nature and

[1] Preface to the second edition of *The Life of Reason,* x.

life gathers around them, and to point to the ideals of thought and action which are approached by this gradual mastering of experience by reason.[2]

It is easy to see why Santayana's Life of Reason appealed so strongly, and still does so to those who feel with him that intelligence is life understanding its conditions, and a rational life one which turns the natural conditions of existence into ideals and one which harmonizes those ideals into a just and equitable proportion. They respect in him his own respect for the natural conditions and the ideal possibilities of existence. They admire his own admiration for those formations in science, religion, and art which are expressive of the basic circumstance of life, men's central interests and their ultimate concerns. They are persuaded by his own sobriety with respect to the obdurate animal facts of existence, and his lyric sensibility to their possible ideal flowerings, and by his dramatic sympathy with other people's formulations of these possibilities.

Readers of Santayana are persuaded, too, by detecting that in Santayana the ideal, as the mean in Aristotle, is declared to vary. Santayana does not seek to impose one code upon all men, one way of life upon all societies. He asks only that each man read the oracles of his own heart, and interpret with that scrupulous dialectic, "the conscience of discourse,"—his own intuitions.

I wish individuals, and races, and nations to be themselves, and to multiply the forms of perfection and happiness, as nature prompts them. The only thing which I think might be propagated without injustice to the types thereby suppressed is harmony; enough harmony to prevent the interference of one type with another, and to allow the perfect development of each type.[3]

The judgments passed, then, upon philosophies and religions are based upon a criterion recurrent in *The Life of Reason* and almost throughout Santayana's writings. An ideal is the perfecting of a life; the ideal is the perfect and harmonious adjustment of all phases and interests of life. Harmony is the formal condition of the ideal and the only end, and harmony is an

[2] *Reason in Common Sense,* 32.

[3] "On My Friendly Critics," in *Soliloquies in England and Later Soliloquies,* 258.

abstract summary of the manifold harmonies which different lives under different conditions generate. The story, as Santayana himself puts it, is romantic, but the moral is classical. Common sense in science, the ordered and responsible in art, the morally expressive and significant in religion, the conditions of a society which organizes the instruments of industry and government so that friendly minds may play together or, better, play alone over the symbols of science, religion, and art,—these are illustrations of the same moral theme in the different aspects of the human scene and the human enterprise.

The ideal may be said to be common sense throughout, but common sense tinctured with generous sympathies even for treacheries to it, and more than a little home-sickness for belief in the existence of realms of efficacious moral powers, of Platonic and Platonized values that common sense would deny. There is a sympathy—almost reluctant—with those aspects of Platonism and of Plato which identify the realm of good with the realm of existence. There is a longing for a literal belief in that beautiful world beyond phenomena which religion promises and which common sense denies, as he himself early put it:

> Bid, then, the tender light of faith to shine
> By which alone the mortal heart is led
> Unto the thinking of the thought divine.

Santayana does not allow the tender light of faith to lead him beyond the realm of matter which is itself merely an object of faith, a convenient and a necessary practical allegation. The realm of matter is the name for the circle of objects and events by which action is both limitated and facilitated. The realm of matter is the realm of action. All else is conditioned by it. All else is a sublimation or a flowering or a dream spun out of it. All else, that is, save essences. Even if these be dreams, they are dreams whose character at least cannot be denied, and whose indentifiable characteristics become, in Santayana's later writings, their sole claims to being.

The criterion is common sense which is thought to be manifest where science is mechanistic, where religion is instructively poetic, where art is expressive of ultimate interests and is a minister to happiness. But the humanism even in these earlier writings is conditioned in several important respects. It is, in the first place, not a program, but a retrospect, a summary estimate, not a working hypothesis. A moral philosophy, if it is to be serious, must be seriously offered as a way of life. How can it be so offered when it is only a bland review of the ways in which intelligence has failed or succeeded in the past, when it is but an ironic commentary on the ways in which, from the high vantage ground of a detached spirit, all human enterprise is failure or foolishness? One cannot at once say that moral philosophy is one's chosen subject and practically deny any efficacy to intelligence save that of disinterested and disillusioned reflection on its failure to be anything but a disinterested commentator. There is nowhere, I believe, in the whole *Life of Reason*, a program of work which includes a program, even a generalized one, for humanity. Santayana is not a lost leader. He is rather one who regards all leaders as lost and as the victims of what he accused Dewey of having—a near-sighted sincerity. All action is a qualification of contemplation, and contemplation, we are eventually informed, can behold with directness and absoluteness only non-existent essences. Awareness in any authentic and indubitable sense turns out to be, in Santayana's own phrase, only "a by-play with the non-existent." The realm of matter is only one of many possible worlds, and its urgencies and interests are simply the accidents of a harassed animal who may, through philosophy, at moments be educated to freedom, the freedom of surveying the human scene as one set of essences among the many that might have been its spheres of burdens and opportunities.

There is a second sense in which the persuasive humanism of Santayana's philosophy is qualified, in which Santayana's classical ideal of harmony is both less inclusive and less tolerant than at first appearance it seems. He proudly boasts that he wishes all creatures to be happy in their own way. He cannot refrain, however, from repeatedly showing what, in the light of his own classicism, he thinks of certain ways of happiness. Santayana once wrote a now-famous essay called "The Genteel Tradition in American Philosophy;" he wrote another one called *The*

Genteel Tradition at Bay. His scorn was lavished upon the provincialism of Puritanism, and the innocent fanaticisms of a colonial imitation of a European culture. The persistence of Calvin in idealistic metaphysics and of Hegel at Harvard, the thin verbal moralities, the shallow metaphysical optimism, the subjectivism of the transcendental approach to nature, come in for his amused, but not altogether amused, condemnation.

Now no one can accuse Santayana of being a Calvinist or a metaphysical idealist or a Puritan in his thinking, though he admits to transcendentalism as a dramatic method. But there is one aspect of the Genteel Tradition, a moral aspect of it, that he does share with those he disdains. Like the eighteenth-century French writers he invokes the name of Aristotle; and a certain genteel distrust of all excess, even when it is that of genius, is apparent in all his writing. He sees the excess rather than the vitality of Whitman, and dismisses mystics as infantile, and romantics as barbarians. What is this barbarism of which he is contemptuous? It is vitality that asserts itself and does not fall into the respectable pattern of harmony. But the harmonies in any life are what and where they are exemplified. Vitality when it asserts itself is egotism; energy is worldliness, libertinism, or fanaticism. Since happiness lies only in harmony, where is that harmony found or how is it practiced or to be achieved?

Santayana says in *Reason in Art:*

> A rational pursuit of happiness—which is one thing with progress or with the Life of Reason—would embody that natural piety which leaves to the episodes of life their inherent values, mourning death, celebrating love, sanctifying civic traditions, enjoying and correcting nature's ways.[4]

Correcting nature's ways in the light of which or of what standards? All standards, he declares, are themselves natural and expressive, or, as he says, are expressive of the human heart. Art he describes as an adequate industry, and science is essentially that union of mechanism with dialectic that is the synonym for effective human art. But harmony is the orchestra as it occasionally sounds; there are no prescriptions for the composition of the music or for the playing of it.

[4] P. 222-223.

There is, however, still another qualification to the humanism of Santayana's moral philosophy. For despite his sense of art as adequate industry, he is singularly unsolicitous in examining the ways in which intelligence functions in the mending of nature's ways. An exploration of the methods of science in specific activities, an examination of the techniques of creative intelligence and the inventive improvement of man's estate have never been part of his special concern. Art is effective and science is man's sole reliance, but a specific analysis of the way in which intelligence functions or the way in which values are discriminated have never received adequate attention from his pen.

Finally, each man to his ideal, but the common man, unhappy under all conditions, has never been the source of his solution. "Promiscuous bipeds who blacken the face of the planet," is what he has to say of human beings; and democracy is a society in which the "tragedy of self-government" is "the tragedy of those who do as they wish, but do not get what they want." (*Dialogues in Limbo*, 93.)

Granted these qualifications of a philosophy that offers itself as human wisdom, one can recognize throughout Santayana's writings a broad and controlling sense of the human scene, and a controlling sense of the human perspective. All philosophies express themselves from a given human station. All ideals have their human roots; they are the dreams of half free and half harassed animals whose psyches are conditioned complexes in the realm of matter. Industry, government, science, and art are estimated by the extent to which they enable this perplexed and dreaming animal to recognize his condition and express luminously and coherently his relevant and characteristic ends. Santayana has, perhaps, nowhere more eloquently and aptly stated his own sense of man's fate than in the conclusion to *Reason in Science:*

> If science then contains the sum total of our rational convictions and gives us the only picture of reality on which we should care to dwell, we have but to consult the sciences in detail to ascertain, as far as that is possible, what sort of a universe we live in. The result is as yet far from satisfactory. . . . The moral sciences especially are a mass of confusion. . . . Yet exactly the same habits and principles that have secured

> our present knowledge are still active within us, and promise further discoveries. It is more desirable to clarify our knowledge within these bounds than to extend it beyond them. For while the reward of action is contemplation, . . . there is nothing stable or interesting to contemplate except objects relevant to action—the natural world and the mind's ideals.[5]

Thus speaks the author of *The Life of Reason.* It is, he assures us, the same author who speaks in his later works, and doubtless it is. But it is a philosopher who thinks there is something more stable than any existence, and not less interesting to contemplate than any "objects relevant to action," than any precarious existences posited by animal faith. Indeed the *only* objects of contemplation are only incidentally relevant to action. They are essences which may serve as signs and portents, but which, as objects of contemplation, have nothing to do with action at all. Indeed, it is only when they are beheld—"intuited" is Santayana's word—freed from any context of hope or fear, prospect or regret, usefulness or injury, that they can be beheld in their own character at all.

It is not within the scope of this paper to consider all the ambiguities which one may find in Santayana's doctrine of Essence. One may take the Realm of Essence in its simplest terms, as that realm of eternally possible characters, of the dateless, timeless self-identifying forms, the realm of all conceivable and inconceivable possibilities, the realm of eternal, non-existent objects of intuition which Santayana declares them by definition inalienably to be. What is interesting and perhaps perturbing to a good many of Santayana's readers is the shift in emphasis which *The Realm of Essence* seems to effect in his moral philosophy. The objects upon which contemplation is to be expended are, in *The Life of Reason,* the natural world and the mind's ideals. But the essences discoursed upon so lovingly—albeit with a love allegedly disenchanted of any particular affection for any particular essence—are not in their own character expressive of man's ideals, nor, in the strictest sense, are they denizens of the natural world. The Realm of Matter is by definition the realm of action; the Realm of Essence is by definition the realm of the

[5] P. 319.

non-existent, and can only be beheld in its purity when action is not involved. Santayana is very careful to distinguish his essences from those adumbrated by Platonists. For his essences are not only the good, the true, and the beautiful; they are the realm of all possibility, including the horrible, the monstrous, the hateful, the fantastic, the contemptible, the absurd. For hateful and lovable, reasonable and absurd, terrifying and delightful, are all attributions of the human perspective. Our philosopher thinks we have not genuinely beheld an essence unless we see it purged of its accidental dress, and are ourselves purged of any accidental interest. We have passed from the Life of Reason to the spiritual life, to the life of detachment in which Spirit is free.

Santayana is not the first to have identified spirituality with unworldliness, if not with otherworldliness. But it is worth noting that spirituality, defined in *Reason in Religion* as living in the light of an ideal, is not so defined in *The Realms of Being*. In the former Santayana says: "The spiritual man, fixing his eyes on them [the ideals of life] could live in the presence of ultimate purposes and ideal issues."[6] Not so is spirituality defined in Santayana's later writings; spirituality is there the activity of spirit, and spirit is the psyche when it forgets its origins and its conditions and is absorbed in timeless forms. Now a writer has a perfect right to vary his terms in a long career, but the fact that spirituality is defined in *The Life of Reason* in terms of ultimate purposes and ideal issues, and is otherwise defined in *The Realms of Being*, is more than a shift in the use of a word. It is a shift in perspective, and a shift that qualifies Santayana's humanism so much that one is tempted to call it "post-humanism," in much the same way as he speaks of certain moralities as "post-rational."

There were symptoms very early in Santayana's writings to indicate that thinking in any serious sense was identified with consciousness and that consciousness was a lyric cry. The practicality of thought referred to in *The Life of Reason* is a Pickwickian practicality. All thought had use insofar as it became a theme for soliloquy or an object for reflection. Ideal society was

[6] *Reason in Religion*, 213.

a living among the images suggested by the circumstances of society, the myths of religion, or the terms of dialectic. But in *The Life of Reason,* also, art was an activity of remaking the natural conditions of life so that they were more appropriate to, and more expressive of, ideal interests. Science was a technique of efficacious control, religion was an art of moral expression and significant metaphor or myth. Spirituality was the name for a life lived in terms of a comprehensive ideal called harmony, and harmony was an equitable realization of natural interests.

Spirituality, in *The Realms of Being* is a different story. The ideal itself is detachment—only one, Santayana admits, among many ideals, but obviously, for him, the ideal of a free mind and an emancipated thinker. In *The Life of Reason* we are constantly reminded of the responsibilities of the artist to the conditions of life, and of the triviality of art that is a mere play with appearance. Science, we are told, serves human ends; religion expresses them. Spirituality is the name for a living continuously and consistently in the realm of ideals, confronted with one another and rendered harmonious. Spirituality is human action turned toward its goals; it is human. In *The Realms of Being,* spirituality is episodic, irresponsible, post-human, "fixed instinctively on the countless moments that are not this moment, on the joys that are not this sorrow and the sorrows that are not this joy. . . ." Spirituality is disinterested; it is detached, indiscriminate. It ignores its origins and is committed to no ends. All human ideals are now seen to be founded in a human bias, and all human bias is a failure to be free. Spirituality is the transcendence of the human bias. The objects of intuition, in beholding which the whole activity of spirit consists, are indifferent. There are no greater or lesser goods, no relevant ideals, no criterion of harmony which is always relevant to a given life, no criterion of evil or of good, which is always the function of a merely human station.

What is the character of this spirituality that entitles it to be called spiritual? Is it not in the very fact that it has emancipated itself from precisely that sphere of conditions and the aspirations which those conditions make possible, which is the theme of *The Life of Reason?* The monk has taken the place of the moralist, the saint the place of the statesman; but a special kind of monk and a special kind of saint—a monk without a religion and a saint without a god. For spirituality in these later writings is marked, it must be noted, by one characteristic trait—detachment: "understanding too much to be ever imprisoned, loving too much to be ever in love." Contemplation is focussed on an essence, not for its truth or its goodness or its beauty, not for its efficacy or for its delightfulness, not as a landscape or as an instrument, but for its own neutral sake. Partial detachment would release us from existence to survey essences; complete detachment would release us from any specific essences to that identification with pure Being which is present in all being, but which interest in one essence rather than another would obscure.

Spirituality, in this sense of disenchantment and disintoxication, is itself a moral idea, and one that human beings have tried to practice in emulation of a god. But it is hardly the human ideal Santayana had preached in *The Life of Reason.* It is not a steady contemplation of all goods in a harmonious order of worth. Disinterestedness is not the ideal of the rational animal; Santayana confesses as much:

> As for me, I frankly cleave to the Greeks and not to the Indians, and I aspire to be a rational animal rather than a pure spirit.[7]

But disinterested contemplation is none the less the only ideal he himself alleges to be without intellectual illusion; it is the only aim of a free mind and its only occupation. Disinterestedness and contemplation indeed! But what is it that contemplation beholds and that disinterestedness is interested in? Essences. These are by definition non-existent. They are by definition irrelevant to human interests as human interests are irrelevant to them. Spirit can observe Essences just insofar as spirit has detached itself, if only for a short time, from the interests of the psyche, from the interests of other human beings, from the organs which make it possible, from the objects and circumstances which bring an essence into its ken. Spirit is an uncaring interest in the non-existent, a detached beholding of pure Being which can, from the point of view of human interest and social con-

[7] *The Realm of Essence,* 65.

cern, be identified only with pure Nothingness. The highest ecstacy is identification with nothing in particular, that is with nothing at all; no wonder that the ecstacy is cold, that the vision is quiet, and that nothing in spirit is obligatory.

Now Santayana is careful to assure us that he neither counsels any one to choose, nor does he himself choose, the spiritual life in this completely emancipated sense. But it is perfectly clear that all other types of interest, types of life, types of achievement, seem, in his later writings, provincial and secondary compared with these ultimates of spiritual deliverance and emancipation.

"The spiritual life, then," writes Santayana, in *Platonism and the Spiritual Life,* "is distinguished from worldly morality and intelligence not so much by knowledge as by disillusion. . . . This eternal aspect of things summons spirit out of its initial immersion in sensation and in animal faith and clarifies it into pure spirit."[8]

I waive the question of the epistemological complexities and the logical ambiguities which haunt this hypostasis of sensations into intuitions, the logical difficulties involved in the insistency on the character of an essence apart from its context, its occasions, and its uses. I chose the passage rather because of the contrast specifically made in Santayana between spirituality and worldly morality and intelligence. Is not what he here calls worldly what he would previously have called rational? Are not morality and intelligence, as here distinguished from spirituality, precisely that directed consideration of conduct by a rational animal (that is, an enlightened human being) which was the predominant interest of *The Life of Reason?* Was not spirituality once in Santayana's thinking the name for intelligence come into a steady vision of its ends? Was not spirituality once continuous with and a flowering of intelligence? Santayana himself, in the eloquent chapter on "Pure Being" in *The Realm of Essence* is aware of the impression he may give that he has deserted the Life of Reason for contemplation of the navel of pure Being with the Indian saints. He says in *The Realm of Essence:*

Those who have spirit in them will live in the spirit, or will suffer hor-

[8] P. 83.

ribly in the flesh; but this very insight into pure Being and into the realm of essence shows that both are absolutely infinite . . .; they therefore release the mind from an exclusive allegiance to this or that good. It is only by the most groundless and unstable of accidents that any such good has been set up, or any such world as that to which this good is relevant. . . .[9]

Whatever the aspirations of the author are, the direction of his thought seems to me to leave no doubt that his later writings, despite his denials, show internal evidence of a departure from his humanistic account of morals and of nature in his earlier work. He describes spirituality, as he defines it, as difficult for most men, but the most sublime ambition open to man. In just what does its sublimity consist, however? To call it sublime is surely to give it a hierarchical moral status. The most sublime activity of man must surely be rated as morally superior to the less sublime, to worldly morality and intelligence, to art, religion, science, and society. And how indeed is it sublime? To survey essences, the indelible self-identifying character of forms, not their use or beauty or delight, but simply for the tautological pleasure of identifying them—why is that sublime? Why is it even characteristically human? Santayana repeatedly suggests that the quality of a toothache is as much intuited as the idea of God, and mud and blood are just as much instances or exemplifications of pure Being as are Beauty and Truth.

Spirituality may be sublime, but this sublimity is somewhere beyond humanity. For it is characterized, on the one hand, by detachment, a detachment so complete that it recognizes neither any special source nor any special object. "In the spiritual life," he writes, "there is nothing obligatory." It beholds all essences or any essence with equal interest, or, more precisely, with equal lack of interest. Spirit has no commitments, no allegiances, no preferences, no scale of values. It has no associations and is a member of no society.

Thus a mind enlightened by scepticism and cured of noisy dogma, a mind discounting all reports, and free from all tormenting anxiety about its own fortunes or existence, finds in the wilderness of essence a very sweet and marvellous solitude. The ultimate reaches of doubt and re-

[9] P. 65.

nunciation open out for it, by an easy transition, into fields of endless variety and peace, as if through the gorges of death it had passed into a paradise where all things are crystallised into the image of themselves, and have lost their urgency and their venom.[10]

It has not, I think, been sufficiently observed how the idea of spirituality in Santayana is tinctured with the celebration of solitude and the exaltation of soliloquy. Is not the criticism he himself levels against egotism in philosophy, if one is to be just, to be levelled in part at least against his own? The detachment which is the acme of liberation turns out to be not the detachment of a saint worshipping a god, but of an aesthete playing with images, with a waking dream, with all the joys and griefs of illusion. Reason which was once celebrated as the ordering of life becomes at its acme the escape from it into the timeless, bodiless images of life. Essence now alone is said to be indubitable. Good and evil, seen from the perspective of the free spirit are seen to be merely the political compromises, the biological provincialisms of a plagued and perplexed animal. The whole world of matter is simply a systematic and working illusion, which from the viewpoint of the free mind is interesting only for the pictures it makes to the uncaring, liberated mind.

There is a kind of deliverance in this, the consolation of a poet's Nirvana, or the detachment of the aesthete playing irresponsibly over an anarchy of images. This post-humanism is a kind of post-impressionism in Santayana. Intuitions are impressions of essences, but the essences themselves have no significance in their own terms and no essential significance to the free spirit. The humane philosophy of *The Life of Reason* has become the disillusioned, ascetic aestheticism of *The Realms of Being.*

What is the connection between the architectonic humanism of *The Life of Reason* and the anarchic detachment of *The Realms of Being?* It seems to me that the nexus lies in one quality of Santayana's thinking that runs through the whole of it—the imagination of the artist and the primarily visual imagination of the painter even more than the poet. The harmony preached in *The Life of Reason* as the human ideal is itself almost a visual

[10] *Scepticism and Animal Faith,* 76.

image of an architectural order. The essences intuited by the free spirit of *The Realms of Being* are the images of the pictorial minded thinker for whom all perspectives are simply pictures, all goods and evils merely images, failures and successes, triumphs and defeats; are only forms beheld by the disenchanted and unanxious mind.

A purified taste in images is a pleasant release from the problems of existence. It is a way of escaping beyond good and evil. But it is implicitly a denial of that very humanism which has been Santayana's most impressive claim to wisdom; the vision of human ideals and their possible accomplishment turns into an ironic disdain for them. All existence comes to have the status of a theme for a soliloquy. All institutions, religions, arts and systems of thought are companions for a soliloquist's society. Santayana defines post-rational moralities as those which have imaginatively tried the Life of Reason and found it wanting. These systems are a refuge from an intolerable situation, they are experiments in redemption. Might not the same judgment be made of the spiritual life as Santayana has of late enunciated it? Moreover, is not abstention from commitment to any ideal a wilfulness in morals; is not the attempt transcendentally to escape Nature a subjectivism in thought? And are not subjectivism in thought and wilfulness in morals Santayana's own characterization of "cgotism in philosophy?"

If one judges Santayana's new spirituality (as old as Hinduism, by the way) as he judges all ideals in *The Life of Reason*, is one not privileged to examine its source and its value? Aesthetic beholding of images is a pleasure. Detachment from responsibilities is a release. But neither the pleasure nor the detachment constitutes a moral philosophy or a comprehensive morality. Absorption in an essence may be intense; is it, therefore, sublime? It is post-humanism, an abdication of humanism, to make all human enterprises provincial as compared with it. Spirituality is a flight to another world, one that is not even, like that of traditional religion, alleged to exist. In the phrase Santayana uses in concluding his account of post-rational morality: "It could never become a mould for thought or art in a civilized society." But civilized society, perhaps, is not the pre-occupation of that free spirit which Santayana celebrates in *The Realms of Being*. It was once the pre-occupation of *The Life of Reason*, in which wisdom was held to be responsible and spirituality addressed to possible human good.

IRWIN EDMAN

DEPARTMENT OF PHILOSOPHY
COLUMBIA UNIVERSITY

11

Eliseo Vivas

FROM *THE LIFE OF REASON* TO *THE LAST PURITAN*

11

FROM *THE LIFE OF REASON* TO *THE LAST PURITAN*

I.

IF WE consider *The Life of Reason* in respect to the time at which it was written we must judge it a very high achievement. For it was published in 1905, at a time when a man seeking for a philosophy had only two very poor choices before him: on the one hand there were the German and English traditions which were, so to speak, the official philosophies cultivated in the universities; but whatever form they took, they were but more or less disguised apologetics for bankrupt religious dogmas; and on the other hand there was the less academic but no less illiberal mechanistic materialism; but materialism crushed the will to happiness by denying meaning to human effort. In contrast to these, Santayana undertook to defend the conviction that human life could be, and to some extent had been a self-justifying and a self-regulating enterprise. This was true humanism. Santayana held that a critical survey could show that in those instances in the past in which life had achieved a modicum of rationality the forces back of that achievement were natural forces. To establish this point satisfactorily was to show that if we want to coax life into rational fruition it is enough to fall back on those forces which are at hand and which can be mastered. In short he offered in *The Life of Reason* a philosophy of history and a moral philosophy. The moral philosophy demonstrated that values must spring from a material ground; and the philosophy of history illustrated this thesis by analysis of concrete historical data.

Thirty-five years have elapsed since the publication of *The Life of Reason*. In no small measure through Santayana's own efforts the philosophic climate of America has changed radically from what it was at the beginning of the century. We no longer need to rout idealism; naturalism won the day long ago. Idealists, intuitionists, and those who believe there are powers outside of nature which interfere with the fortunes of men, are still to be found, and it is pleasant to consider that nature is gentle enough to leave in the intellectual world as much room for the archaic and the obsolescent as she leaves in the biological for armadillos and lung-fishes, even if these creatures no longer flourish in their pristine splendor. But now that we have won, we must re-examine the earlier formulations of our views. When we criticize Santayana, however, we must not forget that we are under an immense debt of gratitude to him. We are not likely to realize the intellectual daring and the moral courage that it took to beard idealism at the turn of the century. Forgetting this, we cannot appreciate at its true value what Santayana contributed to the development of American philosophy. He was one of those who, some thirty years ago or more, begged his colleagues to quit warming their sluggish blood by the low heat of academic controversies and to gaze out of their lancet windows past the familiar orchards beyond the moat, to the busy world of cities and of men they had long ago forgotten. It is not ignorance on my part, I hope, that accounts for my conviction that with *The Sense of Beauty* American aesthetic theory may properly be said to have been born. I remember the names of other thinkers before him, but I do not remember anyone whom we can credit with the influence that can be attributed to him. Santayana also took religion from the hands of apologists and theologians and thus enabled us to see its significance for humane living. He re-routed moral speculation and insisted that a man did not deserve the honorific title of philosopher who, for all the experience he might have of personal goodness and for all the standards of character and right conduct he might have discovered, possessed only a thin and barbarous notion of "what might render human existence good, excellent, beautiful, happy and worth having as a whole."[1]

These contributions give Santayana an eminent position in American philosophy as one of the pioneers of a new era which

[1] *Character and Opinion in the United States*, 85.

no internal criticism of his system can impugn. He oriented us towards our century. Yet his philosophy, if seen in the perspective of three or four decades, leaves much to be desired when we consider it intrinsically. Compared with what naturalism has become, his appears to be split by internal contradictions, to be hesitant, still embryonic. It is necessary therefore to scrutinize it with some care. If we do so, I fear we shall be inclined to say of the author of *The Life of Reason* what he said of Royce: on the surface Santayana seems to be an eminent logician, for he is dialectical and fearless in argument, but all his logic is but a screen for his heart, and in his heart there is no clearness.[2] The reason for this lack of clarity was revealed by himself when he told us that he has sought to build a system of philosophy out of disparate and complex allegiances, "combining them as well as logic allowed, without at heart ever disowning anything."[3] The trouble was that logic allowed much less than his heart advised him to retain and unfortunately Santayana took counsel with his heart.

The novel, *The Last Puritan*, confirms the judgment that Santayana did not succeed in putting together the various philosophic strains which he endeavored to erect into a system of moral philosophy in *The Life of Reason*, for we find in the novel these strains accepted as mutually incompatible elements and embodied in the contrasting personalities of the chief characters of the story. This then is our task in this paper: to analyze some aspects of the theoretical structure of *The Life of Reason* considered as moral philosophy, in order to discover in some detail why Santayana could not carry out successfully the synthesis which he attempted; having done so we shall turn to *The Last Puritan* to see hastily how these incongruous elements issue forth into the moral bankruptcy which finds expression there.

II.

Santayana holds an epiphenomenalist theory of mind, and one of the fundamenal difficulties his readers encounter and

[2] *Ibid.*, 101.

[3] "Brief History of My Opinions," in *Contemporary American Philosophy*, II, 239.

one which was noticed immediately after the publication of his work, is the inconsistency between Santayana's faith in reason and his belief in epiphenomenalism.[4] For according to the latter, mind or reason is impotent to change the flow of events in the natural world. This, however, seems to make nonsense of the life of reason, since on this theory reason cannot be applied to life. In so far then as we identify men with their reason, we have to acknowledge that they are impotent before their blind fate. If accidentally nature achieves in us what recording mind may feel is a happy harnessing of forces, we live in harmony. But we cannot say we are living the life of reason if we mean that, as reasoning beings, we are confronted with alternative ways of living and are able to choose and modify some of these. The choice is made by the blind movement of matter itself and mind merely expresses it. Goods come to us as everything does in due time, as part of the blind procession of nature, and so do evils; from the flood we grasp our share of both; nor does thought have any more to do with effectively directing us from evil towards good than it had with endowing us with an organism that calls that which thwarts it 'evil' and that which fulfills its needs 'good.' "That same spontaneity in nature which has suggested a good must be trusted to fulfill it."[5]

In defense of his epiphenomenalism Santayana offers the stock arguments. It is impossible, he tells us, to assume that thought can influence the course of events, when one recollects that "consciousness is not itself dynamic, for it has no body, no idiosyncracy or particular locus, to be the point of origin for definite relationships."[6] How then can we assign it power to gear in with the machinery which produces it? "All force, implication, or direction inhere in the constitution of specific objects and lives in their interplay."[7] We must also consider the evidence that introspection reveals:

If we look fairly at the actual resources of our minds we perceive that

[4] A. W. Moore, Review of Volumes I, II, III, and IV of *The Life of Reason* in *The Journal of Philosophy*, III (1906) No. 8.

[5] *Reason in Common Sense*, 214.

[6] *Ibid.*, 220.

[7] *Ibid.*

we are as little informed concerning the means and processes of action as concerning the reasons why our motives move us. To execute the simplest intention we must rely on fate: our own acts are mysteries to us.[8]

Back of these arguments, I believe, is to be found deeply lodged a psycho-physical dualism which Santayana never questions. Of course he rejects its obvious formulation, and being a naturalist he will have no truck with a substantialistic theory of mind. Santayana believes that mind cannot be conceived outside of nature, nor can it exist but for its material ground. "That the mind is not the source of itself or its own transformations, is a matter of present experience," and "men, like all things else in the world, are products and vehicles of natural energy."[9] Psychic events are subject to mechanical laws which provide for the transition between them.[10] But, though he rejects the obvious errors of dualism, his epiphenomenalism grows out of his failure thoroughly to transcend its implications. Mind cannot be the source of its own transformations, but it obviously is a something, and that something is unlike its source. He is a materialist, but he does not believe that we can reduce mind to matter.[11] While we can heartily agree with him in this, we would submit that his error consists in his having done away with mind-substance and yet having failed to place mind adequately in nature. To do so he would have had to repudiate the term "mind," with all the old errors to which it commits us, and would have had to open new paths in philosophy, as the instrumentalists are doing.

I must own that if it were a question of a choice of errors I would feel inclined to Santayana's modified dualism, for it allows him to be a materialist while eschewing the materialist error of virtually denying mind through reductionism, and it enables him to avoid the puzzles of interactionism, of parallelism, and of neutral monism. But in order to achieve these desirable results, Santayana ran counter to his conception of the function of reason and was also forced to deny what seems to the plain sense of mankind—a witness to which he himself is

[8] *Ibid.*, 214.

[9] *Ibid.*, 215-216.

[10] *Ibid.*, 217-218.

[11] *Ibid.*, 206.

not above appealing sometimes—an undeniable fact of human experience, namely that occasionally, if seldom, intelligence is effective in action. This fact was often acknowledged by Santayana himself when he was not expounding epiphenomenalism, for more than once he expressed the thought that "the function of reason is to dominate experience."[12]

When in 1905 one of the reviewers of *The Life of Reason* criticized Santayana for his inconsistency, our author tried to make more clear than he had before in what sense precisely we could say thought was practical.[13] I am one of those, however, who believe that his second attempt for all its subtle refinements was no more satisfactory than the first. The error of epiphenomenalism is inherent in the position and no multiplying or subtilizing of distinctions can avoid it. It consists, let me reiterate, of the deeply rooted habit of thinking of "minding" or "consciousing" (it is advisable to put up, here, with this ugly coinage) as if it were a thing or entity. Our reification of "minding," however aware we may be that it is a reification, carries with it subtle implications which the verbal instruments ordinarily employed by traditional philosophers not only sanction but foster. Thus the problem arises, what relation exists between body and "mind?" But we have not yet unravelled the knot, for the epiphenomenalist has what he takes to be an empirical warrant for the formulation of his problem, since surely consciousness does in some sense exist. I feel it in myself, impute it to others, and I am as certain of its existence as I am of anything. How then did that consciousness of mine come about? What relation has it to those successful or botched enterprises of my body which, when scrutinized, turn out to be hardly related to that warm feeling of mine which is the pith of my personality? Surely this puzzle is not an artificial one, nor can it be done away with by denying substantiality to that warm

[12] *Ibid.*, 204. See also *Ibid.*, 2: "To the ideal function of envisaging the absent, memory and reflection will add . . . the practical function of modifying the future. . . . Man's rational life consists in these moments in which reflection not only occurs but proves efficacious." Let these two references suffice; expressions like them occur frequently in the five volumes of *The Life of Reason* and throughout the works of Santayana.

[13] "The Efficacy of Thought," *The Journal of Philosophy*, III (1906) No. 15.

feeling. The epiphenomenalist may concede that his solution of the mind-body problem may not be correct, but that the problem itself can be disposed of merely by substituting minding for mind—how can anyone make such a claim?

I do not suppose that we can deny that consciousness exists in the sense that our experience has a felt quality which is private to the individual experiencer and is attributed to someone else only by analogy. The position, however, from which my criticism of epiphenomenalism is launched does not deny this fact. It merely asserts that this fact is not relevant to the problem at hand in the sense in which the epiphenomenalist takes it. For the quality of my felt experience is what it is, is in itself ineffable. The fact that as felt it does not reveal its connection with the flow of events does not prove that the minding process, of which it is only an analytic product, is impotent to direct those events efficaciously, since it is no wonder that we should find it difficult to discover the connections of something which we have severed from its matrix. Minding is a complex of activities of various sorts which take place in the body and which, when carried on in conjunction with objects in the environment, actually leaves traces, sometimes ineradicable ones, on them. Only a philosopher committed to a mind-body dualism could deny this. For it is only he who would assert that if, through thoughtful search for food, I take an apple from the branch, the complex process, which of course includes the taking of the apple, leaves the tree unchanged. I cannot be said to be thinking when, abstracting from this process some of its terms, I am left finally with the subjective side of the complex activity which is minding. In order to isolate the subjective side of thought, I must perform an analytic act, a highly sophisticated act of thinking. When I do so, I find that the subjective side of the minding process is not in itself any more important in minding or thinking than the objective terms which analysis discovers to constitute its components. By itself it is not efficacious, and it must be admitted that philosophers, adept at isolating the subjective side from the total complex, often think to no purpose whatever. Nevertheless thinking can often be and indeed often is purposive and efficacious.

Considered intrinsically, epiphenomenalism involves the acceptance of a rather luxurious complex of *ad hoc* assumptions essential to sustain it. In order to see how this is the case, let us take as a spring-board an admirably lucid formulation of its essential contention made by Santayana in the chapter from which we have been quoting:

> The mind at best vaguely forecasts the result of action: a schematic verbal sense of the end to be accomplished possibly hovers in consciousness while the act is being performed; but this premonition is itself the sense of a process already present and betrays the tendency at work; it can obviously give no aid or direction to the unkown mechanical process that produced it and that must realize its own prophecy, if that prophecy is to be realized at all.[14]

Notice that in this passage, in order to make its contents consistent with the plain facts of experience, we have to distinguish "impressions" or "sensations" from "mind." Or if we include them as part of "mind," as Santayana does in his discussion a few pages before the passage under examination, we have to distinguish between their mental character and their physical aspect. This means that the epiphenomenalist, at the level of impressions and sensations, must inject into this doctrine a parallelism or a double-aspect assumption from which, at the mind-body level, he takes pain to disengage his theory. Impressions and sensations are, in their physical aspects, the net-work of stimuli that connect the body with the environment. On their mental side, they are the report or sign or transcript—Santayana uses all three terms—of the physical process which takes place through the mediation of the physical net-work. Unless he makes some such assumption he finds himself arguing with Leibnitz as if the body had no connection with the world and acted harmoniously with it by pre-establishment. Now I do not mean to argue that this view is on its face not tenable; for, if all we had against it were only the top heavy elaboration of hypothetical machinery to which it commits us, it would not be enough to turn it down. In these ranges of nature it should not surprise us that events and processes are complex, and that

[14] *Reason in Common Sense,* 214-215.

no simple theory can do them justice. One cannot, however, escape the impression that the machinery is elaborated in a purely hypothetical fashion, that we have no direct evidence for all our inventions, and that the elaboration is done in favor of a doctrinal assumption which we are determined to save at all costs. For consider what an epiphenomenalistic description of a fairly ordinary human transaction would demand. Let us imagine that my body is going downtown this afternoon at 2:15. I cannot say "my body wants to go," for how can the body strictly speaking want anything? It does things and it suffers, but it cannot want. The want is the mental report of blind processes at work. Mind then reports the process and I say to myself, wrongly of course, that I am going to take myself downtown this afternoon at 2:15. When the short hand of the clock is at two and the long at three—since we do not believe in preestablished harmony—we must assume the clock sends some sort of physical shock to the body, which on arrival not only sets the body going but also sends a transcript of its arrival to mind. Mind of course, incurably megalomaniac, believes itself an executive and says, "Now I must go." Of course we must assume that body-processes have a time indicator, and as 2:15 approaches, the body tunes in on the clock, so that when it is 2:15, the message is received as a cause of action, whereas previous messages did not lead to action. Else we cannot explain the fact that at 2:08, and again at 2:13, I looked at the clock, saw it was not time yet to go, and, as I imagined, I decided to stay. The clock then has caused me to go at 2:15. I get my hat and open the door, while a schematical verbal sense is reporting what is happening. The body leaves the apartment and somehow the elevator cage, which is six floors below, sends subtle currents which cause the fingers to press the button which throws the switch and sends the cage up. In a similar way I cross the street with the traffic light. In the subway platform, I pass up the first train that comes along because the train announces to the body, as it pulls in, in some sort of subtle physical way, that it is not taking the body to the place towards which the body's tendencies are driving it. Whereas the next train that comes along three minutes later is distinguished by the body, not by my reading of the sign, but by some subtle mechanical process emanating from the train and affecting my body machinery in such a way that it causes me to go towards the doors when it stops and they open. . . We can stop here in our description. It could have been made more detailed without much difficulty, but it is not necessary to do so to make my point, which is that the effective difference between this view and pre-established harmony is that the latter appeals to a non-natural agency, for which there is no empirical evidence, in order to connect the two worlds, whereas the epiphenomenalist appeals to physical, but no less hypothetical, agencies, all seemingly invented for the occasion, in order to connect the body and the environing world. The philosopher who appeals to pre-established harmony frankly falls back on miracle. The epiphenomenalist appeals to a world that is virtually no less miraculously interrelated. The difference seems to be purely verbal, since the machinery to which the one appeals seems no more open to inspection than that of the other.

The doctrine of epiphenomenalism has been discussed not only on account of its intrinsic importance, but also because of the fact that it has pervasive consequences for Santayana's philosophy. The most important of these is to be found in his treatment of the problem of knowledge. Is knowledge direct or mediate? Do I know only my own ideas or do I know their ground or cause outside? Can I know matter, or must I believe in it instinctively, by virtue of some sort of mysterious faith with which I am endowed? These are questions which, as Dewey has shown by means of elaborate analysis, do not arise on an adequate conception of mind.[15]

If the problem of transcendence and its attendant problems arise in any form whatever it is simply because, though we may be wary of the fact that in saying that mind contains ideas we are using a metaphor, we cannot for all that avoid the compel-

[15] Santayana has dealt with the problem of knowledge extensively in various essays and books. The sections in *The Life of Reason* which bear more directly on this question are in *Reason in Common Sense*, chs. III, IV, VII. I imagine, however, that he would prefer his readers to go to *Scepticism and Animal Faith* for his mature epistemological doctrine.

ling power of the metaphor. As we saw above, we do not have *a* mind. We mind things, using the word now as a transitive verb. This is to say that we respond to things in certain complex ways. Analysis of the complex process involved in our responding will reveal certain types of behavior on our part when in certain dynamic relations with the environment. Considered in abstraction from that environment we call these types of behavior "ideas." But these ideas are not "mental." When we analyze them they turn out to be generalized complex activities, chiefly manipulatory, verbal, and visual in character, which we can carry out implicitly and in a telescoped way and which possess a felt quality for their owner. To say that "ideas are in the mind" is to use a very dangerous expression, fraught with confusion. It would be more correct to say that ideas are the mind, if we must cling to both substantives; but even this expression is not quite exact, since it fails to suggest that the term "mind" refers also to potential processes. To say that ideas are about objects is correct, in the sense that ideas are abstracts from an organism in complex interaction with an environment and they are the products of the impact of environmental objects. We know this because we can trace them back to the total interactive situation from which, for the purposes of analysis, we abstracted them. This indicates, however, that the knowing activity does not start with ideas. Our knowing activity starts from an interactive situation within which, when we wish to know about that activity, we distinguish an organism which does the knowing from an environment about which the organism knows. But the terms are analytic products and the formulation is somewhat false, for the organism by itself, if we can imagine it to be capable of existing by itself, does not do any knowing. Again, neither organism nor environment can be considered prior to the other. Finally, neither is more certainly there than the other. Psychologists, intent on analyzing the subjective side, bring forward towards the footlights the organism, and push the objective towards the back drop; to the psychologist the objective appears under the name of "stimulus." The physicist analyzes the objective, disregarding the idiosyncratic variations which result when we compare in an abstract way several subjective accounts of the objective. Whatever side we attend to involves a neglect of the other; but this is no reason for doubting the 'thereness' of the neglected side in respect to the total situation, nor for attributing to the side in which we are interested an absolute primacy over the other. The side we are interested in is more important, but only in respect to our interests. No animal faith is required to know the world; nor are essences required to mediate between our minds and the external physical world.

On this theory of mind, as on any other, the problem of the validity of knowledge still confronts us; but in a different way from that in which it does for subjectivistic theories of mind. One of the peculiarities about ideas is that once they have been aroused they may afterwards be aroused in the absence of the original stimulus, and seemingly from predominantly subjective causes quite different from the objective ones which originally aroused them. This gives rise to the problem of memory in its most general setting, and to the problem of dreams and of hallucinations. In one of its aspects this is a strictly psychological problem. It also gives rise, however, to the question as to what techniques we shall use in order to distinguish between responses which are aroused by objective stimuli and those which are not and which therefore deceive us as to their reference. Whatever may be the techniques we may finally devise in order to distinguish between imagined objects and real ones, we must not forget that the whole problem is a practical, a methodological one and not a philosophical or epistemological one. The fact that there is pseudo-knowledge trying to pass off for genuine does no more indict the validity of all knowledge than the fact that there is counterfeit money makes all money worthless; but it does burden us with the need to devise proper techniques to distinguish the genuine from the spurious.

Another serious consequence of Santayana's inadequate theory of mind is the split it forces him to make between literary and scientific psychology.[16] Although of less importance than the

[16] *Reason in Science*, ch. V. But see also *Scepticism and Animal Faith*, ch. XXIV, and *The Realm of Matter*, ch. VIII.

former, the split is nevertheless to be regretted because it restricts arbitrarily the principle of the unity of science which Santayana champions in *Reason in Science*.[17] That scientific psychology is behavioristic is something which Santayana has asserted with admirable clarity and vigor. But to the scientific he has been forced to add "literary psychology," because he considers that while behaviorism gives us an account of the *causa fiendi* of immediate experience, he thinks the cause is distinct in its mode of being from the experience.[18] On the theory of mind here suggested, which is behavioristic but not in the narrow Watsonian sense, the split between scientific and literary psychology does not arise, since this theory holds that thinking is a form of behaving and the felt quality of experience—which is, I suppose, what is meant by "immediate experience"—does not give rise to a cognitive problem different from that to which any other felt quality gives rise. As to qualities, all we can investigate are the conditions which bring them about, and this holds as much for the felt quality of experiencing as it does for any other quality. We can investigate the red we see when we look at *The Realm of Truth* on my table, in terms of the physical conditions required to bring it about, or in terms of the physiological conditions required to see it. The red is not in either case "reduced" to the conditions found by our investigation, in the sense that it is identified with its causes. But neither can it in itself be "known" in any other way than by discovering the conditions required to see it and the laws of its behavior in specific situations. I do not "know" it when I see it, I just have it, experience it. The problem of the felt quality of experiencing is a similar problem. The felt quality of experiencing is what it is; we have it, or feel it, if you prefer, but as a felt quality it is a private possession, quite ineffable and incommunicable, and in itself unknowable. We can, however, investigate the conditions necessary for its emergency, and in fact some of these we already possess. To "know" the felt quality of experiencing is to know its causes. To know it and to have it are two different things, however.

[17] *Reason in Science*, 318ff.

[18] "Brief History of My Opinions," in *Contemporary American Philosophy*, II, 253-254.

This hasty sketch is not intended as a definitive or adequate elucidation of the problems to which it refers. It is meant only as a reminder of solutions which already have been elaborated in detail by others.

III.

Another radical ambiguity from which *The Life of Reason* suffers, and one which has fatal consequences for Santayana's conception of the moral life, can be stated succinctly in the form of a question, namely, Is the rational standard of morality a postulate or is it deduced by means of analysis from the psychological makeup of human nature? In *The Life of Reason*, it would seem, the second alternative is favored, but passages are not lacking where a reading which is favorable to the first seems to be called for. The fact that there is ambiguity about this question indicates that when he undertook his ambitious project Santayana had not entirely clarified the theoretical issues on which the validity of his enterprise depended. The upshot, as I hope to show in this section, is that *The Life of Reason* rests on a relativism which is incompatible with the dogmatic conclusions which Santayana sought to establish in his work, and which robs of objective authority his eloquent condemnation of barbarism and of "pre-rational" morality.

Santayana, we must remember, insists that "every genuine ideal has a natural basis," and that an ideal which cannot own up its basis lacks all claim to rational loyalty.[19] From this it follows that the moral philosopher needs but "an analytic spirit and a judicious love of man" to distinguish the forward from the backward steps in the "confused experiment of living."[20] We must try to grasp clearly the important point of this passage for our purpose, namely, that the philosopher does not drag from the outside the standard by means of which he distinguishes progress from regress in the life of reason, but discovers the standard by means of analysis of living situations. The philosopher, therefore, if he would avoid impertinence or irrelevance, must find these standards analytically by deducing them or ex-

[19] *Reason in Common Sense,* 7, 21, etc.
[20] *Ibid.,* 8.

tracting them from the historical period or the people whose progress or regress he wishes to determine.[21]

If we take this condition seriously we run into a radical difficulty for which I cannot find a successful resolution in the text. For in *The Life of Reason* Santayana does not undertake to describe what men, in their purblindness and their partisan ignorance, have called the good. This account would tell us no more than we already know, that men have gone after all sorts of miscellaneous objectives and pursued with admirable loyalty the most contemptible ideals. The moral philosopher, Santayana tells us in an explicit and unequivocal way, must attempt to give us more than mere description, he must be dogmatic. The word "dogmatic" is his own.[22] "What ethics asks is not why a thing is called good, but whether it is good or not, whether it is right or not so to esteem it."[23] He must tell us not what we desire or find pleasure in, but "first of all . . . in what things pleasure ought to be found."[24] This is the critical, as contrasted with the descriptive task, the moralist's as contrasted with the sociologist's, and it requires a "dogmatic background, else it would lack objects and criteria for criticism."[25]

Where, then, does the moralist go for his standard? If he is not to court impertinence and irrelevance he must find it, we saw, in the interests themselves. But can we find standards in nature? Of course we can. If there are interests there are values, and if there are values there must be standards by which to measure them. Which, however, among the multitude of conflicting standards that we actually find in nature is the one which can tell us, not what men have called the good life, but what the good life in truth has been? For the difficulty is not

[21] *Ibid.*, 259-260; see also 13, where, speaking of Protestant bodies he says: "The Life of Reason has no existence for them, because . . . [they] will not suffer extant interests which alone can guide them in action or judgment, to define the worth of life." Also 270, "Nor can the ideal of one man or one age have any authority over another, since the harmony existing in their nature and interests is accidental and each is a transitional phase in an indefinite evolution."

[22] *Reason in Science*, 245.

[23] *Ibid.*, 215.

[24] *Ibid.*, 258; also 215, 216.

[25] *Ibid.*, 245.

that the moralist does not find standards in nature, but that he is embarrassed by their overabundance and their mutual incompatibility. Each man has his own standards and each culture and each age. How then can we choose rationally from among all those standards? Remember that the moralist must not only be dogmatic but he must be rational, and in order to fulfill this requirement he must somehow deduce his standard from the same ground to which it will apply. Only then does it commended itself to reason. Otherwise it will be unjustified, the dogmatism back of it will be arbitrary, and the judgment will be clearly prompted by interests intrinsic to the situation, and therefore irrelevant to it.

Can we accomplish this deduction? Obviously not, for if we do not know what the good is, we cannot choose it from among the mutually incompatible goals which confront us and each of which calls itself the good. Without a criterion, which is what we are looking for, we cannot select from the multiplicity of criteria which press for adoption. But if we are to be moralists and not merely describers of what is called good, we must make a choice. And if we make it it would seem that our choice will have to be an irrational one. Santayana himself recognizes this explicitly in several passages throughout *The Life of Reason.* For instance, he tells us, "All survey needs an arbitrary starting point; all valuation rests on an irrational bias."[26]

We must look into this contradiction a little more closely. A warning first lest the above remarks be taken to assert more than they intend. I do not mean to say that, because the source of valuation is to be found in an irrational impulse, significant moral judgments are not possible. The phrase, "the irrational basis of valuation," may be taken to refer solely to the fact that values are determined by interests and interests are found by the moralist, discovered, not created, by him. In this case moral judgments are significant for the area from which their standard was extracted, and it is an empirical question, when there are conflicts among various systems governed by different criteria, what is the range of their applicability. However, in that case

[26] *Reason in Common Sense,* 43.

the moralist must be ready to give up his dogmatism, and this is what I meant to call attention to. He cannot tell us in what we ought to find pleasure, unless he is ready to show somehow that this is indeed what we do really find pleasure in but do not know. In short, the recognition of the arbitrary basis necessary to a moral survey does away with the possibility of significant moral judgments, if we demand of the moralist that he recognize that all the likes and dislikes that are to be found in the world are intrinsically justified, and yet demand of him at the same time that he tell us which ones we should like and which ones we shouldn't. For what rational authority can the word "should" or "ought" claim in this case? If it were to turn out, as it is likely, that we do not in fact give a hoot for an alien "ought," we can answer the dogmatic moralist that his arbitrary starting point is none of ours, and we see therefore no reason why we should bow to his judgment.

The difficulty is not appreciated by Santayana because he uses as a basic notion the term "harmony," and on scrutiny it turns out that the notion of "harmony" screens the contradiction and thus adds it own share to the confusion. We must therefore examine the notion of "harmony."

The ideal of the life of reason is to set up a perfect harmony among the extant forces of human nature.[27] But since each ideal, considered from its own standpoint, is its own justification, "the only sense in which an ultimate end can be established and become a test of general progress is this: that a harmony and co-operation of impulses should be conceived, leading to the maximum satisfaction possible in the whole community of spirits affected by our action."[28] The question that we must ask about this notion of harmony is the following: Is the harmony sought by the rational man itself the expression of an intrinsic interest? For if it is not, it can have no voice in determining a rational result. The reason for this is that we shall then have to introduce the demand for harmony into our moral economy from the outside, and this would mean that we are attempting to regulate our native impulses in terms of alien forces for the

[27] *Ibid.*, chs. X, XI, XII; *Reason in Science*, chs. VIII, IX, X.

[28] *Reason in Common Sense*, 256.

sake of an ideal which, since it does not emerge from the situation itself, cannot expect the situation to recognize it. But on Santayana's theory this would not be morality but slavery. He tells us:

> Rational life is an art, not a slavery; and terrible as may be the errors and the apathy that impede its successful exercise, the standard and goal of it are given intrinsically. Any task imposed externally on a man is imposed by force only, a force he has the right to defy so soon as he can do so without creating some greater impediment to his natural vocation.[29]

Harmony then, to be authoritative, must somehow itself be the result of the interests in conflict. Now we do not find anywhere in *The Life of Reason* an adequate analysis of the term "harmony;" nor do we find, for that matter, an adequate analysis of the other basic terms on which Santayana's construction rests, terms like "order," "happiness," and "reason." In a passage in the first volume he tells us that "reason as such represents or rather constitutes a single formal interest, the interest in harmony."[30] I do not understand exactly what may be meant by a formal interest, for an interest which is not a concrete interest in something concrete is not a formal interest but merely a vague one and as it becomes defined it becomes clear and distinct and concrete. Be that as it may, Santayana seems to maintain that the interest in harmony arises when conflict is rife and we become conscious of the conflict. The need for harmony emerges spontaneously, it would seem, and according to the conditions laid out it must be an intrinsic need, demanded by the situation itself, not extraneous to it.[31] At this point we must ask two questions: (1) What basis is there for a moral judgment in those cases in which a demand for harmony does not exist among human animals? Or are there no such cases? (2) What gives the interest in harmony authority to legislate over all the other interests?

There is no explicit answer in Santayana to the first ques-

[29] *Reason in Science*, 248; also 240.

[30] *Reason in Common Sense*, 267.

[31] *Ibid.*, 257-259, 267-268.

tion, and this is much to be regretted, because it was rather important for him to be as clear and as precise as he could be on this matter. On his own theory, however, since we must admit that there are cases in which interest in harmony is non-existent or too weak to be noticed, I can only see one answer to our question. If in the midst of conflict no intrinsic demand for harmony should arise, or rather to the degree to which the demand is intrinsically lacking, no valid judgment can be passed on such a conflict. But this amounts to saying that no valid moral judgment can be passed on a situation except where, or to the extent to which, the judgment can be favorable; no adverse judgment can be binding or have rational authority. The reason for this is that an adverse or negative judgment indicates that there is no intrinsic need for harmony in the situation; but to that extent we must suspend judgment, for otherwise the judgment would be based on extrinsic demands, and this would be a slavery which we have a right to defy. This makes the moralist a sort of yes-man whose business is to applaud and never to reprove. When the moralist is confronted by anarchy, all he can do is to appeal to what he, the moralist, calls the best side of the anarch's nature in the hope that he has a better side to his nature.

Which, then, is the best side of an anarch's nature? "Best" according to whom? The difficulty we have been struggling with will not down. There is a passage in *The Life of Reason*, moreover, in which it seems as if Santayana almost grasps it himself, and which we should therefore look into.

> Ethics, if it is to be a science and not a piece of arbitrary legislation, cannot pronounce it sinful in a serpent to be a serpent; it can not even accuse a barbarian of loving a wrong life, except in so far as the barbarian is supposed capable of accusing himself of barbarism. If he is a perfect barbarian he will be inwardly, and therefore morally, justified. The notion of a barbarian will then be accepted by him as that of a true man, and will form the basis of whatever rational judgments or policy he attains. . . . But the degree to which moral science, or the dialectic of will, can candemn any type of life depends on the amount of disruptive contradiction which, at any reflective moment, that life brings under the unity of apperception. The discordant impulses therein confronted will challenge and condemn one another; and the court of rea-

son in which their quarrel is ventilated will have authority to pronounce between them.[32]

We must remember that *The Life of Reason* is an indictment of barbarism, and that for Santayana the term is not a purely descriptive one. Nevertheless, in this passage we are told that we cannot condemn the barbarian if he is a perfect barbarian. This leaves us in the horns of an Irish bull, I am afraid. For what then does perfection mean, if a barbarian can be perfect after his kind? If it is in the nature of the barbarian to be disrupted by mutually contradictory impulses, he could plead that perfection in the barbarian consists in being so disrupted, and the more disrupted the more perfect the barbarian would be after his kind. The disrupted barbarian then could look down on the harmonious barbarian, who is imperfect after his kind and perfect only after Santayana's kind, and accuse him of being imperfect. At this point I can hear the reader calling me back to fundamentals and asking me what in the name of reason is perfection? This is of course the very point of these remarks; moral dogmatism loses its authority when wedded to relativism; in such circumstances terms like "perfection" become dens of logical iniquity.

We also asked what gives the impulse to harmony, when it exists, the authority to regulate all other interests. To this question, fortunately, we do find an explicit answer in Santayana. The interest in harmony has authority because it does not impose new sacrifices on those interests which it brings into harmony, but rather minimizes the sacrifices which a conflict, if allowed to take place, would bring in its wake.[33] It were well to note before proceeding that in Santayana's answer "reason" on the one hand and "conflict" and "force" on the other, are implicitly accepted as mutually exclusive.[34] Now the difficulty with the answer Santayana returns to our question is the un-

[32] *Reason in Science*, 234.

[33] *Reason in Common Sense*, 266.

[34] *Ibid.*, 262. The opposition is also expressed in this statement of the distinction between reason and conscience. *Ibid.*, 265; also 279. In an interesting passage, we are told that a rational society can grow after conflicting ideals have fought it out and one of them has won. Nature brings the selection about, but when the selection has taken place, a moral integration develops and spiritual unity is the

realistic optimism that animates it. Santayana is convinced, or was at the time he wrote *The Life of Reason,* that "the conflict of desires and interests in the world is not radical . . . for every particular ideal, being an expression of human nature in operation, must in the end involve the primary human faculties and cannot be essentially incompatible with any other ideal which involves them too."[35] Hence, he believes, it is "perfectly possible" to live the life of reason, "to adjust all demands to one ideal, and adjust that ideal to its natural conditions."[36]

If we challenge the optimism of *The Life of Reason* we strike at its foundations. And today, and not necessarily in the lurid light of contemporary madness, though it is well-nigh impossible to discount it at this moment, but rather in the light of what we have learnt from the new psychology, there are serious grounds for calling for a better justification of Santayana's youthful optimism than that which he offers. As a result of his confidence Santayana underestimates the absolute sacrifices which rational deliberation often demands of impulses if harmony is to be achieved. Often serious sacrifices are involved in all living; and from rational living, I imagine, often the most serious sacrifices of all are exacted. This is recognized by Santayana when he speaks of the need for "discipline" which is felt by anyone who would live rationally. What discipline does to his optimistic conception of harmony is however not recognized by him. Now the extent of the sacrifice which is involved in the resolution of a crisis is at least in part a function of the animal urge which animates him who would live rationally. It is easy to live rationally for one who has no strong urges, no ardor, in whom the fires of life burn low because for some reason they were banked for him from the start. But in a man of passion, who is alive, who is energetic, who is driven by strong impulses, when these run into conflict with one another, such a man must make serious sacrifices in favor of harmony, often, indeed, terrible ones.

---

natural product. Rationality however does not appear until struggle disposes of threatening forces. Force and reason remain mutually exclusive, though the latter builds on ground prepared by the former. *Ibid.*, 281-282.

[35] *Reason in Common Sense,* 267.

[36] *Ibid.* See also *Reason in Science,* 252, 253, for instance.

The recognition of the different impulses at play forces a complete change in the picture which Santayana gives us of the life of reason. It confronts us with the fact that sacrifices may be necessary for the sake of harmony, and that unless we are somehow endowed with an interest in harmony which is preeminently strong we cannot achieve it. If the interest in harmony is weak it is not capable of whipping the rest of the conflicting interests into shape. But if it must purge the counter-revolutionary soreheads and push the grumblers into their place, we must scrap the pretty picture of an angelic choir following Lord Harmony about in an orderly entourage and singing sweetly at his bid. Harmony is possible, but it can only be brought about through force. On Santayana's theory, however, a harmonious resolution of conflict is brought about only when each interest is allowed the right to be heard. He tells us that in such cases the result is sacrifice on the part of all equally for the sake of all. It would be nice if it were possible, but it just does not work that way. It involves, moreover, the logical confusion of the two meanings of "all." For the "all" for whose sake harmony is sought is a collective, not a distributive "all."

The only conclusion at which we can arrive from these considerations is that the distinction between rational morality and the morality of barbarism, as well as the distinction made by Santayana between reason and conscience, both of which are the very heart of the notion of the life of reason as he proposes it, must be given up. Yet, if we erase these distinctions *The Life of Reason* falls into a heap of limp words. This is all the more the case if we remember that Santayana is an uncompromising individualist, and that one of the consequences of this position is an utterly atomistic moral relativism, according to which each living thing is itself the measure of its own good; indeed not each living thing, but each living stage in its growth, and each moment. For this moral atomism which makes an integration through time impossible Santayana sometimes shows great inclination,[37] but he never embraces it consistently. Yet he should do so, if he were willing to accept the logical implications of one part of his moral philosophy.

[37] *Reason in Common Sense,* 280, 281.

That dogmatic moral standards which are also rationally exclusive cannot be deduced from a psychological account of human nature seems to have been clearly perceived by Santayana some eight years after he wrote *The Life of Reason.* In a book review he stated the problem with all the sharpness and clarity which could be demanded.[38] But I cannot see that even then he resolved it with the same clarity with which he stated it. "Moral comparisons," he tells us in this piece, "are possible only in view of each ideal, and after some ideal has been virtually set up." Before the ideal is set up there is parity and independence among the various perfections. From the standpoint of the ideal which has been set up the universe can be surveyed, and its perfection, and imperfection can be estimated. So far Santayana. We must remember, however, that perfection and imperfection here mean that some aspects of the universe are congenial or beneficial and others inimical to the ideal which has been set up. And it needs to be underscored that a postulational theory of ethics must allow perfect freedom as to the postulates we select and that the postulated ideal has no claim to respect from any other ideal elsewhere set up nor has it any power of rational persuasion over it. The naturalist then may be a dogmatist, "for he has a nature of his own." But he cannot claim nature's preference for his ideal. He may call his way of life by some eulogistic term, like the life of reason, but the term expresses only a set of parochial prejudices, and no more describes the nature of the life to which it refers than the names a lover gives his mistress in their moments of tender intimacy describe objectively the lady's character.

As should be expected from the preceding discussion, the contradiction between dogmatism and relativism in Santayana's thought also vitiates his estimate of progress. For that estimate depends on the discovery of an objective criterion by means of which progress can be measured. This criterion Santayana discovers in Aristotle's conception of human nature: "everything ideal has a natural basis and everything natural an

[38] "Dr. Fuller, Plotinus, and the Nature of Evil," *Journal of Philosophy,* X (October 23, 1913), 589-599.

ideal development."[39] Yet, when he applies this conception to history, it somehow becomes transformed into a Spencerian notion of adaptation: we can say that progress has taken place when man's interests are adequately satisfied by the conditions under which he lives.[40]

In securing his criterion—whether Spencerian or Aristotelian—Santayana got more than he bargained for and also less. For the conception of human nature with which he is working distinctively involves the notion of potentialities with which men are pre-natively endowed. There are some ideals which, as humans, we can fulfill because we are born with certain potentialities to do so. We can tell whether progress or regress has taken place if these potentialities are realized. If not all men had the same potentialities it would make no sense to say that the Greeks were at a higher stage of development than the Medes, or that the Arapesh were at a lower stage than we are.

I take it that it is not necessary today to demonstrate that this doctrine of potentiality is not acceptable. But if we repudiate it, I am afraid, there is very little of *The Life of Reason* that we shall be able to save—certainly nothing of that aspect of it in which the author undertakes to estimate human progress. Now the interesting thing about this is that Santayana himself repudiates the notion of a fixed "personality,"[41] but does not see that on an evolutionary approach to human nature the notion of potentialities also has to be jettisoned. Had he realized this he might have been in a position to give us a correct account of the rôle which the social factor plays in the development of value, and would not have run into the contradiction which leads him to assert on the one hand that the ideal of one man or an age can have no authority over another,[42] and, on the other hand, announce as his intention to demonstrate in his work that the life of reason has in "the ideal world a creative and absolute authority."[43]

[39] *Reason in Common Sense,* 21, 28.

[40] *Ibid.,* preface to second edition, xi.

[41] *Ibid.,* ch. XII.

[42] "Dr. Fuller, Plotinus, and the Nature of Evil," *Journal of Philosophy,* X (October 23, 1913), 589-599.

[43] *Reason in Common Sense,* 290.

IV.

When Santayana, harking back to Spinoza who would call things good because desired, undertook to demonstrate that human needs account for the appearance of ideals without residue, he took an important step forward in value theory. There is, however, a serious defect to the manner in which Santayana sought to develop his insight, a defect which to some extent frustrated the results he sought to achieve.

In order to elucidate this defect we must remind ourselves again of the foundation on which Santayana sought to rear the moral life. One formulation, convenient in the light of what follows, reads: "the varying passions and duties which life can contain depend upon the organic functions of the animal."[44] This is of course a variant statement of the naturalistic principle that all ideal developments must have a natural basis. However, in describing the relationship between morality and its material ground, Santayana was predominantly influenced by the biological approach current in his day, and therefore misconceived the rôle which the social factor plays in the development of the life of reason. Since this is a question of omission rather than of commission no single quotation could be brought forward to justify the charge. But we can find a few statements, like the one just quoted in this paragraph, in which Santayana makes explicit the bias with which he interprets the relationship between ideals and their ground.[45]

I do not of course intend to challenge the fact that moral phenomena have a biological basis. The intention of this criticism is rather to call attention to the fact that the transition between biological and moral phenomena cannot so easily be made as our author makes it, that it is far more complex, since ideals do not grow out of a purely biological ground but out of a social one. Santayana does not apprise the reader that he was adequately aware of this complexity when he wrote *The Life of Reason.*

There are perhaps several reasons for Santayana's under-

[44] *Reason in Society*, 13.

[45] For instance, "all life is animal in its origin and all spiritual in its possible fruits." *Ibid.*, 9.

estimation of the institutional or social ground of morality; an important one no doubt is his youthful connection with Spencer's philosophy, but another is the deep rooted individualistic habit of thinking of the biological individual as the primary element of the social complex and hence of the values it expresses. Although of course in a legitimate sense these assumptions cannot be denied, when we import them into moral inquiry without qualification they give us a vague and incomplete picture of the origin and specific character of the values of men in culture. It is the social factor, not directly reducible to biological terms, that gives biologic needs the specific character that they have, and which therefore determines the specific character of a culture's values. Biological reduction falsifies the picture because it assumes it can account for values directly in terms of organic needs. The biologic roots of the needs are not denied, but by themselves they cannot account for the diversity of cultures and values. Indeed, with Dewey and Mead we can argue that apart from society neither intelligence nor the values expressed in the life of reason are conceivable. The living individual does not, in a purely biological way, create his values. He does modify the values he inherits socially, but only to some extent, by refracting them through the somewhat idiosyncratic prism of his own biological structure. What he adds of his own, however, is partial and limited; essentially his values are social values. Not even in a logical sense, then, and certainly not in a temporal one, is the human individual prior to society. As a purely biological organism, were it conceivable that the human animal could survive outside of society, it is not unsafe to guess that his values would be minimal and hardly distinguishable from those of beasts.

The lack of adequate emphasis on the social determinants of value is particularly evident throughout the whole of *Reason in Society*. It accounts for his treatment of political instrumentalities as if these were *mere* instrumentalities external to the ends they serve; being external they can be substituted for one another as expedience dictates without affecting the character of the ideal they maintain. There may be occasional advantages in being conquered, we are informed, since the foreigner may enable us to realize ideals that the native government could not bring about.[46] This statement is false because it disregards the fact that the ideals which flower in a particular social organization are specific and concrete and are possessed or realized through the specific quality of daily living, not with the aid of external instrumentalities, but by means of and through institutions that are the very filaments of the life they sustain. Men do not distinguish in their daily lives the instruments by which they live and the ideals which the instruments serve, and the reason for this is that in the concrete experience of living the distinction is impossible to make. Insofar as conquest destroys the instruments it destroys the possibility of the ideals they serve. It may substitute other ideals. But the victims will consider these *Ersatz*, since it is the old quality of living, no longer possible, that was the object of their piety. The error appears again when he tells us that "All just government pursues the general good; the choice between aristocratic and democratic forms touches only the means to that end."[47] The only truth this statement may be said to have is a highly abstract one; but unfortunately the social problem does not present itself, except to the academic mind, in such a form. To any but an academic mind it would be obvious that the aristocratic ideal is in its specific character essentially different from the democratic, and abstractions like "the general good," which submerge the specificity of mutually incompatible ideals, are vicious. We see the same fallacy clearly infecting the chapter on "Love."[48] In this beautiful essay, Santayana illustrates most convincingly the relationship between the ideal and its biologic ground. He points out that social factors determine the way in which love finds expression in different cultures, but does not explicitly recognize that love as a value has a social as well as a biological ground.

There is another consequence of the failure to reckon social factors which is so important that we cannot neglect it. Santayana gives the impression that morality lies primarily within the

[46] *Ibid.*, 75ff.
[47] *Ibid.*, 121.
[48] *Ibid.*, ch. I.

sphere of the individual and concerns society only insofar as the individual's choices and actions are impinged on by those of others. This is not to say that Santayana makes the same erroneous absolute split between politics and ethics which is so common in our day. Nor is it to say that Santayana fails altogether to see that the social factors determine the moral situation. What is meant is that because of the extrinsic relationship which the social factors are said to have to values, according to Santayana's theory, the center of gravity of the moral life is essentially within the subjective self. And this I take to be the choicest source of infection for ethical theory. For it is of the essence of the moral judgment to intend a universalistic appeal. Only in terms of this appeal can the moral condemnation of an action be acceptable to the actor. Otherwise the condemnation must appear arbitrary and hence immoral, or at least merely irrelevant. Unless our ethical speculation starts from the social standpoint no satisfactory account can be given of it. We have to fall back then on an instinctive universal sympathy or benevolence which we have no ground for assuming, and which in any case cannot be counted on as a stable foundation for the moral life. Let us, however, try to clarify this criticism by more specific reference to Santayana's theory.

Santayana's ethical theory seeks to achieve, as the moral ideal, a harmony which issues forth in happiness. Harmony, and hence happiness, are the goals of the rational mind, one of whose distinctive traits is the power to consider other impulses than those of the individual in its search for harmony. "To stop at selfishness is not particularly rational. The same principle that creates the ideal of a self creates the ideal of a family or an institution."[49] This is to say that reason is somewhat universalistic, that it tends to transcend the nucleus of individual passion and impulse which it arose to serve. With this opinion there is no quarrel. The quarrel is directed at the fact that Santayana cannot on his theory account for the universalistic scope of reason and hence must account for it by the method of assertion. When we ask why must reason go beyond the range of the self, the only answer we seem to get is that it is

[49] *Reason in Science*, 250.

so because the dialectic development of reason makes it so. But this is no answer for a theory which also insists on the primacy of impulse in the moral life. Such a theory cannot condemn a parochial morality, as we have already seen, if in the parish there happens to be no interest or sympathy for anything beyond its boundaries. I am, however, not really able to come to any clarity on this important point, because there are passages in which Santayana seems to give the impression that what leads reason to consider the claims of alien impulses is an enlightened selfishness.

V.

Some time ago Santayana interrupted the transcendental labors involved in writing *The Realms of Being* to write a novel, and he wrote a most unusual book, full of wisdom and of pathos, of malice and of tenderness, and studded with some of the best epigrams he has ever written. To the student of Santayana's philosophy this novel is of cardinal interest, because he managed by means of it to unite at last those forces which he once sought to synthesize and failed. The union he thus accomplished, however, was not a logical synthesis, but the only type of union that such disparate forces could ever achieve, a dramatic one. A study of *The Last Puritan* should then be a rewarding task. For it gives us an insight into the forces which went to make up *The Life of Reason*, presented by their author not as concepts, but as plastic personalities who define themselves dramatically, and viewed from the vantage point of ripened experience.

For our purposes the most important characters in the novel are Oliver and Mario. Some of the others are also of interest, for some of them represent forces which had found a place in the scheme of *The Life of Reason.*

We must remember that in *The Life of Reason* Santayana has marked out three stages in the development of morality, the pre-rational, the rational, and the post-rational.[50] Now the interesting thing is that pre-rational and post-rational morality are both found embodied in *The Last Puritan*, each through a

[50] *Ibid.*, chs. VII, IX, X.

single character. It is not difficult to see that Jim Darnley represents the same attitude towards the world that Santayana had, in 1905, called pre-rational. In Jim, as in pre-rational morality, the flesh has not yet begun to flower into spirit. He is completely a natural man, unburdened with introspective needs. He is sensuous, fleshly, and "shady."[51] It is not difficult to see, either, that in Peter Alden we have an embodiment of the post-rational attitude, for his is the attitude of the man who has tried the life of reason, at least in imagination, and found it wanting.[52]

Neither Peter nor Jim constitute a problem for us, however, unless the fact that Santayana shows a great deal of sympathy for Jim can be considered a problem. But the personalities of Oliver, of Mario, and of the Vicar do constitute a problem. The reason for this is that neither of the three, by himself, represents a type of living which Santayana could approve of as rational and satisfactory, but the three taken together, if we could imagine them compounded into a single personality, do correspond to the picture of the rational man which he painted in 1905.

Let us begin with Oliver. The reviewers did not allow us to forget that Oliver is the last puritan in the sense that he convinced himself on puritan grounds that it was wrong to be a puritan. But, however much Oliver objected to the strong moral bent of his own nature, he never succeeded in overcoming what his friend Jim once called his "blooming principles," and his "moral tantrums."[53] Before Oliver could accept experience at

[51] *The Last Puritan*, 285. No direct statement is made, so far as I remember, that Jim is responsible for at least two cold-blooded murders, that of the mate and one of his mistress's husbands; but the hints are pretty plain. Cf. 229, 261ff, 272. For Jim's character, personality, values, see 152-158, 230ff, 272, 319, etc.

[52] The quotation comes from *Reason in Science*, 266. Peter, at a time when he was still a boy, reflects that "it was the dreadful nature of life . . . that if you avoided doing one thing because it wasn't worthwhile you were thereby caught doing another, which wasn't worthwhile either." So, having had to flee his country after accidentally killing a man while at Harvard, he drifted the rest of his life in a luxurious yacht, and put himself to sleep with a bit of dope. As one of Santayana's reviewers somewhere remarks, this novel is a beautiful illustration, on the dramatic plane, of what an epiphenomenalist, whose life has been epiphenomenal, would write.

[53] *The Last Puritan*, 169.

all he had to digest it morally. And before he could make a choice he had to be sure that it was the best that he was selecting. In a sense, however, he was really incapable of making a choice, for "he felt bound, . . . as it were, in his present duties, and *couldn't* choose otherwise."[54] Thinking of his friend Jim, who had a way of brushing aside labored scruples and false shams,[55] and remembering how Jim could find comfort and jollity in drink, in sensuality and rowdiness, Oliver said to himself: "But I couldn't. I hate pleasure. I hate what is called having a good time. I hate stimulants. I hate 'dope.' It's all a cheat."[56]

Oliver does not seem to have realized, nor does Santayana himself, that this kind of search for perfection is the very best way to achieve moral frustration. For Oliver's concern was with the form of morality emptied of all content, since the content of the moral life is made up of human impulses, ambitions, reachings towards goals towards which we drive with passion and with joy. Oliver was enamored of the idea of perfection but had no real drive to be anything in particular, except to be perfect. He lacked therefore anything to be perfect about. He studied philosophy almost in the same way in which he played football, out of a somewhat abstract sense that he should; but even though Santayana seems to be, the reader is not convinced that Oliver really loved philosophy. And though we must take the biographer's word for it, it is difficult to believe that anyone could excel as Oliver did when engaged in activities out of a sense of duty and not out of love for the activity itself. Whether one can or not, this much is clear; namely, that the way to lose perfection is to seek it. A person approaches perfection when he wants to improve his game because he loves it and wants to enjoy it even more; or when he wants to master some field of human knowledge, or when he wants to increase his power, because mastery or increase is the objective realization of his love. But to be a perfect being *überhaupt*, morally perfect without being perfect in anything—a man on that road is bound to

[54] *Ibid.*, 227; italics in original.
[55] *Ibid.*, 173.
[56] *Ibid.*, 371.

meet with frustration. We may therefore say that Oliver was the last puritan in another sense besides the one recognized by his biographer. For he was a puritan without anything to be puritanical about. His ancestors, the New England puritans, loved specific forms of perfection. They had their own orthodoxy, and to be right was to be loyal to the principles which they knew to be true. Hence they knew exactly what they wanted to enact or to bring about. Nor were they therefore afraid of being called reformers. Oliver loved perfection but hated reformers and thought them the most odious of beings.[57] He did not want a specific kind of purity or righteousness, was indifferent to social justice, did not care about human dignity, and sought studiously to let everything develop perfectly after its kind. In short, he substituted an abstract verbal goal for a specific form of living, and tried in vain to actualize the form without the matter. Such a life is sheer idolatry of means and neglect of ends; it is an empty life, irrelevant to human goals, and because idolatrous, not moral but essentially immoral. It is one road to disintegration. It should not be surprising therefore that in remaining true to himself Oliver found no adequate self-realization. His biographer speaks of his tragedy. Oliver was essentially a sad, and in a sense, a deeply frustrated person. Because he could not go after the gaiety and the joy for which he longed, he sought to persuade himself that what he missed was not worth having. But he made a poor success of his efforts, since his deep yearning for freedom from his subjective moral monitor was as real as his abstract love of the best.

In spite of Oliver's desolation and sadness, however, Santayana has a very deep respect for him. He may not wish to emulate him—on the contrary. But he is constrained to express in all sorts of direct and indirect ways Oliver's superiority. He knows that a man ruled by a strong conscience is condemned never to enjoy the spontaneity which gives gaiety to life and sweetness. Yet, for all that, it is to Oliver that the best of his respect and admiration goes. For Oliver, as the young man himself realized, may have been "burdened, but [he was] strong, groping but faithful, desolate but proud."[58] He failed at happi-

[57] *Ibid.*, 244.
[58] *Ibid.*, 319.

ness. But he failed because he would not buy it at the price of his integrity.

If Oliver is frustrated, so is the Vicar, Jim's father. His son, who sees through him, tells Oliver that his father is a mystic, because people who fail in the world always say the world isn't a fit place to live in.[59] In the pulpit, Jim's father was all ease, all inspiration and calm eloquence. But out of the pulpit these qualities disappeared and he seemed like a "raw, bony, rather rude schoolmaster who said only the most conventional things in the most conventional see-saw."[60] As Jim tells Oliver, his father "can't come down gracefully out of his element; feels dreadfully out of it in this world, doesn't honestly belong here at all."[61] He is the spiritual man; and such a man, as the Vicar himself puts it, "lives tragically, because his flesh and his pride and his hope have been withered early under the hot rays of revelation."[62]

In contrast to the attitude which Santayana has towards Oliver and towards the Vicar, he is all admiration and love for Mario. For unlike Oliver, Mario is gay and untroubled and natural. He is refined by nature, clear as crystal, merry without claims, brave without armour. He danced his way through the show with graceful ease. Men liked him, women adored him. He made love assiduously to all the young women he met, because that is the way of a gentleman. He was infectiously charming, worldly. Above all, however, he was "a gentleman." Like Jim, he was unburdened and knew the world's values and had no quarrel with them. Unlike Jim however he had no steep and shady crimes to confess. He lives "irresponsibly, even licentiously," and yet within the limits of kindness and honor. Oliver loved him as everybody else did, and thought there was something enviable about him—but enviable only "if you wished to be happy;" not if you wished to do right, "to make yourself and the world better."[63]

We must try to see how these three characters, Mario, Oliver, and the Vicar, represent the three elements which Santayana

[59] *Ibid.*, 233.
[60] *Ibid.*, 251.
[61] *Ibid.*, 252.
[62] *Ibid.*, 255.
[63] *Ibid.*, 289, 311, 319, 447, 508.

sought to bring into synthesis in *The Life of Reason*, but failed to do so. To take first the Vicar, let us remember that for Santayana thought is the entelechy of being.[64] But thought has its roots in matter. Although in his official philosophy Santayana seems still to maintain this point of view, in his dramatic vision of the world this does not turn out to be the case. For the man of spirit does not express the energies of the world: indeed he is not at all at ease in the world, and seems out of the pulpit a rude and commonplace schoolmaster. But haven't schoolmasters always been thought a little ridiculous? The Vicar, at any rate, is; he is a little queer, a little odd, ill at ease. He has not been blessed with worldly goods, but was blessed with a cantankerous wife who nags all day about their poverty and has no inkling of the inner riches of her husband, nor of the climate in which he lives. The whole worth of ideas then may be ideal, and thought may be the entelechy of being, but Santayana now seems to be a little skeptical of the connection on which he once insisted between "spirit" and "matter." He is still a materialist, but thought does not seem as clearly as it once did to express the energies of the world. If we can read the lesson of the Vicar, spirit remains spirit, matter matter, and the integration once insisted on, he now seems to say, is not possible; spirit does not find itself at home in the world, and the spiritual man, his hope and his flesh withered, is, outside of the artificial circumstances of the pulpit, queer and a bit ridiculous.

If the Vicar represents the failure of the spiritual man, Oliver represents the failure of the moral man. The moral dogmatism, which, as we saw, he endeavored in 1905 to incorporate in his conception of reason in order to have both contribute to happiness, is here by his own admission seen to be an obstacle to the proper flowering of personality. This means that the distinction between reason and conscience has been abandoned. Happiness and morality do not seem compatible. The moral man dies frustrated, exhausted in a losing war against himself. There seems to be, as Oliver suspects, something in nature which condemns nature.[65] On the other hand, by some

[64] *Reason in Common Sense*, 233.

[65] *The Last Puritan*, 520.

happy accident nature may achieve through some men like Mario an amoral freedom and gaiety which are a full realization of enviable happiness. Happiness was the keystone of the life of reason as he conceived it in 1905. But he then thought that happiness and dogmatism, natural impulse and morality, could be made to pull together. In the edges of the life of reason lurked, according to the picture, the frightful spectre of "conscience." This spectre was a perversion of the moral drive which could be moral and yet allow for the expression of each impulse as in itself justified. We have seen that the synthesis he then thought could exist was not actually to be found in his conception of the life of reason. And now, it would seem, he agrees with us and no longer thinks the synthesis possible. Morality and happiness are clearly incompatible; morality is always conscience. Oliver is no fanatic as the type had been defined earlier; but though he was admirable he is pitiable. It is the young fop, capable of living licentiously and irresponsibly, who is the ideal type of person whom the author now really loves.

This is not all, however. For Oliver is a fully realized personality; we know him inwardly and become acquainted with the poignant reality of his motives. He seems overdrawn at times; but at no time does the reader lose the conviction that Santayana is portraying a living man. Of Mario, whom Santayana loves, the same cannot be said. Mario is not real at all. He is no more than a concretion of a dream. Oliver himself does not quite believe in Mario's reality when he meets him. He was "so merry, so unconcerned about everything, so innocently sparkling, that to Oliver he hardly seemed human at all: more like some Chinese figurine, all ivory and silk. . . ."[66] Too good to be true, it takes no great perspicacity to see that this precocious Mediterranean imp educated in Eton is the latest version of a dream Santayana once was fond of dreaming in another disguise; for the "Hellas" of whom he often has spoken is neither to be found in maps nor in histories, it is a literary perpetration, an invention into which he projected all his aspirations.

[66] *Ibid.*, 289.

This then is what *The Life of Reason* turns into in the short span of three decades or a little over: utter moral bankruptcy and a louring despair which is held precariously at bay. A sad ending for so brave a beginning.

Does this mean that all morality is a sham? Or does it mean that naturalism is a failure? Neither. Santayana's transitional naturalism is not the only naturalism possible, nor is his account of the life of reason the only account that can be given of it. It does mean, however, that if we are to retain our naturalism we must abandon our pre-naturalistic notion of mind, and must repudiate the split between matter and spirit it involves. It also means that a theory of the life of reason is not possible when we undertake the task of rearing one with unanalyzed notions of "reason" and of "harmony."

ELISEO VIVAS

DEPARTMENT OF PHILOSOPHY
UNIVERSITY OF WISCONSIN

12

Horace L. Friess and Henry M. Rosenthal

REASON IN RELIGION AND THE EMANCIPATED SPIRIT

12

REASON IN RELIGION AND THE EMANCIPATED SPIRIT: A DIALOGUE

*H.L.**—Of course, Henry, you know that Santayana is occupied with a still unpublished book on *The Realm of Spirit*† which will no doubt bring further important clarification of his views on religion. Do you feel constrained on this account or do you enjoy with me the feeling that it permits us to express our thought the more freely without obligation to define the position of one who is still to be his own interpreter?

H.M.—But are you persuaded we may await this forthcoming work with fair hopes? Will it not bring more evidence of his avowed sympathies with the infra-Machiavelli?

H.L.—However the case may stand with his politics, I suspect *The Realm of Spirit* will reveal some deepening of his thought on religion. I have heard that after completing *The Last Puritan* he was drawn to the theme of "The First Christian," by way of venturing on certain interpretations of Christ. Now I imagine that his mature reflections today about things of Caesar's and things of the spirit, if carried out in consonance with his later philosophy, would necessarily constitute a very significant part of his thought on religion. Indeed, it is not impossible that you might find it more satisfying than anything of his hitherto on this subject.

H.M.—It is a tenable hypothesis.

H.L.—In any case, I myself am truly happy to be absolved for the present from any need of fixing his position. That can

* The initials used throughout this essay are those of the first and middle (given) names of the participants in this dialogue. H.L., then, stands for Horace L. Friess, and H.M. represents Henry M. Rosenthal. *Ed.*

† At the time this essay was completed *The Realm of Spirit*, which has since appeared (Scribner's, New York, 1940), was still unpublished. *Ed.*

be left to Santayana and we can pursue our own thoughts about him the more freely.

H.M.—Where will your thought take hold of his thought, I wonder?

H.L.—Well, his ideas first took hold of mine with that pregnant statement of the relations between poetry and religion in his early essays called *Interpretations of Poetry and Religion.* Do you remember the formula: "Religion is an imaginative echo of things natural and moral,"[1] and the brief Preface in which he said:

> the excellence of religion is due to an idealization of experience which, while making religion noble if treated as poetry, makes it necessarily false if treated as science. Its function is rather to draw from reality materials for an image of that ideal to which reality ought to conform, and to make us citizens, by anticipation, in the world we crave.[2]

H.M.—Yes, and I also recall the illuminating way in which that same Preface describes his position in relation to the "apologists of theology" and to "its critics" in those days. Among the former he includes not only the orthodox but also the liberal school, pointing out to them that "mythology cannot become science by being reduced in bulk, but it may cease, as a mythology, to be worth having."[3] On the other hand, against the "apathetic naturalism" of "the positivistic school of criticism," he urges that "all the errors and follies of religion are worthy of indulgent sympathy, since they represent an effort, however misguided, to interpret and to use the materials of experience for moral ends, and to measure the value of reality by its relation to the ideal."[4] Santayana thus proposed to save religion from both its friends and enemies for positive purposes in the work of reason.

H.L.—I have always wondered whether what you call Santayana's saving of religion for positive purposes in the work of reason has a prospective future reference as well as retrospective historical significance, or not. Is Santayana's theory of religion

[1] *Interpretations of Poetry and Religion*, 235.
[2] *Ibid.*, vi.
[3] *Ibid.*, viii.
[4] *Ibid.*, ix.

part of philosophy's wisdom as the Owl of Minerva, a vision granted only as the shades of night are falling on religion? Did he mean it to be more?

H.M.—At the beginning of *Reason in Science,* he wrote: "Religion and art have had their day."[5] Did not Hegel say something similar? But Santayana's theory, while not perhaps a creative principle generative of future religion, would have just as much critical function and validity in the future as in its present application to tradition, would it not?

H.L.—Yes, it would. It is perfectly clear that Santayana did intend his theory to aid in clarifying the positive rôle of religion with respect to the history of civilization hitherto. But I have sometimes thought that he showed a marked and conscious lack of sympathy for heretical and unborn religion. Still on the very page of *Reason in Science* which you cite, he added that a critic might "venture to hope that religion and art may assume in the future forms far nobler and more rational than any they have hitherto worn."[6] His aversion to the confusion and lack of standards that attend the disintegration of a great tradition is, however, unmistakable. Perhaps it is in this light that one should understand his recent statement, in explaining "the unity of his earlier and later philosophy," when he again declared: "I have always disliked mystics who were not definite in their logic and orthodox in their religion."[7]

H.M.—Besides being a matter of temperament, do you not suppose this attitude relates to the fact that his thought unfolded in a special atmosphere at the end of the nineteenth century? In "Brief History of My Opinions" he refers to "the historical spirit of the nineteenth century, and to that splendid panorama of nations and religions, literatures and arts, which it unrolled before the imagination," as having been particularly liberating.[8] Obviously he was also deeply influenced by the critical currents of that century, by the special forms which the

[5] *Reason in Science,* 3.

[6] *Ibid.,* 3.

[7] Preface to Vol. VII of the Triton Edition of *The Works of George Santayana,* xi.

[8] "Brief History of My Opinions," in *Contemporary American Philosophy,* 244-245.

conflict of religion and science assumed for men in Spencer's time and in the flood-tide of the elder Huxley's brand of positivism. Of course, it is clear today with what great success Santayana's genius found a way beyond the restrictions and tangles of that positivistic naturalism into a world of larger orbit and horizon. Still such was the milieu from which his thought sprang.

H.L.—Yes, what you say certainly helps to illumine the double character of positive appraisal and of emancipation which his thought on religion has throughout. He has wanted at one and the same time to point out the positive rôle of religion in the life of reason, in human progress, and also to free us from its errors. Remember his statement: "In no sphere is the contrast clearer between wisdom and folly; in none, perhaps, has there been so much of both," as in religion.[9]

But now in the light of Santayana's recent writings—those of his later philosophy—one sees the way he has come from intellectual emancipation and from appraisal in terms of rational morality to a still more exacting form of spiritual appraisal and spiritual emancipation. Has he not travelled from the attempt to tell us about reason in historical religion to a concern with that "ultimate religion . . . proper to a wholly free and disillusioned spirit?"[10]

H.M.—*Reason in Religion* itself seems to contain a prospectus of that itinerary, in its voyage from "the Christian epic" to the realm of "ideal immortality" at the end, which indeed is a certain pre-figuring of the later realm of essence. The stages of his itinerary, as you name them, are surely impressive. But must we not consider also how they were carried through?

H.L.—Yes, of course, we must. And I suggest that we should attend first and last to Santayana's concern with intellectual and with spiritual emancipation, while in between we may follow his course through various phases of moral and spiritual appraisal.

H.M.—I believe I follow you in distinguishing these different functions of his thought. But does not the same founda-

[9] *Reason in Religion,* 274.

[10] "Ultimate Religion," in *Obiter Scripta,* 280.

tion, his materialism, serve the purpose of both his intellectual and his spiritual emancipation? This viewpoint, I mean, is the ground not only of his critique of belief, but also of his freedom to confront the world, as he puts it "martially . . . with courage and good humor, rather than supplications and fears."[11]

H.L.—Very true. But let us consider first his critique of belief. For I wonder how far you and I would agree as to the issues of that first phase of his work which we have called one of intellectual emancipation.

I.

H.M.—Well, as far as the criticism of theological beliefs is concerned, do you not think that he has stated his principle admirably in *Reason in Religion*, when he says that:

> To regain moral freedom—without which knowledge cannot be put to its rational use in the government of life—we must rediscover the origin of the gods, reduce them analytically to their natural and moral constituents, and then proceed to rearrange those materials, without any quantitative loss, in forms appropriate to a maturer reflection.[12]

It is a principle of dissolving theological doctrines and beliefs by analysis into their natural and moral constituents.

H.L.—I think you have put your finger on the principle of his method, and I often return in thought to that very passage. As you read it, however, I could not help being struck by the fact that Santayana here feels concerned with more than intellectual emancipation, namely with "regaining moral freedom." Let us not forget that point. But let me first ask you to what limits you think Santayana intends to carry the dissolution of theological beliefs, and what is the meaning of intellectual emancipation in this regard? Is it only the traditional, anthropomorphic beliefs of the popular faiths that are to be analyzed into their "natural and moral constituents?" Or is the same method, as I think, to be applied to the more philosophical theologies as well?

H.M.—It is his virtue to apply it to them all. As far as I

[11] Preface to Vol. VII of the Triton Edition of *The Works of George Santayana*, viii, xiv.

[12] *Reason in Religion*, 61.

can see there is neither shred nor core of theological doctrine that remains immune to the kind of analysis he proposes.

H.L.—And so theological belief goes into the discard?

H.M.—How so? The analysis gives back those beliefs at least as symbols of the natural and moral facts it discovers to be their constituents. But critical reflection, Santayana says, emancipates him "from the horrid claim of ideas to literal truth," in science and philosophy no less than in religion.[13] "My matured conclusion," he writes, "has been that no system is to be trusted, not even that of science in any literal or pictorial sense; but all systems may be used and, up to a certain point, trusted as symbols."[14]

H.L.—Up to what point, I wonder; and how is that to be decided? Religious faith generally implies other trust than Santayana's materialism renders appropriate, does it not?

H.M.—That depends on the religion, I suppose. Santayana's respect for Power and Truth seems large and deep. Is it less so for Good, I wonder, because he takes that to be relative to each kind of sentient creature?

H.L.—Yet your own view would emphasize a fuller likeness between man and his Maker? I must confess that what you say in that essay of yours about our being able to reach into the structure of reality along the lines of the emotional structure in life and faith seems rather vague to me. Would not Santayana find here a philosophical version of that pathetic fallacy which his materialism is determined to avoid?

H.M.—He probably would. But perhaps there are some outworn dogmas—dating from that *fin de siècle* whence we said he sprang—in the form of materialism he holds. It has certainly been remarked at what price to intelligibility he combines that bare materialism with his many-colored coat of humanism.

H.L.—Still, is Santayana's concept of being what you mean by the structure of reality? And if I say on my part that the emotional structure of life and faith leads us into the structure

[13] Preface to Vol. VII of the Triton Edition of *The Works of George Santayana*, xiii.

[14] "Brief History of My Opinions," in *Contemporary American Philosophy*, II, 244.

of our real existence and its surrounding world by many most significant clues, again I am not sure that what I mean by this is what you mean by "reality." Life has many emotions and many faiths. Is it so evident that its deepest and fullest relations are caught up in some version of theism?

H.M.—Why should I say how evident it is to those who won't hear Moses and the prophets? But coming back to Santayana, do you remember his early "theological tragedy" with its sympathetic portrayal of Lucifer's denial of God's sovereign omniscience? What I want to know is whether such an inclination toward the side of Lucifer is of the essence of intellectual emancipation. Or is it just part of Santayana's revulsion against the infinite mind of Royce's theodicy, about which he says: "It would be hard to exaggerate the ire which [it] aroused in my youthful breast."[15]

H.L.—Whatever its personal genesis, it seems to be a very stable and essential component of Santayana's intellectual freedom, does it not? I doubt if he himself would regard it as separable from his inclination toward the truth. In rereading *Lucifer* lately I was struck by its continuity with Santayana's later philosophy. The conception of unfathomable being underlies the whole, whereas both Greek and Christian deities appear there only as special symbols.

It occurs to me, however, that we have been talking of intellectual emancipation in the usual manner as meaning deliverance from the constrictions of false and inadequate beliefs. In so far it is a condition of disillusion and Lucifer is a magnificent symbol for it. But one may also think of it as a process of liberating the intellectual powers for significant performance. And from this point of view I find it impossible to conceive that the intellectual powers of mankind could be given maximum liberation under the dispensation of any one posture of metaphysical faith, were it entertained by all, however luminous in itself. I cannot, for instance, disengage the work of Bach's mind from his faith in Christian Providence, just as it is difficult to imagine, let us say, the work of Freud or Marx combined with such faith. In this sense actual emancipations of the mind

[15] *Ibid.*, 246.

are specific and relative rather than complete, and Lucifer is no preferred symbol for them all.

My persuasion on this point is one of the reasons why I cannot take to the idea of one single faith by which all are to be saved, nor feel well when Catholics, Protestants, and Jews propose a common front against the atheists on behalf of civilization. On the other hand, it equally prevents me from identifying the cause of universal enlightenment with the triumph of atheism and the City of Moscow.

H.M.—What you say recalls to me that no small part of Santayana's motivation may have been to remove the discussion of religion from the rather waste yet blood-caked sand of that nineteenth-century arena in which "theism" and "atheism" were the main issues, and to establish it on a more decent platform where "religion" and "irreligion" should be the real ones. Though not himself a theist I doubt whether Santayana would consider a man much concerned to deny or negate theism to be intellectually emancipated.

For this reason I propose we consider that concern for "moral freedom" which Santayana expressed when he spoke of "analyzing theological doctrines and beliefs into their natural and moral constituents." I confess the discussion of religious belief runs thin when abstracted from that fuller ground of practice and emotion which supplies so many determinants of it.

H.L.—I like your suggestion. But what do you take Santayana to mean by "moral freedom" in this connection? Surely it includes the critical aspect of freeing conduct from the tyranny of superstitious beliefs. But more than that I think he has in mind the positive conception of a rational morality on natural grounds which he sets over against the various forms of absolutistic conscience so generally associated with religious conviction. Achieving such a morality he takes to be a matter of relative polity, that is of adjusting the various natural interests of men to each other and to the specific circumstances that obtain in the given case. However, have you considered how far his theory of religion—and especially what we have called his appraisal of its historic rôle in terms of rational morality—how far this contributes to an understanding of practice, and illumines the nature and requirements of such polity?

II.

H.M.—As a matter of fact I have been thinking much on this point. And I must admit that Santayana's thought seems to me to suggest much more than it fulfills in this regard. His interest in describing the rôle of historic religion as a phase of the life of reason, in assessing its contributions to human progress, has deeply fascinated me, but I cannot help concluding that his way of characterizing religion is too incomplete for him to accomplish this splendid humane purpose in a satisfying realistic manner.

I do not know how I can best communicate the difficulties I find, so I shall venture to suggest them in a number of different ways. Santayana says that "poetry is called religion when it intervenes in life, and religion, when it merely supervenes upon life, is seen to be nothing but poetry."[16] Now one way of stating my question would be to ask in how far Santayana has explored and understood the nature, the way, I might almost say the mechanism, of that intervention in life which makes religion of poetry. Santayana says explicitly enough, and certainly he knows that "the core of religion is not theoretical."[17] Yet his own way of exploring the subject seems to fall short of conducting us truly and altogether into the nature of its practicality. *How* religion *is* practical is what I should like to understand better; through what conditions it accomplishes whatever it does accomplish.

In *Reason in Religion* the practical side of religion seems to fall into two spheres: ritual and morality. Yet despite all his sympathetic interest in mythology, and feeling for its nature, Santayana gives surprisingly little attention to ritual. Though there is ample historic justification, of course, for his treatment of ritual together with magic, he surely must know better than to dismiss it together with superstition. One might expect from him some further consideration of the ceremonial arts, their underlying conditions and their significance in life's economy.

H.L.—But how much attention to the dynamics of ritual should be expected from one so greatly devoted to essences?

[16] *Interpretations of Poetry and Religion*, v.

[17] *Reason in Religion*, 178.

Perhaps Santayana takes this aspect of the matter for granted. And perhaps church services bore him or make him feel uncomfortable.

H.M.—That may well be. He is entitled to be bored. (For that matter, who is not bored?) As one might be, unhappily, and for one reason or another, with the ritual of love; yet it is only a semi-divine Plato who may forget, and he too at his peril, that there is no love without ritual. So that, however Santayana may feel personally about contemporary rituals, as a writer on the whole sweep of religion he surely should not take this aspect of the subject for granted.

Santayana has written movingly and memorably of piety and spirituality, of reverent attachment to the sources of our being and of spiritual vision of its goals. Has he, however, sufficiently examined religion as a phase of life as it is reared and lived in the middle between its natural bases and its ideal fulfilments? Perhaps the task did not suit his contemplative and aesthetic humor. And perhaps he rationalized this aversion by the doctrine that "consciousness was created by the muses; but meantime industrious nature, in our bodily organization, takes good care to keep our actions moderately sane, in spite of our poetic genius."[18] I know it does not always seem so, but is not sanity in some measure a function of culture also?

We must be indebted to Santayana—especially those of us who live in a culture dominated so largely by Protestant traditions—for his great emphasis on the rôle of the imagination in religion. But just because I find this emphasis so welcome, I regret that the nature of the imagination and its relations were not more steadily explored.

H.L.—You remind me of something that Nilsson said who came over from Lund last fall and lectured to us on Eleusis. He raised the question whether northern people ever really had understood the Greek experience connected with the ancient myth of Kôre, the corn-maiden. He told us about the Greek calendar and the seasonal occupations. And it seemed to him likely that it was not in winter that Kôre was underground, but

[18] Preface to Vol. VII of the Triton Edition of *The Works of George Santayana*, xiii.

in the parched summer months when the grain had been cut and stored in underground silos as the wealth of Pluto. His whole exposition preserved no less the poetry of the myth, but showed its force within the actualities of existence and of the cult as a practical institution. Now is it your contention that Santayana passes by such insights and treats the religious imagination as more freely fanciful in its dramatization of nature's changes?

H.M.—No, I do not claim that such observations have escaped Santayana, for it is obvious from many passages that they have not. But I do not find his theory aligned to a sustained pursuit of them. And without this the appraisal of religion in relation to rational morality can scarcely be solid.

H.L.—What you say touches a large part of what has stirred me for many years. I remember the group in 1917 with Professor B. when I first read *Reason in Religion*. B. told us that he had been reading *The Life of Reason* (and especially this volume) annually for a long time. His appreciation of the work was both full and fine. But he kept emphasizing to us constantly—who found the cup running over as it was—that there was an immense amount to be added to what Santayana had said from all the stores of anthropology, and sociology, and psychology. One of his own additions came I think from his acquaintance with the school of Durkheim, for he liked to say that religion might be viewed as "the world of the imagination when it functions socially, that is to integrate a group."

Professor B. was not thinking to rest with this, or any such generalization, as a formula. But he wanted to elaborate Santayana's emphasis on the imagination and its intervention in life with a view to understanding the development and rôle of religion and art and philosophy in their social context. So you see that Santayana really brought thoughtful readers close to the ways of inquiry that you have in mind.

H.M.—Oh, of course, I realize that. In fact, it is just because Santayana is so frequently travelling in or near those ways himself that I regret their features and implications do not more completely inform his general theory. There are many fine passages for the analysis of religion in different cultures in Santayana's writings. Yet I do not find that he gives us a theory of religion as adequate as one might wish to sustain or guide such analysis. This is a pity, for one certainly needs theoretical instruments and focus to assimilate what anthropologists and historians serve to us in the way of information. Santayana is one who might have given us even more help than he did in this regard.

H.L.—After all, do you expect a writer to do single-handed the work of all generations? Consider not only the setting in which Santayana began his work, but still more the fact that his own genius led him toward quite a different horizon, as I think, than to cultural history and social analysis. We must talk of that presently.

But since you feel as you do, why not yourself take up the work where you find it left off? Why not devote some attention to the anthropologists and sociologists and to recent psychological literature, observing moreover what that literature has had to say about the nature and functioning of emotional symbols. Then come back to Santayana's theory of religion and see what needs to be subtracted, added, or otherwise amended.

H.M.—I already see myself proposing a new hypothesis about the nature and function of religion in culture, namely, that religion is the central art in culture for the control of the emotional system.

H.L.—Your haste to this conclusion gives me as much pause as does Santayana's light passage over rational to "post-rational morality." Were we to explore your hypothesis as fully as I should wish eventually to do, I think we would now be led considerably off the course of Santayana's own line of progress.

H.M.—Let us return to that then, if you know the way.

III.

H.L.—Well then, I might suggest that Santayana in his comments on historical religion has really been less interested in the history of culture than in a phenomenology of spirit. Would you not agree to that, if this last ponderous phrase be taken broadly and not in the sense of any special German system of philosophy? I mean that he likes to characterize and appraise different dispositions toward the world, in a manner that reminds me of the transcendentalists' interest in attitudes. I find this interest running through not only his major works but also his shorter essays on a great variety of themes. We are not apt to forget, however, that he soliloquizes in English, and that he is not like some contemporary philosophers translating the German "Geist" when he uses the word "spirit."

H.M.—I should say his comments on historical religion are often of a rather hybrid nature, a mixture of cultural history and spiritual appraisal, phenomenology of spirit, if you want to use such terms. Hegel, of course, systematically combined the two because in his view the history of culture is essentially the self-realization of *Geist.* But with Santayana who is very far from taking this view the proportion or relation between the two seems without plan. I also often wonder whether Santayana has really achieved a clear conception of spirit. If such is to be found in his recent works, do you think his characterizations of human genius in various attitudes should be called a phenomenology of "spirit" in the more exact sense he now gives that term? I remember, for instance, that he speaks of the "Protestant determination to wash the world clean" as "very unspiritual."[19] Is this merely a matter of terms or do you see questions here for *The Realm of Spirit* to answer?

H.L.—There may well be real questions. But in the absence of Santayana's own answers let us regard it for the present as a matter of terms, and let us speak of the phenomenology of spirit in a broad sense to include his account of even such attitudes as he might call predominantly unspiritual. This will not prevent us from discussing his own conception of "spirit" attentively either.

First, I must agree with you that cultural history and phenomenology of spirit are combined in what Santayana has written about the Greeks, and about "the Christian compromise," as well as about modern nations, such as Germany, England, and the United States. But does it not grow more obvious all

[19] *Platonism and the Spiritual Life,* 85.

the time that a description of dispositions of mind has been the predominant interest? Of course, I must repeat, it has not been pursued in any systematic way as if to achieve a comprehensiveness which in the nature of the case I believe Santayana would not consider possible. I remember a remark which he included in a review of Spengler to the effect that it would be ungracious to assume there could be but a limited number of types of culture or of spirit, as if one were to speak of nine kinds of possible mountains, rivers, and so on.[20]

The same review, by the way, contained several very interesting paragraphs on the "Magian soul" in comparison with other strains affecting Catholicism, together with some autobiographical musings as to whether Santayana was not really closer to the former than to the latter in his own makeup. Sometimes he gives us these remarkable impressionistic glimpses, and then again more sustained treatments of certain themes like that of "the Christian compromise" in its various main phases, Catholic and Protestant. For my own part I gladly read and reread these descriptions and spiritual appraisals, be they great or small, and am not disposed to tax him with being himself wilful and romantic merely because of the unevenness of his treatment.

But I must confess that a more serious question arises at this point. Do you think that a phenomenology of spirit can be objective in the sense of having no special, partisan point of view, no particular inclination of spirit of its own? You may remember the late Edmund Husserl claimed for his phenomenology that it is a discipline of "presuppositionless" intuition or contemplation, and Santayana refers to Husserl in his *Realm of Essence* as being on a path akin to his own.[21] Perhaps Husserl, however, meant only a form of contemplation without ontological postulation but not without noetic viewpoint or orientation. What is your thought about this?

H.M.—Well, whatever Husserl meant, and also without committing myself in one and the same breath as to what may be possible, I should just like to remark that Santayana's talk

[20] "Spengler," *The New Adelphi*, II, 210-214.

[21] *The Realm of Essence*, 172ff.

about spirit often seems to be his favorite way of damning what he doesn't like, for instance, Protestantism, Wordsworth's "black coat and white choker," the modern philanthropist, and most of the U.S.A.

H.L.—Many people have been damned before as enemies of the spirit. But do you hold that what Santayana says about these *bêtes noires* of his is not true?

H.M.—We must allow him these *bêtes noires* as a special gallery of black essences. Much is very good that he says about them.

H.L.—And often hits home as truth? Let us allow also his observation that "there is a clarifying and satiric force in the discrimination of essences," as he knows how to practice it.[22]

Nevertheless, I do think that Santayana is pretty casual at times in his characterizations, in what I have called his phenomenology of spirit, and sometimes when important issues are at stake. He will occasionally fire a double-barrel of buckshot quite beside the mark. I find a case of that, for instance, at the close of *The Genteel Tradition at Bay*, and feel the more let down because of satisfaction with much of the book to that point.

H.M.—I do not seem to recall the passage.

H.L.—Well, now and again in the last twenty pages of the book Santayana goes for Professor Norton and other representatives of a form of absolutistic conscience he is characterizing—not impartially and not carefully, I should say. "Can the way of Matthew Arnold and of Professor Norton be the way of life for all men for ever?" he asks.[23] Thank God or Nature: No. I do not question, as some might, these thrusts at particular autocrats; for I find the point of them palpable enough. But at the close of the essay Santayana delivers the following broadside, aimed presumably at absolutistic conscience in general:

The commandment *Thou shalt not kill*, is given out on divine authority, and infinite sanctions are supposed to confirm it in the other world. . . . In its human atmosphere the thunder of that precept is not hollow;

[22] Preface to Vol. VII of the Triton Edition of *The Works of George Santayana*, xiii.

[23] *The Genteel Tradition at Bay*, 69.

> the sharp bolts of remorse and ruin follow closely upon it. But in the cosmos at large is killing forbidden? If so, the fabric of creation must be monstrous and sinful indeed. . . . Had it been the Creator who said *Thou shalt not kill,* and said it to the universe, existence would have been arrested. . . . A morality frankly relative to man's nature is worthy of man, being at once vital and rational, martial and generous; whereas absolutism smells of fustiness as well as of faggots.[24]

I am really amazed at this passage. At precisely what conscience east or west of Suez is Santayana aiming his hypothetical absurdity when he says "Had it been the Creator who said *Thou shalt not kill,* and said it to the universe, existence would have been arrested?" Surely Professor Norton knew as well as Santayana that the Bible represents The Lord saying this to man.

H.M.—I wonder if either of them observed that the Hebrew sense of the commandment is more accurately rendered by the expression *Thou shalt not murder.* Several recent translations both by Christian and Jewish scholars have adopted this rendering.

H.L.—How very pertinent! Of course, Santayana's whole statement is plainly built on a correct understanding of the commandment. But wanting to damn a certain way of taking commandments, an attitude of moral absolutism, he distorts this attitude by associating it with a purely fictitious absurd injunction to the universe. And then glibly substituting his own way of taking the commandment, he begs the whole basic question of *what is* "the human atmosphere in which the thunder of that precept is not hollow." A rather serious question to beg in the present murderous atmosphere of the world, don't you think?

Of course, I can understand how black and indistinguishable everything must look to him when he thinks of Professor Norton or Matthew Arnold wanting to make everybody like themselves. Still, in order to attack moral snobbery one need not distort and travesty man's disposition to think that his rôle in the whole scheme of things bids him abstain from murder. A better discrimination of essences at this point would certainly

[24] *Ibid.,* 72, 73, 74.

have more clarifying and also greater satiric force, I should think.

IV.

H.M.—I should like to think twice about what you were saying. Does not Santayana after all pursue a way of his own pretty consistently through all his spiritual appraisals which you call his phenomenology of spirit? On the one hand, he acknowledges the sphere of relativistic human politics and ethics, while over against this he perceives the universality of a "truly free and disillusioned spirit," disintoxicated of values. As he himself has explained, his later writings are consistent enough with his earlier, but represent a change of emphasis and interest from human to cosmic natural perspectives. The humanism of his first works, as he says, remains standing, but foundations have been supplied "by a more explicit and vigorous natural philosophy."[25]

H.L.—Yes, I think there is this large consistency in his own position. The confusion I pointed to arose in his momentarily unfair characterization and criticism of another position. And such distortions that a critic will make are generally in some degree revealing of his own bent. But I want to ask you something further about Santayana's idea of "spirit." You asked earlier whether I found it clear.

H.M.—Yes.

H.L.—I have been much struck by the determination of Santayana's attempt to define "spirit" in trans-human terms. "Spirit itself," he says in his essay on *Platonism and the Spiritual Life*, "is not human; it may spring up in any life; it may detach itself from any provincialism; as it exists in all nations and religions, so it may exist in all animals, and who knows in how many undreamt of beings, and in the midst of what worlds." Again, spirit is "an overtone of animal life, a realization, on a hypostatic plane, of certain moving unities in matter." It is "a hypostatic unity which makes actual and emotional the merely formal unities and harmonies of bodily life." It is

[25] Preface to Vol. VII of the Triton Edition of *The Works of George Santayana*, vii.

not the living psyche, but a wayward child of this psyche.[26] Is not all this pretty clear?

H.M.—Not very. This wayward child or this hypostatic unity—as you prefer—what kind of a unity, what kind of a child is it? At one time he speaks of "the flitting life of this winged thing, spirit, in this old, sordid maternal earth," and says too that "spirituality is only a sort of return to innocence, birdlike and childlike." But then again he says "The perfect spirit must be a patient hearer, a sober pupil, not an occasional automatic sky-lark." "Its eye, indeed, has virtual omniscience," for "spirit is the conscience of nature that sees the truth of nature." "Spirit is awareness, intelligence, recollection . . . the act of making light actual, of greeting, observing, questioning, and judging anything and everything." "To have spirit is to understand" with "perfect candour and impartial vision." It is also "to aspire," yet "without ulterior interest," since it "lives in a continual sense of the ultimate in the immediate."[27]

I do not know how well I understand how all this goes together. I think I comprehend well enough when he says "spiritual life is *disintoxication* from the influence of values."[28] But there is a kind of intoxication—an ecstatic element—that remains in realizing and expressing all this. And I am not too clear where it leaves us!

H.L.—Surely it is not intended to take or leave us anywhere, only to illumine whatever may be present to us. And I certainly think you must allow Santayana the ecstatic element, the rapture of things.

You know, when you put side by side these various facets of Santayana's thought on "spirit" just now, they made a more unified impression than I had expected, for I too have wondered whether there were not some incongruities compounded in his deliverances on this theme. But perhaps it is simply the great range which he perceives open to the spirit that made us suspect incongruities. Spirit is always innocently witnessing and recognizing without ulterior motive, burden, or claim, yet how

[26] *Platonism and the Spiritual Life*, 56, 47, 57, and 52.

[27] *Platonism and the Spiritual Life*, 85, 56, 53, 83; *The Genteel Tradition at Bay*, 64; Preface to Vol. VII of the Triton Edition of *The Works of George Santayana*, xii.

[28] *Platonism and the Spiritual Life*, 30.

infinitely varied are the events and the essences to be witnessed and recognized. There is a difference between what lights up in the face of a child and of a saint, to be sure, and it may be this difference between what is apprehended by the childlike and by the disciplined spirit that gave us pause regarding the clear unity of Santayana's conception. But we must not on this account miss the pervasive unity which his conception of spirit has as spontaneous, ultimate, universal and free vision.

And how spacious and untrammelled a view it is! What a relief and liberation it is to be carried once more beyond the bounds described by the categories of physics and by anthropocentric perspectives! And not on some dubious vehicle of speculation or of faith, but on the light wings of spiritual sight!

H.M.—Hold on!—or I shall be as transported as you are. I can see this free and infinite realm of spirit from the point of view of Santayana's natural philosophy too. Nature does not care whether spirit sees this or that, and this impartiality of nature is, it is evident, a large portion of the truth which Santayana wishes to convey.

But we have been talking about religion, and in religion there is a caring for the difference between a childlike and a disciplined spirit. Consequently, is it not the crucial thing for us to consider what Santayana has to say about the character of this caring and this discipline?

H.L.—No doubt you remember that some utterances of religion have taken little children as a symbol of heaven. Still you properly take us back from nature to the human perspective with your question about discipline.

Have Santayana's views changed on this matter, I wonder? I seem to recall that *Reason in Religion* indicated two main vehicles of a reasonable discipline of religion. The one is piety conceived as "reverent attachment to the sources of one's being."[29] And the other is the steadying of spirituality in terms of those symbols of eternal good that the religious imagination has supplied, and without which spirituality, except in moments of deep original inspiration, tends to be reduced to "a cultivated sympathy with the brighter scintillation of things."[30] Now is

[29] *Reason in Religion,* 179.
[30] *Ibid.,* 211.

there anything in Santayana's later writings to suggest a different opinion? In his address on "Ultimate Religion" at the Spinoza Tercentenary he repeats, does he not, that spirituality must be joined with piety to make up the two essential components of a sound religion? You may recall that he spoke there of the quest for "a sure foothold and a sublime companionship."[31] I take it these might be designated as ultimate objectives of piety and spirituality.

H.M.—Yes, but I could not help observing that the symbolic world of the religious imagination was passed over as silently as by Spinoza himself. And at the close of the essay on *Platonism and the Spiritual Life* he says that such a world "floating like a bubble in the flux of things, would almost certainly dissolve. It is not there that an enlightened heart would lay up its treasure. The flood itself is a nobler companion, and the spirit moves at ease upon the waters."[32] Does this mean that the "sublime companionship" of ultimate religion is one between the spirit and the flood? You may remember that, when we were discussing Santayana's appraisals of historic religion in terms of rational morality, I mentioned my regret that he had not explored the bearings of the religious imagination more basically and more thoroughly. I may now add that he seems to express in his final view much respect for Power, and much ideality, but a rather reserved amount of what has been called the love of God and man.

H.L.—I remember you suggested that he failed to investigate sufficiently the living unity of religion in its essentially practical character. And so you think that this is not merely a defect in his historical method but one grounded in his total attitude? Perhaps there are certain queries of my own that apply here, though it is not altogether clear to me how well they combine with your criticisms. I suspect that from my point of view they would combine very advantageously, but I cannot judge whether they do so from yours.

H.M.—Neither can I without knowing what you mean.

H.L.—Well, in that brief address on "Ultimate Religion" Santayana says, near the close, that "what I come to is not

[31] "Ultimate Religion," in *Obiter Scripta*, 281.

[32] *Platonism and the Spiritual Life*, 94.

religion; nor is it exactly philosophy."[33] Now though I am not bent on calling names, you know I could not help thinking all this while that what he represents is perhaps a species of Gnosticism, such as once sprang up in ancient Alexandria on the boundaries of religion and philosophy, though his is an inverted, naturalistic kind of Gnosticism, of course, and a deeply conceived one. I have in mind not only the subtle mixture of scepticism and Platonism, the easy use of all mythologies, the contemplative attitude of an élite detachment that "mocks the runner's heat," and similar traits which all belong to the picture. But I am thinking at the moment of his outlook upon an infinite realm of the spirit that is human only by accident, as it were.

The controversies of bygone times come to life again as soon as some party to the dispute reappears on the scene in vital form. So when Santayana the Gnostic looms into view I seem to see afresh the significance of the discussions about the Incarnation. Not that I mean to defend a traditional Christian form of that dogma; please do not misunderstand it so. But I realize the momentousness of the question anew: what have the spirit and humanity to do with one another? The universality in Santayana's conception of spirit I find good, because a narrow humanism is unsatisfying. Yet I think that man's "sure foothold and sublime companionship" even in relation to the non-human must be sought through the development of his humanity, and that ecstatic contemplation is a moment within this and not an alternative to it. Very likely Santayana would agree to this, if I do not misunderstand his lines in explaining "the unity of his earlier and later philosophy," where he says:

There is a certain option and practical incompatibility between spirituality and humanism . . . but the conflict is only marginal, the things are concentric, and spirit merely heightens and universalizes the synthesis which reason makes partially, as occasion requires, in the service of natural interests. . . . Between the spiritual life and the life of reason there is accordingly no contradiction: they are concomitant: yet there is a difference of temper, and level, as there is between agriculture and music.[34]

[33] "Ultimate Religion," in *Obiter Scripta*, 295.

[34] Preface to Vol. VII of the Triton Edition of *The Works of George Santayana*, xii, xi.

Thus, in Santayana's ideal, spirit does not furnish an alternative but adds a natural grace to the life of reason.

Surely there is no desertion of humanism in this. Still I feel the need of a more adequate humanistic principle. I seem to be looking for a term of intermediate scope, and of dynamic character, between the two Santayana gives us, namely the universal vision of spirit, on the one hand, and the relative moralities of human beings in their polities and communities, on the other. Christianity has such an intermediate term in Christ, the God-man, and Judaism in Torah, the God-given law. These indeed intend, but do they adequately suggest to us the preserver and savior, that is the saving principles of humanity that come to man's realization in the course of his experience?

H.M.—Perhaps I do not follow you. But what I seem to hear suggests an expanding realm of good-will, such as was invoked in the eighteenth century under the name of *humanité*.

H.L.—I shall not debate names with you now, but I should like to add that the saving principles of humanity—call them by what name you will—must necessarily associate with much different company in the course of human history, both from the side of what is generally called religion and from the secular side of culture. They travel with prophets of God and of machines, with civil and ascetic moralists, with scientists and poets. In actuality they cannot be separated from such companions, since they can only survive and grow in manifold relationships.

H.M.—You speak very generally. You surely are not overlooking the fact, are you, that Santayana has stated a general humanistic principle which is quite sturdy and well-travelled? I mean the principle of the life of reason, that, though rational morality in its specific content will vary relatively to circumstances, it must always and everywhere represent a harmony, an equilibrium, an adjustment of human impulses to one another and to the circumstances in which they must function.

H.L.—No, I neither overlook nor wish to minimize this formal principle of reason. Moreover, Santayana's way of stating it, which you cite, certainly has its advantages over Kant's, though not all the advantages are on his side, in my opinion.

H.M.—Well, then, are you forgetting that Santayana devoted five volumes to a more concrete account of reason in common sense, in society, in religion, in art, and in science? Would he not claim to have said something about what you call the saving principles of humanity in those volumes?

H.L.—Yes, and we have said a little about his treatment of one of those spheres. Do you think if we examined his account of the others everything would be made good?

H.M.—As a matter of fact, in *Reason in Society* I have noticed a tendency to set humanitarian social ideals in the abstract over against presumably necessary compromises of power politics in the concrete. I have wondered whether there is not a false dialectic in this, whereas a truer analysis would draw a comparison between various ideals and again between the concrete alternatives present in a given case.

H.L.—Exactly so. You know, with regard to religion, I do not ask any guarantee of the increasing realization of humanity in the world. I only wish that the possibilities of such increase were more decisively espoused.

H.M.—I doubt if Santayana is your man for that. Perhaps some feelings similar to yours came to the surface in my dream the other night.

H.L.—Why—what did you dream?

H.M.—Mr. Santayana was writing in his study, when the form of the devil entered through a picture on the wall.

The devil held a page of *Lucifer* which glowed, and the devil said he used to read it annually at midnight on New Year's eve.

They climbed onto the thatched roof of an odd squat building which began to move and carry them upward through the air where winged angels, wheeled cherubim and forked seraphim came down to meet them. Mr. Santayana regarded them sadly—noting the quaint but ineluctable mechanism of their activity, and that here and there an angel had lost a feather—but he was not insensible to the bright scintillation they made. The building on which he and the devil were perched appeared to me to be the synagogue that Marc Chagall had painted flying through the air.

It descended in the loveliest of green fields, where people walked on Elysian grass. Mr. Santayana recognized some, such as Plato, Democritus, and Avicenna, but was puzzled at the oddly assorted moderns that mingled with them. The devil said some indistinction of essences indeed prevailed here, but it was all quite familiar. St. Francis and Cervantes were pleased to hear Bucephalus explain to Democritus: "I crop this succulent grass with joy, but I was even happier when I prophesied as Balaam's ass."

Mr. Santayana avoided Professor Norton and Arnold, who were seated on a little mound, but the devil thought their "venom of absolute pretensions" quite innocuous in all this company.

Now a voice that was Theodore Roosevelt's called for followers to climb a mountain from which there was one of the most important views in the whole world. The green fields were blacked over, and the peak of the mountain began to shine like a point of pure light against absolute blackness. The devil and Mr. Santayana ascended, by some mysterious levitation, toward the supernal point of light, and presently distinct voices were heard from there, though no forms became visible. The men of the past were beholding anew the agony of the world, and their voices spoke as they had spoken before.

Finally, the blackness lifted; the point of pure light vanished into a frail but beautiful daylight. The figures of the devil and Mr. Santayana descended the mountain, and as they came to the lower slopes they saw in the distant meadow a vast concourse of people pressing about a great fountain whose streams flowed off in many channels to the plains. It could be observed (as the two came nearer) that the proportion of crippled people and of children in the throng was large; and their eagerness for the water was apparent in the clamor of their voices. Mr. Santayana said to the devil, "How vigorous the air this morning! I should like to stand for a while by the power and glory of this fountain, which is very like that of Trevi." The devil merely observed that all these were needy and lusty people, and that he himself after all was no materialist. He seemed to vanish. And as my dream ended, I had a sense of the great human throng waiting, and a last glimpse of Mr. Santayana watching the fountain.

Horace L. Friess
Henry M. Rosenthal

Department of Philosophy
Columbia University

13

Paul Arthur Schilpp

SANTAYANA ON *THE REALM OF SPIRIT*

13

SANTAYANA ON *THE REALM OF SPIRIT*

I

WITH this, *The Realm of Spirit*,[1] Professor Santayana has concluded the grandly conceived metaphysics of his later years, entitled *The Realms of Being*, to which the *Scepticism and Animal Faith* of 1923 was the fitting introduction and which included three other "realms of being," those of matter, essence, and truth. It can now perhaps even be said that both, *Scepticism and Animal Faith* and *Platonism and the Spiritual Life* (1927), quite adequately foreshadowed the ultimate intent and meaning of *The Realm of Spirit*. If the references to "spirit" there were felt to be vague and more an expression of a direct intuitive sensing than of rigorous psychological or philosophical analysis, the three hundred pages of the present work will do little to dispel that feeling. Logical positivists in philosophy, for example, will hardly get beyond the brief (6 pp.) Preface of this volume (if any one of them should "stoop" to pick it up at all). But many other philosophers who are far from being classifiable as logical

[1] On September 3, 1940, the first copy of Santayana's *The Realm of Spirit* (New York, Scribner's) reached the desk of the editor of this volume. At that time all save one of the contributed essays to the present volume were already in type. At such short notice it was, obviously, impossible to secure an outside philosophical critic to give our readers an account of this latest of Mr. Santayana's contributions to philosophy; nor did it seem fair to ask Messrs. Friess and Rosenthal to revise their dialogue at this late moment in the light of the new book. At the same time, it seemed quite unthinkable that our volume on *The Philosophy of George Santayana* should come off the press—about two months after the appearance of *The Realm of Spirit*—without any reference to "*Book Fourth of Realms of Being*," looked upon apparently by Mr. Santayana himself as the capstone of his mature thought. It was with this in mind that the editor finally decided to jump into the breach by writing on this work himself. He does not, however, desire to have the above essay looked at as much more than a book-review. In view of the brevity of time, nothing more was possible.

positivists will have little less trouble with *The Realm of Spirit*. There is no denying the fact that Mr. Santayana's "Fourth Realm of Being" does not fit into the dominant moods of most contemporary philosophy.

When, for instance, Mr. Santayana introduces his reader to the realm of spirit by saying:

> What I call spirit is only that inner light of actuality or attention which floods all life as men actually live it on earth. It is roughly the same thing as feeling or thought; it might be called consciousness; it might be identified with the *pensée* or *cogitatio* of Descartes or Spinoza.[2]

it will at once be granted by any reader familiar with contemporary philosophy that such language and description—despite its beautiful literary expression—appears to the average philosophically trained mind not merely as meaningless, but as definitely confusing, not to say misleading. For here, within the space of two sentences (and in the second paragraph of the Preface to this new book), Mr. Santayana succeeds in throwing together, helterskelter, such concepts as feeling, thought, consciousness, Descartes' *pensée*, and Spinoza's *cogitatio*, and to equate all of these not merely with each other, but also with "spirit." About the only assignable meaning that the average contemporary philosopher might be able to give to those two sentences, therefore, would be to assert that what Mr. Santayana is really trying to say is that spirit is as mysterious as are most of these other terms with which he wants to identify spirit, with the possible exception of feeling. But, if this is what Mr. Santayana is really trying to say, the inevitable question is: Why does he not simply and directly come out and say so? Besides, why write a three-hundred page book about a mystery anyway? Or, if one writes such a book, why suppose that it could possibly be of any interest to serious-minded philosophers, theologians, scientists, or other scholars?

Nor are such objections readily dispelled by other descriptions, definitions, and identifications of "spirit" or by analogies with the "spiritual."

When, for example, a page further on, we read:

[2] *The Realm of Spirit*, Preface, vii.

> This inner light is indeed requisite for focussing impressions and rendering them mentally present, but it is biologically prior to them, vital and central, a product of combustion, a leaping flame, a fountain and seat of judgment. I therefore call it spirit; not that I think it either a substance or a physical power, or capable of existing by itself, but that it is a personal and moral focus in life, where the perspectives of nature are reversed as in a mirror and attached to the fortunes of the single soul.[3]

one cannot, in honesty, say that one feels greatly enlightened on the precise nature of Spirit by these sentences. Or, rather, what light they do shed is much more obvious and meaningful in the negative assertion that spirit is neither a substance nor a physical power than in any of its positive statements.

On the other hand, however, I am inclined to think that Mr. Santayana's claim that "a study of the realm of spirit is . . . an exercise in self-knowledge"[4] is indeed a revelatory remark. It frankly points to the introspective character of this entire study and thereby places it at once in a category in which, at the moment, it stands almost by itself among serious contemporary philosophical treatises. Whatever else may be said about Santayana and his work, no one certainly could accuse him of being a fashionable philosopher. Whereas some may take this remark as an opprobrium, I feel confident that a philosopher of the stature of Mr. Santayana will—in my opinion rightly—take it as a compliment. He can stand on his own feet. The philosophical fashions of the moment leave him—almost completely—untouched. He goes his own—unperturbed and imperturbable—way.

Spirit, Mr. Santayana insists, must be "conceived in spiritual terms."[5] Since it is *sui generis* in its essential character, though not of course in its origin or background which is solidly found in physical nature, it is absurd and misleading to attempt to conceive of it in any other than its own—spiritual—terms. At this point too Santayana's negative darts, hurled at materialists and religious philosophers alike for their respective denial of spirit's existence or their "love to materialize spirit," (p. 3) are

[3] *Ibid.*, viii.
[4] *Ibid.*, ix.
[5] *Ibid.*, p. 3.

far sharper and more specific than is his positive exposition. Of course, we are repeatedly told that "spirit is immaterial and transcendental," and that it becomes "a transcendental centre for making a survey of everything."[6] Moreover, spirit's "own essence is an invisible stress; the vital, intellectual and moral actuality of each moment."[7] And again: "Spirit is the witness of the cosmic dance,"[8] and "a moral force of recollection, discrimination and judgment."[9] Yet even these positive affirmations do not by any means seem to be as clear as the assertions that "Spirit is not a seed, it is not a potentiality, it is not a power. It is not even . . . a grammar of thought or divine Logos."[10]

If, however, the reader of *The Realm of Spirit* has a never quite ceasing feeling that, on its positive side, spirit is something vague and indistinct, he does not have to wait long for a free and frank admission to the same effect by Mr. Santayana himself. Says our author:

"Spirit has an initial vagueness; it awakes, it looks, it waits, it oscillates between universal curiosity and primeval sleep. . . . Spirit is infinitely open."[11] "Spirit is eventually hospitable to all sorts of things. . . . It is . . . open to all truth, even to all fiction and to all essence. . . . It is the most volatile of things, and the most evanescent, a flame blown or extinguished by any wind: but no extinction here can prevent it from blazing up there, and its resurrection is as perpetual as its death."[12]

And, since "spirit is a product of the psyche,"[13] the "specific function of the spirit, which it lives by fulfilling, and dies if it cannot somehow fulfill,"[14] is to feel a "vicarious sympathy with its native psyche and her native world, which [psyche] it [namely, the spirit] cannot bear to feel dragged hither and thither in tragic confusion, but craves to see everywhere well-ordered and beautiful, *so that it may be better seen and under-*

[6] *Ibid.*, p. 6
[7] *Ibid.*, p. 7.
[8] *Ibid.*, p. 8.
[9] *Ibid.*, p. 9.
[10] *Ibid.*, p. 12.
[11] *Ibid.*, p. 12.
[12] *Ibid.*, p. 13.
[13] *Ibid.*, p. 13.
[14] *Ibid.*, p. 14.

stood."[15] And, finally, "whilst spirit is physically the voice of the soul crying in the wilderness, it becomes vicariously and morally the voice of the wilderness admonishing the soul,"[16] a sentiment which also found its expression already in the Preface, where Santayana writes:

> . . . actual spirit is well acquainted with solitude, with insulation, and with chasms, and this not by any accident; . . . it dwells, not in setting suns, but in human bodies, bodies breeding a thousand passions and diseases by which the spirit also is tormented, so that it congenitally longs at first for happiness and at last for salvation.[17]

Mr. Santayana concludes his opening chapter on "The Nature of Spirit" with a glossary of terms, in which he attempts to explain to his reader the peculiar meaning of the major terms with which *The Realm of Spirit* is mainly concerned. Nothing, I think, could more quickly or more conclusively prove my first major point in this discussion—namely that Mr. Santayana's language, though beautiful, rich, and meaning-conveying (if intuitively grasped), is nonetheless anything but clear or precise—than for me here to reprint his glossary of terms in toto.[18]

> Let me tabulate, as briefly as possible, the principal words and ideas that mark the differences, the bonds, and the confusions that exist between matter and spirit. Such a glossary may help the reader to criticize his favourite modes of expression and to be patient with those of other people.
>
> *Body.* Ancient usage identifies a man with his body, as Homer in the first lines of the Iliad: and in English we still speak of *nobody* and *everybody*. This places man quite correctly in the realm of matter amongst other bodies, but it treats him and them summarily and externally as gross units and dead weights, ignoring their immaterial properties and their subtle physical substance and relations.
>
> *Organism.* This word still designates the body, since the organization of an organism must exist somewhere and on a particular scale, if it is to exist at all. But a body is an organism only by virtue of its vital power of nutrition and reproduction. By these functions bodily life becomes continuous with the ambient forces on which it feeds and theoretically

[15] *Ibid.*, 13-14; *italics* are Mr. Santayana's.

[16] *Ibid.*, p. 14.

[17] *Ibid.*, Preface, ix.

[18] I do so with the express permission of Charles Scribner's Sons, New York.

with the whole dynamic universe. Thus an organism is both a closed system of vital tropes and a nucleus in the general cosmic process.

Psyche. The forms of inorganic matter, though distinct from matter logically, are clearly passive: matter may fall into them innumerable times, yet if anywhere disturbed, they show no tendency to reinstate themselves. This tendency defines an organism: its actual form hides a power to maintain or restore that form. This power or potentiality, often concentrated in a seed, dwells in the matter of the organism, but is mysterious; so that for observation the form itself seems to be a power (when locked in that sort of substance or seed) and to work towards its own manifestation. The self-maintaining and reproducing pattern or structure of an organism, conceived as a power, is called a psyche. The psyche, in its moral unity, is a poetic or mythological notion, but needed to mark the hereditary vehement movement in organisms towards specific forms and functions.

Animal. All natural organisms have psyches, and are at the same time in dynamic relations to the whole physical world. When the organism waits for favourable opportunities to unfold itself, the psyche is vegetative; when it goes to seek favourable opportunities, it is animal.

This is an important step in laying the ground for spirit. The unity of the organism subtends the moral unity of the spirit, which raises that unity to an actual and intense existence; the impulse of the psyche, making for a specific perfection of form and action, underlies the spiritual distinction between good and evil; and the power of locomotion gives the spirit occasion for perception and knowledge. Will is no doubt deeper than intelligence in the spirit, as it is in the animal; yet will without intelligence would not be spirit, since it would not distinguish what it willed or what it suffered. So that the passage from vegetation to action seems to produce the passage from a dark physical excitability to the *qui vive* of consciousness.

Soul. The same thing that looked at from the outside or biologically is called the psyche, looked at morally from within is called the soul. This change of aspect so transforms the object that it might be mistaken for two separate things, one a kind of physical organization and the other a pure spirit. And spirit is in fact involved in feeling and knowing life from the inside: not that spirit is then *self*-conscious, or sees nothing save its own states, but that it is then the medium and focus for apprehension, and imposes on its objects categories and qualities of its own. A psyche, when spirit awakes in it, is turned into a soul. Not only can the career of that psyche now be reviewed in memory, or conceived in prophecy, but many a private impulse or thought never exhibited to the world can now be added to one's history; so that oneself is now not merely the body, its power, and its experience, but also an invisible guest, the soul, dwelling in that body and having motions and hopes of its own. This soul can be conceived to issue out of the body, to pass into a different body, or to remain thinking and talking to itself without a body at all. This, for the psyche, would have been inconceivable; for, as Aristotle shows, the psyche, or specific form of organization and movement, in an elephant, can no more pass into the body of a fly, than the faculty of cutting can pass from an axe into a lyre, or the faculty of making music from the lyre into the axe. The soul, however, having an apparently independent discoursing and desiring faculty, and a power to imagine all sorts of non-existent things, may easily be conceived to pass from one body to another, as by a change of domicile, and to have had forgotten incarnations, with an endless future.

Self or Person. If memory, dreams, and silent musings seem to detach the soul from bodily life, social relations and moral qualities may re-attach the soul to the world, not now biologically but politically. Politically a man cannot be separated from his body; but it is not by his bodily faculties that he chiefly holds his own in society, or conceives his individuality. He is a person, a self, a character; he has a judicial and economic status; he lives in his ambitions, affections, and repute. All this again, as in the notion of the soul, cannot come about without the secret intervention of spirit: yet these ideas, although spirit must be there to entertain them, are not spiritual ideas; the interests chiefly concerned are those of animal or social bodies. Even moral worth or immortal life are ideals borrowed from animal impulses and animal conditions. In a different biological setting, or in a realm of pure spirits, those social duties and services would be impossible: and the will to live forever is nothing but the animal will to go on living expressed reflectively and transferred, somewhat incongruously, to the social self or historical person.

Spirit. Psyches, we have said, take on the character of souls when spirit awakes in them. Spirit is an awareness natural to animals, revealing the world and themselves in it. Other names for spirit are consciousness, attention, feeling, thought, or any word that marks the total *inner* difference between being awake or asleep, alive or dead. This difference is morally absolute; but physically the birth of spirit caps a long growth during which excitability and potentiality of various kinds are concentrated in organisms and become transmissible. The *outer* difference between sleeping and waking, life and death, is not absolute; and we may trace certain divergences between the path of transmission for the psyche and the basis of distribution for the spirit. Life follows the seed, through long periods of unconsciousness and moral nonexistence; whereas spirit lives in the quick interplay of each sensitive individual and the world, and often is at its height when, after keen experience, the brain digests the event at leisure, and the body is sexually quiescent or reduced by old age to a mere husk. In the spirit, by definition, there is nothing persistent or potential. It is pure light and perpetual actuality. Yet the intensity and scope of this moral illumination, as well as the choice of characters lighted up, the order of the scenes and how long each shall last, all hang on the preparations nature may have made for this free entertainment.[19]

Some of the terms discussed in this glossary are, obviously, much more precisely formulated than are others. Foremost among the clearer ones are "body" and "organism." For the balance of the terms it will, I think, be admitted that the nearer we get to "spirit" itself the vaguer the statements become and the more one has the feeling that one's understanding of the terms treated is much more an intuitive sensing or following the leadership of the author than a reasoned or critical comprehension of any precise meanings. The glossary suffers, moreover, from another rather far-reaching defect. It fails to include such important terms as "moral," "morality," "intelligence," *et al.*, terms into which Santayana puts new (or, at any rate, different) meanings; meanings, different not only from their usual employment by intelligent men of "common sense," but different also from Santayana's own earlier use of those terms in *The Life of Reason.*[20] Morality, for example, is now practically equated with spirituality; and spirituality is taken as super-rational or trans-rational. Whereas, in *The Life of Reason,* the nature of morality was essentially and significantly rational.

Although the first of the ten chapters in this book was obviously intended by Mr. Santayana to furnish the reader with an explanation of "the nature of spirit," and although I have tried to bring together here most of Mr. Santayana's most significant—both positive and negative—assertions concerning

[19] *The Realm of Spirit,* pp. 14-18.

[20] This fact is also observed and discussed in the essays by Messrs. Edman, Vivas, and Friess-Rosenthal above.

spirit, and although the reader may be getting rather tired of endless quotations, my fundamental purpose requires still more quotations from later chapters of *The Realm of Spirit*. For this purpose is to bring together here, insofar as possible, all of the more significant assertions about and characterizations of spirit as they are to be found in this "Book Fourth of the Realms of Being," in order that the reader may have an opportunity to convince himself from these quotations of the validity of the two main conclusions I desire to draw from this book. The first of these conclusions, as must already have become clear, is the proposition that, despite the many and significant things which Mr. Santayana is saying about spirit, even his own final conclusions are by no means very clear or precise. I trust, however, that my second conclusion is no less significant than the first one. This is to the general effect that, although Mr. Santayana is perhaps mainly groping rather than putting his finger on anything very definite, he is after all groping after something highly important and significant. A conclusion, this latter, which will attempt to show that we ought to be grateful for the presence in our midst of a philosopher who is not afraid to take his readers—even unwilling and in this particular area today altogether unprepared readers—into his confidence as he engages in a search which, for its very uncommon character, is all the more important; and in a search where intuitive flashes of insight may indeed prove finally more significant than careful critical analysis and examination. With this I am, however, getting ahead of myself.

Let us, then, get back to our first point again. I think, for example, that the very opening two sentences of Chapter II are quite revelatory in more ways than one. "Let us admit," Santayana begins, "that something called spirit exists, and exists invisibly, in a manner of its own, by virtue of an intrinsic moral intensity. Its essence lies in willing, suffering, looking, being pleased, absorbed, or offended."[21] Here Mr. Santayana, obviously tired of the necessity of arguing the point and anxious to get on with his major purpose, says to the reader: Let's admit (1) "that something called spirit exists," (2) that it "exists in-

[21] *The Realm of Spirit*, p. 19.

visibly," (3) that it exists "in a manner of its own" and is therefore not to be explained in terms of anything else, but must be grasped in its own manifestation in its own realm, (4) that it exists "by virtue of an intrinsic moral intensity" (whatever this may mean), and that (5) and finally it is essentially a conscious reaction of mind, such as "willing, suffering, looking, being pleased, absorbed, or offended." A few pages further on he adds: ". . . without expectation, memory, and impulsive preference we should hardly give to intuition the name of spirit,"[22] thus giving additional confirmation to his insistence that spirit is the intuitive reaction of conscious mind. All of which may be clear enough as far as it goes. It certainly is quite in line with the initial identifications made by Mr. Santayana in the first paragraphs of his Preface.[23] But the criticisms I urged at that point would seem just as applicable to these second chapter passages. And yet one hesitates to press the criticism of "uncritical philosophy" too far against Mr. Santayana. For, despite his admissions of vagueness, intuitive apprehension and his disclaimer of scientific analysis,[24] it is perfectly clear from Santayana's own words that he is definitely considering himself as engaged in the task of "critical philosophy" in this book. It is in his arguments against positive materialism that we find Santayana saying:

> . . . if we define spirit in the primitive materialistic manner, as the principle and cause of motion, it becomes a truism that matter is everywhere instinct with spirit. But *such ways of speaking are intolerable in a critical philosophy*, and I have already discarded any definition of spirit that identifies it with physical motions or physical forces. The potential and the dynamic, according to my use of terms, are by definition material; while spirit possesses activity or energy only in the Aristotelian sense of being a perfect realization or ultimate fruition of function . . . and we know in our own case that the fortunes of a living organism have a moral import; in other words, carry consciousness or spirit with them.[25]

Yet, despite this outspoken claim for "critical philosophy," it is difficult to take the claim too seriously, especially in view of

[22] *Ibid.*, p. 28.
[23] Quoted previously on page 380 above.
[24] Cf. on this the quotation cited in footnote 31 on page 390 below.
[25] *The Realm of Spirit,* 35-36; *italics* are mine.

the fact that this very passage ends on the same broad identifications—viz., "moral import" equals "consciousness" equals "spirit"—to which we objected in the first place.

On the other hand, it is quite undeniable that, *within* those broad identifications, Mr. Santayana is and remains thoroughly consistent in his delineations of spirit. Take, for example, the following quotations from Chapter III, which only re-emphasize some of the claims for the nature, locus, and activities of spirit which we have already met in earlier passages.

> The place of spirit is in a psyche. . . . Spirit is incarnate by nature, not by accident. Otherwise it would not possess the lyrical, moral, impassioned character that makes it spiritual. It is intellectual, it thinks ideas; but it is not a realm of ideas hypostasized. It is alive, nothing if not transitive, always on the wing, watching, comparing, suffering, and laughing. It is the consciousness proper to an animal psyche . . . a spiritual symptom of vital strains.[26] . . . spirit is a form of life, not a hypostasis of logic . . . in its outlook, spirit rests in essences, in its origin it springs from matter; . . . An actual moment, or moment of spirit, possesses an internal intensive unity.[27] For spirit all times are equally present. . . .[28] The impossibility of other than moral relations between the moments of spirit follows from their immaterial nature.[29] The potentialities of spiritual life are infinite and no revolutions in nature can exhaust them.[30]

All of these quotations appear to me to support each other. But beyond this I am none too sure about the precise meaning of any one of them. They startle one by the categorical character of this way of being stated. But, despite the detailed and expanded argument of the book, I do not feel that they are argumentatively supported. They are, I repeat, intuitively grasped and, in terms of direct pointing, perhaps ably supported. But, if one fail to see the pointers, it will be just too bad.

However, this must suffice on our first point. Save, perhaps, to put down here a sentence from pp. 49-50, in which Santayana specifically states "the proper subject of this book." He writes:

[26] *Ibid.*, p. 43.
[27] *Ibid.*, p. 49.
[28] *Ibid.*, p. 51.
[29] *Ibid.*, p. 50.
[30] *Ibid.*, p. 51.

"How moments of spirit may spiritually support, contradict, or fulfil one another is in fact the proper subject of this book." Unfortunately, we shall not be able, in the present discussion, to take our readers along into this absorbing and, under Santayana's leadership, exceedingly profitable and even exciting undertaking. For purposes of this brief analysis we had to restrict ourselves to the more limited task of trying to see just what Mr. Santayana means by spirit and how he conceives of its nature. From the standpoint of practical significance, I feel certain that Chapters IV to IX (incl.) are the most important chapters in the book. But from the standpoint of philosophical and theoretical underpinning, it is also quite clear that the book will largely stand or fall in terms of the analysis of spirit contained in the Preface and in the first three chapters.

II

At the same time, as I have already intimated, I do not think that it will do to pass off this latest work from the pen of Mr. Santayana as lightly as our discussion up to the present point might indicate. In the first place, Santayana, himself, not merely admits but goes out of his way to insist that this volume is *not* a scientific treatise.[31] Anyone, therefore, who insists on reading or treating it as such has failed not merely to heed the warning of its author but also to enter into the meaning and intent of what Mr. Santayana is trying to say. In fact, if there is one thing clear on which Mr. Santayana seems to insist throughout it is the proposition that "things of the spirit must be spiritually discerned." To try to get at the things of spirit, therefore, with the methods of the physical sciences or with basically non-spiritual tools would be like trying to dip water with a net; only worse! For the net and the water, however unsuitable the net for the specific immediate purpose of getting water, are at least objects within the same realm of physical nature. Whereas spirit is, after all, a realm by itself.

If these two demands of Santayana—namely that the realm

[31] Even in his Preface, Mr. Santayana states: "My subject is not experience surveyed impartially, as a book of descriptive psychology, but experience viewed at a certain angle. . . . Nor is my subject the whole of moral philosophy or the life of reason. . . ." Preface, viii.

of spirit is a unique realm of being, and that, therefore, spiritual things must be spiritually discerned—are kept in mind, it will readily be seen that most of the criticisms which are bound to be hurled at this book by the professional philosophers and psychologists will be greatly beside the point. Mr. Santayana will be able to say of them that they are trying to comprehend and deal with one discussion in terms of not merely another discussion, but of an incommensurable one. In this way most of their criticisms can leave him entirely unaffected.

I have already ventured to suggest that, in the volume under discussion, Mr. Santayana is engaged in a search for and in an intuitive delineation of an aspect of immediately felt and experienced conscious life, which, just because it lies in a realm or dimension thus far inaccessible to the ordinary methods of scientific analysis and description, has been quite generally neglected. But general neglect is a poor reason for inattention, especially when something is involved which, as Mr. Santayana suggests, is the very appex of the flowering of conscious mind in the human organism. As he, himself, puts it: "Our habitual ignorance cannot abolish what happens to be unknown to us, or forbid it to exist."[32] Precisely. *"Du sprachst ein grosse Wort gelassen aus!"* One could wish that Mr. Santayana's remark at this point might become an academic proverb. If so, it should work miracles in academic, yes even in philosophical, circles. For, there is no denying the fact that, especially since about the last third of the nineteenth century, it has become the fashion among academicians and scholars to delete first from polite vocabulary and thereafter to bow out of existence entirely anything which did not "happen to be known to us" or which did not yield to certain predetermined methods of analysis and investigation. A very bad habit indeed, this; and never worse than when practiced by those who, under the cloak of being seekers after truth, use their official capacity as savants in the intimidation of others who refuse to admit that any obvious fact of experience is tabu, even though it may as yet be shrouded in mystery and refuse to yield to pre-conceived methods of investigation.

[32] *The Realm of Spirit,* p. 20.

I need not take back anything I have said in Part I of this essay to venture now the remark that Santayana's willingness to tackle the realm of the spirit in a serious treatise marks him as one of the most heroic philosophers of our age. His heroism, so far from being diminished by the fact that he still is as much as ever a naturalist, yes even a materialist,[33] is actually enhanced by that fact. For, although I might venture no too cocksure brief for spirit, it seems almost silly to attempt to deny that the types of action, attitude, etc. which Santayana in his book takes together under the head of the spirit do as a matter of fact constitute definite and easily observable aspects of conscious human experience. And Mr. Santayana, as a real philosopher, is simply not satisfied to leave these real and significant aspects of conscious human experience lie on one side undiscussed, even though those experiences in their fundamental nature may still "happen to be unknown to us," yes, may even have been "forbidden to exist" by those who simply will not listen to the existence of anything *was nicht in ihren Kram passt.*

I am, for example, not at all sure that I can approve of the use of spirit in its substantive (grammatical substantive) form; and this not because I am a stickler for words, but because—especially in view of the specific demands made by Santayana, to the effect that spirit is *not* a substance, *not* a power, *not* a thing, not even "a grammar of thought or divine Logos"—it seems to me a bit too misleading to talk constantly about spirit or about *the* spirit. At the same time, speaking about, say, a

[33] The third sentence of Mr. Santayana's Preface to the book here under discussion contains this clause: "I am intellectually a convinced materialist." (Preface, vii.) It ought, moreover, to be added here that, from the standpoint of the origin and foundation of the spiritual in the existence of man, there is nothing whatsoever anywhere in *The Realm of Spririt* to contradict this confession of the materialistic faith. I am not here raising the question as to how possible it is to be both a "convinced materialist" and equally as convinced a spiritualist (in matters of the spirit). To take up this problem would, I take it, require an essay by itself, or perhaps a book. And any such essay or book would itself, of course, be written from the standpoint of a more or less definite position or metaphysics. Besides, the question as to wether or not it actually is possible to be a materialist and a spiritualist at the same time and in the same person has already been answered for us in the affirmative. Mr. Santayana is the living demonstration of this possibility and *The Realm of Spirit* constitutes the proof in print.

"spiritual outlook on life" or a "spiritual attitude" not merely makes sense but says something rather important. Moreover, it would seem highly important to attempt to put some rather definite content into such terms, especially so long as the terms are fairly generally in use. Although I should, of course, be one of the first to admit that the merely general usage of those terms does not in itself or *ipso facto* justify their use. If the use of the terms is justifiable to rational and critical minds at all, this justification must, obviously, take place in pointing to aspects of human experience which do not yield to some other—simpler or more common—interpretation. Now I find myself quite in agreement with Mr. Santayana that there are actually many such aspects of conscious human experience. And I repeat that I think we may count ourselves singularly fortunate that one philosopher at least has been engaged in the process of tracking those experiences down.

What, in Part I above, I have taken exception to is *not*, then, the nature of the project, nor the aim of the undertaking; I have not objected to the task itself nor even questioned the worthwhileness of the search. Rather I have objected to what seems to me to be quite unfortunate: the fact, namely, that the entire book seems to be an unconscious but none the less powerful demonstration for the assumption that just because the spiritual comes to the fore basically in *enthusiastic* and passionate conscious living and thinking, therefore, the critical examination of that enthusiastic and passionate aspect of human life need also be carried on enthusiastically and passionately. Of course, if Mr. Santayana means to say that no really critical analysis of the passionate aspect of human life (i.e., of spirit) is at all possible, then that is another matter. Perhaps, in other words, only an enthusiast can say anything significant about enthusiasm. But, if that is the case it would seem that every scholar in almost any field is in a bad way. What, then, can the physicist ever say that is really significant about electrons, protons, and neutrons, etc.? I fear that to go to such lengths is going too far. I am perfectly willing to admit that no one except he who himself has actually had—and therefore directly and immediately *felt*—an experience can really know just what the experience *felt like.* But this, I submit, is by no means the same thing as saying that an untutored person, say, falling down on the street, can give a better physical and psychological explanation of the falling down than can a reputable physicist or psychologist, merely because neither of the latter had actually ever had the *experience* of "falling down." I feel reasonably certain that Mr. Santayana himself would agree with this judgment. After all, *understanding* and, in so far as possible, explaining an experience—although it is not, of course, the same thing as *having* the experience—may, at any rate, from a critical and analytical standpoint, be just as important as having the experience. That the two procedures are *different,* no one but a fool would deny. But their difference does by no means make *one* of the tasks either impossible or unnecessary. And, perhaps, those two functions ought not only to be distinguished in theory but kept distinct in practice. This might save much confusion.

Be this as it may—and I do think that Santayana errs gravely at this point (just discussed)—I desire to repeat that I, none the less, consider the job Mr. Santayana undertook in this treatise to be very much worth doing and of great importance. Nor do I think for one moment that the way he chose to discuss the realm of spirit is one of mere floundering in phrases of passionate enthusiasm and of mystical enjoyment. In fact, there is much here to shed light on this "inner light" of the spiritual attitude; much more than I shall be able to mention in this all too brief discussion. The book is full of great and significant flashes of (intuitive) insight and will well repay the reader who is willing to follow the inspired leadership of Santayana through the discussions on "Will," "Freedom," "Intuition," "Distraction," "Liberation," and "Union." Unfortunately, the best I can do here is briefly to point to two or three aspects of Mr. Santayana's treatment of the spirit which appear to me to be particularly fruitful and worthy of more than passing attention. Even the *discussion* of these few points I must leave either to other students of the problem or, at any rate, to another occasion.

In the first place, I am inclined to think that Mr. Santayana's suggestion of what he calls the "transcendental" character of the spiritual can hardly be taken too seriously by honest students of this realm. Moreover, this transcendental nature of the spiritual is not only an immediately felt fact or one which is easily pointed out, but one which is psychologically demonstrable in the life of every normal human being. There is, in other words, some specific aspect of the conscious life of man which is better characterized in terms of self-transcendence than in any other terms. And I see no good reason why these particular—self-transcendent—aspects of human conscious experience should not be identified with the spiritual. In fact, it seems to me that an excellent—demonstrative—case can be made for the proposition that such precisely is the very essence of spirituality.

For example, it seems to me that the conscious human capacity to transcend the immediacy of the present moment, in the directions both backward into the past and forward into the future, belongs here. So does the ability to transcend space. So also do the aspirational and idealizing capacities of man. Not to speak of man's reach for whatever he may think to be the infinite.

Even the strange but exceedingly important capacity of man to put himself, at least to a degree, into the place and position of another of his fellow-human beings seems to me to belong here and to partake essentially of this spiritual aspect of man's conscious life. Here, then, in this "transcendental" aspect of the nature of the spiritual lies an exceedingly helpful and worthy—yes, important—suggestion in this latest book from the pen of Santayana.

Moreover, although I find it impossible (personally) to follow Santayana in his simple identification (in *The Realm of Spirit*) of morality with spirituality, I do agree most heartily with his insistence that morality too is quite unthinkable without this transcendental aspect or capacity of man. Certainly no man who permits himself to be shut up in himself, who is unable to burst the chains of immediacy in time and space and individuality, can ever in any significant sense of the term be called moral. Self-transcendence would appear to be one of the first and prime prerequisites of even the *possibility* of morality. And to the extent to which spirituality and self-transcendence are to be identified, to that extent I should say, then, that morality is dependent upon spirituality. (But dependence of one thing upon another is by no means the same thing as identity!) Here too, then, Santayana seems to have come to a highly significant insight; one which can stand a good deal of analysis, but also one which ought to be most seriously considered by students of ethics and of morals.

Santayana's claims for the "open-ness" of spirit and for what he says is the character of spirit as being "on the wing" are two other contributions of this book which are worthy of further attention. Although I rather feel that both of these characterizations of the spiritual owe their existence to the basically transcendental nature of spirituality, it is nevertheless worth while to pick them out—even though they be only *derived* from the other—for a separate look and for independent emphasis. But it would be foolish for the present writer to attempt here to discuss them; they are so well brought out and so inimitably treated by the matchless pen and mind of Santayana that anything I would try to say on these subjects would, by comparison, appear to profane them.

I want to close this discussion by quoting once more from the Preface to *The Realm of Spirit.* Introducing next to the last paragraph, Santayana utters a sentence which I cannot refrain from doctoring up, by the addition of three words in brackets. "The Indians and the mystics [and George Santayana] are inspired people, and their language does not always bear critical examination."[34] Well said! The only fault one could find with this remark is that it is probably an understatement. Instead of saying, "not always," Mr. Santayana might well have said, "not very often." Nor need such a correction necessarily imply a derogatory criticism; as indeed Mr. Santayana's paragraph introduced by the above sentence well bears out. In other words, critical examination of language undoubtedly has its place. But its place is not at every point or time where language is used. Sometimes, surely, it is the function of language more to convey certain immediately *felt* intuitive impressions than to stand up to precise, scientific, critical examination. One is, more-

[34] Preface, x.

over, likely to agree with Mr. Santayana that language which does bear critical examination seldom (if, indeed, ever) leaves the reader or listener with any sense of inspiration. Language which is felt to be inspired and which carries a sense of inspiration to the witness seldom yields to critical examination. Though I trust that no reader of these lines will from this—generally true—observation jump to the generalization that all language which does not bear critical examination is, therefore, inspired language; a generalization, this latter, which is so absurd that it would be difficult to utter one which could be charged with greater absurdity.

There is, however, also another problem involved here. Does the rational thinker ever have the right to let himself completely be carried away even by inspired language? Everyone knows the tale concerning Immanuel Kant's iron-clad regularity and about the punctuality of his daily walks. And almost everyone has heard that only the reading of Rousseau's unquestionably inspired *Émile* is said ever to have roused and disturbed Kant sufficiently to have caused a break in that regularity and punctuality. Few, however, are aware of Kant's own statement concerning Rousseau to the effect that "I have to read Rousseau until the beauty of his expression no longer disturbs me; only then can I really view him rationally."[35] If the reader will put the name of Santayana into this quotation from Kant where the name of Rousseau stands now, the quotation will come very close to the present writer's reaction to *The Realm of Spirit* and to many other of Santayana's works. Yet, part of this reaction may be a case of "sour grapes." Which writer of English prose —more particularly, which philosopher (with the possible exception of Bertrand Russell)—does not wish that he could use the King's English with the finesse and beauty of George Santayana?

Yes, *The Realm of Spirit* is a book to be appreciated, felt, intuited, rather than a book to be analyzed, dissected, or criticized. And who will rise up and set himself up as judge of such

[35] Kant in Fragmentary Notes (datable c. 1764-1765) written by him into an interleaved copy of his *Beobachtungen über das Gefühl des Schönen und Erhabenen.* Reproduced in Hartenstein's, *Kants Sämmtliche Werke,* VIII, 618.

a book? Who will say that it is better to be a botanist surrounded by the dissected particles of a rose than a lover of flowers in possession of a rose? How many human beings would trade the ultimate results of the botanist's painstaking labors for the possession of the full beauty and fragrance of a bouquet of flowers? There certainly is no doubt in this particular reader's mind that the Santayana of today wants to be read, not by the critic or analyst, but rather by the devout, sympathetic, understanding person; not by one whose understanding is coldly rational, logical, or critical, but by him who can bring to his reading the warm, direct, immediate, intuitive insight which shares and enters into the feeling-tone of what Santayana is saying, without worrying too much about logical analysis or precision of statement or of meaning. In this, Santayana, like Mary of old, may have chosen "the better part."

Paul Arthur Schilpp

Department of Philosophy
Northwestern University

14

Edward L. Schaub

SANTAYANA'S CONTENTIONS RESPECTING GERMAN PHILOSOPHY

14

SANTAYANA'S CONTENTIONS RESPECTING GERMAN PHILOSOPHY

I

OF Hegel Santayana alleges that his "historical insight is not really sympathetic; it is imperious, external, contemptuous, feigned."[1] "What we know little or nothing about," he writes, "seems to us in Hegel admirably characterized: what we know intimately seems to us painted with the eye of a pedantic, remote, and insolent foreigner. It is but an idea of his own that he is foisting upon us, calling it our soul" (79).

Of German philosophy in general Santayana alleges that "subjectivity in thought" is a conspicuous feature, and that romantic egotism is part of its very spirit. Into the nature of the latter, he maintains, Goethe affords a perfect insight when he makes Faust, in emulation of Luther, deal with the first verse of Saint John in such wise as "not prosaically to discover what the Evangelist meant, but rather what he must and shall have meant" (40). Thus, then, do we learn that *Im Anfang war die That.*

Now a study of Santayana's account of what he calls German Philosophy, more specifically in his book *Egotism in German Philosophy,* leave one with the conclusion that he executes his task pretty much in the spirit which, correctly or otherwise, he attributes to Hegel, and that in its performance he manifests himself as a devotee of that subjectivity and that romantic egotism which, rightly or wrongly, he affirms to be of the essence of German Philosophy. Indeed, he does more than merely exemplify those characteristics which, in the passages referred to above, he ascribes to Hegel and to the representatives of Ger-

[1] *Egotism in German Philosophy,* new ed. (1940) 78. Unless otherwise stated all further page references in this essay are to this edition of Santayana's book.

man philosophy in general. Of the manner in which he deals with his subject, he is definitely conscious. Nay more: he even defends it as morally justifiable. Recognizing that he has "failed at many points, since human faculties are limited and it is impossible altogether to overcome the bias of temperament and tradition," he adds: "Nor is it morally desirable to do so" (vi). "Reflection and description are things superadded, things which ought to be more winged and more selective than what they play upon" (ix).

Doubtless, to be sure, Santayana would resent being thus explicitly bracketed with Hegel and the leading representatives of German philosophy. The contention that in his treatment of them he associates himself with the figures as he portrays them, would be to him most repugnant. For, with the typical German thinkers Santayana would have no social commerce. "The aroma of German philosophy that has reached . . . [his] nostrils" (ix) he finds most foul.

Paradoxical indeed is this exemplification, on the part of Santayana, of the very traits which it is one of his concerns to castigate. What may be the source of this paradox? Some there are who would account for it by the apologetic contention that *Egotism in German Philosophy* first appeared in 1916 and that it was written under emotions aroused by a war which threatened to destroy the ideals and the civilization highly prized by the author of the book. Supporting this contention are the impassioned tones of numerous passages and various allusions to contemporary events, such, for example as one that is introduced in a reference to Goethe's love-affairs.[2] To quote: "Every pathetic sweetheart in turn was a sort of Belgium to him; he violated her neutrality with a sigh; his heart bled for her innocent sufferings, and he never said afterwards in self-defence, like the German Chancellor, that she was no better than she should be" (38).

The contention to which we have referred, however, ill serves

[2] With reference to these passages and allusions Santayana, in the recent edition of his book, confesses: "I should not now repeat them, but I leave them unaltered, in order that the text may stand absolutely as it was written and that there may be no suspicion of sentiments or prophecies re-edited after the event" (vii).

the purpose of apologetics. By virtue of the intellectual privileges enjoyed during the period of their training, and by virtue of the opportunities and the responsibilities of their office, philosophers of all men are least justified in utterance distorted by passion. Nor can the contention be brought into harmony with Santayana's own statements. Does he not declare, in the very first sentence of his preface to the original edition, that his volume represents "the fruit of a long gestation" (viii)? This declaration he reinforces in the new preface of twenty-three years later when he says of his work: "Although it passed for a war-book, it was really philosophical" (v). "It seemed to many," he writes, "that I was taking an unworthy advantage of public resentment against particular acts of the German Government in order to justify my prejudice against German philosophy. Few people[3] had actually read the German authors to whom I referred or could see the care or even the sympathy with which my brief commentary was composed. . . . I am not sure that my difficulties with German philosophy should be called prejudices, since I have always wished to overcome them, and to understand this philosophy, and every other, sympathetically from the inside" (v f.). An early fear that the secret of German philosophy might be eluding him, he explains, spurred him "to great and prolonged efforts to understand what confronted . . . [him] so bewilderingly" (viii). "I wished," he asserts, "to be as clear and just about it as I could—more clear and just, indeed, than it ever was about itself" (viii).

Fairly common has been the belief that Santayana indicts the German philosophers for having injected iron into the blood of the German people, for having intensified if not indeed generated their cultural and national conceit, and for having at least abetted, if not even aroused, their aggressive ambitions. For this belief also the book affords some bits of evidence, including Santayana's statements that under "the obscure and fluctuating tenets" of German philosophy, he felt "something sinister at work, something at once hollow and aggressive"

[3] Concerning these few Santayana is of the opinion that "some of the most competent were perhaps wounded in their own hearts by my criticisms, and found it easier to dismiss than to discuss them" (vi).

(viii), and that the "glorified and dogged egotism" which he discovered in it "might now . . . be evident to the whole world" (x). Thus also he closes his chapter on Hegel with the sentence: "The die is cast, the war against human nature and happiness is declared, and an idol that feeds on blood, the Absolute State, is set up in the heart and over the city" (83).

In objection it may be urged that philosophers and their books may not be claimed to exercise nearly so potent an influence on public attitudes or on national policies and acts as this implies; also, that Santayana himself admits that

> if we counted the Catholics and the old-fashioned Protestants on the one hand, and the materialists (who call themselves monists) on the other, we should very likely discover that the majority of intelligent Germans held views which German philosophy proper must entirely despise, and that this philosophy seemed as strange to them as to other people (p. 1)

—and how could those who are but a minority in that group which represents only that particular section of the German people who are "intelligent" in the sense here meant, be the dominant influence on public thought or the controlling, or even a very considerable, factor in the realm of social and political institutions and forces?

Now, though it must be admitted that Santayana has given some provocation for these objections, it is likewise the case that he has committed himself as follows: "Not that the German philosophers are responsible for the war, or for that recrudescence of corporate fanaticism which prepared it from afar. They merely shared and justified prophetically that spirit of uncompromising self-assertion and metaphysical conceit which the German nation is now reducing to action" (x).

It is therefore not unfitting to deal with *Egotism in German Philosophy* as though it were intended to be a serious philosophical treatise, and to consider its interpretations of German thinkers from the point of view of validity, quite apart from the question as to the extent to which these thinkers were responsible for such evil (or good) actions as are attributable to the German governments or people. That Santayana's book has been so regarded is evidenced by the fact that it was the first of his works ever to have been translated, and that its translators into French and Italian were Catholics. With reference to them Santayana, in the Postscript to his new edition, writes as follows:

> The ground on which I stood might be naturalistic; but they felt instinctively how much naturalism, supernaturalism, and Platonism are at one in recognizing the dependence and deceitfulness of the senses and the vain if not sinful character of worldly passions. I therefore seemed to them to be criticizing in modern terms the radical arrogance of modern philosophy, and I might prove a useful ally (152).

II

By German philosophy Santayana does not mean philosophy in Germany. Many, perhaps even most, of the Germans who may properly be included within the ranks of philosophers, even as the majority of intelligent Germans, he recognizes as espousing doctrines essentially opposed to the tenets of that "original and profound philosophy . . . [which] has arisen in Germany" (1) and which, apparently for this reason, he calls German.

What, then, is the nature of the philosophy of which it is said that it has thus arisen and which presumably is therefore distinguished as German? In answer one might survey the various characteristics and tenets which Santayana ascribes to it throughout his book. Or, one might glance at the list and at the interpretations given of those whom he singles out for discussion as its progenitors, contributors, or leading representatives. For, Santayana offers abstract and general characterization, on the one hand, and, on the other, expositions of the philosophies of particular thinkers. Herein, indeed, lies one source of his difficulties, methodologically speaking, and one cause of the fact that his accounts of the various philosophical systems are, to say the least, frequently out of focus. His abstract characterization motivates both his selection of the particular thoughts by reference to which he expounds the philosophers of whom he treats, and also his tendency to take these thoughts independently of their nexus and of the central aims of the thinkers to whom they are ascribed. No one who pursues such a course could find it at all difficult to uncover some degree or another of egotism, or for that matter of almost anything else that might be mentioned, in any selected list of thinkers, particularly if the definitions were left vague, made flexible, and allowed to shift. But is it likely that the resulting generalizations or that the interpretations of the several thinkers included in the list would be more than *prima facie* sound?

Be it remarked also that Santayana deals with his problem within chronological limits. As respects the philosophers, he begins with Leibniz and ends with Nietzsche. The intervening thinkers given particular attention are Goethe, Kant, Fichte, Hegel, Max Stirner,[4] and Schopenhauer. Few indeed are those others of whom there is some passing note, and these do not include even such prominent philosophers as Schelling and Herbart, though both, however distinctive their views, would certainly be caught up in any net whose meshes are sufficiently close to confine all those thinkers to whom Santayana gives attention, and though both have continuously been more widely read and influential, in intellectual circles, within even as without Germany, than, certainly, has Kaspar Schmidt.[5] Surprising also is the fact that Santayana gives so relatively large an allotment of space to a man of letters, and even more that his choice fell on Goethe.[6] Not only was Schiller, for example—to say nothing of Lessing and Herder—more philosophically minded and active than his literary and personal friend, but he drew heavily from the fonts of Kant (whom Santayana portrays as a

[4] Santayana's account gives no indication of the fact that Max Stirner is a pseudonym used by Kaspar Schmidt in the publication of his rather strange book, *Der Einzige und sein Eigentum.*

[5] It is very doubtful whether his philosophical book—for he wrote but one such—was known even to that German philosopher whose thought most closely follows in its course, namely Nietzsche. (Cf. Paul Lauterbach's Introduction in the Reclam edition of *Der Einzige,* p. 8, note 2.) What Santayana says of German philosophy in general, it might be pointed out, holds more fully of Kaspar Schmidt's book than of any other work by a German writer. But even *Der Einzige* is very far from teaching solipsism.

[6] Santayana attributes only "hints of egotism" to Goethe, and he recognizes that Goethe's "contact with philosophical egotism was but slight" (33). However, he goes on to say, there is in this writer much that is "so full of the spirit of German philosophy, that it would be a pity not to draw some illustration for our subject from so pleasant a source" (33).

seminal figure in German philosophy) whereas Goethe derived more satisfaction, sustenance and strength from Spinoza than he did from any other single philosopher, whether German, of Germany, or foreign.[7]

Adverting now to the features in terms of which Santayana characterizes German philosophy, the following would appear, and would call for comment, in a general and a running inventory. (*a*) "Wilfulness in morals" (ix). [This of Kant! Or of Hegel, whose ethics assuredly must be said to differ fundamentally from that of Kant! Yet both thinkers are taken as exponents of German philosophy!] (*b*) "Subjectivity in thought" (ix); "deliberately subjective" (1); limitation "to the articulation of self-consciousness" (2). [Yet Leibniz and Schopenhauer are included among its representatives, and in Schopenhauer—we have the words of Santayana himself for it—"Will . . . is a metaphorical term, and stands for all physical or vital energies" (170). Further to quote Santayana against Santayana, without subscribing to the truth of the generalization: "Yet this Will, this psychological name for matter, plays the leading part in all German systems, and in most of those composed abroad under German influence" (170).] It "probes the self—as unaided introspection may—with extraordinary intentness and sincerity. In inventing the transcendental method, the study of subjective projections and perspectives, it has added a new dimension to human speculation" (2). [But how can one possibly equate the transcendental method with that of unaided introspection? How can it be called a study of subjective projections and perspectives if the reference is (as numerous other passages clearly indicate) to empirical human individuals and their experiences *qua* private? Was it not for the express purpose of establishing and characterizing a public world, the world of intelligible discourse and of science, that the transcendental method was adopted and designed? And was it not precisely because he deemed it inadequate in this respect as in others, that Hegel—cited by Santayana as a repre-

[7] See "Goethe and Philosophy," an essay contributed by the present writer to *Goethe Centenary Papers*, ed. by Martin Schütze, Open Court Publishing Company, 1932.

sentative of German philosophy—parted company with Kant?] (*c*) "Uncompromising self-assertion" (x) [Is Schopenhauer's doctrine of morality forgotten?]; and "metaphysical conceit" (x) [An exceedingly strange thing to ascribe to Kant. Of him Santayana himself writes: "To this contrite attitude of Kant's agnosticism his personal character and ethics corresponded" (43).] (*d*) "Against liberty and reason" (xi). [But see the next following quotations and (*m*) below. And, as regards reason, shades of Leibniz and of Hegel!] (*e*) Solipsism. Its "fundamental conviction is that there are no existing things except imagined ones: God as much as matter is exhausted by the thought of Him, and entirely resident in this thought" (2).

> My Will or Spirit, the rumble of my unconscious appetitions, thus absorbs my ideas, my ideas absorb their objects, and these objects absorb the world, past, present, and future. Earth and heaven, God and my fellow-men are mere expressions of my Will, and if they were anything more, I could not now be alive to their presence? My Will is absolute (28).

Je suis, donc tu n'es pas was subtly placed by the French translator on the title page of his rendering of Santayana's book on German philosophy, approvingly reports its author. (Cf. 153.) [The contentions here advanced are too far fetched to deserve comment, even if the description in the first of the passages were not of its "conviction" but of the import of its teachings. More reasonable, even though itself not true in the case of all who are included among the builders of German philosophy, is the statement (153): The "ego enlarged and made exclusively real by the egotist is not his physical person or self. It is a far subtler and more impersonal entity, namely the spirit to whom this whole world appears." Compare what is said about Will, in the second of the passages quoted, with the contention quoted above, under (*b*).] (*f*) Discards altogether the "notion that knowledge can *discover* anything, or that anything previously existing can be revealed" (2). [An excessively bold statement in the face even of Hegel alone—Hegel, of whom Santayana in one passage himself says that he "drew an outline portrait of things, according to what he thought their ideal essence" (5).] (*g*) "Accepts the total relativity of the human mind and luxuriates in it" (4). [But Hegel is deemed a representative! The word "total," if nothing else, makes inacceptable the next sentence of Santayana's "This sort of agnosticism in a minor key is conspicuous in the *Critique of Pure Reason*."] (*h*) Doctrines "that the very notion of truth or fact is a fiction of the will" (17), and that human beings "are limited to the autobiography of . . . [their] illusions" (4). [Doctrines, we would say, which can be ascribed in common to those who are singled out by Santayana as German thinkers, only through a fiction of the writer's will. He arrives at his interpretation, apparently, mainly in consequence of his belief that these thinkers are committed to solipsism. "I am solitary, says the romantic egotist, and sufficient unto myself. The world is my idea, new every day: what can I have to do with truth?" (111).] (*i*) "Contempt for happiness, for one's own happiness as well as for other people's" (133), in contrast with "Judaism and Christianity" which "like Greek philosophy, were singly inspired by the pursuit of happiness, in whatever form it might be really attainable" (133). [A contention which is very puzzling if one holds before one's mind the group called German philosophers, especially inasmuch as the concept of happiness is left undefined. Nevertheless it would be a safe guess that the statement is invalid if "happiness" is taken in that very broad connotation in which alone it can be said to be that by which Judaism, Christianity, and Greek philosophy were alike "singly inspired."] (*j*) Antipathy to the recognition of "the dependence and deceitfulness of the senses and the vain if not sinful character of worldly passions" (152). [*Pace* Leibniz and especially Kant!] (*k*) The thought that "if the spirit in them is divine, it lends its supreme sanction to all their desires" (156). [One would be glad for a single reference in, let us say, Leibniz, Kant, Fichte or Hegel, that even by a *tour de force* might be said to embody or even to imply this doctrine.] (*l*) Belief that "the one God remained their special national God; so that the creator of the world and the providence ruling over history was pledged, according to their insane persuasion, to ordain everything solely for their ultimate triumph" (161; cf. also 10). [Though this is offered in general characterization of German philosophy, it was doubtless a mere slip that no exception was explicitly made of those thinkers who espoused atheistic views. Even of the theists, however, the contention is a perversion of historical facts. For Hegel, world history is subsumptive of the life of every actual State,[8] and God is the Lord of the universe. Of Fichte Engelbrecht has well said that he strove for a "synthesis of patriotism and cosmopolitanism" and that his "cosmopolitanism created a cultural-Jacobin nationalism, while his patriotism produced an embryonic internationalism;"[9] this ethical passion was ever focussed on the universally human and on the circle inclusive of all "who bear a human countenance;" his God stood for the realization of moral requirements and values both in nature and in history.]

(*m*) "Pronounced egotism, psychological, moral, historical, and political" (154). Not natural egoism or self-assertion, such as is "proper to every living creature" (151) but something "spuri-

[8] In so far as the Additions in the *Philosophie des Rechts* may be trusted, Hegel indeed said that the "state is the march of God in the world; its ground or cause is the power of reason realizing itself as will." (*The Philosophy of Right*, tr. by S. W. Dyde, 247.) Following immediately hereupon, however, are the sentences: "When thinking of the idea of the state, we must not have in our mind any particular state, or particular institution, but must rather contemplate the idea, this actual God, by itself. . . . The state is not a work of art. It is in the world, in the sphere of caprice, accident, and error."

Much later in his book Hegel mentions "the northern principle of the Germanic nations" as the fourth and last of the principles of the "world-historic empires" and as the one that brings "to completion" the evolution of the State. At first blush this might seem to afford at least some measure of substantiation to Santayana's contention, as well as to the charge very commonly made that Hegel apotheosized the Prussian State in which he lived. Contentions and charges of this sort, however, lose sight of the fact that Hegel referred to the *principle* which he found exemplified in the *Germanic* nations and of the further fact that he proceeded at once to add: "The internal aspect of this northern principle exists in feeling as faith, love, and hope. . . . But as it is yet not thought out, and still is veiled in the barbarism of picture-thinking, it exists as a spiritual force, which exercises over the actual mind a despotic and tyrannical influence." (Ibid., 349.)

[9] H. C. Engelbrecht, *Johann Gottlieb Fichte: A Study of his Writings with Special Reference to his Nationalism*, 154. Even in his *Reden an die deutsche Nation* Fichte expressed himself as follows concerning the noble man: "His faith and his endeavor to plant what is imperishable, his conception in terms of which he understands his own life as an eternal life, is the tie by which he binds most closely to himself his nation, in the first instance, and through it the entire human race, and takes up into his expanded heart all their needs until the end of days." (*Sämmtliche Werke*, ed. by I. H. Fichte, VII, 382f.)

ous and artificial" (151), "diabolical in its courage" and "satanic in its loftiness," "subjectivism become proud of itself and proclaiming itself absolute" (152). Egotism "assumes, if it does not assert, that the source of one's being and power lies in oneself, that will and logic are by right omnipotent, and that nothing should control the mind or the conscience except the mind or the conscience itself" (151). If we probe into it we will discover Protestantism, even as the doctrine of Fichte and Hegel concerning "a providential plan of the world" is "Protestant theology rationalized" (11). Also[10] may it be said that in "their tentative, many-sided, indomitable way, the Germans have been groping for four hundred years towards a restoration of their primitive heathenism" (131), this heathenism consisting in a disregard of the possible teachings of history,[11] "a sincere revulsion against the difficult and confused undertakings of reason; against science, institutions, and moral compulsions" (129). [It is difficult to see how the attitude which "assumes, if it does not assert . . . that will and logic are by right omnipotent" should be deemed a continuation of a groping for the restoration of what is "a sincere revulsion against the difficult and confused undertakings of reason;" difficult also to understand how Santayana can identify with a movement that opposes "science, institutions and moral compulsions" such philosophers as Hegel, who is described as having declared "war against human nature" and set up the "Absolute State" "in the heart and over the city" (83). How can one who is guilty of the latter belong among those whose characteristic teachings are "wilfullness in morals," "uncompromising self-assertion," "subjectivism," and "solipsism"? Or how can any thinker be said thus to belong who, as is claimed of Fichte, insists that if "the people are disinclined to obey the Idea, the Government must constrain them to do so" and that all "the powers of all the citizens must be absorbed in the State" (66)? Against German philosophy and those taken to be its representatives Santayana hurls the charge now of advocating un-

[10] For, declares Santayana, the "rebellion of the heathen soul is unmistakable in the Reformation" (132).

[11] The verb used by Santayana in describing the attitude of the German philosophers to the "lessons of experience" is "rejected." (20).

mitigated license on the basis of an egoism become self-conscious and fanatic, and now of sponsoring tyrannical discipline and the effacement of individual choices and judgments! Egotism seems to be the central doctrine and spirit from which stem the various characteristics of German philosophy that he sets forth. But what conception can be formed of that which can in any wise unify such incompatible elements? In whose system of philosophy are all these to be found, whether as assumed, implied, or pronounced? And, if the name of some German philosopher were mentioned, could one not readily point to others who, ever since the days of the Sophists, have in equal degree exhibited the same traits and teachings?]

Now it might be claimed that our comments on these various items of Santayana's characterization are at least in some measure unfounded. Thus, we have more than once raised objections by calling attention to Schopenhauer, and yet does not Santayana, in one passage, explicitly say that "Schopenhauer was not an egotist" (102)? So indeed he does; however, he deals with Schopenhauer throughout as a representative of German philosophy, and the latter is described as implicitly, if not avowedly, egotistic and characterized by the other features to which we have made allusion. Further, our attention might be called to the fact that to Kant Santayana attributes only the "seeds of egotism" (cf., e.g., the heading of Chapter V) and that of him he says that as there was much in his "personal belief which this critical method of his could not sanction, so there were implications and consequences latent in his critical method which he never absorbed" (42). Nevertheless, we would reply, it is contended that "One of these latent implications was egotism" and explained that Kant's failure to absorb this was due to the fact that he was an "old man" when he adopted his critical method. Actually, Kant was forty-six when he wrote his *De Mundi Sensibilis atque Intelligibilis Forma et Principiis*, and much else that later found inclusion in his *Kritik der reinen Vernunft* was written before he reached the age of fifty-seven. That he had not yet become mentally old by 1781 is abundantly clear from the number and the quality of the works that came from his pen subsequently to his first Critique. Or, still again, we might be reminded of a paragraph in which Santayana writes:

> The beauty and torment of Protestantism is that it opens the door so wide to what lies beyond it. This progressive quality it has fully transmitted to all the systems of German philosophy. Not that each of them, like the earlier Protestant sects, does not think itself true and final; but in spite of itself it suggests some next thing. We must expect, therefore, that the more conservative elements in each system should provoke protests in the next generation (13).

These observations are not without subtlety and truth. But how, then, may one logically group together and ascribe common teachings to the thinkers who appeared successively in such protest?

Santayana implies that at least one reason why he labels as German the philosophy contained in the systems he interprets is the fact that it arose in Germany (cf. 1). Concerning this but few words need be said. For, Santayana himself states that a dominant motif of German philosophy, "The notion of spirit," was "present in European philosophy" "ever since Descartes uttered his *cogito*" (155). He himself calls attention to the fact that Kant's "mind had been more open than that of Leibniz to the influences of English psychology" (23), though more might and should have been made of Kant's indebtedness to Hume and other British thinkers as well as to Descartes and the continental rationalists. On Santayana's authority we have it that Fichte was ungrateful for calling Locke the worst of philosophers, "seeing that his own philosophy was founded on one of Locke's errors" (21). Respecting egotism he says: "It was the ancient Hebrews that first invented egotism, and have transmitted it to the rest of the world" (160; cf. 162). One of his statements includes the observation that the "sophistication" which "is the first principle of German philosophy" was "borrowed . . . from non-Germans" (9). Such being Santayana's own admissions and assertions he is debarred from the contention that the philosophy which his book portrays, though indeed obnoxious to many thinkers in Germany, may nevertheless be called German by reason of the fact that, in distinction from other philosophies espoused by Germans, it arose in Germany.

Santayana's accounts of the particular thought systems comprised within German philosophy differ widely in their merits. Incidentally to our comments on his general characterization, some of their defects have come to light. More than to any other single cause they are due to a false view of the teachings of Kant, Fichte and Hegel respecting the human self. "Duty, will, or the grammar of thought" were not for them "the most personal and subjective parts of the mind" (2); of what Kant meant by the "postulates of practical reason" one may not say that they "are no less subjective than knowledge, and far more private and variable" (49); nor is it the case that German idealism did or possibly could accept the proposition that it "is for the ego who posits to judge what it should posit" (49). Likewise is it untrue that, in the Fichtean system, the reason for the positing of a material world by the ego is its experience of "the categorical imperative," of "an absolute duty" required of it (148). Santayana goes astray because he seems to be completely insensitive to the fundamental distinction made by Kant, Fichte, and (less directly) Hegel between the transcendental self, the absolute ego, and reason, on the one hand, and on the other, the empirical, personal, and private self, as well as he is to Fichte's distinctions between the Absolute Ego, the practical ego, the ego *qua* theoretical, and the Idea of the Ego. Fichte, for example, was by no means a solipsist, belonging among those (if any there have been) who maintain that their interest in genealogy created their great-grandfathers. (Cf. 30.) As early as 1796 he presented what, in his meaning of the term, is a "deduction" of fellow-humans—of beings to whom we owe respect and have moral duties. Only a rollicking caricaturist should venture to ask, as was done by a writer of Fichte's day, how this philosopher's wife could possibly tolerate his pretensions to be the supreme and indeed the sole reality. As for his subjectivistic teachings, we need not take very seriously the imputation implied in a remark made by Goethe at the time when the enraged student societies of Jena stoned the windows and demolished the doors of Fichte's house—a remark which, reminiscent of Samuel Johnson's refutation of Berkeley, called attention to the fact that the student's actions certainly offered a forcible demonstration of the existence of a non-ego. In so far as Fichte may be called subjectivistic, it is fundamentally because of his doctrine of the primacy of the practical reason, of his teaching that what is absolute for the finite individual is the *ought* and that reason is operative and becomes vocal in man fundamentally in its call that he do his part in the realization of the principles and the ends of reason. Wide indeed is the gulf between this sort of subjectivism and that with which Santayana charges Fichte. Furthermore it should be noted that even the subjectivism of Fichte's doctrine of *Sollen*, which stresses the dualism and the conflict between the actual and the ideal, was very early made a target by a somewhat younger contemporary who, even as Fichte, is represented by Santayana as an outstanding egotist and representative of German philosophy.[12]

The nature of Santayana's treatment of German philosophy forced upon us the ungracious task of criticism. This does not preclude us from gladly acknowledging the beauty and force of Santayana's style nor from paying our appreciative tribute to the numerous shafts of light which he has thrown into the recesses of human nature and on the principles of human action.

EDWARD L. SCHAUB

DEPARTMENT OF PHILOSOPHY
NORTHWESTERN UNIVERSITY

[12] For a somewhat detailed discussion of the matters alluded to in this and the immediately preceding sentences we would refer to our essay "Hegel's Criticism of Fichte's Subjectivism," *The Philosophical Review*, XXI, 5, 566-584 and XXII, 1, 17-37.

15

William Ray Dennes

SANTAYANA'S MATERIALISM

15

SANTAYANA'S MATERIALISM

IN *The Realm of Matter* Mr. Santayana formulates "the great axiom of materialism, to which this whole book is only a corollary" as asserting "the dominance of matter in every existing being, even when that being is spiritual."[1] If *The Realm of Matter* is but a corollary to this "great axiom," would it be fair to describe the whole of Santayana's philosophical work as an elaborate illustration of the same principle—as an explication of its meaning by way of interpretations of various stretches and phases of natural and human history? Is his position rightly understood as a "materialistic world-view:" as the metaphysics of one who confesses himself "a decided materialist—apparently the only one living?"[2] And do the emphatic passages in which he describes the goal of inquiry as to "discover behind this glorious chaos a deeper mechanical order,"[3] and those in which he insists that, in natural philosophy (which for him is the philosophy of all existence), "Mechanism is not one principle of explanation among others . . . mechanism is explanation itself"[4] —do such passages justify us in calling his position not only materialism but also mechanism?

But how does such an interpretation of his philosophy as materialistic metaphysics square with Santayana's outspoken empiricism and positivism? How well does it accord with his description of his own critical method as being transcendental in the sense that it is a challenge to produce the factual evidence (if there is any) which would support human beliefs, and par-

[1] *The Realm of Matter*, 100.
[2] *Scepticism and Animal Faith*, vii.
[3] *Reason in Common Sense*, 124.
[4] *Ibid.*, 17.

ticularly the more lordly of human beliefs?[5] How well does such an interpretation agree with his insistence that everything thinkable must be experienceable?[6] How does it accord with the principle that it is impossible to believe in anything not intuited—a principle upon which he seems to rely when he argues that, if nothing persisted, "There would be no intuition of change, and therefore not even a possible belief in it?"[7] How is such an interpretation to be squared with his insistence that there is no knowledge beyond, or different in method and authority from, the sort called scientific;[8] and with his doctrine of the material emptiness of all *a priori* principles—their irrelevance to the content or the probability (let alone the truth) of beliefs, in spite of their convenience in indicating intent and in clarifying the language by which intentions and opinions are communicated?[9] How is it to be reconciled with his frequent denunciations of metaphysics as "idolatrous,"[10] as a confusion of natural science with dialectic and a mixture of both with myths,[11] and with his many disclaimers that his own system is metaphysical?[12]

It is indeed difficult to ascribe a metaphysics, either materialism or any other, to one who writes: "But my materialism, for all that, is not metaphysical. I do not profess to know what matter is in itself. . . . But whatever matter may be, I call it matter boldly. . . ."[13] And in the very passage in which he formulates "the great axiom of materialism" Santayana goes on to say

[5] *Scepticism and Animal Faith*, 4 and 5. Compare also *The Realm of Matter*, 8: "My survey of the realm of matter will accordingly be merely transcendental. . . . By transcendental reflection I understand reversion, in the presence of any object or affirmation, to the immediate experience which discloses that object or prompts that affirmation. Transcendental reflection is a challenge to all dogmatism, a demand for radical evidence."

[6] *Reason in Common Sense*, 182; *Reason in Science*, 13.

[7] *Scepticism and Animal Faith*, 30.

[8] *Reason in Science*, 18-36; Cf. also *Realm of Matter*, 196.

[9] *Cf. Reason in Science*, 35; *Winds of Doctrine*, 122; *Scepticism and Animal Faith*, 3; *The Realm of Matter*, 13, 85; *The Realm of Truth*, *passim*, but especially chapters 1 and 2 and p. 110.

[10] *The Realm of Matter*, 5.

[11] *Reason in Science*, 318; *Scepticism and Animal Faith*, vii; *The Realm of Essence*, 175.

[12] *Scepticism and Animal Faith*, vii.

[13] *Ibid.*, vii, viii.

But this axiom would not be consonant with the life of nature if it did not involve a complementary truth which *takes away all its partisan bias* and half its inhuman sting: I mean the complementary truth that matter is no model devised by the human imagination, like Egyptian atoms or the laws of physics, but is a primeval plastic substance of unknown potentiality, perpetually taking on new forms; the gist of materialism being that these forms are all passive and precarious, while the plastic stress of matter is alone creative and, as far as we can surmise, indestructible.[14]

Further on in the same work Santayana gives notice that "By the word matter I do not understand any human idea of matter [presumably not even any idea of his own as to what matter is] popular or scientific, ancient or recent. Matter is properly a name for the actual substance of the natural world, whatever that substance may be."[15]

It is plausible to deny that any metaphysical system is either expressed or implied by statements that matter is all that exists, if we mean by "matter" nothing restricted or specific, but simply whatever exists. The more serious question is whether such "statements" have any significance at all (metaphysical or other), except as illustrations of a definition of the term "matter"—as manifestations of the resolution to call any and every existent "matter" or "material." And upon this definition the terms become redundant synonyms for "existent," in the substantive and adjectival senses of that word. Such rather elaborate developments as the "finding" that "There is no such thing as mental substance, mental force, mental machinery, or mental causation,"[16] give emphasis to the above question; since if *any* substance, force, machinery, or causation were found, inferred, or considered, it would, on Santayana's definition, but merely by definition, have to be called material (and hence non-mental, if by "the mental" is meant that which, among other things, is not material). To be sure, Santayana does not use "matter" as a term to apply to everything whatever. Essences and spirit (the latter not as occurrent awareness, but as the light of awareness, and also sometimes as the objects [essences] upon which

[14] *The Realm of Matter*, 100; *italics* mine.

[15] *Ibid.*, 140.

[16] *Ibid.*, 188-189.

that light plays) contrast with matter. The essences are self-identical and eternal. Matter, on the other hand, is perpetual flux or, as is sometimes very darkly asserted, is that which is in flux and also animates or moves the flux.[17] No man can notice or intuit it. Its existence and its nature are both of them objects of animal faith; and our beliefs about it are, on Santayana's account, in one plain sense beliefs in we know not what. But the relevant point here is that in *Scepticism and Animal Faith*, *The Realm of Essence* and *The Realm of Matter* "existent" is defined to mean that which comes-to-be, endures, and passes away, *i.e.*, the flux; and "matter" is also defined to mean flux, or that which is in flux. Therefore, to say of minds or of anything else that they exist is (by definition) to say that they are in process and are material; and to deny that they are material is simply (and by definition) to deny that they exist at all.

A materialism that gives no further specification of what it means by "matter" than that it means anything and everything that exists, and excludes nothing but the non-existent, is, we may grant, free from dogmatism. But is it thus free only because it says nothing, expresses no particular opinion, is not (although it was so offered to us) "one more system of philosophy"[18] at all? Has a materialism that describes matter as a "dark principle" which it would be "frivolous to attempt to define"[19] and which is "necessarily inexplicable"[20] purchased intellectual chastity at the price of emptiness and sterility? And how is such a materialism to be reconciled with what has been called the "forthright Democritean materialism" of *The Life of Reason*—the doctrine that "His [Democritus'] was an indefensible faith in a single radical insight, *which happened nevertheless to be true;*"[21] that "existing nature is a system of bodies long antedating sentience;"[22] "in natural philosophy . . . mechanism is explanation itself,"[23] and the function of reason the clarification

[17] Cf. *ibid.*, ix and 89. Compare also C. J. Sullivan's statement in this volume, —: "What Santayana calls matter, the natural and dynamic force at work in the world, the one being. . . ."

[18] *Scepticism and Animal Faith*, v.

[19] *The Realm of Matter*, 14, 18.

[20] *Scepticism and Animal Faith*, 208.

[21] *Reason in Science*, 82, *italics* mine.

[22] *Reason in Common Sense*, Preface to Second Edition, viii.

[23] *Ibid.*, 17.

of mythical notions "until nature is seen to be a mechanism?"[24]

In view of the statements just cited, it has been natural that two questions should, characteristically, be raised by students and critics of Santayana's philosophy: (1) Has there been a shift in Santayana's position from an earlier naturalism (expressed in the five volumes of *The Life of Reason*) specifically and even dogmatically materialistic and mechanistic, to a later and chastened naturalism (expressed in *Scepticism and Animal Faith* and in the three *Realms of Being* thus far published), still called by Santayana materialism, although it can say of existence (or matter) only that it is flux, that it is any and all events whatsoever, that we cannot directly inspect any section of it, or instance of it, and that we cannot legitimately hold that it is restricted to "atoms" or other bodies and their motions, or to *any other particular sorts of processes or endurants?* (2) Has such a chastened naturalism (or materialism) any positive theoretic content at all, either as metaphysics or as a particular distinguishable philosophic system? (And is such self-immolation, as specific theory, the inevitable fate of metaphysics or philosophy that is honestly critical of itself?)

The present writer believes, and will try to show, (1) that there has been no such shift as that just described in Santayana's position from *The Life of Reason* to *Scepticism and Animal Faith* and the three books on *Realms of Being*, although there has been precisely such a shift in the development of much critical naturalistic philosophy during the last fifty years; (2) that Santayana's consistently maintained philosophical position does in fact lack any specific and positive theoretical content—adds no beliefs about existence and the ways and history of nature to the hypotheses of the sciences and to those beliefs of common sense which are their soil and seed.[25] But, if Santayana's philosophical position lacks positive theoretic content, it will be argued in what follows that it does effectively expose some of the chief confusions and pretensions which have obstructed (and do still obstruct) the development and the interpretation of human sciences and arts, and that it thereby makes to man's intellectual enterprise a contribution of the one kind of which

[24] *Ibid.*, x.

[25] *Reason in Science*, 18; *The Realm of Truth*, v.

dialectic or criticism or philosophy, as contrasted with science, is capable.

First a word about the terms "metaphysics" and "metaphysical." Mr. Santayana has always interpreted with understanding and with a genuine, if somewhat ironic, sympathy, the yearnings which have impelled men to construct metaphysical systems of the nature, the structure, the limits, and the "purpose" of the universe. But no one has criticized more sharply than he the claims of such systems—of such mixtures of science, dialectic, and myth—to contain more theoretical enlightenment or truth or probability than is expressed by the various definitions and bits of scientific hypothesis that are woven into them. Nevertheless, Santayana writes also of a "legitimate metaphysics"—which consists in the acceptance of science "while its present results are modified by suggesting speculatively what its ultimate results might be;"[26] and in this sense much of Santayana's philosophy is metaphysics and is legitimate, although he prefers to give it the name of natural philosophy. In *The Realm of Matter* (p. 3) he writes that "a theoretical refusal to trust natural philosophy cannot absolve the most skeptical of us from framing one, and from living by it." It is hard to understand what difference in living one natural philosophy could make as against any other—if, that is, all of them accept the results of science and if their further speculations are not merely whimsical but are probabilities grounded in evidence. Again, as Hume used the term "metaphysics" to denote the analysis and indication of the intent of key terms and principal distinctions employed in every-day and scientific explanation, much of Santayana's work would fairly be called metaphysical. But for such analysis Santayana prefers the name dialectic. We shall, on the whole, follow his preference and drop the terms "metaphysics" and "metaphysical" in referring to his position. Since, however, most of Santayana's critics contrast his "earlier metaphysics:" Democritean materialism, with his "later metaphysics" of essence and flux, we shall sometimes employ their terms while exploring (and exposing) their opinions.

Is the doctrine of essence and existence a positive account

[26] *Reason in Science*, 301.

of the cosmos? Does it in *any* way—even hypothetically—specify what is supposed to exist? Does it assert or entail any traits of, or relations among, existents? Does it exclude anything from existence, or from the possibility of existence? Does it differ from the materialism of *The Life of Reason?*

Santayana says that he means by the existent anything determinately charactered that comes-into-being, endures, and usually does (as it always may or may not) pass away. Like Aristotle, he holds that anything not determinately charactered would differ from nothing else—indeed, would not be different from nothing. But unlike Aristotle, he burdens himself with what seems to the present writer the quite arbitrary and gratuitous—indeed, indefensible— epistemological dogma that the occurrent, the existent, can never be noted. Nothing given to attention, to intuition, to awareness, exists. The datum is always essence or character, never an existent. Animal faith posits the existent in flux, and posits also the existence of itself. In such faith we believe in something which Santayana calls substance, with the like of which we have never been, and can never be, acquainted. "We may enjoy it, we may enact it, but we cannot conceive it; not because our intellect by accident is inadequate, but because existence, which substance makes continuous, is intrinsically a surd, a flux, and a contradiction."[27]

We may leave the merits and faults of this dogma to those who discuss Santayana's theory of knowledge. At all events, Santayana argues that, as active animals, we do and must believe in, and also perceive (which, on his account, is itself a kind of believing), stirrings of the flux which come to be, and endure briefly or lengthily, or it may be (although in no case could this be necessary) forever. Although no animal can confront a section of the flux in direct intuition, nor know with certainty what characters any stretches of the flux embody, yet no active (*i.e.*, living) animal can actually doubt that there are such particular stirrings—can believe that there are only timeless characters—since we can imagine no way of accounting for the varying shocks that fill our experiences except by supposing that particular characters and configurations, now these, again

[27] *The Realm of Matter*, 27.

those, pass from the status of possibilities to that of traits of the recalcitrant, arbitrary flux which we believe to constitute the environment, and also the careers, of animals.

> Whatever else its [*i.e.*, substance's] intrinsic essence may be, it is certainly complex, local, and temporal. *Its secret flux involves at least as many contrasts and variations as the course of nature shows on the surface.* Otherwise the ultimate core of existence would not exist, and the causes of variation would not vary. But how shall that which puts on this specious essence here and not there, be in the same inner condition in both places? Or how shall that which explodes now, have been equally active before? Substance, if it is to fulfil the function in virtue of which it is recognized and posited, must accordingly be forever changing its own inner conditions. It must be in flux.[28]

The flux, Santayana thus argues, is not merely events, for animal faith is bound to posit continuity, persistence, in something that undergoes events and moves and changes. This something Santayana calls substance and, adding scarcely anything to the meaning of that term, also matter. However, those philosophers who invite us to interpret all existence as events with their qualities and relations, insist that every event must have some endurance—none is or could be instantaneous. They therefore conclude that, since Santayana does not ascribe necessary indestructibility to substance, events with their durations and overlappings may quite well supply all the continuity which Santayana thinks animal faith must infer, or posit, in the flux. There would thus seem to be no more than a difference in notation between those who speak of nature as substance (in Santayana's sense) and those who speak of nature as events. Critics have pointed out that nothing in logic, and very little in physics and physiology, supports Santayana's view, just quoted, that the parts or phases of substance must vary as much as do the changing things of our experience. The cause of much—or all—variety in experience might lie in us, and not in "external nature." But since, as existents, we are parts of the flux, if variations in our organisms caused differences in our experience, then those variations would still be variations in material substance—in nature external to experience. However, the general notion that whenever there

[28] *Ibid.*, 15, *italics* mine.

is variation in one stretch of existence there *must* be variations elsewhere that are its causes and effects—that it would be *unnatural* for anything to alter simply of itself, that everything is *naturally* lazy and *naturally* continues at rest or in its old routine unless something else disturbs it—this notion, while pragmatically justified as a heuristic principle in scientific investigation where correlative variations can be explored, is of most dubious relevance in arguments from the whole of observable phenomena to an utterly transcendent substance which, it is said, *must* exist and *must* vary as the phenomena do, although no man can ever observe it as either existent or changing.

Critics put much stress on the fact that in *Scepticism and Animal Faith* and in the *Realms of Being* Santayana treats as the defining traits of matter—or substance or existence—not spatial shape or extension or solidity, but flux, process, coming-to-be, enduring, and passing away.[29] Santayana's later position would thus seem to be much closer to Aristotle than to Democritus, at least in so far as Aristotle treats matter not as bodies, but as the surd factor in substances (whether extended or not) by virtue of which they move and change and harbor within themselves potentialities not actually realized. Critics of Aristotle—those who are sane enough not to try to deny that change and motion are real—have long asked what it adds to the mere facts of change and motion to say that these occur by virtue of a material cause or factor in substances. Santayana seems to oscillate between regarding matter as flux itself, as that which is in flux, and as something originative or creative in the flux.[30] A critic is somewhat held back from pressing against Santayana the same question that is commonly raised with respect to Aristotle's doctrine, since not only the matter of which Santayana speaks, but also the flux which it suffers (or is), are something wholly closed to inspection, and one could not say what would be evidence for or against their possessing any particular trait. What, then, except for continuity with certain traditions of philosophic discourse, is added to the mere admission that things as we experience them are in flux, by

[29] *Ibid.*, 38, and indeed *passim.*

[30] Cf. *ibid.*, 100.

saying that these things are in some sense manifestations (or effects) of a matter—a substance—which we cannot experience, and which is flux, or is in flux, or is the dynamic factor in nature?

The other chief category, in what Santayana's critics call his latter-day metaphysics, is essence. We note—intuit—various qualities and relations, and we believe that flux exists and constantly embodies various qualities and relations which might be some of those we intuit, but most likely are not. Now the qualities and relations cannot themselves change, in the sense, say, of the range of qualities usually called black becoming those usually called white, or an instance of the relation called "greater than" becoming an instance of that called "less than," or of any other. Such changeless qualities and relations, such "eternal" characters, Santayana calls essences. And if motion, or any other sort of change, is either to be or to be conceived, then whatever pattern or quality marks one phase must be self-identical and distinct from all others. Existence, as stirring in the flux, is not required for the being of any essence, since anything must be self-identical and distinct, and thus have the being proper to essence, even in order to lack existence or to have existence doubted or denied of it. More than this, existence is irrelevant to essence, since no self-identical character could in itself contain or imply a reference to any setting in space or time, or indeed to anything (even another essence) distinct from itself. And since nothing could be excluded from the realm of essence that was not something self-identical and hence an essence, the realm of essence is infinite.

As a matter of fact, however, any area of the flux is quite as changeless as any essence, in the sense that *it* cannot possibly be-itself-and-become-something-else. It is a stretch of process —say, the career of an apple—that is in this phase green, in that phase red. But the green-qualitied processes are quite as self-identical as green is, and they could no more themselves become the red-qualitied processes than green itself could become red. However, it is useful to distinguish qualities and relations which could appear repeatedly and identically, from the appearings, the precedings, and the followings-after which cannot be identically repeated. A man might have a second son indistinguishable in every trait and quality from his first, but he could not possibly have a second first-born. And no matter how uniformly any qualities appear, we can never say of existence that it is confined to those qualities. It might never embody them again. No number of repetitions in the appearance of a trait entails, or requires, so much as one single additional manifestation of it. Everything is possible. Nothing is impossible except that whose being would be its own non-being, and the assertion of it its denial—that is, precisely nothing. Neither from a history (even ideally complete) of nature down to date, nor from a consideration of the logical status of essences, can we exclude any event (or the manifestation of any character) as impossible, or represent any as necessary.[31]

Santayana expresses these insights by saying that the realm of essence is infinite; and his critics have frequently supposed that he meant thereby that there is (perhaps even *somewhere*) an infinite subsistent realm of universals, like that of Plato's theory but devoid of the authority, the intrinsic order, and the activity which Plato seems sometimes to attribute to the Forms.[32]

What is gained, except a certain continuity with some of the traditions of philosophical discourse, by speaking of a realm of essence? Does not a little attention to elementary logic suffice to make it clear that possibilities are infinite;[33] that no proposition that is not self-contradictory, that does not unsay precisely what it says, *i.e.*, that asserts *anything, i.e., that is a proposition at all,* could assert something of which we can say significantly that it could not possibly be the case; and that no proposition that states what is, or what is believed to be, the case, could rule out any other proposition but its contradictory—could rule out, as untrue or improbable, propositions ascribing other qualities and other relations to other existents than those de-

[31] Cf. *Scepticism and Animal Faith*, 100, 137; and *The Realm of Essence*, 78, 82, 86, 98, 103.

[32] Nearly all the textual evidence would support the view that it is not Plato but his interpreters (including Santayana in *Platonism and the Spiritual Life* and other writings) who teach that Platonic forms are active forces.

[33] A principle recognized and formulated by Santayana in *The Life of Reason*, for example, *Reason in Science*, 146.

scribed by the first proposition—or even to those very existents in others of their areas or aspects?[34]

On the realm of spirit Santayana's work, reportedly long ago completed, is not yet published. But what he has thus far given us on spirit as awareness of essences seems to describe material processes—the occurrences of awareness in organisms—and to refer to the essences intuited in such awareness, but to give us no more than a name for the light of awareness as distinguished (if indeed it can be distinguished) from the occurrence of that light and from its objects (essences).

On truth Santayana has given us much good sense, but also two challenging deliverances. One, that the realm of truth is that tragic segment of the realm of essence that is embodied in existence;[35] that "the universe must have a form which we call the truth of it."[36] The other, that the truth about anything would be that absolutely complete description of it which there is no reason to suppose any man will ever achieve, and which it would be quite impossible for him to know to be true and complete even if he should achieve it.[37] There is no logical fault to find with the definition of truth as the segment of essences embodied in existence. But the definition does seem to make "truth" a synonym for "fact"—for "all the facts," or else a name for what that phrase means, namely all the characters embodied in existence and their embodiment—quite apart from any beliefs or assertions about them. Is it useful to speak of truth or falsity except where some animal believes or asserts that some specific qualities or relations are embodied in existence—and believes truly if they are, and falsely if they are not? The characters, and their embodiment in existence, are surely, in every useful sense of the terms, neither false nor true. Such an account of truth in contrast to the doctrine just criticized, Santayana has expressed frequently and clearly.[38] As for the complete description of anything, covering all its traits and relations:

[34] *Ibid.*, 155.

[35] Cf. *The Realm of Essence*, xv.

[36] *The Realm of Truth*, 110. Compare *Reason in Science*, 9 and 31.

[37] Cf. *Scepticism and Animal Faith*, 267-268.

[38] As in *Character and Opinion in the United States*, 153-156, and in many places in *The Realm of Truth*.

would it not be better to call that a truth more comprehensive, but not truer, than a true but partial description? For in what sense is the more comprehensive account truer? If it is true at all that Napoleon Bonaparte is now dead, then no possible description of Napoleon Bonaparte (or of the universe) could be any truer than is the sentence that asserts that fact about him. Indeed, the complete description of Napoleon Bonaparte's career (or of the universe's) could only be a system of such statements of particular facts about him (or it), and the truth of the complete description would be nothing over and above the truth of its constituent lemmas.

The materialism of *Scepticism and Animal Faith* and of the *Realms of Being* does not assert that nature is composed of moving bodies whose actions and reactions exhibit mechanical regularity as that was conceived in classical mechanics. Rather it asserts that nature is processes (or temporally and spatially and qualitatively variegated process), is whatever is going on; that we can never be sure that anything is going on, or what it is that is going on; that we can never pretend that existence must be confined to the traits and patterns we suppose it to embody—even if our supposition were (as we could never know) correct for its finite range. For the realm of essence is infinite; *i.e.*, the fact that some qualities and relations are embodied here or there in existence in no way prevents others from being embodied elsewhere. Santayana's peculiar epistemology requires us to say that it is impossible for us to intuit any stretch of existence—to know certainly that anything exists, or what any of its properties are. But, like all other strict impossibilities, this one depends upon definitions which render self-contradictory the statement of what is said to be impossible. Santayana's definitions are clearly illustrated and, on the whole, consistently respected in his work; but it is more than disputable whether they are reasonably convenient and more likely to aid than to obstruct understanding. There are respects in which it is appropriate to say that my perception that a ring is on my finger and my belief that there will be an eclipse of the sun visible in Central Europe on August 11, 1999, are both *equally* notions of animal faith. But a qualification which applies to all perceptions and beliefs whatever makes extremely little difference to any of them—we may as well discard the adverb "probably" as to introduce it into all declarative sentences without exception. And much more important than any identity of character between observations and hypotheses are the differences between them. But such questions are for epistemologists to consider. Sufficient to the sane balance of scepticism and belief which Santayana seeks are the simple principles (elaborated in their own terms by Leibniz and by Hume) that no fact—no existent—either entails or excludes any other, and that no character or structure entails any other or entails any existent. His later materialism is not so much an account of bodies and their motions as it is an invitation to explore nature as the (supposed) processes that are going on, to explore so far as possible without restricting preconceptions as to what the traits of those processes may be, and to recognize with proper humility that it is only belief (or hypothesis) that goes beyond what is now present to our attention. This last recognition is fully shared by those philosophers who hold, as against Santayana, that stretches of events, and not merely essences, may be directly present to attention.

Of the contemporary philosophers usually called naturalists, empiricists, or positivists, the most critical and careful have, in the last decades, and rather laboriously, won their way to precisely such a position as that just outlined as Santayana's—except for the dogma that "nothing given exists," which dogma rests upon definitions of "existence" and "datum" that render any denial of the dogma simply self-contradictory. They have shifted from basic categories like matter, motion, sensations, mechanism to such relatively neutral categories as event, quality, and relation.

Just what, then, is the rôle of categories in interpretation, philosophical or other? "Categories" is a term sometimes used to mean such other terms as "space," "time," "matter," "mind," "cause," "purpose;" and sometimes used to mean the sorts of entities (various kinds of qualities, structures, configurations of events) for which terms like "space," "time," "matter," "mind," "cause," "purpose," etc., are the names. An immense amount of confusion results from our frequent failures to make clear when we are dealing with categories as terms and when we are dealing with them as traits or patterns of existents named by certain terms, and from the consequent judgments about the one, which would be suitable only if made of the other. But "categories" has not been used to name just any terms, or to refer to just any set of traits named by any terms. Men have set off from others as categorial certain traits or certain sorts of existent, because they have made some one, or all, of the following suppositions: (1) that instances of those traits (or of those sorts of existents) are exceptionally widespread in the universe; (2) that many other traits and existents can be reduced to them—that is, that they *are* in reality, whatever they may appear to be, identical with those called categorial; (3) that the categorial traits and existents are the chief, or the sole, constituents of many entities apparently different from them; (4) that instances of the categorial traits or existents are the causes of many other states of affairs; (5) that the categorial traits or kinds of existents are such that their instances are either of great value, or else contribute largely to the being of other entities that are of outstanding value and importance. When philosophers have dealt with categories as terms, they have usually conceived of them as names for such traits or patterns of existents as had some or all of the properties set forth in (1), (2), (3), (4), and (5). They have believed that the most satisfactory explanation, or evaluation, of any materials whatever would be expressed in statements finally translatable into sentences in which such categorial terms were pivotal.

But if any categorial term is used to mean some specific and limited sort of thing—and if it is not so used, it has no theoretical meaning, whatever emotional or propagandist effects its use may have—then the question how numerous the instances of that sort of thing are and in what pattern they are distributed is one we have no serious way of answering except by the ordinary scientific procedures of exploration, experiment, and induction. If we are responsible intelligences, we accept the results of such investigation, and it can make no difference to the theoretical contents of those results in what categorial terms we express them. That is to say, if science establishes the probability that instances of X are thus and thus distributed, it will make no difference whether we treat X as categorial or whether we describe it (or its instances) in terms of relations to instances of some other trait or configuration of existents, named Y, which we take to be categorial. As for supposition (2)—that some entities can be reduced to others because those entities are *really*, though not apparently, what the entities are—this supposition makes sense only if it is construed as meaning (as often it does in fact mean) what is meant by (3) or (4) or other suppositions like them. It is never intelligible to speak of anything as strictly identical with—as actually being—anything other than itself. To say that the smooth ivory and ebony keys of the piano are *really* not smooth at all but are roughly bounded sets of jumping molecules or of shifting forces and potentials—to say this cannot mean that smooth things are really not smooth, but only that they may have constituents or causes to which there would be no grounds for ascribing (as indeed there might be no sense in either ascribing or denying) the character of smoothness. And if our opinions about the constituents and causes of anything (suppositions of types [3] and [4] above) have any serious grounds, then those opinions will remain quite the same in theoretical content, and quite the same in degree of probability, whatever terms we employ as categorial when we state them.

Something very much the same holds of values. A man may choose to signalize his interest in some aspect or character of existence by using its name as a categorial term—that is, as a term of which other terms will be derivative functions. He may thus interpret other traits and processes by stating what he supposes to be their relations to instances of the aspect or character of existence which he prizes, or feels that men generally prize, or would come to prize if their understandings were enlarged, or would be happier if they prized. But is not this a clumsy and, on the whole, misleading way to express his interest and his convictions about the interests of other human beings? Would he not do better to interpret sorts of occurrences and configurations by the discovered (or inferred) correlations of their instances with instances of such other sorts of events and patterns as are themselves best known, rather than by their relations to those sorts that happen to be dearest to him? He could then conjoin to the interpretation, and with much less likelihood of being misunderstood, a statement of the relations of the materials thus interpreted to needs, hopes, and interests (his own and those of other men). The great point is, however, that, if scrupulously carried out, the theoretical content of interpretations in terms of relations to what is valued, and of causal interpretations to which a record of appreciations is conjoined, is precisely the same. The statements of such interpretations differ in notation, but not in what they state.

So long as we mean something determinate by whatever categories we use, anything found, imagined, or inductively inferred from evidence, can be described quite as well in terms of its relations to what is meant by one category (or set of categories) as it can in terms of its relations to entities referred to by any other category or set of categories. The choice of categories, metaphysical or other, employed in explanation can make no legitimate theoretical difference, but only a notational difference, to the results achieved. For wherever any Y whatsoever can be interpreted as a function (say Φ) of some sort of X, then that X can, with identical meaning, be interpreted as a certain function (say Ψ) of that Y. Even if one's categorial terms named null classes—sorts of presumable non-existents like unicorns—one could describe and interpret all existents by specifying the ways in which they differed from imagined unicorns, and the ways in which, as thus differing, they were related to one another. If a choice of basic categories in terms of which to discuss the ranges of existents is really the expression of hypotheses to the effect that what is named by the categories is widespread, causally important, or otherwise interesting feature of nature, is it not far better simply to say so? We should then make clear, what is in any event the case, that our hypotheses stand or fall according to the supporting evidence, and would retain precisely the same meaning and degree of probability whether expressed in terms of the categories selected or in terms of any other categories whatsoever.

It is a recognition of these points that has impelled most contemporary naturalists to look for basic categories as neutral as possible, in terms of which to interpret those configurations of existence ordinarily called instances of occurrence, endurance, causation, purpose, explanation, and the like—configurations that have a central rôle in almost all human theories. The minimum categorial requirement would seem to be the recognition and distinction of, and the categorial naming of, the formal and non-formal factors in existence and discourse. Whether to call the formal, repeatable factors by a single name—such as essence or character—or whether to distinguish among them relations and qualities, may be a matter of verbal convenience. Among characters some, often called relations, have converses, as others, often called qualities, do not. Less is the converse of greater, to-the-right-of the converse of to-the-left-of; but what sense is there in speaking of a quality that would be the converse of what is meant by "willow green" or "F-sharp" or "the fragrance of the tea rose on the table?" Of course, the distinction of formal from non-formal factors is, in Hume's phrase, a distinction of reason. We never find an instance of one without the other. To find a character is, at the very least, for that character to *come-into* attention. And, as Aristotle and Hegel have both borne witness, any process that was characterless, indeterminate, would not be distinguishable from nothing. To take as basic categories existence (or flux or matter) and essence, or event, quality, and relation, is not to commit oneself to, or to estrange oneself from, any science or any metaphysic that is a positive characterization of existence. It is merely to clear the decks for the task of discovering and inferring what specific sorts of qualitied and structured processes we are actually dealing with under such names as mind, body, force, cause, purpose, value, order, history, explanation. There are, moreover, no serious methods for carrying out such discovery and inference except those of experiment, observation, and induction.

Such is the position of the majority of careful naturalists, empiricists, and positivists to-day—a position very close to that of Santayana in *Scepticism and Animal Faith* and in the

Realms, although in most cases approached, it would appear, without much attention to his writings. Is it a sound philosophical position? Or is it a confession of the bankruptcy, not only of metaphysics, but also of philosophy generally? And how much does the "forthright Democritean materialism" of *The Life of Reason* differ from this position? To answer the second question first: I do not believe that Santayana's earlier materialism differs at all (except to some extent in the choice of language) from the later position, which most naturalists of the present day are coming to accept,—although as a result of such considerations as we have just traced rather than through study of Santayana's work. In passages on pp. 221 and 182 of *Reason in Common Sense* and on pp. 7 and 100-101 of *Reason in Science*, Santayana makes it clear that the nature he calls material is quite as characteristically exhibited in the activities of minds and of gods (if there are any) as in the motions of solid bodies—in other words, that by "matter" he means simply all existence, whatever it may be. His minimum requirement for actual material existents is that they be occurrent, be somewhere in time and space (but in a time and space their flux generates, not in some sort of transcendental container)—and to this requirement he finds that a "state of mind" conforms quite as fully as could anything else. He seems to choose the phrases of Democritus and Epicurus in order to stress that atomicity of distinguished and demarcated ranges of existents that is indispensable to attention and discourse, but not in order to accept or to suggest any metaphysical atomicity of indestructible bodies. This insight concerning atomicity finds development and expression in Santayana's later writings, as in the doctrine that "nature shows . . . no privileged partitions."[39] Above all, his use of the phrases of Democritus, and his deliberate allegiance to ancient materialism, expresses important negative convictions, as contrasted with positive opinions about the shapes, hardness, number, etc., of little bodies that make up the universe. Those negative convictions are: that the processes of nature do not require for their occurrence or for their explana-

[39] *The Realm of Matter*, 11; cf., e.g., *ibid.*, 77 on historical events as "conventional stretches."

tion any support or control by, or any reference to, purposes, causes, orders, values, ends, creators that are transcendent of them. The processes of nature require, for their reality, nothing but their own occurrence. And to explain them is not to refer them to something beyond themselves, but is to discover or infer their own mechanism. To explain a limited section of these processes is, indeed, to develop hypotheses with respect both to their internal mechanism and to the larger mechanism of nature in which they are themselves factors. It is to explore and infer relationships between some stretches of events and others—relationships that may be stated in laws and principles. But it is *not* to appeal to factors behind, beyond, or in any way distinct from stretches of events, as grounds for their occurrence and bases for the explanation of them.

Now what did Santayana mean in *The Life of Reason* by saying that to understand is to conceive nature as a mechanism —that explanation as such—and not just one sort of explanation among others—is mechanistic? Plainly no more than this: that we are merely having experience, and not doing anything that we could usefully signalize as understanding it, until we distinguish some objects, characters, events as similar to others, and notice (and infer) correlations between transactions of some specific sorts and those of other specific sorts.[40] Some philosophers have preferred to define the understanding of anything as the thorough-going absorbed intuition of the thing itself and its structure; others as skill in practically operating upon and transforming the kind of thing that is to be understood; still others as the appreciation of the value of the entity; and many have held that all these kinds of explanation are more like a sympathetic participation in the career of a unique and growing organism than they are like a classification of entities by their similarities and differences and a tracing of correlations in their changes. Now in following Aristotle and describing understanding as "knowledge of the causes" of things, Santayana is not denying that the other sorts of activity just mentioned (which others have preferred to call understanding or explanation) occur, or that they are interesting or

[40] *Reasons in Common Sense*, 16; *Reason in Science*, 69.

important. But is not appreciation best called appreciation? And are not manipulation and transformation best called manipulation and transformation—and not explanation? And, although the absorbed intuition of an object and the sympathetic—even the empathetic—grasp of a living organic process, may be important factors in the understanding of objects and processes, is it satisfactory to say that they themselves constitute explanation? Have we explained until we have found and stated correlations among processes—correlations of types which we expect to find recurrent? It is often said that our understanding of history is an exception to this principle, because historical processes are never repeated. But unless we rely upon approximate general notions as to how men generally would act if they had gone through careers such as, say, Caesar's, and had written statements like those in Caesar's "Commentaries," how are we to infer from Caesar's statements, even in the most tentative way, what Caesar intended? Such general notions are, of course, for the most part, habits of expecting which we have not formulated verbally, and of which we are not very clearly conscious.

One can define terms like "understanding" and "explanation" as one will. But defining them in any one way neither denies the occurrence or the importance, nor implies a denial of the occurrence or the importance, of any other sorts of activities which others may define the terms to designate. Santayana, as it seems to me, has chosen a definition of "explanation" which specifies precisely the kind of thing which the long tradition of western science has developed under the name, and which is characteristic of the vast body of unlearnëd and unformulated everyday habits and beliefs upon which science depends and which (as Santayana brilliantly argues) science and metaphysics can only extend and clarify, but never replace by any profounder kind of knowledge. That Santayana in *The Life of Reason* called explanation mechanistic does not allow us to infer that he thought the world (or even the phases of it studied by physics) is a mechanism in the strict sense of necessarily conforming to the principle of equality of action and reaction. It does not justify us in inferring that he thought nature, or any stretch of it, consisted in identically (mechanically) repeated atoms or sensible qualities. What the world, or any part of it, is like—what its structure, conditions, context, effects may be—Santayana insists we can only infer by the methods of scientific observation, experiment, and induction. If we thus inferred that it had no repetition in it but was an affair of ever novel organic growth, he would presumably still call our explanation of it mechanistic—an affair of inferring what follows what, namely, that which is different from anything found before—and not an affair of referring natural processes to controlling grounds, causes, purposes, orders that are alleged not to be merely further stretches or patterns of natural process.

To be sure, Santayana uses such rhetoric as "the efficacious infallible order"[41] in referring to the mechanical processes which we infer in our quest for explanation. Critics have taken such phrases to mean that Santayana conceives, beyond (or within) events, necessitating forces that control them. But I think it is clear from the context, and from the whole direction and pressure of *The Life of Reason*,[42] that Santayana means, when he writes of any order as "necessary" or "inevitable," only to express the strength of his (and of most other men's) conviction that the order has been regularly manifested and will be regularly manifested in the future—not that, besides the stirrings of the flux, there are ontological necessities that govern them. Similar comments are relevant, I think, to Santayan'a statements[43] that an orderly cosmos *must* lie beneath the apparent chaos of nature and experience. In *Reason in Common Sense*, p. 35, he makes it quite clear that anything any man could conceive, or refer to, as chaos, could only be some particular order, in itself as orderly as any other, but probably an order inharmonious with his (or with many, or with all, men's) interests. Hence, if Santayana argues that under chaos there must lie order, he expresses thereby no principle of ontological necessity, but only the speculative conviction that we shall find (or plausibly infer) more and more regularity in nature as we explore her further and further.

[41] *Reason in Common Sense*, 126; *Reason in Science*, 76.

[42] Cf., e.g., *Reason in Science*, 154-155. Compare *The Realm of Matter*, 85.

[43] As in *Reason in Science*, 76.

In connection with Santayana's conception of explanation, many students (including the present writer) have been puzzled by his recent and repeated observations to the effect that "Existence is necessarily . . . inexplicable" and "irrational."[44] Does he mean by calling existence irrational that (formed process as it is) it is not pure transparent form or essence? But that, on Santayana's definitions, is a truism. Does he mean that no *a priori* logic or mathematics controls the pattern of existence? On Santayana's own analysis of the *a priori* it would not even make sense to say that any did. Does he mean that beyond existence there are no causes, powers, forces operating, to which we might appeal for explanation? This again is a truism, for on Santayana's definitions any and every operating cause or force must itself be a strand in the flux of existence. Does he mean that explanation in terms of causal hypotheses —mechanistic explanation—is never certain? And never certain in the sense that it can be no better than belief (inductive inference) and even as such may always be upset by new and recalcitrant evidence? But this is the predicament of all knowledge whatever on Santayana's definitions. If anything called explanation were indubitable, then, on Santayana's definitions, it could not be knowledge. Does he mean that we explain existents only by beliefs about their relations to further stretches of existents which are themselves not self-explanatory but are as much in need of explanation as were the primary explicanda? To say that existents are inexplicable in any of these senses would seem to reflect a hankering after something (as explanation) which, on Santayana's own grounds, is not even conceivable—a something one knows not what.

We have considered some of the factors which convince at least one student of Santayana's writings that there is no doctrinal cleavage between what critics have called the materialistic and mechanistic metaphysics of *The Life of Reason* and the more neutral position of *Scepticism and Animal Faith* and the *Realms of Being*. Running through all the works alike is the insight that *a priori* logical or rational necessity can in no way determine any but truistic beliefs (and those are very mislead-

[44] *Scepticism and Animal Faith*, 208, 211; Cf., *The Realm of Matter*, 32, 57.

ingly called by the name "*beliefs*"); that non-truistic beliefs are still propulsions of habit and feeling, no matter how extensive the "supporting evidence" may be; that anything experienced or imagined, while it cannot be said to be controlled by mathematical or logical principles, must yet embody form, all form is susceptible of mathematical or logical statement (so far as *anything* can be stated), and such statement in no ways denies or disparages any of the qualitative richness or dynamic go there may be in what is experienced or imagined;[45] above all, the insight that we cannot strictly make theoretical sense of, let alone justify the probability or necessity of, theories that natural existence depends for its being or requires for its explanation the operation of ends, forces, purposes, causes, creators, intelligences, which are not themselves part and parcel of natural existence. To this last insight Santayana has joined great gifts of imagination and great patience and diligence in exploring the humanly important needs and hopes and fears that prompt men to seek beyond nature for the grounds and the explanation of the processes of nature. No one has offered more genial and enlightening interpretations of the fantasies and attitudes which the mythologies of metaphysics (as Santayana calls them) express through image and allegory.

The upshot of Santayana's materialism and naturalism, and of his criticisms of metaphysics, would seem to be a recognition and correction of the misleading effects which our language produces when we depart from the expression of frankly tentative beliefs and the development of honest dialectic, and try by definition and by dialectic to determine hypotheses about the ways of existence, and dogmas about values as having a higher authority than that conferred upon them by their satisfaction of human needs and interests. Such analysis and correction seems to me to be the major function of philosophy or, if one

[45] This insight, which can, I think, be defended against all relevant objections, cuts the ground from under many of the constructions upon which the Bergsons, the idealists, the "rationalists," and some of the pragmatic contextualists have been engaged through the last sixty years—provided those constructions are interpreted, not as expressions of moods, nor as emphases (for one purpose or another) upon selected aspects or areas of existence, but as alternative theories, different from scientific theories and more profound than they, about the structure of nature.

likes the word, of metaphysics, so far as these are in any way distinguished from science. But it is to science, and not to metaphysics, that Santayana looks for the development of opinions which may better and better satisfy our curiosity and serve our techniques and arts (including the moral and political). It is to poetry, in the widest sense, and not to metaphysics, that Santayana looks for the best expression, and much of the development and discipline, of feeling and imagination. With all this, critical naturalists, empiricists, and positivists in our own times must heartily agree. They must admire his actual practice of philosophy as criticism, and covet some of the gifts and learning that have enabled him to interpret human civilization at once as scientist, as poet, and as critic. There is nothing in naturalistic or empiricist or positivist principles that is incompatible with thorough—and properly unpretentious—work in the history and evaluation of any factors in human culture. But lack of interest or of capacity or of learning has prevented most who hold such principles from dealing with such matters. To them, as supplementing the deficiencies of their own studies, as well as to other literate persons, the combination of critical clarity and unpretentiousness with scope and richness of materials, which characterizes Santayana's work, must make it for a long time, and even under conditions that may bc so changed as to lie beyond all present imagining, an important source of guidance, enlightenment, and intellectual joy.

William Ray Dennes

Department of Philosophy
University of California

16

C. A. Strong

SANTAYANA'S PHILOSOPHY

16

SANTAYANA'S PHILOSOPHY*

MY TASK is a delicate one. Mr. Santayana and I have been friends since we were students at Harvard and together founded the Harvard Philosophical Club. Later we divided a Harvard fellowship and lived together in Berlin. After a separation of some years, during which he taught at Harvard and I at Cornell, Chicago, and Columbia, we rejoined forces in Paris, inhabiting the same apartment.

His preparation for philosophy had been mainly historical and logical, while mine had been psychological and medical; so that in discussing questions we approached them from somewhat different points of view. The arguments I used were based on physiology and analysis, but they met with opposition from his Platonism, which must I think have been already fixed. In time, having made up my mind that there were *three* things to be distinguished in perception—subject, datum, and object—I too readily accepted a Platonic essence as the proper account of the nature of the datum.

This conclusion I have since seen reason to abandon; and that is the first criticism which I must offer on my friend's philosophy. The point goes pretty deep; in its ultimate consequences it makes all the difference between a naturalistic and a (so to speak) anthropomorphic outcome; between the view that universals are prior to particulars in the nature of things and the contrary view.

In a second criticism I feel less sure of having correctly understood Mr. Santayana's meaning. I refer to what I am accus-

* This MS. was sent by Dr. Strong from Fiesole, Italy, on January 1st, 1940. Twenty-three days later, on January 23rd, 1940, Dr. Strong died at the age of seventy-seven. It is very likely, therefore, that this MS. constitutes the last literary effort in which Dr. Strong engaged. *Ed.*

tomed to think of as his "agnosticism"—a view also to be found in the philosophy of Bertrand Russell. They hold that reality is in time and space, but say that real time and space may be totally different from the time and space we experience, that what is common to reality and the experienced may be only "structure." This attitude leaves knowledge open to Humian doubts. I should like to ask them *how they know* even that experience and reality have the same structure, or that real things are in time and space at all? I myself think it can be proved that real space is much the same in quality as experienced space, and am prepared to prove it on demand.

I told my good friend not long since that it looked to me as if his philosophy might impose itself by its reasonableness in the near future, and said that it would be a great improvement on the philosophies that had gone before. The idea of discriminating clearly the chief Realms with which thought has to do, and making it more certain that thinkers will not be continually "slipping into another genus," is a great idea, which I heartily approve. I do not object to the inclusion, with the three others, of a fourth Realm—so important is Truth. I found nothing to dissent from in the book on that Realm—unless it should be, the continued presence of Truth in a world without minds.

But I should wish to be told how the four Realms hang together, and form a Universe. Which Realm, if any, is fundamental? To put it as I once did in a letter: in replacing the Christian Trinity by that of Matter, Essence, Spirit, you have omitted the "procession" of the Holy Ghost, as well as the begetting of the Son by the Father. No doubt Mr. Santayana will have no difficulty in unifying his Creed, if he has not already done so in some passage which I ought to remember.

As a final question I would ask him: Is your Platonism really consistent with your Materialism? It depends on how he conceives the former. If Platonism means simply the recognition of essences, the tracing of their logical relations to one another, the celebration of their importance in human life and thought, it is consistent; if Platonism means that essences are prior to and determinative of existents rather than posterior to and expressive of existents, that essences have a being independent of the being of existents and would continue to be if all existents were annihilated, then it is inconsistent. The latter view is a species of Idealism, the goodness of which may serve conveniently to balance the badness of Materialism, without there being any logical tie between them.

But Mr. Santayana has not concluded the exposition of his philosophy; the *Realm of Spirit* is still unpublished. From that work we may hope for further enlightenment both as to the bases and as to the final outcome of his system of thought, and probably all the points I have raised will receive satisfactory answers.

C. A. STRONG

FIESOLE, ITALY

17

Bertrand Russell

THE PHILOSOPHY OF SANTAYANA

17

THE PHILOSOPHY OF SANTAYANA

IN attempting to characterize philosophers, no uniform method should be adopted. The method, in each case, should be such as to exhibit what the philosopher himself thinks important, and what, in the opinion of the critic, makes him worthy of study. There are some—of whom Leibniz is the most important example— who stand or fall by the correctness of their reasoning and logical analysis; the treatment of such philosophers demands minute dissection and the search for fallacies. There are others—e.g. Democritus and Descartes—who invent imaginative hypotheses of a sweeping kind, which act as a spur to detailed scientific investigation; these men owe their importance, not to the adequacy of their own grounds for their hypotheses, but to their subsequent fruitfulness. Another large group of philosophers—of whom the German idealists are the classic examples—derive their merit or demerit, according to the opinions of the critic, from an attempt to humanize the universe; these men are important if their metaphysics are correct, and unimportant if not.

Apart from the attempt to understand the world, philosophy has other functions to fulfill. It can enlarge the imagination by the construction of a cosmic epic, or it can suggest a way of life less wayward and accidental than that of the unreflective. A philosopher who attempts either of these tasks must be judged by a standard of values, aesthetic or ethical, rather than by intellectual correctness. Lucretius and Spinoza may be taken as illustrative of these two types; each has a metaphysic, but neither loses his importance when his metaphysic is discredited.

Santayana, like Spinoza, is to be read, not so much on account of his theoretical doctrines, as on account of his view as to what constitutes the good life, and of his standard of values in art and morals. I do not mean to suggest that either his opinions or his values resemble Spinoza's. Spinoza, he says, failed to reconstitute the life of reason, because "everything impassioned seemed to him insane, everything human necessarily petty. Man was to be a pious tame animal, with the stars shining above his head." The likeness to Spinoza consists in concern for the life of reason, not in the theory as to what it consists of.

When a philosophy is in this sense fundamentally ethical, the question whether, as a whole, it is to be accepted or rejected is not amenable to argument, and reduces, when honestly considered, to the question: "Do I like or dislike it?" This, however, is not the only issue for the critic. There is also the question of internal consistency: has the system in question been so deeply felt and thought as to possess a comprehensive subjective harmony? And there is another matter, less definite, namely what we may call the *importance* of the point of view. A lunatic's judgments, even if they achieve consistency, remain unimportant; Spinoza's, though not wholly consistent, are important.

As regards these three problems, I will, to begin with, briefly state my own view of Santayana's system. To a certain extent, though not wholly, I am in agreement with it; it is exceptionally self-consistent; and I have no doubt that it is important.

To understand Santayana, it is necessary to bear in mind some general features of his circumstances and temperament. While his environment has been mainly American, his tastes and preferences have remained predominently Spanish. This clash, it would seem, produced a rare explicitness and self-knowledge as regards values. Those who have always lived in sympathetic surroundings have had no occasion to become aware of the impersonal part of their springs of action, since no one has questioned it. Unsympathetic surroundings, on the contrary, generate, in a reflective mind, an intellectual defensive system. In a world of pragmatism, democracy, mechanism, and Protestant modernism, Santayana remained a Platonizing scholastic,[1] a

[1] "My position is the orthodox Scholastic one in respect to pure logic, but freed from Platonic cosmology and from any tendency to psychologism." *Realm of Essence*, 93 *n*. "I might almost say that my theory is a variant of Platonism,

theoretical believer in aristocracy, unmoved by the trumphs of scientific technique, aesthetically and politically, though not theologically, a Catholic. Perhaps his negative reaction to the modern non-Mediterranean world contains more of passion than appears in his writings, which have a possibly deceptive stylistic calm. His literary taste is incompatible with controversy, and his most incisive criticisms are aphoristic rather than argumentative. Take, for example, his judgment on Kant's ethics: "The 'categorical imperative' was a shadow of the ten commandments; the postulates of practical reason were the minimal tenets of the most abstract Protestantism. These fossils, found unaccountably imbedded in the old man's mind, he regarded as evidences of an inward but supernatural revelation." Most professorial philosophers would develop this sentiment into a volume, but Santayana is content with a polished expression of contemptuous distaste. It may well be doubted whether greater length would have added anything of value.

But it is time to leave these generalities and consider Santayana's system in more detail.

His views on metaphysics and theory of knowledge are most explicitly set forth in *Realms of Being*. Essences, matter, and truth are the three realms. (A fourth, *The Realm of Spirit*, has just been published, since the writing of this essay.) The realm of essence is "the infinite multitude of distinguishable ideal terms." An essence does not exist as such, but may be exemplified in what exists; absolute truth is "merely that segment of the realm of essence which happens to be illustrated in existence." "Sometimes," he says,

> sensation and language, instead of being passed over like the ticking of the telegraph, may become objects in themselves, in all their absolute musical insignificance; and then animals become idealists. The terms in which they describe things, unlike the things they are meant to describe, are purely specious, arbitrary, and ideal; whether visual, tactile, auditory, or conceptual these terms are essentially *words*. They possess intrinsically, on their own ontological plane, only logical or aesthetic being; and this contains no indication whatever of the material act of

---

designed to render Platonic logic and morals consistent with the facts of nature." *Ibid.*, 155.

speaking, touching, or looking which causes them to appear. All possible terms in mental discourse are essences existing nowhere; visionary equally, whether the faculty that discovers them be sense or thought or the most fantastic fancy.[2]

Thus essences are not mental; they are objects which may be apprehended by minds, but which are in no way affected by being apprehended, and have the kind of being appropriate to them even if they never become objects to any minds. They constitute a world of Platonic ideas, but purified from all such contact with the world of existence as sullied their purity in Plato's system.

The substance of what actually exists Santayana calls "matter." It would be verbally correct, though very misleading, to call him a materialist; it would be misleading, both because he uses the word "matter" in a somewhat peculiar sense, and because he is less interested in the material world than in the realm of essence. Essence, he says, "is a sort of invitation to the dance." "However monistic physics may choose to be, the realm of essence is the home of eternal and irreducible plurality." "Essences are definite and thinkable: existence is indefinite and only endured." This is a sentiment with which, in feeling, I find myself completely in sympathy, though it is of the South rather than of the misty North. If the world is to be conceived in terms of substance and attribute, then everything, or almost everything, that Santayana says about essence commands my assent. Whether the world should be so conceived has been often questioned, but in *The Realm of Essence* there is no controversial defence of this fundamental assumption. Whatever may be the correct view, any adequate discussion of this question must be very technical and must be influenced by modern logic. It is, however, a fixed practice with Santayana to avoid everything that cannot be discussed in literary form. This imposes certain limitations upon his writing, and also, I think, upon his thought. He has, for instance, a chapter on "Pure Being," which would have been different if he had taken account of logical technique. Perhaps, however, the difference would not have been as to anything that he thinks important. When a pre-

[2] *Realm of Essence*, viii.

viously philosophical question becomes technical, he might say, it is shown to have been not genuinely philosophical; philosophy conceived as a means to the Life of Reason must be capable of being set forth in literary as opposed to technical language.

The question as to what can and what cannot be expressed in philosophy without the use of a crabbed and difficult vocabulary and syntax is an important one, which has more influence than might be thought upon the actual content of a writer's opinions. Broadly speaking, old conceptions have acquired pleasant literary clothes, whereas new ones still appear uncouth. An aesthetic bias in favour of good literary form is therefore likely to be associated with conservatism. This does not always happen; Hume is an instance to the contrary. But Hume's innovations were only in opinion, not in the concepts applied to the understanding of the world. No one has ever surpassed Plato in the literary expression of new ideas, but even he felt compelled to abandon charm of style as he grew older. As a result of many centuries of Platonism, the language of educated men can now express even the most difficult of Plato's ideas without crabbedness; but this was not the case in his own day. The scholastics were notorious for their barbarous jargon, which caused the renaissance to despise them; yet whatever had value in their systems can be expressed by Santayana in the most smooth and exquisite English. The mathematical concepts of the seventeenth century—function, differential, integral, etc.—though immeasurably useful in understanding the world, have no means of literary expression, with the result that philosophers still think of causation in the discrete form "A causes B," and finance ministers introducing a graduated income tax cannot say "the tax shall be proportional to the three-halfth power of the income." In such ways those who insist upon elegant literary form are compelled to lag behind—often far behind—the best thought of their time. Per contra, conservatives have a great aesthetic advantage over innovators, for ideas, unlike animals, grow more beautiful as they grow older.

Every philosopher has limitations, and Santayana frequently acknowledges his own. What he has to say about the Realm of Matter is less interesting than what he has to say about the

Realms of Essence and Truth. His volume on *Reason in Science*, though full of valuable material, contains very little about science, and almost nothing to console the man who has "doubts" about scientific method, in the sense in which Victorians had "doubts" about religion. This is one instance of the bearing of difficult technical discussions upon questions of value. If scientific knowledge is possible, the pursuit of it is part of the Life of Reason; if not, not. Confronted with this issue, Santayana appeals to "animal faith." I think it highly probable that there is nothing better to be done. Santayana sighs as a lover (of knowledge), and obeys as a son (of nature). But a more passionate lover of knowledge will not obey until he has explored every avenue of escape, and some of these lead into the tangled forests of probability and induction; he may even prefer to perish philosophically in the attempt to blaze a trail through these pathless wilds, rather than acquiesce in a renunciation which saps the springs of hope. To attempt the impossible is, no doubt, contrary to reason; but to attempt the possible which *looks* impossible is the summit of wisdom. Only the issue can decide whether a man is wise or a fanatical madman, and fanatics of certain kinds should therefore be treated with hypothetical respect. All this will be found admitted in various passages of Santayana's books, but it is the admission of an onlooker, not an actor. "We live in this human scene as in a theatre,"[3] he says. But it is not so that the actors and the dramatist live.

There is in Santayana's system a very complete dualism between "essence" and "matter." The category of substance—which, unlike most recent philosophers, he sees no reason to reject—applies, in his view, only to "matter," which includes "the gods." (Does it include God? And is there a God? I am not sure what his answer would be.) All natural knowledge, he says, rests on the assumption that there are things and events prior to the discovery of them and independent of this discovery; these things are "substance." All causal efficacy is ascribed to matter; the causes of mental changes are material. Substance which is not material is only grammatical. He makes fun of Leibniz and Berkeley as "muscular idealists;" in their

[3] *Realm of Truth*, 66.

systems, "God was comfortably pledged never to act otherwise than as if matter were acting for him." Their religiosity was "purely official; their idealism was, and was intended to be, perfectly mundane." Spirits thought of as powers "are simply mythological names for certain operations of matter, poetically apprehended, and turned into dramatic units with reference to the observer's interests or emotions." As criticism, what is said against idealism is admirable, but considered as ground for materialism it suffers from the assumption that there is no third possibility.

The divorce of essence from existence, in which I formerly believed as completely as Santayana does, has come to seem to me questionable. I re-read recently his criticism of me in *Winds of Doctrine* (1913), and found myself, broadly speaking, in agreement with him whenever he thought me in the wrong, but not when he thought me in the right. My views have changed so much that I could read what he said with almost as much detachment as if it applied to some one else. The only element that has remained constant is a certain method, notably Occam's razor, of which he disapproves as "the weapon of a monstrous self-mutilation with which British philosophy, if consistent, would soon have committed suicide."[4] This, however, is by the way; the problem with which we are concerned at the moment is the relation of essence to existence. In his discussion of me he says:

> Nothing can ever exist in nature or for consciousness which has not a prior and independent locus in the realm of essence. When a man lights upon a thought or is interested in tracing a relation, he does not introduce those objects into the realm of essence, but merely selects them from the plenitude of what lies there eternally.[5]

Let us consider a particular application of this theory. Suppose—what would be quite possible—that in every spectrum a certain small finite region is dark, and that nowhere in nature is any colour to be found which has its place within this region. Are we to say that the shades of colour which would occupy

[4] *Realm of Truth*, 104.

[5] *Winds of Doctrine*, 119.

this region if they existed have a timeless being in the realm of essence? I see no reason why we should say so. Words of which the meaning is universal are used in describing what exists, and if a word cannot serve this purpose I do not see in what sense it has meaning. This question, however, is too vast to be pursued further in the present connection.

The realm of Truth, as Santayana conceives it, involves both matter and essence; it depends upon the essences that happen to be exemplified in the actual world. All truth is contingent, since it describes existence. The view that truth consists in coherence is rejected as arrogant, and as yet involving impotence, since it abandons the hope that truth may really tell us something about the world. In regard to truth, "animal faith" is again very convenient so long as we can trust it, but there seems no good reason, except of a practical kind, in favour of doing so. "The only belief that I myself entertain," we are told, "because I find it irresistible, is the belief in a realm of matter, the expectation of persistence and order in a natural world; and this is a belief which I am confident the reader shares." I have not anything better to offer; I am, however, less contented with this solution than Santayana appears to be. For, after all, "animal faith" is only a name for a certain kind of blind impulse. Why, then, should we trust it?

The pragmatic answer is foreign to Santayana's whole outlook, which demands a more or less ascetic submission to a truth supposed independent of our desires and volitions. In *Scepticism and Animal Faith*, all *rational* arguments for any kind of belief are dismissed. "Belief in the existence of anything, including myself, is something radically incapable of proof, and resting, like all belief, on some irrational persuasion or prompting of life." "For all an ultimate scepticism can see, there may be no facts at all, and perhaps nothing has ever existed."

There are certain motives . . . which render ultimate scepticism precious to a spiritual mind, as a sanctuary from grosser illusions. For the wayward sceptic, who regards it as no truer than any other view, it also has some utility: it accustoms him to discard the dogma which an introspective critic might be tempted to think self-evident, namely, that he himself lives and thinks. That he does so is true; but to establish that truth he must appeal to animal faith. If he is too proud for that, and simply stares at the datum, the last thing he will see is himself.[6]

It is not quite clear what is intended by these passages. That belief in existence, speaking generally, is incapable of *proof*, is obvious to all who do not accept the ontological argument, since a conclusion cannot assert existence unless there is an assertion of existence among the premisses. But to call an unproved premiss "irrational" is hardly warranted. All unproved beliefs are, to begin with, mere expressions of animal faith, but the problem of theory of knowledge is to find some way of selecting some of these as more worthy of credence than others. This cannot be done by ultimate scepticism, which rejects them all, nor by animal faith, which accepts them all. If we are going to accept some and reject others, which is what every philosopher does, we need some principle intermediate between animal faith and complete scepticism. Perhaps this principle may be merely the power of resistance to scepticism, which is greater in some cases than in others; but if so, the above argument against Descartes' *cogito* loses its force. However that may be, there is, I think, a problem in regard to the rejection of scepticism which cannot be solved by an appeal to animal faith alone.

I come now to Santayana's judgments of value, as set forth in *The Life of Reason.* Although, having begun with his last comprehensive work, I am going backwards chronologically, this fact has little importance, as he is a remarkably consistent thinker, and has travelled, in his books, from the outworks of his system to the citadel. His judgments as to what parts of human life can be considered rational, which are set forth in *The Life of Reason,* are based upon a metaphysic which, in that book, is implicit, but becomes explicit in *Realms of Being.* That is why, in exposition, it has seemed best to reverse the chronological order.

Reason is considered by Santayana in five different spheres, Common Sense, Society, Religion, Art, and Science. "*The Life of Reason,*" we are told, "will then be a name for that part of experience which perceives and pursues ideals—all conduct so controlled and all sense so interpreted as to perfect natural hap-

[6] *Scepticism and Animal Faith,* 35, 40-41.

piness."[7] His ideals, like those of all ages and classes before the industrial revolution, are contemplative rather than active.

> This world of free expression, this drift of sensations, passions, and ideas, perpetually kindled and fading in the light of consciousness, I call the *Realm of Spirit*. It is only for the sake of this free life that material competence and knowledge of fact are worth attaining. Facts for a living creature are only instruments; his play-life is his true life.[8]

This is the kind of ideal which is nowadays called "aristocratic," because it values things which, hitherto, have only been open to aristocrats. For my part, I am in agreement with Santayana on this matter, as against the critics whom I can imagine pointing out the class origin of such an ethic. As a matter of fact, the Marxist ideal of honest toil is one taken over by intellectuals from employers. The genuine proletarian ideal is obviously one of idleness, as expressed in the swan-song of the dying washerwoman:

> I'm going where anthems for ever are ringing,
> But as I've no voice I get out of the singing.

Christianity has been called a religion for slaves, and its heaven is one of contemplation rather than action. It is in hell—according to *Paradise Lost*—that industrial activity is practiced. Those who are, or imagine themselves, in power have a motive for trying to cause others to accept honest toil as an ideal, but those who have always had a plethora of work will consider rest an essential part of the good life. All this, however, is strictly irrelevant. There is no reason to suppose that the social systems which have prevailed hitherto have permitted what is best to be enjoyed by the many, nor, conversely, to condemn as not really good whatever, hitherto, has been the privilege of the few. It may be the temporary duty of the fortunate to renounce their privileges pending the creation of a better social system, but that is a question of morals, not of ultimate ideals; it is analogous to rationing during a siege.

Santayana distinguishes three stages in the development of ideals: prerational morality, rational ethics, and post-rational

[7] *The Life of Reason*, vol. I, Intro., 3.
[8] *The Realm of Essence*, x-xi.

morality. The first precedes philosophy, the second has existed only in Greece, the third is that of the great religions of India and Christendom The difference between rational and post-rational morality is, roughly speaking, the same as the difference between the artist and the ascetic.

> The Life of Reason is the happy marriage of two elements—impulse and ideation—which if wholly divorced would reduce man to a brute or to a maniac. The rational animal is generated by the union of these two monsters. He is constituted by ideas which have ceased to be visionary and actions which have ceased to be vain. Thus the Life of Reason is another name for what, in the widest sense of the word, might be called Art.[9]

I think—though in this I am no longer verbally following Santayana—that the difference between the rational and the post-rational may be regarded as a difference as regards matter. To the artist, matter is raw material for the embodiment of his ideals; to the ascetic, it is the alien power by which his spiritual life is enslaved. The man who is enjoying a good dinner or carving a statue out of marble is not thinking of matter as his enemy, but as his opportunity. The ascetic, on the contrary—who, if he is logical, is a Manichaean—condemns all pleasures that depend on matter, and regards them as due to the material part of himself, from which he strives to be liberated. This condemnation applies not only to the pleasures commonly called sensual, but to the whole realm of art, since art is bound up with sense. Such a morality is an outcome of despair, and arises only when the primitive zest for life is extinct.

Reason, Santayana says, expresses impulses reduced to harmony, and its sanction is happiness.[10] Nevertheless, he continues, democratic hedonism is mistaken, because we should not value silly pleasures.[11] I do not quite understand how he arrives at this conclusion. Impulses are easier to harmonize if they are few and simple than if they are many and complex; therefore reason, by his own definition, should favour paucity of impulses. A man, he says

[9] *The Life of Reason*, vol. I, Intro., 6.

[10] *Reason in Science*, 248ff.

[11] *Ibid.*, 256-257.

> need not limit his efforts to spreading needless comforts and silly pleasures among the million; he need not accept for a goal a child's caprices multiplied by infinity. . . . A conscience is a living function, expressing a particular nature; it is not a passive medium where heterogeneous values can find their balance by virtue of their dead weight and number.[12]

This seems to imply that the harmony of impulses which the rational man will seek is purely personal; he need only take account of his own impulses, and may condemn those of children or of the million as silly. Perhaps he would say that they are silly only because they cannot lead to satisfaction. "Ideals," he says, "are legitimate, and each initially envisages a genuine and innocent good; but they are not realizable together, nor even singly when they have no deep roots in the world."[13] This seems to me a groundless dogma. The pleasure of seeing a football match or a cinema can be provided at less cost per head than that involved in a good performance of Hamlet or the C minor symphony, and I rather think that the pleasure of an uncultivated person at a cinema is greater than that of a cultivated person critically observing a production of Hamlet. Culture, I should say, subtracts more pleasures than it adds; moreover those that it adds are more expensive and less intense than those that it subtracts. If this is the case, no form of hedonism can justify the pursuit of culture.

It is natural to look for the solution of this problem in the volume on *Reason in Society*. But here we find culture frankly accepted as an ideal, regardless of the definition of Reason as a harmonizing of impulses. Thus: "Culture is on the horns of this dilemma: if profound and noble it must remain rare, if common it must become mean. These alternatives can never be eluded until some purified and high-bred race succeeds the promiscuous bipeds that now blacken the planet."[14] "Civilization has hitherto consisted in diffusion and dilution of habits arising in privileged centers. . . . To abolish aristocracy, in the sense of social privilege and sanctified authority, would be to cut off

[12] *Ibid.*, 257-258.
[13] *The Life of Reason*, vol. I, Intro., 8.
[14] *Reason in Society*, 111.

the source from which all culture has hitherto flowed."[15] All these statements, as history, appear to me undeniable; but if taken as ethics, they imply that culture is to be sought even at the cost of a vast accumulation of human suffering. This view is compatible with one of Santayana's definitions of the Life of Reason, as "practice guided by science and directed toward spiritual goods,"[16] provided it is understood that goods are "spiritual" when such as are enjoyed by men of culture; but it is not compatible with the definition of Reason as harmonizing impulses, nor with the statement that its sanction is happiness.

Santayana's attitude to democracy, as the foregoing would lead us to expect, is somewhat critical. He distinguishes between social democracy on the one hand and democracy as a governmental expedient on the other. The former is the democracy of Arcadia, Switzerland, and the American pioneers; the latter that of modern America or England. Social democracy, if any cultural goods are to survive, demands a limitation of labour and luxuries, and a general return to a simple way of life; for if all have long hours of work, none will have leisure to enjoy the product. "What sort of pleasures, arts, and sciences would those grimy workmen have time and energy for after a day of hot and unremitting exertion?"[17] Santayana does not point out, what is nevertheless true, that with modern technique all that reasonable men could want in the way of commodities could be produced by a very moderate amount of work, so that social democracy is more compatible with culture now than at any previous time.

The dangers of a democracy which aims at merely material progress are forcibly portrayed. In such a community, with aristocratic influences removed,

> would any head be lifted above a dead level of infinite dulness and vulgarity? Would mankind be anything but a trivial, sensuous, superstitious, custom-ridden herd? There is no tyranny so hateful as a vulgar and anonymous tyranny. . . . A headless people has the mind of a worm

[15] *Ibid.*, 125.
[16] *Reason in Common Sense*, 256.
[17] *Reason in Society*, 127.

and the claws of a dragon. . . . The only freeman in it would be one whose whole ideal was to be an average man.[18]

All this may be true of a bad democracy, but it is at least equally true of a bad despotism. I will not adduce recent instances, which are controversial. But take (say) the government of the Neapolitan Bourbons from 1815 to 1860; is there one word in the above that would not be applicable to it? I have taken this example because, since the fall of the dynasty, no human being has had a word to say in their favour; but every reader can think without difficulty of scores of absolute monarchies that were disastrous, not only to happiness, but to culture. Santayana concludes: "If a noble and civilised democracy is to subsist, the common citizen must be something of a saint and something of a hero."[19] Very true; but, in view of the corrupting influence of power, this miracle is less improbable than an absolute monarch who is "something of a saint and something of a hero."

One of the most interesting of Santayana's volumes is the one on *Reason in Religion.* It is made interesting by his profound understanding of Catholic Christianity from Constantine to the present day, and by his hostile but penetrating analysis of the spirit and tendency of Protestantism. He points out first that unfortunately Christianity and Islam took over the doctrine, previously peculiar to the Jews, that only one religion is to be regarded as deserving respect. If this had not happened, he says, "the nature of religion would not have been falsified among us and we should not now have so much to apologize for and to retract."[20] In an attempt to recapture the spirit of antiquity, he does not discuss the truth or falsehood of any religious dogma; indeed, he takes it for granted that none is literally true. Religion, to him, is essentially myth, which may be useful or harmful, noble or ignoble, beautiful or ugly, but which it is somewhat Philistine to regard as true or false.

Nietzsche and his successors have accustomed us to the view that Christianity was one of the products of decay in the ancient world, and that we ought to throw over Christian ethics in order

[18] *Ibid.*, 127-128.
[19] *Ibid.*, 136.
[20] *Reason in Religion*, 77.

to recover barbaric vigour. What Santayana admires is not barbaric vigour, but the urbane and disciplined vigour of Socrates and Plato. Early Christianity, like the later Pagan philosophy, is judged by him as inferior to what the great age of Greece produced, because it is founded on despair. Stoicism, Platonism after Plato, and Christianity were all, he says, post-rational, "as befitted a decadent age." But this post-rational despair was inevitable, and Santayana is sympathetic to the way in which the Church dealt with it. He dislikes, in Christianity, every innovation from the eleventh century to the present day, all of which he regards as due to the inability of Northern nations to assimilate the ancient wisdom which inspired the doctrine of Christian resignation. Medieval people were only superficially Christian; they admired valour and honour, which to any true Christian would be vanity. Gothic art, chivalry, and even scholastic philosophy, he says, "barbarised Christianity, just as Greek philosophy and worship and Roman habits of administration had paganised it in the beginning."[21]

I think this goes too far. It is of course true of chivalry, from which the Church always held aloof with a certain hostility. It may, though with less certainty, be admitted as regards Gothic architecture, which was inspired less by faith than by worldly pride. But to consider scholastic philosophy as part of the revolt of the North against the Mediterranean tradition seems to me an inadmissible paradox. The Church had certainly less vital connection with antiquity in the tenth century than in the thirteenth, and the change was largely due to the schoolmen and their revival of Aristotle. It is true that many of them lived north of the Alps and Pyrenees, but Thomas Aquinas came from the kingdom of Naples, and wrote in conscious opposition to the *furor teutonicus* of Frederick II. The Mohammedan influence, so far as it was operative, worked in the same direction, for the Arabs and (later) the Moors of Spain preserved much more of the Greek tradition than had survived in any part of Western Christendom.

Whatever may be thought of scholasticism, there is no doubt that Santayana is right in speaking of Protestantism as "the na-

[21] *Ibid.*, 111.

tural religion of the Teutons raising its head."[22] Protestantism, for which he feels a contemptuous hatred, inspires some of his most scathing satire.

> It is convinced of the importance of success and prosperity; it abominates what is disreputable; contemplation seems to it idleness, solitude selfishness, and poverty a sort of dishonourable punishment. . . . Swayed as it is by public opinion, it is necessarily conventional in its conception of duty and earnestly materialistic; for the meaning of the word vanity never crosses the vulgar heart. In fine, it is the religion of a race young, wistful, and adventurous, . . . vaguely assured of an earthly vocation, and possessing, like the barbarian and the healthy child, pure but unchastened energies.[23]

With the exception of the word "pure," is there anything in this description which would not apply to Mussolini and the Fascisti? Santayana never mentions anything economic; but for my part I believe that "the meaning of the word vanity" is understood in communities whose average income is diminishing, but not in those whose average income is increasing. Therefore to give a man a "vulgar heart" it is only necessary to make him rich. I have adopted this view, not from Marx, but from the Gospels.

There are passages in *Reason in Religion* which show a praiseworthy desire to do justice to the merits of Protestantism. It is characterized, we are told, by personal integrity, conscience, and human instinct courageously meeting the world.

> Such a religion is indeed profoundly ignorant, it is the religion of inexperience, yet it has, at its core, the very spirit of life. . . . It was this youthful religion—profound, barbaric, poetical—that the Teutonic races insinuated into Christianity and substituted for that last sigh of two expiring worlds.[24]

This is very well said, and its historical truth is undeniable. But perhaps the word "Teutonic" suggests a wrong causation. The outlook of the Cathari who led the rise of financial capitalism in the Lombard cities of the twelfth century was very

[22] *Ibid.*, 115.
[23] *Ibid.*, 116-118.
[24] *Ibid.*, 125.

similar to that of the Calvinist business men of the North in the sixteenth and seventeenth centuries. Thinking in national terms, though it may have some justification, is dangerous, and encourages generalizations which look more profound than they are.

Fairness to Protestantism quickly gives place to satire in Santayana's discussions. Animals and plants, he says, if they could speak, would be Protestants. This applies especially to aggressive animals: "We may well imagine that lions and porpoises have a more masculine assurance that God is on their side than ever visits the breast of antelope or jelly-fish."[25] "Protestants," he continues, "show some respect even for an artist when he has once achieved success."[26] All this, however true, has, I believe, no essential connection with Protestantism, but only with economic success. Men and nations come to resemble lions when they prosper and antelopes or jelly-fish when they fail. Respect for artists is, as a social force, derivative from the desire of the great for immortal fame; it is part of the overflow of an income too large to be wholly spent on comforts. In spite of the difference of their religions, Augustus, Julius II, and J. Pierpont Morgan (Senior) patronized the arts in very similar ways, because of the similarity in their economic circumstances.

Leaving aside these historical questions, and returning to Santayana's own religious opinions, we find him reaching a conclusion surprisingly reminiscent of Spinoza.

> The better a man evokes and realises the ideal the more he leads the life that all others, in proportion to their worth, will seek to live after him, and the more he helps them to live in that nobler fashion. His presence in the society of the immortals thus becomes, so to speak, more pervasive. He not only vanquishes time by his own rationality, living now in the eternal, but he continually lives again in all rational beings. . . . By becoming the spectator and confessor of his own death and of universal mutation, he will have identified himself with what is spiritual in all spirits and masterful in all apprehension; and so conceiving himself, he may truly feel and know that he is eternal.[27]

[25] *Ibid.*, 123.
[26] *Ibid.*, 124.
[27] *Ibid.*, 272-273.

I do not know how far this passage is to be taken literally. If so taken, it would seem to imply that (using Santayana's language) a man can, by living wisely, progressively transfer his identity from his substance to his essence, and therefore progressively acquire the eternity of the latter. This seems contrary to what is said in *The Realm of Matter*, according to which every man's essence is wholly eternal and every man's matter wholly transitory. Nor do I quite understand what is meant by "worth" or by "living in a nobler fashion." It was Santayana's criticism (in *Winds of Doctrine*) that caused me to abandon the belief in the objectivity of "good," and yet, in the above passage, he uses language which seems to imply that doctrine. It is evident that Santayana considers a life spent in contemplation of the eternal—i.e., of essence—better than one spent in more mundane activities, and he does not *seem* to mean by this merely that he prefers such a life. There is no doubt an answer to these objections, but I have been unable to think of it, and I look forward to learning what it is.

Both *The Life of Reason* and *Realms of Being* are important books—more important than they appear on a cursory reading. The extraordinary excellence of the style has a soothing effect, which makes it easy to read on without fully apprehending the purport of what is said. The delightful aphorisms which occur from time to time temporarily dispel the reader's seriousness, and make him happy instead of earnest. But when these pleasant obstacles have been overcome, it appears that a comprehensive view of life and the world has been presented, which is all the more valuable because it is very different from any of those that are prevalent in the present age. It is urbane, historical, free from fanaticism, and the expression of an exceptionally sensitive intellectual perception.

These merits, however, inevitably entail certain limitations. They could hardly exist in a man with any originality of technique. Like almost everything aesthetically delightful, they depend upon a degree of continuity with the past which is not likely to be found in a man who makes important innovations. The temptation to hate in the present the same sort of thing that we value in the past, and to respect men in proportion to their antiquity, is one which Santayana perhaps does not always resist. He remarks, for instance, that Heraclitus was a "freer and wiser" man than Hegel. This may be true, and for my part I find Heraclitus delightful and Hegel disgusting. But how would it be if we possessed as little of the works of Hegel as those of Heraclitus? Or, conversely, what should we think if, like Plato in the *Theaetetus*, we were irritated beyond endurance by glib young men assuring us that all modern minded people agreed with Heraclitus? Heraclitus favored aristocracy against democracy in the politics of Ephesus, but this is an ancient issue, and we can allow ourselves to enjoy his invective without sharing his opinions. But Hegel's glorification of the Prussian State made him an ally of the modern governments which are attempting to enslave intelligence, and we, who are participants, can hardly view this struggle with historic detachment. I think that, if we were as remote from present-day politics as from those of ancient Greece, and knew as little of Hegel as of Heraclitus, we might see nothing to choose between the two men. I often think with envy how full of ripe wisdom I should seem if I had lived two thousand years ago, written in a dead language, and remained known only through a few of my more ponderous aphorisms. But these advantages, alas, can only be enjoyed by my "essence."

Santayana is fond of myths, and I offer him one to embody what I have been saying. Dr. Johnson said the devil was the first Whig; I suggest that he was the first Tory. When the Lord decided to create Man, He acted as a revolutionary; to Satan, when he got wind of the project, it seemed a wild and foolish innovation, since the angelic universe was well ordered, had an ancient mellow ritual, and was long since purged of all the crudities that had marred its earlier aeons. The only solution that occurred to him was to bring death into our world; he did not foresee that death would come too slowly to prevent our first parents from leaving progeny who would perpetuate the legacy of confusion. In all this dislike of rash and chaotic novelty, I feel sure that Santayana would have agreed with Satan; I should have agreed myself if I could have foreseen what Man would make of his planet. Nevertheless, it is *possible* that we should have been in the wrong.

Santayana's discussions of philosophy in America[28] illustrate his attitude towards vigorous contemporary innovation. He speaks of himself as "not an American except by long association," but the association was so long and so intimate that his knowledge is to be trusted, though his feelings about what he knows remain those of a European. He is struck, as every foreigner in America must be, by the gulf between academic values and those of daily life. I have felt it myself to be typified by the preference of universities for Gothic architecture, and have sometimes thought that professors would be more respected if their work were carried on in skyscrapers, and I find that Santayana has expressed a similar idea.[29] Universities in Europe were an important part of the State from the early Middle Ages to the end of the nineteenth century. Now this has ceased to be the case in Germany and Russia, and, at least temporarily, in France. In America they have never had the same governmental significance, because, in culture though not in science, they were endeavouring to keep alive an ancient tradition of which most people felt no sincere need. This tradition, in philosophy as in religion, was based upon the emotional realization of human impotence in face of natural forces. Men gave thanks to God for their daily bread; now, when not dominated by convention, they give thanks to the government or to a new fertilizer. Other men, not Nature or God, must be propitiated or restrained in order to secure prosperity. For economic reasons, this modern outlook is especially developed in America, although it is kept from explicitness by inherited piety. In philosophy, it shows itself as a revolt against what Santayana calls the "genteel tradition"—a revolt which, as he rightly recognizes, was led by William James.

Santayana's essay on William James is as sympathetic as he can make it, and filled with scrupulous fairness. But at moments

[28] *Character and Opinion in the United States*, 1921. Also: "The Genteel Tradition in American Philosophy," in *Winds of Doctrine*, 1913.

[29] "The American Will inhabits the skyscraper; the American Intellect inhabits the colonial mansion. The one is the sphere of the American man; the other, at least predominantly, of the American woman. The one is all aggressive enterprise; the other is all genteel tradition." *Winds of Doctrine*, 188.

his feelings are too strong for him. James, he says, tried to help his students to live a good life.

> But what is a good life? Had William James, had the people about him, had modern philosophers anywhere, any notion of that? I cannot think so. They had much experience of personal goodness, and love of it; they had standards of character and right conduct; but as to what might render human existence good, excellent, beautiful, happy, and worth having as a whole, their notions were utterly thin and barbarous. They had forgotten the Greeks, or never known them.[30]

I think the idea that the Greeks knew how to live the good life has very little to support it. Would Harvard have been better than it was if Boston had been engaged in a long and disastrous war with New York, if William James had been executed on a charge of atheism, and his disciples had established an abominable tyranny? For my part, I am persuaded that no Athenian, not even Plato, understood the good life as well as William James did. I admit that Plato could have defined the good life with more eloquence and precision; but that is another matter. I admit also that I, as a European, feel at home with the culture inherited from the Greeks as I do not with the nascent pragmatic culture of America. Nevertheless it seems to me probable that, from a historical standpoint, and ignoring the question of relative truth or falsehood, we are seeing the beginnings of a new and vigorous philosophy, which, in the market place as well as in the schools, will replace Hellenism and Christianity, and may, two thousand years hence, have acquired all the beauties of age that now make us reverence those other equally erroneous orthodoxies which have been its predecessors. The world has changed too much to be content with the philosophies of the past, and even those who cannot adapt themselves to what is new must admit that, in time, it may become as delightful as what it is superseding—at any rate to those who will be accustomed to it.

I have refrained from speaking of the important section of Santayana's writings which is concerned with aesthetics and literary criticism, not because I undervalue it, but because I

[30] *Character and Opinion in the United States,* 85-86.

think that other contributors can deal with it more competently. Many years ago I derived great pleasure from his *Three Philosophical Poets,* at any rate from his discussion of the two who were Italians. As for Goethe, I have been told that he is a great poet, "and do in part believe it." But I do not *feel* it, except as regards a few lyrics. I think Santayana is in the same case, and would, but for authority, treat Goethe with less respect than he forces himself to express.

Santayana's general outlook is one which is not likely to be widely influential in America, because it is aristocratic, not only politically, but philosophically. He is himself a sceptic, but believes that mankind in general has need of myths. His social values are thus different from his intellectual values; the latter are for the esoteric few, the former for the multitude. For my part, I prefer this view to that which rejects the best on the ground that only a minority can appreciate it, but I shrink—perhaps irrationally—from the admission that, not only here and now, but always and everywhere, what is best worth having can only be enjoyed by a cultural aristocracy. Those who take this view have the advantage of avoiding conflict with the mob, but I would rather rouse its hostility in attempting to serve it than secure its tolerance by concealing a contemptuous aloofness. From a personal point of view, aloofness may be wiser philosophically and practically, but the opposite attitude is a heritage of Christianity, and one which is essential to the survival of intelligence as a social force.

BERTRAND RUSSELL

FALLEN LEAF LODGE
LAKE TAHOE, CALIFORNIA

18

Antonio Banfi

THE THOUGHT OF GEORGE SANTAYANA IN THE CRISIS OF CONTEMPO-RARY PHILOSOPHY

18

THE THOUGHT OF GEORGE SANTAYANA IN THE CRISIS OF CONTEMPORARY PHILOSOPHY*

NOTHING is less philosophical, I believe, than dogmatic criticism of a system of philosophy, in the sense of mere condemnation of errors about matters of fact, or logical incongruities or contradictions unless indeed the purpose be to reduce to absurdity precisely the dogmatism found in that system. Before the philosophy of a Santayana, such a criticism is destined to struggle in the dark, since rarely does one find a mind so agile in avoiding all manner of abstract conceptual rigidity and always ready for and hospitable to the innumerable forms of experience. His being sceptical on principle, his criticism of discursive knowledge, his hypothetical procedure, the comprehensive elasticity of his definitions, his renunciation of any system of absolute values, his sense of an immanent contradictoriness of the real—all make it impossible to submit his thought to rigid analysis or to judge it according to some dogmatic criterion of truth. I would even say that, notwithstanding the ancient and modern sources which such thought clearly betrays, it is all but impossible to fit its course into the traditional speculative problematics. For the various problems and motives have in Santayana so much been re-lived, broken up, differentiated, and removed from their original context by an energy of research so acute and scholarly, by an affluence of data always new and always viewed afresh, by personal vision which does not uncompromisingly impose its judgments but lets them emerge, as it were, of themselves out of the same theoretical distance to which experiences and concepts, prob-

* Translated from the Italian by Arturo B. L. Fallico.

lems and solutions have been relegated by a purely speculative disinterestedness.

To one who comes from another philosophical climate, bringing with him not only other methods and instruments of measurement and appreciation, but also a different system of planes of knowledge, many of Santayana's perspectives may seem wrong, many definitions arbitrary, and many standards insecure or not sufficiently coördinated. Nevertheless, without counting the special charm of Santayana's free and vital exposition and the deep echo which the vision of his world calls forth in his spirit, Santayana does not fail to recognize the validity and efficacy of many speculative positions, the attraction of many discoveries, even though their normal meaning and implications may not be those which they suggest to a Spaniard educated in America. It then becomes for him a question of transposing them into the dimensions of his own thought, translating them into his own language, and grafting their truth upon his own world of truth. I am well aware that what I am about to undertake is neither faithful exposition nor objective criticism. At the same time it may, at least for me, be something far more important. For our intellectual sympathy permits the construction not merely of one truth but of a level of truth or, better still, of a law of integration binding together the various levels of truth, so that one thinker's search may prove fruitful to the other, each making his own whatsoever may serve to lend a greater significance and universality to his labors.

I

First of all, an observation on the method of approach which Santayana has in common with almost all recent American philosophy: it consists of placing oneself in direct contact with experience, with the minimum of theoretical and methodological presuppositions. The richness of experience, freely received, leads one to dissolve its practical crystallizations, and to extend and renew concepts, now in one field and now in another, now in one and now in another direction, without any prefixed plan. It is a research, so to speak, innocent and free, aided by the fact that its corresponding American culture and experience have as yet suffered little from internal conflict and, in the reflective realm, still have undergone little schematization or speculative interpretation. Thus the datum is frank and immediate, the problems are concrete and living in their particularity, the methods of analysis are varied and adapted from time to time to the subject at hand, and the concepts still uncoördinated in the variety of intuitions that enter into them to render them extremely elastic. Now all this might very well convey to one the impression of disorganization if, to unify these researches, there did not arise hypotheses, at times bold, often genial, hardly demonstrable, but intuitively alive and produced by a speculative imagination, emptied at least in intention of all dogmatic stress and metaphysical pretension.

For us of the old continent, experience and culture in particular come to us more full of conflict, more clearly distinguished and internally organized, and deeper in meaning and value. They are, in a certain sense, already schematized and signified for speculative interpretation, and speculative thought is in turn already formed and prepared to give relief to their dominant structures. The speculative tradition has infused itself into life, and life has given it efficacy and continuity, so that it would be very much more difficult for us, and, I might say, even scandalous, to use the characteristically free procedures of the new world, breaking up the abstract but universal problematics of our philosophical experience into a series of concrete, particular problems. Yet, if there is in our contemporary European philosophy a need universally felt, it is precisely that of freeing itself from the speculative schemas, from the formulas of traditional problems, and to give to thought a greater subtlety and freedom, so that it may come in direct contact with experience and follow the living complexity of its movements without becoming rigid in abstract dogmatic hypostatizations.

But as much as we, or at least some of us, admire and even envy the free procedure of American philosophy, so uninhibited by scruples and without excessive systematic preoccupations, we cannot follow it on its own path. We cannot renounce the continuity of our traditional speculation without renouncing, at the same time, our very experience and our culture with which it is imbued. In order to free ourselves from its schemas and from its formulas, we have to review it and renew it in the light of history as new motives and new problems emerge and mature in our experience. In order to give thought more elasticity, and experience a securer right to be valued in its complexity, we must guarantee this freedom and this concreteness by a radical critique of dogmatic theoretics, and of the hypostatization of concepts into realities. Further still, we must guarantee it in an open systematics of knowledge which will offer to the various methods of research, points of departure, or hypothetical solutions, a criterion of definition, of procedure, and of integration which will, in resolving in principle all the forms of empirical and metaphysical dogmatism, permit experience to assert itself.

The determination of an open systematics of knowledge in the sense above indicated is perhaps today the deepest and most general need of contemporary European philosophy, and we find it in neo-criticism as well as in neo-idealism, neo-realism and in phenomenology. And it is not to be thought that such determination implies either the definition of ontological principles or the deduction of absolute categorial forms, that is, in other words, that it leads back to some more or less explicit rationalistic metaphysics. I believe, rather—and this seems to me the most radically pure form of transcendental method—that it must take shape in the recognition of the essential nature of the problematics of knowledge, or, if you like, in the idea of reason as the problem of the autonomous theoretical and universal organization of experience and, in its various moments, as the constitutive and developmental principle of the various directions of knowing determining themselves by contact with the infinite multiplicity of experiential data. In any case, it seems clear that only in such an open systematics of knowledge can European thought find the guaranty of its freedom from all dogmatic limitations, and so also from every sort of metaphysical mythology.

At the same time, it needs to maintain the criteria of an organic dialectic, of consecutiveness, of the internal differentiation of knowledge, of the recognition of its various methods, and the possibility of an ever-increasing adherence to experience—in short, of all the penetrating and free conditions for a radical empiricism. The truth of the various anti-dogmatic directions of contemporary thought lies in this critical rationalism. Regarding, in the first place, scepticism, the fact is that sceptical doubt is not distrust of thought or of knowledge generally, since, as doubt, it is *thought*, and not in a generic sense but in an eminent sense: it is, in fact, doubt of the validity of the dogmas of thought, and of every object of thought taken as absolute limit. Thus, it is thought which, in this attitude, posits itself as free, that is, as actually able to think beyond every datum. Thus scepticism is and stands essentially as the affirmation of the autonomy and universality of theoretical reason. In the second place, the empirical, pragmatic, and conventional or symbolical conceptions of knowledge put in relief, not its essentially theoretical moment or aspect, which posits the problematics of knowledge, founding its structure and guarantying its continuity, but rather the elements which determine its particular aspects and justify its limitations. And in doing this, while offering a great deal of material for a phenomenology of knowledge, they empty dogmatism of all of its theoretical value.

II

I have insisted on this point because it is in this that I seem to find the fundamental motive for an accord as well as for a clear distinction between what I take to be the more living and fruitful currents of European and of American thought. The anti-dogmatism is common to both, meaning by dogmatism, the naïve conception of truth as correspondence of the subjective concept with an absolute being real in itself. But while the second of these currents derives from this the legitimacy of miscellaneous empiricism, the former suspects that in this procedure may be lurking the danger of a new dogmatic form of thought which may gather as data, and hypostatize as truths, immediate crystallizations of a conceptual sort which have not been critically sifted. It sees, moreover, as I have mentioned, the only guaranty possible in an open systematics of knowledge or, more precisely, in a transcendental method emptied of all metaphysical pretensions. So far as Santayana is concerned, therefore, our interest and our approval are secured by the anti-dogmatic motives of his thought. I can here do little more than mention the free and varied method of his researches, his careful and always attentive hypothetical procedure; but I want especially to insist on two fundamental principles. The one is his scepticism on principle against all hypostatizations of abstract thought, which he develops with much subtle penetration and good sense. It is not to be confused with some kind of tragic scepticism that discredits the profoundest human hopes, but a scepticism rather which accompanies and enriches life, and, in the end, breeds new certainty in it. The other principle is the concept of "animal faith," or of an atheoretical force which, from the data of experience, constructs and guarantees and extends the world of man, or, as Santayana says, the "life of reason." There is no doubt, in fact, that all that we feel and value as reality, is such not in the function of mere theoretical reflection, but in its complex relation to our existence, in an activity and faith of constructivity. And it is even more certain that our knowledge is always defined and objectified in the function of this pragmatic energy and in the valuational choice which accompanies it.

But is it really true that, as Santayana maintains, a transcendental critique of knowledge, in the sense of a recognition of the law of the theoretical resolution of the datum whose mere being-in-itself comes to be denied by scepticism, is impossible? A law, I mean, not psychological, nor methodological, but transcendental, intending by this the formula which expresses the essential problematics of knowledge no matter what the psychological forms or methods by which it is actuated. And is it really possible to conceive of a "life of reason" without thinking a certain unity at the basis of such a problem? And if the recognition of this unity can be understood as the freeing of experience from its personal limitations, for the purpose of universalizing it in a radical way, such a demand and endeavour being present in each one of the infinite forms and aspects of spiritual life in its variations of meaning and of value, it would seem to me that it finds its pure and unlimited expression precisely in the theoretical idea of knowledge or, in other words, in the transcendental conception of reason. Therefore, theoretical activity is the level on which spirituality has the consciousness and the guaranty of its freedom, and for this reason, in fact, the theoretical system is open and infinite. In this way, the principle of scepticism, the concept of a pragmatic-valuational determination of knowledge, as well as "animal faith" and the idea of a "life of reason," taken in themselves as anti-dogmatic positions of Santayana's thought, do not seem to exclude a transcendental method of defining and analyzing spirituality in general and theoretical activity in particular.

Putting aside for the moment the conception of spiritual life, let us here take into consideration only the theoretical sphere. Certainly the idea of a pure theoretical problem—or the idea of reason—is a mere hypothesis, and hypothetical is also the systematics of knowledge derived from it. But it is a necessary hypothesis. Not only do, as we have noted, the guaranty of an order and of a coherent progressivity in the world of knowledge, and the criteria of its differentiation depend on this hypothesis, but it also furnishes a unitary and total principle of definition for knowledge, clearly anti-dogmatic, which covers every degree and aspect of it, keeping thought from hypostatizing its positions as forms of absolute reality. Notwithstanding its positions in principle, the philosophy of Santayana, unless I am mistaken, relapses, without wishing or knowing it, into a dogmatic attitude from which its own refined and transparent form of dogmatism cannot save it.

In this connection an initial observation must be made regarding Santayana's epistemological realism, a realism which is critical, and which posits itself as an hypothesis which the process of scientific thought establishes and justifies. This is enough to tell us that we cannot in any way—at this point—define the nature of this reality of the object of knowledge as such, particularly as we know that it determines itself for us always in the function of an extra-theoretical activity, or "animal faith." Moreover, Santayana himself admits that from this reality of the object he cannot possibly derive knowledge, and I would say that the case here is not one of mere difficulty, but of logical impossibility to derive a relation from one of the terms of a relation, that is, of the same relation. This is an impossibility which, of course, tells us nothing about the nature of said relation and of its terms, which latter are purely conceptual positions; so it cannot serve as proof for idealism.

As a matter of fact, realism, for Santayana, does not conceal or does not intend to conceal any metaphysical hypothesis, as a certain naïve European realism is frequently inclined to do. Santayana's is simply an analysis of knowledge, a bringing into relief of certain of its fundamental aspects. In fact, it can be summed up in the two characters of knowledge itself: transitivity and relevance; this means that knowledge is determined, in its psychological concreteness, by a *quid* extraneous to the empirical subject or ego, and, in its advance, refers to it and puts in relief its aspects. As long as we remain within the limits of this analysis, it is all very well. Against the claims of idealism that it resolves the real in knowledge, or in one of its forms (consciousness, sensation, the idea, thought, all abstractly set up as absolute being), realism affirms, and with good reason, the character of relativity and relationality of knowledge and of its forms, reveals the infinity of its process, in the positing and resolving of its determinations by various degrees; it recalls, in other words, the infinite and complex problematic character of knowledge. But precisely this problematic character, this unlimited positing and resolving of a determinate relation between a subject and a determinate object, depends on the ideal autonomy and universality of theoretical knowledge itself, which does not permit itself to be fixed in any position as final, but continuously resolves all positions towards a limit, which remains always the limit of an absolute theoretical resolution of the datum. Now it is precisely this other aspect of knowledge that dogmatic realism forgets. So that if idealism could not account for the complexity of knowledge and for its actual movement, except by introducing surreptitiously an extraneous principle, realism cannot account for either the unity or the continuity of knowledge itself. It is precisely this unity and continuity of knowledge, this autonomy and universality of knowledge in principle, that idealism, in its profound meaning and freedom from metaphysical dogmatism, expresses. This is the theoretical significance of both Platonic and Kantian idealisms, if we take away from them other elements which determine them in a metaphysical sense. Realism and idealism, therefore, in their essential significance, express the two correlative moments of knowledge, resulting from a transcendental analysis of it. Transported on the level of metaphysics—aside from the fact that they necessarily disappear the one in the other—they impose an abstract limit to knowledge itself, hypostatizing either its empirical content or else its form. They both, instead, possess a critical value since only in their dialectic can a theory of knowledge justify the nature of knowledge, and establish the foundations for an open systematics of knowledge. For here is not involved the question of explaining knowledge in such a way as to imply that the resolution of the problem of knowledge or the definition of the real has already happened, but simply to guarantee to knowledge itself its freedom as infinite theoretical systematization of experience, which systematization is identified with reality only at its limits.

III

Notwithstanding the fact that the realism of Santayana is cautious and thoughtful, it remains weighted down by a certain implicit sense of dogmatism which adulterates his whole conception of knowledge. Of course Santayana knows very well that the object as conceived by common sense or by science can not be assumed as the absolute reality. He says, in fact, that this reality is posited by "animal faith," and that its objectivity rests on its pragmatic value. Since this object is variable and is so in many ways, the objectivity which discursive thought continuously traces and weaves, always combining it in new relationships, must also be variable in many ways. All this is a phenomenological description of concrete knowledge, profoundly vital and interesting. Since to discursive thought, which is rational thought in general, no theoretical autonomy, such as would permit us to define the problem of knowledge in its purity and to recognize the process of unlimited integration of experience, is conceded, not even in principle, it becomes necessary for Santayana to conceive of knowledge as pure knowledge outside of discursive thought. This knowledge has an absolute objectivity and is in itself absolute and immediate: it is, in other words, intuition, and its objects are the "essences."

The concept of intuition designates an immediate knowledge in which all problematical character is either suppressed or resolved. In effect, it arises in the history of philosophy to express the overcoming of discursive thought, the inquiry into the simple, and the definitive vision of the real, from Plato through Spinoza to Schelling, or, in contemporary philosophy, as a swimming against the stream; it denotes not completion or overcoming, but antithesis to discursive thought (in Bergson and Klages, for instance), as an act of participation in life. In Santayana intuition seems to have, in his own original way, both meanings, since it is the opposite of discourse, yet not so much an act as a passivity of the mind, which takes up in itself the real in absolute immediateness, mere contemplation. Now that which is contemplated is not a true universal in itself, but the datum of experience divested of all addenda, of all interpretation by animal faith, and of all the particularity which characterizes its objects, in short it is the pure "essence." The intuition is not therefore an exceptional position of the mind, it is rather the immediacy on which the mind laboriously constructs its world; the kind of immediacy, therefore, which cannot be reached except as the mind detaches itself from its construction, doubts it, and abandons it to its own destiny, thus placing itself in an act of simple contemplative receptivity.

Concerning the concept of "essence" as object of pure thought, this is nothing new; we can find its antecedents or correspondents, as an anti-rationalistic element, in the rationalistic sphere; in the Platonic ideas, and in the pure phenomena of Hume, and in the phenomenological essences and "images" of Klages, where alternately a universal-rational and an individual-sensible character is accentuated. The "essence," in any case, is the object of knowledge emptied of all the problematical character which makes it concrete, resolving it in the relationship with all others, as the intuition is the knowledge which has resolved in itself all problematical character, and therefore all discursiveness. In Santayana, the essence is both individual and universal, the mere datum of pure sense and of pure thought, without external references or relations, the immediate datum as such, in which the sensible and rational, individual and universal moments are perfectly fused. Now this concept of pure immediate knowledge, or intuition of the essence, presents not a few difficulties. It is, in the first place, a limitation-concept which is not definable nor determinable in itself, but only the limit of a mere demand, and for this reason purely hypothetical. The demand comes from the fact that the criticism of dogmatic positions regarding discursive knowledge as determined by "animal faith" leads Santayana to seek for the theoretical reality of knowledge in the function, not of the definition of its ideal law, but in the immediate annulment of its problematical character, or in the intuition of the essence. This, however, must remain, it seems to me, knowledge in the dogmatic sense, as a static identity of the subjective and the objective; and this even more so because here not only subject and object but also their relation are emptied of every concreteness, and it can be said, therefore, that knowledge is no longer knowledge, no longer theory, but, as Santayana himself says, mere aesthetic contemplation.

This pure knowledge or limit of the solution of the problem of knowledge is no longer knowledge; it is the extreme refuge of a dogmatic conception of knowledge which denies itself. It is therefore, from one point of view, an idea-limit which eliminates and does not resolve the problematic character from which it emerges. Nor do I see, on the other hand, any possibility for its psychological realization. For, an intuition deprived of all faith, as Santayana says, and deprived of every existential position and activity of the ego—an essence which is neither mere logical form nor mere sensible quality and implies no relation to the world of objects—may be conceivable as position in a dialectic of thought, but cannot be recognized as feature in an experience of knowledge.

Finally, if the intuition of the essence, inconceivable as theoretical activity, comes to be defined on the level of aesthetic activity, are we not here subject to a grave illusion? It may be true that the aesthetic experience is, as compared with empirical experience, free from the determinations and connections which define this letter in an existential sense, but this does not mean that it lacks a law of its constitution. The aesthetic image is not theoretical representation free from all objective determination: it implies a construction according to connections on which depend the universality and individuality peculiarly characteristic of such image and generally of the structure of the aesthetic experience. The intuition of the essences is, therefore, not even aesthetic contemplation, even though it might appear to possess a similar character of boundless freedom as over against existential experience. To have confused the two concepts without giving concreteness to the one, obscures the other by limiting it to a particular acceptation. It bars, I believe, an integral comprehension of the sphere of the aesthetic, of its spiritual sense as function in a culture, which is a great deal more complex than the cathartic function which Santayana ascribes to it, barring, at the same time, its more exact recognition in connection with the world of art.

Having brought out these difficulties incidentally, we must recognize that the idea of the "intuition of the essences" implies a series of fundamental speculative positions which have an entirely different meaning when they are freed from the residuum of dogmatic presuppositions.

We can note in every act of knowing an intuitive and a rational moment. The intuitive moment corresponds to the concrete determination of knowledge itself as it functions in the particularity of the subject, of the object, and of their relations. The immediateness which characterizes the intuition comes from the fact that the problem of knowledge is here not resolved, but annulled by the existential determination, in which knowledge itself is placed. And the intuition can be of various forms, according to the variety of the existential determinations, of the concrete relation between determined subject and object in various degrees, from the sensible intuition to the conceptual, since every concept is always in its determinateness given by a very complicated intuition which unifies and signifies in a variable equilibrium the experience which underlies it. The rational moment is that which is properly theoretical, by which knowledge is posited as universal resolution and systematic organization of the datum. It is an absolute infinite mediation also of various degrees and on various levels. Every intuition, insofar as it is posited for knowledge, is posited for this resolving mediation by which it is freed from its existential particularity and tends to enter into an order of absolute universality and theoretical autonomy. The concept, in its rational moment, is the potential symbol of this infinite mediation of the datum or data of experience, which are unified in it; a mediation which expresses itself in the judgment, and, generally, in knowledge.

The formula, therefore, "the intuition of the essences," corresponds, in its true epistemological sense, to this unity in the general datum of knowledge, namely, to the intuitive and rational moments, the one, a moment of individual mediation because existentially determined, the other, a moment of universal mediation because it is infinite resolution of such determinateness. For this reason, the "intuition of the essences," which in Santayana represents the last refuge of a dogmatic conception of knowledge, and stands for the absolute completion of knowledge itself, in which, as we have seen, it is annulled, is rather the point of departure of knowledge or the *terminus a quo*, the abstract origin of the process which unfolds in the theoretical mediation ever-increasing its limits, and in a certain intuitive determination, ever-enriching itself up to a limit which may be conceived as the systematic integration of all experience. Here, if I am not mistaken, is the explanation of the secret of this formula, and the element of truth which it contains, together with the deviation of meaning which it has undergone, and the difficulties which must follow.

We have followed so far the development of the dogmatic element implicit in Santayana's theory of knowledge. Notwithstanding the fact of the anti-dogmatic presuppositions and method, from his epistemological realism, through his pragmatic critique of discoursive knowledge, we have arrived at the conception of the intuition of the essence, an extreme and in itself contradictory position of epistemological dogmatism. But this conception is contradictory not only as regards the conception of knowledge which it is supposed to define, but dissolves instead; it is contradictory regarding the first and fundamental anti-dogmatic presupposition of Santayana's thought, which supports his realism and colors it throughout with an undertone altogether different from that of the theory of the essences. I refer to his naturalism. I am myself more than disposed to accept and affirm the value of a philosophical naturalism. The inebriation of idealism and of spiritualism from which contemporary European philosophy has not yet emerged, about a century or so ago, had profound historical and cultural reasons, as we all know. But today it is like the morning after a carnival, cluttered with torn masks and trampled trinkets. Moreover, it has given, in the theoretical field, all that it could possibly give; its present sentimental and sad falling back on metaphysical and religious motives confirms this judgment. Today a naturalistic sense means a taste for the kind of thinking which has been purified from the contamination with beautiful souls, it means mental and spiritual sanity, balance in concrete judgment in view of action, without despondent pessimism or exaggerated optimism; it means freedom and richness of theoretical research, with an eye for problems, and for the problematical character of life itself. The naturalistic attitude has to do with a declaration of a firm and vigorous principle similar to that of the pre-Socratic philosophers or the thinkers of the Renaissance. But a naturalism today can have neither the naïve metaphysical form of the older ones, nor the abstractly unilateral form of the scientific naturalism of the Eighteenth and Nineteenth centuries. A naturalistic metaphysics is, to be sure, —and meritoriously so—the least acceptable of metaphysics; on the other hand, the connection between naturalism and scientism which feeds the life of positivistic philosophy, has been refuted by science itself.

A naturalism, if it is to introduce into thought all of its valid motives without limiting such thought to metaphysical or scientific finalities, must today be extremely critical and phenomenological. In other words, the need is not to define a natural reality as absolute reality, but to recognize a naturalistic experience intersecting and interacting with a spiritual experience, determining the structure and justifying in such interaction the principles, methods, limits, and development of natural science and of a philosophy of nature. Just as realism and idealism represent in their essence the two moments of knowledge, so also naturalism and spiritualism represent the two moments of experience, which result in its concreteness from their interaction, each according to its own principle and its own universal and autonomous law. Certainly the principle of transcendental autonomy—autonomy not of being, but of law—the autonomy of mind, has been the presupposition requisite for the revivification and analysis of spiritual and cultural experience. The merit of idealism is to have grasped this principle. But its limitation was to have transposed it in a metaphysical sense, turning the rational notion of mind into the abstract concept of an absolute reality. In this way, idealism denied itself the justification and comprehension of the complex phenomenology of mind, and denied its own principle, personality, overlooking the natural moment which determines both. In this way, the meaning of both spirituality and history was defaced, the vision of the world was narrowed down to the level of a mediocre anthropocentrism.

But Santayana's naturalism tends to be a little too much like a theory of absolute reality and, as such, I admit that it may justify animality; I do not see how it can justify faith, to say nothing of the universality of such faith which Santayana calls reason. Nor can Santayana's naturalism serve as the criterion for the analysis of the life of reason and of culture. Such a criterion can be nothing but a mere negativity of all the concrete and constructive spiritual life. At the limit of this the only remaining positive thing, in fact, is the mere contemplative disposition to suffer reality, a reality, however, which is no longer nature, but image, essence, a reign of dream and a phantasy. The efficacy of the naturalism seems in this way to be lost in such a dialectic; the natural vanishes, while the spiritual also disappears, resolving themselves in a realm of shadows where not even the person can find himself or justify himself.

The researches which, in Santayana, throw light on the life of reason and on the process of culture, are certainly among the most penetrating and freed from rhetorical dead-weight that contemporary philosophy has yet seen. There is no doubt that the very negativity of the analytic criteria illuminates them with a light particularly frank and penetrating; but it also confuses the levels and directions of the life of culture. One of the major conquests of European thought since Kant—due also to profound crises—has been the more and more clear relief given to the ideal autonomy of the various spiritual forms and directions that converge and fuse in the interconnections of culture. This principle alone makes it possible for us to enter deeply into the structure of cultural reality without superimposing on our analyses the bias of partial evaluations. Now it is precisely this relief and this purity of analysis that seems to be missing in Santayana. The same undertone, a sense of the same rhythm, dominates the various degrees of the life of reason, and they are distinguished only as grades of disillusionment. The same pure contemplative quality confuses the theoretical and the aesthetic moments, placing them on a plane which is neither the one, nor the other, denying both art and knowledge. What remains of Santayana's naturalism is a sense of the absolutely incoherent and negatively problematical character of the spiritual life—even if the refined taste of the author does not accentuate the pessimistic note. The resolution of such futile effort is mere contemplation, free from all activity and from all faith. But, while this contemplation refers to the aesthetical and the theoretical, it is only an abstract moment of these; for the one and the other are really contemplative evasions from life and from empirical reality, and at the same time, a construction of another reality and of another life. Therefore, at this limit of essential intuition, the mind and its problematical character are annulled, and with it also nature. We do not here want to judge this ideal of life, but will only say that it is a metaphysical ideal behind existence and experience; that it is a solution which denies the very data of the problem; an imaginative idealism which destroys or makes futile the realism and the naturalism which justify its existence.

There is no doubt that the spiritual life has a problematical character, which has no determinate solution; culture is a living process which does not end in any ideal; still less is it a solution or an ideal which negates itself; the suffering of this problematic nature is real and present everywhere, but real and present everywhere is also a positive sense, however weak, of joy, of fullness, of activity, and of freedom which corresponds to it. Pessimism and optimism find here their justification, their connection, and their limit. Now, the position of philosophical thought is precisely in overcoming this antithesis while justifying it. And this it can do only if, from a transcendental point of view, it can define the law or laws of the problematical situation, conceiving it as life which only in the infinity of its aspects and phenomenological processes can realize the fullness of reality. Such fullness of reality is never given except as a myth—the myth of the Spinozistic Substance—which guides and sustains thought in its obstinate will to comprehend, in its denial of every limitation, in the consciousness of freedom which is diffused throughout the spiritual life. Only this ideal terminus, it seems to me, can be hypothetically thought by the act of pure contemplation, free from the world and at the same time participating in its very essence to which every single aspect is present in the harmonious equilibrium of a total unity. Of such an act we can have some premonition only in the sense of serene liberation which comes to us in the search for the truth, a search in itself infinite.

Let us now conclude. The spirit of contemporary philosophy in its profound crisis, breathes powerfully in the thought of Santayana. His very method of research, his fundamental points of view: the scepticism, the epistemological realism, the naturalism, the theories of animal faith and intuition of the essences, illuminate motives which are profoundly and essentially innovating in speculative thought. His very position permits a profound, unprejudiced, and fresh view of the problematics of the mind, which makes our life and culture pass before it, alive, multiform, but without illusions.

A refined sense of unruffled scepticism frees him from the toils of doubt, a scepticism which is light, without passion, and which guides him to an ideal, not of wisdom, but of imaginative contemplation and freedom. On our part, we do not wish to refute either the fruitfulness of this analysis without illusions, nor the nostalgic value of this ideal of escape from a world which today, more than ever, seems hard and burdensome.

But it did seem to us that all these motives, fruitful as they are for thought, crystallize in a sense of dogmatism and end by contradicting themselves, paralyzing one another. Such a crystallization can be undone only by a critical attitude in a transcendental sense, without falling back into the forms of metaphysical idealism. And it seems to us also that only such a method, permitting as it does, full freedom to thought, can make for a radical and organic analysis of the spiritual life and of the world of culture, such as to take into consideration its differentiations and interactions, its autonomy, and its phenomenological determinations; a method, in short, that would gather the positive vitality of problematical development, without illusions, but also without disillusions. It seems to us, then, that no evasion from the problematical is possible, except in the very act in which we know it in its radical positivity, and we accept the necessary relativity of every one of our acts, of every volition, and of the sorrow and joy which derive from them, with absolute and free willingness. This is an act of faith and of love which, the more it is concrete, the more it can ideally construct our humanity and renew it in the profound and fresh currents of life.

ANTONIO BANFI

REGIA UNIVERSITÀ DI MILANO
MILAN, ITALY

George Santayana

APOLOGIA PRO MENTE SUA

Apologia Pro Mente Sua

I. Early Criticisms

Josiah Royce, who had kept a kindly but troubled watch over my youth, once said to me that the gist of my philosophy was the separation of essence from existence. This was one of those rare criticisms that open one's eyes to one's own nature. It was also, perhaps, one of those prophecies that help to fulfil themselves; because it came long before I began to make any special use of the word essence, or attempted to analyze the concept of existence. But in Interpretations of Poetry & Religion, then just published, I freely referred to "ideals," insisting that Platonic Ideas and the deities and dogmas of religion were ideal only; that is to say, they were fictions inspired by the moral imagination, and they expressed unsatisfied demands or implicit standards native to the human mind. Ideals belonged to poetry, not to science or to serious hypothesis. They were better than any known or probable truth. Far from being less interested in them than if I had thought them true, I was more keenly and humanly interested, for I found them essentially poetical and beautiful, as mere facts are not likely to be. They were acts of worship on the part of the real addressed to the good.

FACSIMILE OF PAGE ONE OF SANTAYANA'S "APOLOGIA PRO MENTE SUA"

APOLOGIA PRO MENTE SUA

I. Early Criticisms

JOSIAH ROYCE, who had kept a kindly but troubled watch over my youth, once said to me that the gist of my philosophy was the separation of essence from existence. This was one of those rare criticisms that open one's eyes to one's own nature. It was also, perhaps, one of those prophecies that help to fulfil themselves; because it came long before I began to make any special use of the word essence, or attempted to analyse the concept of existence. But in *Interpretations of Poetry and Religion*, then just published, I freely referred to "ideals", insisting that Platonic Ideas and the deities and dogmas of religion were ideal only: that is to say, they were fictions inspired by the moral imagination, and they expressed unsatisfied demands or implicit standards native to the human mind. Ideals belonged to poetry, not to science or to serious hypothesis. They were better than any known or probable truth. Far from being less interested in them than if I had thought them true, I was more keenly and humanly interested, for I found them essentially poetical and beautiful, as mere facts are not likely to be. They were acts or worship on the part of the real addressed to the good.

Now these sentiments showed an attachment to Platonism and to Catholicism (which was the religion most familiar and congenial to me) entirely divorced from faith, an attachment confirmed rather than dispelled by scepticism. It was a philosophical appreciation, not an accidental prejudice of birth or education, as belief in such objects would probably have been. I saw, or thought I saw, *why* those ideas had been formed and cherished, and *what function* they exercised in moral life.

Royce, like everyone who has fallen under the spell of Hegel, conceived philosophy, and everything else, historically; and he was too learned and too expert dialectically not to feel that the contrast between essence and existence (which is not a division among existences) is inevitable and axiomatic; and that the neglect of it has led to the worst paradoxes and extravagances of Eleatic, Platonic, German and Indian metaphysics. Moreover, unlike Hegel, Royce was deeply interested in mathematics, and followed the development of symbolic logic and of the contemporary doctrine that regards mathematics as hypothetical and not in itself true; that is to say, not necessarily applicable to natural facts. Here was essence zealously separated from existence by the logicians, as since the Renaissance it had been contemptuously banished from philosophy by the humanists. Why, then, did Royce complain—for it was a complaint—that I also should separate the two? The reason probably was that, if logic had no coercive authority over facts, his religious and political convictions could not be enforced by pure logic, but would have to be advanced on empirical evidence (notoriously not available) or else posited with sporting risks by a desperate act of faith.

I remember another occasion on which Royce spoke to me with some warmth about the error of my ways. It was apropos of a dialogue entitled *The Two Idealisms*, in which I made the *Spirit of Socrates*, in Dante's *Limbo*, utterly disown the ethics of the German idealists. Royce felt how much I hated the worship of a Calvinistic God; and he said he would entirely agree with me, were it not for the logical necessity of a Universal Mind, knowing and sanctioning everything. Royce himself escaped Calvinism by denying that the Universal Mind was a power. It was what I should call the truth, but personified and turned into a psychological entity. In separating essence from existence I avoided this myth, which Royce's psychologism caused him to think essential to the being of truth.

For quite different reasons, my thesis about poetry and religion also made an unfavourable impression on William James, who declared it to be "the perfection of rottenness." James, I need hardly say, was ready enough to snap his fingers at dialectical proofs, and deeply consented to appeal to faith, and to take sporting risks in the most serious matters. But he overlooked the fact that I too relied on animal faith in science and common life; what arrested his attention was my aestheticism, that seemed to find the highest satisfaction in essences or ideals, apart from their eventual realisation in matters of fact. What he hyperbolically called perfection was, I suppose, my way of spying the self-deceptive processes, *la fonction fabulatrice,* of the inspired mind; what he called rottenness was my apparent assumption that in the direction of religion and morals imagination was all, and there was nothing objective. Mine, he also said, was the most anti-realistic book he had ever read. I reported this saying to Royce, who observed, "That is just the side of it I agree with."

The judgments of William James were indeed impulsive, and his descriptions impressionistic, based on a penetrating but casual spurt of sympathy or antipathy. He smelt my aestheticism, and naturally enough identified it with the aestheticism of the day. He felt that I was detached; and he may well have had a shrewd medical suspicion to the effect that detachment is likely to spring from some suppressed attachment, and that if the real world displeased me, I must be in love with some false world. Yet he was no less quick in generously revising his judgments than in first forming them. Soon, when the first two volumes of the *Life of Reason* appeared, he stopped me one day in the street, aglow with encouragement—a paternally humorous encouragement such as athletic English dons shout to their pupils in a race. He had been reading my new book, and proceeded to give me a hardly recognisable version of what it *meant,* turning it into a sort of Bergsonian vision of a miraculous human evolution. When I looked doubtful, and said that this was only his interpretation, he asked what, then, was my own view; and when I explained that progress, to my mind, was wholly moral, and signified improvement or approach to perfection in some specific direction, not physical creation or evolution of fresh beings and new purposes, he exclaimed "But then you are a Scholastic!" I pleaded guilty to the horrid charge. Hadn't James himself declared that Scholasticism was nothing but common sense carried out consistently? And we parted laughing and in the best of humour.

I dwell on these early criticisms of my views partly because their source lends them a certain historical interest, and partly because they seem to mark the radical lines of divergence between my mind and that of my readers and critics down to the present day. There is now much denunciation of my theory of essence, with some misunderstanding of it, and greater emphasis laid on it than I should lay myself; for to my mind it is something perfectly clear and obvious, hardly worth quarrelling about; although I can see why the mention of it is disliked or even resented. It dethrones the family idol of British home-philosophy. An essence is an "idea," but an idea lifted out of its immersion in existing objects and in existing feelings; so that when considered in itself and recognised as a pure essence its very clarity seems to strip both objects and feelings of their familiar lights: reality becomes mysterious and appearance becomes unreal: an intolerable thought to pictorial realists and pictorial idealists. But no analysis can threaten the reality of appearances *as appearances:* that is just the reality that the theory of essence proclaims, and places in its proper logical sphere. In denying that appearances are existences or powers this theory merely banishes superstition and idolatry. Essences are not ghosts that someone says he has seen in the dark: they are precisely that which is clearest and most indubitably present in the brightest light. They are, in any "idea," all that can be observed, retained, recalled, or communicated. Mystery and obscurity invade the psychological notion of "ideas" only when we consider them to be unrecoverable acts of thought, moments in a flux of existence that stretches beyond the obvious, and is saturated with the unseizable, the dynamic, and the unknown. For then we have turned towards the realm of matter, towards all those intricate and infinitely extensible processes that no doubt underlie our chaotic "ideas" and bring them into existence.

My theory ought to be intelligible to poets and artists who have not bothered with modern philosophy, a radically subjective and sophistical thing. For there is a natural transition between focussing attention and perceiving that what thereby comes to light is an essence and not a fact. This transition gives the artist his liberty. He may yield to inspiration. There will be enough relevance to the world in his originality, if this originality springs from his deeper self, which is a living part of that world, existing only in constant contact with the rest. He lives immersed like everyone else in the current of automatic events; but his psyche has an unusually retentive, imitative and inventive power, with the knack of reproducing, with variations, the impression received; and in this quick transition from sensibility to art, intuition grows pure and reveals a clear essence to the mind. Vegetation in the psyche is marvelously rapid, and flowers may spring up as soon as seeds are planted; but whether sudden or deferred there is always this material pregnancy bursting out at last into a spiritual birth, in the rapid intuition of an essence, momentary but capable of being indefinitely renewed.

There is affinity to art in intuition in as much as the result is, in one sense, a fiction, something not pre-existent in the world; but art proper is that organic or external rearrangement of matter by which a *monument* or a *maxim* is established in the world, and an element of traditional form is added to culture. Intuition flashes often in the artist as he works; but it flashes also in all the passions and in all spontaneous sensation and play; so that the *aesthetic* character can be attributed to my theory of essence only in the Kantian sense of *Aesthetik*. Intuition of essence is *Anschauung*, but not necessarily sensuous; it may be conceptual or intellectual. In my own case, aestheticism blew over with the first mists of adolescence; I very soon tired of aesthetic affectations and archeological pedantry: nor has my love of the beautiful ever found its chief sustenance in the arts. If art *transports*, if it liberates the mind and heart, I prize it; but nature and reflection do so more often and with greater authority. If ever I have been captivated it has been by beautiful places, beautiful manners, and beautiful institutions: whence my admiration for Greece and for England and my pleasure in youthful, sporting, ingenuous America. It is certainly essences that I love in these things, and not the gross things in their material totality and ramifications; but essences are non-existent, they cannot manifest themselves of their own initiative; and it is only in matter, or in a mind fed on matter, that they can shine in all their concreteness and splendour. For my essences are not washed out; they are *the whole* of what is actually visible, audible, imaginable or thinkable; and these manifestations in their pungency can come only to a warm soul from a world of matter.

This was my interest in composing the *Life of Reason*, with an eye open to all concrete perfections, such as what I knew of Greece and England powerfully evoked in my imagination. It was the same interest, if on a different scale, and less concentrated, that has now inspired my *Realm of Spirit*. In both, I have been looking for the high lights that here and there, in various directions, might shine in the revolutions of nature and of history. This interest may still be called aesthetic in as much as it is a joy in perfection; yet it is also intellectual, when this perfection has been approached in the clarification of thought, and it is also moral, when perfection is approached in the political sphere.

Here, before the pattern of my philosophy was fully disentangled, I find in the mouth of my Harvard teachers, full as they were of kindness towards my person, the latent and permanent principle of almost all the hostility I encounter. This principle is what I call moralism, and has two forms. One, moralism proper, asserts the categorical imperative of an absolute reason or duty determining right judgment and conduct. In the other form, moralism becomes a principle of cosmology and religion; it asserts the actual dominance of reason or goodness over the universe at large. It was moralism and not logic that led Royce to deprecate my separation of essence from existence. They are separable and even contrary logically, since any essence is eternally identical with itself, while existing things suffer continual and treacherous mutation. But Royce demanded that a particular eternal essence should solve the perpetual charade, and should dominate and explain every vital puzzle. Essence therefore must be narrowed to the humanly rational, and existence must be raised to the ideally necessary. As against this, my view seemed an intolerable diminution of the claims of reason and conscience. Not that I denied their supremacy in logic and morals: they were like mathematics, autonomous at home. But how should conscience or reason arise in me or gain the least ascendancy over my heart, if I had no natural needs, interests, or affections? These with their truly categorical imperative might then lend reason and conscience some vital force to oppose to a no less natural madness and vice. Rational life could be nothing but natural life becoming harmonious. The principle of harmony itself, if disembodied, is as impotent as any other essence to govern existence or to manifest itself as a prescribed end to a mind not organically directed upon it.

Moralism was likewise the preconception that led James to think my aestheticism corrupt. In reality his own allegiances were more aesthetic than mine, since they were romantic; and romance has a moral inspiration and looks for miraculous events satisfying the affections, and opening out into unpredictable enticing adventures. My aestheticism, on the contrary, seemed deathlike and pessimistic, being based on everywhere dismissing the fact and retaining only the image. Mine was indeed a modest Epicurean humanism, that invited mankind to profit morally as much as possible by the course of natural events, without pretending to subject them to any secretly moral principle. So my description of the life of reason could be welcomed only if it was misunderstood romantically; it would have to be condemned as soon as it was understood naturalistically, as I had meant it.

This same moralism, sometimes political, sometimes romantic or pseudological, sometimes humanitarian, animates the more severe strictures passed upon me in this book. I see these strictures to be amply justified from those alien points of view; but criticism is double-edged, and exposes the critic in turn to criticism. Recrimination in this way may become endless; and the better way is to approach any system, as well as the criticisms of it, from within, beginning with what was their vital foundation, and proceeding to its corollaries. Now I feel that the vital foundation of my philosophy has escaped almost everybody: whence a certain sense of insecurity even in the most friendly comments. The blame is often thrown upon the notion of essence; but I think that is historically a mistake, and I am happy to see that, at least in one place, the real foundation has been indicated. I will therefore begin my review with that indication, hoping that the element of misunderstanding or dislocation contained in the criticisms may be better discriminated, in that light, from the element of sympathetic analysis.

II. Materialism

In the dialogue between Professor Friess and Mr. Rosenthal, the latter writes: "Does not the same foundation, [Santayana's] materialism, serve his intellectual and his spiritual emancipation? This view-point, I mean, is the ground not only of his critique of belief, but also of his freedom to confront the world, as he puts it, 'martially . . . with courage and good humor, rather than supplications and fears'?" Exactly: this hits the nail on the head, but I think the nail might be driven in still further. My materialism indeed corroborates and justifies my analysis of knowledge, that it is faith mediated by symbols; since bodily life is, for the naturalist, the perfectly evident basis of moral emotions, pain, fear, attachment, and all kinds of desire; while patent and inevitable tensions between the animal organism and the rest of the world render those moral emotions indicative and extroverted, and turn them into knowledge. But this sensibility cannot create within the animal a feeling existentially similar to the material object that provokes that feeling. The feeling can be only a sign, a signal; so that both the transitive indicativeness and the subjective animal status proper to all mind are corollaries of materialism. Yet that is not all: from the transcendental nature of mind follows also, that it cannot figure among the objects it surveys, yet is essential to their moral presence. For the realm of matter cannot admit mind into its progressive structure and movement; each trope or rhythm must be complete before sensation can arise; so that this sensation is intrinsically a result and not a cause, a comment and not an agent, an occurrence not physical but spiritual and moral. It is in an ideal synthesis impossible in a flux, in spanning relations in the realm of truth, that mounting animal passions attain this hypostatic individuality, and become feelings. Events have then given birth, in a living organism, to experience of events. My whole description of the spiritual life is thus an extension of my materialism and a consequence of it.

But if my materialism be the ground of so much in my philosophy, what, you may ask, is the ground of my materialism? I have indicated it in passing at page 12f. My philosophy is not an academic opinion adopted because academic tendencies seemed at any moment to favour it. I care very little whether, at any moment, academic tendencies favour one unnecessary opinion or another. I ask myself only what are the fundamental presuppositions that I cannot live without making. And I find that they are summed up in the word materialism. This word denotes and confesses in the first place that I find myself carried along by a great automatic engine moving out of the past into the future, not giving me any reason for its being, nor any reason why I should be. Existence is groundless, essentially groundless; for if I thought I saw a ground for it, I should have to look for a ground for that ground, *ad infinitum*. I must halt content at the *quia*,[1] at the brute fact.

The world I find myself in is irrational, but it is not mad. It keeps moving in fundamentally constant ways, so that experience of it accumulates and work in it counts. In contrast with it, however, madness is possible in myself; as if, for instance, I insisted on finding a reason for existence, and started a perpetual and maddening vortex in my head. For there is an intensive inner life going on within me together with my familiar bodily contact with material things, a life peopled with surviving images, with true or false anticipations, and with altogether vain fancies. Even unnecessary and materially objectless ideas may be interesting, as a novel may be interesting, because they may excite dramatically the same passions that active life excites; but if these interesting but objectless ideas interfere with our actions or seem to be perceptions, we are deceived, we are dreaming, we are moving toward the madhouse.

My materialism is therefore simply ordinary perception, sustained in its impulsive trust but criticized in its deliverance. It is the presupposition of all natural investigation and science, a presupposition rather than a conclusion, and the presupposition not only of all natural science but of all deliberate action. Whenever I look, act, or judge I assume that there is a continuous dynamic world that I am momentarily looking at, acting upon, or thinking about; for if the world were not continuous and external, but the figment of a dream, retention or reconsideration of it would be morbid, since there would be

[1] DANTE: *State contenti, umana gente, al quia.*

nothing existent to be perceived more clearly or possessed more safely. Materialism marks the down of intelligence in the animal mind. I am not sure that there may not often be vapours in the mind earlier, as there are later: but with life in the open, and instinctive action, sensibility naturally becomes objective, expectant, and full of assurance and transcendent intent. It becomes knowledge; and it becomes knowledge, not of itself, but in its own sensuous or conceptual terms it becomes knowledge of the real material world of which the sensitive body is an integral part.

Professor Banfi, in his desire to be courteous, very much understates this position when he laments that there should be in my treatment of knowledge "an implicit dogmatic tendency" and that I should "relapse into a dogmatic attitude without noticing or intending it." He thinks my first principle an unintentional lapse, because (as he says) he is reviewing my theories from his own point of view and not from mine; and he finds that even I "seem not to exclude transcendental logic," from which it would be a relapse to revert to vulgar trust in perception.

Certainly I do not exclude transcendental logic; but I admit it only in what I think its place, consistently with materialism; just as, consistently with materialism, I admit the authority of grammar over language when a particular language has developed a particular grammar, and thereby has become coherent internally and communicative. Yet a language, however organically developed, cannot impose its grammar on things or on other languages. Similarly transcendental logic serves to render articulate certain special perspectives necessarily confined to the subjective or poetic sphere. Whether it shall have any validity or appropriateness in relation to further facts remains an open question. Every mental development has *some* material significance, since it cannot help being an index to its material ground. In its inner genesis transcendental logic is like poetry and religion, spinning itself out quite freely in the open, that is to say, in the realm of essence, until the vital impulse that sustains it subsides, and the spiritual winds begin to blow from some other quarter. Whether, in any instance, this logic corresponds at all to the articulation of events or even to the history of ideas, can never be discovered by this logic from the inside. The appositeness of so much of the criticism and dialectic to be found in Hegel, for instance, comes from side-glances continually taken by him surreptitiously towards the facts; and this true appositeness (which renders the logic arbitrary as logic) is reinforced by an illusion of appositeness, created dramatically, as in telling a ghost-story, by selecting and distorting such facts as can lend themselves to that fiction and ignoring the rest.

That this logic should claim to be a *universal law*, as Banfi proposes, betrays its non-logical origin. There is, especially in the younger Italians, an efflorescence of spirituality, which cannot entirely graft itself on the Catholic tradition, although among the truly learned it might easily do so; and there is also, coming from Germany and England, a transcendental idealism or dialectical eschatology, which are simply Protestant theology attenuated. The right of private judgment has become absolute inwardness and universal mentality; and the cries of the Hebrew prophets have become a moralistic philosophy of history, always flattering to the nationality or politics of the historian.

We hear on every side that science has now finally refuted and buried materialism, while the most stalwart activists, like Mussolini, call themselves idealists. How then, can I say that materialism is presupposed in all natural science and in all deliberate action? Evidently a word in common use, like materialism, must take on various meanings in various mouths; and science may be said to refute materialism when it abandons one idea of matter for another. This is its business, to investigate and to understand the material world better; but if it ceased to investigate things by experiment and lapsed into the description of experience as a drama, it would cease to be science and would become autobiography. Science—I am speaking of natural science, not of mathematics or philology—is the study of *nature;* the description of *experience* is literature. Any study or description of natural objects on their own plane is a study or description of matter: and any philosophy is materialistic that, like mine, regards this study, physics, as alone competent to reveal the secret source and method of gross events, or the ways of power. There might be said to be as many materialisms as there are stages of discovery in natural science; and the most recent notions, for instance about the disjointed character of minute events, are perfectly materialistic, jumping being as material an act as gliding. What should prevent matter, if it likes, from existing in pulses, and being atomic in time as well as in space? In any case a principle of continuity could not be absent if the separate strokes were not to form entirely separate universes. That existence should be intermittent therefore would add little to the axiom that it is transitory. Such new suggestions merely serve to refresh the salutary feeling, never lost by sceptics, that science is something human and that its language should not be hypostatised. It represents only the effect that surrounding reality produces at any moment upon us, accordings to our sensibility and equipment at that time.

For this reason I have sometimes used the word naturalism instead of materialism to indicate my fundamental belief: but that word is open to even worse equivocations. Naturalism might include psychologism or, as Banfi suggests, it might mean only one moral interest or one logical perspective open to absolute thought. The term materialism seems to me safer, precisely because more disliked; and the cruder notions of it are so crude that they may be easily distinguished and discarded. The theoretical sensualist, for instance, who thinks only sensations true or real, is evidently no materialist, but a psychological idealist; else Democritus would be an idealist, in believing in geometrical atoms. He was in fact a rationalist; and in this, to my mind, he was not materialistic enough, because there is ideolatry and conceptual dogmatism in attributing geometrical forms to matter absolutely, simply because they are clear essences to our intuition. All the appearances of matter including the geometrical, are *relatively* true of it, since it evokes them; but they all are conventional and qualified by the nature of the animal psyches in which they are evoked. These psyches are organizations in matter, seeing they are reproduced by seeds and sustained by food; and it is the marvellous physical energies released in well-knit and healthy psyches that produce those revolutions in the world which activists attribute to their mighty spirit. The spirit, Sir Oliver Lodge once said, was made of ether; and he thought he had refuted materialism. Ether might well be a name for the material agency that explodes in intuition and in action; but Lodge was a gross materialist in identifying *spirit* with ghosts or with invisible magicians that might discover hidden treasure or make tables dance.

Supernaturalism is indeed a phase of materialism, where imagination anticipates marvellous and morally interesting material discoveries; as we see in all the wonders of the Arabian nights, and in the orthodox notions of hell, of heaven, and of the resurrection of the body. There is nothing physically *inconceivable* in such miraculous extensions or complications in the cosmos: only they become *incredible* to an unprejudiced science. When in boyhood I liked to entertain such supernatural conceptions of nature, I was therefore quite as much a materialist in principle as I am now: the difference was that I was inclined to trust the picture of the material world painted by revelation rather than the pictures of it in the daily press.

Materialism by no means implies that nothing exists save matter. Democritus admitted the void to an equal reality, with all the relations and events that motion in that void would involve: he thereby admitted what I call the realm of truth. He also admitted appearances, bred in a material psyche by contact with other currents in matter; he thus recognised the moral presence of essences in themselves unsubstantial and not forms of matter. If he did not explicitly admit spirit, which is also involved in the presence of appearances, this was not because his principles forbade it but because Greek philosophy was physical and political rather than spiritual, and had not yet turned to that transcendental contrition which played so great a part in Indian and afterwards in Christian speculation. That matter is capable of eliciting feeling and thought follows necessarily from the principle that matter is the only *substance*, *power*, or *agency* in the universe: and this, not that matter is the only *reality*, is the first principle of materialism.

Initially, as the recognition of a single overpowering automatic process within us as well as without, materialism coincides with pantheism, or even with theism of that Islamic and Calvinistic kind which conceives God as omnificent. Divergence begins with the ways of acting attributed to this single force. The more minute, repeated, and constant the tropes discovered, the more materialistic or mechanical our dynamic monism will seem to grow; but I think there has been unnecessary rhetorical heat in the traditional quarrels on this subject. The entire history and destiny of the universe, if they could be surveyed, would in any case remain what they are, and contingent. They would make a total dramatic impression which imagination might regard as the moral *reason* (not the antecedent cause) of the whole reality. In the same way, imagination might regard particular parts of the process, such as human choices or human works of art, as *justified* (not produced) by the rightness or beauty or intention discernible in them. Teleology would thus be a sympathetic moral method of appreciating mechanism, and not an alternative natural process.

The elements of mechanism must in any case be single tropes, contingent and repeatable. If all existence were spanned by a single trope, like the plot of a novel, that trope would not be called mechanical, being unique; but if, according to an ancient fancy, cosmic history repeated itself in cycles for ever, even the total burden of history would become mechanical. Yet why, if one rehearsal of a play seem a jet of free life, should it become forced and mechanical if it executed itself an infinite number of times?

III. Dogmatism

In ordinary conversation we are said to be dogmatic when we assert too many private opinions too stubbornly. It would not be dogmatic to assert that it was raining, when this merely anticipated what anybody else would say on looking out of the window. Nor would it be dogmatic to express even a private opinion, if this were done modestly, giving a reason, or with the prefix "I think" or "I believe." And yet, logically, every belief or opinion is a dogma; and the prefix "I think" or "I believe," far from removing the dogmatism of the assertion, expressly declares that dogmatism to be intentional; so much so that the phrase "I believe" introduces the most dogmatic creeds, and is echoed at the end with a loud *Amen.*

Now my first principles are cases of such deliberately reaffirmed belief, dogmatic as every opinion has to be dogmatic, but not dogmatic, I hope, in being unreasonable or, to my own mind, avoidable. I should prefer not to believe anything, if I could manage it: but life forbids, and when I am forced to judge, I judge, and am not ashamed to confess that I believe what I actually believe. It would be ridiculous, when questioned by the census-taker, to reply: "*Perhaps* my name is John Smith, I *might* be sixty years old, and *it seems to me* that I live in Brickville." Doubt is something secondary, the conflict of two dogmas; and any philosophy not respectful towards our inevitable primary dogmas, and not built upon them, condemns itself to be artificial, and not quite honest. Its logic may carry the mind spontaneously and even passionately to any paradox; but when the heat of the argument cools, the natural man is left without a philosophy, or the philosopher becomes a mad tyrant over the man.

There are thus two kinds of dogmatism, although both preserve this fundamental presupposition of animal intelligence, namely: that apprehension is informative, that antecedent or hidden facts exist to be discovered, and that knowledge of them is possible. But the initial kind of dogmatist, having only sensation and fancy to guide him, assumes that things are just as they seem or as he thinks they ought to be: and if this assumption be challenged, the rash dogmatist hotly denies the relativity of his knowledge and of his conscience. Now I have always asserted this double relativity; it is implied in my materialism. I am not, then, a dogmatist in this first popular sense of the word, but decidedly a sceptic. Yet I stoutly assert relativity; I am a dogmatist there; for I see clearly that an animal cannot exist without a habitat, and that his impulses and perceptions are soon directed upon it with a remarkable quickness and precision: he therefore has true and transitive knowledge. But I also see clearly that this knowledge, if it takes an imaginative or moral form at all, must take a form determined by his specific senses and instincts. His true knowledge must then be, in its terms, relative to his nature, and no miraculous intuition of his habitat as it exists in itself.

This inevitable relativity of knowledge and interest, far from abolishing their assertiveness, justifies this assertiveness in its intellectual confidence and in its moral warmth. For it is some soul that is being touched, that is finding its level, and building its nest. My perceptions and my preferences are my own; but they are just as relevant to the facts as those of other creatures, and just as true to my nature as their different sentiments are to theirs. In this way I confirm myself in a dogmatism of a deliberate, qualified, and critical kind, not built on sense or imagination, but on faith, a faith in which active impulse is redirected by reflection and judgment. I need not, like Kant, remove knowledge to make room for faith. He removed knowledge by reducing it sophistically to elaborate intuition; and the faith he substituted was not an inevitable rational faith such as materialism justifies, but only a moral dogmatism of the first kind, hypostasising a few traditional maxims, local and unnecessary. Instead, with St. Augustine and with nature in me, I would retain faith to give breath to knowledge: a faith imposed on every living creature by the exigences of action and justified in the natural interplay of each animal with his environment. Such faith accumulates sufficient and trustworthy knowledge of "things-in-themselves," that is, of the substances, powers, or agencies that actually breed and support animal life; but this is *natural* knowledge, not unnecessary intuition of the depths of the world or of its entirety. It is knowledge inevitably limited to the range of the natural or artificial instruments that convey it, and couched, in each case, in the language of a special experience. Therefore, as a foundation for speculation, I accept all ordinary beliefs, including belief in the history of philosophy, which would not be belief, but only make-believe, if I did not first accept belief in the history of the material world, with India and Greece, England and Germany within it. I am far more firmly convinced of the physical existence of the great philosophers, although I have never seen one, than of the truth of any of their tenets. These tenets existed *in them* and may be repeated *in me*; and being unavoidably dependent on the workings of our respective minds, they may easily have deceived us; but I cannot honestly doubt that we have existed. On this principle I also believe firmly in some of the sciences, such as geography, elementary mechanics, and the astronomy of the solar system: all this has been steadily verified in my travels and ocular observations. When it comes to more speculative physics, I am not competent to form a personal opinion, and am not sure how far anybody is competent. The experts no doubt know their *theory* perfectly, as do the transcendental logicians: but what does their theory help them to know? I am not envious of science that is knowledge only of science, or of experience that is experience only of experience. It was unnecessary, and it may be vicious.

Dogmatism is out of place in the ideal sphere, where essence is studied and endlessly traced freely because the spirit moves, as in music, mathematics, and poetry. Such pursuits may be progressive and may consistently or inconsistently develop a chosen theme; but alternative themes, with other developments, always remain possible; so that it would be mere narrowness of mind to posit one's own idealism as the only *right* one. There is indeed a connection between such pursuits and morality, because they occupy human attention and qualify the tone and tendency of the mind: and they may also be more or less useful or applicable in education and in the practical arts. But they convey no knowledge of fact, and to suppose that they do is an abuse of dogmatism.

Banfi is therefore quite right in saying that, *in his own philosophy*, the term of a relation can never be separated from that relation, so that matter, for instance, being a term in thought, contrasted perhaps with mind or with appearance, matter cannot be hypostasised into an antecedent to the thought that defines and impossibly projects it.

We presuppose in this argument that we are talking of the terms of thought in themselves, as essences, which have eternal intrinsic relations to one another, and no further significance. We are ignoring altogether that thought goes on in an animal, and that the terms of it are signs for facts surrounding that animal or existing within his body, and that it is only in this capacity, as signs and not as dialectical terms, that essences can convey *knowledge.* Knowledge is always about the not given, it is faith justified by its material ground or by its material verification. The notion that objects are data hypostasised is a false reading of human intelligence. Nobody thinks the dog Toby to be the *sound* Toby wagging its tail; nor does anybody think the tail to be the *sight* of the tail wagging. Objects are goals of thought, of action, or of intent: they are not data. Data, and intuition of data, are prerequisites to knowledge and furnish the terms of it; but they are not focussed in rapid thought, as the sounds of words are not focussed in interested speech. Nevertheless, in calmer moments, the pure datum may be distinguished; and it may even be elaborated into some great vision or vast study of essence, like mathematics. Yet it is only as somehow relevant to material existence that mathematics or poetry or dialectics can be knowledge of anything, except—if you will—knowledge of themselves. When an ideal discipline, such as theology, has become traditional, its logic can be taught as a fact (a fact of doctrine or revelation) to minds quite innocent of logic; and in this way, by their social objectivity, many purely ideal figments become, for the vulgar, objects of knowledge, to be studied externally, as if they were material facts; but the letter then becomes an idol, and kills the spirit.

Idealists, on the contrary, who tend to deride convention and to retract faith in favour of intuition and dialectics, end if they are consistent in an opposite extravagance. William James used to ridicule their arguments by saying that according to them the pedestrian could never ride and the rider could never walk. In other words, they try to live in the realm of essence, which is dead and eternal. If the man riding were only the essence of equestrianism, he could never get off his horse: and on this principle Banfi accuses me of self-contradiction when I assume that matter existed before the idea of matter came into anyone's head. Matter, he thinks, is only the idea of materiality hypostasised. Such is not the case. The word matter *means* an object of belief, not an essence given in intuition. It *means* something that fills the world of which I am a part, not a part of the ideal or moral excitation which that world arouses within me. Consider a particular instance. A father cannot be a father before he has a child. Therefore, says the dogmatic logician, my father could never have existed before I was born. But this logic, even as logic, is not perfect, because if my father had not existed before I was born, he could not, in the nature of things, ever have been my father. The word father is not a mere term in logic but the name for a natural fact, for a man who has begotten a child. The logic of the word can never abolish the history of the action: yet this odd pretension, that data, which people human intelligence as signs, cannot be signs but only data, is what idealists call *criticism.*

To abolish dogmatism would be to abolish intelligence. Intelligence enables faith to discern the elements in things that are relevant to the action on foot or to the subject in hand. It precipitates the opportune dogma, and thereby helps to furnish the imagination with safe and clear ideas, so that the spirit that has to endure this world may also enjoy and understand it.

IV. Scepticism

I am a dogmatist, yet I have raised my system on a sceptical foundation: how is this to be disentangled?

Before developing my reply, let me indicate in a few words what it turns upon. My dogmatism asserts that, in an observable biological sense, knowledge is possible, and, on the same biological grounds, that knowledge is relative. My scepticism confirms this dogma, from the inside and analytically, by pointing out that knowledge, for the spirit, involves a claim that the spirit may always challenge; whereas self-evidence, or contemplative possession of a datum, collapses logically into tautology, and is not knowledge. Intellection without dubious claims can be found only in some self-limiting sensation, intuition, or definition.

Thus my dogmatism and my scepticism are complementary views of the same fact of natural history, namely: that organisms are affected and react as wholes according to the total customary operation of the object, as in hunting, fighting, and fleeing. Meantime on these occasions animals *feel* the excitement they undergo and *imagine* the object that excites them. Such feeling and imagination is something private and original to the organism; it is a spiritual event; and it becomes true knowledge, or spiritual dominion over the object, in so far as feelings and images express faithfully the relevant relations between the object and the organism. Such knowledge cannot be literal or exhaustive because it expresses the violently selective and transmuting sensibility of one vital atom in a vast world; yet because it is natural, such knowledge cannot be irrelevant to its occasions, and brings timely tidings of the real world, in appropriate moral perspectives, to each vital atom.

So much being premissed in general, I will consider two or three special points.

A great source of misunderstanding is the impression that scepticism means disbelief. But disbelief is not sceptical; it is *belief* in the falseness of a previous assertion. The true sceptic merely analyses belief, discovering the risk and the logical uncertainty inherent in it. He finds that alleged knowledge is always faith; he would not be a sceptic if he pretended to have proved that any belief, much less all belief, was *wrong*. The notion that scepticism means disbelief has a social origin. Unbelievers in traditional religion were called sceptics out of courtesy or because they were subject to waves of unbelief without knowing what belief they could cling to. Common unbelievers are probably materialists, whatever else they may call themselves; they are not likely to be sceptical at all. Extraordinary heroism would be required to turn scepticism into a final philosophy, as some of the ancients tried to do. We should have to suspend all belief, and confine ourselves to dialectic in a kind of self-denying solipsism: for if we nursed our solitude and idealism as a superior state of mind we should be romantic egotists and not sceptics at all. Modest dogma with the prefix "I think" becomes the most arrogant of dogmas when "I think" means not "I believe" but "I create my objects and nothing else can exist." Although I am not afraid of solitude, I have no predilection for any acrobatic pose, sceptical, transcendental, or prophetic; and my scepticism remains merely the confession that faith is faith, without any rebellion against the physical necessity of believing. It enables me to believe in common-sense and in materialism and, like Landor, to warm both hands before the fire of life; and at the same time it gives me the key to the realms of dialectic and fancy, which I may enter without illusion.

A second point regards the alleged artificiality of introducing a dogmatic view, already settled, by an elaborate pretense at scepticism. Banfi thinks that I am desperately searching for certitude, and finally embrace unmeaning essences as if they were the ultimate truth. Many other critics feel that I *substitute* essences for facts, and that I condemn myself to idiotic contemplation, entirely abandoning my materialism and my knowledge of the world. All this is a mare's nest. I think I understand the world better and certainly judge it more tolerantly now than when I was young; and in the preface to *Scepticism and Animal Faith* I proclaimed my materialism. My sceptical analysis of human opinion, ending in solipsism of the passing moment, was as sincere as I could make it. It was not an invitation to the public to become solipsists or a pretence that I had become one, but a demonstration that demonstration in matters of belief is impossible, that the terms of experience are unsubstantial, and that life would be a vain dream, if faith did not interpret it. The interpretation, obviously, will be existentially only a further idea: but if nature is not dead within us, and we have the courage to trust the natural impulse of faith, we may be restored by it to peace with nature and with ourselves. Our conventional knowledge will then possess a double authority, as poetry in form and as science in function.

The stages of possible scepticism do not represent the order of genesis in human ideas: we do not begin with solipsism and end with common sense. These stages represent only a possible order of evidence, or depths of assumption and presupposition involved unawares in what we call reason. The deepest presuppositions, for a naturalist, are the most trustworthy, since they express the primary adjustment of the psyche to the world; but for a critic looking for demonstration the deepest presuppositions are the most arbitrary. Indeed, nothing can be more arbitrary than existence, and therefore than the truth about existence; and it will be only by docility to nature, within us and without, that we shall be at all able to approach the truth.

There is a further tangle, again due to preoccupation with religious controversies, in confusing scepticism with agnosticism. Agnostics were people who were emptily austere, because they could frame no credible idea of God. They demanded literal knowledge, and they thought, in their surviving image-worship, that science gave them literal knowledge, or if not science, at least history. But *knowledge ceases to be knowledge if taken literally;* so that what is called agnosticism, say in Kant, far from removing knowledge removes only idolatry, and enables the sceptical mind to purify both its science and its religion by regarding them only as symbols, without destroying their natural and traditional texture. That these natural signs have a real object is the first and truest of all presuppositions; and they reveal this reality to us in the only way in which revelation or knowledge is possible to a mind, namely, by faith mediated by some feeling, image, or concept. We are a part of the reality, but cannot, in body or mind, be or become any other part of it. We can only *think* the rest and believe in it. Faith is accordingly gnostic. Only the demand for literal knowledge makes knowledge impossible.

This is not to say that the same essence that appears in intuition may not be exemplified also passively in objects. When the object is another man's thoughts, this similarity between datum and object becomes natural and normal: whence the often literal truth of psychological insight. Yet even here similarity is not the nerve of knowledge. Doubtless I repeat constantly feelings and ideas that mankind has had for ages; but this is not *knowledge* of history or psychology, unless physical objects or occasions justify me in attributing those feelings and ideas to mankind, or to particular existing persons. So too in material objects. This table has four legs, and I may bring my image of it to show four legs also, if I take pains: but this image will not become my *knowledge* of the table more than the other perspectives I may take of it. Knowledge begins when the element "four" contained in the given essence is attributed to the material table by my understanding: that is, by my instinctive trust in the consistence and consecutiveness of a world in which I move.

V. Physics, Metaphysics, and Psychology

If the word physics be used, as the ancients did and as I do, for all natural science or natural philosophy, does physics thereby become metaphysics? When Aristotle added his first philosophy or theology to his physics, did he merely continue his physics or did he introduce other postulates and presuppositions? I think he did the latter: he introduced hypostatically the Socratic or Platonic element of the good to be the secret of the real. This good was partly moral, the self-sufficing, perfect, or blessed, and partly intellectual, the clear, the definite, the eternal. Physics was now backed by a moral and logical reason for the facts that it described: it had become metaphysics.

Taking the word metaphysics in this sense I have always regarded it as false physics, or humanism materialised. But I have no wish to quarrel about words, and I quite understand why idealists, who also use the word in a derogatory sense, call materialism too metaphysics. Of late, however, the word seems again to be used respectfully; and my theories of essence, truth, and spirit are certainly not parts of physics, and metaphysical in a literary sense. This label at present has rather lost its glue and may harmlessly flutter down upon anything. Thus Professor Collingwood, in his recent *Essay on Metaphysics*, tells us that metaphysics is a part of history; the history of the various ultimate presuppositions made unconsciously by people at various times. And in the present volume Professor Dennes writes at length about my "metaphysics," although he tells me in private that I "have consistently, from the earliest writings, held that there is no serious method except the scientific (and that wholly continuous with everyday thought)—no metaphysical method—of developing beliefs (or hypotheses) let alone profounder beliefs about existence." My metaphysics would therefore not regard the existent at all, or else would be contained in everyday beliefs or be an extension of them identical with science. The latter is precisely what I maintain in respect to my fundamental presuppositions: they are the assumptions involved in living. I presuppose, for instance, a real future coming, a real past gone, and a physical universe surrounding and containing me. Then, if we adopt Collingwood's definition, I should indeed have a metaphysics; not my materialism, for that would be only my physics or scientific speculation; but my metaphysics would be the belated history or analysis of my presuppositions contained in this very *Apology*. Personally, I should prefer to call such a retrospect self-criticism or the pursuit of self-knowledge. It is certainly historical in being reflection upon thoughts once actually entertained, recovered as well as may be in a new perspective. Yet historical accuracy is not attainable absolutely in such a review, nor is it important in what is essentially a moral exercise or examination of conscience. I am not guided by any urgent desire to recover the past, but by the impulse to understand myself and to achieve integrity.

Essence and spirit are certainly metaphysical in the sense of being immaterial or non-physical; yet nobody calls mathematics metaphysical, which has exactly the same status as my logic of essence. The conceptions involved, in both cases, are suggested by natural objects and natural relations; but here the mind, instead of incorporating those conceptions in matter, as if they actually happened to be found there, considers the suggested idea or ideal in itself: something falsely described as an abstraction. You cannot abstract from anything something that isn't there; and the mathematical point and mathematical line form no material part of a dot or a stick, but are seen *instead* of the gross dot or the straight stick by the mind's eye, by the actual intellect. They are the *only* terms in which position and straightness can be given at all. Logical thoughts are not abstract but constructive, like poetry: they seem abstract only to persons incapable of attending to them, and interested only in something else. Yet essences become metaphysical in my sense of the word when they are supposed to be powers, and are invoked superstitiously, as names are invoked in magic; and in that sense mathematics was metaphysical for the Pythagoreans and perhaps for Plato. In the same way spirit becomes metaphysical when its immaterial character and ultimate status are not understood and it is regarded as a physical agent.

As to spirit, I am sorry that my volume on that subject had not appeared when these essays were composed; yet I had previously said enough about spirit to make clear the status I assign to it. In reaching a definition of existence, I had expressly reserved it for physical objects and for intuitions, intuitions being moments or instances of spirit. Dennes seems to have overlooked this in alleging that I regard matter as the only existent. I regard it as the only power, as composing the groundwork or scaffolding on which everything is stretched and supported; but the great characteristic of matter as known to us is its potentiality; an *existing* potentiality, definite in its possibilities and distribution, so that all its ulterior manifestations give knowledge of it. It determines the character, order, and tempo of all events: but in itself this potentiality, like the pregnancy of any seed, is unpictured and blind. The appearances and the perceptions that it is destined to breed do not pre-exist in it explicitly; yet it would not be the potentiality that it is were those developments not forthcoming on the appropriate occasions. And how should this ultimate phase of explicitness, in which potentiality becomes actuality, be less existent than the primary phase? In animals the ultimate phase is moral. Nature, which was dynamic in matter then becomes actual in spirit; it becomes the sense and the knowledge of its own existence. And how should this moral actualisation of existence be less existent than the physical potentiality of it?

However, I can well understand the modern feeling that spirit is nothing, that essence is nothing, and that even matter is nothing. Modern philosophy, as it became psychological, became essentially literary: it first neglected and then discarded the units of physics and logic in favour of the humanistic dramatic units of discourse. Theology had always done the same thing, at the moral, religious, or mystical level: so that lay philosophy, in Germany at least, became a theology universalised, a literary view of all human experience turned into a cosmic fable. In England, with characteristic partiality and caution, theology was left to cultivate its own garden; and an elementary empiricism was introduced, reducing all facts to sensations and ideas, to correspond with such common names as green, sharp, loud, pleasant, and painful. These names, taken logically, denote essences: and this was ultimately perceived by James, Russell, and those others that now speak of "neutral entities;"

but their predecessors took the fact designated to be a psychological atom, an essence hypostasised into an intuition. Out of such atoms it behoved them to construct the universe; but not even a mind can be constructed out of them, and the issue was a literary or historical description of "experience," more positivistic in tone and range than the German fable, but no less conventional and subjective.

Thus when I object to Dewey's philosophy that it contains no cosmology, he replies that it is not the philosopher's business to rediscover all the sciences: cosmology, if I do not misunderstand him, belongs to natural science. But the cosmological problem is the problem of existence, of the source and conditions of all experience: so that if philosophy must leave that question to be solved by the specialists, philosophy confesses, as I do, that only physics, not metaphysics and not "experience," must reveal the structure of the world to us, in so far as we can discover it. Empiricism is current literary convention hypostasised, and only the sciences study reality.

An advantage of literature over science is that it puts everything on one plane, that of dramatic experience or report: it indulges the journalistic mind. Everything can be talked about, and nothing need be understood, because in this field language is more real than its meaning. From this comfortable vantage-ground it will seem reactionary and perverse to revert to specific logic and specific physics or even to specific psychology. My essences must then be rejected without examination, because they dissolve "ideas" or "neutral entities" into logical terms incapable of existing by themselves. They may indeed be exemplified, either in the flux of matter, as forms of events, or else for the spirit, as distinguishable features in a total field of apprehension, always infinitely extensible and open to variation. It will then be only by virtue of inclusion in the material or in the spiritual chain of contingent events that these neutral entities will exist at all. So long as they are neutral they will remain essences, or sheer possibles: they cannot begin to exist until they figure in one or the other of these two orders. Even then they will be only characters of existence or appearances to spirit, not substantive existents by themselves. The stress of matter flowing through those forms and linking them in the life of nature will alone lend them, for a moment, a place in the history of things: and this place will be moral, and they will become themes of interested thought, only when some animal psyche evokes them imaginatively in its struggles with itself and with an ominous world. We cannot say that neutral entities exist by themselves, so that, in James's example, the leaping fire in the hearth is one fact, merely *called* material or mental by virtue of *simultaneous* relations in two different directions, in one path physical and in the other biographical. That pictorial essence is one and the same only logically: it is a universal that may be seen again and again, painted, remembered, symbolised and recalled by a word, or by some happy poetic description. It never exists in the material fire at all, which is a chemical process of combustion expressible perhaps in algebraic terms but not paintable; it is a sensuous essence, evokable only to human vision and charged there with emotional and sentimental values. These neutral data are not neutral; they are psychical in quality and status, as might be expected *a priori* in view of their ancestry, since they are the shy children of those robust British entities, actual perceptions and obvious ideas. In Russell's theory they are truer to their origin, since they exist in the head. The pictorial fire is no longer in the hearth at all, as James wished to believe; it is *only* in the *brain*, the fire being inhabited by other, non-human, neutral entities, existing only in that physical medium. So transformed and corrected I gladly accept the theory, except that my neutral entities are essences only, and not, after the manner of Leibniz, at once perceptions and atoms. I cannot conceive truly neutral entities *composing* either mind or matter: but I can admit them as figuring in the history of one or the other, or in some cases in the history of both. They may then be loosely said to exist; but they will exist as properties or themes, and in neither case as self-grounded facts.

This divergence is partly a question of words, in that I define existence as essence lying in external or non-essential relations. Temporal relations, for instance, within an essence compose a picture, a view, an ideal synthesis of time, a memory, a prophecy, or a story. All the given parts of it are essential and internal to that essence, which is a universal capable of being repeated, like old men's good stories. But the temporal relations of these repetitions lie in physical time and are irrelevant to the story ideally; the tale may be told once a year or once a month or once a week, according to the force of automatism in the old man's psyche, without changing the story itself. The tellings therefore are real events, but the story and the reported events within it are only essences. If the story happens to be true historically, the reported events will have existed in their contingent relations at the time and in the world in which they occurred; but they will not exist again in the story; only the telling and the hearing of that story will exist now; and any story essentially contains a certain ideal sequence of ideal events, equally capable of being false or true. In other words, a neutral monism represents accurately the intuitive field congenial to a mathematical and logical mind; but for a system of the universe it is too simple and clear. Definition, whether sensuous or verbal, does not individuate: that which individuates is precisely the contingent position of the neutral entity, now in the chain of material events, now in that of perceptions. The neutral event therefore is only a possible event, the essence of a story, until its place in a medium external and prior to it is determined. In beginning to exist it ceases to be neutral.

My account of the psyche has hardly been noticed by my critics in this book. One of them condemns my distinction between scientific and literary psychology; this is a distinction in depth, between the dynamic and the phenomenal. Evidently for a phenomenalist there can be no such distinction; for him nothing can exist but surfaces, and no connection between events can be other than accidental. My distinction certainly implies other principles. Yet in making it I am not intending to deny for a moment that the episodes reviewed in literary psychology and in dramatised history are natural events, biologically conditioned. I everywhere insist that mental events have physical grounds. Yet biology and behaviouristic psychology have no direct means of discovering the character of feeling or even its existence. The man beneath the psychologist must interpret the evidence by natural divination: he must become sympathetic.

Such instinctive imitation yields the imaginative psychology of common mutual understanding or misunderstanding; and later, after being buried for a while in the psyche and fructifying there, those seeds may yield the spontaneous imaginative psychology of novels and dramas. Literary psychology is therefore not at all divorced from the processes that scientific psychology may study. These must supply the scaffolding for that interpretation; then sympathetic intuition may build a dramatic fiction upon them, that may be trusted to be historical and, in the relevant measure, true to the spiritual facts.

VI. Misunderstandings of Essence

A. Transcendental Absolutism

If there was insight in Royce's saying that I separated essence from existence, there was not absolute accuracy. I do not *separate* the two, I merely distinguish them. It is axiomatic that a thing can have no existence if it has no character: only things with *some* character can exist. Yet existence involves change or the danger of change: things may be transformed, or in other words they may drop one essence and pick up another. The lost essences then seem to be actually separated from existence, like dead leaves from a tree; but this too is not accurate. We may separate things that lie on the same plane, as England and France are separated by the Channel. Perhaps they were once continuous, and a change in the sea level might make them continuous again. But nothing can ever make existence and essence continuous, as nothing can ever make architecture continuous with music: like parallels such orders of being can never flow into one another. But they may be conjoined or superposed; they may be simultaneous dimensions of the same world. A changing world is defined at each moment or in each movement by the essence of that moment or of that movement; and when it drops that pattern or that trope, the essence then dismissed remains, in its logical identity, precisely the essence that it was during that manifestation and before it. Were it not the same essence throughout, *it* could not be picked up or dropped, recognised, or contrasted with the forms that existence might wear earlier or later. The eternal self-identity of every essence is therefore a condition for the possibility of change; and complete as the realm of essence is in its ideal infinity, and unaffected there by the evolution of things, yet it is intimately interwoven, by its very eternity, with this perpetual mutation. Allowing matter a dynamic priority (matter and not essence being the seat and principle of genesis) we might describe in a myth the temporal discovery of eternity. Becoming, we might say, in the fierce struggle to generate he knew not what, begat Difference; and Difference, once born, astonished its parent by growing into a great swarm of Differences, until it exhibited all possible Differences; that is to say, until it exhibited the whole realm of essence. Up to that time Becoming, who was a brisk bold lusty Daemon, had thought himself the cock of the walk; but now, painful as it was for him to see any truth whatever, he couldn't help suspecting that he lived and moved only through ignorance, not being able to maintain the limitations of any moment nor to escape the limitations of the next, like a dancing Dervish that must lift one foot and then the other from the burning coals.

It is by its very ideality, non-existence, and eternity, then, that essence is inwardly linked with existence, not by being an extension or a portion of that which exists. This seems to me so simple and clear that I hardly know what to say to those who find it unintelligible. Is it perhaps *too* simple and clear, and are people led astray by expecting something more pretentious and difficult? Remembering and resenting imposture, do they then assume that I am wickedly inventing a metaphysical realm of essence to take the place of the natural world and of real life? This was the misunderstanding into which William James was led by my *Interpretations of Poetry and Religion* and into which the mere word essence has led many readers since. For instance, in the first volume of this series,[2] Professor Savery, in a remarkably fair and penetrating essay on Dewey observes incidentally that I call myself a materialist but am something else, since *I believe in eternal essences.* The word "believe" is unfortunate here, though natural enough in the colloquial sense in which some

[2] *The Philosophy of John Dewey,* 512.

worthy reformer of hygiene might believe in fresh air and one apple a day. The diet would be thin but disinfecting, and for that ascetic purpose I certainly believe in essences. Technically, however, to believe in anything means to believe that it exists; whereas an essence is what anything turns into in our eyes when we do not believe in it. We do not cease to conceive that which we explicitly deny, and for us then this conceived but denied thing is an essence; so that if my critics, when they deny essences, clearly conceived what they are denying, they would have admitted all that I assert. An essence is anything definite capable of appearing or being thought of; the existence of something possessing that essence is an ulterior question irrelevant to logic and to aesthetics. Misunderstanding is therefore redoubled if you say that I believe in *eternal* essences; because the reader, if not the writer, is likely to take "eternal essences" to mean everlasting substances; whereby my doctrine is blown sky-high into the Platonic heaven of magnetic forces, intelligences, or deities, astrologically guiding the fortunes of men and of nations. I am thus turned into a friend of outworn superstitions, when I am no friend even of the superstitions that prevail today.

An insidious remnant of such Platonic mythology adheres to the notion of essences when these are said to *subsist*. Subsistence means latent duration, and duration means steady persistence in time; but the eternity intrinsic to all essences is timeless. The same essence may therefore recur any number of times; and when this happens, or when some essence is exemplified continuously, as the laws of nature or morals are supposed to be exemplified in our world, we may say that these essences subsist: not, however, by virtue of their own timeless eternity, but by virtue of a certain alleged constancy in things, that keeps those essences in office for the time being. The rules of chess, for instance, subsist in that chess-players continue to observe them. If the game were obsolete, the rules would have subsided into merely possible rules or essences; and all that would then subsist in regard to them would be the truth that they had once been established and obeyed. Truth may be said to subsist because even when the facts concerned are past or future, they lend to the essences manifest in them an eternal relevance to existence: for let existence change as fast and as radically as it will, it cannot expunge either its past or its future.

While more important than chess in the economy of nature, mathematics, logic, and all laws formulated by the sciences are not essentially in a different case. Matter or mind may have adopted these rules and may continue to observe them: but their prevalence is contingent, and they are essentially necessary only to themselves, in the realm of essence. In nature they are, at best, only factually dominant.

I should say, then, that subsistence is something proper to matter and to the phases of matter, astronomical, anthropological, or social. It is not proper to essence. To make any essence properly *subsist,* to give it a lasting empire over events, is ideolatry. Thus mathematical terms and the laws of nature are often taken for forces controlling the world, or imposing their material truth upon all mind. But no essence imposes itself on the mind unless the mind is led by material circumstances to think of it; even the intrinsic relations of a given essence to other essences are never noticed until a vital impulse leads the mind to perceive those implications: else all mathematics would be familiar to everybody. And no essence imposes itself on nature, unless nature falls of its own accord into that special shape. That whatever has always been the way of the world must always continue to be so is a merely empirical presumption; and in the measure in which it is verified, it reports the inertia of matter, not the self-identity of essences or the power of any of them over things.

Ideolatry is also common in morals, when certain precepts are felt to coerce the conscience by their intrinsic authority, without any vital or rational backing. Categorical imperatives, such as "*Do what is right*" or *Fiat justitia* are indeed coercive because they are tautologies; but the concrete action called right or just in any instance cannot justify its title except by concrete considerations. The clear discrimination of essence blasts all these superstitions.

A subtler misunderstanding clings to the status of essences when they appear in intuition. Whenever a new essence is seen or conceived, an event has occurred: there is a fresh natural moment in the natural world. But is that which has come into existence the given essence itself? Appearance is an ambiguous term. It may mean a false appearance, contrasted with a true one, or it may mean any positive presence. The green after-image of a red stamp is a false appearance, since no green stamp exists; yet the optical illusion by which a green stamp appears is an illusion that occurs, and in that psychological sense is perfectly real. It has a biographical status, being part of the experience of a physically extant person, with physiological causes in that person; but the green stamp itself has no physical status, such as the red stamp has. Thus givenness does not confer existence on that which is given. Whenever a perception or an illusion arises that which comes into existence is not the datum but the perception or illusion itself. We are in the realm of spirit.

The spirituality of spirit and the ideality of data follow directly from materialism; and I think that it was by convinced materialists, by men thoroughly disillusioned about the course of nature and the decrees of fate, as the Indians were disillusioned, that the true quality of spirit was first discerned. For a materialist the mind will be simply sensibility in bodies; things that stimulate that sensibility will be the inevitable objects of pursuit, attention, and passion; but how should the feelings thereby aroused in the organism present the *intrinsic* character of the surrounding things? Evidently they will transcribe only the effects of those things on the organism; and this in aesthetic, moral, or verbal terms, not in the diffused and complicated form of the physical processes concerned. Mind, for a materialist, will therefore seem necessarily poetical, and data fictions of sense. If you are a materialist in respect to matter you will be an idealist in respect to mind. Commonly materialists no doubt ignore mind altogether; they are seldom competent philosophers, and when they are they may express the quite special quality of mind perhaps in some disparaging way, by calling it illusion as the Indians did, or appearance with Parmenides, or convention with Democritus. Attaching myself to this ancient tradition, without neglecting more modern spokesmen of the spirit, I call it intuition, and note that it possesses qualities that render it necessarily original in respect to the physical world. Matter is in flux; spirit, while existentially carried along in that movement, arrests some datum, lending it an ideal unity, fixity, and moral colour such as neither the organ of sensation nor the stimulus can possess in themselves. We are, in the texture of our impressions, in the realm of essence; and it is only in the language of essence that spirit can describe its fortunes. It is a poet, a singer, a sufferer, it is memory and imagination, living in a pedestrian world that cannot suffer or sing.

By disregarding this open-air materialistic setting of my analysis, some critics, who do not expect such an atmosphere in philosophy, draw the most incongruous inferences from my discrimination of essence, as if it were an exotic plant forced in the subjective greenhouse. Thus Banfi finds that my essences are not data but hypothetical ideals, invented to satisfy dogmatic certitude. He then points out, as if I had not perceived it, that intuition of essence is not that dogmatic knowledge which I am supposed to be longing for. And he adds that such contemplation would not even be aesthetic, in the sense of revealing the beautiful or being relevant to the history of the fine arts.

In the 1890's the history of art excited all aspirants to "culture," and all rich collectors; but it forms only a phase of general history, as do various fashions in dress, with much the same basis in circumstance and in instinct. For intuition and for the spiritual life the arts are parts of nature, reflecting nature at second hand: and if sometimes they enlighten and exalt, more often, especially when their day is past, they detain uselessly and become curiosities. My theory of essence and of intuition of essence has nothing to do with aestheticism. Intuition is *Anschauung* and aesthetic only in the Kantian sense, as in the transcendental *Aesthetik*. Images, judged morally, seem neutral or ugly as easily when they proceed from works of art, as when they proceed from natural objects. When the moral reaction is suspended, as Schopenhauer explains so eloquently in his account of the Idea, there is indeed a great liberation from care, from the vanities of culture no less than from the horrors of history; but this is only a momentary relief, not a positive acquisition; and when habitual intuition becomes purer, as it does in poets, the themes that most attach and most liberate the spirit are drawn from nature and life directly, never from the arts and their history. The notion that a theory of essence *ought* to generate the history of arts belongs to the romantic dream of a "phenomenology of spirit," as if spirit were a social or divine psyche pregnant with wonderful visions and tragic passions, which when unrolled would display the panorama that idealists call reality and the mental fiction that they call truth. From that point of view Banfi naturally finds that even my naturalism must evaporate and leave me, with my realm of essence, idiotically plunged in an unmeaning trance; for he cannot conceive naturalism otherwise than as a department of pure logic. But my naturalism asserts that I am a part of nature. How, then, could any development internal to my mind contradict my naturalism? The mystic and the madman merely complicate the fact of the world.

Finally, as his own solution, Banfi proposes a view which I have always maintained, namely, that essences are not ultimate objects of knowledge but initial terms in all thought; and he suggests—what ignores my whole reliance on action, intent, and environment in generating knowledge—that knowledge is a concretion of essences into theories, according to the laws of transcendental logic.

This travesty of my motives and of the moral issue of my philosophising is explicable in so good a critic only by the arbitrary perspective in which he has chosen to cast his criticism. He takes me for a representative of the New World, and wishes to indicate the youthful virtues and the technical faults that characterise American speculation, as seen from a transcendental point of view which he calls European. He forgets that I and many of the older American professors were pupils of Royce and students of Bradley and were brought up—thank God, not exclusively—on Kant and Hegel; and he forgets Emerson. There was little need of reminding the New World of transcendentalism. As for me my Catholic background and Latin mind placed me in conscious and sometimes violent contrast with old Boston, and also with the new America that has grown up for the most part after my day. This did not exclude innumerable warm friendships and, I hope, some lessons learned from both those circles; I have tacitly acknowledged my debt in *The Last Puritan*. But what I owe to America is naturally not that which my critics, even Banfi himself, censure in me. They deplore rather my personal views, of which America is guiltless.

Now it was precisely against the transcendental denial of transitive knowledge and of the dogmatic intellect that my honest convictions asserted themselves from the beginning. I could easily reduce all alleged knowledge to illusion, and intrench myself in solipsism of the present moment; and this even in my adolescence, as my lines on *Solipsism* testify, written in the 1880's. But that was a blind alley; and its blindness proved the incompatibility of idealism with any claim to knowledge. Knowledge presupposes faith, a faith that when intelligent perceives that its terms are symbolic. Faith may then be justly dogmatic, as intuition should never be; for faith is addressed to external realities, realities that are truly revealed to it in their relevant relations to the believer, when, as happens in perception and in natural science, his faith is closely controlled by contact between his organs and their objects.

With such trustworthy human *knowledge* I have always been perfectly content, discontented as I may have been with the realities that it reports. I have never been curious to make more accurate the rough views that common information gives us of the physical world and of human history. Increase in such worldly knowledge may enlarge and strengthen the mind, or may distract and confuse it. The use of philosophy, and in particular of the discrimination of essence, is to distil the wine out of those trodden grapes, in order that in whatever kind of world we may be living, we may live freely in the spirit. The relief that I find, when in the presence of facts I can discern essences, does not come, as in religious faith, through trust in any higher facts. It comes through liberation from anxiety, from the need of faith, and from the very problem of knowledge. I then espouse precisely the transcendental logic that Banfi recommends; only it never crosses my mind to mistake this play of ideas for *knowledge*, or to suppose that it miraculously reveals to me the logic of history or the necessary problems of all thought. That would be dogmatism indeed, and in the wrong place: the childish dogmatism of intuition, not the competent dogmatism of the sailor's eye or of the doctor's judgment.

The use of experience, to my mind, cannot be to prepare us for further experience; somewhere this experience must be self-rewarding, else all would be a democracy of unhappy tyrants making slaves of one another. There is a concomitant fruit to be gathered during this journey, experience at another level, the level of reflection, of spiritual self-possession, of poetry, of prayer. This is not a parasitic growth or expensive luxury that need not be added or that might exist elsewhere by itself. It could never exist elsewhere by itself, and the life here could never be complete naturally or spontaneously without it; not that it *adds* any energy or gives any new direction to the vital process, but that it *is* that vital process brought to a head and becoming a moral reality instead of a merely physical one. This moral reality or spiritual life will of course be peopled only with such images and sentiments as crude experience has elicited in each particular soul. I cannot transcend the scope of my faculties; but within these limits I am content to trace and to recast freely those special images and conceptions which the world or the arts happen to arouse in me. In the sphere of essence I lose nothing of my lessons learned from the facts, except precisely the wagers that at first I may have made about them. I can now smile at my losses, and at myself; but when the clock strikes, I instantly recover my dogmatic readiness in the requisite direction, and confidently skimming over all essences and appearances, I make my way back to school as directly, if not so fast, as any urchin. But I am no longer merely a distracted automaton; spirit in me has laid up some immaterial treasures in its own depths.

B. Pragmatist Propaganda

A cruder hostility to essence, a sort of political hostility, was to be expected in the empirical, nominalistic, positivistic camp. Transcendentalists at least preserve the notion of spirit, which enables them to conceive essences without hypostasising them. Indeed, hypostasis is their pet aversion, and they refuse to hypostasise even substance, power, or cause, which thereby lose their meaning and have to be rejected ostentatiously, but in vain; because if we hypostasise nothing in spontaneous faith we must ultimately hypostasise spirit in reflection, turning it into the absolute substance, power, and cause. But by philosophers belonging politically to the Left, spirit and essence are gaily jettisoned together; there is a note of triumph and contempt in their glee, as they fancy themselves pulling the long false beards off those old imposters. This must be allowed to go on, it belongs to the ritual of intellectual insurrection; but there are technical misunderstandings that might be cleared up, without asking the positivists to change their radical allegiance.

One misunderstanding appears in the notion that essences are abstract ideas, whereas they are the direct data, and the only possible data, of sensation and thought. The *objects* from which they are alleged to be abstracted are objects posited and never given, whether these objects be material things or other men's thoughts or one's own past or future experience. The less hypothetical a view is the more it dwells upon essence. Berkeley, for instance, was a nominalist and a great enemy of abstract ideas; yet the ideas (images) that he recognised, and the notions (concepts) that he was obliged to admit, were precisely my essences. They were inert, unsubstantial, individual, and perfectly distinct; and they composed the whole "furniture of the mind" and the "divine language" in which spirits spoke to one another. Unfortunately Berkeley began by calling these natural signs the only *objects of human knowledge;* when evidently the *objects signified and partly discovered* were the spirits that used those signs and whose wills governed the flow of that language. The mere intuition of a word is not knowledge, it is an odd unmeaning sensation, if the word is not understood; and all the ideas in the mind are not knowledge if they are not intelligently interpreted.

This ambiguity about the objects of knowledge involves another ambiguity about the distinctness of ideas. A datum cannot be other than it is, and a fact must be exactly what has happened; but a datum may have any degree of vagueness as the sign or description of a fact.

When empiricism attempts to reduce facts to data, it therefore runs up against this terrible paradox, that every idea must be perfectly clear and every object must be thoroughly well known. The perfect self-determination of essence and the perfect self-determination of fact thus yield to the utter confusion of the one by the other. Professor Hartshorne reproaches me for not taking account of this Neglected Alternative. His alternative also contains an interesting cosmology or theology of which I shall say a word presently; but the point in regard to essences is put most clearly by Bergson where he says that nothing is possible before it happens, but only afterwards. Suppose I have cut an apple in two. Before the cutting there were no two specific halves to the apple: it was only a whole apple. Afterwards I may say that it was possible for me to cut it in halves, because I took that free determination; whereas to have cut it in thirds would have required a good eye for an angle of 120 degrees, with which, owing to laziness in the study of mathematics, I am not provided. Grant, now, all the absence you choose of division in the apple, and all the freewill and guiltiness you like in myself: does it follow that the essence ½ became ½ when I divided the apple, and that previously it had been indistinct and no more ½ than ⅓ or than 1? Had not this neglected alternative better remain neglected?

The force of nominalism comes from the appeal to facts; its absurdity comes of perpetually substituting these facts for the differences that distinguish them. These differences cannot occur before the facts that manifest them; therefore the nominalist, who is a hard-headed fellow, swears that differences are nothing except their occurrence. Things like essence, matter, truth, and spirit, which my philosophy talks about, are therefore for him nothing; or at most the ambiguous burden of some word used to name a number of separate facts, as many persons are called John, though apart from each John, the word John designates nothing. Proper names are indeed almost wholly improper, since they evoke no essence attributable to their object except the most generic, as the name John only implies a male Jew or Christian; beyond that it carries no idea, unless we turn back reflectively to the sound and history of the word. Only the names of essences are truly proper, in that they designate a single and precise object; and this just as singly and precisely when the essence is simple as when it is complex. The notion that, for instance, "the triangle" is abstract or indeterminate, but "the equilateral triangle" at least relatively precise, is a sheer prejudice. The three-corneredness indicated by the one word is just as definite as the equality designated by the other. It is just as recognisable as sight, or more so; because the terms of sense and thought are distinct inwardly almost in the inverse ratio to their adequacy as descriptions of material facts. Good and evil are perfectly definite: no one misses the difference; but nature and history are utterly unseizable, both in their totality and in their detail. When nominalists say that an essence, before it is exemplified, has no identity, so that reference to *it* is impossible, they are as usual reversing the relative status of essences and facts. It is the facts that cannot be identified or divided before they arise and are caught in some net of essence, at least in the net of chronology and topography; but essences supply the very definitions by which the facts may be said to define themselves, and may become possible themes for discrimination. Events are determinable physically by their antecedents and by the inherent contingency of all change; essences are the types and standards of that determination.

The epithet *universal,* justly given to all essences in as much as each may be exemplified in any number of instances, when that epithet is confused with the epithet *general,* leads to a great deal of false refutation. "John" is a general name for all Johns, but not for any essence. As the old nominalists said, it is only a sound. As such it no doubt has a modest musical essence, but it names no essence of Johnniness. Universal terms such as man, green, or good, on the contrary, are names of essences. They evoke a determinate character, having a determinate moral range; and it is for possessing this character, or others of the same universality, that any fact can be perceived and distinguished. They are forms of being, not names for groups of particulars. "Being" itself, the highest universal, it not a name for all particular beings but a name for their very sensible common essence, by which each being and all beings together are weighted and distinguished emphatically from nothing. Pure or universal Being, far from being empty, is pregnant with all characters and distinctions, and its essence cannot be fully exhausted by anything less. But it is an essence, not a substance or a principle of existence. Infinite essence excludes existence by admitting all contraries, rising above their contrariety by embracing them all. Existence endeavours, as it were, to make up for being contingent and onesided by being unstable, as if dying to be all things at least in turn; but it has to die in order to be born again, and can probably never exhaust the variety of essence even in infinite time.

A worse confusion, fostered by a deeper passion, overtook this subject in the seventeenth century, when the word idea began to change its meaning and to designate not a datum but a perception, not an essence but a moment of spirit, not a universal but an event. There was indeed an event, a moment of spirit, or a perception involved in *seeing* an idea; and this personal and subjective circumstance, in a Protestant or romantic age, became absorbingly interesting, to the exclusion of logic, and ultimately even of physics. Nominalism then passed into psychologism. Spirit was explained away, as well as matter, and the universe was reduced to turbid psychological atoms, conceived by drowning spirit in each given essence, and at the same time hypostasising this essence into a moment of spirit, a moment that felt, saw, and knew itself. The mystery now was, whence any of these moments drew the knowledge that it evidently had of the others, and of the order, and the many parallel lives, in which they all seemed somehow to find their places. Technically there ought to have been only a greater or lesser complexity in each sensation, as in the monadology of Leibniz; and transcendentalism would logically follow. But this new philosophy was not technical, rather literary, humanistic, and above all anticlerical; it had ample means of thriving in its logical impotence, for it always kept one foot planted in common materialism and common assumptions about the course of nature, while the other foot stirred the shallows of prevalent sentiment. These appeals were more cogent in fact than they may seem in theory; they were virtually an appeal to materialism, capable of bringing philosophy round to its sound beginnings in antiquity. For after all, what is feeling but some strain in living matter, raised by the endeavour after specific form into a moral unit?

Professor Edman, Professor Vivas, and Doctor Munitz represent this historic movement in the form it has taken in America under the influence of Dewey. In what they write I feel the pressure of subterranean forces, not only legitimate in themselves but on the whole such as I should look to for healthy progress in the life of reason; only that the negative part of their position is narrowly partizan and the positive side rudimentary. Their personal animus against me is the more noticeable in that Edman and Munitz had previously published appreciative studies of my writings, showing a proper independence of judgment on their part, without impatience or misrepresentation. Perhaps the times have brought on a fresh wave of zeal in political and racial matters that sweeps aside superficial sympathies and exposes the hidden lines of cleavage in the depths. Or perhaps views that in some ancient author would have seemed merely commonplace or antiquated are resented in me, because these critics had found other things in my books that sounded modern, and that they had innocently appropriated as if compatible with their own principles; so that now they attribute to incoherence or to treason in me what is due to an old misapprehension of theirs. Taking this line, Munitz in particular has ingeniously refuted me out of my own mouth, searching in the most out-of-the-way corners for something of mine that might seem to contradict me, and subjecting me to a retrospective cross-examination. He does it admirably, and if ever he should wish, like me, to abandon the thankless teaching of philosophy, I am sure he might make his mark as a prosecuting attorney. He almost persuades me that, without feeling it, I may have become a different person, intensely and clearly as I seem to myself to have remained the same. I should say that, during a long life, I have expressed in turn different sides of my nature, and developed different parts of my innate philosophy. But let us suppose with James that I was rotten in 1900 but sound in 1905, and with Banfi and Munitz that I was rotten again in 1920, and doubtless much more so in 1940. Nevertheless this method of invidious comparisons of oneself with oneself, leaves me under the form of eternity, like the curate's egg, "excellent in parts;" and what more can a human being aspire to?

However, let me examine one or two of the spots that, to the pragmatist, seem so diseased. I somewhere sigh at the sad contrast between the opinions of mankind and the real course of nature. On this, Munitz asks: "What does it *mean* to compare beliefs with nature?" It certainly couldn't mean that the *acceptance* of an opion by anybody at any moment was not a part of the course of nature, if this be understood to comprise the whole flux of existence, physical and psychological. But the interesting thing about opinions is not their numerical existence and position in the natural world, like trees in a wood, but the remarkable fact that they are opinions about something not themselves; so that when these opinions are reported to a third person he may easily compare them, *in their ideal deliverance*, with their intended objects, provided that these objects have been independently reported to him also by perception or science or history. In this way every man continually compares people's opinions, including his own, with the facts; and this without instituting any ultimate criterion either for the truth of memory and history, which report the opinions, or for the truth of perception and science, which report the facts. We inevitably assume a sufficient indicative truth in both reports, without minding their conventional symbolism and extreme inadequacy. Opinions have to be symbolic and inadequate because they are phases of animal life and not reproductions of their objects. Nature reproduces itself by generation or derivation on the material plane. When it creates feeling and thought it passes to the moral plane of comment and enjoyment.

This fact furnishes an answer to the further question as to what it can mean to judge all opinions to be fictions. They are all creations of some living psyche, of human senses and passions stimulated and controlled by external facts. They therefore are indicative, first, of the life of the organism, its well-being or distress, and secondly of the character of the environment, expressed in the language of psychic life. All thinking is originally poetic in texture, but not all is equally penetrating or wise in describing the course of nature, not even of that part of nature formed by the accompanying flux of opinions.

All this follows from materialism, which regards appearances as derived from realities and indicative of them, but not as substantial in themselves. Such is the great *lesson* of experience; but it imposes discriminations and discloses derivations; whereas for a hurried empiricism everything is grist for the verbal mill, and there is a perfect democracy of items, as in a popular newspaper. Experience abounds, and teaches us nothing.

In regard to essences in their own sphere, Munitz asserts that the notion of pure Being and that of a realm of essence are errors. Can a concept be an error? If I do not predicate it of anything existent, am I not free to entertain it? And can I help entertaining it, if it distinctly presents itself to my thought? It is an old story that the concept of Being is the concept of nothing. But the word nothing has itself a definite meaning: it denotes the absence of something expected. Taken absolutely, it denotes the absence of everything expectable. Everything expectable would be a fair synonym for the whole realm of essence; so that if when I mention pure Being pure Nothing were in my mind (which is not the case) this specific datum, Nothing, would involve a reference to all possibles, that is, to all other essences. I need not pursue this subject. Bergson has elaborately shown us the psychological antecedents that make Nothing mean emptiness; and Heidegger, another "living philosopher," has traced the dialectics of this notion. I will only observe that the whole force of this obstinate controversy lies in taking Being to mean existence. "Nothing" *existing*, any universal, any eternal essence, *existing*, would indeed be a contradiction in terms; when we say that essences exist we mean that they appear, that something moving and existing has put on that form. Thus the whole Eleatic and mystically monistic tradition is open to the nominalist refutation, because it confuses Being with substance. Some persons, both nominalists and realists, seem congenitally unable to distinguish a particular from a universal, an occurrence from a character. Thus Munitz repeats that I propose a "metaphysics" of essences, and that I "hypostasise" them, although he has quoted my definition of them as non-existent. Further words would be wasted.

My type of philosophy is perhaps better described by Vivas than by Edman and Munitz. He looks at me more coolly and from a greater distance; and while he denounces my principles as leading to a total bankruptcy of his own, and as now happily superseded by those of nobler and younger philosophers, yet he sees what my principles are, and I am condemned without being misrepresented. Only in some points not adequately developed in *The Life of Reason* does the interpretation go astray. When, for instance, I say or assume that reflection and reason have important consequences, I am not contradicting my doctrine of the material inefficacy of consciousness or spirit. Reflection and reason are forms taken by life, they are psychic processes in organisms, involving all sorts of physical relations and potentialities. They are not clear hypostatic *results* of these processes such as consciousness and spirit are. That a man is reflective or rational appears in his whole behaviour during long stretches of time; an idiot does not speak or act like intelligent people. Yet who knows what intuitions, what moments of spirit, may not sometimes visit an idiot or a wild animal? These are things that God only knows; they are laid up in the treasury of truth. In a word, the psyche must not be confused with the spirit. Spirit has in my view the status that Dewey assigns to "consummation;" only that I think this consummation is not rare or occasional but accompanies the whole orchestration of life, often discordant and distressful, sometimes pure and harmonious. Clear data are the high notes, the distinguished recognisable phrases, caught in this complex and unstable moral resonance, where all is actual and nothing is potential; for the whole is a voluminous drift of sensation, the *feeling* of what we are doing, suffering, or thinking. The thinking, suffering, and doing, on the contrary, as organic processes, are integral part of the dynamic world. The psyche, in my system, belongs to the realm of matter. Only the spirit is immaterial, being the moral fruition of existence, as incapable as an essence or a truth of modifying the movement that evokes it. At the same time, the psychic synthesis or redirection of action that subtends that spiritual sensibility and is often called by the same name naturally works out its consequences in the material world where it belongs. Sensation, passion, and thought are therefore efficacious materially in so far as they are material, but not in so far as they are spiritual.

In conclusion, I would point out a general psychological reason for the recalcitrancy of positivistic minds on the subject of essences. Spinoza says that the idea of a horse involves belief in the existence of that horse. It does, I should say, if you have an irresistable impulse to get out of the horse's way or to mount it. In other words attention, if wholly directed by the exigences of action, hypostasises its data. The active man therefore cannot understand that something given in idea should not exist in fact. And yet it never exists simply because it is given, although it often is given because, in some object, it exists. More often, however, it has no such embodiment, and borrows existence, as pain does, only from the wholly dissimilar life of its organ. Therefore in a disillusioned analytic mind attention intently fixed on the given, far from inducing belief, induces definition of the given, and suspension of all belief; for now what in animal life was a mere incident in action has become absorption in intuition, and belief in existence has turned into contemplation of essence. I happen to be able to do this trick and to enjoy doing it; which by no means implies that I refuse ever to trust perception or to believe in facts, when the facts really impose and justify such belief, which is not always. I do not, then, substitute essences for things *in rerum natura;* but as Aristotle says, the the mind can absorb only the forms of things. It is for the body to deal with their matter.

VII. Relation to Platonism

Here let me put in a word about some inaccuracies or partialiities pointed out by Professor Sullivan in my apprehension of Platonism. He shows a perfect understanding of my essences, but thinks that I have exaggerated the difference between my doctrine and that of Platonic Ideas, in as much as I allege that these Ideas were turned into powers and limited to moral or zoological norms. In fact, Plato explicitly introduced souls or deities looking at the Ideas as models and fashioning things after their image; and it was these souls or deities, not the Ideas, that were regarded by him as powers. Moreover, Plato identified Ideas with numbers, and in this direction admitted an infinity of them, and did not limit them to forms of the good.

Verbally, except perhaps in regard to the "infinite," these emendations are necessary, and I plead guilty to having treated Plato (and all other philosophers) somewhat cavalierly, not at all from disrespect or quarrelsomeness or lack of delight in their speculations, but because my interest has seldom been strictly philological or historical. I have studied very little except for pleasure, and have made my authors a quarry or a touchstone for my own thoughts. My lesson from Plato in particular was learned in 1897 and in the years immediately following, when the experts did not tell us what they tell us now, and when I was meditating the *Life of Reason* and intent on ethics to the exclusion of ontology. I therefore overlooked almost on purpose the Pythagorean side of Platonism and dwelt only on the Socratic side, as if doing Plato the justice to retain the part of him that seemed sound. I have since seen the egotism of that procedure, and the danger of it. The non-Socratic cosmological elements in Plato were the most influential and perhaps the most profound.

Granting this, does it follow that Platonic Ideas were not conceived to be powers or to exercise any attraction over the material world? I confess that merely to put the question seems to me to answer it. The gods and the souls that intervened were a part of the cosmological machinery conceived to transmit the vivifying and moralising influence of the good to this nether world. Nor did I overlook these intervening deities or souls merely because they were mythical. Myths were not meant to be false; they were to be as true as conjecture could make them. Plato was in the same case in his cosmology as Dante in describing his *Inferno:* he unhesitatingly believed that something of the kind existed, yet was well aware that his account was poetically inspired and not revealed to inspection, like sensuous or mathematical objects. The Ideas themselves, which were originally pure essences, became mythical when they were set up to be existences and models. We learn in the *Timaeus* that the first of all distinctions is that between what is always identical with itself and immutable and what, on the contrary, is in flux and indefinable. This is the precise distinction I should make between essence and existence; and then power would belong only to the latter, since for me eternity and ideality, by definition, remove essences from the dynamic cycle. But for Plato the distinction lay rather between reality and appearance, between substantial being and elusive phenomena; for he was a disciple of Parmenides as well as of Socrates. For him Ideas were formative principles at the heart of things, ruling alike over gods and men. And if we use the words "make" and "govern" in a logical sense, this is actually the case: for only the recognisable ideal characters dominant in things can lift a knowable or habitable world out of the waters of chaos. The danger is that in a mind intent on these "formal causes" that "make" things and virtues to be what they are, language and reverence are apt to slip into a teleological myth, in which the *logical character* or essence that renders the cosmos a cosmos will be turned into a *dynamic agent* imposing that character upon it. And when once characters or essences are conceived to exist prior to things and apart from them, it becomes difficult not to personify them: for how should an Idea not embodied in matter work or even seem to exist except by presence to a mind? Yet the operation of Ideas through minds is just as metaphysical and miraculous as their operation would be through an intrinsic magic; and this dynamic idealism has always been my bugbear in traditional philosophy.

When anybody sees or thinks anything, does the idea impose itself on the mind or does the mind form the idea? In a purely literary psychology, for which mind means the passing consciousness and idea the passing datum, those two expressions would be synonymous; for then neither that mind nor that datum could have pre-existed or could have exercised any power; nor could either of them survive the flash of actuality in which they arose together. But if we assign to the idea not merely logical self-identity and eternity, but a privileged and everlasting seat in heaven with a quasi-divine ascendency and claims to recognition, then it might seem that, as in Neo-Platonism, the Ideas poured influence down upon all souls, and imposed themselves on human reason, whenever a soul came, so to speak, within their range, just as material objects are conceived to impose themselves on the senses. The Ideas would then be the constant and guiding powers over thought; yet the soul too would be a condition of their manifestation to us. A blind man cannot see the sun, and an irrational soul cannot see the necessary relations between one essence and another. The cause of blindness or of intelligence would then be found in the soul. The soul, like a seed, would possess a heritage: and Plato, like the Indians, was rich in myths to explain this heritage as the fruit of a previous influence exerted by the Ideas upon the soul, as in the *Phaedrus*, or of previous free but ignorant choices made by the soul, as at the end of the *Republic*. It would be only in the latter case that any power not that of the Ideas would be manifested in the world; but this power of blind choice in souls, like the power of matter, would seem to be wholly negative. It was the power to fail. I think, then, that at bottom Platonism assigns all creative power to the magic attraction of Ideas.

My naturalism pursues the opposite course. Sense and reason unfold themselves according to the endowment of the psyche; and this endowment is due, not to the influence of ideal objects, which are non-existent, but to the spontaneous formation, in living nuclei in matter, of organs fit for action and observation. All power lies in the inner unrest of matter, finding some momentary equilibrium, and establishing the slow and tentative life of nature, within us and without.

When the ideas were identified with numbers, did they become "infinite?" I know nothing of ancient mathematics and little of modern; but certainly what Plato called infinite, boundless, or indeterminate cannot be identified with the infinite series of whole numbers as we conceive it today. The infinite, for him, was the logically indistinct and therefore detestable; whereas I understand that the infinite series of numbers, though not itself a number, is a perfectly exact concept or Idea, such as may figure unambiguously in calculation, with eternally fixed ideal relations; and such an Idea would not have been open to the reproach of being "infinite" in the sense of ill-defined. Nor is my realm of essence "infinite" in that evil sense; on the contrary, my intention is to clarify and render perfectly distinct all the characters conceivable or noticeable, and thereby to remove from Platonic Ideas and Pythagorean numbers the important element in them that was not ideal and not numerical. For in being represented as the substance of things and the ruling principles in nature and morals, those terms became partly opaque, potential, and material. The Idea of justice, for instance, might exhibit a number, one having a special configuration and harmony in it; but then it would prove much more than a mere number, by virtue of the consequent aesthetic virtue and moral signification; and we know how privileged even such modest numbers as 3, 7, or 10 could be and what empire they could exercise over fate. If there seems to be something superstitious about this magic assigned to particular numbers, their preeminence would become an honest matter of fact recognisable by natural science, had those numbers been actually adopted by nature and were they the specific ratios essential to the stones of an arch or the strings of a lyre. Form unmistakably governs the world when it is the form of matter. In this direction Pythagorean speculation, intent on the secret mathematics of nature, with the Greek love of purity of line and of vital harmony, foreshadowed the most exact physics and the least superstitious morality. I admire the insight of those poetic sages, when having observed that numbers solved the mystery of the planetary courses and the mystery of music, they extended the empire of number to the whole universe, even to the depths of the soul and of matter. This is what I mean by saying that the Pythagorean strain in Plato was perhaps the most profound. It made for the roots of life, it was *physical* investigation; whereas the Socratic strain played with the facets of words and of moral sentiment and failed ignominiously in natural science and in political practice. It had neglected matter and failed to trace *there* the particular mathematical ratios that are vital to real things.

A further point made by Sullivan, if pressed, might penetrate to the heart of the Platonic philosophy and of mine also. I had said that "to this descendant of Solon the universe could never be anything but a crystal case to hold the jewel of a Greek city." As if in opposition to this, Sullivan urges that "Plato's ideal state was meant to serve the interests of its members and specifically in the case of the rulers, their interest in pure science." Yes, indeed: that is axiomatic; and when I spoke of a Greek city I too was thinking of the life of the spirit there, not of the walls. My point was that those walls circumscribed the spirit too tightly, oppressed it with pervasive terror and a vain ambition never to be conquered, never to change, never to disappear. If that Nocturnal Council ever looked at the stars, it was for omens of danger, or for favourable conjunctions; and if those withered old astrologers thought they had fathomed the secret ratios and proportions from which the good might flow, they did so as priests, inquisitors, and fatherly physicians of the soul. They were *Guardians*, not poets, lovers, or free philosophers. They were sad Greeks. We may catch a glimpse of this in the legislation against irreligion proposed by Plato in the *Laws*. There were three kinds of impiety: to deny that the gods existed; to assert that they took no thought for mankind; and to pretend that by gifts or incantations they could be won over to protect evil-doing. Those who might have fallen into these errors through ignorance or sophistry were to be segregated and subjected to a fresh education. The incorrigibles were to be put to death and their bodies cast unburied beyond the limits of the state. The third kind of impiety in particular, when it was deliberate imposture, deserved a thousand deaths, because it brought ruin on the city, the family, and the individual soul. Be it observed that in distinguishing these three kinds of impiety Plato shows scant respect either for tradition or for speculative probability. According to universal tradition it is far from impious to implore and to propitiate the heavenly powers in the hope of particular favours: and who shall draw the line between divine favours granted to our aspiration and those granted to our weakness? And as to speculative probability, the philosophers and the poets, for once in agreement, had spoken at pleasure of numberless gods and of only one, often identified with the All. Nor was it philosophically impious to conceive superhuman spirits happy and perfect in themselves, and unmoved by human troubles: Aristotle and Epicurus were soon to come to this conclusion. A disinterested worship of perfection and a spiritual union with it composed, however, only a speculative religion, and one politically futile. It promised nothing to the people, and it threatened nothing. Therefore in Plato's ideal city it was to be suppressed: and legislation guided by political considerations was to impose, under terrific sanctions, the only authorised conception and cultus of the gods. Gods not enlisted in the service of the city-state, though nature might seem to be full of them, were to be banished from the universe and from the heart. Thus the exclusive sovereignty of the Socratic Ideas, or forms of the good, as established by law, was to be preached persistently, in the trembling hope that it might never be questioned, at least not within those walls.

I think, then, that my metaphor about a jewel in a crystal case was not unjustified. A jewel is something natural and precious, and so is any traditional polity or morality; the artifice lies only attributing to it an absolute price, and demanding that, encrusted as we have encrusted it, it should be preserved and worshipped for ever by posterity. Had Plato admitted that essences are infinite in variety, and that nature may flower at different times and places into different forms of the good, his ideal republics need not have been so tight and harsh in their moral economy, so artificial, or so tormented by a thousand fears. If we think that our moral ideas govern the world, or ought to govern it, we shall endeavour to give to our institutions and to our thoughts the fixity of essences; we shall study hygiene and politics not on earth by experiment but in utopias evoked by irresponsible eloquence; and we shall imagine that the heavens watch over our efforts, and crown them with approval if not with success. Such illusions are not necessary to the simple integrity of good people and of brave nations; they were not necessary to the many lawgivers and reformers in those real and flourishing Greek cities that Plato looked back upon; but in desperation at their inevitable decline, he dreamt of substituting for them an eternal city. Had he been more docile to the ways of nature, he might have retained in his ideal more of what had rendered those many cities so beautiful in their youth: the spontaneous spirituality of intuition (which he certainly loved) and the measured expression of all the passions. Then the ideal good need not have been realised only by a few desiccated doctrinaires entrenched in a tower. The young and the inspired might have realised their perfection also; it would not have been denied to women and children and slaves: they might all have touched it, I mean, in passing, which is all that the wisest soul can ever do, or the happiest city.

VIII. Criticism

I am glad that at least one of my critics in this book has criticised my criticism. A critical habit is perhaps more spontaneous in me than a constructive one. I like to lean on the works and opinions of others, as a civilised man prefers cooked food to raw. This does not absolve the private stomach from its digestive functions; and the critic, unlike the passive disciple, cannot depute to others his responsibility for his judgments; but at least he is not guilty of inventing his subject-matter, and the free play of his mind, buffeted by other minds, runs less risk of becoming absolute. This secondary place of criticism, like that of reflection in general, has its prerogatives. Without laying claims to genius, the critic gains a certain comprehensiveness, and the spontaneity of taste in him, without being suppressed, is challenged and enlightened. He becomes social, yet intercourse for him never reverts to a mere contagion between persons; it turns into a contact btween divergent minds, where his own character and intellect remain as dominant as in soliloquy. He is free to be as selective, as humorous, as satirical as he likes, and as rich in comparisons. He is placing other men in a medium of which they were not aware, and yet which, in the realm of truth, really surrounded them. Any foray into that realm, however limited and momentary, makes its little discoveries not only about others but about ourselves. It sharpens our wits and clarifies our allegiances, and it makes a beginning in putting our own principles, as well as those we are criticising, where they respectively belong in the family of possible principles.

When no criticism exists, as in ages of faith, there may be any amount of genius and learning. Then studious minds will produce anthologies, compendiums, paraphrases, or orthodox commentaries and concordances of the received texts; while inspired minds will catch and continue the inspiration of the prophets with an originality that humbly thinks itself pure fidelity to the primitive revelation. The sense of continuity will drown the sense of divergence to an extent astonishing to the eventual critic. Yet the new prophets, each claiming to be orthodox, will inevitably quarrel with one another, until criticism finally awakes, to comparate them with their common sources, and to judge these sources themselves, not taking them at their word, but placing them again in the common world in which they had arisen. Knowledge of this common world, and of the human passions that govern it, is presupposed in all criticism; and this implicit criterion must be acceptable to the public addressed, if the whole criticism is not to fall flat, or to seem a mere exhibition of dogmatism.

This, I suspect, has happened to Professor Schaub in regard to my little book about *Egotism in German Philosophy*. He says that the only egotist is myself; and it is quite true that I was writing as a critic, not as an expositor, and my criticism had a clear criterion, namely, my naturalism; so that my problem was to make precise, within the frame of my naturalism, the place and quality of this remarkable philosophy. When I said that I endeavoured to understand German philosophy, I by no means intended to lay aside, even for a moment, my own dogmas, which I had already examined and reduced to the minimum compatible with honest living, that is, to materialism. But materialism is a humble philosophy, and cannot wish to dictate to matter, like rationalism, what it shall be and what it shall do; so that the devout materialist endeavours to understand every part of nature from within, being sure that nothing existing, not even German philosophy, when truly understood, can alienate him from the heart of nature. This principle leads me to conceive life, knowledge, and spirit as absolutely natural growths, and not to grudge them their exuberance, as a partisan materialist might do. I gladly observe, for instance, the transcendental relation of spirit to all feeling and knowledge; on this point my sympathy with German philosophy is complete.

But when this philosophy proceeds to rescind the dogmatism inherent, and justly inherent, in knowledge (since knowledge truly indicates the relation of the knowing animal to other things) and when consequently knowledge is subjectified and conceived to be intuition of its terms rather than discovery of its objects, and when finally spirit is declared to be absolute and the only possible form of existence, then I smile at the fatuity and blindness of such a pretension and I call it egotism.

Criticism, by a transcendental necessity, is thus internal to each logical organism or rational mind; and the choice between different ultimate criteria cannot be made critically but must be spontaneous and sanctioned only by the material and moral consequences. That these follow and that they are good or bad must be a direct dictum of the intellect or the heart; and the expression of such first principles cannot be criticism but only confession or propaganda. Criticism is therefore confined, in a certain sense, to the circle of one's intellectual kindred, and can display the dialectic of other assumptions only vicariously and within one's home logic; although the brilliancy and humour of this logic may win over less nimble minds, as the dialectic of Hegel has done in so many quarters, not by its cogency but by its spice. This would not happen to minds not previously at sea and adrift in their allegiance. Firm minds and complete philosophies are as incapable as rival actresses of being disturbed by the criticism they may pass on one another.

It is with such unclouded and innocent conviction that Schaub rebuts my criticisms. He thinks them insults, and naturally resents them. It never occurs to him to ask what presuppositions and preferences in my mind could have led me to say those unmannerly things. In fact, he appears to have no notion of the sort of criticism I have been describing, and seems not to regard my sketch as criticism at all, but thinks it was meant to be, or ought to have been, exposition. I wrote a monograph on *Egotism*, in order to define that principle and show its relation to transcendentalism and to subjectivism in general; an inquiry that constitutes a criticism of German philosophy and, at least in intention, not a superficial criticism. But if taken for a general history or treasury of philosophy in Germany my book becomes indeed incredibly bad. What could have induced me to undertake so laborious and needless a task? The truth is that the nordic imagination has always interested and attracted me, because of a certain romantic mystery or aroma, as I called it in my preface, that hangs about it: and Schaub is entirely misled by his feelings when he thinks that this aroma is *foul* in my nostrils. On the contrary, it has the purity of a wintry atmosphere, rarefied but dark and comfortless, spiritual yet not bringing any sense of liberation or peace. This was the ambiguous character that I wished to explain to myself and to disentangle. But my reviewer demands the familiar tone of the texts, and when he finds something so utterly different he thinks I am denying the breadth of professed dominion over nature and history that characterised the German philosophers, or even that I had never heard of the distinction between the universal and the private self, as if my old teacher Royce had ever stopped talking about it, and as if that projection of the ego into the universe or the empyrean were not the height of egotism. But the nature of egotism apart, I freely confess that it forms only one strain in German philosophy, which I expressly select for study; I therefore discuss one minor writer in whom that strain was vulgarised and perverted, as it naturally tends to be in politics and morals; and I omit more important writers in whom it was comparatively absent; I make many observations about German philosophy that the German philosophers themselves never made about it, although they may have made such observations about one another; and if one of them wrote under a pseudonym I fail (is it from ignorance?) to mention that fact, which would have been such a plum for the puzzled student preparing for examinations.

If some good critic in sympathy with German idealism, such as Croce or Collingwood, had chanced to notice my criticism, he could easily have refuted it from the idealistic point of view. He would have understood that what I call *Egotism,* like what Hegel called *The State,* is an Idea, and that I conceive it to be a misplacement or corruption of transcendentalism. If now this good critic had been an absolute transcendentalist, he would at once have pointed out that my criticism was based on inadmissible assumptions, namely, on the alleged independent reality of nature and of truth; whereas every transcendentalist knows that nature and truth are also Ideas, and that all we can legitimately do with them is to develop their dialectical relations to other Ideas, without ever dreaming of hypostasising them dogmatically into independent realities. What I call egotism, therefore, would not be an abuse of transcendentalism but transcendentalism itself consistently carried out. It would be criticism made absolute.

Yes, that is just what I maintain; but the argument of the first part of my *Scepticism and Animal Faith* is precisely that no criticism can be absolute, and the same is the virtual thesis of my *Egotism*. Criticism is necessarily relative to presuppositions which must be accepted on faith; and the absolute critic or egotist would be reduced to solipsism of the passing moment (as he will never admit that he is reduced) unless at least he believed dogmatically in his own past; while in fact all egotists believe dogmatically in the independent reality of all the rest of human experience, apart from their Idea of it. They are therefore wretched critics of themselves in thinking they are pure critics, and they ought to begin by beating their breasts and confessing that they are dogmatists.

However, not all lovers of German idealism are absolute transcendentalists. Many religious people accept or admire this philosophy as a sublime dogma; and what they place beneath the open spectacle of nature and history is not the transcendental ego, with its categories and postulates, as described by Kant, but rather the Platonic Ideas or Logos, which being imperfectly manifested in nature and history, may in turn be dimly apprehended by human observers. A good critic taking this view could also have refuted my criticism, without denying its justice in respect to absolute transcendentalism; for in his eyes my error would lie not in being a dogmatist but in cleaving to the horrid dogmas of materialism instead of being a good dogmatic Platonist or Christian. And he would defend the Germans for their speculative breadth and courage, while admitting that they were too romantic and too much given to a cloudy pantheism.

This position is not inwardly suicidal, as absolute transcendentalism is; but it is hard to maintain critically together with other dogmas that are indispensable in life. It is like the position of Catholics in regard to criticism of the New Testament. This criticism rests on the same naturalistic assumptions as my criticisms of the Germans. Catholics are perfectly free to reject it, if their faith in Catholic dogma transforms for them the criterion of probability, and they can think it not only possible but an all-solving truth that God should have become man in Galilee and that miracles should rain down upon earth thicker than bombs. It is a question of good sense and sincerity. When these have laid a dogmatic foundation, it becomes possible for criticism, on that basis, to study the infinite dialectic of the accredited Ideas.

IX. Humanism

My earlier manner, humanistic and historical, was speculatively vague. It might seem sometimes to substitute literary psychology and criticism for physics or natural philosophy. In my first prose book, *The Sense of Beauty*, as Professor Boas shows, I skirted psychologism rather dangerously; my Catholic and pagan affinities kept me from being immersed in it, but I was somewhat besprinkled. Besides, I was still a young man and never naturally a prophet or reformer. It would have been unsuitable for me to parade my fundamental allegiance to matter and to spirit in a way offensive to the prevalent optimisms; nor was this allegiance as yet quite explicit in my own mind. There remained, therefore, only literary psychology and criticism for a common stamping-ground. After all, both spirit and matter were implied in what was termed "experience." Reasonable things might be said about the ways of mankind without metaphysical commitments and without much positive knowledge. That first aesthetical book of mine was not about the arts nor about the criterion of excellence in them. Something in me has always rebelled against the priggish habit of drawing up an honours-list of poets and philosophers, and proclaiming who is the winner. They were not running a race, and though they may have thought so they were not really practising the same art.

A relative rank may be assigned to artists of a single school by a public that has no other standards; but who shall judge that school or that public? Nor was my book even about the beautiful, in its dialectical relations, perhaps to the real or to the good; I wrote only about the *sense* for the beautiful. Literary psychology was therefore in its place here, and I followed some quaint old English treatises, Schopenhauer, and Taine.

The danger of slipping into psychologism thus became imminent, and I even used the word "association," though certainly without intending any myth about "states of mind" mating and breeding in a vacuum. Literary psychology is but a way of speaking about processes not understood at all in their genesis, but perhaps understood in their meaning, that is, in their moral relevance to one another. Now the apprehension of this relevance, as between a motive and an action, is not literary psychology, but behaviouristic knowledge of human nature. It is actions, occasions, physical events that are seen conspiring towards one Idea, which arrests and satisfies us; and we describe the process, in a dramatic fiction, by attributing a love of this Idea to the persons who were concerned in that process. It is as if we attributed a love of sunsets to the sun; because although the persons concerned were men like ourselves, and given to the same fabulations, they stood in an entirely different relation to their labours from that in which we stand to their works. Sometimes some of them may have become retrospective critics like ourselves, and judged their works somewhat as we judge them; yet how rarely this occurs, even in the most reflective artists, may be gathered from the sayings of Leonardo, so different from those of our aesthetes, so much the materialistic sayings of a workingman and a scientific inquirer.

My psychology of aesthetics and morals, even at first, was not wholly verbal, being supported by the theory of psychophysical parallelism, and by attachment to Spinoza; but I had not yet studied Aristotle or formed my present notion of the psyche. That the whole mind at each moment is wholly dependent on the existence and health of the body was indeed obvious to me; and James's psychology, in spite of his own spiritism, seemed to breathe nothing else. His neglected or abandoned theory of the emotions was an instance of this truly naturalistic and radical insight. Anger, for example, observably arises by a perfectly physical tension mounting and holding one by the throat, a blinding rush of blood, like the vertigo. The *reasons* for being angry, which might justify the feeling in subsequent argument, would never have produced it if the physical intoxication had failed. The reasons are steadily at hand, before and after the fit assails us, while the actual anger is a wave rising and spending itself materially; it initiates that violence which the reasons are supposed to bring about though not by any conceivable derivation. The genesis of that wave may be traced by observation to the primary impatience of the organism, stimulated by untoward events: an impatience that may be restrained by contrary impulses, and then suddenly let loose, not by a mere thought, but by a fresh unbidden but sensible confluence of currents in the body, producing passion, action, and eloquence.

Thus it is nature in contact with nature, and not any ideal relation between ideas, that governs human action, and the actual flow of the ideas themselves. Then, when the ideas have come, borne on the vital currents of the moment, spirit may perceive their discord or their harmony; and the absurdity or grandeur of that effusion will become clearer and more firmly fixed in reflection, as the wave of passion that brought it subsides. This makes the fifth act of the tragedy, Delphic wisdom supervening upon Bacchic rage.

Literary psychology, with its dramatic plausibilities, was indispensable to me in composing *The Life of Reason.* To have treated that subject realistically infinite information and universal sympathy would have been requisite; and ignorant as I was of concrete history and without much experience of human affairs, I had no resource but imagination, and was reduced to conceiving more or less vividly what *might have been* the feelings and the thoughts of people at certain cross-roads in their moral travels. As Mr. Cory observes, "sometimes the description is in terms of the mental history of the individual at other times it refers to the general dawning of knowledge in . . . the race." My historical manner, he thinks, did not permit a closer description or analysis of knowledge; and he finds my epistemology a little "in the air." There was also another reason for my subject-matter being in the air. My interest was not fundamentally psychological but moral; I wished to select such turns in human sentiment as poetically if not intellectually rendered mankind wiser and nobler. I was collecting materials for a utopia. I actually wrote (to the scandal of a British critic, doubtless a disciple of Hegel), that, although I studied to make my account of facts as accurate as possible, fictitious instances might have served my purpose equally well, since this purpose was to show how natural passions are fertile in moral principles. I might indeed have gone further, and maintained that fictitious instances would have been better, as the fable of the lion and the lamb with its final argument, *quia nominor leo,* is far better than any invective against some historical case of prepotency; a case where the pure essence of insolence would surely be clouded by qualifying motives, and where the historian too would probably be venting casual passions of his own, and not an impartial and tragic sense of defeated justice.

My interest being moral, the historical manner exposed me to a worse danger than that of not formulating a scientific theory of knowledge; for I might have seemed to favour the then popular notion that historical sequence is equivalent to moral progress. Yet from my earliest youth, this notion was my pet aversion: it seemed an insult to vanished honour and vanished beauty. It was precisely the taint I wished to wash out from Hegel's phenomenology of spirit. "You give great attention," a French professor once said to a friend of mine, "to the logical sequence of ideas in Greek poetry. Are you quite sure that there is any?" I was quite sure that even if the sequence of ideas in history might be called dialectical, in the sense that no prevalent idea is stable, but slips according to the suggestions of the moment into a somewhat different idea, yet this instability presupposes neither logical implication nor moral advance. Reason lives *within* each movement towards some chosen end or perfection; it does not live *between* these movements. Thus, for instance, a rapid development occurs in each language and literature towards its golden age; but no moral progress exists between each language or literature and the next; only confused material readjustments, until some new type of order begins to assert itself somewhere in the vast chaos. Moreover, these disparate civilizations need not succeed one another in single file; they may be simultaneous, if only the physical contagion and blind egotism of each of them do not lead it to devour the others, and thereby probably to lose its own integrity of soul.

The notion that a single universal vocation summons all mankind and even all the universe to tread a single path towards the same end seems to me utterly anti-natural. It has come into modern opinion as a heritage from religion; and I respect it in religion when it expresses the genuine aspiration of some particular race or, in the best instance, of spirit in anybody; but I cannot respect it as a view of history; and I positively deplore it when it undertakes to coerce spirit in everybody into the worship of some insolent local, temporary, material ambition.

Here I come to a paradox in my *Apology*, in that on this point I must excuse myself for not deserving the good opinion of some of my judges. William James was not alone in taking a romantic view of *The Life of Reason*, as if it described an evolution of human experience *in vacuo*, the world being nothing but the growing subject-matter of that experience itself. This subject-matter might indeed be naturalistic, political, biological, even material; yet it was all cooked in the angels' kitchen, and reason, like yeast in the dough, perpetually swelled the universe into a human birthday-cake, with one more bright candle every year. My historical manner no doubt lent itself to such an interpretation, legitimate in particular directions, since civilization has certainly grown (where it has grown) out of small beginnings; yet my whole purpose was to mark the *natural* origin of these improvements and their *natural* sanctions and fate. The reason I talked of was not a law or a trope describing the flux of events, but a harmony attainable at any point by the elements which the flux, at that point, might have juxtaposed. Progress was therefore not forward but upward; and it moved not toward any one form of life, but centrifugally towards every diametrically contrary form of life that nature might produce.

Progress could not, then, be universal or endless, but only episodic, divergent, and multifarious. Each development was good in its own eyes; but if they became rivals for the same matter, they became evils for one another. The only possible progress was moral or spiritual, even when rational arts were employed in transforming matter, since the *benefit* of such transformation could be only spiritual in the last resort. My humanism was entirely confined to man.

How could this humanism ever be taken for a cosmic fable or for a dogmatic morality, when the relativity of morals, learned from Spinoza, has always been the first principle of my ethics? If I am not mistaken an old equivocation reappears here which has played a great part in history. Naturalism and humanism mean order and firm precepts for a man who believes in an ordered universe and a moderately stable human nature; but for a man who thinks his passing ideas and wishes absolute, they mean anarchy. Anarchy might have been inference drawn from these principles by a radical genius, like Nietzsche, whose subjectivism had been free from prejudice; but my readers were hardly of that stamp, and for them naturalism and humanism rather meant no popery, the rights of man, pragmatism, international socialism, and cosmopolitan culture. My naturalism and humanism seemed to them to give *carte blanche* to revolution: and so they do, if the revolution represents a deeper understanding of human nature and human virtue than tradition does at that moment; but, if we make allowance for the inevitable symbolism and convention in human ideas, tradition must normally represent human nature and human virtue much better than impatience with tradition can do; especially when this impatience is founded on love of luxury, childishness, and the absence of any serious discipline of mind or heart. These are the perils that threaten naturalism and humanism in America.

Now I am far too naturalistic and humanistic in temper to rebel against luxury, international culture, or cosmopolitan socialism if they fell to my lot. If I had lived under the Roman Empire I should not have rebelled against it, and I should not have been converted to Christianity. Yet I might have seen Christianity coming, or some kindred spiritual revolution, because human nature demanded it. Luxury and culture are not self-supporting; the master-currents and trade-winds ignore them; they are the rather bitter foam of an occasional wave. And it seems to me a strange way of honouring nature and mankind to detest and denounce precisely the characteristic works of nature in man, namely, the traditional forms of his languages, religions, and governments. Such customs no doubt have their day, and it would be an unphilosophical though not ignoble passion to cling to them out of season. We must welcome the future, remembering that soon it will be the past; and we must respect the past remembering that once it was all that was humanly possible.

X. Rational and Post-Rational Morality

It is especially in regard to morals that Edman, Vivas, and Munitz feel that I have deserted the truth for the very errors that I denounced when I was a good humanist. My explanations (repeated here in the third part of my *General Confession*) far from allaying the resentment of my critics seems to have embittered it. It has become an *idée fixe*. I understand this resentment because there has really been a change in my sentiment, though none in my theory or in my allegiance to the life of reason; but I no longer tend to identify rational life with any single *Kultur*, such as the Greek. I see the truth of what Vivas says about my Hellas being a mere dream; it is not even an ideal in the sense of being a programme for action or a goal to propose for all men's aspirations. It represents only one possibility, one type of approachable harmony, such as the ideal of chivalry was also, or that of Franciscan brotherhood. Such ideals have the defect of not being realisable permanently or on a large scale. The Jeffersonian ideal of democracy might perhaps be such a dream in the minds of my critics; but they live in modern New York, where everything is miscellaneous, urgent, and on an overwhelming scale, and where nothing counts but realisation. They naturally despise any ideal that is not a living purpose. Living purposes confront them on every side in conservative phalanxes and in revolutionary hordes; and reason for them can mean only to find means for realising those purposes, or to devise some compromise for realising as much of them as can be realised together. This is exactly how the principle of moral rationality works when the premises have been accepted; but reason is also competent to criticise those premises, appealing to the voice of nature, to the aroused and clarified conscience, in each individual. This is what Socrates compelled his interlocuters to do, who in the bevy of sophisticated Athens hankered for all sorts of unrewarding things. Have my critics ever questioned the purposes of their environment? Have they ever questioned their own standards? If I had been born by chance among the Israelites in Babylon when Cyrus permitted them to return from exile, probably I should have abandoned that advanced civilization in order to return to the arid solitude of home and to the studious chants of the temple. Would my critics have done so? Or would they have remained with the majority to help carry on the important and varied business of the age? Would they not naturally have supposed, though mistakenly, that it was on that important business that the future of mankind depended?

Edman thinks that my view of the spiritual life is open to the very charge of egotism which I bring against the German idealists; and he paints a melancholy picture of the vacuity of the life to which I have condemned myself. The withered Indian gymnosophist (whom I do not much resemble in belief or in way of living) chooses death out of self-love, and by losing his individuality in Brahma or in Nirvana abandons all distinction between good and evil. This is the opposite of what I call egotism, which consists in imposing one's special categories and standards, as alone right or possible, upon all mankind and even upon God and nature. But that is perhaps a matter of words. As to the fact, I am not sure that this interpretation of salvation, according to the Indians, is correct. The texts seem to speak rather of enlightenment and bliss than of annihilation; and certainly they regard *reaching* salvation as the highest good, although it made them, or because it made them, "free from good deeds, and free from evil deeds," that is, free from the heritage that an accidental past imposes on the spirit. But to Edman it is apparently axiomatic that to lose individual existence and an accidental heritage of good and evil would be itself the greatest of evils. I should not dispute that judgment, if it be deliberate and sincere; but on the same conditions I should not dispute the Indians' judgment, either. We are at the level of radical elementary preferences, at the level of pre-rational morality.

As for my own judgment, since the first principle of my ethics is relativity, I cannot admit that such elementary differences might be reconciled morally, from the point of view of either party. They may, however, be collated by the natural philosopher, and explained by their natural conditions, the first of which is the existence of living animals with irrepressible instincts and specific capacities. It would be cruel and stupid to wish to suppress the voice of nature in any creature. If circumstances allow it to live, philosophy must suffer it to seek its appointed good. Yet this moral liberty allowed by the sceptic to others, he preserves also for himself. Scepticism no more pledges me to indifference than it does to disbelief: it pledges me only to justice and to self-knowledge. Maintaining, as I do, that morality is relative, and that the ideal moves like the zenith above the head of the traveller, I respect and require pre-rational preferences to be the nerve of all contrasts between good and evil, and of all virtue. Yet such preferences are vital not rational, psychic not spiritual; they express particular interests, that are legitimate relatively but are expressed absolutely, as befits a call to arms for the home forces. By this moral rhetoric eventual conflicts with contrary interests become actual conflicts for a critical conscience; since such absolutism in pre-rational morality condemns those who know only their own class, their own country, and their own religion to intellectual provinciality. They may be beautifully virtuous, but they do not understand the world nor their place in it. This becomes obvious to the critic, like Socrates, who loves his moral traditions, yet lives in a sophisticated or enlightened age; and then he institutes rational ethics.

It may be useful to remind the reader that by rational ethics I do not understand a set of reasonable precepts contrasted with another set that are unreasonable; I understand rather reasonableness itself, something intellectual, prudential, or even aesthetic, rather than some new or "higher" moral impulse to be substituted for the old impulses of human nature. It is *prudent* to be rational up to a certain point, because if we neglect too many or too deeply rooted impulses in ourselves or in the world, our master-passion itself will come to grief; but too much rationality might be fatal to that passion at once, before it ventured to take its chance and win the prizes that were possible. So too, the impulse to be rational and to establish harmony in oneself and in the world may be itself a "higher" impulse than others, in that it presupposes them; yet the romantic impulse to be rash, or the sudden call to be converted, might be thought "higher" than rationality by many people. Reason alone can be rational, but it does not follow that reason alone is good. The criterion of worth remains always the voice of nature, truly consulted, in the person that speaks.

I may notice, in passing, the suggestion that I confuse harmony, drawn from Plato, with adaptation, drawn from Herbert Spencer. Spencer may have given greater currency for a time to the word adaptation; but harmony as the essence of the good is a profoundly naturalistic principle: it is akin to organic health and to mystic union with the universe. Adaptation is simply the process by which parts of nature that moved at cross purposes may so modify each other as to move in harmony. It is not a question, as sentimentalists might think, of the *sense* of harmony. A drug may produce that; but real harmony, by which eventual conflicts and mutual destruction are obviated, must be partially established in the realm of matter before the feeling or the love of harmony can become a guide to rational ethics.

Now you cannot have a harmony of nothings, and rational ethics would be impossible if pre-rational morality were annulled. And as the impulse to establish harmony, and the love of order, are themselves natural and pre-rational passions, so an ulterior shift to post-rational morality introduces a new natural and pre-rational passion, the demand for harmony not merely within the human psyche or within the human world, but between this world and the psyche on the one hand and the universe, the truth, or God on the other. We have passed from morality to religion; but not so as to destroy morality, because religion itself only adds a fresh passion (reason raised to a higher power and taking a broader view) to the passions that reason undertakes to harmonise. And religion, unless it takes the bit in its teeth and becomes fanatical, will admit the need of harmonising its inspirations with the counsels of good sense: often it goes so far as to regard itself as the only safe guardian of conventional morals. That is not my view; but I see the perfect continuity of post-rational with rational and with pre-rational morality. We begin with the instinct of animals, sometimes ferocious, sometimes placid, sometimes industrious, always self-justified and self-repeating; we proceed to a certain teachableness by experience, to a certain tradition and progress in the arts; we proceed further to general reflection, to tragic discoveries, to transformed interests. For instance, poets begin to be elegiac and to insist that everything is transitory; all is vanity; even our virtues and our prayers, before God, are impertinent. All this, that might occur to Solomon, would not have occurred to Joshua. Joshua would have been sure that God was on the side of pre-rational morality, and against the foreigner. And Solomon would have agreed that, on whatever side the Lord might be, the fear of the Lord was the beginning of wisdom.

There is one suggestion that I should remove, if I could, from the account given of these matters in *Reason in Science*, the suggestion, due to my historical manner, that these phases of morality are successive, and as it were, abolish one another. The post-rational phase, I there observe, comes of despair and belongs to ages of decadence. I was thinking of the Stoics and Epicureans in contrast to the previous spirit of Greek politics; yet the fourth century B.C. was hardly an age of decadence in general, and for Rome it was a school-age. I was perhaps thinking also of Leopardi, whose pessimism certainly expressed despair; yet the nineteenth century did not pass for an age of decadence, and Leopardi's shepherd so post-rationally questioning the moon about the uses of life, represents an adolescent sentiment, a sentiment very strong and persistent in myself when I was a schoolboy. To draw the sum total of our account, and ask what do we gain, what do we lose, is possible at any moment of reflection, whatever the wealth or paucity of our experience. But it is the impulse to reflect, not the impulse to acquire or to venture, that is here at work; and reason, instead of looking for means to achieving given ends, has become an autonomous interest capable of criticising those ends. To itself therefore it seems reason liberated rather than reason abandoned; but I think that in fact reason here has lost its judicial peace-making function (which was constantly in mind in my *Life of Reason*) and has become a separate pre-rational impulse, like any other original factor in morals. Judicial political reason therefore may well turn upon reason emancipated and ask it to take its place among the constituent interests that a life or reason should harmonise.

This has always been, and remains today, my conclusion on this subject. I respect, sometimes I venerate, the philosophers or saints that have renounced the ordinary life of the world for a special vocation. They have the same perfect right, at their own risk, to do this, as artists, poets, or explorers have to sacrifice all else to a single ambition. On the other hand, the world too has a perfect right to judge and to control the ways of these inspired people; and although putting them to death is a harsh and imprudent policy, gentler and more efficacious means are not wanting for domesticating and humanising them. Rulers in disturbed countries sometimes incorporate the bandits and turn them into police; and sometimes it will suffice to give the prophets a church and a stipend for them to become the best allies of the government.

I should therefore ask Edman, Vivas, and Munitz to admit post-rational sentiment into their life of reason as an element, and to coördinate it with all the other profound and perennial elements in human nature. If they refuse to do so, it seems to me that rational life in them would itself sink to the pre-rational level. They would be fighting for a closed circle of accidental interests, established by them as absolute and alone legitimate, and fighting in the pre-rational jungle, like cats and dogs, or like prophets crying anathema to all other prophets.

This does not overlook the vital necessity of limitation and of specific moral character in each man and in each age and nation; it does not even preclude a certain intolerance, because a certain practical intolerance goes with integrity. Unlimited tolerance, in an organic society, would open the way to disintegration. But the ground on which post-rational teachings may, on occasion, be condemned by the statesman is not that those teachings are false or wrong; the statesman has no competence to pass such a judgment. The ground will be that those teachings might withdraw or withhold energies that otherwise would help to secure the common good pursued at that time and in that society. The pacifist will not fight, the mendicant friar will not earn his living, the Carthusian will refuse even to do good, as the statesman does, by talking. Yes, many a privately cherished but inopportune ideal has to be suppressed in a perfectly integrated society or totalitarian state; and as Plato banished the poets, so Edman and Munitz would banish Buddha and Christ. It is an old story. Yet the poets and the prophets, in a regimen that recognised the interests of the spirit among human interests, might unintentionally coöperate with the statesman by offering mankind a holiday from the statesman's world; and I think that as mankind is now constituted it would be most impolitic to force the engine to work under still higher and higher pressure, while closing the safety-valves that religion and post-rational philosophy would open towards the non-human. The spirit in man cannot live for man alone, and man is never happier than when the spirit carries him beyond himself. Nor need this non-human *Lebensraum* be any fictitious supernatural sphere. My personal philosophy, so severely blamed for turning its eyes away from human society, is a strict materialism; and this materialism about the universe makes it easier for me to endure and even to enjoy the materialism of the world.

Professor Lamprecht, too, dislikes the phrase "spiritual life" and thinks I was better inspired when I spoke instead of "spirituality," by which he understands "that quality which life has when it is most sensitive to the varied goods available." What does "available" mean? There would be no spirituality, though there would have to be spirit, in enjoying the food and drink on the table. Spirituality would appear if we began to enjoy these things disinterestedly and impersonally, in view of the *ultimate good* that might flow from their substance and their appearance; in other words, if we enjoyed them convivially, pictorially, intellectually. In the passage referred to I was speaking of religion and contrasting piety, or reverence for the sources of life, with spirituality, or sense for what I called ideals. In saying grace at table, we should be regarding the available goods piously: if we enjoyed them intellectually, pictorially and convivially, we should be regarding them spiritually, or as ideals. The contrast between ideals and essences forms the subject of the whole criticism levelled at me by Munitz; but I am afraid he misunderstands what I meant by ideals as much as he misunderstands what I mean by essences. In the first page of this *Apologia,* without reference to this particular controversy, I have indicated how "ideals" came to figure in my speculation. They were the stuff of poetry and religion, in contrast to material or historical facts. They were ideal negatively in being imaginative and in that sense *unreal.* But they were also ideal positively in being *better* than the reality, and expressing demands made by human nature but not fulfilled by nature at large. Now I remember a young pragmatist telling me long ago that ideals were means to ends: they were useful blue-prints for machinery to be constructed. They were plans. They were, he might have added, the good intentions with which the road to hell is paved. Undoubtedly plans, forecasts, and good resolutions are often prophetic, and when the event realises them, they are conventionally reputed to cause or to facilitate that event; although I think they merely indicate the readiness of the psyche, and of other conditions, to bring that event about. More often, however, plans, forecasts, and good resolutions go awry; the psyche and the other conditions were not really ready for such an issue. If ideals meant merely programmes they would therefore be morally futile; for a blue-print or a printed programme may be practically useful or even necessary; but as an end in itself, as a possession, it would be trivial and worthless: the sort of thing that fools collect.

Had my "ideals" not been poetic and religious, had they not

been essences more interesting than any facts, because more perfectly corresponding to the demands of human nature, there would therefore have been the strangest silliness in dwelling upon them; and perhaps my critics would not have accepted them so kindly (as right where essences are wrong) had they not kept an eye on the practical function of programmes in bringing performances about. Yet that was remote from my thoughts. The question regarded the value of the performances, when they actually took place. Did this value lie in the material assault of the fact, in the possible irrevocable pleasure of it, in its possible effects in bringing about other material assaults? I was maintaining that the value of it *for the spirit* lay rather in the "ideal" *essence* that might be evoked by that performance, when this essence actualised in thought what the labouring psyche was pregnant with, and what would remain her joy as long as she had eyes to see it. My "ideals" were therefore not means but ends; and not ends in the sense of forming the final state of an object, such as a finished poem, but in being the *good* of that finished work, that is to say, the vision and emotion that it could awaken in the mind that, at some supreme moment, understood it best. Ideals were essences, and the opposition imagined by Munitz turns only on the senses in which essences may become ideals. All are ideal in being universals, not particulars; not events but forms of events. But not all realise the demands of some psyche, not all fill the top moments of some life; so that in a moral sense the infinite stretches of essence contain few ideals. This moral ideality, being relative to appreciation, may accrue or may lapse; we may see a thing a thousand times with indifference, and then, by the maturing of an interest within us, we may see it with a sudden emotion. The essence given was at first graphic only: later it was re-exemplified in a form of beauty, containing the original essence but suffusing it with a new magic: it had become an ideal. When I say, for instance, that pure Being is the ultimate ideal for pure spirit, I am recording the infinity of the one and the infinite openness of the other; as if I had said that the ideal of knowledge was omniscience. This does not mean that we are or should be equally interested in knowing everything or in conceiving every possibility. Spirit, being a psychic faculty, cannot exist without an organ at a particular place and time, with a specific range. It would cease to exist, if it could embrace every view and every preference at once. The Indians I was following (because they are the true masters of this subject) actually aspire to the suspension of life and the equilibrium of a divine repose, something that I can sympathise with; but they sometimes identify that final peace, which is an ideal, with a longing to be merged in primeval substance, which is an unlimited potentiality; and here I cannot follow them, because the peace of the sea is treacherous, and potentiality is not an ideal, but a blind commitment.

Spirituality, then, was a word for the quality of spiritual life; and if there be any choice between the two expressions, I incline to prefer the second. Spiritual lives are facts. Psalmists, evengelists, saints, poets, philosophers in the ancient sense, have actually existed, who lived by a special light in a special fashion. Spirituality, on the other hand, is only an attribute in the air; and I doubt that it can be discerned with any clearness except in those moments of life that have a transporting quality, and that assimilate the least spiritual of us, for a moment, to those exceptional spirits. Moreover, although rare, this transporting movement of thought is intimately natural to all of us: when it comes we feel that for the first time we are ourselves; and we return to our common preoccupations as if to the routine of a prison. Nor is this taste of liberty altogether momentary. I think that the most desultory spiritual insights induce a new habit, open a path to a deeper stratum of the soul. The heart has found a truer good, and does not forget it.

Lamprecht also wonders how at one time I avow a preference for being a rational animal rather than a pure spirit, and at another time profess to have no passionate love of existence and no desire for immortality. These sentiments are personal, and if they were contradictory it would be no great matter. Who has not said of life, *Odi et amo?* But if you choose to exalt these feelings into maxims, I see no contradiction. Pure spirit does not exist, spirit according to my theory being a function of the psyche; but if you conceive a spirit without any natural place, time, or point of view, and without any moral bias, it would seem to me a useless reproduction of the truth absolute, which actual spirit lives by seeing only in perspectives and on actual occasions. The first maxim would therefore merely assert that life is acceptable: that its variability and other essential limitations do not disgrace it but enable it to be a natural enjoyment of its natural good. The second maxim affirms the same thing seen from above rather than from within. Each life has its day and its quality: it is surrounded by other lives, no less real, no less good and evil in their own eyes. Each therefore counts for something, but not for much; and a judicious mind will not think itself absolutely important or never to be superseded, or worthy of being imitated and continued by all other minds. Yet as I say, sentiments of this kind are not precepts; they belong to poetry rather than to morals. You see the force of them, as you might that of a proverb; and then you pass to something else.

For those who demand a complete code of ethics, as I do not, there is an orthodox way of reconciling the morality proper to lay life and that peculiar to a consecrated spirit. The Catholic Church, for instance, distinguishes Commandments imposed on everybody from Evangelical Counsels of Perfection, like turning the other cheek, taking no thought for the morrow, or loving your enemies, not only a little theoretically, but practically and as much as you love yourself. These counsels are ideals, and even an approach to putting them into practice would bring human life to an end. Yet they are authoritative not only for believers but for any reflective mind, because spirit suffers and enjoys as truly in one man as in another, and is equally helpless and innocent in all: at least if you conceive spirit to be, as I conceive it, the witness and not the actor in the soul. The actor is the psyche in which the spirit lives; and it is this animal psyche that *acts* even in the spirit. The spirit merely perceives and endures that action, become for it emotion and light. The more this cognisance of self and of the world gains upon the animal interests of the particular psyche, the nearer that psyche will come to putting those Evangelical Counsels in practice and the greater saint the man will be.

Another version of the relations between rational and post-rational morality may be found in the Mahabharata, in the well-known scene where two armies face each other with drawn swords, awaiting the signal for battle. But the prince commanding one of the armies has pacifist scruples, which he confesses to his spiritual mentor—a god in disguise—in the most eloquent words I have ever read on that theme. His heart will not suffer him to give the word. And then the sage, while the armies stand spell-bound at arms, pours forth wisdom for eighteen cantos; yet the conclusion is simple enough. The tender prince must live the life appointed for him; he must fight this battle, *but with detachment.*

This version has the advantage of not separating natural virtue and spiritual insight into two different lives or two strands of action or interest: the two may be lived together and in the same moment. Just as rational ethics would have no materials if pre-rational preferences were abolished, so post-rational detachment would have no occasion and no reality if men and nations had no natural passions and ambitions. You cannot be detached without being previously attached; you cannot renounce or sacrifice anything significantly unless you love it. And if you withdraw from any action it must not be from timidity or laziness; that would be giving up one vain impulse for another still vainer and more physical. Your detachment will not be spiritual unless it is universal; it will then bring you liberation at once from the world and from yourself. This will neither destroy your natural gifts and duties nor add to them; but it will enable you to exercise them without illusion and in far-seeing harmony with their real function and end. Detachment leaves you content to be where you are, and what you are. Why should you hanker to be elsewhere or someone else? Yet in your physical particularity detachment makes you ideally impartial; and in enlightening your mind it is likely to render your action also more successful and generous.

Such at least would be the case if human psyches were well-balanced, instead of screechingly one-sided, if education and custom were judicious, so that each faculty might be cultivated in the natural order and in due season, and above all if religion and morals were free from superstition, so that nothing true should be denied and nothing possible excluded. But nature is abundant and imperfect. The Indians have established castes, and Christianity has segregated the clergy and the religious orders, as society has segregated the rich and the poor. Perhaps nothing could have been achieved otherwise; yet the system involves terrible suppressions here and great corruption there. The Romans sometimes almost united in one noble figure the soldier, the statesman, and the philosopher: yet Cicero was fatuous, and Augustus and Antonines, though they did their best, were rather oppressed by their burden and almost begged to be pitied and excused. The younger Brutus and the younger Cato seem perfect heroes to many, but like all puritans in a decadent age they were rebels against destiny and thought themselves better than the gods: not a good foundation on which to build anything. Piety must never be dislodged: spirituality without it is madness. We must be content with the benefits and insights that the times afford, and suffer reflected light from other ages or from better minds to lighten a little our inevitable darkness.

This reconciliation of spirit with nature does not rest, in my view, merely on moral grounds. It is inherent in my theory of the origin and place of spirit in nature. It follows from my materialism. So long as life is only tactile and digestive, it seems to remain unconscious; but when physical sensibility stretches to things at a distance and action can be focussed upon them, impressions become signals and reports, and a sense develops for the whole field of action, in which distinct movements and qualities begin to be discerned. Spirit from the beginning has the whole world and all events for its virtual object. The particular psyche that has bred this spirit has done so in the act of adapting action to distant things; this field of action then appears to the spirit, with that psyche and the body it animates strangely central and powerful in the midst of that field. Thus the child has a different allegiance from that of the parent. The parent is Will, local, specific, blind, and indomitable; the child is Intelligence, plastic, extroverted, impartial, and universal. Up to a certain point it is useful for a busy-body to mind external things, yet it becomes disconcerting to learn too much and to begin to care for seeing for its own sake or even (worst of treasons) for the sake of the things seen. And still this disinterested speculation sends a breath of free air, a wonderful tragic light, into the dark convolutions of the psyche, always a little insecure and blustering in her egoism. She can begin to understand her housekeeping, to love it with a modesty and truth unknown before. She can become truly human, because something superhuman within her has made her peace with what is non-human outside.

XI. Physical Impression, Feeling, and Intuition

Professor Dennes complains of my "indefensible dogma that the occurrent, the existent, can never be noted;" and he thinks that, in my view, animal faith is directed upon "something with the like of which we can never be acquainted." The words "noted" and "acquainted," which are not my words, here serve to obliterate the distinction between intuition and belief, or in Dewey's language, between that which is "had" and that which is known. Mind cannot be "acquainted" with matter in the sense of "having" or becoming matter, as the voice cannot be acquainted with the throat; but mind may know matter by feeling its presence—especially in one's own body—and by forming all sorts of ideas of it, pictorial and scientific. Matter cannot be understood from within by mind, as another mind might be understood, yet it is continually and most abundantly "noted" in being minded and named. You cannot point to a dog or call him "dog" without first having your attention called to him by a physical impression; yet the image and the name so supplied by your vital faculties are not parts of the dog, and do not repeat in your intuition the probable absolute texture either of the dog's body or of the dog's mind.

This reply, though consonant with common sense, will probably seem unsatisfactory, because it involves a Scholastic revulsion from the first principles or habits of English and German philosophy. These principles or habits (for they were not adopted with eyes open to their consequences or even to their radical meaning) are implicit in that saying of Berkeley's which I have already quoted, that all the objects of human knowledge are ideas in the mind. This, understood as later idealism understood it, issues in the conviction that feelings feel themselves, that perceptions perceive themselves, that experience can touch nothing but experience, and that knowledge can know nothing but knowledge. This seems to me a self-contradictory denial of the cognitive function of intelligence; yet I could easily make Berkeley's maxim my own by a slight change of vocabulary, and say that all the *terms* of human knowledge are *essences* present to *spirit*. I almost think that Berkeley himself would have accepted this language; because the *objects* of human knowledge, for him as for me, were not really those inert essences, but self-moving substances like ourselves, establishing our existence and fortunes. They were objects of belief, of rational or moral demonstration, and by no means data of sense; they were, for him, God and other spirits. For me they are not that; but they are still the dynamic agencies that Berkeley called spirits and that I call matter.

Dennes is further scandalised by the view he attributes to me that "no animal can confront a section of the flux in direct intuition." To confront seems to mean to face physically; and intuition does not seem here to be distinguished from physical impressions; so that I should be denying that anybody could stand in the street and see a procession passing. But I am so far from denying this possibility that watching things in motion is something that still fascinates me as when I was a child, and only toys with wheels could please me; and the pleasure of watching motion comes, I should say, precisely from the challenge that motion gives to intuition, and the mastery that intuition is able to acquire over it. For your "section of the flux" cannot be given piece-meal, in discrete instants embracing no motion; it can be given only in an idea of motion. The movement occurs successively, it can be given only at once. That it is given in idea and at once follows from the fact it is given at all, that the man *sees* the motion and does not merely undergo it. In nature each moment is gone when it is past; in memory, for spirit, it is only when past that it can be present, and is then essentially present for ever. We are not always thinking about it, but we know it is true; and it is the very nature of mind, even in rapid sensation or perception, to see all things under the form of truth. Under the form of truth change and motion become visible; in precipitation, in self-abolishing flux from instant to instant, they are perfectly invisible and unconscious of themselves. In order to be present to sense, motion and transition must first be synthesised in the organism, and reported all together, as successive, to the spirit. This does not mean that a second observer, called the spirit, must exist in the brain, or in no place, and must glance so rapidly, as in the films, at traces of successive impressions, that he thinks he sees them all at once. That would eliminate succession, both in the supposed record and in the datum to the mind. A spiritual substance or ego storing successive impressions or images is perfectly unnecessary; all that is requisite is that, when the physical impressions have been successive in fact, they should appear as successive in a single intuition, arising at the end, continuing for a shorter or longer time, or perhaps not arising until long afterwards. It is such an intuition that is an instance of spirit in act; there is no spirit before such intuitions occur. The accumulated stimulus, the tensions of old and new movements superposed, the impulse to prepare for, or even to anticipate, fresh events, all gather in the psyche; and the concomitant act of the intellect is to *see* the order of those past, present, and future events, with their momentum, transitions, and proper sequence, all given as parts of one picture.

The date or duration of this intuition is irrelevant to the temporal sequence that it embraces ideally. It will last as long as the vital interest that calls it forth, or until the organ is fatigued; but however momentary and irrevocable or however familiar and often repeated, the intuition will reveal the stretch of specious time that it reveals, with the speed and direction proper to that adventure. That adventure has been lifted out of existence in being perceived, and is perceived as a part of history, real or imagined. Is it not a commonplace that sequence cannot be given in a sequence of perceptions, but only in a perception of sequence? That is only another way of saying that things as they exist cannot be data, and that in being given they have become ideas.

Suppose now that while I am idly watching a procession, a boy, too eager not to miss the useless spectacle, falls from a roof. If my eyes catch that briefer "section of the flux," the image of the boy falling may remain with me and may haunt me for years; or if the impression was only physical and marginal, and at the time I did not notice it at all, perhaps in a dream it may come to consciousness and seem to me an inexplicable creation of my whimsical psyche. My doctrine, then, is not that it is impossible to see a boy fall, but, that it is impossible without having eyes capable of *seeing*, that is of translating a physical accident into an eternal essence.

The flux of sensation, itself, in any man or society, could never be seen in perspective, with dramatic progress in it, if "sections" or "areas" of that flux had not been synthesised in some organism, becoming seminal there, to be re-evoked on occasion within a single intuition. That there exists any perception or conception of a flux proves that a knot or lump has been formed in that flux, a new self-repeating trope called life or the psyche, with spirit in it; so that a dualism arises within that monism, not a dualism of substance or dynamic process, but a dualism of quality and function. Matter, in creating mind, has discovered how it moves, and time, in discovering itself, has conceived eternity.

Professor Pepper is an appreciative critic and distinguishes my natural manner and intention in philosophising from what he calls "literal" views. Literal views, to my mind, cannot be cognitive of matters of fact: therefore, as he very justly perceives, the looseness and variety of my language indicate my sense of the seriousness of my subject, and my respect for it. I do not delude myself into thinking that I can thrust it bodily into my pocket or into my mind. When on the contrary I choose to be literal—as in talking about essence or distinguishing the meaning of the word "Is"—I am consciously playing with definitions, ramifying transcendental "problematics," like the Italian idealists, and laughing up my sleeve. I am examining the lens of our telescope, an important instrument to possess and not to make misleading; I am not examining the stars. Yet the two inquiries, in us if not in their object, inevitably affect and confuse each other; and Pepper finds my "theory of value" ambiguous. It is so ambiguous that, under that name, I was not aware that I had one. I certainly have a doctrine concerning the good, borrowed from Socrates and his School: a doctrine rather than a theory, since it professes to be a judgment rather than the description of a fact. And it concerns the good, the object of desire, rather than "value." Value is an economic and secondary term like "use." Things have or acquire values in different connections from different points of view; and a universal history of ethics and economics would no doubt contain a theory or description of values, which might be abstracted from the total picture. But I confess that when Pepper goes on to distinguish various literal theories of value, I hardly know what he is talking about. In respect to me, he ends by finding two incompatible views, one that the principle of value is interest and the other that it is rationality or harmony. On this point I may be able to make some reply.

The *source* of values, I take it, lies in the specific potentialities and demands of life in various individuals. This natural demand or affinity may be called an interest, although the word interest belongs rather to politics or trade, and it might run deeper to speak of the passions. Passions and interests in themselves are not goods, they are commitments; they may be painful and biologically erratic. If the whole soul is absorbed in any one of them, they no doubt set up a great good, which they probably miss; so that reflection and the vital aspiration for success and dominion ultimately condemn them. The master-passion, if it survives, will in turn condemn reflection and the desire for harmony as tyrants and enemies of "life." There are, then, intense values that are evils in one another's eyes. To harmonise them is simply impossible; all that the interest in harmony (itself only one of the passions) can aspire to do is to separate, to alternate, or partially to sacrifice all the passions, or some of them, so that they may collide as little as possible and that each may not fanatically call evil that which another finds good.

I should therefore say that interest, if you identify interest with all passions or valuations, was the *source* of value; while interests conceived objectively, as the ends or goals of aspiration were *identical* with value or with what Whitehead calls Importance.

As a rationality, or harmony, my critics should remember that I maintain the relativity of morals as well as of knowledge. The value of harmony or rationality, in my philosophy, can therefore be only a natural and relative value. It is the condition of any specific perfection, but not the totality of all good. Even the most narrow and rebellious passion may find its chosen good perfect, if that passion is inwardly integrated and harmonious. Harmony turns out, in this way, to be a prerequisite to precision in interest or passion itself: a physical prerequisite, not an inevitably chosen end for the world at large or for each individual. We may prefer discord, if none of our passions consents to surrender anything; or we may love harmony, and prefer that our natural hopes should enter halt and blind into the kingdom of heaven rather than that they should, all but one, perish in mortal combat.

Professor Lamprecht, in spite of his desire to be just and my desire to be clear, is puzzled by my summary way of talking about matter and essence, animal faith and intuition, as if there were nothing between, no formed things and no turbid feelings. Perhaps in my mind those summary terms are both more radical and more concrete than he takes them to be. Thus he puzzled me in turn by speaking of the *art* of intuition; but after some correspondence with him and some reflection, I think I see how he regards as a sort of eventual achievement what I regard as the common property of all mental life or as the light of consciousness itself. Yet light sometimes dazzles, we see and we do not see; sound deafens, we hear and we do not hear; and so the intuition of violence or confusion is intuition and is not intuition. Were there no intuition, we should be unconscious; yet as what we are conscious of has no name, no distinction, no permanence, intuition is frustrated in its function, and tells itself nothing, as if like the early Christians it spoke with tongues, and didn't know what it was saying. Let me call such balked intuition feeling; this term will have two advantages: it will bring out the element of intensity in all moments of spirit, which are essentially moments of life, not collections of data, essences, or objects; and it will indicate also the variable degree of articulation, clearness, or material significance possible in intuition.

Feeling I have habitually defined in my reflections—I am not sure whether I have done so in my writings—as intuition of the inarticulate. Feelings may be perfectly clear, perfectly distinct, as savours and smells are, from others that only lack of intuition fails to distinguish from them; but if they have graphic or describable form they have become "ideas," and intuition has passed from evoking a pure emotion or state of the psyche, as in pain, to evoking a character that might perhaps be the character of a lifeless thing, and a fit symbol for objects about us. This advance in descriptive power, however, does not imply an advance in importance. Intuition of the good remains, in one sense, the only important intuition, since without it all the others would be worthless: yet this is a pure feeling, and however delicately its quality may be felt in each of its instances, it always remains a direct transcript of the will, that is to say, of the total direction of life at that moment in the psyche. Subjective as it is in its source, feeling may also be of the greatest significance in action. The knowledge that men of action possess may be indispensable for executing their decisions; but the decision comes from a deeper source that can be expressed only in feeling. When we say, the die is cast, perhaps not one of our motives, not one of the circumstances, is clearly present to us; but we feel that the hour has struck, that the decision has finally been made within us, and that, come now what come may, we are in for it.

Feeling may also dominate through the multitude of articulations offering themselves, as a multitude of voices becomes a mere noise. So in daily life, intuition lights up a path, a prospect, a vaguely familiar world in its entirety, rather than any precise objects or ideas; and the masculine pragmatist may manipulate the most intricate business, as he might drive a four-in-hand, competent without theory and decided without a purpose, while the feminine idealist floats gloriously through life on the utter feeling of utterness.

These hints may suffice to show that if I neglect sensation and emotion in my analysis of knowledge it is only because I take them for granted, as I also take for granted the will and the whole complex life of the psyche. But what comes to the surface in that region is trivial unless it is dreadful, and my interest has gone rather to conceiving or learning how something worth having may take its place in the mind. My materialism regards the mind as purely expressive; there is no mental machinery; the underground work is all done by the organism, in the psyche, or in what people call the unconscious mind. I leave that to the scientific psychologists; but in *The Realm of Spirit* I have studied some of the phases through which intuition may pass in growing pure and being liberated from useless pain and distraction. I entirely agree with Lamprecht in thinking that there is an art of clarifying intuition, although this art would seem proper rather to spiritual directors than to their catechumens; for nothing can be more artless than actual intuition, as for instance the intuition of a joke, and the laughter that comes with it. But there is an art of comedy and of telling good stories well; so that we might establish an art of eliciting intuition, though hardly one of being intuitive.

About animal faith Lemprecht and others again see too much artifice, as if I had been speaking of arguments and not presuppositions. I will return to this point in replying to Russell: but the fact that animals have the confidence that we have in expecting things to remain where they are put, or to be found where they appear, does not constitute an argument, either against transitive knowledge (as being a mere prejudice and brutish) or in favour of it (as being a practical guide); it merely shows that such faith is a prerequisite to the claim to knowledge, and that life renders it inevitable. Life also vindicates and verifies it substantially; but this could not be discovered unless we trusted animal faith in the first place, so as to accept as valid the picture that it has led us to frame of the world. Undoubtedly if we took animal faith abstractedly, in a soliloquy, as a groundless instinct promopting us to pass from sheer poetry into a realm of alleged facts, it would be pertinent to ask for evidence that we might justly do so; but that is not the case; we are not called upon to issue from pure intuition into belief, but at most to discern in our actual beliefs an element of pure intuition. I neither wish to reverse this process nor think it possible logically to reverse it. We were not made out of pure spirit (which is not a material) but out of the dust of the earth. The motions of that dust, when organised, produce our sensations, with our *consequent* faith in them; we believe because we act, we do not act because we believe; a true faith, since those sensations can occur only in organisms having a real habitat. Animal faith therefore requires no special philosophical evidence of its validity. All experience, all knowledge, all art are applications of it, and reason has no competence to defend this faith, because it rests on it.

Nothing, for instance, could be more out of focus than the comment that Banfi makes when he says that my naturalism might perhaps account for animals but not for faith, and when he adds that animal faith works upon the data of experience and builds the world out of them. To understand experience and to understand faith it would be well to close your Locke and your Kant, your Pascal and your Newman, and spend a few studious hours in a zoological garden. Robert Bridges, in his *Testament of Beauty* considers what might be the sentiment of birds building their nests. He thinks it might be that they *must* gather those twigs and *must* weave them carefully together into a hollow bowl. Such is the animal basis of duty and honour; and as to faith, what could be more decided, more prospective, more fearlessly sacrificial than what every wild animal does throughout his career? When the fledglings take their first flight, has their faith first needed to build the world out of the data of experience? Does that faith not launch them rather into an existing world, a hard but tolerably stable world that has bred those instincts and encouraged that faith in the race of birds for millions of years? What data of experience do you suppose ever appear to those slight and ineffectual spirits? We ourselves, amid our thousand cross-purposes and perverse discussions, need that instinctive faith and pure courage for our simplest acts, those that we do well, such as throwing a missile, or making tools, or wooing a mate, or defending ourselves and our friends and families. Even in being startled and looking to see what's up, animal faith appears in all its purity, and shows itself to be the presupposition of all curiosity and discovery. This readiness and this pre-established reaction of the organism, given the appropriate stimulus, launch virgin courage on its course with assurance, and if consciousness transcribes that assurance, it will surely not be by giving a reason for it, nor for choosing the purpose that so suddenly possesses the soul. Reason can only trust nature within us not to be wholly out of harmony with nature round about us; and then, when the experiment is made, if we and reason in us survive, we may have learned something about the truth or error of our ways.

It is *only* animal nature that is capable of faith. Reason, if it did not assume some natural creed, could never persuade itself to believe anything.

XII. Substance

In Russell's essay, as was to be expected, his well-known incisiveness and wit have been softened by kindness, and also enlightened by old acquaintance. He can interpret my writings by his direct knowledge of my ways, where other criticis must piece out my spirit for themselves out of the letter of my books. Yet even when Russell's insight is keenest, as when he speaks of my feeling for Goethe, the very intensity of his vision concentrates it too much. The focus is microscopic; he sees one thing at a time with extraordinary clearness, or one strain in history or politics; and the vivid realisation of that element blinds him to the rest. It is true that I feel no such affinity to Goethe as I feel to Lucretius or to Dante: yet my effort to overcome this private bias was not due to deference for current opinion. I did not defer to current opinion at all in respect to Kant or Hegel or Browning or William James or Bergson; but in respect to Goethe my deliberate judgment really differed from my instinctive taste. I felt how much at home Goethe was in nature and in human life; and though such moral conformity with the non-moral might be unspiritual and even unintelligent (since spirit is the specifically human faculty in man, through which alone he can be victoriously reconciled with nature) yet moral dominion over nature requires us in the first place to conceive nature naturalistically, not morally. Then the spiritual man may become inflexible in his integrity, as Goethe was not, because he is already, like Goethe, sympathetic in his apprehension. I recognise therefore in Goethe a great master in naturalism, precisely in that moral and sentimental sphere in which the northern nations sometimes remain superstitious.

Russell himself cannot see in nature a rational support for morals, for (according to Mr. T. S. Eliot) although he has ceased to be a Christian he still belongs to the Low Church. I am aware that something of the sort, *mutatis mutandis*, has been said about myself; but my affection for the Catholic system is justified naturalistically because I regard it as a true symbol for the real relations of spirit within nature. Of Russell's religious conservatism I see signs in this paper. He appeals to the (post-rational) Gospels to support a (pre-rational) disapproval of privilege; and he evades altogether my point, in speaking of William James, regarding the difference between a (pre-rational) love and practice of goodness and a (rational) conception of a good life. A good life for mankind would require sacred institutions to canalise human interests and to enrich them. But William James was a romantic individualist, generously sympathising with cranks, weaklings, and impostors; they were entitled to prove themselves right, if they could, and to blaze a new trail through other people's gardens. This spontaneous democratic love of mankind overlooks the nature and fate of mankind in deference to their wishes; it overlooks the need of tradition and team-work. Club-spirit was odious to James; yet the faculty and the joy of clubbing together, if only for the fun of beating another club, seemed to me the one ray of genuine social freedom in the United States of his day. It brought not only a jolly "moral holiday" from commercial moralism, but it bred natural virtue, and tested it; it produced friendship. Charity without home discipline would be anarchical. We must have an exclusive order and exclusive friendships first, as Christianity had the Law and the Prophets; and then, with that fulcrum, the lever of infinite charity may perhaps move the world. When once we are sure of ourselves, we may recognise without dishonour the equally natural needs and pleasures of other creatures.

I should not have stopped to repeat these commonplaces, had not Russell expressly asked me a question that, from this moral ground, leads to the cosmological problem that I wish to discuss here. I evidently prefer contemplation to action and essences to things or people. Is this a personal preference only, or do I profess that it is right, and the contrary preference wrong? And by living, according to Aristotle's precept, as much as possible in the eternal, do I think that a man may "progressively transfer his identity from his substance to his essence"? I think (to answer the second question first) that a man can live only in time, "living in eternity" being a phrase that signifies being absorbed for a time in the view of eternal things. One of these things may be a man's own career or intelligible character, as the souls in Dante, by poetic license, are represented as able to peruse their temporal lives when themselves dead and past into eternity; or rather when living on, without yet having got their bodies back, in a second twilight world. This perusal, whether made with or without a body, is evidently a temporal event. The man or the soul cannot therefore be "transferred" into eternity or become an essence. He may merely, on occasion, forget his temporal status and peruse both temporal and eternal things in their truth, that is, under the form of eternity.

Now to answer the other question, whether a preference for this practice of "living in the eternal" is a private preference of mine and of Aristotle's, or is a universal duty or vocation, I say: neither. Every animal prefers the activity proper to his nature and organs, and it cannot be his duty or vocation to prefer any other. To say that fishes miss their vocation if they don't fly or pragmatics if they don't contemplate the eternal would be a piece of egotism in birds or in contemplative people. But within the "art of intuition," by which even the images of sense are drawn from the flux of matter, there is a natural and vital tendency to clarify images, to broaden landscapes, to put two and two together in every direction; and this, as far as it goes, evokes an essence, and trains the mind to "live in the eternal." Is it *better* to do this than not to do it? It is certainly better if you are committed to that task, or love that employment; but if you ask me whether it is better to be so committed, or so to love, I am speechless. Is it better to live than not to live? Public opinion thinks it better when we are growing richer and not when we are growing poorer; but Russell says that when we are growing rich we are growing vulgar, and I suppose it would be better not to do that. My own feeling rather prompts me to think life and to think contemplation and to think riches a good when they come spontaneously, and an evil when they are constrained or distracted; but this is only a way of avoiding the question, and leaving it to each spirit at each moment to judge for itself. I am not a dogmatist in ethics.

I am, however, a dogmatist in physics, yet not as the innocent realist is, who supposes appearances to be substantial; for my interest in essences, aesthetic or intelligible, has a curious effect on my interest in nature. I have no wish that things should be as they seem. They are, no doubt, like their appearances, or closely analogous, in some respects, such as duration, number, and distribution; but that applies only to gross aggregates on the human scale. The finer structure, the inner potentialities, the ultimate extent, origin, and end of matter escape us. Russell says of me, with wonderful sympathy: he "sighs as a lover (of knowledge) and obeys as a son (of nature)." Only this sigh is not, as Russell's more masterful intelligence leads him to suppose, a sigh of unsatisfied longing, but the warm sigh of a satisfied love (since I possess the beautiful appearance) yet a love that has not banished trepidation and wonder (since I do not possess the will of the substance). But without trepidation and wonder would love still be love? And is it not better and holier not to know all one's mother's secrets? There is also trepidation and wonder, for a different reason, in the love of any manifest essence. The vision cannot be arrested: it is a mere glimpse of something eternal. Intuition, being the perfection of life, preserves this tantalising insecurity, proper to the flux of existence; while at the same time, by supplying terms for knowledge, it reassures the spirit in regard to the dark world of nature; because the psyche reacts instantly on the relevant features of each physical impression, while unconsciously shedding the bright flower of consciousness as a useless husk.

It is a pleasant surprise that Russell should be so patient with my allegiance to substance; especially when, in regard to essence, he brings up an argument that Whitehead thinks fatal to the notion of substance, namely, that this notion rests exclusively on the grammatical dualism of subject and predicate. But neither in respect to substance nor to essence has this argument any value in my eyes. Substances and essences alike become subjects (or in modern parlance become *objects*) whenever a mind happens to think of them; and essences become predicates when they are assigned to some substance or to some more complex essence as a formal feature, or as a quality accruing to them in relation to something else. But intrinsically, according to Spinoza's definition, substance is that which exists in itself and is conceived through itself; so that nothing could be more adventitious to it than being made occasionally the subject (or object) of some assertion. Nor has grammar, to my mind, anything to do with the origin or necessity of this category. Its obvious origin and justification lie in the fact of transformation. Throughout nature change is neither complete, total, nor untraceable. Observation spans it in perceiving it; otherwise change could not be perceived nor conceived to exist, since each moment would be absolute and without relations. Existence flows, and preserves continuity in place, time, and quantity, with specific potentialities. Specific potentialities existing at specific places and times are precisely what substance means. I should adopt that for a definition of matter. This is what Mill ought to have said, putting potentiality, a physical term, in the place of "possibility," an irrelevant logical one; since everything is always possible, but only specific eventual things are *grounded* in matter; and Mill also ought not to have spoken of "sensation" as the realisation of that definite and local potency, because sensation almost always is absent in the evolution of matter, that in which the potentiality is developed being all the ensuing events.

It was doubtless a challenge to choose so brutal a term as animal faith for what I might have called cognitive instinct, empirical confidence, or even practical reason; but I think that Russell hardly perceives how fundamental a thing I was describing. He thinks it a *pis-aller,* a bad substitute, for knowledge in its principle, much as Banfi thinks essences a *pis-aller* for the unknowable objects of knowledge. But essences are nearer and clearer to me than anything that needs to be investigated, asserted, or respected; and animal faith, far from being a substitute for something more informative is the very source and principle of inquiry. Because I have animal faith, and believe there is something to discover or to obtain, I can regard my perceptions as knowledge, and can frame hyphotheses. Without such faith, all would be intuition of data and there would be no such thing for me as signification, indication, or experiment. Experience would all be idealistic experience, experience of experience, and never experience of a world.

When Russell says that, for his part, he still hopes for something better than faith, I wonder if he is not pining for those essences that, as essences, he no longer is sure of. It was he and Moore that helped me, in 1897, to grind fine and filter Platonic Ideas into my realm of essence; but now that these pure logical entities have recovered, in his eyes, their metaphysical bodies, and have become constituents of nature, does he hope to reduce nature to evident data? Some neutral entities, some essences, are data; and by hypostasising them into substances or into moments of spirit, we might turn them into constituents of nature, probably as strains or movements in the brain; yet the vast majority of neutral entities would never be given, and how, without faith, could they be posited or believed to exist? I prefer to leave substance to be what it likes, including the atoms or the seeds of ideas in my brain, and to appropriate only these ideas when they appear. Our love of appearances—and science, like sense, can yield only appearances—should be somewhat light, like the appearances themselves. They may be charming and may fulfil their function perfectly, like lady-loves of an hour, to be embraced with pleasure but not with passion and dismissed with thanks but not with tears. Grave loyalty and love can go only elsewhere, to mother nature, our true wife and also daughter; because while our knowledge is only a part of us, we are an integral part of nature, and leave our traces there as all things do; whereas appearances or data, unless materialised, as in a phonograph, in institutions or works that may serve to re-awaken them, perish in the very act of coming to light. Spirit lives in these manifestations and in the emotions that come with them; its proper themes are essences and harmonies in essence; yet its faith and confidence regard the continuity and perpetual resurrection proper to life, now in one psyche and now in another. So led by the hand of nature, I am not troubled because not well informed about her history; and as to what the gossips may say of us, we laugh if we overhear it. It may be true, or it may be absurdly invented; if true, we virtually knew it already, and if invented it cannot touch us, although as gossip it may be entertaining enough.

I have deliberately called this familiar communion with nature *animal faith,* in order not to be taken (as my earliest sonnet has been taken) to advocate religious illusions feebly appended to science; yet this faith of mine is religious precisely in the Protestant sense of religious faith; for if in other respects Protestant sentiment often seems to me rather a religious cloak for worldliness, as to the nature of faith it seems to me admirable and profound. For whereas faith among Catholics (except for the mystics) means intellectual assent to traditional dogmas, among Protestants it means an unspoken and sacrificial trust in an unfathomable power; not, in the deeper souls, confidence that we shall materially or personally prosper under it, or be publicly vindicated or saved, but rather willingness to have been born, to have drunk our cup to the dregs, and even to be eternally damned, because such was the will of God, intent on his own glory. *Worship* of this non-moral absolute Will seems to me canine and slavish, and excusable only as the sheer greatness of this universal power carries us with it dramatically, like a storm or an earthquake which we forget to fear because we identify ourselves with it and positively enjoy it. This is a precarious aesthetic or intellectual rapture on which it would be rash and unmoral to build our religion; but *faith* and *trust* in that universal dispensation are signs of healthy life in ourselves, of intelligence and mastery; they bring, if we are reasonably plastic, a justified assurance of fellowship with reality, partly by participation and partly by understanding.

This brings me once more to Hartshorne and his notable and elaborate essay, nominally about my essences but really about his system of cosmology. He explains this by saying that criticism is worthless unless it avows the criterion to which it appeals. Yet we expect this criterion to be relevant; and while cosmology is certainly relevant to potentialities in evolution, it seems quite irrelevant to ideal possibilities, intrinsically timeless, such as my essences are. He remembers at the beginning of various paragraphs that he is supposed to be talking about my theory, and quotes something of mine; but immediately he reverts to what he calls the Neglected Alternative. This is an alternative, perhaps, to my theory of matter and of the psyche, but not to my theory of essence. My essences are first politely invited to put their head into a physical system, but not their tail. Then the guillotine drops, cuts the heads off, and the executioner explains that no harm has been done, because the heads were always nothing but features of existence, and the tails were never anything at all.

In the first place, in both spheres, I must admit and apologise for neglecting the thousand elaborations, qualifications and transformations that I conceive stronger heads than mine to be busy with. Russell, too, being an expert, naturally feels my ignorance in these matters. Yet both spheres are superhuman and we must in any case be satisfied with partial explorations, and I for my part gladly bow beforehand to what others may discover there. Abstraction is difficult for me. Unless I can move with a certain volume of miscellaneous notions in mind, I lose my interest and my direction. I could never play chess: the problems fatigue me without rewarding me. I know that this is a fatal laziness or incapacity not only in logic but in physics, which advances only by growing abstract: therefore both in the realm of essence and in that of matter I give only some initial hints, and like an acolyte sing only the first verse of the psalm, *Introibo ad altare Dei.* I leave the rest of the Mass to the consecrated priests, who know the lawful words to be spoken. But that I am a true believer and at home in both temples, I am intimately convinced; and nothing could trouble me less than the greater wisdom of the experts or the future transformations of their science. If I could have understood those things I should, of course, have written very differently. But my effusions were not meant as contributions to science, but as confessions of faith; and this faith is not self-indulgent but carefully reduced to a minimum. It is only as perhaps needlessly or too dogmatically exceeding this minimum that the speculations of others seem to me questionable. They may be right: but for exciting wagers and poetic luxuries I prefer to look in other directions.

If this limited range of my powers in physics had not prevented me from working out my view of matter and especially of the psyche, I think Hartshorne would have perceived that I do not neglect his Alternative, but merely express it in other words and regard it, not as a dogma, but as a free speculation, essentially theological and mythical, like those of the Indians and the Neo-Platonists. The dangerous transition from logic to cosmology is made by Hartshorne in the second phase which he chooses to distinguish in my theory; but my theory knows nothing of these distinct phases, and sees in them, taken as logic, nothing but tautologies. The real distinction lies in passing from the logically possible to the physically realised or potential; and in logic, as I conceive it, a determinable has as much definition in it as a determinate. Only nature or the mind, which is a part of nature, may have got as far as determining the triangle and not so far as determining the equilateral triangle; but the triangle could never have been indeterminate in respect to the equality or non-equality of its sides, if the equilateral triangle had not been self-determined eternally. The choice of essences for comparison is an accident of discourse; but discourse would be lost in irrevocable abysses if the essences by chance evoked had no fixed relations among themselves. To say that essences *become* determinate when they are exemplified seems to me only an egotistical way of saying that there had been no occasion to distinguish them before; egotistical, not because the development of nature or of thought may not be more important for us than the pure logic of ideas, but because, even so, there is usurpation of the divine by the human in reducing what we discover to the fact that we have discovered it.

You may say, and I think it is quite possible, that the time for what I call pure logic is past, and that now we must cultivate a method of thinking more sympathetic to the movement of things, more supple, more human, and in a word more physical. Very well: and if you said, "It is raining, it is chilly, let us go indoors and sit by the fire," I might also agree; but I shouldn't think that I was changing the weather or adding to the dignity of the mind.

There is a view of "cosmic weather" akin to Hartshorne's Alternative which far from neglecting, I have heartily adopted, although it was contrary to the spirit of my favourite Democritus, Spinoza, and Lucretius, and the science of the nineteenth century. This is the view that nothing existent is necessary, but that nature and all events in nature are thoroughly contingent. And, curiously enough, it has been precisely my strictly Scholastic logic of essence that brought me to this conclusion, and not at all the moral, biological, or introspective arguments usually invoked for indeterminism; for I constantly recall the saying of Schopenhauer that thinking indeterminism essential to life or to morals is the great sign of incapacity for speculation. But contingency runs so deep that it does not exclude any contingent order: and the world *may* be as regular as any mechanism or as chaotic as any chaos. This is merely a question of fact.

Nor is the conception of indeterminism in nature separable intrinsically from the logic of essence. If essences have no identity until nature exhibits them, *choice*, choice between definite alternatives, becomes inconceivable. The dictum of Bergson that I have already quoted has helped me to see this. Possibles, he says, become possible only after they are realised; and Bergson elsewhere has given us a careful description of the manner in which, absolutely in the dark, various currents of potentiality meet and combine in the psyche (for instance in literary composition) until some definite phrase or conclusion suddenly asserts itself: a perfectly unforeseen and unforseeable birth, until just those currents have met, and that unpredicted thought has appeared. Had it been predicted, as sometimes happens, the process of spontaneous generation would have occurred in forming that prediction, and the performance later would merely have filled out that partial rehearsal. Excellent, this seems to me, as a description of life as it is lived or existence as it flows;

and the frequent repetition of tropes or the presence of laws, which Bergson neglects because he dislikes it, does not at all remove the spontaneity and contingency of each instance of change, even if such changes are habitual. But now the great motive for insisting on indeterminism has usually been the horror of necessity or fate: we were morally nullified unless we could freely choose between alternatives, *both equally possible*, both clearly conceived, duty here, temptation there, with our deepest allegiance victoriously asserting itself in the issue. We demanded to live in the light and to decide in the light; to choose between eternal essences, to identify ourselves for ever with what we loved, and not with what we hated. And what do the vitalists and temporalists tell us? That nothing is possible or distinguishable or nameable before it occurs, that what we are now can never determine what we shall do next, that each action and decision shapes itself unpredictably by a conjunction of vital forces, and was not preformed either in any one of those forces or in their mutual relations, but fell out so, for no reason, like a bolt from the blue. Does this vindicate our rational freedom? Does this leave any decision to the mind? Apparently not. Everything comes about blindly, and choice is equally impossible for God or for man, because both must *grow* into what they are to be before they can conceive where they are going. The mind finds itself like the dead Polonius, at supper, not where it eats but where it is eaten. A politic convocation of worms are e'en at it.

I think that the old controversy about freedom and necessity was always morally futile, because whether, in physical genesis, there be continuity or fresh beginnings, law or chance, the spirit is equally the sport of fact. The freedom and dominion morally possible are of another kind, touching not the genesis of facts but the wisdom of the affections. Affections may liberate the heart or they may enslave it. This is not a question of good or ill fortune supervening, but of being or not being deceived in the original choice of our interests. Does the object correspond to the true demands of our nature? Such demands are ideals, implicit or explicit. They are definable by some essence. To say that they possess no ideal determination until they are realised in events would abolish the possibility of intelligent foresight. It would condemn us to live in the dark. In the dark, I mean, in respect to the future, because Bergson and Hartshorne make up for the utter formlessness they assign to the future by the perfect and indelible actuality they assign to the past. They not only allow us to look backward and to find distinct essences exemplified there, but they represent the past as actually enduring and always at hand, both as images recoverable in memory exactly as they appeared in experience and also as a structure and momentum enduring in the world, and forming a basis for all future developments.

This, in the realm of matter, belongs to the assumption of common sense and science; but these philosophers, who reject any clear division between matter and mind, run here into what seems to me an excess of conservatism. The past conditions the future materially; it persists in the present, according to the old idea of the conservation of energy, quantitatively and dynamically, although there remains much uncertainty as to whether this persistent matter or energy remains available for perpetual motion or life. But the notion that *history*, with all the actions, feelings, and living ideas that have diversified the past, endures unchanged and unchangeable and continues to control the future for ever—this notion seems a materialisation of the truth of the past, and utterly non-natural. What effect have the thoughts of extinct races, or the cries of extinct animals upon the world now? Where, in their pictorial and moral essence, are the snows of all past years? This is a pretty, irresponsible fancy, transposed from psychic recollection and telepathy to the general march of nature, where the gradual but radical destruction of organisms and of traditions renders it incongruous.

Incongruous physically, and religiously strangely naturalistic. In making the past morally persistent and morally indelible, temporalism has surrendered half its charm. Religions have often announced the end of the world, the coming of the Kingdom of Heaven, the forgiveness of sins, resurrection in another world, as if awaking from a bad dream, and the total extinction of Karma, or the dreadful burden of a guilty past. All this is now swept away, not because it is too fantastic but because it is not fantastic enough. The real moral discontinuity of religions and civilisations is to be denied in the interests of an imaginative idea that happens to please us.

I will not dwell on the theological difficulties that this system involves. A fuller explanation might attenuate them. But I confess that I drew a long breath when I read that God, throughout infinite past time had perpetually chosen the best course possible, under the conditions that primeval substance, found extant within himself, imposed on his divine goodness. If after that infinite number of improvements the world is what it is today, what must it have been to begin with? Is this not a kind of Manichæan doctrine, where infinite evil is posited in order that infinite good may vanquish it? Yet if ever totally vanquished, the evil would leave the good with nothing to do; so that this victory must never be an ultimate fact, but only a concomitant judgment made by those who find life good on the whole, to the effect that the good has secretly commissioned the evil to appear, in order to enable the good to assert itself. And has it been observed that, in this case, if the devil were allowed a hearing, he might employ the very same reasoning, and proclaim himself eternally victorious, because he allowed the good to revive, after he had each time destroyed it, only in order to have the pleasure of destroying it again?

I believe that a sound cosmology, unconcerned initially to be edifying and intent only on discovering the truth, would lay the most solid possible foundations for religion and morality. It would save both from the illusions that discredit them. But let us not have an exchange of illusions. The Fathers of the Church were very wise men; they had a vast experience of religious needs and religious speculation. If they turned their backs on natural science, it was not by false readings of nature, but by invoking, through faith, a background for nature responsive to the spirit of man. They put the drama of moral life, as it is really unfolded, on a finite stage. They gave it an absolute beginning and an absolute end. It could thus remain a moral drama. Had they adapted their eschatology to the analogies of physics, without miracles and without another world where the human conscience might triumph, they would never have lent mankind either courage to face a moral chaos or light eventually to discover the truth of nature.

XIII. Personalities and Personal Remarks

More is said in some of these essays about my person than perhaps was strictly pertinent to my philosophy; but personalities, introduced as if to throw light on theory, are often a relief from theory. The public likes them better, and so does the lower semi-public part of each of our minds. I am here engaged in a semi-personal apology, and I need not apologise further for adding something in reply to animadversions upon my person.

Charles Augustus Strong

The shortest notice in this book comes from the friend who had known me longest; and these are presumably the last words that he ever wrote. He had come to Harvard during my Senior year, after graduating from the University of his native Rochester, New York. His father was President of the Baptist Theological Seminary in that town; and it would have been natural, with his studious habits and most serious and speculative turn of mind, that he should have followed in his father's footsteps. Harvard, even the Harvard Divinity School, would then have hardly been the right place in which to complete his preparation for the ministry. But this preparation had already been a little too thorough, or had carried him too far afield; for he had studied for several years at a German Gymnasium, in the province of Hannover, where the atmosphere was strictly religious, but where the too knowing pupils, if not the teachers, may have inoculated him with critical and unsuitable notions. At any rate, when he returned home, he had discovered by his own collation of the Greek Gospel texts, that he could no longer believe in the material resurrection of Christ, or in the other miracles. The greatest prudence and reserve could not permanently conceal this sad fact from his father; and a terrible conflict followed, suppressed but life-long and embittered, between father and son. For it was not only the old man that was uncompromising.

Very characteristically, young Strong himself had transferred his complete conviction from Revelation to naturalism and Darwinian evolution. His whole interest and single ambition henceforth centred on proving the truth of his new faith and especially its moral sufficiency. This last point was a great bond between us, differently as we might picture the face of the moral world; for he had not the least dread of moral discouragement, supposed to attach to naturalism. He found, however, a most grave problem in what never has troubled me, namely, in the origin of consciousness within an unconscious world. And in the end he had the satisfaction of thinking that he had solved this problem scientifically, and discovered the true and necessary derivation of mind from an unconscious substance. This substance, though unconscious in the sense of not being aware of itself or of anything else, and having no *knowledge,* nevertheless was essentially sensitive, or as he said, *sentient:* and the derivation of "awareness" from the "sentience" was the subject of his minute and prolonged investigations. At first, under the influence of empirical idealism and of the theory of Clifford, he called this sentience "mind-stuff," and conceived it to be composed of very dim sparks of actual feeling; but later he changed his conception radically, and mind was conceived to arise, not by the juxtaposition of elements already mental, but by a movement or function acquired by elements in themselves not mental. The inner intensity or (as he sometimes called it) the luminosity of these elements, when they were engaged in the movement of an organism, was fused or summed up into an actual feeling. When this movement was one of action or reaction upon things external to the organism, actual feeling could become an image of those things and sentient existence could become knowledge.

In a series of books and articles Strong worked out this discovery, and the slowness of the learned world in taking note of it distressed but did not discourage him. Never was fortitude more entire than in this man. Sure of his vocation, if not always of his steps and his method, he continued undaunted by neglect and comparative isolation, never losing confidence in the importance and ultimate success of his labours. Nor was he turned aside by the hopeless and protracted afflictions that affected first his wife's health and then his own. Crippled and physically helpless for twenty years, he kept a single eye upon his chosen task, tirelessly revising and perfecting every detail of his theory.

Unfortunately my fundamental agreement with his general view and my willingness to entertain some such solution for the problem of mind in nature, could not be of much technical use to him, because I could seldom accept the arguments by which he supported his theory. These arguments were based on presuppositions that I was inclined to question. They were rationalistic arguments applied to matters of fact, and involved a conceptual dogmatism like that of Leibniz; whereas it seems to me that, since nature has found some means of eliciting mind out of matter, this mind may live content without dictating, out of its own resources, how nature could or could not have done it. The miracle recurs in us every morning and at the birth of every child; and the difficulties we find in conceiving it arise from our prejudices, not from the miracle itself. Everything is a miracle, until we call it natural, and everything is equally natural that actually happens. My philosophy was thus strangely different from Strong's in spite of our large agreement. He was meagre, persistent, scientific; I was rapid, sceptical and ironical. He had zealously preserved his allegiance to a traditional morality and a precise scientific truth as the heart of religion; whereas I tolerantly observed religion always superposing itself upon truth and morality upon nature. In practice we both loved simple regular ways of living and quiet surroundings, where nature had been purified yet not concealed by the arts of man. We never left Europe if we could help it; yet Strong was not an expatriate at heart, but always absolutely rooted in his native country and his professional tasks. In contact with the foreign world he was courteous and well-informed yet unyielding: marooned abroad by a series of accidents and minor conveniences, until his anchor buried itself and was too heavy to raise. Places after all were indifferent to his mind, if only his mind could work there; and no wanderer was ever truer to a fixed vocation or carried his high thoughts more sternly hidden and unpolluted through the streets of Babel.

My Poetry

Professor Rice attributes the mediocrity of my verses to philosophy, to Platonism, and to nineteenth century America; but here he seems to be considering my hackneyed prosody rather than my lack of inspiration. The nineteenth century was favourable to the poetry of rebellion, and might not philosophy and Platonism have given wings to that rebellion, if I had felt it? Rice seems to me to come nearer to the root of the trouble when he says that my poetic imagination did not mature until after I had stopped writing verse. Why did I stop? I should say that I felt—as so many recent poets have felt—that what I had to say could be said better without the traditional poetic form, that is, in prose; because the invention of typographical devices for turning prose into poetry did not occur to me. And this leads me to observe that I meant rather more than I said when I spoke of English not being my mother-tongue. It is not the vocabulary only that is concerned; I could have enriched my vocabulary by learning a trade, or by reading the metaphysical poets, which I have never done. I mentioned the language not being quite native to me; but that was only a symbol for the much more hopelessly foreign quality of the English sort of imagination, and the northern respect for the inner man instead of the southern respect for the great world, for fate, for history, for matter. I could not be a good poet after the English fashion; and as I was compelled to use the English language, I had better not be a poet at all. Moreover, versifying was fast becoming a dead art, easy and pleasant still, perhaps, as writing Latin hexameters might still be easy and pleasant, but no longer a medium for the inspired effusion of thought. True poetry could now be written only in prose, for which in English the Bible and Shakespeare and the whole sixteenth and seventeenth centuries furnish such excellent precedents. Indeed, except when meter remains instinctive, like good manners, a fresh graphic phrase, a profound original metaphor, slips more easily and freely into liquid prose than into the meshes of verse.

This brings me to a mistake that both Rice and Professor Howgate seem to me to make about my poetry. They study it too technically, they think it more artful and voluntary than it ever was, because in one sense I was a born poet, like Ovid, and lisped in numbers, for the numbers came. Of course I re-read the scrawl, said to myself that's good or that's bad, and often had a new inspiration, the best things being perhaps my second thoughts, as also in my prose; but that is because my mind works by making variations on a given theme or congruous extensions. I tend to repeat myself like a refrain; I do not pass to something else that suggests itself by chance. In a word, I move in the realm of essences, not in that of accidents. One reason for this may be limitation of experience but another reason may be the intensity of what experience I have. And my poetry is for that very cause not a poetry of words or concepts, but a poetry of things; for if according to Virgil things have their tears, so they have their poetry: and by "things" I understand events and interests as well as objects. I notice how insensible Howgate is, for instance, to the poetry of the subject-matter of my verses, which he studies with such unmerited attention as to their forms. He despises my little *Athletic Ode* because it is about sports, and my *Spain in America* because it is about geography and politics; but whatever technical defects these pieces may have, they are inspired by the charm of the tragedy of their subject-matter; and it was that in its actual intensity that I was thinking of, and not of my composition. So in *Lucifer*, Rice says that it reads like the translation of a Greek tragedy. Very likely; but who wrote the original? And wasn't it worth translating? He also says that it contains some good passages. That is the technical judgment of a professor of rhetoric; the real poetry of the poem lies in its subject-matter, as seen in a vision, the *Heavenly Truce*, or the naturalness, the glory, and the pity of rival religions and rival ideals. Of course, if you don't feel the poetry of things, you will not feel it in some verbal reflection of it caught by a poet; but I am a true poet in feeling that poetry, and the critics are not good critics if they fail to perceive it. For this reason it is important, in judging any rendering of the poetry of things, to have some knowledge of those things. Howgate, again, who is remarkably accurate in reporting all the facts about my life, happens not to know Spain or old Boston or Harvard or the spots in England, France, and Italy that have been my favourite haunts. Naturally it was impossible for him to have known me as a young man, or my contemporaries, and even in my old age he has seen but little of me. This is not his fault, but it is a handicap for a biographer. He therefore makes ill-informed criticisms about my verses, not seeing, for instance, the need of not having the "bark" and the "bight" in the same tragic line, or the "garden rear;" and attributing to trite convention the mention of a ship in the sonnets to my young friend W.P. who had died in one. This could not be known, of course, beyond a limited circle; but it illustrates the false impressions that poetry may make when the poetry of things is not perceived beneath the jingle of rhyme. Worst of all is the lack of understanding for Platonism when Platonism is the whole secret and substance of a poem: and it is a most suitable and inspiring subject, because like a religious conversion it reviews and recasts all emotional experience into a new mould, giving it a moral unity and intensity that it never had before. Now Platonism was a vivid experience of mine when I wrote those Platonising sonnets. They were not imitated from the Italians without knowing what the Italians had felt. They express both a personal emotion and a moral conviction. But Howgate imagines that *two ladies* must have existed to explain the difference between love satisfied but not satisfying and love denied and sublimated! Otherwise he could not turn my philosophy of love into biographical material. And this shows, to return to Rice, how much less dangerous Platonism is for poets and ignorance of Platonism for critics.

My Americanism

Professor Brownell proclaims in large letters that I am an American. It is a true honour to be claimed when one might so easily be disowned; and what Brownell says about me marks sufficiently the limitations of my Americanism as well as its source and quality. This quality he finds present and important in my philosophy, in something he calls naturalism, but which he does not describe clearly. It is evidently not my professed cosmological naturalism or materialism, which I consciously draw from Democritus, Lucretius and Spinoza. It must be something rather social or psychological; perhaps the habit of reducing ideas to their human origin, to expressions of human nature, rather than to truths or errors to be tested by logic or by external facts. I believe profoundly in the animality of the mind; this is my critical, as distinguished from my cosmological or dogmatic naturalism; and if this be what Brownell refers to, I agree that it characterises my philosophy and my instinctive way of thinking in a marked degree. But is this critical, satirical naturalism of mine distinctively American? Perhaps in the last thirty years, in an America unknown to me save by report, a naturalistic, pessimistic, infra-moral spirit may have been abroad; but I have seen no signs of it in American philosophy; and my naturalism, on the moral side, tends to sanction discipline, organisation and tradition as the natural conditions of any notable or fertile achievements. In my time, this would have sounded un-American. If I had had to name in those days a representative of American naturalism, I should have chosen Walt Whitman. He wished to turn and live like the animals; and he had vast cosmic intuitions, rather idealistic and mystical, but still not narrowly human. And his democratic enthusiasm was not opposed to anything; it was genuine openness to all men, and to all sides of human nature. There were to be no exclusions and no compulsions: things that since his day have taken root in America, and made the spirit of the nation less naturalistic.

If I were to describe my Americanism I should divide it into two parts, the involuntary and the voluntary. The involuntary part comprises long residence, education, and twenty years of teaching in the United States. This was all due to circumstances; if I had been free to choose, I should not have lived there, or been educated there, or taught philosophy there or anywhere else. There was no hardship in any of these things; they had good sides and I sometimes enjoyed them frankly and unfeignedly; but they were not done by choice. There is, however, an eminently voluntary side to my Americanism which I may sum up in a single word: Friendships. From the age of sixteen to the present time, when I am not far from eighty, I have had American friends more numerous, more loyal, more sympathetic, and with two or three exceptions more beloved than my friends of other nationalities; and this has inevitably made American manners and tastes more natural to me than any others. The people with whom I feel most at ease—again with a few exceptions—are Americans, especially Americans who live or have lived in Europe, or who are in other ways somewhat exotic. Reversible points of view must be understood and liked, if I am to feel entire sympathy with anybody. Friendships, then, in abundance; but with the deeper layers and broad currents of American life I never had any contact. I believe that on the whole they are healthy, and free from the worst vices and dangers that oppress mankind; but there was nothing in them in my time to interest me, nor had I any opportunity to explore them. Harvard College, a part of Boston, an occasional glimpse of New York made up my America.

The limitations of my Americanism are easily told. I have no American or English blood; I was not born in the United States; I have never become an American citizen; as soon as I was my own master I spent every free winter and almost every summer in Europe; I never married or kept house or expected to end my days in America. This sense of belonging elsewhere, or rather of not belonging where I lived, was nothing anomalous or unpleasant to me but, as it were, hereditary. My father had done his life-work in a remote colony; my mother had had no home as a child, her first husband had been of one nationality and her second husband of another, and she had always been a stranger, like me, wherever she was. This is rather consonant with my philosophy and may have helped to form it. It is not a thing I regret. So that my intentional detachability from America is balanced by an equal detachability from every other place. As to my native Spain, it has never crossed my mind to renounce my formal allegiance to it; that would be like attempting to change one's parents; and Spain is a great country for the imagination with a great power over the spirit. From 1883 to 1930 it remained for me a constant place of pilgrimage. At Avila, first at my father's house and later at my sister's, during all those years, I could always live as if at home; and that would not have been a bad place to retire to from the world;

but Spanish society and public life were most unattractive to me, a positive barrier. It was not only that I was too foreign, but also that Spain was not Spanish enough. My lot happens to have been cast in the very worst and most ignoble epoch of her history, when she was least herself. A hundred years earlier or a hundred years later there might have been no occasion for such estrangement.

In England, on the contrary, the way of living and the temper of society, in public and in private, entirely pleased me, as did the countryside and the older towns, such as Oxford and Cambridge. But when the possibility of living there more or less permanently at last presented itself, I was already fifty years of age: too old to form new ties, and to begin a different life; especially as by that time my closest English friends were declining in years, in spirit, in fortune, and sometimes even in kindness; and however faithfully one may love one's friends for what they were, too often it is only possible to pity them for what they become. The mirage of lovely England had begun to dissolve before my eyes. On the other hand, for a man of my traditions and tastes, Italy, Rome especially, has an eternal dignity. Materially too it was more convenient, milder than Spain, more in the current of travel and of affairs; and chiefly in Italy I have lived ever since, perfectly free, busy enough, and sufficiently accompanied. Yet as this book shows, my intellectual relations and labours still unite me closely to America; and it is as an American writer that I must be counted, if I am counted at all.

In spirit, therefore, I gratefully accept Brownell's cordial compliment as to my genuine Americanism. Yet there are other compliments that I must accept with equal thanks and would wish to think no less justified. One distinguished friend, Boutroux, once said that I was an antique sage; and another distinguished friend, Marichalar, has said that I am a Castilian mystic. I have written harsh things about mysticism, and had I been called a mystic simply it might have sounded surprising or even offensive. But that happy restriction, Castilian, removes all those unpleasant suggestions. Castile can breed nothing nebulous. No danger there of thinking oneself God or thinking that God is oneself. That word Castilian dries the wind, clears the jungle, lays bare earth and sky alike, infinitely apart yet separated by nothing, as the soul and God should always remain. The mere mystic might be anything, good or bad; but the Castilian mystic is vowed to an unflinching realism about the world and an unsullied allegiance to the ideal. He is Don Quixote sane.

Last Words

My first care in replying to these numerous criticisms was to acknowledge their legitimacy, when once any element of misunderstanding should have been removed from them. So now the last word of my apology must be to beg my critics in turn to remove from my reply any elements of misunderstanding that it may contain, and for the rest to acknowledge the legitimacy of my defence. As to the contrary principles or preferences that dictate our different views, it would be chimerical and ill-natured to argue. You cannot refute a principle or rebut a preference, you can only indicate its consequences or present alluringly the charms of a rival doctrine. I am aware of the rigidity and untimeliness of my views, and rather wonder that they should have now received so much careful consideration. That they should often be misunderstood is rather my fault, because I have clothed them in a rhetoric that, though perfectly spontaneous and inevitable in my own thoughts, misleads at first as to their character, and in some readers may induce an assent that afterwards has to be rescinded. I am a Scholastic at heart, but I lack the patience and the traditional training that might have enabled me to discuss every point minutely, without escapades or ornament or exaggeration or irony. My books would then have been much more solid, and nobody would have read them. For better or for worse, I am a Scholastic only in my principles not in my ways. I detest disputation and distrust proofs and disproofs. Nor do I expect or desire that everybody else should think as I do. The truth is not impatient; it can stand representation and misrepresentation. The more we respect its authority, the more confidently and familiarly we may play round its base. The plainest facts, such as the existence of body and of spirit, may be explained away, if we like to do so and to keep house with the resulting paradoxes. A view becomes untenable only when seen to contradict some conviction ineradicable from one's own mind; and not the same convictions are irradicable from all minds, at least not in mature years. Thoughts go to seed. If by chance a group of persons anywhere were brought to accept my philosophy, I am surc this would be done at the cost of misrepresenting it; I mean, by not understanding it as I do, but giving it some other twist, perhaps nearer to the truth of the matter. Heartily as I enjoy the pleasure of intellectual friendship, where it is spontaneous and sincere, I dislike perfunctory compliments and mincing praise. It is honour enough to be read and studied, even if only to be combated; and I send my critics back to their respective camps with my blessing, hoping that the world may prove staunch and beautiful to them, pictured in their own terms.

G Santayana

ROME, OCTOBER, 1940

Grand Hotel, Rome
October 21, 1940

Dear Professor Schilpp

Your review of *The Realm of Spirit* arrived yesterday. It is at once friendly and remote, and I think it was as well to have decided before hand not to attempt to reply to it. You have more than carried out my idea of quoting from the book, and the Glossary of Terms alone makes, to my mind, an ample reply to your chief criticism. Would anyone not immersed in a particular contemporary movement think my terms not clear? This is the first time I have heard that allegation. Certainly they are much clearer than the scraps of Logical Realism that I have read, that needed to be translated into ordinary language to be at all intelligible. You yourself indicate the cause of this divergence in criteria, but perhaps without seeing how deep it runs. It was in the second part of your paper that I was confirmed in thinking that you are interested only in *concepts*, not in *things*; for you select transcendence as the chief character of spirit, actuality and moral intensity seeming to you meaningless. Now transcendence is proper to intent; intuition does not transcend the given; it is not faith but sight. And transcendence, intent, or intelligence (all names for the same thing) is inconceivable except in spirit; so that there you find a trait of spirit that begins to give you a notion of what the *concept* of spirit might be. But the *concept* of spirit doesn't interest me, except as a technicality: it is the *life* of spirit that I am talking about, the question what good, if any, there is in living, and where our treasure, if any, is to be laid up. It is a religious question. It is not a question of words. You seem to feel this, yet it takes you a long time to discover it. — I hope the rest of my *Apologia* has reached you safely. Yours sincerely G Santayana

NOTE. As the above letter indicates, the Editor's review of *The Realm of Spirit* (cf. pp. 377-398 above) reached Professor Santayana in Rome, Italy, on October 20th, 1940. By that time, the last part of Santayana's "Apologia" had already been forwarded by him by trans-Atlantic clipper to the United States. It was, therefore, impossible for him to reply to said review within the confines of the "Apologia" itself. However, since the above letter, written one day after Mr. Santayana received the review, constitutes in itself perhaps a sufficient reply to the review, it has seemed best to include it here in facsimile reproduction, after the close of Professor Santayana's "Apologia."—*Ed.*

BIBLIOGRAPHY OF THE WRITINGS OF GEORGE SANTAYANA

To October, 1940
(With Index)

Compiled by

Shohig Terzian

PREFATORY NOTE

THIS Bibliography aims to present a comprehensive list of Santayana's published and unpublished writings. Supplementing it is a Special Index, which was prepared to serve as a title guide, and to facilitate the location of references to Santayana's writings.

Part I covers published material, and Part II unpublished manuscripts, exclusive of personal or business correspondence, which do not fall within the present scope. The arrangement of entries is essentially chronological, but within specific years, references to single volumes precede those to periodicals, which are inserted according to the month of publication.

Part II and the incidental references to manuscripts in Part I are a record far from complete of those extant. It is hoped, however, that their inclusion will induce individuals and libraries to make known their possession of similar material.

The lists of reprints of individual poems and essays in anthologies are, by no means, exhaustive: only a limited number were included to indicate the widespread appeal of certain selections. Additional references to the appearance of various poems will be found in Granger's *Index to Poetry*. For selected quotations, such works as L. P. Smith's *Treasury of English Aphorisms*, Stevenson's *Home Book of Quotations*, and Bartlett's *Familiar Quotations* may be consulted. Several editions of Santayana's works have been reissued by the same publisher at intervals with varying imprint dates, but no attempt was made to record them in this Bibliography.

Entries in the Index refer, by dates of publication, to Part I, unless otherwise indicated. For each entry, only the original date of publication is specified, except when the first line of a poem varies in a previous or later publication; in these instances, additional references are included with corresponding dates. Succeeding publication dates of any title may be found by consulting the bibliographic entry designated. For all titles, initial articles were omitted in the alphabetical arrangement, whereas the first lines of verses were classified strictly under the first word. Wherever possible, book reviews were listed according to the titles assigned to them, appearing in the Bibliography, and all were combined under the main heading. Similarly, references to letters by Santayana are grouped together, arranged alphabetically by recipients' names.

The material for this Bibliography was gathered and assembled from a variety of sources, too numerous to mention. Its preliminary basis was the list of Santayana's published writings in *Obiter Scripta* (1936), edited by Messrs. Buchler and Schwartz.

It would be impossible for me to acknowledge here all of the assistance I have received both verbally and through correspondence. My thanks cannot be extended adequately to individuals in this country and abroad who have responded generously to my inquiries. I am particularly indebted to Messrs. John Hall Wheelock, Thomas P. Fleming of the Columbia University Libraries, and Luis E. Bejarano of the New York Public Library for their gracious assistance in various matters. At the beginning of this enterprise, a cordial letter from Mr. Santayana informing me of obscure translations, was a considerable source of inspiration.

Communications will be most welcome for the purpose of including any necessary corrections and omissions in subsequent versions of this Bibliography. Such correspondence may be addressed to the Editor of this volume, or directly to the undersigned compiler.

SHOHIG TERZIAN

130 POST AVENUE
NEW YORK, N.Y.
October 1, 1940

WRITINGS OF GEORGE SANTAYANA TO OCTOBER, 1940

Part I

PUBLISHED WRITINGS

1880

Lines; on Leaving the Bedford St. Schoolhouse. [Boston?] [1880] [privately printed], 4 unnumbered p.

The caption serves as title page. The author's name is not mentioned.

Originally read to members of the Debating Society of the Class of 1882, and privately printed *in toto* shortly thereafter. Expurgated edition (i.e. first part only) delivered as a "poem of farewell" . . . "before the assembled school in the old hall at the Bedford Street building on Dec. 24, 1880—the last gathering in that building. . . ." (Mendum, Samuel M., "When Santayana Was a Boy," *The Christian Leader,* v. 39, no. 48, Nov. 28, 1936, p. 1526.)

Copies available in the Boston Latin School Library and in the Treasure Room at Harvard University, which also has a 5 p. typewritten copy.

Reprints. Brief extracts from latter part. In: *Summer School News* (pub. by students at Harvard Summer School), Friday, July 30, 1937, p. 3-4, in an article headed, "Santayana's Poems on Exhibition in Poetry Room," [by Shohig Terzian].

First part. In: Howgate, George W., *George Santayana,* Phila., University of Pennsylvania Press, 1938, p. 10.

1881

President Garfield. *Latin School Register,* v. 1, no. 1, Sept., 1881, p. 1.

Note: In each issue of the *Register* for 1881-1882 appears a short, unsigned poem of which this "sonnet" is the first. Mr. Lee J. Dunn, Librarian of the Boston Latin School, informed the present compiler that, according to the recollections of a prominent alumnus, Santayana had once been questioned about his authorship of these poems. It is reported that he replied he thought he did, but would hesitate to claim the credit. Despite this hearsay evidence, Santayana is entitled to the benefit of the doubt; and they are listed below, with a note indicating that they are unsigned. Moreover, only a few of the contributions during these years bear signatures. Santayana was probably responsible for more of the writing with which it is not possible now to credit him, due to the lack of authoritative evidence.

Reprinted. In: Howgate, G.W., *George Santayana*, Phila., 1938, p. 11-12.

THE CLASS OF 1882. *Latin School Register*, v. 1, no. 1, Sept., 1881, p. 1; no. 2, Oct., 1881, p. 1.

Unsigned. History of the class from 1874.

RHYMES OF THE DAY. *Latin School Register*, v. 1, no. 2, Oct., 1881, p. 1.

Unsigned.

A THANKSGIVING EPISODE. *Latin School Register*, v. 1, no. 3, Nov., 1881, p. 1.

Unsigned.

CLASS SONG. (Which will NOT be sung on the 22d of February). *Latin School Register*, v. 1, no. 4, Dec., 1881, p. 1.

Unsigned.

1881-1882

THE AENEID. *Latin School Register*, v. 1, nos. 1-10, Sept., 1881-June, 1882.

Unsigned. Each contribution on p. 2.

Book First: "Aeneas comes to land
(Sept.-Jan.) On Afric's torrid strand"

Book Second: "Which shows what latent forces
(Feb.-June) May be in wooden horses"

Reprinted. In: Holmes, Pauline, *A Tercentenary History of the Boston Public Latin School*, 1635-1935, Cambridge, Harvard Univ. Press, 1935. Book I, p. 506-513; Book II, p. 513-521.

Excerpts. In: Howgate, George W., *George Santayana*, Phila., 1938, p. 11.

1882

THE SCHOOLBOY'S EARNEST CRY FOR FREEDOM. *Latin School Register*, v. 1, no. 5, Jan., 1882, p. 1.

Unsigned.

ASPIRATIONS OF A COUNTRY LAD. *Latin School Register*, v. 1, no. 6, Feb., 1882, p. 1.

Unsigned.

THE BOY AND THE FROGS. *Latin School Register*, v. 1, no. 7, March, 1882, p. 1.

Unsigned.

AMERICA. *Latin School Register,* v. 1, no. 8, April, 1882, p. 1.
Unsigned.

A CALM. *Latin School Register,* v. 1, no. 9, May, 1882, p. 1.
Unsigned.

EXEUNT OMNES. *Latin School Register,* v. 1, no. 10, June, 1882, p. 1.
Unsigned.

1883

Cartoon entitled TIMELY WARNING. *The Harvard Lampoon,* ser. 2, v. 4, no. 10, Feb. 9, 1883, p. 91.

Cartoon entitled FEMININE SUBTLETY. *The Harvard Lampoon,* ser. 2, v. 5, no. 1, Feb. 23, 1883, p. 8.

Cartoon entitled TAKING MEMORIAL HALL SOUP. *The Harvard Lampoon,* ser. 2, v. 5, no. 3, March 23, 1883, p. 29.

Cartoon entitled LADIES' DAY. *The Harvard Lampoon,* ser. 2, v. 5, no. 4, April 6, 1883, p. 31.

Cartoon entitled THOSE TIGHT BOOTS! *The Harvard Lampoon,* ser. 2, v. 5, no. 4, April 6, 1883, p. 38.

Cartoon entitled MAKING HIM FEEL AT HOME. *The Harvard Lampoon,* ser. 2, v. 5, no. 5, April 20, 1883, p. 49.

Cartoon entitled ANOTHER PLEA FOR TARIFF REFORM. *The Harvard Lampoon,* ser. 2, v. 5, no. 6, May 4, 1883, p. 55.

Cartoon entitled FAITH. *The Harvard Lampoon,* ser. 2, v. 5, no. 7, May 18, 1883, p. 69.

Cartoon entitled WHAT WE HAVE TO PUT UP WITH. *The Harvard Lampoon,* ser. 2, v. 5, no. 8, June 1, 1883, p. 78.

Cartoon entitled LOVE THYSELF AS THY NEIGHBOR. *The Harvard Lampoon,* ser. 2, v. 5, no. 9, June 15, 1883, p. 81.

Cartoon entitled A CLASS-DAY HORROR IN HOLYOKE HOUSE. *The Harvard Lampoon,* ser. 2, v. 5, no. 10, June 22, 1883, p. 98.

Cartoon entitled IMPERTINENCE. *The Harvard Lampoon,* ser. 2, v. 6, no. 3, Nov. 16, 1883, p. 28.

Cartoon entitled Hollis Holworthy's Courtesy. *The Harvard Lampoon*, ser. 2, v. 6, no. 4, Nov. 30, 1883, p. 34.

Cartoon entitled A Confession. *The Harvard Lampoon*, ser. 2, v. 6, no. 5, Dec. 7, 1883, p. 41.

Cartoon entitled Obejoyful Binks. *The Harvard Lampoon*, ser. 2, v. 6, no. 6, Dec. 21, 1883, p. 56.

1884

Cartoon entitled Choice of a Profession. *The Harvard Lampoon*, ser. 2, v. 6, no. 8, Jan. 18, 1884, p. 77.

Cartoon entitled Commendable Industry. *The Harvard Lampoon*, ser. 2, v. 6, no. 9, Feb. 1, 1884, p. 81.

Cartoon entitled A Double Game. *The Harvard Lampoon*, ser. 2, v. 6, no. 9, Feb. 1, 1884, p. 87.

[Initial for Valentine's Day.] *The Harvard Lampoon*, ser. 2, v. 6, no. 10, Feb. 15, 1884, p. 92.

Cartoon entitled Very Nice. *The Harvard Lampoon*, ser. 2, v. 7, no. 1, Feb. 29, 1884, p. 9.

Cartoon entitled O! Tempora! O! Mores! *The Harvard Lampoon*, ser. 2, v. 7, no. 2, March 14, 1884, p. 14.

Cartoon entitled Poor Snod. *The Harvard Lampoon*, ser. 2, v. 7, no. 3, March 28, 1884, p. 28.

Cartoon entitled An Unpopular Belt. *The Harvard Lampoon*, ser. 2, v. 7, no. 4, April 11, 1884, p. 33.

Cartoon entitled His Tile. *The Harvard Lampoon*, ser. 2, v. 7, no. 4, April 11, 1884, p. 35.

Cartoon entitled A Distinction. *The Harvard Lampoon*, ser. 2, v. 7, no. 5, April 25, 1884, p. 48.

Cartoon entitled No Chance. *The Harvard Lampoon*, ser. 2, v. 7, no. 6, May 2, 1884, p. 58.

Cartoon entitled Not His Meaning. *The Harvard Lampoon*, ser. 2, v. 7, no. 7, May 16, 1884, p. 61.

Cartoon entitled SIMPLEBOY'S BOLDNESS. *The Harvard Lampoon*, ser. 2, v. 7, no. 8, May 30, 1884, p. 71.

Cartoon entitled SHE BUILDED BETTER THAN SHE KNEW. *The Harvard Lampoon.* ser. 2, v. 7, no. 9, June 13, 1884, p. 88.

Cartoon entitled CLASS DAY. *The Harvard Lampoon*, ser. 2, v. 7, no. 10, June 20, 1884, p. 94-95.

Cartoon entitled THE RISE OF THE CURTAIN. *The Harvard Lampoon*, ser. 2, v. 8, no. 1, Oct. 17, 1884, p. 4-5.

Cartoon entitled A HORRID PUN. *The Harvard Lampoon*, ser. 2, v. 8, no. 1, Oct. 17, 1884, p. 8.

Cartoon entitled A HOPELESS CASE. *The Harvard Lampoon*, ser. 2, v. 8, no. 2, Oct. 24, 1884, p. 19.

Cartoon entitled LAMENTABLE CONCLUSION. *The Harvard Lampoon*, ser. 2, v. 8, no. 3, Nov. 7, 1884, p. 24.

Cartoon entitled HARD. *The Harvard Lampoon*, ser. 2, v. 8, no. 4, Nov. 21, 1884, p. 31.

Cartoon entitled QUITE ANOTHER THING. *The Harvard Lampoon*, ser. 2, v. 8, no. 5, Nov. 28, 1884, p. 42.

Cartoon entitled REPARTEE. *The Harvard Lampoon*, ser. 2, v. 8, no. 6, Dec. 22, 1884, p. 58.

1885

Cartoon entitled CATECHISM MODERNIZED. *The Harvard Lampoon*, ser. 2, v. 8, no. 7, Jan. 9, 1885, p. 61.

Cartoon entitled A BIG GUN. *The Harvard Lampoon*, ser. 2, v. 8, no. 8, Jan. 23, 1885, p. 71.

Cartoon entitled TOO YOUNG FOR SUSPICION. *The Harvard Lampoon*, ser. 2, v. 8, no. 9, Feb. 13, 1885, p. 81.

THE PROBLEM OF THE FREEDOM OF THE WILL IN ITS RELATION TO ETHICS. A Junior Forensic. *The Daily Crimson*, v. 7, no. 15, Feb. 25, 1885, Supplement, p. 2-4.

Cartoon entitled JUST OUT. *The Harvard Lampoon*, ser. 2, v. 9, no. 1, March 6, 1885, p. 9.

Cartoon entitled EVOLUTION OF THE GREAT ANNEX IDEA; COMPULSORY CHAPEL MADE EASY. *The Harvard Lampoon*, ser. 2, v. 9, no. 2, March 20, 1885, p. 19.

KING LEAR AS A TYPE OF THE GOTHIC DRAMA. A Junior Theme. *The Daily Crimson*, v. 7, no. 40, March 26, 1885, Supplement, p. 2.

Cartoon entitled THINGS ONE WOULD RATHER HAVE LEFT UNSAID. *The Harvard Lampoon*, ser. 2, v. 9, no. 4, April 17, 1885, p. 38.

Cartoon entitled A NATURAL MISTAKE. *The Harvard Lampoon*, ser. 2, v. 9, no. 7, May 22, 1885, p. 69.

Cartoon entitled FINE ARTS. *The Harvard Lampoon*, ser. 2, v. 9, no. 10, June 26, 1885, p. 99.

SONNET. *The Harvard Monthly*, v. 1, no. 1, Oct., 1885, p. 11.

"I would I might forget that I am I"

Reprinted, with changes, as Sonnet VII. In: *Sonnets and Other Verses* (1894), (1896), (1906); *Poems* (1923), p. 9; Edman, I., ed., *The Philosophy of Santayana* (1936), p. 22; *Triton Ed.*, v. 1 (1936), p. 218.

Other reprints. In: Ritterhouse, J. B., ed. *Younger American Poets*, Boston, 1904, p. 98-99; Ritterhouse, J. B., ed. *Little Book of Modern Verse*, Boston, [c1913], p. 177-178; Zeitlin, J. and C. Rinaker, eds., *Types of Poetry*, New York, 1927, p. 675-676; Van Doren, M. and G. M. Lapolla, eds., *World's Best Poems*, New York, [c1929] p. 651; Van Doren, M. ed., *American Poets from 1630-1930*, Boston, 1933, p. 344; Van Doren, M. ed., *Anthology of World Poetry*, New York, [c1939] p. 1375-1376.

For mss., cf. entry, part II, 1890.

SPANISH EPIGRAMS. *The Harvard Monthly*, v. 1, no. 1, Oct. 1885, p. 22.

SONNET. *The Harvard Monthly*, v. 1, no. 2, Nov. 1885, p. 49.

"Dreamt I to-night the dream of yesternight"

Reprinted, with changes, as Sonnet V. In: *Sonnets and Other Verses* (1894), (1896), (1906); *Poems* (1923), p. 7; *Triton Ed.*, v. 1 (1936), p. 217.

For mss., cf. entry, part II, 1890.

Cartoon entitled DISTINCTION WITH DIFFERENCE. *The Harvard Lampoon*, ser. 2, v. 10, no. 2, Nov. 6, 1885, p. 18.

Cartoon entitled FROM HER POINT OF VIEW. *The Harvard Lampoon*, ser. 2, v. 10, no. 3, Nov. 20, 1885, p. 21.

THE MAY NIGHT. *The Harvard Monthly*, v. 1, no. 3, Dec. 1885, p. 96-101.

From the French of Alfred de Musset.

REVIEW of John Fiske, *The Idea of God as Affected by Modern Knowledge. The Harvard Monthly*, v. 1, no. 3, Dec. 1885, p, 134.

Cartoon entitled SOME CLASS PHOTOGRAPHS. *The Harvard Lampoon*, ser. 2, v. 10, no. 5, Dec. 11, 1885, p. 48.

In collaboration with C. C. Felton, '86.

Includes self-portrait.

1886

Cartoon entitled REVENGE. *The Harvard Lampoon*, ser. 2, v. 10, no. 9, Jan. 29, 1886, p. 84.

SONNET. *The Harvard Monthly*, v. 1, no. 5, Feb. 1886, p. 206.

"Love not as do the phantom-driven men"

Reprinted, with changes, as Sonnet VI. In: *Sonnets and Other Verses* (1894), (1896), (1906), *Poems* (1923), p. 8; *Philosophy of Santayana* (1936), p. 22; *Triton Ed.*, v. 1 (1936), p. 217.

For mss., cf. entry, part II, 1890.

Cartoon entitled AN EPITAPH. *The Harvard Lampoon*, ser. 2, v. 10, no. 10, Feb. 12, 1886, p. 98.

Cartoon entitled AMBIGUOUS. *The Harvard Lampoon*, ser. 2, v. 11, no. 2, March 12, 1886, p. 18.

SONNET. *The Harvard Monthly*, v. 2, no. 2, April, 1886, p. 68.

"O World thou choosest not the better part"

Dated 1884, and listed as Sonnet IV, in *Earliest Verses . . .* (1890, Part II), p. 8. Cf. letter to William Lyon Phelps from Rome, Nov. 2, 1928 (in which 1884 is mentioned) for Santayana's criticisms of this Sonnet. (Phelps' *Autobiography With Letters*, New York, 1939, p. 343.)

Reprinted, with changes, as Sonnet III. In: *Sonnets and Other Verses* (1894), (1896), (1906), *Poems* (1923), p. 5; *Philosophy of Santayana* (1936), p. 21; *Triton Ed.*, v. 1 (1936), p. 216.

Other reprints. In: Warner, C. D., ed., *Library of World's Best Literature, Ancient and Modern*, v. 41, 1897, p. 16881; Hill, C. M., ed., *World's Great Religious Poetry*, New York, 1923, p. 216; Carman, B., ed., *Oxford Book of American Verse*, New York, 1927, p. 510; Clark, T. C. and E. A. Gillespie, *Quotable Poems*, Chicago, 1928, p. 7; Untermeyer, L., *Modern American Poetry*, New York, 1930, p. 136; Lieberman, E., ed., *Poems for Enjoyment*, New York, 1931, p. 254; Braddy, N., ed., *Standard Book of British and American Verse*, Garden City [c1932], p. 672; *The Homiletic Review*, v. 103, no. 4, April, 1932, p. 322; Phelps, W. L., ed., *What I Like in Poetry*, New York, 1934, p. 352; Blair, W. and W. K. Chandler, eds., *Approaches to Poetry*, New York, [c1935], p. 333; *Scholastic*, v. 25, no. 13, Jan. 5, 1935, p. 11; Hubbell, J. B. and J. O. Beaty, eds., *Introduction to Poetry*, New York,

1936, p. 291; Hubbell, J. B., ed., *American Life in Literature*, New York, 1936, p. 415; Untermeyer, L., ed., *Critical Anthology*, New York, [c1936], p. 126; Stevenson, B. E., ed., *Home Book of Verse*, New York, [c1937], v. 2, p. 2907; Benet, W. R., and N. H. Pearson, eds., *Oxford Anthology of American Literature*, New York, 1938, p. 1110.

For mss., cf. entry, part II, 1890.

Cartoon entitled SOME DINNERS. *The Harvard Lampoon*, ser. 2, v. 11, no. 7, May 21, 1886, p. 64-65.

In collaboration with H. Dike, '86 and L. L. Hight, '86.

THE ETHICAL DOCTRINE OF SPINOZA. *The Harvard Monthly*, v. 2, no. 4, June, 1886, p. 144-152.

SONNET. *The Harvard Monthly*, v. 2, no. 4, June, 1886, p. 152.

"Oh would we had been born in nature's day"

Reprinted, with changes, as Sonnet IV. In: *Sonnets and Other Verses* (1894), (1896), (1906), *Poems* (1923), p. 6; *Philosophy of Santayana* (1936), p. 21; *Triton Ed.*, v. 1 (1936), p. 216.

For mss., cf. entry, part II, 1890.

Cartoon entitled FAREWELL FANCIES. *The Harvard Lampoon*, ser. 2, v. 11, no. 10, June 25, 1886, p. 94-95.

In collaboration with L. L. Hight, '86 and C. C. Felton, '86.

1888

TWO VOICES. *The Harvard Monthly*, v. 6, no. 3, May, 1888, p. 94-95.

For mss., cf. entry, part II, 1890.

1889

THOMAS PARKER SANBORN. *The Harvard Monthly*, v. 8, no. 1, March, 1889, p. 35.

This obituary differs from the one published in *Harvard College. Class of 1886. Secretary's Report. No. VII.*
Cf. entry, 1911.

[AUTOBIOGRAPHICAL REPORT]. In: *Harvard College. Class of 1886. Secretary's Report. No. II.* June, 1889. Cambridge, Mass., W. H. Wheeler, Printer, [1889?], p. 50.

In section entitled, "Record of the Class."

Relates activities since June, 1886: European travels and studies on a Walker fellowship, return to Harvard for graduate work and writing thesis on Lotze.

REVIEW of William A. Leahy, *The Siege of Syracuse: A Political Drama. The Harvard Monthly*, v. 8, no. 4, June, 1889, p. 166-168.

1890

SOUVENIR. *The Harvard Monthly*, v. 10, no. 1, March, 1890, p. 8-14.

From the French of Alfred de Musset.

Reprinted, with changes. In: *A Hermit of Carmel and Other Poems* (1901), p. 144-155. In: Van Doren, M., ed., *Anthology of World Poetry*, New York, [c1939], p. 748-753.

LOTZE'S MORAL IDEALISM. *Mind*, v. 15, no. 58, April, 1890, p. 191-212.

Modified abstracts of Ph.D. thesis.

Cf. entry, part II, 1889.

WALT WHITMAN; A Dialogue. *The Harvard Monthly*, v. 10, no. 3, May, 1890, p. 85-92.

1891

JAMES'S PSYCHOLOGY. *The Atlantic Monthly*, v. 67, no. 4, April, 1891, p. 552-556.

Unsigned review of William James, *The Principles of Psychology*.

Listed as by Santayana. In: *Harvard College. Class of 1886. Secretary's Report. No. VII.* Cambridge, The University Press, [1911?], p. 327.

Excerpts. In: Perry, Ralph Barton, *The Thought and Character of William James . . .*, Boston, Little, Brown, 1935, v. 2, p. 110-111.

1892

AT NOON. *Scribner's Magazine*, v. 11, no. 1, Jan., 1892, p. 67.

FIVE SONNETS. *The Harvard Monthly*, v. 13, no. 4, Jan., 1892, p. 153-155.

I. There was a time when in the teeth of fate, p. 153.
II. A thousand beauties that have never been, p. 154.
III. There may be chaos still around the world, p. 154.
IV. Blaspheme not love, ye lovers, nor dispraise, p. 155.
V. Above the battlements of heaven rise, p. 155.

Reprints. I as XVII, II as XVI, III as XIV, IV as XVIII, V as XIX. In: *Sonnets and Other Verses* (1894), (1896), (1906), *Poems* (1923), p. 19, 18, 16, 20, 21. In: *Triton Ed.*, v. 1 (1936), p. 223, 222, 221, 223, 224.

Other reprints. I. In: Hall, H. J., *Types of Poetry*, New York, [c1927], p. 311; II. In: Ritterhouse, J. B., ed., *Younger American Poets*, Boston, 1904, p. 95-96.

For mss. of Sonnet IV, cf. entry, part II, 1890.

REVIEW of William Morton Fullerton, *In Cairo*. *The Harvard Monthly*, v. 13, no. 4, Jan., 1892, p. 172-174.

WHAT IS A PHILISTINE? *The Harvard Monthly*, v. 14, no. 3, May, 1892, p. 89-99.

A GLIMPSE OF YALE. *The Harvard Monthly*, v. 15, no. 3, Dec. 1892, p. 89-97.

THE PRESENT POSITION OF THE ROMAN CATHOLIC CHURCH. *The New World* (Boston), v. 1, no. 4, Dec., 1892, p. 658-673.

1894

SONNETS AND OTHER VERSES. Cambridge and Chicago, G. S. Stone and Kimball, 1894. 90 p.

500 copies; 450 in cloth, and 50 large paper in vellum binding.

Border and lettering in the title on the title page by the author.

Other eds. *Sonnets and Other Verses* (1896): Contents identical, with the addition of Sonnets, and series, XXI-L. *Sonnets and Other Verses* (1906): *Lucifer, A Prelude*, omitted; Sonnets, 2nd series, added.

Contents. I. I sought on earth a garden of delight—II. Slow and reluctant was the long descent—III. O world thou choosest not the better part—IV. I would I had been born in nature's day—V. Dreamt I to-day the dream of yesternight—VI. Love not as do the flesh-imprisoned men—VII. I would I might forget that I am I—VIII. O martyred Spirit of this helpless Whole—IX. Have patience: It is fit that in this wise—X. Have I the heart to wander on the earth—XI. Deem not, because you see me in the press—XII. Mightier storms than this are brewed on earth—XIII. Sweet are the days when we wander with no hope—XIV. There may be chaos still around the world—XV. A wall, a wall around my garden rear—XVI. A thousand beauties that have never been—XVII. Gone is the time when in the teeth of fate—XVIII. Blaspheme not love, ye lovers, nor dispraise—XIX. Above the battlements of heaven rise—XX. These strewn thoughts, by the mountain pathway sprung—On a Volume of Scholastic Philosophy—On the Death of a Metaphysician—On a Piece of Tapestry—The Power of Art—Gabriel—To W. P. Odes: I. What God will choose me from this labouring nation—II. My heart rebels against my generation—III. Gathering the echoes of forgotten wisdom—IV. Slowly the black earth gains upon the yellow—V. Of thee the Northman by his beachèd galley.

Various Poems: Easter Hymn—Good Friday Hymn—Cape Cod—Lenten Greeting; to a Lady—Decima—A Toast—Chorus—Lucifer, A Prelude.

Reprints. "Lucifer, A Prelude." In: *Sonnets and Other Verses* (1896), p. 101-122. With changes, as Act I of *Lucifer, A Theological Tragedy* (1899), p. 1-34. (In 2nd ed. (1924), p. 1-23; *Triton Ed.*, v. 1 (1936), p. 297-319.)

In: *Poems* (1923). Sonnets I-XX (1883-1893), p. 3-22; On a Volume of Scholastic Philosophy, p. 57; On the Death of a Metaphysician, p. 58; On a Piece of Tapestry, p. 59; To W. P., p. 60-63; Odes, p. 71-82; Cape Cod, p. 91; A Toast, p. 92.

In: *Philosophy of Santayana* (1936). Sonnet III, p. 21; IV, p. 21; VI, p. 22; VII, p. 22; XI, p. 23; XIII, p. 23; On a Volume of Scholastic Philosophy, p.

25; On the Death of a Metaphysician, p. 26; To W.P. [Sonnet II], p. 26. In: *Triton Ed.*, v. 1 (1936). Sonnets I-XX, p. 215-224; On a Volume of Scholastic Philosophy; On the Death of a Metaphysician, p. 240; On a Piece of Tapestry, p. 241; To W.P., p. 242-244; Odes, p. 246-252; Cape Cod, p. 257; A Toast, p. 257-258.

For previous and later publication, and for reprints of the following Sonnets, cf. entries under dates listed. Sonnets III, IV, VI, 1886; V, VII, 1885; XIV, XVI, XVII, XVIII, XIX, 1892.

Other reprints. Sonnet I. In: Hall, H. J., ed. *Types of Poetry*, New York, [c1927], p. 311. II. In: Van Doren, M., ed., *American Poets*, Boston, 1933, p. 344. IX. In: Hill, C. M., ed., *World's Great Religious Poetry*, New York, 1923, p. 596-597; Van Doren, M., ed., *American Poets*, Boston, 1933, p. 344-345. X. In: *Scholastic*, v. 15, no. 13, Jan. 5, 1935, p. 11. XIII. In: Van Doren, M., ed., *American Poets*, Boston, 1933, p. 345. XV. In: Phelps, W. L., *What I Like in Poetry*, New York, 1934, p. 351. XX. In: Ritterhouse, J. B., ed., *Younger American Poets*, Boston, 1904, p. 103; Carman, B., ed., *Oxford Book of American Verse*, New York, 1927, p. 511.

On a Volume of Scholastic Philosophy. In: Untermeyer, L., ed., *American Poetry Since 1900*, New York, 1923, p. 289-290; Phelps, W. L., *What I Like in Poetry*, New York, 1934, p. 352; Hubbell, J. B., ed., *American Life in Literature*, New York, 1936, p. 415.

On the Death of a Metaphysician. In: Stedman, E. C., ed., *American Anthology, 1787-1900*, Boston, 1900, p. 761; Carman, B., ed., *Oxford Book of American Verse*, New York, 1927, p. 509; Aiken, C., ed., *American Poetry*, New York, [c1929], p. 207-208; *Latin School Register*, v. 49, no. 4, 1929-1930, p. 7; Untermeyer, L., ed., *Critical Anthology*, New York, [c1936], p. 125.

On a Piece of Tapestry. In: Stedman, E. C., ed., *American Anthology, 1787-1900*, Boston, 1900, p. 761-762; Carman, B., ed., *Oxford Book of American Verse*, New York, 1927, p. 509-510.

The Power of Art. In: Howgate, G. W., *George Santayana*, Phila., 1938, p. 70. To W.P. In: Carman, B., ed., *Oxford Book of American Verse*, New York, 1927, p. 512-514.

Odes. I. In: Aiken, C., ed., *American Poetry* (Modern Library ed.), [c1929], p. 209-210. II. In: *Ibid.*, p. 210; Blair, W. and W. K. Chandler, eds., *Approaches to Poetry*, New York, [c1935], p. 375-376; Hubbell, J. B., *American Life in Literature*, New York, 1936, p. 416. III. In: Aiken, C., ed., *American Poetry*, [c1929], p. 211-213; Kreymborg, A., ed., *Lyric America*, New York, 1930, p. 232-234. IV. In: Aiken, C., *American Poetry*, [c1929], p. 213. V. In: *Magic Carpet*, Boston, 1924, p. 409-411; Hall, H. J., *Types of Poetry*, New York, [c1927], p. 290; Horan, K., *Parnassus en Route*, New York, 1929, p. 222-223; Aiken, C., ed., *American Poetry*, [c1929], p. 213-215; Kreymborg, A., ed., *Lyric America*, New York, 1930, p. 234-236.

Odes set to music. IV. as no. 38, *The Ploughman*. Songs, by Reginald C. Robbins. (For bass or baritone.) Paris, Editions Maurice Senart, 20, Rue du Dragon, [c1924], 3 p. V. as no. 47, *Ode to the Mediterranean*. *Ibid.* 7 p.

For mss. of Sonnets I, X, XI, XIII, Easter Hymn, and Good Friday Hymn, cf. entry, part II, 1890.

REVIEW of John Owen, *The Skeptics of the Italian Renaissance. The New World* (Boston), v. 3, no. 9, March, 1894, p. 190-192.

THE SPIRIT AND IDEALS OF HARVARD UNIVERSITY. *The Educational Review*, v. 7, April, 1894, p. 313-325.

PHILOSOPHY ON THE BLEACHERS. *The Harvard Monthly*, v. 18, no. 5, July, 1894, p. 181-190.

TWO MORALITIES. *The Harvard Monthly*, v. 19, no. 1, Oct., 1894, p. 30.

1895

SONNETS. *The Harvard Monthly*, v. 21, no. 1, Oct., 1895, p. 4-9.

I. Among the myriad voices of the Spring, p. 4-5.
II. 'Tis love that moveth the celestial spheres, p. 5.
III. But is this love, that in my hollow breast, p. 5-6.
IV. As in the midst of battle there is room, p. 6.
V. Let my lips touch thy lips, and my desire, p. 6-7.
VI. Out of the dust the queen of roses springs, p. 7.
VII. A perfect love is nourished by despair, p. 7.
VIII. Thou hast no name, or if a name thou bearest, p. 8.
IX. When I survey the harvest of the year, p. 8.
X. Though utter death should swallow up my hope, p. 8-9.

Reprints. In: *Sonnets and Other Verses* (1896), (1906), *Poems* (1923) as Sonnets XXI, XXII, XXIII, XXV, XXX, XXVIII, XXXIII, XLVII, XLVI, L., p. 25, 26, 27, 29, 34, 32, 37, 51, 50, 54. In: *Philosophy of Santayana* (1936), II and IV, p. 24. In: *Triton Ed.*, v. 1 (1936), p. 225, 226, 227, 229, 228, 231, 238, 237,239.

Other reprints. II. In: Richards, W., ed., *Love's High Way*, Boston, 1927, p. 182; Van Doren, M., ed., *American Poets, 1630-1930*, Boston, 1933, p. 345. IV. Ritterhouse, J. B., ed., *Little Book of Modern Verse*, Boston, [c1913], p. 153; Le Gallienne, R., ed., *Le Gallienne Book of American Verse*, New York, [c1925], p. 259; Zeitlin, J. and C. Rinaker, eds., *Types of Poetry*, New York, 1927, p. 676; Van Doren, M. and G. M. Lapolla, eds., *World's Best Poems*, New York, [c1929], p. 651-652; *Latin School Register*, v. 49, no. 4, 1929-1930, p. 7; Aiken, C., *American Poetry*, [c1929], p. 208; Van Doren, M., ed., *American Poets, 1630-1930*, Boston, 1933, p. 345-346; Markham, E., ed., *Book of American Poetry*, New York, 1934, p. 350; Untermeyer, L., ed., *Critical Anthology*, New York, [c1936], p. 125; Van Doren, M., ed., *Anthology of World Poetry*, New York, [c1939], p. 1376.

1896

THE SENSE OF BEAUTY; BEING THE OUTLINES OF AESTHETIC THEORY. New York, Charles Scribner's Sons. ix, 275 p.

Published in London by A. and C. Black, 1896, and Constable and Co., Ltd., 1918.

Republished by Scribner's [c1936]. xi, 210 p.

Reprinted. In: *Triton Ed.*, v. 1 (1936), p. 3-205.

Translation. *Bi-ishiki ron*, by Ukô Washio, Tokyo, Shunjû sha, 1936.

Contents. Preface (dated Sept., 1896)—Introduction; The Methods of Aesthetics—Part I. The Nature of Beauty—Part II. The Materials of Beauty—Part III. Form—Part IV. Expression—Conclusion.

Other reprints. Introduction and part of Part II. In: *Philosophy of Santayana* (1936), p. 27-39. Part II. In: Burgum, E.B., ed., *The New Criticism; An Anthology of Modern Aesthetics and Literary Criticism*, New York, 1930, p. 75-106.

Certain excerpts from "The Sense of Beauty." In: Carritt, F.F., ed., *Philosophies of Beauty from Socrates to Robert Bridges; Being the Source of Aesthetic Theory*, London, 1931, p. 198-204.

Certain portions of the following noted pages appear in *Little Essays* (1920): p. 3-4 as essay no. 1, "Spirit the Judge," p. 3-4; p. 189-191 as no. 33, "Christ and the Virgin," p. 76-77; p. 215-221 as no. 49, "Utility and Beauty," p. 119-123; p. 260-262 as no. 50, "Glimpses of Perfection," p. 123-125; p. 211-214 as no. 52, "Costliness," p. 125-126; p. 100-106 as no. 53, "The Stars," p. 126-129; p. 69-70 as no. 54, "Music," p. 129-137; p. 63-65 as no. 73, "The Unhappiness of Artists," p. 184-186; p. 16-20 as no. 88, "Value Irrational," p. 224-226; p. 41-42 as no. 94, "Relativity of Values," p. 240-242; p. 39 as no. 96, "Pleasures Ingenuous," p. 246-247; p. 66-68 as no. 97, "The Lower Senses," p. 247-248; p. 23-25 as no. 98, "Pleasure and Conscience," p. 248-249; p. 241-242, 244-245, as no. 112, "Detachment," p. 280-282; p. 29-31, p. 263-264 as no. 113, "The Profits of Living," p. 282-285; p. 267-270, as no. 114, "Beauty a Hint of Happiness," p. 285-286.

SONNETS AND OTHER VERSES. New York, Stone and Kimball, 1896. 122 p.

Border and lettering in title on title page by the author.

Contents. First series I-XX. (cf. entry 1894 ed.) Second Series XXI-L.
XXI. Among the myriad voices of the Spring—XXII. 'Tis love that moveth the celestial spheres—XXIII. But is this love, that in my hollow breast—XXIV. Although I decked a chamber for my bride—XXV. As in the midst of battle there is room—XXVI. Oh, if the heavy last uttered groan—XXVII. Sleep hath composed the anguish of my brain—XXVIII. Out of the dust the queen of roses springs—XXIX. What riches have you that you deem me poor—XXX. Let my lips touch thy lips, and my desire—XXXI. A brother's love, but that I chose thee out—XXXII. Let not thy bosom, to my foes allied—XXXIII. A perfect love is nourished by despair—XXXIV. Though destiny half broke her cruel bars—XXXV. We needs must be divided in the tomb—XXXVI. We were together, and I longed to tell—XXXVII. And I was silent. Now you do not know—XXXVIII. Oh, not for me, for thee, dear God, her head—XXXIX. The world will say, "What mystic love is this?—XL. If,

when the story of my love is told—XLI. Yet why, of one who loved thee not, command—XLII. As when the sceptre dangles from the hand—XLIII. The candour of the gods is in thy gaze—XLIV. For thee the sun doth daily rise, and set—XLV. Flower of my world, bright angel, single friend!—XLVI. When I survey the harvest of the year—XLVII. Thou hast no name, or, if a name thou bearest—XLVIII. Of Helen's brothers, one was born to die—XLIX. After grey vigils, sunshine in the heart—L. Though utter death should swallow up my hope. (The rest of the contents, as in 1894 ed.)

For previous and later publication, and for reprints of the following Sonnets, cf. entry under 1895: XXI, XXII, XXIII, XXV, XXVIII, XXX, XXXIII, XLVII, XLVI, L.

Reprints. Sonnet XXIX. In: Cooper, A.C., ed., *Poems of To-day*, New York, [c1924], p. 153; Le Gallienne, R., ed., *Le Gallienne Book of American Verse*, New York, [c1925], p. 259-260; Markham, E., ed., *Book of American Poetry*, New York, 1934, p. 349-350; Stevenson, E. G., ed., *Home Book of Verse*, New York [c1937] v. 2, p. 2907. Sonnet XXXV. In: Ritterhouse, J.B., *Younger American Poets*, Boston, 1904, p. 109; Ritterhouse, J. B., *Little Book of Modern Verse*, Boston, [c1913], p. 172; Carman, B., ed., *Oxford Book of American Verse*, New York, 1927, p. 511-512. Sonnet XLI. In: Ritterhouse, J.B., *Younger American Poets*, 1904, p. 108-109. Sonnet XLII. In: Van Doren, M., ed., *American Poets, 1630-1930*, Boston, 1933, p. 346; Blair, W. and W. K. Chandler, *Approaches to Poetry*, New York, [c1935], p. 333. Sonnet XLIX. In: Untermeyer, L., *American Poetry Since 1900*, New York, 1923, p. 289; Van Doren, M., ed., *American Poets, 1630-1930*, Boston, 1933, p. 346; Untermeyer, L., ed., *Critical Anthology*, New York, [c1936], p. 125. Sonnet L. In: Hubbell, J. B., *American Life in Literature*, New York, 1936, p. 415.

PLATONISM IN THE ITALIAN POETS. Buffalo, Paul's Press, [1896?], [privately published], 31 unnumbered p.

Written for the Contemporary Club, and read at the meeting of Feb. 5, 1896.

Reprinted, with changes. In: *Interpretations of Poetry and Religion* (1900) as Ch. V, p. 118-146; *Triton Ed.*, v. 2 (1936), p. 85-105.

In William James's copy, kept in the Treasure Room at Harvard University, there are several textual corrections in Santayana's handwriting.

BERENSON'S FLORENTINE PAINTERS. *The Psychological Review*, v. 3, no. 6, Nov., 1896, p. 677-679.

Review of Bernhard Berenson, *The Florentine Painters of the Italian Renaissance with an Index to their Works.*

THE ABSENCE OF RELIGION IN SHAKESPEARE. *The New World* (Boston), v. 5, no. 22, Dec., 1896, p. 681-691.

Condensed version. In: *Public Opinion; a Weekly Journal*, v. 22, no. 9, March 4, 1897, p. 275.

Reprinted. In: *Interpretations of Poetry and Religion* (1900), as Ch. VI, p. 147-165; *Triton Ed.*, v. 2 (1936), p. 106-118.

1897

CERVANTES (1547-1616). In: Warner, Charles Dudley, ed., *A Library of the World's Best Literature, Ancient and Modern.* (The University Edition) The International Society, 1897, v. 8, p. 3451-3457.

Also in: Cunliffe, J. W. and Thorndike, A. H., *The World's Best Literature* (Warner Library), New York, Warner Library Co., 1917, v. 6, p. 3451-3457.

Reprinted. In: *Columbia University. Course in Literature.* v. 8, *The Great Literature of Small Nations.* New York, Columbia University Press, [c1929] p. 82-87.

REVIEW of Giuseppe Sergi, *Psicologia per le Scuole. The Psychological Review,* v. 4, no. 5, Sept., 1897, p. 538-539.

BEFORE A STATUE OF ACHILLES. *The Harvard Monthly,* v. 25, no. 1, Oct., 1897, p. 1-2.

3 Sonnets. I. Behold Pelides with his yellow hair. II. I gaze on him as Phidias of old. III. Who brought thee forth, immortal vision, who.

Reprinted, with changes. In: *A Hermit of Carmel* (1901), p. 117-119; *Poems* (1923), p. 64-66; *Triton Ed.*, v. 1 (1936), p. 243-244; Stevenson, B. E., ed., *Home Book of Verse,* New York, [c1937], v. 2, p. 3212-3213.

REVIEW of Otto Willmann, *Geschichte des Idealismus. Zweiter Band. Der Idealismus der Kirchenväter und der Realismus der Scholastiker. The Philosophical Review,* v. 6, no. 6, Nov., 1897, p. 661-664.

1898

KING'S COLLEGE CHAPEL; An Elegy. *The Harvard Monthly,* v. 26, no. 1, March, 1898, p. 1-5.

Dated King's College, Cambridge, Nov., 1896.

Reprinted, with changes. In: *A Hermit of Carmel* (1901), p. 99-106; *Poems* (1923), p. 105-109; *Triton Ed.,* v. 1 (1936), p. 265-269.

1899

LUCIFER; A THEOLOGICAL TRAGEDY. Chicago and New York, Herbert S. Stone and Co., 1899. 187 p.

Contents. Invocation—Act I. A Mountain Top—Act II. The Garden of the Hesperides—Act III. Hell; Subterraneous Hall, with a great Hearth—Act IV, Scene I [The Gate of Heaven]; Scene II, Heaven—Act V, Scene I. The Palace of Zeus; Scene II, Lucifer's Island, as in Act I.

Reprints. Invocation and excerpts. In: An unsigned review, *Literature; an International Gazette of Criticism,* n.s. no. 32, Aug. 18, 1899, p. 138-139.
2nd ed., 1924.

MEMORIES OF KING'S COLLEGE, CAMBRIDGE. *The Harvard Monthly,* v. 28, no. 1, March, 1899, p. 1-14.

Autobiographical essay, describing experiences at King's College during a year's leave of absence, 1896-1897.

IN GRANTCHESTER MEADOWS; On First Hearing a Skylark Sing. *The Harvard Monthly*, v. 28, no. 3, May, 1899, p. 85-86.

Reprinted. In: *A Hermit of Carmel* (1901), p. 114-115; *The Book Buyer*, v. 23, n.s. no. 5, Dec., 1901, p. 384; *Poems* (1923), p. 116-117; *Triton Ed.*, v. 1 (1936), p. 272-273.

REVIEW of George Santayana, *Lucifer; A Theological Tragedy*. *The Harvard Monthly*, v. 28, no. 5, July, 1899, p. 210-212.

Signed "H.M." Listed as having been written "by myself." In: *Harvard College. Class of 1886. Secretary's Report. No. VII*, [1911?], in the Bibliography, p. 327.

Excerpt. In: Howgate, G. W., *George Santayana*, Phila., 1938, p. 74. Footnote by Santayana on how he came to write this review.

GREEK RELIGION. *The New World* (Boston), v. 8, no. 31, Sept., 1899, p. 401-417.

Review of Lewis Campbell, *Religion in Greek Literature*.

Reprinted, with changes. In: *Interpretations of Poetry and Religion* (1900), as Ch. III, p. 49-75; *Triton Ed.*, v 2 (1936), p. 40-58.

1900

INTERPRETATION OF POETRY AND RELIGION. New York, Charles Scribner's Sons, 1900. xi, 290 p.

Published in London by A. and C. Black, 1900.

Reprinted. In: *Triton Ed.*, v. 2 (1936), p. 3-201.

For previous and later publication, and for reprints of certain chapters, cf. entries under dates immediately following titles listed in the contents.

Contents. Preface—I. Understanding, Imagination, and Mysticism—II. The Homeric Hymns—III. The Dissolution of Paganism (1899)—IV. The Poetry of Christian Dogma—V. Platonic Love in Some Italian Poets (1896)—VI. The Absence of Religion in Shakespeare (1896)—VII. The Poetry of Barbarism—VIII. Emerson—IX. A Religion of Disillusion—X. The Elements and Function of Poetry.

Ch. VII was originally read before the Browning Club of Boston.

In Ch. V appear incidental translations from Michelangelo, Cavalcanti, and Lorenzo de' Medici.

Reprints. Ch. VIII. In: Hillyer, R.S. *et al.*, eds., *Prose Masterpieces of English and American Literature*, New York, [c1931], p. 390-400.

Certain portions of the following noted pages appear in *Little Essays* (1920): p. 28-29 as essay no. 2, "The Origin of Morals," p. 4-5; p. 246 as no. 3, "Ideals," p. 5-6; p. 1-3 as no. 4, "Intellectual Ambition," p. 6-8; p. 252 as no. 13, "What People Will Put Up With," p. 27-28; p. v-ix as no. 24, "Prosaic

Misunderstandings," p. 51-53; p. 47 as no. 26, "Pathetic Notions of God," p. 54-56; p. 85-86, 285, 88, as no. 29, "The Convert," p. 60-62; p. 90-98 as no. 30, "Christian Doctrine a Moral Allegory," p. 62-67; p. 57, 113-117 as no. 34, "Orthodoxy and Heresy," p. 77-80; p. 112-113 as no. 35, "Protestantism," p. 80-83; p. 137-141 as no. 43, "Platonic Love," p. 100-102; p. 268-270 as no. 56, "The Need of Poetry," p. 139-140; p. 258-263 as no. 58, "The Elements of Poetry," p. 144-146; p. 219-220, 248, as no. 69, "Transcendentalism," p. 176-178; p. 166-170 as no. 72, "Modern Poetry," p. 182-184; p. 131-132 as no. 74, "Poetry of Latin Peoples," p. 186; p. 153-156 as no. 76, "Absence of Religion in Shakespeare," p. 188-190; p. 185 as no. 77, "Romantic Ignorance of Self," p. 190-191; p. 231-233 as no. 81, "Emerson," p. 199-203; p. 192-194; 199-207 as no. 83, "Browning," p. 206-212; p. 21 as no. 90, "Sadness of Naturalism," p. 230-234; p. 249-250 as no. 91, "Happiness in Disillusion," p. 234-235; p. 101 as no. 113, "The Profit of Living," p. 282-285.

THE DECAY OF LATIN. *The Harvard Monthly*, v. 30, no. 1, March, 1900, p. 1-13.

REVIEW of Lucien Levy-Bruhl, *History of Modern Philosophy in France. The New World* (Boston), v. 9, no. 34, June, 1900, p. 356-357.

REVIEW of James Haughton Woods, *The Value of Religious Facts; a Study of Some Aspects of the Science of Religion. Ibid.*, p. 357-359.

REVIEW of William Wells Newell, *Sonnets and Madrigals of Michelangelo Buonarroti. The New World* (Boston), v. 9, no. 37, Sept., 1900, p. 584-585.

YOUNG SAMMY'S FIRST WILD OATS: Lines Read at the Thirtieth Anniversary of the Signet. *The Harvard Lampoon*, v. 40, no. 4, Nov. 20, 1900, Supplement, p. 1-4.

Reprinted, with subtitle, "Lines Written before the Presidential Election of 1900." In: *A Hermit of Carmel* (1901), p. 204-215.

1901

A HERMIT OF CARMEL, AND OTHER POEMS. New York, Charles Scribner's Sons, 1901. vi, 234 p.

Published in London by R. B. Johnson, 1902; new ed. in London by T. Fisher Unwin, 1907.

Contents. A Hermit of Carmel—The Knight's Return; A Sequel to A Hermit of Carmel—Elegiac and Lyric Poems: Premonition—Solipsism—Sybaris—Avila—King's College Chapel—On An Unfinished Statue; by Michael Angelo in the Bargello, Called an Apollo or a David—Midnight—In Grantchester Meadows—Futility—Before a Statue of Achilles—Odi et Amo—Cathedrals by the Sea; Reply to a Sonnet beginning "Cathedrals are not built along the Sea"—Mont Brevent—The Rustic at the Play—Resurrection—Translations: From Michael Angelo—From Alfred de Musset: Souvenir—From Théophile Gautier: Art—Convival and Occasional Verses: Prosit Neujahr—Fair Harvard —College Drinking Song—Six Wise Fools—Athletic Ode—The Bottles and the Wine; Lines Read at the Reunion of a College Club—The Poetic Medium —Young Sammy's First Wild Oats—Spain in America—Youth's Immortality.

Reprints. In: *Poems* (1923). Premonition, p. 93-94; Solipsism, 95-96; Sybaris, p. 97-100; Avila, p. 101-104; On an Unfinished Statue, p. 110-113; Midnight, p. 114-115; Rustic at the Play, p. 67; Art from Theophile Gautier, p. 138-140; Athletic Ode, p. 83-87; Spain in America, p. 118-129.

In: *Triton Ed.*, v. 1 (1936). Premonition, p. 258-259; Solipsism, p. 259-260; Sybaris, p. 260-262; Avila, p. 262-265; On an Unfinished Statue, p. 269-271; Midnight, p. 271-272; The Rustic at the Play, p. 254; Art from Theophile Gautier, p. 286-287; Athletic Ode, p. 253-256; Spain in America, p. 273-282. For previous and later publication, and for reprints of the following, cf. entries under dates listed: Before a Statue of Achilles (1897); King's College Chapel (1898); In Grantchester Meadows (1899); Young Sammy's First Wild Oats (1900); Translations from Michael Angelo (Sonnets, 1901).

Other reprints. Solipsism. In: Aiken, C., ed., *American Poetry* (Modern Library ed.), New York, [c1929] p. 208-209.

Midnight. In: *The Living Age*, 7th ser. v. 19, no. 3065, April 4, 1903, p. 64. Mont Brevent as The Brevent. In: *The Living Age*, 7th ser., v. 36, no. 3292, Aug. 10, 1907, p. 322.

The Rustic at the Play. In: *The Living Age*, 7th ser. v. 18, no. 3064, March 28, 1903, p. 824; Untermeyer, L., ed., *Modern American Poetry*, New York, 1930, p. 135; Quiller-Couch, A., ed., *Oxford Book of Victorian Verse*, Oxford, [1935] p. 988; Untermeyer, L., ed., *Critical Anthology*, New York, [c1936] p. 126; Stevenson, B. G., ed., *Home Book of Verse*, New York, [c1937] p. 2908. From Théophile Gautier: Art. In: Van Doren, M., *Anthology of World Poetry*, [c1939] p. 755-756.

For mss. of *Solipsism* and *Premonition*, cf. entry, Part II, 1890.

The Lampoon from 1883-1886. In: *Reminiscences and a List of Editors of the Harvard Lampoon, 1876-1901*. Cambridge, [privately printed], [1901], p. 9-11.

Sonnets. *The Harvard Monthly*, v. 31, no. 4, Jan., 1901, p. 133-134.

Translations from Michael Angelo.

I. Non so se s'è la desiata luce, p. 133.

II. Il mio refugio, p. 133-134.

III. Gli occhi miei vaghi delle cose belle, p. 134.

Reprinted. In: *A Hermit of Carmel* (1901), p. 141-143; *Poems* (1923), p. 135-137; *Triton Ed.*, v. 1 (1936), p. 284-285.

Other reprints. In: Van Doren, M. and G. M. Lapolla, eds., *World's Best Poems*, New York [c1929], p. 231; Van Doren, M., ed., *Anthology of World Poetry*, New York, [c1939], p. 586-587.

[AUTOBIOGRAPHICAL REPORT]. In: *Harvard College. Class of 1886. Secretary's Report. No. V.* Part I. June, 1901. New York, The Calumet Press, [1901?] p. 78.

Includes a list of books published to date.

REVIEW of Jules Martin, *Saint Augustin. The Philosophical Review*, v. 10, Sept, 1901, p. 515-526.

Reprinted, with changes. In: *Reason in Religion* (1905), as part of Ch. IX, p. 148-177.

1902

THE SEARCH FOR THE TRUE PLATO. *The International Monthly; A Magazine of Contemporary Thought*, v. 5, Feb., 1902, p. 185-199.

THE DIOSCURI; Two Interludes. *The Harvard Monthly*, v. 34, no. 4, June, 1902, p. 141-144.

THE TWO IDEALISMS; A Dialogue in Limbo. *The International Quarterly*, v. 6, no. 1, Sept., 1902, p. 13-28.

Reprinted. In: *Obiter Scripta* (1936), p. 1-29; *Triton Ed.*, v. 6 (1936), p. 253-273.

1903

THE FLIGHT OF HELEN; A Fragment. *The Harvard Monthly*, v. 36, no. 2, April, 1903, p. 53-56.

CROCE'S AESTHETICS. *The Journal of Comparative Literature*, v. 1, April, 1903, p. 191-195.

Review of Benedetto Croce, *Estetica come scienza dell' espressione e linguistica generale.*

EMERSON'S POEMS PROCLAIM THE DIVINITY OF NATURE, WITH FREEDOM AS HIS PROFOUNDEST IDEAL. *Boston Daily Advertiser*, May 23, 1903, Special Emerson Supplement, p. 16, col. 1-5.

Text of an address delivered on Friday, May 22, 1903, at Harvard University during Emerson Memorial week.

1904

REVIEW of E. Hershey Sneath, *Philosophy in Poetry; A Study of Sir John Davies' Poem 'Nosce Te Ipsum'*, and *The Mind of Tennyson; His Thoughts of God, Freedom and Immortality. The Journal of*

Philosophy, Psychology, and Scientific Methods, v. 1, no. 8, April 14, 1904, p. 216-217.

WHAT IS AESTHETICS? *The Philosophical Review*, v. 13, no. 3, May, 1904, p. 320-327.

Reprinted. In: *Obiter Scripta* (1936), p. 30-40.

PHILOSOPHERS AT COURT, From Act IV. *The Harvard Monthly*, v. 38, no. 4, June, 1904, p. 129-133.

THE ILLUSTRATORS OF PETRARCH. *The Atlantic Monthly*, v. 94, no. 7, July, 1904, p. 135-138.

Review of Prince d'Essling and Eugene Muntz, *Pétrarque: ses études d'art, son influence sur les artistes, ses portraits et ceux de Laure, l'illustration de ses écrits.*

TRADITION AND PRACTICE. *The Oberlin Alumni Magazine*, v. 1, no. 1, Oct., 1904, p. 4-14.

Oberlin Commencement address, 1904.

1905-06

THE LIFE OF REASON; OR, THE PHASES OF HUMAN PROGRESS. New York, Charles Scribner's Sons, 1905-06. 5 vols.

Published in London by Constable and Co., Ltd., 1905-06.

2nd ed., Scribner's, 1922; Constable, 1923.

For contents and reprints of the volumes forming the set, cf. analyzed entries under 1905-06.

Dr. Antonio Banfi has informed the present compiler that an Italian translation is in progress.

1905

THE LIFE OF REASON; OR, THE PHASES OF HUMAN PROGRESS: INTRODUCTION AND REASON IN COMMON SENSE. [The Life of Reason, v. 1] 1905. ix, 291 p.

Contents. Introduction—I. The Birth of Reason—II. First Steps and First Fluctuations—III. The Discovery of Natural Objects—IV. On Some Critics of This Discovery—V. Nature Unified and Mind Discerned—VI. Discovery of Fellow-Minds—VII. Concretions in Discourse and in Existence—VIII. On the Relative Value of Things and Ideas—IX. How Thought is Practical—X. The Measure of Values in Reflection—XI. Some Abstract Conditions of the Ideal—XII. Flux and Constancy in Human Nature.

Reprinted. In: *Triton Ed.*, v. 3 (1936), p. 3-223. (With the inclusion of the Preface to 2nd ed., 1922) Introduction, part of Ch. IX and XI. In: *Philosophy of Santayana* (1936), p. 46-83.

Certain portions of the following noted pages appear in *Little Essays* (1922): p. 50-52 as essay no. 5, "The Suppressed Madness of Sane Men," p. 8-9; p. 40, 44, 42, 45-47, as no. 6, "The Birth of Reason," p. 10-12; p. 59, 57-58, 53-54, 60 as no. 7, "The Difference Reason Makes," p. 12-14; p. 205-213, as no. 8, "Body and Mind," p. 15-18; p. 248-251, 253-255, 252, as no. 11, "False Moral Perspectives," p. 24-26; p. 224-225 as no. 12, "Pain," p. 27; p. 78, 81, 130 as no. 15, "The Transitive Force of Knowledge," p. 29; p. 152-154, 149-150, 175-176, as no. 19, "Mind Reading," p. 34-35; p. 155-158 as no. 20. "Knowledge of Character," p. 35-37; p. 121-123 as no. 23, "Imaginative Nature of Religion," p. 47-51; p. 11-12 as no. 35, "Protestantism," p. 80-83; p. 9-10 as no. 63, "The Dearth of Great Men," p. 159-162; p. 180-182, 171-172 as no. 65 "Essence and Existence," p. 165-167; p. 84-86 as no. 66, "Malicious Psychology," p. 168-169; p. 112-114 as no. 67, "On Esse Est Percipi," p. 169-170; p. 94-97 as no. 68, "Kant," p. 170-176; p. 29-30, 219-220 as no. 69, "Transcendentalism," p. 176-178; p. 198-202 as no. 70, "Precarious Rationalisms," p. 178-180; p. 106, 108-109, 222, as no. 71, "Unjust Judgments," 180-181; p. 262, 231-233 as no. 78, "The Barbarian," p. 191-193; p. 189-193 as no. 90, "Sadness of Naturalism," p. 230-234; p. 16-17 as no. 92, "The True Place of Materialism," p. 235-236; p. 32 as no. 94, "Relativity of Values," p. 240-242; p. 236-239, 55-56 as no. 99, "The Worth of Pleasures and Pains," p. 249-252; p. 30 as no. 111, "Happiness," p. 278-280; p. 229-230 as no. 113, "The Profit of Living," p. 282-285.

THE LIFE OF REASON; OR, THE PHASES OF HUMAN PROGRESS: REASON IN SOCIETY. [The Life of Reason, v. 2] 1905. viii, 205 p.

Contents. I. Love—II. The Family—III. Industry, Government and War.—IV. The Aristocratic Ideal—V. Democracy—VI. Free Society—VII. Patriotism—VIII. Ideal Society.

Reprinted. In: *Triton Ed.*, v. 3 (1936), p. 227-375. Ch. I, VI, VIII. In: *Philosophy of Santayana* (1936), p. 84-139. Part of Ch. III as "War." In: Vallance, R., ed., *Hundred English Essays*, London, [1936], p. 571-573.

Translations. In 1940, the firm of Editorial Losada of Buenos Aires secured permission from Scribner's to publish a translation in Spanish.
Mr. Santayana informed the present compiler that the Beck'sche Verlagsbuchhandlung of Munich, in their *Yearbook* or *Calendar* of a year or two ago, published a translation of a part of Ch. I. No copy has been available to date. (Oct. 1940.)

Certain portions of the following noted pages appear in *Little Essays* (1920): p. 140-146 as essay no. 10, "Self-Consciousness, Vanity and Fame," p. 20-24; p. 37, 36 as no. 14, "Advantages of a Long Childhood," p. 28-29; p. 201-204 as no. 16, "Knowledge of Nature is Symbolic," p. 31-32; p. 147-149 as no. 21, "Comradeship," p. 37-39; p. 26-34 as no. 22, "Love," p. 39-44; p. 61 as no. 71, "Unjust Judgments," p. 180-181; p. 193 as no. 77, "Romantic Ignorance of Self," p. 190-191; p. 195 as no. 91, "Hapiness in Disillusion," p. 234-235; p. 70-72, 80, 79, as no. 102, "Origin of Tyranny," p. 259-260; p. 81-85, as no. 103, "War," p. 260-262; p. 171-184 as no. 104, "Patriotism," p. 263-266; p. 67-68, as no. 105, "Industrial Idealism," p. 266-268; p. 133-134, 52-53 as no. 106, "Collectivism," p. 268-269.

THE LIFE OF REASON; OR, THE PHASES OF HUMAN PROGRESS: REASON IN RELIGION. [The Life of Reason, v. 3] 1905. ix, 279 p.

Contents. I. How Religion May Be an Embodiment of Reason—II. Rational Elements in Superstition—III. Magic, Sacrifice, and Prayer—IV. Mythology—V. The Hebraic Tradition—VI. The Christian Epic—VII. Pagan Custom and Barbarian Genius Infused into Christianity—VIII. Conflict of Mythology with Moral Truth—IX. The Christian Compromise (cf. entry, 1901)—X. Piety—XI. Spirituality and Its Corruption—XII. Charity—XIII. The Belief in a Future Life—XIV. Ideal Immortality—Conclusion.

Reprinted. In: *Triton Ed.*, v. 4 (1936), p. 3-204. Ch. I, part of III, IV, VI, Ch. X, XI, parts of XIV. In: *Philosophy of Santayana* (1936), p. 140-211.

Certain portions of the following noted pages appear in *Little Essays* (1920): p. 3-6, 52, as essay no. 23, "Imaginative Nature of Religion," p. 47-51; p. 131, 24 as no. 25, "The Haste to Believe," p. 53-54; p. 34 as no. 26, "Pathetic Notions of God," p. 54-55; p. 89-98 as no. 31, "The Christian Epic," p. 67-73; p. 99-104 as no. 32, "Pagan Custom Infused Into Christianity," p. 73-76; p. 115-118, 125-126 as no. 35, "Protestantism," p. 80-83; p. 179, 184-185, 189-192 as no. 36, "Piety," p. 83-86; p. 193-195 as no. 37, "Spirituality," p. 86-88; p. 44-48 as no. 38, "Prayer," p. 88-91; p. 232-234 as no. 40, "Psychic Phenomena," p. 93-94; p. 243-247 as no. 41, "A Future Life," p. 94-97; p. 254-255 as no 42, "Disinterested Interest in Life," p. 97-99; p. 260-267, 268-273 as no. 44, "Ideal Immortality," p. 102-107; p. 200-204, 210 as no. 100, "The Voluptuary and the Worldling," p. 252-255; p. 186-187 as no. 104, "Patriotism," p. 263-266.

THE LIFE OF REASON; OR, THE PHASES OF HUMAN PROGRESS: REASON IN ART. [The Life of Reason, v. 4] 1905. ix, 230 p.

Contents. I. The Basis of Art in Instinct and Experience—II. Rationality of Industrial Art—III. Emergence of Fine Art—IV. Music—V. Speech and Significance—VI. Poetry and Prose—VII. Plastic Construction—VIII. Plastic Representation—IX. Justification of Art—X. The Criterion of Taste—XI. Art and Happiness.

Reprinted. In: *Triton Ed.*, v. 4 (1936), p. 204-374. Ch. I, X, XI. In: *Philosophy of Santayana* (1936), p. 212-251.

Certain portions of the following noted pages appear in *Little Essays* (1920): p. 208 as no. 2, "The Origin of Morals," p. 4-5; p. 8-10 as no. 9, "The Self," p. 19-20; p. 175 as no. 26, "Pathetic Notions of God," p. 54-56; p. 166-174 as no. 45, "Justification of Art," p. 111-115; p. 181-184, 177-178 as no. 46, "The Place of Art in Moral Economy," p. 115-117; p. 193-195 as no. 47, "Rareness of Aesthetic Feeling," p. 117-118; p. 222-223 as no. 48, "Art and Happiness," p. 119; p. 211-212 as no. 51, "Mere Art," p. 125; p. 45-49, 56-60 as no. 54, "Music," p. 129-137; p. 82-84 as no. 55, "The Essence of Literature," p. 138-139; p. 99-104 as no. 59, "Poetry and Prose," p. 146-149; p. 87-94, 201-202 as no. 60, "Primary Poetry," p. 149-153; p. 169 as no. 90, "Sadness of Naturalism," p. 230-234; p. 168-169 as no. 96, "Pleasures Ingenuous," p. 246-247; p. 21 as no. 105, "Industrial Idealism," p. 266-267; p. 188-190 as no. 110, "The Need of Discipline," p. 277-278.

1906

THE LIFE OF REASON; OR, THE PHASES OF HUMAN PROGRESS: REASON IN SCIENCE. [The Life of Reason, v. 5] 1906. ix, 320 p.

Contents. I. Types and Aims of Science—II. History—III. Mechanism—IV. Hesitations in Method—V. Psychology—VI. The Nature of Intent—VII. Dialectic—VIII. Pre-rational Morality—IX. Rational Ethics—X. Post-Rational Morality—XI. The Validity of Science.

Reprinted. In: *Triton Ed.*, v. 5 (1936), p. 3-231. Chs. I, III, VII, XI. In: *Philosophy of Santayana* (1936), p. 252-326.

Portion of Ch. X entitled, "Its Moral Value is Therefore Contigent" as "Mathematics a Vice." In: Read, H. and B. Dobrée, eds., *London Book of English Prose*, London, 1936, p. 301. P. 307-309 of Ch. XI as "On the Relativity of Science." In: Vallance, R., ed. *Hundred English Essays*, London, [1936], p. 574-575.

Certain portions of the following noted pages appear in *Little Essays* (1920): p. 209 as no. 3, "Ideals," p. 506; p. 307-309 as no. 17, "Relativity of Science," p. 32-33; p. 194-195 as no. 18, "Mathematics and Morals," p. 33-34; p. 312 as no. 69, "Transcendentalism," p. 176-178; p. 89-94 as no 89, "Emotions of the Materialist," p. 227-230; p. 218-223 as no. 93, "Intuitive Morality," p. 237-240; p. 231-232, 249-250, 244-245, 248, 266-268, as no. 95, "Authority of Reason in Morals," p. 242-246; p. 233-238 as no. 101, "Moral War," p. 255-258; p. 281-286 as no. 107, "Christian Morality," p. 269-272; p. 290, 291, 297-300 as no. 108, "Supernaturalism," p. 273-275; p. 266-268 as no. 109, "Post-Rational Morality," p. 275-277; p. 251-253 as no. 111, "Happiness," p. 278-280.

SONNETS AND OTHER VERSES. New York, Duffield and Co., 1906, 97 p.

For other eds., cf., entry for 1894 ed.

Contents. With the omission of *Lucifer, A Prelude*, identical with that for 1896 ed. For previous and later publication, and for reprints, cf. entries for 1894 and 1896 eds.

THE EFFICACY OF THOUGHT. *The Journal of Philosophy, Psychology, and Scientific Methods*, v. 3, no. 15, July 19, 1906, p. 410-412.

Reply to review by A. W. Moore of *The Life of Reason* in *ibid.*, no. 8, April 12, 1906, p. 211-221.

1907

[TRANSLATION]. *The Complete Writings of Alfred de Musset.* v. 2, *Rolla, Novels in Verse, Silvia, Stories in Verse, The Nights, Simone.* Done into English by George Santayana, Emily Shaw Forman, Marie Agathe Clarke. illus. by M. Bida, Henry Pille. rev. ed. New York, Edwin C. Hill, 1907.

REVIEW of Thomas Davidson, *The Philosophy of Goethe's Faust. The Journal of Philosophy, Psychology, and Scientific Methods,* v. 4, no. 4, Feb. 14, 1907, p. 106-108.

REVIEW of Edith Henry Johnson, *The Argument of Aristotle's Metaphysics. The Journal of Philosophy, Psychology, and Scientific Methods,* v. 4, no. 7, March 28, 1907, p. 186-187.

1908

INTRODUCTION TO HAMLET. In: *The Complete Works of William Shakespeare;* with Annotations and A General Introduction, by Sidney Lee. New York, Harper and Brothers, [c1906-c1908] (The Harper Edition of Shakespeare's Works). v. 15, *Hamlet,* with a Special Introduction by George Santayana, [c1908] p. ix-xxxiii.

Appears also in the following editions: *The Complete Works of William Shakespeare.* Boston and New York, Jefferson Press [c1908], *Hamlet,* v. 15, p. ix-xxxiii. *The Complete Works of William Shakespeare* (The Renaissance Edition). New York, George D. Sproul, 1908. *Hamlet,* v. 30, p. ix-xxxiii.

Reprints. With minor changes as "Hamlet." In: *Life and Letters,* v. I, no. 1, June, 1928, p. 17-38.

Also in: *Obiter Scripta* (1936), p. 41-67; *Triton Ed.,* v. 2 (1936), p. 205-224.

SCULPTURE. *New England Magazine,* n.s. v. 38, no. 1, March, 1908, p. 103-111.

1909

REVIEW of James Adam, *The Religious Teachers of Greece. The Journal of Philosophy, Psychology, and Scientific Methods,* v. 6, no. 1, Jan. 7, 1909, p. 23-25.

REVIEW OF G. LOWES DICKINSON, *Is Immortality Desirable? The Journal of Philosophy, Psychology, and Scientific Methods,* v. 6, no. 15, July 22, 1909, p. 411-415.

1910

THREE PHILOSOPHICAL POETS; LUCRETIUS, DANTE, AND GOETHE. Cambridge, Harvard University Press, 1910. viii, 215 p. (Harvard Studies in Comparative Literature, v. 1).

Six lectures read at Columbia University and the University of Wisconsin in Feb. and April, 1910, based on a regular course given at Harvard.

Published in London by the Oxford University Press, 1910.

Contents. Preface—I. Introduction—II. Lucretius—III. Dante—IV. Goethe's Faust—V. Conclusion.

Reprinted. In: *Triton Ed.*, v. 6 (1936), p. 3-142. Introduction. In: *Philosophy of Santayana* (1936), p. 327-335.

Certain portions of the following noted pages appear in *Little Essays* (1920): p. 98 as essay no. 3, "Ideals," p. 5-6; p. 63-64 as no. 27, "Greek Religion," p. 56; p. 51-54 as no. 39, "Fear of Death," p. 91-92; p. 54-56 as no. 42, "Disinterested Interest in Life," p. 97-99; p. 8, 10-14, 123-124, 142 as no. 57, "Poetry and Philosophy," p. 140-144; p. 212-215 as no. 61, "The Supreme Poet," p. 153-155; p. 20 as no. 62, "Against Prying Biographers," p. 159; p. 132-135 as no. 75, "Dante," p. 186-188; p. 143-148, 196-199 as no. 79, "Romanticism," p. 193-196; p. 181-185 as no. 80, "The Politics of Faust," p. 196-199; p. 32-34 as no. 87, "Moral Neutrality of Materialism," p. 223-224; p. 210-211 as no. 90, "Sadness of Naturalism," p. 230-234; p. 27 as no. 92, "The True Place of Materialism," p. 235-236.

Translation. In 1939, the firm of Editorial Losada, Buenos Aires, received permission from the Harvard University Press to publish a Spanish translation.

INTRODUCTION. In: Spinoza, Benedict de. *"Ethics" and "De Intellectus Emendatione,"* New York, E. P. Dutton and Co., 1910 (Everyman's Library, 481), p. vii-xxii.

Certain portions of the following noted pages appear in *Little Essays* (1920): p. xv as no. 2, "The Origin of Morals," p. 4-5; p. xviii, xix as no. 44, "Ideal Immortality," p. 102-107; p. viii as no. 89, "Emotions of the Materialist," p. 227-230.

REPLY to a review of *Three Philosophical Poets. The Nation,* v. 91, no. 2368, Nov. 17, 1910, p. 471.

Letter dated Cambridge, Mass., Nov. 8, 1910, with editorial caption, "Professor Santayana's Philosophy."

1911

THOMAS PARKER SANBORN. In: *Harvard College. Class of 1886. Secretary's Report. No. VII. Twenty-Fifth Anniversary, 1911.* Cambridge, Printed for the Class, The University Press, [1911?] p. 200-201.

[PUBLICATIONS]. *Ibid.*, p. 327-329.

The period covered is from 1890 to 1910. 38 items are listed, beginning with *Lotze's Moral Idealism,* and ending with *Three Philosophical Poets.*

RUSSELL'S PHILOSOPHICAL ESSAYS. *The Journal of Philosophy, Psychology, and Scientific Methods.* I. *The Study of Essence,* v. 8, no. 3, Feb. 3, 1911, p. 57-63; II. *The Critique of Pragmatism,* v. 8, no. 5, March 2, 1911, p. 113-124; III. *Hypostatic Ethics,* v. 8, no. 16, Aug. 3, 1911, p. 421-432.

Review of Bertrand Russell, *Philosophical Essays.*

Reprinted, preceded by a new section, "*A New Scholasticism*," as Ch. IV. In: *Winds of Doctrine* (1913), p. 110-154. In: *Triton Ed.*, v. 7 (1937), p. 91-127.

THE GENTEEL TRADITION IN AMERICAN PHILOSOPHY. *The University of California Chronicle*, v. 13, no. 4, Oct., 1911, p. 357-380.

Address delivered before the Philosophical Union of the University of California, Aug. 25, 1911.

Reprinted as Ch. VI. In: *Winds of Doctrine* (1913), p. 186-205. In: *Triton Ed.*, v. 7 (1937), p. 127-150.

Excerpts in: Hackett, F., *Horizons; a Book of Criticism*, New York, 1918, p. 47-48.

1913

WINDS OF DOCTRINE; STUDIES IN CONTEMPORARY OPINION. New York, Charles Scribner's Sons [1913]. v, 215 p.

Published in London by J. M. Dent and Sons, Ltd. [1913].

Reprinted, with a new preface, by Scribner's, 1926.

For previous and later publication, and for reprints of certain chapters, cf. entries under dates following titles, listed in the contents.

Contents. I. The Intellectual Temper of the Age—II. Modernism and Christianity—III. The Philosophy of M. Henri Bergson—IV. The Philosophy of Mr. Bertrand Russell (1911)—V. Shelley: or The Poetic Value of Revolutionary Principles—VI. The Genteel Tradition in American Philosophy (1911). Reprints. Ch. V. In: *Triton Ed.*, v. 2 (1936), p. 217-252. Ch. I-IV, VI. In: *Triton Ed.*, v. 7 (1937), p. 3-150. (Includes Preface to 1926 ed.)

Certain portions of the following noted pages appear in *Little Essays* (1920): p. 183-184 as no. 16, "Knowledge of Nature is Symbolic," p. 30-32; p. 33-38 as no. 28, "Original Christian Faith," p. 56-60; p. 20-22, 109 as no. 63, "The Dearth of Great Men," p. 159-162; p. 17-20, 23-24 as no. 64, "The Intellect Out of Fashion," p. 163-165; p. 197-200 as no. 81, "Emerson," p. 199-203; p. 158-160 as no. 82, "Shelley," p. 203-205; p. 151-152 as no. 94, "Relativity of Values," p. 240-242; p. 6 as no. 104, "Patriotism," p. 263-266.

Translation. Ch. I, III, IV, VI. In: Santayana, Giorgio. *Il Pensiero Americano e Altri Saggi; con una introduzioni di Antonio Banfi.* (Traduzioni di Carol Coardi.) Milano, Valentino Bompiani, 1939, 299 p.: p. 9-36; 193-248; 251-299; 64-96.

DR. FULLER, PLOTINUS, AND THE NATURE OF EVIL. *The Journal of Philosophy, Psychology, and Scientific Methods*, v. 10, no. 23, Oct. 23, 1913, p. 589-599.

Review of B. A. G. Fuller, *The Problem of Evil in Plotinus.*

Reprinted. In: *Obiter Scripta* (1936), p. 68-87, as "Plotinus and the Nature of Evil;" *Triton Ed.*, v. 6 (1936), p. 277-291.

1914

THE COMING PHILOSOPHY. *The Journal of Philosophy, Psychology, and Scientific Methods*, v. 11, no. 17, Aug. 13, 1914, p. 449-463.

Review of E. B. Holt, *The Concept of Consciousness.*

Abstract. In: *The Philosophical Review*, v. 24, no. 1, Jan., 1915, p. 117-118, by Raymond P. Hawes.

THE LOGIC OF FANATICISM. *The New Republic*, v. 1, no. 4, Nov. 28, 1914, p. 18-19.

1915

GOETHE AND GERMAN EGOTISM. *The New Republic*, v. 1, no. 9, Jan. 2, 1915, p. 15-16.

Reprinted, with changes, as Ch. IV. In: *Egotism in German Philosophy* (1916), p. 43-53; *Triton Ed.*, v. 6 (1936), p. 169-176.

SOME MEANINGS OF THE WORD IS. *The Journal of Philosophy, Psychology, and Scientific Methods*, v. 12, no. 3, Feb. 4, 1915, p. 66-68.

Cf. entry under 1924 for reprints and later publication of expanded version with identical title.

SHAKESPEARE; MADE IN AMERICA. *The New Republic*, v. 2, no. 17, Feb. 27, 1915, p. 96-98.

Reprinted. In: Conklin, Groff, ed., *The New Republic Anthology, 1915: 1935*, New York [c1936], p. 13-17.

PHILOSOPHIC SANCTION OF AMBITION. *The Journal of Philosophy, Psychology, and Scientific Methods*, v. 12, no. 5, March 4, 1915, p. 113-116.

SPANISH OPINION ON THE WAR. *The New Republic*, v. 2, no. 23, April 10, 1915, p. 252-253.

HEATHENISM. *The New Republic*, v. 2, no. 25, April 24, 1915, p. 296-297.

Reprinted, with changes, as Ch. XIV. In: *Egotism in German Philosophy* (1916), p. 144-153; *Triton Ed.*, v. 6 (1936), p. 233-240.

THE INDOMITABLE INDIVIDUAL. *The New Republic*, v. 3, no. 29, May 22, 1915, p. 64-66.

Reprinted. In: *Obiter Scripta* (1936), p. 88-93.

GENTEEL AMERICAN POETRY. *The New Republic*, v. 3, no. 30, May 29, 1915, p. 94-95.

NATURAL LEADERSHIP. *The New Republic,* v. 3, no. 39, July 31, 1915, p. 333-334.

CLASSIC LIBERTY. *The New Republic,* v. 4, no. 42, Aug. 21, 1915, p. 65-66.

Reprinted as soliloquy no. 40. In: *Soliloquies in England and Later Soliloquies* (1922), p. 165-169; *Triton Ed.,* v. 9 (1937), p. 165-168.

GERMAN FREEDOM. *The New Republic,* v. 4, no. 43, Aug. 28, 1915, p. 94-96.

Reprinted as soliloquy no. 41. In: *Soliloquies in England* (1922), p. 169-173; *Triton Ed.,* v. 9 (1937), p. 169-173.

LIBERALISM AND CULTURE. *The New Republic,* v. 4, no. 44, Sept. 4, 1915, p. 123-125.

Reprinted as soliloquy no. 42. In: *Soliloquies in England* (1922), p. 173-178; *Triton Ed.,* v. 9 (1937), p. 173-178.

PHILOSOPHICAL HERESY. *The Journal of Philosophy, Psychology, and Scientific Methods,* v. 12, no. 21, Oct. 14, 1915, p. 561-568.

Reprinted. In: *Obiter Scripta* (1936), p. 94-107; *Triton Ed.,* v. 8 (1937), p. 197-207.

GERMAN PHILOSOPHY AND POLITICS. *The Journal of Philosophy, Psychology, and Scientific Methods,* v 12, no. 24, Nov. 25, 1915, p. 645-649.

Review of John Dewey, *German Philosophy and Politics.*

1916

EGOTISM IN GERMAN PHILOSOPHY. New York, Charles Scribner's Sons, 1915. xii, 173 p.

Published in London by J. M. Dent and Sons, Ltd. 1916.

Reprinted, with additions in contents, by Dent in 1939, and Scribner's, 1940. For previous and later publication, and for reprints of Ch. IV and XIV, cf. entries listed under 1915.

Contents. Preface (dated 1916)—I. The General Character of German Philosophy—II. The Protestant Heritage—III. Transcendentalism—IV. Hints of Egotism in Goethe—V. Seeds of Egotism in Kant—VI. Transcendentalism Perfected—VII. Fichte on the Mission of Germany—VIII. The Egotism of Ideas—IX. Egotism and Selfishness—X. The Breach with Christianity—XI. Nietzsche and Schopenhauer—XII. The Ethics of Nietzsche—XIII. The Superman—XIV. Heathenism—XV. German Genius—XVI. Egotism in Practice.

Reprinted. In: *Triton Ed.,* v. 6 (1936), p. 145-249.

Certain portions of the following noted pages appear in *Little Essays* (1920):

p. 6 as essay no. 16, "Knowledge of Nature is Symbolic," p. 30-32; p. 154-155 as no. 23, "Imaginative Nature of Religion," p. 47-51; p. 161 as no. 54, "Music," p. 129-137; p. 54-60 as no. 68, "Kant," p. 170-176; p. 167-168 as no. 69, "Transcendentalism," p. 176-178; p. 116 as no. 71, "Unjust Judgments," p. 180-181; p. 137 as no. 77, "Romantic Ignorance of Self," p. 190-191; p. 127, 134-135 as no. 84, "Nietzsche," p. 212-214; p. 109-111 as no. 85, "Intrinsic Values," p. 214-215; p. 144-149 as no. 86, "Heathenism," p. 215-219; p. 70 as no. 92, "The True Place of Materialism," p. 235-236; p. 152-153 as no. 111, "Happiness," p. 278-280.

Translations. *L'Erreur de la Philosophie Allemande.* ("Je suis, donc tu n'es pas.") Trans. by Guillaume Lerolle and Henri Quentin. Preface to the Fr. ed. by Émil Boutroux. Paris, Nouvelle Librairie Nationale, 1917. 217 p. Note by the translators: Additions and changes in the French text made with the author's assistance.

L'Io Nella Filosofia Germanica. Transl. by Luciano Zampa. Lanciano, R. Carabba, 1920. 187 p.

In 1940, the firm of Editorial Losada of Buenos Aires secured permission from Scribner's to publish a Spanish trans.

SONNET. In: Gollancz, Israel, ed. *A Book of Homage to Shakespeare; to Commemorate the Three Hundredth Anniversary of Shakespeare's Death,* MCMXVI. Humphrey Milford, Oxford University Press, [1916] p. 377.

THE ALLEGED CATHOLIC DANGER. *The New Republic,* v. 5, no. 63, Jan. 15, 1916, p. 269-271.

THE HUMAN SCALE. *The New Republic,* v. 5, no. 65, Jan. 29, 1916, p. 326-328.

Reprinted as soliloquy no. 19. In: *Soliloquies in England* (1922), p. 73-77; *Triton Ed.,* v. 9 (1937), p. 65-70.

THE WAR AS WE SEE IT. *The New Republic,* v. 6, no. 69, Feb. 26, 1916, p. 99-100.

Letter dated Oxford, Jan. 5, 1916 to *The New Republic* on its pro-Germanism. Reply by the editors, p. 100-104.

TWO RATIONAL MORALISTS. *The Journal of Philosophy, Psychology, and Scientific Methods,* v. 13, no. 11, May 25, 1916, p. 290-296.

Review of John Erskine, *The Moral Obligation To Be Intelligent,* and E. B. Holt, *The Freudian Wish.*

1918

PHILOSOPHICAL OPINION IN AMERICA. In: *British Academy* (London). *Proceedings,* v. 8, 1917-1918 [1918], p. 299-309.

Third Annual Philosophical Lecture; Henriette Hertz Trust, delivered Jan. 30, 1918.

Published separately for the British Academy, by Humphrey Milford, Oxford University Press, [1918], 13 p.

Reprinted, with changes, as Ch. V. In: *Character and Opinion in the United States* (1920), p. 139-164; *Triton Ed.*, v. 8 (1937), p. 79-93.

Trans. "De Wijsbegeerte in Amerika," by Dr. Antoon Vloemans. In: *Erasmus* (Rotterdam), v. 6, no. 4, July-Aug., 1938, p. 137-152.

A SHORT PREFACE [TO THE LIFE OF REASON]. *The Journal of Philosophy, Psychology, and Scientific Methods*, v. 15, no. 3, Jan. 31, 1918, p. 82-83.

Preceding note: "The Brick Row Book and Print Shop of New Haven was offering recently for sale a copy of the *Life of Reason* . . . in the volumes of which the author had written various prefatory notes, dated, Cambridge, April 18, 1907." This Preface was written in a copy of *Reason in Common Sense.* Three other selections, which appear with this Preface in the same journal, are listed below.

In this preface, Santayana relates how the first impulse to write *The Life of Reason* came to him in 1889.

PAGANISM INEVITABLE. *Ibid.*, p. 83.

Written in a copy of *Reason in Religion.*

REPLY TO A CRITICISM. *Ibid.*, p. 84.

Written in a copy of *Reason in Art.* In reply to an observation that as a younger man, he used to be more idealistic and more a friend of the arts, Santayana transcribed some verses to explain this deterioration. (Cf. following entry.)

APOLLO IN LOVE; OR THE POET LOST IN THE PLATONIST. *Ibid.*, p. 84.

Verses addressed by Apollo to Venus in an unpublished play called, *The Marriage of Aphrodite.*

LITERAL AND SYMBOLIC KNOWLEDGE. *The Journal of Philosophy, Psychology, and Scientific Methods*, v. 15, no. 16, Aug. 1, 1918, p. 421-444.

Captions. The Problem—Alleged Self-Contradiction of Transitive Knowledge—Alleged. Unknowability of the Real—Alleged Incompetence of Sense and Intellect—Knowledge of Existence is Normally Symbolic—Nature of the Symbol—Conclusion.

Reprinted. In: *Obiter Scripta* (1936), p. 108-150; *Triton Ed.*, v. 13, (1936), p. 299-330.

Parts of the first, second, and third paragraphs of "Knowledge of Existence is Normally Symbolic" and the first paragraph of the Conclusion, are reprinted, with changes. In: *Scepticism and Animal Faith* (1923), as part of Ch. XI, p. 99-108.

1919

MATERIALISM AND IDEALISM IN AMERICA. *The Landmark, The Monthly Magazine of the English-Speaking Union* (London), v. 1, no. 1, Jan., 1919, p. 28-38.

According to a report in the *Cincinnati Enquirer,* this address was delivered at the Bedford College for Women, Oct. 20, 1918.

Published also. In: *The Living Age,* v. 300, no. 3896, March 8, 1919, p. 589-595.

Reprinted. In: *Character and Opinion in the U.S.* (1920), as Ch. VI, p. 165-191; *Triton Ed.,* v. 8 (1937), p. 93-107.

LOW VISIBILITY. *The Athenaeum,* no. 4640, April 4, 1919, p. 133-134.

Reprinted as soliloquy no. 1 entitled, "Atmosphere." In: *Soliloquies in England* (1922), p. 11-13; *Triton Ed.,* v. 9 (1937), p. 15-18.

THE TWO PARENTS OF VISION. *The Athenaeum,* no. 4641, April 11, 1919, p. 168-169.

Reprinted as soliloquy no. 4. In: *Soliloquies in England* (1922), p. 17-18; *Triton Ed.,* v. 9 (1937), p. 21-22.

PRAISES OF WATER. *The Athenaeum,* no. 4642, April 18, 1919, p. 199-200.

Also in: *The Living Age,* v. 301, no. 3908, May 31, 1919, p. 538-539.

Reprinted as soliloquy no. 3. In: *Soliloquies in England* (1922), p. 15-16; *Triton Ed.,* v. 9 (1937), p. 19-21.

THE BRITISH CHARACTER. *The Athenaeum,* no. 4643, April 25, 1919, p. 231-232.

Reprinted as soliloquy no. 9. In: *Soliloquies in England* (1922), p. 29-32; *Triton Ed.,* v. 9 (1937), p. 35-38.

Other reprints. In: Archbold, W. A. J., ed. *20th Century Essays and Addresses,* London, 1927, p. 78-81; Hastings, W. T. ed., *Contemporary Essays,* New York, [c1928], p. 336-339; Shackelford, L. B. and F. P. Gass, *Essays of Our Day,* New York, [c1931], p. 299-301. A portion as "The Weather in His Soul." In: Quiller-Couch, A., ed., *Oxford Book of English Prose,* Oxford, [1930], p. 1002-1005.

GRISAILLE. *The Athenaeum,* no. 4644, May 2, 1919, p. 262.

Reprinted as soliloquy no. 2. In: *Soliloquies in England* (1922), p. 13-14; *Triton Ed.,* v. 9 (1937), p. 18-19.

HAMLET'S QUESTION. *The Athenaeum,* no. 4645, May 9, 1919, p. 296-297.

Reprinted as soliloquy no. 8. In: *Soliloquies in England* (1922), p. 27-29; *Triton Ed.,* v. 9 (1937), p. 32-35.

AVERSION FROM PLATONISM. *The Athenaeum, Ibid.*, p. 297.

Reprinted as soliloquy no. 5. In: *Soliloquies in England* (1922), p. 18-19; *Triton Ed.*, v. 9 (1937), p. 23.

PRIVACY. *The Athenaeum*, no. 4660, Aug. 22, 1919, p. 773-774.

Reprinted as soliloquy no. 11. In: *Soliloquies in England* (1922), p. 35-38; *Triton Ed.*, v. 9 (1937), p. 41-44.

Other reprints. In: Hastings, W. T., ed., *Contemporary Essays*, New York, [c1928], p. 339-344; Shackelford, L. B. and F. P. Gass, *Essays of Our Day*, New York [c1931], p. 301-305.

APOLOGY FOR SNOBS. *The Athenaeum*, no. 4661, Aug. 29, 1919, p. 805-806.

Also in: *The Living Age*, v. 303, no. 3927, Oct. 11, 1919, p. 88-90. Reprinted as soliloquy no. 14. In: *Soliloquies in England* (1922), p. 45-49; *Triton Ed.*, v. 9 (1937), p. 51-55.

CLOUD CASTLES. *The Athenaeum*, no. 4664, Sept. 19, 1919, p. 905-906.

Reprinted as soliloquy no. 6. In: *Soliloquies in England* (1922), p. 19-22; *Triton Ed.*, v. 9 (1937), p. 23-27.

JOHN BULL AND HIS PHILOSOPHIES. *The Athenaeum*, no. 4666, Oct. 3, 1919, p. 969-970.

Reprinted as soliloquy no. 44. In: *Soliloquies in England* (1922), p. 190-194; *Triton Ed.*, v. 9 (1937), p. 191-196.

OCCAM'S RAZOR. *The Athenaeum*, no. 4669, Oct. 24, 1919, p. 1058-1059.

Reprinted as soliloquy no. 45. In: *Soliloquies in England* (1922), p. 194-197; *Triton Ed.*, v. 9 (1937), p. 196-199.

EMPIRICISM. *The Athenaeum*, no. 4672, Nov. 14, 1919, p. 1178-1179.

Reprinted as soliloquy no. 46. In: *Soliloquies in England* (1922), p. 198-201; *Triton Ed.*, v. 9 (1937), p. 199-203.

1920

CHARACTER AND OPINION IN THE UNITED STATES; WITH REMINISCENCES OF WILLIAM JAMES AND JOSIAH ROYCE AND ACADEMIC LIFE IN AMERICA. New York, Charles Scribner's Sons, 1920. ix, 233 p.

Published in London by Constable and Co., Ltd., 1920.

Reprinted; as *Character and Opinion in the United States* (White Oak Library), New York, W. W. Norton and Co., Inc., [1934]. x, 233 p.

Reprinted. In: *Triton Ed.*, v. 8 (1937), p. 3-130.

The major part of this book is composed of lectures originally addressed to British audiences.

For previous and later publication, and for reprints of certain chapters, cf. entries under dates following titles, listed in the contents.

Contents. Preface—I. The Moral Background—II. The Academic Environment—III. William James—IV. Josiah Royce—V. Later Speculations (1918) —VI. Materialism and Idealism in American Life (1919)—VII. English Liberty in America.

Reprints. Quotations by Santayana in an unsigned reply to a review. (Cf. entry listed under 1921.) Ch. II. In: Hubbell, J. B., *American Life in Literature*, New York, 1936, p. 408-415. Ch. III. In: Van Doren, C., ed., *Modern American Prose*, New York, [c1934], p. 180-193. 2 passages from Ch. VI as "The American." In: Beston, H., ed., *American Memory*, New York, [c1937], p. 482-483. Ch. VI. In: Johnson, A. T. and A. Tate, eds., *America Through the Essay*, New York, 1938, p. 136-148.

Trans. Passages from Ch. III and IV. In: Müller, Gustav E., *Amerikanische Philosophie* (Frommanns Klassiker der Philosophie XXXI), Stuttgart, 1936, p. 138-139, 184, trans. by Dr. Müller.

Santayana, Giorgio. *Il Pensiero Americano e Altri Saggi;* con una introduzioni di Antonio Banfi. (Traduzioni di Carlo Coardi.) Milano, Valentino Bompiani, 1939. 299 p. Ch. I, III, IV, V, VI. In section, "Il pensiero americano," p. 39-63, 97-189.

LITTLE ESSAYS; DRAWN FROM THE WRITINGS OF GEORGE SANTAYANA BY LOGAN PEARSALL SMITH, WITH THE COLLABORATION OF THE AUTHOR. New York, Charles Scribner's Sons. [1920]. ix, 290 p.

Published in London by Constable and Co., Ltd., 1920.

Note: For the exact source of each essay, cf. notes in entries for the following works: *The Sense of Beauty* (1896); *Interpretations of Poetry and Religion* (1900); *The Life of Reason* (1905-06)—*Three Philosophical Poets* (1910) —*Spinoza's Ethics and De Intellectus Emendatione* (1910)—*Winds of Doctrine* (1913)—*Egotism in German Philosophy* (1916).

Contents. Preface (by Logan Pearsall Smith). *Part I. Little Essays on Human Nature:* 1. Spirit the Judge—2. The Origin of Morals—3. Ideals—4. Intellectual Ambition—5. The Suppressed Madness of Sane Men—6. The Birth of Reason—7. The Difference Reason Makes—8. Body and Mind—9. The Self —10. Self-Consciousness, Vanity, and Fame—11. False Moral Perspectives— 12. Pain—13. What People Will Put Up With—14. Advantages of a Long Childhood—15. The Transitive Force of Knowledge—16. Knowledge of Nature is Symbolic—17. Relativity of Science—18. Mathematics and Morals— 19. Mind-Reading—20. Knowledge of Character—21. Comradeship—22. Love.

Part II. Little Essays on Religion: 23. Imaginative Nature of Religion —24. Prosaic Misunderstandings—25. The Haste to Believe—26. Pathetic Notions of God—27. Greek Religion—28. Original Christian Faith—29. The Convert—30. Christian Doctrine a Moral Allegory—31. The Christian Epic—32. Pagan Custom Infused into Christianity—33. Christ and the Virgin—34. Orthodoxy and Heresy—35. Protestantism—36. Piety—37. Spirituality—38. Prayer—39. The Fear of Death—40. Psychic Phenomena—41. A Future Life—42. Disinterested Interest in Life—43. Platonic Love—44. Ideal Immortality.

Part III. Little Essays on Art and Poetry: 45. Justification of Art—46. The Place of Art in Moral Economy—47. Rareness of Aesthetic Feeling—48. Art and Happiness—49. Utility and Beauty—50. Glimpses of Perfection—51. Mere Art—52. Costliness—53. The Stars—54. Music—55. The Essence of Literature—56. The Need of Poetry—57. Poetry and Philosophy—58. The Elements of Poetry—59. Poetry and Prose—60. Primary Poetry—61. The Supreme Poet.

Part IV. Little Essays on Poets and Philosophers: 62. Against Prying Biographers—63. The Dearth of Great Men—64. The Intellect Out of Fashion—65. Essence and Existence—66. Malicious Psychology—67. On *Esse Est Percipi*—68. Kant—69. Transcendentalism—70. Precarious Rationalisms—71. Unjust Judgments—72. Modern Poetry—73. The Unhappiness of Artists—74. Poetry of Latin Peoples—75. Dante—76. Absence of Religion in Shakespeare—77. Romantic Ignorance of Self—78. The Barbarian—79. Romanticism—80. The Politics of Faust—81. Emerson—82. Shelley—83. Browning—84. Nietzsche—85. Intrinsic Values—86. Heathenism.

Part V. Little Essays on Materialism and Morals: 87. Moral Neutrality of Materialism—88. Value Irrational—89. Emotions of the Materialist—90. Sadness of Naturalism—91. Happiness in Disillusion—92. The True Place of Materialism—93. Intuitive Morality—94. Relativity of Values—95. Authority of Reason in Morals—96. Pleasure Ingenuous—97. The Lower Senses—98. Pleasure and Conscience—99. The Worth of Pleasures and Pains—100. The Voluptuary and the Worldling—101. Moral War—102. Origin of Tyranny—103. War—104. Patriotism—105. Industrial Idealism—106. Collectivism—107. Christian Morality—108. Supernaturalism—109. Post-Rational Morality—110. The Need of Discipline—111. Happiness—112. Detachment—113. The Profit of Living—114. Beauty a Hint of Happiness.

Reprints. no. 22. In: Van Doren, M., ed., *Oxford Book of American Prose,* New York, 1932, p. 459-464. A portion of no. 36 entitled, "Religio Stoici." In: Quiller-Couch, A., ed., *Oxford Book of English Prose,* Oxford, 1930, p. 1005-1006. no. 44. In: Tanner, W. M. and D. B. Tanner, eds., *Modern Familiar Essays,* Boston, 1927, p. 190-196. no. 45. In: Benet, W. R. and N. H. Pearson, *Oxford Anthology of American Literature,* New York, 1938, p. 1104-1106. no. 57. In: Brown, S., ed., *Essays of Our Times,* Chicago, [c1928], p. 377-381. no. 58. In: Morley, C., ed., *Modern Essays,* New York, 1921, p. 241-245; Baird, A. C., ed., *Essays and Addresses Toward a Liberal Education,* New York, [c1934], p. 187-189. no. 81. In: Alden, R. M., ed. (rev. by Robert M. Smith), *Essays, English and American,* Chicago, [c1927], p. 508-513. no. 86. In: Rhys, Ernest, ed., *Modern English Essays,* London, 1922, v. 5, p. 41-49.

no. 103. In: Bachelor, J. M. and R. L. Henry, *Challenging Essays in Modern Thought*, New York, [c1928], p. 289-291; Pritchard, F. H., ed., *Great Essays of All Nations*, London, [1929], p. 966-968; Pritchard, F. H., *From Confucius to Mencken*, New York, [c1929], p. 966-968; Baird, A. C., ed., *Essays and Addresses Toward a Liberal Education*, New York, [c1934], p. 339-341. Selections from nine "little essays," several retitled, appear in: Lewisohn, Ludwig, ed., *Creative America; An Anthology*, New York, 1933, p. 409-418.

THREE PROOFS OF REALISM. In: *Essays in Critical Realism; A Co-operative Study of the Problem of Knoweldge* by Durant Drake, Arthur O. Lovejoy, James Bissett Pratt, Arthur K. Rogers, George Santayana, Roy Wood Sellars, C. A. Strong. London, Macmillan and Co., Ltd., 1920, p. 163-184.

In 5 parts: Definition of Realism—Biological Proof—Psychological Proof—Logical Proof—Conclusion.

2nd part reprinted with changes. In: *Scepticism and Animal Faith* (1923) as part of Ch. XVIII, p. 164-181.

THE LION AND THE UNICORN. *The Athenaeum*, no. 4712, Aug. 20, 1920, p. 231-233.

Reprinted as soliloquy no. 12. In: *Soliloquies in England* (1922), p. 39-42; *Triton Ed.*, v. 9 (1937), p. 45-49.

SEAFARING. *The Athenaeum*, no. 4714, Sept. 3, 1920, p. 295-296.

Also in: *The Living Age*, v. 307, no. 3981, Oct. 23, 1920, p. 233-235. Reprinted as soliloquy no. 10. In: *Soliloquies in England* (1922), p. 32-35; *Triton Ed.*, v. 9 (1937), p. 38-41.

MASKS. *The Athenaeum*, no. 4716, Sept. 17, 1920, p. 366.

Also in: *The Living Age*, v. 307, no. 3988, Dec. 11, 1920, p. 669-671.

Reprinted as soliloquy no. 31. In: *Soliloquies in England* (1922), p. 128-135; *Triton Ed.*, v. 9 (1937), p. 125-128.

THE WORLD'S A STAGE. *The Athenaeum*, no. 4719, Oct. 8, 1920, p. 464.

Reprinted as soliloquy no. 30. In: *Soliloquies in England* (1922), p. 126-128; *Triton Ed.*, v. 9 (1937), p. 123-125.

CROSS-LIGHTS. *The Athenaeum*, no. 4726, Nov. 26, 1920, p. 720-721.

Reprinted as soliloquy no. 7. In: *Soliloquies in England* (1922), p. 23-27; *Triton Ed.*, v. 9 (1937), p. 27-32.

QUEEN MAB. *The Athenaeum*, no. 4728, Dec. 10, 1920, p. 800-802.

Reprinted as soliloquy no. 35. In: *Soliloquies in England* (1922), p. 144-149; *Triton Ed.*, v. 9 (1937), p. 142-147.

1921

THE TRAGIC MASK. *The Athenaeum,* no. 4732, Jan. 7, 1921, p. 6-7.

Reprinted as soliloquy no. 32. In: *Soliloquies in England* (1922), p. 131-135; *Triton Ed.*, v. 9 (1937), p. 128-132.

A CONTRAST WITH SPANISH DRAMA. *The Athenaeum,* no. 4737, Feb. 11, 1921, p. 146-147.

Reprinted as soliloquy no. 36. In: *Soliloquies in England* (1922), p. 149-155; *Triton Ed.*, v. 9 (1937), p. 147-153.

SOCIETY AND SOLITUDE. *The Nation [and the Athenaeum]*, v. 28, no. 22, Feb. 26, 1921, p. 734-735.

Also in: *The Living Age,* v. 309, no. 4005, April 9, 1921, p. 109-111. Reprinted as soliloquy no. 28. In: *Soliloquies in England* (1922), p. 119-122; *Triton Ed.*, v. 9 (1937), p. 115-118.

THE COMIC MASK. *The Dial,* v. 70, June, 1921, p. 629-632.

Reprinted as soliloquy no. 33. In: *Soliloquies in England* (1922), p. 135-139; *Triton Ed.*, v. 9 (1937), p. 132-136.

CARNIVAL. *The Dial,* v. 71, July, 1921, p. 43-47.

Reprinted as soliloquy no. 34. In: *Soliloquies in England* (1922), p. 139-144; *Triton Ed.*, v. 9 (1937), p. 136-142. Also in: *The Golden Book Magazine,* v. 16, no. 93, Sept. 1932, p. 263-265.

DONS. *The Dial,* v. 71, Aug., 1921, p. 143-145.

Reprinted as soliloquy no. 13. In: *Soliloquies in England* (1922), p. 43-45; *Triton Ed.*, v. 9 (1937), p. 49-51.

PROFESSOR MILLER AND MR. SANTAYANA. *The Harvard Graduates' Magazine,* v. 30, no. 117, Sept., 1921, p. 32-36.

Unsigned reply to review by Rev. Miller in March issue. This reply consists of an explanatory note preceding parallel passages drawn from Rev. Miller's article and *Character and Opinion in the U.S.* Each page is divided into two parts, headed, "Professor Miller in 'Mr. Santayana and William James'" and "Mr. Santayana in *Character and Opinion in the U.S.*"

THE IRONY OF LIBERALISM. *The Dial,* v. 71, Oct., 1921, p. 407-417.

Reprinted as soliloquy no. 43. In: *Soliloquies in England* (1922), p. 178-189; *Triton Ed.*, v. 9 (1937), p. 178-191.

DICKENS. *The Dial,* v. 71, Nov., 1921, p. 537-549.

Reprinted as soliloquy no. 18. In: *Soliloquies in England* (1922), p. 58-73; *Triton Ed.*, v. 2 (1936), p. 255-271.

Other reprints. McCullough, B. W. and E. B. Burgum, eds., *A Book of Modern Essays,* New York, [c1926] p. 349-364; MacLean, M. S. and E. K. Holmes, eds., *Men and Books,* New York, 1930, p. 23-38.

On My Friendly Critics. *The Journal of Philosophy*, v. 18, no. 26, Dec. 22, 1921, p. 701-713.

Reprinted, with changes, as soliloquy no. 54. In: *Soliloquies in England* (1922), p. 245-259; *Triton Ed.*, v. 9 (1937), p. 251-266.

1922

Soliloquies in England and Later Soliloquies. New York, Charles Scribner's Sons, 1922. viii, 264 p.

Published in London by Constable and Co., Ltd., [1922].

Contents. Prologue includes 3 sonnets: A Premonition, Cambridge, Oct., 1913; The Undergraduate Killed in Battle, Oxford, 1915; The Darkest Hour, Oxford, 1917.

Soliloquies in England, 1914-1918: 1. Atmosphere—2. Grisaille—3. Praises of Water—4. The Two Parents of Vision—5. Aversion from Platonism—6. Cloud Castles—7. Cross-Lights—8. Hamlet's Question—9. The British Character—10. Seafaring—11. Privacy—12. The Lion and the Unicorn—13. Dons—14. Apology for Snobs—15. The Higher Snobbery—16. Distinction in Englishmen—17. Friendships—18. Dickens—19. The Human Scale—20. English Architecture—21. The English Church—22. Leaving Church—23. Death-Bed Manners—24. War Shrines—25. Tipperary—26. Skylarks—27. At Heaven's Gate.

Later Soliloquies, 1918-1921: 28. Society and Solitude—29. Imagination—30. The World's a Stage—31. Masks—32. The Tragic Mask—33. The Comic Mask—34. Carnival—35. Queen Mab—36. A Contrast with Spanish Drama—37. The Censor and the Poet—38. The Mask of the Philosopher—39. The Voyage of the Saint Christopher—40. Classic Liberty—41. German Freedom—42. Liberalism and Culture—43. The Irony of Liberalism—44. John Bull and His Philosophers—45. Occam's Razor—46. Empiricism—47. The British Hegelians—48. The Progress of Philosophy—49. The Psyche—50. Reversion to Platonism—51. Ideas—52. The Mansions of Helen—53. The Judgement of Paris—54. On My Friendly Critics—55. Hermes the Interpreter.

Entire contents. In: *Triton Ed.*, v. 9 (1937), p. 3-271, except "Dickens," which appears in *Triton Ed.*, v. 2 (1936), p. 255-271. Nos. 26, 28, 38, 44, 48, 50. In: *Philosophy of Santayana* (1936), p. 336-337.

For previous and later publication, and for reprints of the following soliloquies, cf. entries after dates listed: 1-9 (1919); 10 (1920); 11 (1919); 12 (1920); 13 (1921); 14 (1919); 18 (1921); 19 (1916); 28 (1921); 30-31 (1920); 32-34 (1921); 35 (1920); 36 (1921); 40-42 (1915); 43 (1921); 44-46 (1919); 54 (1921); 55 (1922).

Other reprints. no. 16. In: Hastings, W. T., ed., *Contemporary Essays*, New York, [c1928], p. 344-347. no. 17. In: White, I. H., ed., *Essays in Value*, New York, [c1938], p. 71-73. no. 26. In: Shepard, O., ed., *Contemporary Essays*, New York, [c1929], p. 290-298. no. 27. *Ibid.*, p. 299-302; Williams, B. C., ed., *Book of Essays*, New York, [c1931], p. 385-388; Benet, W. R. and N. H. Pearson, eds., *Oxford Anthology of American Literature*, New York, 1938, p. 1108-1109.

THE LIFE OF REASON; OR, THE PHASES OF HUMAN PROGRESS. Second Edition, with a New Preface. New York, Charles Scribner's Sons, 1922. 5 v.

Published in London by Constable and Co., Ltd., 1923.

Preface to 2nd ed., [dated May, 1922], v. 1, p. v-xiii. Reprinted. In; *Philosophy of Santayana* (1936), p. 40-46; *Triton Ed.*, v. 3 (1936), p. 3-9. For previous and later publication, and for contents and reprints, cf. entries for first ed., 1905-06.

HERMES THE INTERPRETER. *The London Mercury*, v. 5, no. 28, Feb., 1922, p. 374-377.

Reprinted as soliloquy no. 55. In: *Soliloquies in England* (1922), p. 259-264; *Triton Ed.*, v. 9 (1937), p. 266-271. Also in: Scott, F. W., and J. Zeitlin, eds., *Essays Formal and Informal*, New York, [c1927], p. 380-385.

AMERICA'S YOUNG RADICALS. *The Forum*. v. 67, May, 1922, p. 371-375.

Mr. Santayana once informed the present compiler that this title was not his own, but was inserted by the editor.

Reprinted. In: Bachelor, J. M. and R. L. Henry, eds., *Challenging Essays in Modern Thought*, New York, [c1928], p. 88-91.

MARGINAL NOTES ON CIVILIZATION IN THE UNITED STATES. *The Dial*, v. 72, June, 1922, p. 553-568.

Review of Harold Stearns, ed., *Civilization in the United States, An Inquiry by 30 Americans.*

Note: "These marginal notes . . . are published in place of a formal review. . . ."

Contents. "Marginal notes" on the Title Page—Contents—Preface—The City—Politics—Journalism—Education—Scholarship and Criticism—School and College Life—Science—The Literary Life—Music—Economic Opinion—Radicalism—The Small Town—The Family—Advertising—Business—Sport and Play—Humour.

PENITENT ART. *The Dial*, v. 73, July, 1922, p. 25-31.

Reprinted in: *Obiter Scripta* (1936), p. 151-161, *Triton Ed.*, v. 7 (1937), p. 219-226.

Also in: Zabel, Morton Dauwen, *Literary Opinion in America* . . . New York, 1937, p. 122-129.

LIVING WITHOUT THINKING. *The Forum*, v. 68, Sept., 1922, p. 731-735.

Review of John B. Watson, *Psychology from the Standpoint of a Behaviorist.*

1923

SCEPTICISM AND ANIMAL FAITH; INTRODUCTION TO A SYSTEM OF PHILOSOPHY. New York, Charles Scribner's Sons, 1923. xii, 314 p.

Published in London by Constable and Co., Ltd. 1923.

For previous and later publication, and for reprints of certain chapters, cf. entries under dates following titles, listed in the contents.

Contents. Preface—I. There Is No First Principal of Criticism—II. Dogma and Doubt—III. Wayward Scepticism—IV. Doubts About Self-Consciousness—V. Doubts About Change—VI. Ultimate Scepticism—VII. Nothing Given Exists—VIII. Some Authorities For This Conclusion—IX. The Discovery of Essence—X. Some Uses of This Discovery—XI. The Watershed of Criticism (1918)—XII. Identity and Duration Attributed to Essences—XIII. Belief in Demonstration—XIV. Essence and Intuition—XV. Belief in Experience—XVI. Belief in the Self—XVII. The Cognitive Claims of Memory—XVIII. Knowledge is Faith Mediated by Symbols (1920)—XIX. Belief in Substance—XX. On Some Objections to Belief in Substance—XXI. Sublimation of Animal Faith—XXII. Belief in Nature—XXIII. Evidences of Animation in Nature—XXIV. Literary Psychology—XXV. The Implied Being of Truth—XXVI. Discernment of Spirit—XXVII. Comparison with Other Criticism of Knowledge.

The *Realms of Being*, 1927-1940, is a sequel to this volume.

Reprinted. In: *Triton Ed.*, v. 13 (1937), p. 3-275. Preface, Ch. VI, parts of Ch. VII, IX, Ch. XI, parts of XIV, XVI, Ch. XVIII, part of XIX, Ch. XXIV, parts of XXV, XXVI, XXVII. In: *Philosophy of Santayana* (1936), p. 368-441.

Other reprints. Ch. IX. In: Robinson, D. S., comp. *Anthology of Recent Philosophy; Selections for Beginners from the Writings of the Greatest Twentieth Century Philosophers*, New York, [c1929], p. 327-332. "Preface" as "Preface to a New Philosophy." In: Van Doren, C., ed., *Anthology of World Prose*, New York, [c1939], p. 1522-1524.

Dr. Antonio Banfi has informed the present compiler that an Italian transl. is in progress.

Manuscript. Deposited in the Treasure Room at Harvard University by the Delphic Club of Boston. Part I: [223] p.; Part II: [450] p.

POEMS; SELECTED BY THE AUTHOR AND REVISED. New York, Charles Scribner's Sons, 1923. xiv, 140 p.

Published in London by Constable and Co., Ltd. 1923.

In London ed.: "An essay on the work of George Santayana written by Edmund Gosse is . . . reprinted overleaf." [Entitled, "A Spaniard in England"], p. 2-4.

Contents. (For previous and later publication, and for reprints, cf. entries under dates listed.) Preface, [dated Nov., 1922]—Sonnets, 1883-1895, I-L (*Sonnets and Other Verses,* 1894, 1896)—Miscellaneous Sonnets: On a Volume of Scholastic Philosophy—On the Death of a Metaphysician—On a Piece of Tapestry—To W.P. (*Sonnets and Others Verses,* 1894)—Before a Statue of

Achilles (1897)—The Rustic at the Play (*Hermit of Carmel,* 1901)—Odes (*Sonnets and Other Verses,* 1894)—Athletic Ode (*Hermit of Carmel,* 1901)—Various Poems: Cape Cod—A Toast (*Sonnets and Other Verses,* 1894)—Premonition—Solipsism—Sybaris—Avila (*Hermit of Carmel,* 1901)—King's College Chapel (1898)—On an Unfinished Statue—Midnight (*Hermit of Carmel,* 1901)—In Granchester Meadows (1899)—Spain in America (*Hermit of Carmel,* 1901)—A Minuet, on Reaching the Age of Fifty, [December, 1913] (1923)—Translations: From Michael Angelo (Sonnets, 1901)—From Théophile Gautier: Art (*Hermit of Carmel,* 1901).

Reprints. Contents, including preface. In: *Triton Ed.,* v. 1 (1936), p. 209-287.

Trans. *A Minuet* . . . into Latin. Cf. entry below.

THE UNKNOWABLE; The Herbert Spencer Lecture Delivered at Oxford, October 24, 1923. Oxford, At the Clarendon Press, 1923. 29 p.

Reprinted. In: *Obiter Scripta* (1936), p. 162-188; *Triton Ed.,* v. 13 (1937), p. 333-352.

Other reprint. p. 6-13, 16-21, 27-29 as "The Unknowable of Herbert Spencer." In: Robinson, D.S., comp. *Anthology of Recent Philosophy* . . . New York, [c1929], p. 576-586.

A MINUET, ON REACHING THE AGE OF FIFTY, *The Century,* v. 105, March 1923, p. 684-685.

Reprinted. In: *The Literary Digest,* v. 77, no. 1, April 7, 1923, p. 40; *Poems* (1923), p. 130-132; *Triton Ed.,* v. 1 (1936), p. 282-284; Benet, W. R. and N. H. Pearson, eds., *Oxford Anthology of American Literature,* New York, 1938, p. 1112; *National Review* (London), v. 110, no. 660, Feb., 1938, p. 222 and 224.

Trans. Into Latin, by A. N. St. John-Mildmay. In: *National Review* (cf. above), p. 223 and 225.

A LONG WAY ROUND TO NIRVANA; OR, MUCH ADO ABOUT DYING. *The Dial,* v. 75, Nov. 1923, p. 435-442.

Development of a Suggestion Found in Freud's Beyond the Pleasure Principle.

Reprinted. In: *Some Turns of Thought in Modern Philosophy* (1933) as Ch. IV, 87-101; *Philosophy of Santayana* (1936), p. 563-571; *Triton Ed.,* v. 10 (1937), p. 219-227.

Trans. "Largo rodeo hacia el Nirvana." (Traducción de A. Marichalar). *Cruz y Raya; Revista de Afirmación y Negación (Madrid).* [v. 1] no. 4, July 15, 1933, p. 67-81.

IMITATION OF CALDERON; THE LAMENT OF SEGISMUNDO IN *La Vida Es Sueño. The London Mercury,* v. 9, Nov., 1923, p. 13-14.

1924

LUCIFER; OR, THE HEAVENLY TRUCE; A THEOLOGICAL TRAGEDY. Cambridge, Mass., Dunster House, 1924. xxi, 128 p.

Published in London by W. Jackson. (450 copies).

"This, the second edition—the first with the author's preface and revised text, consists of 450 copies . . ."

Contents. Preface [dated Rome, 1924]—Invocation—Dramatis Personae—Act I-Act V.

Reprinted. In: *Triton Ed.*, v. 1 (1936), p. 291-421. First ed., 1899.

[LETTER TO PROFESSOR MÜNSTERBERG.] Münsterberg, Margaret, "Santayana at Cambridge," *The American Mercury*, v. 1, no. 1, Jan., 1924, p. 69-74.

p. 72, dated 75 Monmouth St., Brookline, Jan. 13; no year given. In postscript, comments briefly on *Also sprach Zarathustra.*

THE SORROWS OF AVICENNA. A Dialogue in Limbo. *The Dial,* v. 76, March, 1924, p. 250-256.

Reprinted, with slight changes. In: *Dialogues in Limbo* (1926), as Ch. IX, p. 162-172; *Triton Ed.*, v. 10 (1937), p. 135-143.

A PREFACE TO A SYSTEM OF PHILOSOPHY. *The Yale Review,* v. 13, no. 3, April, 1924, p. 417-430.

Reprinted, with minor changes. In: *The Realm of Essence* (1927) as "Preface to Realms of Being," p. v-xix; *Philosophy of Santayana,* (1936), p. 461-475; *Triton Ed.*, v. 14 (1937), p. xi-xxv.
For Spanish trans. of Preface, cf. entry, 1927.

SOME MEANINGS OF THE WORD "IS." *The Journal of Philosophy,* v. 21, no. 14, July 3, 1924, p. 365-377.

Paragraph headings: Language is Loose Because Significant—First Meaning of the Word "Is:" Identity (Part of this paragraph is reprinted, with slight changes, in *The Realm of Essence,* 1927, p. 6)—Identity the Principle of Essence (Part of this paragraph and all of the next are reprinted in *ibid.*, p. 23-24)—Notion of the Realm of Essence—Translation to Looser Meanings: Posited or Problematical Identities—Second Meaning: Equivalence—Third Meaning: Definition—Fourth Meaning: Predication—Fifth Meaning: Existence—Existence Means Being in External Relations—Sixth Meaning: Actuality—Seventh Meaning: Derivation.

Reprinted. In: *Obiter Scripta* (1936), p. 189-202; *Triton Ed.*, v. 13 (1937), p. 279-296.

Note by Santayana: "A short article under this title appeared many years ago in this Journal (v. 12, p. 66) [1915]. The present expanded version is designed to form the first chapter of a book entitled, *Realms of Being.*"

Brief passages appearing in *The Realm of Essence (Realms of Being,* Book I), are indicated above in the paragraph headings.

THE WISDOM OF AVICENNA. A Dialogue in Limbo. *The Dial,* v. 77, Aug., 1925, p. 91-103.

Reprinted, with changes. In: *Dialogues in Limbo* (1926), as Ch. X, "The Secret of Aristotle," p. 173-193; *Triton Ed.*, v. 10 (1937), p. 143-159.

1925

ON SELF-GOVERNMENT. A Dialogue in Limbo. *The Dial*, v. 77, March, 1925, p. 181-192.

Reprinted, with slight changes. In: *Dialogues in Limbo* (1926) as Ch. VI, "Self-Government, First Dialogue," p. 89-107; *Triton Ed.*, v. 10 (1937), p. 72-87.

ON SELF-GOVERNMENT. A Dialogue in Limbo. *The Dial*, v. 78, April, 1925, p. 302-312.

Reprinted, with slight changes. In: *Dialogues in Limbo* (1926) as Ch. VII, "Self-Government, Second Dialogue," p. 107-123; *Triton Ed.*, v. 10 (1937), p. 87-101.

THE MUTABILITY OF AESTHETIC CATEGORIES. *The Philosophical Review*, v. 24, no. 3, May, 1925, p. 281-291.

Review of Henry Rutgers Marshall, *The Beautiful.*

The note on p. 284 is reprinted as a note accompanying the essay, "An Aesthetic Soviet," in *Obiter Scripta* (1936), p. 253-255.

DEWEY'S NATURALISTIC METAPHYSICS. *The Journal of Philosophy*, v. 22, no. 25, Dec. 3, 1925, p. 673-688.

Review of John Dewey, *Experience and Nature.*

Reprinted. In: *Obiter Scripta* (1936), p. 213-240, with the omission of a clause stating that knowledge of acquaintance means intuition of essence. For Santayana's present remarks concerning it, cf. *Obiter Scripta*, note, p. 222.

In: *Triton Ed.*, v. 8 (1937), p. 173-193 as from *Obiter Scripta.*

In: Schilpp, Paul Arthur, ed., *The Philosophy of John Dewey*, Evanston and Chicago, Northwestern University, 1939, p. 245-261. (The Library of Living Philosophers, v. 1). ed. note: ". . . with a few minor changes made by Mr. Santayana himself for the present purpose."

1926

DIALOGUES IN LIMBO. New York, Charles Scribner's Sons, 1926. vii, 193 p.

Published in London by Constable and Co., Ltd., 1925.

For previous and later publication, and for reprints of certain chapters, cf. entries under dates following titles listed in the contents.

Contents. I. The Scent of Philosophies—II. Vivisection of a Mind—III. Normal Madness—IV. Autologos—V. Lovers of Illusion—VI. Self-Government, First Dialogue (1925)—VII. Self-Government, Second Dialogue (1925)—VIII. The Philanthropist—IX. Homesickness for the World (1924)—X. The Secret of Aristotle (1924).

Reprinted. In: *Triton Ed.*, v. 10 (1937), p. 3-159. Ch. III. In: *Philosophy of Santayana* (1936), p. 442-457.

Manuscript. Deposited in the Treasure Room at Harvard University by the Delphic Club of Boston. Includes mss., typescripts, and revised texts. [226] p.

WINDS OF DOCTRINE; STUDIES IN CONTEMPORARY OPINION. [New ed.] New York, Charles Scribner's Sons, [1926]. vii, 215 p.

Preface to the New ed. [dated Rome, 1926] p. v-vi.

Reprinted. In: *Triton Ed.*, v. 7 (1937), p. 3-4.

For previous and later publication, and for contents and reprints, cf. entry for first ed., 1913.

[AUTOBIOGRAPHICAL NOTES.] In: *Harvard College, Class of 1886. Secretary's Report. No. X. 40th Anniversary Report, June 1886-June, 1926.* Boston, Printed for the Class by Anchor Linotype Printing Company, [1926?] p. 90.

Includes comments on publications, major undergraduate activities at college (extra-curricular, social, and scholastic), and favorite instructors.

1927-1940

REALMS OF BEING. New York, Charles Scribner's Sons, 1927-1940. 4 v.

For contents and other editions of the volumes forming this set, cf. analyzed entries under 1927, 1930, 1938, 1940.

This set is a sequel to *Scepticism and Animal Faith* (1923).

1927

THE REALM OF ESSENCE; BOOK FIRST OF REALMS OF BEING. New York, Charles Scribner's Sons, xxiii, 183 p., 1927.

Published in London by Constable and Co., Ltd. [1927]

For previous publication of Preface, cf. entry under 1924.

Contents. Preface to Realms of Being—I. Various Approaches to Essence—II. The Being Proper to Essences—III. Adventitious Aspects of Essence—IV. Pure Being—V. Complex Essences—VI. Implication—VII. The Basis of Dialectic—VIII. Essences as Terms—IX. Instances of Essences—X. Essences All Primary—XI. Comparison with Some Kindred Doctrines—Postscript: Corroborations in Current Opinion.

Reprinted. In: *Triton Ed.*, v. 14 (1937), p. xi-179. (Postscript includes *Proust on Essences*, 1929). Preface, Ch. II, part of IV, Ch. VII, part of XI. In: *Philosophy of Santayana* (1936), p. 461-513.

Section entitled, "The estimation in which pure being is held is optional and relative to some finite nature" of Ch. IV as "A Rational Animal." In: Read, H. and B. Dobrée, eds., *London Book of English Prose*, London, 1931, p. 164-165.

Translation of Preface. "Prólogo a *Los Reinos del Ser.*" *Revista de Occidente* (Madrid), v. 48, no. 144, June, 1935, p. 233-254. (with 10 captions.)

Manuscript. Deposited in the Treasure Room at Harvard University by the Delphic Club of Boston. [329 pp.]

PLATONISM AND THE SPIRITUAL LIFE. New York, Charles Scribner's Sons. 94 p.

Published in London by Constable and Co., Ltd., 1927.

In 25 Chapters. Reprinted. In: *Triton Ed.*, v. 10 (1937), p. 163-215. Ch. XXIII as "The Life of this Winged Thing, Spirit." In: *Philosophy of Santayana* (1936), p. 458-460.

Manuscript. Deposited in the Treasure Room at Harvard University by the Delphic Club of Boston. [110 pp.]

OVERHEARD IN SEVILLE; DURING THE PROCESSION ON MAUDY THURSDAY, 1913. *The Dial,* v. 82, April, 1927, p. 282-286.

Dialogues, in 3 parts. I. A street where a procession has halted, carrying an image of Our Lady of the Seven Dolours. II. [Continuation] III. The grand stand in the Square.

Reprinted. In: *Obiter Scripta* (1936), p. 240-248; *Triton Ed.*, v. 1 (1936), p. 425-432.

AN AESTHETIC SOVIET. *The Dial,* v. 82, May, 1927, p. 361-370.

Reprinted. In: *Obiter Scripta* (1936), p. 249-264.

1928

REVOLUTIONS IN SCIENCE. *The New Adelphi,* n.s. v. 1, no. 3, March, 1928, p. 206-211.

Some Comments on the Theory of Relativity and the New Physics.

Reprinted. In: *Some Turns of Thought in Modern Philosophy* (1933) as Ch. III, p. 71-86. In: *Triton Ed.*, v. 7 (1937), p. 190-199.

FIFTY YEARS OF BRITISH IDEALISM. *The New Adelphi,* n.s. v. 2, no. 2, Dec., 1928, p. 112-120.

Reflections on the republication of F. H. Bradley's *Ethical Studies.*

Reprinted. In: *Some Turns of Thought in Modern Philosophy* (1933), as Ch. II, p. 48-70. In: *Triton Ed.*, v. 7 (1937), p. 178-190.

1929

A FEW REMARKS. *Life and Letters,* v. 2, Jan., 1929, p. 29-35.

Remarks On Crime—On Prudence—On Money—On Self-Sacrifice.

Reprinted. In: *Obiter Scripta* (1936), p. 265-272.

REVIEW of Oswald Spengler, *The Decline of the West. The New Adelphi,* n.s., v. 2, no. 3, March, 1929, p. 210-214.

Proust on Essences. *Life and Letters*, v. 2, June, 1929, p. 455-459.

Reprinted. In: *Obiter Scripta* (1936), p. 273-279; *Triton Ed.*, v. 14 (1937), p. 175-179.

Enduring the Truth. *The Saturday Review of Literature*, v. 6, no. 512, Dec. 7, 1929, p. 512.

Published also in: *The New Adelphi*, n.s. v. 3, Dec. 1929-Feb. 1930, p. 120-124.

Review of Walter Lippmann, *A Preface to Morals.*

A footnote to Santayana by Lippmann, p. 513.

1930

The Realm of Matter; Book Second of Realms of Being. New York, Charles Scribner's Sons, 1930. xv, 209 p.

Published in London by Constable and Co., Ltd., 1930.

Contents. Preface—I. The Scope of Natural Philosophy—II. Indispensable Properties of Substance—III. Presumable Properties of Substance—IV. Pictorial Space and Sentimental Time—V. The Flux of Existence—VI. Tropes—VII. Teleology—VIII. The Psyche—IX. Psychologism—X. The Latent Materialism of Idealists.

Reprinted. In: *Triton Ed.*, v. 14 (1937), p. 183-392. Preface, Ch. I-III. In: *Philosophy of Santayana* (1936), p. 514-562.

Manuscript. Deposited in the Treasure Room at Harvard University by the Delphic Club of Boston. [327] p.

A Brief History of My Opinions. In: Adams, George P. and William Montague, eds., *Contemporary American Philosophy;* Personal Statements. New York, Macmillan and Co., 1930, 2 v. v. 2, p. 239-257.

Reprints. Some paragraphs as "Brief History of Myself." In: *The Saturday Review of Literature*, v. 13, no. 14, Feb. 1, 1936, p. 13.

In: *Philosophy of Santayana* (1936), p. 1-20; *Triton Ed.*, v. 2 (1936), p. vii-xxvii.

Headed "George Santayana." In: Fadiman, C., ed. *I Believe; The Personal Philosophies of Certain Eminent Men and Women of Our Time.* New York, Simon and Schuster, 1939, p. 231-252.

As part of the chapter, *A General Confession.* In: Schilpp, Paul Arthur, ed., *The Philosophy of George Santayana*, Evanston and Chicago, Northwestern University, 1940. (*Library of Living Philosophers*, v. 2).

Translations. "Breve Historia de Mis Opiniones" [by Antonio Marichalar]. *Sur; Revista Trimestral* (Buenos Aires), v. 3, April, 1933, p. 7-44.

Excerpts. In: Menéndez, Jaime, "Santayana, Filósofo y Novelista," *Cruz y Raya (Madrid)*, [v. 3], May, 1936, no. 38, p. 134-135; 138-139; 140-141.

"Breve storia delle mie opinioni." In: *Filosofi americani contemporani;* con una introduzione di Antonio Banfi. Traduz. di Carlo Coardi. Milano, Bompiani (Bergamo, Istituto Ital. d'arti Grafiche), 1939, 342 p.

1931

THE GENTEEL TRADITION AT BAY. *The Saturday Review of Literature.* Part I. *Analysis of Modernity,* v. 7, no. 24, Jan. 3, 1931, p. 502-503; Part II. *The Appeal to the Supernatural,* v. 7, no. 25, Jan. 10, p. 518-519; Part III. *Moral Adequacy of Naturalism,* v. 7, no. 26, Jan. 17, p. 534-535.

Published also in: *The Adelphi,* ser. 3, v. 1, Jan., 1931, p. 309-321; v. 1, Feb., 1931, p. 389-400; v. 1, March, 1931, p. 466-479.
Also published as a single volume. Cf. below.

Part I reprinted. In: Canby, H. S., et al., eds., *Designed for Reading; An Anthology Drawn from the Saturday Review of Literature, 1924-1934,* New York, 1934, p. 47-59.

THE GENTEEL TRADITION AT BAY. New York, Charles Scribner's Sons, 1931. 74 p.

Published in London by "The Adelphi," 1931. 43 p.

For contents, cf. preceding entry. Reprinted. In: *Triton Ed.,* v. 8 (1937), p. 133-169.

1932

GLIMPSES OF OLD BOSTON. *The Latin School Register,* v. 51, no. 5, March, 1932, p. 8-10.

Extract in: Holmes, P., *Tercentenary History of the Boston Public Latin School,* 1935, p. 247.

THE PRESTIGE OF THE INFINITE. *The Journal of Philosophy,* v. 29, no. 11, May 26, 1932, p. 281-289.

Review of Julien Benda, *Essai d'un Discours Cohérent sur les Rapports de Dieu et du Monde.*

Reprinted. In: *Some Turns of Thought in Modern Philosophy* (1933), as Ch. V, p. 102-121; *Triton Ed.,* v. 10 (1937), p. 231-242.

1933

SOME TURNS OF THOUGHT IN MODERN PHILOSOPHY; Five Essays. New York, Charles Scribner's Sons, 1933. 121 p.

Published in Cambridge [Eng.] by The University Press, 1933, under the auspices of the Royal Society of Literature.

For previous and later publication, and for reprints of certain chapters, cf. entries under dates following titles, listed in the contents.

Contents. I. Locke and the Frontiers of Common Sense; Paper read before the Royal Society of Literature on the Occasion of the Tercentenary of the birth of John Locke. With some supplementary Notes, 1-8—II. Fifty Years of British Idealism (1928)—III. Revolutions in Science (1928)—IV. A Long Way Round to Nirvana (1923)—V. The Prestige of the Infinite (1932).

Reprints. Ch. I. In: *Triton Ed.,* v. 7 (1937), p. 153-177.

[Letter to Antonio Marichalar]. *Revista de Occidente* (Madrid), v. 2, no. 126, Dec., 1933, p. 273.

Excerpt from a letter dated Aug. 17, 1933, written in Spanish. This excerpt dealing with Spinoza's pantheism, together with explicatory notes by the translator, precedes the translation of *Ultimate Religion.* (cf. following entry).

Ultimate Religion. In: *Septimana Spinozana; Acta Conventus Oecumenici in Memoriam Benedicti de Spinoza Diei Natalis Trecentesimi Hagae Comitis Habiti; Curis Societatis Spinozanae Edita.* Hagae Comitis, Martinus Nijoff, 1933, p. 105-115.

Paper read in the *Domus Spinozana* at the Hague during the commemoration of the tercentenary of the birth of Spinoza.

Reprinted. In: *Obiter Scripta* (1936), p. 280-297; *Triton Ed.*, v. 10 (1937), p. 245-257; *Philosophy of Santayana* (1936), p. 572-586.

Translation. "Religió última" tr. by Antonio Marichalar. In: *Revista de Occidente* (Madrid), v. 11, no. 126, Dec. 1933, p. 274-292.

1934

Alternatives to Liberalism. *The Saturday Review of Literature*, v. 10, no. 49, June 23, 1934, p. 761-762.

Also in: *Life and Letters*, v. 10, Aug., 1934, p. 541-545.

Many Nations in One Empire. *The New Frontier* (Exeter, N.H.), v. 1, no. 4, Sept., 1934, p. 6-10.

1935

Foreword. In: Origo, Iris, *Leopardi; A Biography (With a Foreword by George Santayana)*, Humphrey Milford, Oxford University Press, 1935, p. v-vi.

Reprinted in: *Philosophy of Santayana* (1936), p. 585-586.

Boston Latin School 1635:1935. In [*Program*]. *The Boston Latin School. 300th Anniversary 1635:1935. Symphony Hall: 23 April, 1935.* 4 unnumbered pages. p. [2].

Message to the Boston Latin School on its Tercentenary.

Reprinted. In: *The Boston Herald*, v. 177, no. 114, April 24, 1935, p. 11. In: Holmes, P., *Tercentenary History of the Boston Public Latin School*, 1935, p. 1-2. In: *Proceedings and Addresses of the Boston Latin School Tercentenary 1635-1935*, comp. and ed. by Lee J. Dunn, Boston Latin School Association, 1937, p. 110-111.

[Letters to William James, 1887-1905]. In: Perry, Ralph Barton, *The Thought and Character of William James; As Revealed in Unpublished Correspondence and Notes, Together with His Pub-*

lished Writings. v. 1, *Inheritance and Vocation;* v. 2, *Philosophy and Psychology*. Boston, Little, Brown, and Co., 1935.

The following letters are included; v. 1, "Berlin, Dec. 18, 1887," p. 401-402; "Berlin, Jan. 28, 1888," p. 404; "Avila, July 3, 1888," p. 405-406; v. 2, "Cambridge, [Mass.] Easter, 1900," p. 320-321; "Rome, Nov. 29, 1904," p. 396-397; "Paris, Dec. 5, 1905," p. 399-401; "Paris, Dec. 6, 1905," p. 401-403.

WHY I AM NOT A MARXIST. *The Modern Monthly*, v. 9, no. 1, April, 1935, p. 77-79.

OLIVER CHOOSES TO BE A BOY. *The Saturday Review of Literature*, v. 12, no. 17, Aug. 24, 1935, p. 3-4, 16.

Excerpts from Ch. I of Part II, from *The Last Puritan* (1936).
Title given by the Editor without the author's knowledge.

1936

*THE LAST PURITAN; A MEMOIR IN THE FORM OF A NOVEL. New York, Charles Scribner's Sons, 1936. 602 p.

Published in London by Constable and Co., Ltd., 1935, 721 p. In Toronto by Macmillan, 1935.
Contents. Prologue—Part I. Ancestry—Part II. Boyhood—Part III. First Pilgrimage—Part IV. In the Home Orbit—Part V. Last Pilgrimage—Epilogue.

Reprinted, with a new Preface. In: *Triton Ed.*, v. 11 (1937), p. 3-303; v. 12 (1937), p. 3-345.

Translations. *Der letzte Puritaner. Die Geschichte eines tragischen Lebens.* Aus dem Amerikanischen von Luise Laporte und Gertrud Grote. München, C. H. Beck, 1936. 720 p. Several condensations made in the text.

Den siste Puritanen. En minnenas roman. Översättning av Alf Ahlberg. Stockholm, Natur och kulture, 1936. (published also in Helsingfors by Söderström and Co.), v. 1, 366 p.; v. 2, 744 p.

Den sidste Puritaner; Erindringer i Romanform. [tr.] Krista Jørgensen. Kobenhavn, Jespersen and Pio, 1937. v. 1, 248 p.; v. 2, 328 p.

Saigo no seikyôto, trans. by Tomoji Abé and Chôju Ugai, Tokyo, Kawade Shobô, 1939-1941. 3 v.

Spanish translation to be published by the firm of Editorial Sudamericana of Buenos Aires.

Reprints. Excerpts from Part II appeared as "Oliver Chooses to Be a Boy." (cf. entry, 1935).

Excerpts from Oliver's final soliloquy and the epilogue. In: Phelps, W. L., "As I Like It," *Scribner's Magazine*, v. 99, no. 3, March, 1936, p. 186-187.

Part of the Epilogue. In: *Philosophy of Santayana* (1936), p. 587.

Prologue. In: Anderson, G. K. and E. L. Walton, eds., *This Generation; A Selection of British and American Literature from 1914 to the Present with Historical and Critical Essays.* Chicago, [c1939], p. 95-99.

Excerpts from the Prologue, the conversation between Caleb and Peter on Oliver's education, and the description of Caleb. In: Menéndez, Jaime, "Santayana, Filósofo y Novelista," *Cruz y Raya* (Madrid), [v. 3] no. 38, May, 1936, p. 121-142.

El último puritano, Prólogo, Epílogo, tr. by Antonia Marichalar. In: *Sur, Revista Mensual* (Buenos Aires), v. 7, July, 1937, p. 7-28.

Manuscript. Preface. In the possession of Mr. John Hall Wheelock. [18]p.

OBITER SCRIPTA; LECTURES, ESSAYS AND REVIEWS. Buchler, Justus and Benjamin Schwartz, eds., Charles Scribner's Sons, New York, 1936. xiv, 319 p.

Published in London by Constable and Co., Ltd., 1936.

For previous and later publication, and for reprints, cf. entries under dates following the titles listed in the contents.

Contents. Author's Preface—The Two Idealisms (1902)—What Is Aesthetics? (1904)—Hamlet (1908)—Plotinus and the Nature of Evil (1913)—The Indomitable Individual (1915)—Philosophical Heresy (1915)—Literal and Symbolic Knowledge (1918)—Penitent Art (1922)—The Unknowable (1923)—Some Meanings of the Word "Is" (1924)—Dewey's Naturalistic Metaphysics (1925)—Overheard in Seville (1927)—An Aesthetic Soviet (1927)—A Few Remarks (1929)—Proust on Essences (1929)—Ultimate Religion (1933)—Bibliography.

Reprints. Preface, with minor changes, as part of the Preface to the *Triton Ed.*, v. 1 (1936), p. vii-xi.

PHILOSOPHY OF SANTAYANA; SELECTIONS FROM THE WORKS OF GEORGE SANTAYANA. Edited, with an introductory essay, by Irwin Edman, New York, Charles Scribner's Sons, 1936. lvi, 587 p.

Contents. (The information below indicates the source of the contents and when publication first took place.) Introductory Essay by Irwin Edman—A Brief History of My Opinions (1930)—Poems: [Sonnets]—III. (1886)—IV. (1886)—VI. (1886)—VII. (1885)—XI, XIII (*Sonnets and Other Verses*, 1894)—XXII, XXV (Sonnets, 1895)—XLIX (*Sonnets and Other Verses*, 1896)—On a Volume of Scholastic Philosophy—On the Death of a Metaphysician—To W. P. [Sonnet II] (*Sonnets and Other Verses*, 1894).

Introduction and part of Part II of *Sense of Beauty* (1896)—Introduction, part of Ch. IX, and Ch. XI of *Reason in Common Sense* (1905) [Includes Preface to 2nd ed., 1922]—Ch. I, VI, VIII of *Reason in Society* (1905)—Ch. I. parts of III, IV, VI, Ch. X, XI, part of Ch. XIV of *Reason in Religion* (1905)—Ch. I, X, XI of *Reason in Art* (1905)—Ch. I, III, VII, XI of *Reason in Science* (1906)—Introduction of *Three Philosophical Poets* (1910)—nos. 26, 28, 38, 44, 48, 50 of *Soliloquies in England and Later Soliloquies* (1922)—Preface. Ch. VI, parts of Ch. VII, IX, Ch. XI, parts of XIV, XVI, Ch. XVIII, parts of XIX, Ch. XXIV, parts of Ch. XXV, XXVI, XXVII of *Scepticism and Animal Faith* (1923)—Ch. III of *Dialogues in Limbo* (1926)—Ch. XXIII of *Platonism and the Spiritual Life* (1927)—Preface, Ch. II, part of Ch. IV, Ch. VII, part of Ch. XI of *The Realm of Essence* (1927)—Preface, Ch. I-III of *The Realm of Matter* (1930)—Ch. IV of *Some Turns of Thought in Modern Philosophy* (1933)—*Ultimate Religion* (1933) (from *Obiter Scripta*, 1936)—From the *"Foreword"* in *Leopardi by Origo* (1935)—part of *Epilogue* in *The Last Puritan* (1936).

1936-1940

THE WORKS OF GEORGE SANTAYANA. Triton Edition. New York, Charles Scribner's Sons. 1936-1940. 15 v.

Cf. Frontispiece, v. 2 (1936). Facsimile of a letter from Santayana to John Hall Wheelock, dated Paris, June 23, 1936: ". . . What suggested the word [Triton Edition] to me is that my windows in Rome look down in the *Fontana del Tritone* and *Via del Tritone*. The Triton, by Bernini, is well known, and might be reproduced for a frontispiece or paper-cover. Then there is the association with Wordsworth's sonnet: 'a pagan suckled in a creed outworn,' and 'hear old Triton blow his wreathed horn'."

From the Prospectus to the Edition (1936):

". . . This edition printed from type is limited to 940 copies signed by the author. 20 sets are for presentation, and 920 for subscription. . . . Mr. Santayana has written a special preface for the set . . . he has also prepared prefaces to certain other volumes. . . . Each volume is illustrated by a photogravure frontispiece . . . including portraits of Santayana in his youth, photographs of his home in Spain, of his residence at Harvard, facsimile manuscript pages, etc. . . . Each frontispiece has the approval and interest of the author, and the volumes were arranged in . . . order by him."

For a detailed list of the contents of each volume, see the entries, which follow under the dates 1936, 1937, 1940.

For previous and later publication, and for reprints, cf. entries under the dates immediately following the titles listed in the contents.

1936

THE WORKS OF GEORGE SANTAYANA. [Triton Edition, v. 1]. 1936. xxi, 432 p.

Contents. Preface to the Triton Ed. [Dated Sept., 1936] (*Obiter Scripta*, 1936)—The Sense of Beauty (1896)—Poems (1923)—Lucifer (1924)—Overheard in Seville (1927).

Reprints. Latter half of Preface as part of "A General Confession." In: Schilpp, P. A., ed., *The Philosophy of George Santayana*, Evanston and Chicago, Northwestern University, 1940. (*The Library of Living Philosophers*, v. 2).

Mss. Preface. In the possession of Mr. John Hall Wheelock. [8 pp.]

THE WORKS OF GEORGE SANTAYANA. [Triton Edition, v. 2]. 1936. xxx, 288 p.

Contents. Frontispiece. Facsimile of a letter from the author regarding the Triton ed. [To John Hall Wheelock dated Paris, June 23, 1936.]

Preface; A Brief History of My Opinions (1930)—Interpretations of Poetry and Religions (1900)—Hamlet (1908)—Shelley (1913)—Dickens (1921)—Tragic Philosophy (1936).

THE WORKS OF GEORGE SANTAYANA. [Triton Edition, v. 3]. 1936. xiii, 375 p.

Contents. The Life of Reason: Introduction; Reason in Common Sense (Includes Preface to 2nd ed., 1922)—Reason in Society (1905).

THE WORKS OF GEORGE SANTAYANA. [Triton Edition, v. 4]. 1936. xiv, 374 p.

Contents. The Life of Reason: Reason in Religion (1905)—Reason in Art (1905).

THE WORKS OF GEORGE SANTAYANA. [Triton Edition, v. 5]. 1936. x, 231 p.

Contents. The Life of Reason; Reason in Science (1906).

THE WORKS OF GEORGE SANTAYANA. [Triton Edition, v. 6] 1936. viii, 291 p.

Contents. Frontispiece: Facsimile of a hitherto unpublished Sonnet by the Author. [entitled "On The Three Philosophical Poets"].

Three Philosophical Poets (1910)—Egotism in German Philosophy (1916)—The Two Idealisms (1902)—Plotinus and the Nature of Evil (1913).

[AUTOBIOGRAPHICAL SKETCH]. In: *Harvard College. Class of 1886. Secretary's Report. The Fiftieth Anniversary of the Class of '86 and the Three Hundredth of the College.* Anchor Linotype Printing Co., Boston, 1936, p. 388-389.

For mss., cf. entry under 1935 in Part II.

BERTRAND RUSSELL'S SEARCHLIGHT. *The American Mercury*, v. 37, no. 3, March, 1936, p. 377-379.

Review of Bertrand Russell, *Religion and Science.*

TRAGIC PHILOSOPHY. *Scrutiny* (Cambridge, Eng.), v. 4, no. 4, March, 1936, p. 365-376.

Reprinted. In: *Triton Ed.*, v. 2 (1936), p. 275-288. Also in: Zabel, M. D. *Literary Opinion in America . . .* , New York, 1927, p. 129-141.

SANTAYANA'S VIEW OF AMERICA. *The Saturday Review of Literature*, v. 13, no. 19, March 7, 1936, p. 9.

Letter to the Editor concerning a criticism of *The Last Puritan.*

[LETTERS TO WILLIAM LYON PHELPS]. In: Phelps' column, "As I Like It," *Scribner's Magazine*, v. 99, no. 6, June, 1936, p. 379-380.

Remarks on characterization in *The Last Puritan* (1936).

Reprinted. In: Chapter on Santayana in Phelps' *Autobiography with Letters*, New York, 1939, p. 346-349.

1937

THE WORKS OF GEORGE SANTAYANA. [Triton Edition, v. 7]. 1937. xviii, 226 p.

Contents. Preface; On the Unity of My Earlier and Later Philosophy—Winds of Doctrine (1913) [with Preface to 2nd ed., 1926]—Some Turns of Thought in Modern Philosophy: Ch. I. [with Supplementary Notes]; Ch. III. (1933)—Bishop Berkeley (1937)—Penitent Art (1922).

Mss. Preface. In the posession of Mr. John Hall Wheelock. [18] p.

THE WORKS OF GEORGE SANTAYANA. [Triton Edition, v. 8]. 1937. viii, 207 p.

Contents. Character and Opinion in the United States (1920)—The Genteel Tradition at Bay (1931)—Dewey's Naturalistic Metaphysics (1925)—Philosophical Heresy (1915).

THE WORKS OF GEORGE SANTAYANA. [Triton Edition, v. 9]. 1937. ix, 271 p.

Contents. Soliloquies in England and Later Soliloquies (1922).

THE WORKS OF GEORGE SANTAYANA. [Triton Edition, v. 10]. 1937. viii, 257 p.

Contents. Dialogues in Limbo (1926)—Platonism and the Spiritual Life (1927)—A Long Way Round to Nirvana (1923)—The Prestige of the Infinite (1932)—Ultimate Religion (1933).

THE WORKS OF GEORGE SANTAYANA. [Triton Edition, v. 11]. 1937. xv, 303 p.

Contents. The Last Puritan, v. 1. Preface to *The Last Puritan*—Prologue—Parts I-III (to end of Ch. V). (1936).

Mss. Preface. In the possession of Mr. John Hall Wheelock. [18] p.

THE WORKS OF GEORGE SANTAYANA. [Triton Edition, v. 12]. 1937. 345 p.

Contents. The Last Puritan, v. 2. Part III (Ch. VI to conclusion)—Part IV-V—Epilogue (1936).

THE WORKS OF GEORGE SANTAYANA. [Triton Edition, v. 13]. 1937. viii, 352 p.

Contents. Scepticism and Animal Faith (1923)—Some Meanings of the Word "Is" (1924)—Literal and Symbolic Knowledge (1918)—The Unknowable (1923).

THE WORKS OF GEORGE SANTAYANA. [Triton Edition, v. 14]. 1937. xxv, 392 p.

Contents. Realms of Being: The Realm of Essence (1927)—Proust on Essences (1929)—The Realm of Matter (1930).

BISHOP BERKELEY (1685-1753). In: Dobrée, Bonamy, ed., *From Anne to Victoria; Essays by Various Hands*. London, Cassell and Co., Ltd., [1937], p. 75-88.

Appears also in: *Triton Ed.*, v. 7 (1937), p. 203-216.

AN APOLOGY FOR BEING PRECOCIOUS. *The Harvard Monthly*, v. 65, no. 1, March, 1937. (Revival Issue), p. 3-4, 32.

"A founder of the *Monthly* begins the new series of graduate articles with a reminiscence of our founding."

[LETTER]. *The American Clipper*, The American Autograph Shop, Merion Station, Pa., March, 1937, p. 673.

Excerpts from a letter listed as no. 149 in this catalogue headed, "A Great Letter." Recipient's name is not mentioned; name of purchaser of letter not available. Excerpts touch upon *Lucifer* and *The Last Puritan*.

[LETTER TO THE EDITOR]. *The Harvard Monthly*, v. 65, no. 3, June, 1937, p. 2.

Brief comment on the Revival Issue.

1938

THE REALM OF TRUTH; BOOK THIRD OF REALMS OF BEING. New York, Charles Scribner's Sons, 1938. xiv, 142 p.

Published in London by Constable and Co., Ltd., 1937, and by Macmillan, in Toronto.

Contents. Preface—I. There Are no Necessary Truths—II. Facts Arbitrary, Logic Ideal—III. Interplay Between Truth and Logic—IV. Psychological Approaches to Truth—V. Radiation of Truth—VI. Conventional Truths—VII. Dramatic Truth—VIII. Moral Truth—IX. Truth Supertemporal—X. Cognition of the Future—XI. Truth and Chance—XII. Love and Hatred of Truth—XIII. Denials of Truth—XIV. Beyond the Truth.

To be reprinted. In: *Triton Ed.*, v. 15 (1940), p. 3-144.

[QUOTATIONS FROM LETTERS]. In: Howgate, George W., *George Santayana*, Phila., University of Pennsylvania Press, 1938. viii, 363 p.

Quotations from personal letters to the biographer, appearing in the text, indicated in the Notes, p. 297-325.

[POST CARD TO JAMES C. AYER]. *The New York Times. Book Review Section.* Sept. 18, 1938, p. 26, col. 3.

Excerpts from comments on own writings. Supplementary remarks on the subject briefly summarized.

1939

[LETTER TO LOGAN PEARSALL SMITH]. In: Smith, L. P., *Unforgotten Years*, Boston, Little, Brown and Co., 1939, p. 283-288.

Unsigned. Dated Rome, Dec. 2, 1921.

[LETTERS TO WILLIAM LYON PHELPS]. In: Phelps, W. L., *Autobiography With Letters*, New York, Oxford University Press, 1939.

In Ch., "George Santayana," p. 332-349. The following letters are included: "Paris, Sept. 8, 1920," p. 341-342 (comments on Phelps' review of *Little Essays*); "Rome, Nov. 2, 1928," p. 343; "Hotel Bristol, Rome," Jan. 4, 1932, p. 344-345; "Hotel Miramonti, Cortina d'Amperesso, [d'Ampezzo?] July 10, 1933;" p. 345-346; "Hotel Bristol, Rome, Feb. 16, 1936," p. 346-348 (on *The Last Puritan*); "Hotel Bristol, Rome, March 16, 1936," p. 348-349.

For previous publication of last two letters, cf. entry under 1936.

1940

EGOTISM IN GERMAN PHILOSOPHY [New ed.]. New York, Charles Scribner's Sons, 1940. xii, 178 p.

Published in London by J. M. Dent and Sons, Ltd., New ed. [1939].

For previous and later publication, and for contents and reprints, cf. entry for first ed., 1916.

Additions in Contents. New Preface, pp. v-vii [dated Cortina d'Ampezzo, August, 1939] and a Postscript: The Nature of Egotism and of the Moral Conflicts that Disturb the World. Pp. 151-173.

A GENERAL CONFESSION. In: Schilpp, Paul Arthur, ed., *The Philosophy of George Santayana*, Evanston and Chicago, Northwestern University, 1940. (*The Library of Living Philosophers*, v. 2.)

Consists of the latter half of the Preface of *Triton Edition* v. 1 (1936), Preface to v. 7 (1937), and *Brief History of My Opinions* (1930), with minor corrections made for the present purpose by Mr. Santayana himself.

APOLOGIA PRO MENTE SUA: A REJOINDER. In: Schilpp, Paul Arthur, ed., *The Philosophy of George Santayana*, Evanston and Chicago, Northwestern University, 1940.

Santayana's Reply to his Commentators and Critics.

THE REALM OF SPIRIT; BOOK FOURTH OF REALMS OF BEING. New York, Charles Scribner's Sons, 1940. xii, 302 p.

Published in London by Constable and Co., Ltd., 1940.

Contents. Preface.—I. The Nature of Spirit—II. On Cosmic Animism—III. The Natural Distribution of Spirit—IV. The Will—V. Freedom—VI. Intuition VII. Distraction—VIII. Liberation—IX. Union—X. General Review of *Realms of Being.*

To be reprinted in: *Triton Ed.*, v. 15 (1940), pp. 147-449.

THE WORKS OF GEORGE SANTAYANA. [Triton Edition, v. 15.] 1940. 449 p.

To be published in the fall of 1940.

Contents. Realms of Being: The Realm of Truth (1938)—The Realm of Spirit (1940).

VOLUMES IN PREPARATION

DOMINATIONS AND POWERS

PERSONS AND PLACES: FRAGMENTS OF AUTOBIOGRAPHY

Both vols. to be published by Scribner's in the future.

NOTE: Mr. Santayana has stated that "there may also be" the following volumes:

HELLENISTIC PLAYS

Three plays in verse, written in the 1890's.

POSTHUMOUS POEMS

PART II

UNPUBLISHED MANUSCRIPTS

1885-1886

THE OPTIMISM OF RALPH WALDO EMERSON. By "Victor Cousin." Senior Class ('86) of Harvard College. 23 l., written on both sides.

Unsuccessful Bowdoin Prize Essay, signed "Victor Cousin," and attributed, in pencil, to Santayana.

Kept in the Harvard University Archives.

1889

LOTZE'S SYSTEM OF PHILOSOPHY. [Harvard University]. [1889]. 322 l., written on one side.

Thesis submitted for the Ph.D. degree at Harvard.

Contents. I. Lotze's Problems; His Relation to Natural Science—II. Lotze and the Kantian Philosophy—III. Lotze's Atomism; His Argument for Idealism—

IV. Monism; Causality; Indeterminism—V. Personality and God; Aesthetics; Optimism—Note [on Lotze's Life]—Titles and Dates of Lotze's Works.

Kept in the Harvard University Archives.

Condensed and modified version published as "Lotze's Moral Idealism," in *Mind*, April, 1890. Cf. entry, Part I.

1890?

EARLIEST VERSES OF GEORGE SANTAYANA TRANSCRIBED BY HIS OWN HAND ABOUT THE YEAR 1890, NO EARLIER MANUSCRIPT REMAINING IN HIS POSSESSION, Rome, Nov. 29, 1936. 72 numbered mss. pp.

Note: This Notebook was presented by Santayana to the Lockwood Memorial Library of the University of Buffalo in Dec., 1936. It was sent in response to a request for materials with which to study the creative methods of poetry as illustrated by as nearly complete dossiers as could be provided in the making of individual poems. Santayana replied that he could not supply the Library with exactly what was requested, but that he was happy to present this Notebook to the collection. He instructed the Library that nothing in it may be published, except ". . . if some student should wish to quote some part of it to illustrate any thesis he may be defending."

In the list of contents given below, the date preceding the title indicates the date of composition. First lines, as they appear in the Notebook, are followed by the page number; the pagination is in accordance with the numbering assigned to the Notebook by the University. The date in parenthesis indicates when, if ever, a selection was first published.

The Verses are arranged in six sections:

I. *Sonnets*

1882.	I.	Is there on earth a garden of delight. (*Sonnets and Other Verses*, 1894)	p. 5
1882.	II.	My soul is driven from the good I seek. (Marked "omit" in pencil). Unpublished.	p. 6
1900.		I reverence thy godhead and obey. (An unnumbered sonnet written in pencil on the same page as II.) Unpublished.	p. 6
1883.	III.	O would we had been born in nature's day. (Sonnets, 1886)	p. 7
1884.	IV.	O world, thou choosest not the better part! (Sonnet, 1886)	p. 8
1884.	V.	I did not seek to live when I was born. (Marked in pencil, "leave out"). Unpublished.	p. 9
1884.	VI.	Dream I today the dream of yesternight. (Sonnet, 1885)	p. 10
1884.	VII.	Love not as do the flesh-imprisoned men. (Sonnet, 1886)	p. 11
1885.	VIII.	O would I might forget that I am I. (Sonnet, 1885)	p. 12

1886.	IX.	What worth hath man? Upon some craggy hill. Unpublished.	p. 13
1887.	X.	Have I the heart to wander on the earth. (*Sonnets and Other Verses*, 1894)	p. 14
1887.	XI.	Deem not, because you see me in the press. (*Sonnets and Other Verses*, 1894)	p. 15
1887.	XII.	Sweet are the days we wander with no hope. (*Sonnets and Other Verses*, 1894)	p. 16
1887.	XIII.	Blaspheme not love, ye lovers, nor dispraise. (Sonnets, 1892)	p. 17

II. *Verses Written in 1880, Revised in 1888.*

1880 Day and Night, p. 21-23. Unpublished. Note in pencil: "Boston Latin School Prize Poem, 1880."
1880 Luna. p. 24. Unpublished.
1880 On A Drawing. p. 25. Unpublished.

III. *Verses of 1881 and of 1883.*

1881 Prison Walls. p. 29. Unpublished.
1883 Song, "Love, do not leave me yet." p. 30. Unpublished.
1883 Echo. p. 31. Unpublished.

IV. *1885 and 1886.*

1885 Paradise. p. 35-36. Unpublished.
1885 Solipsismus. p. 37-38. Published as "Solipsism" (*Hermit of Carmel*, 1901).
1885 The Ten Commandments. p. 39-41. Unpublished.
1886 Descende Caelo. p. 42-43. Unpublished.
1886 Mother Earth. p. 44-45. Unpublished.
1886 Awaking. p. 46. Unpublished.

V. *1887.*

1887 Two Voices. (1888). p. 49-51.
1887 At the Church Door. p. 52-55. Unpublished. Note in pencil at bottom of p. 55, "Compare Lionel Johnson's Poem, 'To a Spanish Friend'."
1887 Prayer to the Ocean. p. 56-58. Unpublished.

VI. *1888.*

1888 Easter Hymn. p. 61-63. Dated Berlin, Easter, 1888. (*Sonnets and Other Verses*, 1894).
1888 Good Friday Hymn. p. 64-65. (*Sonnets and Other Verses*, 1894).
1888 The Living Stars. p. 66-67. Unpublished.
1888 Premonition. p. 68-69. (*Hermit of Carmel*, 1901).

Note: Pages, which are not enumerated, are either blank, or contain contents headings. Most of the poems differ from the published version with identical titles; a few bear corrections on the mss. Since the present compiler has not had an opportunity to examine this Notebook personally, she wishes to acknowledge the assistance of Miss Mary Barnard, Curator of the Poetry Collection, and of Dr. C. D. Abbott, Director of Libraries at the University of Buffalo, in securing the information given.

1892

THE JUDGMENT OF PARIS, OR, HOW THE "FIRST-TEN" MAN CHOOSES A CLUB. 1892. 4 l., numbered 1-7.

Dated, Oct. 28, 1892.

Deposited in the Treasure Room at Harvard University by the Delphic Club of Boston.

1895

AT ARLES; Where a picture of the Crucifixion hung in the museum above a bust of Antinöus.

Unpublished sonnet of 1895, presented to the Library of Congress for the Poet's Corner. Accompanying letter dated, Rome, June 10, 1939. Both are kept in the Rare Book Room.

1903?

[MARGINAL NOTES]. In: Russell, Bertrand, *The Principle of Mathematics.* v. 1, Cambridge, at the University Press, 1903. 534 p.

These marginal notes, written in pencil, are scattered throughout the volume. Presented by Santayana as a gift to the Philosophy Dept. at Harvard in Jan., 1912. In 1935, it was transferred to the Treasure Room.

1935

[ANSWERS TO QUESTIONNAIRE]. [*Harvard College*]. [*Class of 1886*]. Circular for Information for the Fiftieth Report. [4 p.]

Date of receipt stamped, July 5, 1935. Comments on present occupation and published works. Information appearing on p. 3-4 published in *Harvard College. Class of 1886. Secretary's Report,* 1936. Cf. entry, Part I.

Kept in the Harvard University Archives.

SPECIAL INDEX TO THE BIBLIOGRAPHY OF THE WRITINGS OF GEORGE SANTAYANA

NOTE: The following abbreviations are used to facilitate the location of items in works listed in the Bibliography. Cf. *Prefatory Note* for additional explanations concerning the arrangement of material in this Index. Since the Bibliography itself is chronologically arranged, the reader will find himself referred, for each indexed item, to the year under which the item may be found, rather than to the page in the Bibliography.

EV	*Earliest Verses . . .*
HC	*Hermit of Carmel . . .*
PR	*Interpretations of Poetry and Religion*
LE	*Little Essays . . .*
SE	*Soliloquies in England . . .*
SOV	*Sonnets and Other Verses*
TE	*Triton Edition*
VP	Volumes in Preparation
II	Refers to Part II of the Bibliography

Art, The Power of, 1894, SOV
Art, Reason in, 1905
Art and Happiness, 1920, LE
Art in Moral Economy, The Place of, 1920, LE
Artists, The Unhappiness of, 1920, LE
"As in the midst of battle there is room," 1895
"As when the sceptre dangles from the hand," 1896, SOV
Aspirations of a Country Lad, 1882
At Arles, 1895, II
At the Church Door, 1890, II, EV
At Heaven's Gate, 1922, SE
At Noon, 1892
Athletic Ode, 1901, HC
Atmosphere, 1922, SE
Authority of Reason in Morals, 1920, LE
Autobiographical Notes, 1926
Autobiographical Report, 1889; 1901
Autobiographical Sketch, 1936
Autobiography, Fragments of, VP
Aversion from Platonism, 1919
Avicenna, The Sorrows of, 1924
Avicenna, The Wisdom of, 1924
Avila, 1901, HC
Awakening, 1890, II, EV
The Barbarian, 1920, LE
Beauty, The Sense of; Being the Outlines of Aesthetic Theory, 1896
Beauty, Utility and, 1920, LE
Beauty a Hint of Happiness, 1920, LE
Bedford St. Schoolhouse; Lines on Leaving the, 1880
Before a Statue of Achilles, 1897
Being, Realms of, 1927-1940
Berenson's Florentine Painters, 1896
Berkeley, Bishop, 1937
Bertrand Russell's Searchlight, 1936
"Blaspheme not love, ye lovers, nor dispraise," 1892
The Birth of Reason, 1920, LE
Bishop Berkeley, 1937
Body and Mind, 1920, LE
Book Reviews:
- Adam, J., *Religious Teachers of Greece,* 1908
- Benda, J., *Essai d'un discours cohérent sur les rapports de Dieu et du monde,* 1932
- Berenson, B., *Floretine Painters of the Italian Renaissance,* 1896
- Bradley, F. H., *Ethical Studies,* 1928
- Campbell, L., *Religion in Greek Literature,* 1899
- Croce, B., *Estetica come scienza dell'espressione e linguistica generale,* 1903
- Davidson, T., *Philosophy of Goethe's Faust,* 1907
- Dewey, J., *Experience and Nature,* 1925
- Dewey, J., *German Philosophy and Politics,* 1915
- Dickinson, G. L., *Is Immortality Desirable?* 1909
- Erskine, J., *Moral Obligation to be Intelligent,* 1916
- d'Essling, P. and E. Muntz, *Pétrarque,* 1904
- Fiske, J., *Idea of God as Affected by Modern Knowledge,* 1885
- Fuller, B. A. G., *Problem of Evil in Plotinus,* 1913
- Fullerton, W. M., *In Cairo,* 1892
- Holt, E. B., *Concept of Consciousness,* 1914
- Holt, E. B., *Freudian Wish,* 1916
- James, W., *Principles of Psychology,* 1891
- Johnson, E. H., *Argument of Aristotle's Metaphysics,* 1907
- Leahy, W. A., *Siege of Syracuse,* 1889
- Levy-Bruhl, L., *History of Modern Philosophy in France,* 1900
- Lippman, W., *Preface to Morals,* 1929
- Marshall, H. R., *The Beautiful,* 1925
- Martin, J., *Saint Augustin,* 1901
- Newell, W. W., *Sonnets and Madrigals of Michaelangelo Buonarroti,* 1900
- Owen, J., *Skeptics of the Italian Renaissance,* 1894
- Russell, B., *Philosophical Essays,* 1911
- Russell, B., *Religion and Science,* 1936
- Santayana, G., *Lucifer; A Theological Tragedy,* 1899
- Sergi, G., *Psicologia per le Scuole,* 1897
- Sneath, E. H., *Philosophy in Poetry; Mind of Tennyson,* 1904
- Spengler, O., *Decline of the West,* 1929
- Stearns, H., *Civilization in the United States,* 1922
- Watson, J. B., *Psychology from the Standpoint of a Behavorist,* 1922
- Willmann, O., *Geschichte des Idealismus,* 1897
- Woods, J. H., *Value of Religious Facts,* 1900

Boston, Glimpses of Old, 1932
Boston Latin School. *The Class of 1882,* 1881

INDEX

(Not including Bibliography)